n
.esh
gar
aprayag
hal
war

TIBET

ARUNACHAL
PRADESH

NEPAL

SIKKIM BHUTAN

ASSAM

Ayodhya

Darjeeling

Goalpara Guwahati

NAGALAND

arnath Ghazipur

BIHAR

Shillong

ranasi

Kashi

Bhagalpur

MEGHALAYA

MANIPUR

Gaya

Simultala

BANGLA
DESH

Bodh Gaya Deoghar

WEST

TRIPURA

BENGAL

Dhaka

ipur

Jayrambati
Kamarpukur Howrah
Antpur Calcutta

MIZORAM

Chandranath

BURMA

ORISSA

Bay of Bengal

ANDAMAN &
NICOBAR ISLANDS

nad (Ramanathapuram)

a

pura

SRI LANKA

THE LIFE OF
SWAMI VIVEKANANDA

THE LIFE OF
SWAMI VIVEKANANDA

HIS EASTERN AND WESTERN DISCIPLES

VOLUME I

Advaita Ashrama
(Publication Department)
5 DEHI ENTALLY ROAD
CALCUTTA 700 014

Published by
Swami Mumukshananda
President, Advaita Ashrama
Mayavati, Pithoragarh, Himalayas
from its Publication Department, Calcutta

© *Advaita Ashrama, Mayavati, India, 1989*
Sixth Edition, January 1989
Third Reprint, December 1997
3M3C

ISBN 81-7505-043-8 (Vol. I)
ISBN 81-7505-042-X (Set)

Printed in India at
Gipidi Box Co.
3B Chatu Babu Lane
Calcutta 700 014

PREFACE TO THE FIFTH EDITION

IT GIVES us great pleasure to place this revised and enlarged edition, which in fact is the ninth impression of Swami Vivekananda's life, in the hands of the readers. Since 1933, when *The Life of Swami Vivekananda* by His Eastern and Western Disciples was revised, much new published as well as unpublished material about the Swami's life has come to our hands. All significant new information has, therefore, been incorporated in this edition in the light of these archives. No pains have been spared to make it informative, up to date, and authentic. Secondly, some material that was omitted in the abridged second edition has been restored in appropriate places for the sake of fuller account. Thirdly, the number of chapters has been increased and the captions of some chapters changed to suit the new set-up. This naturally led to splitting the volume into two. A new chapter on "Setting the Indian Work in Motion" has been added to the first volume.

Furthermore, an effort has been made to make the earlier text read more simply and smoothly, and make the added matter all of a piece with it. Some factual errors, which occurred in the earlier editions owing to the scanty resources available then, have been rectified wherever possible in the light of the recently discovered material. The dates and versions of Swamiji's letters quoted in this edition have mostly been taken from the photostats of the originals. As such, in certain places they may vary from those found in *The Complete Works of Swami Vivekananda* published by us. Besides these, numerous quotations from many hitherto unpublished letters of Swamiji, of his friends and disciples, and some hitherto unknown information about the Swami, have been added, which make this edition unique among all the Swami's biographies available. The portions taken from the Bengali sources are our translations. Occasionally, more than one version of the same incident has been given for the benefit of the readers.

A Glossary, Bibliography, Index, and a few illustrations have been added to this edition for the convenience of the readers.

The authorities of the Belur Math were greatly helpful in various ways in our work while preparing this edition. Special reference may be made in this connection to the learned guidance and inspiration given by Swami Gambhiranandaji, General Secretary of the Ramakrishna Math and the Ramakrishna Mission.

Many hands, both monastic and lay, have contributed to the diverse aspects of the work on the present edition. We particularly wish to mention the contribution of Marie Louise Burke, now named Gargi. She has liberally supplied a substantial portion of the new information from her books as well as from her hitherto unpublished archives. Moreover, she gave much help in the revision of the first four chapters, and all the "Western" chapters. She has thus generously contributed both on the research and the editing side. We are, therefore, thankful to her for her kindness.

We are also thankful to Mrs. Gertrude Emerson Sen and Shri Sankari Prasad Basu, for providing us with some hitherto unpublished material regarding the Swami's life, and to several other friends for collecting material for this edition.

We wish to express our sincere thanks to Professor Jnanendra Chandra Datta, Lecturer in Sanskrit, Women's College, Calcutta, and Shri Nachiketa Bharadwaj, Assistant Librarian, National Library, Calcutta, for preparing the Index to this volume.

It is our hope that the present enriched edition, to be issued in two volumes, will be received with warmth by Swamiji's admirers, devotees, and research students all over the world. The second volume will follow in due course.

MAYAVATI   PUBLISHER
25 August 1978

PREFACE TO THE FOURTH EDITION

This edition is practically a reprint of the earlier one; but the two volumes are now offered to the public in one volume of handy size and good get-up. The price of the book has been lowered to bring it within the reach of a wider public.

Mayavati
September 1, 1949

Publisher

PREFACE TO THE SECOND EDITION

The second edition of *The Life of Swami Vivekananda* comes out after a long pause due to unavoidable circumstances. In this edition the volumes have come under a thorough revision and some inaccuracies which had crept in in the first edition have been corrected in the light of later investigations. Much that was superfluous by way of extensive descriptions of Hindu religious and social ideals, with most of which the Indian reader is already conversant, has been cut short. Only that much has been preserved which is necessary for a Western reader to understand the full significance of the life. So too the chapters dealing with the elucidation of religious and philosophical consciousness have undergone much abridgement. In effecting these alterations, however, care has been taken to see that no fact of importance was omitted and that none of the numerous aspects of that marvellous character was neglected. On the other hand new information has been added, which was not available at first.

Chapters VI–XI, which throw light on the relation between Naren and Shri Ramakrishna, and on Naren, the man in the making, have been rewritten in accordance with that excellent work, in Bengali, of Swami Saradananda, *Shri Ramakrishna Lila Prasanga*, written after the publication of the first edition of this work. We need hardly say anything about the value of these new facts, coming as they do from a rationalistic mind like that of Swami Saradananda, who above all is a direct disciple of the Master. In spite of such additions the condensation above referred to has reduced the bulk of the work to two volumes, thus bringing it within the reasonable limits of a biography for the busy general reader. The price too has been considerably lowered.

We hope the work in its new garb will be heartily welcomed by the reading public.

MAYAVATI   PUBLISHER
January 18, 1933

PREFACE TO THE FIRST EDITION

IT IS now ten years since Swami Vivekananda entered FINAL ILLUMINATION; it is fifty years since his personality was ushered upon earth. It is, therefore, befitting that these events should be conterminous with and celebrated by the publishing of the life he lived. For years it has been the desire of the Eastern disciples at the Advaita Ashrama to publish an authoritative biography of their teacher so as to present to the world at large and to posterity the vision, the ideas, the work and the greatness of that personality which the Swami's life embodied.

In the beginning it was planned to incorporate a biographical sketch in the last volume of the Mayavati Memorial Edition of *The Complete Works of Swami Vivekananda*, but both by reason of the supreme import of the Swami's life to the world and the vast collection of biographical facts of the most interesting nature and of far-reaching significance, gathered during the last seven years, this idea was abandoned. Instead, the life is now presented in three[1] separate volumes.

Much has been written in this work in the way of interpretation, for many of the facts in the Swami's life, without explanation of the Hindu religious and social ideals and without

[1] Actually in four volumes.

some reference to the psychology of the mystical consciousness, would confuse the casual reader and might even seem improbable. The world knows the Swami as a giant intellect, a great scholar and orator, a patriotic Hindu and a powerful preacher of the Vedânta. But that is knowing only one phase of this many-sided genius. Even to those who knew him personally, the Swami, both as a lad and as a man, was too complex a character to be readily understood. He was a man of original thoughts and numerous moods, each a world in itself, and when any single one of them came upon him he was so intense that for the time being he would identify himself solely with that particular state of mind above all others. Thus it happened that many persons saw him from widely varying angles and spoke of him chiefly in the sense in which they personally understood him. This accounts for the many differing presentations of the Swami. Efforts have been made in this work to present the Swami in all his moods and varied illumination so as to reveal the man *as he was*.

Great pains have been taken to authenticate all the private and public sources of information in connection with the biographical facts, and much discretion has been exercised in embodying these, so as to offer to the public a complete and reliable work. An excellent advantage was that most of those who knew the Swami intimately are still alive. There are many disciples, both of the Swami himself and of his Master Shri Ramakrishna, whose reminiscences by means of talks and writings, and whose private diaries and published works have given every opportunity for ascertaining the accuracy of statements. Then there are the numerous letters and writings, published and unpublished, of the Swami himself from which to verify the character and the development of his mind and his entire personality. We heartily acknowledge our indebtedness to all these valuable authorities and sources of information, too numerous to mention individually here. Everything in the way of illuminating anecdote and interpretation has been included, and all accounts have been diligently studied so as to keep within the bounds of legitimate biographical treatment.

In order to facilitate the reading and to render the treatment of the lengthy history of the life easier of approach, it has been presented in a series of short chapters under descriptive headings. The attempt throughout has been to portray the elements of life, character, growth and work in as simple and direct a manner as possible and to picture, in particular, the conditions under which the Swami's life was developed and expressed. This necessitated an exposition of the ideas and activities of the modern transition in India, and a comprehensive sketch of the life and teachings of Shri Ramakrishna who is regarded as the unique spiritual character of Modern India; it necessitated also the recital of the modern religious transition in the West, because of the Swami's multifarious work there, and also the rise and development of the monastic order of which he was the moving spirit, and of the great philanthropic organisation, known as the Ramakrishna Mission, which he founded.

The first volume presents the narrative of his personality until his twenty-fourth year and the training he underwent at the feet of his Master for the attainment of spiritual insight and realisation. It takes into account the theme around which the Swami's life is drawn—the theme of Hinduism, its setting, its basis and its structure. It reveals the growth of a gigantic mind through modern agnosticism into complete saintship. It presents the character of the Swami's Master in the light in which the Swami himself understood him. The reader will become familiar with the Swami in the first volume as "Naren" or "Narendra", the name by which he was known both to the Master and to his brother-disciples and friends, as his proper name was Narendra Nath Datta. The first volume shows how Naren, having become de-Hinduised became re-Hinduised through his perception of the synthesis of Hinduism as lived and realised by his Master. For the sake of a clear understanding of the process by which this was effected, several chapters of the first volume are devoted to the elucidation of the Hindu religious and philosophic consciousness. One sees in the first volume the man, the saint and the prophet in the making.

The second volume deals with the narrative of the Swami's life as the wandering monk, and later on as the bearer of the message of Hinduism to the West. It takes the reader through the scenes of the Swami's life of intense austerities and Sadhanas in the Baranagore Math, of his travels and silent preaching throughout the length and breadth of Hindusthan, prior to his departure for America, and of his triumphant public career as the apostle of Vedântism during his sojourn in the West. It shows how at the Parliament of Religions held in Chicago, in 1893, the Swami became a world-wide figure and the Prophet of Hinduism. And it dwells on the momentous significance of his ideas and of his work as the spiritual teacher.

The third volume speaks of the Swami's attempts at re-modelling the Indian thought-world, of his restating the entire contents of the Sahâtana Dharma and the ancient Aryan culture, and of his bringing about a religious revival in India. It reveals him as the founder of monasteries and centres of public service, as the Man of Sorrows, whose heart bled for the millions of India's poor and distressed, and also as the Man of Joys, thundering at all times in the hearing of his co-religionists the glories of Hinduism and the bright future of his race. It records his activities during his second visit to the West, and gives a vivid picture of his subsequent life in India. Finally, it speaks of the Swami's influence on Indian life, and of his message and mission as a whole; and it also speaks of the end.

The publishers are well aware that this great life has been lived too recently for the public to gauge fully the import and the possibilities it represents; they know that many of the statements and interpretations concerning the Swami, recorded in this work, may not meet with universal acceptance; but they are firmly convinced that time will substantiate their value. It matters not in what light the present generation, by reading this life, may regard the Swami, be it as a teacher, patriot, prophet or saint; it matters not whether they accept his teachings and his ideas only partially or in their entirety; but all will have to admit that in his life there was made manifest a tremendous force for the moral and spiritual welfare and uplifting of humanity, irrespective of caste, creed, nationality or time, and that as such it commends itself for careful study and reflection.

Those who have produced this work are the Swami's outspoken followers; nay, more than that, they are his disciples and co-workers, representing as they do the Brotherhood of the Advaita Ashrama founded by the Swami himself. They have made every endeavour to give a true and comprehensive revelation of their Master. They fully realise that theirs is an enormous undertaking and responsibility. They realise, also, how difficult it is to bring the *man* into the narrow compass of a biography. This is true of every great life, but it is particularly true of Swami Vivekananda. The limitations of biographical treatment and description have been constantly before them. On the other hand, even the telling of this life is sufficiently inspiring, as of itself it affords a *Revelation*. They earnestly believe that the more the life and teachings of the Swami are made known, the more will the spiritual perspective of humanity be widened and the more will the Hindus take up the methods set forth by him for the reorganisation of their Dharma in consonance with modern needs and modern problems. They therefore make no apologies as to their understanding of him or for the method in which they have presented him. They have been actuated by the spirit of discipleship. In sending out this work into the world, they are guided by the hope that many a seeker after Truth, having a deeper knowledge of this great life, may be helped to solve the problem of existence, and having an entrée into a world of richer spiritual insight may be inspired to follow his example to travel upon that Path of Righteousness which the Swami pointed out, in the words of the Vedas, to be—*Âtmano Mokshârtham Jagaddhitâya cha*—"for the Salvation of one's own soul and for the good of the world."

THE

ADVAITA ASHRAMA
MAYAVATI, HIMALAYAS
The 4th of July, 1912

EASTERN AND WESTERN
DISCIPLES

CONTENTS

ILLUSTRATIONS

1

ANCESTRY

Coming from afar are the voices of the Silence. Rarely are they heard, save by mystics and sages. And when one of these voices becomes embodied as sound audible to mortal hearing, blessed is the time and blessed are those who hear. Formless is the Spirit and subjective is the vision thereof; dense is the illusion that hangs as the cosmic veil before Reality! How divine, therefore, must be the personality that makes objective the vision of the Spirit! How priceless the history of one who has lifted even a fringe of the veil! The illusion becomes transparent in the effulgence of such a spiritual personality. Verily, the Spirit Itself becomes revealed; and those who see are brought face to face with Reality!

To introduce the life of Swami Vivekananda is to introduce the subject of spiritual life itself. All the intellectual struggle, all the doubts, all the burning faith, all the unfolding process of spiritual illumination were revealed in him. As a man and as a Vedantist he manifested the manliness that is sanctity, and the sanctity that is manliness; he manifested the patriotism that proceeds from the vision of the Dharma and the universality that comes when God is seen in everything; and through the true insight of divine wisdom, he lived a life of both intense activity and Supreme Realization. Indeed, his life revealed throughout, the glory of the supersensuous life.

To the task of writing his life, we fervently set ourselves, conscious of unworthiness; for who can know the inner self of even the least of men, much less that of a Vivekananda! And who can sound the depths of his realization! The task is, in a way, beyond us, yet the world must know the greatness of the life that has thrilled it through its Eastern heart and Western mind.

The Datta family of Simla (or Simulia), a northern district

in Calcutta, was rich and powerful, renowned for many generations for its charity, learning and strong independent spirit. Rammohan Datta, the great-grandfather of the subject of this chronicle, was the managing clerk and associate of an English solicitor. He amassed a great fortune in the exercise of his profession, and lived happily, surrounded by a large family in a mansion in Gourmohan Mukherjee Lane. The house is still standing, but because of the subsequent straitened circumstances of the family, that part of it which had once been used as a temple has passed into the hands of strangers. The doorway that fronts on the street is massive. The covered hall, with a room on one side and seating space on the other, leads to a second doorway, beyond which are the courtyard and the living quarters. To the right are the rooms for the male members of the family. Across the courtyard and facing the doorway rises the women's quarter, two storeys high, the lower floor containing the kitchens, the upper the living apartments. From the latticed enclosure the purdah ladies in the olden days could look onto the courtyard when religious ceremonies on special occasions were being performed to the beating of drums and the blowing of conchs.

Rammohan Datta left two sons, Durgaprasad and Kaliprasad. Durgaprasad was a gifted youth, well versed in Persian and Sanskrit, and so skilled in law that his father made him a partner in his legal profession. But he had such a strong leaning towards monastic life that after the birth of a son in 1835 he renounced the world, becoming a monk at the age of twenty-five, and was not heard of by any member of the family until the twelve years of spiritual practices prescribed by monastic rule had been completed.

In the meantime his son, Vishwanath, who had been left as an infant with his mother, required bringing up. The mother, Shyamasundari, was fearless, devout and worthy in every way of accepting the great responsibility that had fallen upon her. When Vishwanath was three years old she took him on a pilgrimage to the holy city of Varanasi. As there was no railway in those days, the entire party set out by boat on the five hundred mile trip. What a thrilling adventure that excursion was—a combination of hardships and romance! New cities, new scenes, new customs, new peoples, even new languages, were encountered as the boat with its precious freight glided on. One morning, as Vishwanath was playing about on the deck, he fell into the Ganga. Without a second's hesitation Shyamasundari, though she could not swim, jumped overboard fully clothed, to save him. Fortunately, she was in time and held her tiny son up by the hand until they were both hauled aboard. So tight was her grip on him that he bore the marks of it for many years.

At last Varanasi was reached. Delighted with the holy atmosphere of the place, Shyamasundari visited all the temples, including that of Vireshwar Shiva. One day after she had bathed and was on her way to the temple of Vishwanath she slipped and fell with enough force to make her lose consciousness. A passing monk came to her assistance, picked her up and laid her on the temple steps. When she opened her eyes, what was her amazement to find that the monk was her husband! Instantly, both were overwhelmed with a tremendous emotion. But worldly attachments were not for them. She, as well as he, had renounced. In a moment he disappeared, murmuring "Oh, Maya, Maya!" And she continued her pious round.

An interesting story is told of Durgaprasad's return to his birthplace, one that reveals the essential strength and quality of the man. Quite unostentatiously he made his way into Calcutta and, instead of going to his former home, put up at the house of an old friend, begging him not to let anyone know of his return. But the friend was unable to contain the joyous news and informed Durgaprasad's relatives, who at once came and forcibly took him away with them. The monk, without a word, seated himself in a corner of the room provided for him, the door of which had been locked so that he might not escape. For three days he stayed there without giving any sign or tasting a bite of food. The relatives, fearing that he might die, finally opened the door. Later, the monk disappeared and, except for a rumour that he had become the head of a monastery in Varanasi, was never again heard of by the Datta family. When Vishwanath had come of age and was earning his own livelihood, he once went to Varanasi in search of his father, but could not trace him.

In striving to account for the exceptional genius of Swami Vivekananda, one must not lose sight of the impressive figure of his grandfather, the man who deemed the world well lost in his search for God. Vivekananda's pronounced tendency towards the monastic life was "in his blood"—as we say to explain those inexplicable outcroppings of family traits and tendencies that are at times so remarkable that, in order to satisfy ourselves, we must accept either the theory of reincarnation or that of heredity.

After his father had renounced the world, Vishwanath's uncle, Kaliprasad, became the head of the family. Since he had no income of his own, the Dattas' accumulated wealth had to be spent to maintain the large joint family. Thus they gradually became poorer and poorer. Nor was Kaliprasad a generous-hearted person, which would explain why Vishwanath's courageous mother had to bring up her son in considerable difficulty, though legally he was the inheritor of half the family property. To add to his misfortune, when Vishwanath was ten years old, his mother passed away. Thenceforth, the orphaned boy received at the hands of his uncle the kind of treatment that orphans generally receive in this world. Yet, all through his life Vishwanath reverenced and generously helped the uncle, though he was well aware that he had been cheated by him at every step.

As Vishwanath grew to manhood he became the pride of the Dattas, who, in high hopes and expectation, looked to him to carry on the family tradition of learning. Nor were they disappointed. He became proficient in Bengali, English, Persian, Arabic, Urdu and Hindi. He also studied Sanskrit in a *tol*, a traditional Sanskrit school. History was his forte, but in addition he acquired a fairly good knowledge of astrology, and later on was himself able to cast the horoscopes of some of his children. He was also a great lover of music. Like his father, Durgaprasad, he had a sweet voice, and at one time he took lessons in singing from an Ustad, a music expert. There was a time when, every Saturday and Sunday, he used to hold a musical soirée and entertain his guests with a pilau-feast.

After passing the final examination at Gourmohan Adhya's school (which afterwards came to be called The Oriental Seminary), Vishwanath at first tried his hand at business, but was not successful. He then began apprenticeship under a British attorney, Mr. Temple by name. He passed the attorney-ship examination in 1866 and set up practice in partnership with Ashutosh Dhar, under the firm name of "Dhar and Datta". After some time he settled in the legal profession independently and was enrolled as an attorney-at-law in the High Court of Calcutta.

As an attorney, Vishwanath made a considerable reputation, and his field of work spread over the whole of northern India. His practice took him to such distant places as Lucknow, Lahore, Delhi, Rajputana, Bilaspur, Raipur and so on. In those days journeys were not simple, for the railway line extended only up to Mughal Sarai, from where one had to travel to further distant places by other means. While in Lahore, he performed the worship of the Divine Mother Durga, in a portrait, and entertained many people with the consecrated food.

On the one hand, Vishwanath earned a great deal of money through his professional work of attorney; on the other hand, he spent money liberally. Surrounded by friends and relatives, attended by many servants, owning carriages and horses, he enjoyed living in affluent style. He was a connoisseur of good cooking and was himself expert in the art, preparing various kinds of dishes for his friends and relatives. He was of the opinion that growing children needed to be well fed; otherwise their brains would not develop properly; thus he spared no expense in providing good and nourishing food for his children. He thought it was not necessary to leave behind an enormous patrimony; for if money were spent in giving his sons a taste for a high standard of living, a good education, and healthy bodies, in due course they would be compelled to make suitable arrangements for themselves—and would be able to do so. But if, on the other hand, they were to inherit much wealth, they would remain indolent and would squander all the money. We may well imagine that the experience of his own rise to affluence, together with his observation of the do-nothing members of the joint family, gave him this philosophy of life. He had observed his uncle Kaliprasad, son of an affluent father, engaged in spending the inherited wealth, while earning nothing. Whereas, he himself, a poor orphan, had become wealthy through his own manly efforts.

Aside from his intellectual attainments, Vishwanath was endowed with many good qualities that endeared him to all. In whatever situation he might have been, he never lost the nobility of his nature. He was independent in spirit, generous in disposition, devoted to his friends, a protector of the needy. His keen understanding of his fellowmen resulted in deep compassion and extensive charity. At the sight of anyone in distress he would himself feel afflicted and would help him unstintingly. Many students who were distant relatives used to stay at his house and receive a good education at his expense, all of them becoming successful in life. Nor would any neighbour who sought his help ever go away disappointed. Little wonder, then, that the people of the locality used to call him *dātā* Vishwanath (charitable Vishwanath)! One of his sons later wrote of him: "Extending charity to the poor and the distressed was like a disease with him." Vishwanath used to say, "There is no need to worry about my sons. They will themselves make their own living; but these poor people have not that strength; that is why it is necessary to help them."

Indeed, Vishwanath spent his ample means without thought of the morrow, giving to all who asked. And here it was that he showed a lack of discretion, for he maintained some of his relatives in idleness—even in drunkenness. Criticized at one time by his eldest son, Naren, for bestowing charity upon such worthless persons, Vishwanath replied, "How can you understand the great misery of human life? When you realize it, you will sympathize with the poor creatures who try to forget their sorrows in the momentary oblivion obtained through intoxicants!"

Although Vishwanath's behaviour with people was warm-hearted and sweet, his temperament was basically grave. He would meet contrary or illogical arguments with reasoned answers. His outlook was broad and his knowledge vast. Being a liberal Hindu with a receptive mind, he desired to know the essential and universal teachings of all religions, and thus he carefully studied the Bible and the Dewan-i-Hafiz.

But though liberal-minded by temperament, Vishwanath was averse to indiscriminately rushing into newly started movements. He was, nevertheless, progressive in his views. In 1882 he wrote in both Bengali and Hindi a book entitled *Sishtachar Paddhati* (Canons of Good Conduct), in two parts, in which he stated that during his travels in northern and central India he had noticed that there persisted a lot of social superstitions harmful to the people. Owing to Vishwanath's premature death the second part of the book was not published. This was the second of two known books written by Vishwanath. The first was his Bengali novel *Sulochana*, published in 1880, in the name of his uncle, Gopalchandra Datta. Vishwanath also defended the remarriage of girl-widows, as championed by Ishwar-chandra Vidyasagar. When a strong agitation centring on two such marriages raged in the neighbourhood, Vishwanath and his wife supported the remarriages. In fine, though Vishwanath was like other Hindus in manners and conduct, his catholic outlook, born of his liberal education and acquired culture, saved him from a narrow orthodoxy.

This was a transitional period of India's history. The new civilization that had grown through the intermingling of Hindu and Islamic cultures was still prevalent, but European culture had also entered the stream of Indian life. The educated Indians of the time naturally came under these three influences. Vishwanath was no exception. His profession brought him into intimate contact with high-ranking Muslim families in northern India, many of whom were his clients. As a result, he used to follow, in dress and deportment, eating and drinking, manners and etiquette, traditional Hindu-Islamic ways. He also had many friends among the Europeans, and in some matters of daily life would follow the British, as was the vogue among the *élite*. Hence his conduct was marked by Hindu-Islamic culture on the one hand and European culture on the other. Both Brahmins and Muslim fakirs used to receive alms as well as sympathy from him. The Dattas were Shaktas by faith; and Vishwanath, though so liberal in outlook, did not make any change in the traditional ways of the family, with regard to the practice of religion.

Vishwanath was blessed with a wife who was his peer in every respect. At the age of sixteen, he had been married to Bhuvaneshwari Devi, the only child of Nandalal Basu of the renowned Basu family of Simla, Calcutta. Bhuvaneshwari, born in 1841, was only ten years old at the time of her marriage. Being the only child of her parents, she inherited the paternal property, which afterwards accrued to her children. As she grew older, she became expert in the management of household affairs and cheerfully shouldered the responsibility of her husband's large family. She was exceptionally intelligent and found time, even in the midst of her many chores, for sewing, music and the daily study of the *Ramayana* and the *Mahabharata*. Graceful, devoted and full of the fire of one born to regal estate, she commanded the respect and veneration of all who came in contact with her, and her judgement was followed in all matters of importance. Above all, Bhuvaneshwari Devi was deeply religious in temperament, and used daily to perform herself the worship of Shiva. She was not given to much talking. Calm resignation to the will of God in all circumstances, power, and reserve characterized this noble Hindu woman. The poor and the helpless were the special objects of her solicitude. Like Vishwanath, Bhuvaneshwari Devi had a very sweet voice and could beautifully sing the songs on Sri Krishna as heard in religious dramas. When beggars singing religious songs came to the house to beg, she could learn their songs by listening only once. She was, indeed, noted for her unusual memory and knew by heart long passages from the *Ramayana* and the *Mahabharata*. More important, she had absorbed the essence of these timeless epics, and that essence, together with the culture to which it was the key, she passed on to her children as their great heritage.

It was, then, to these two, Vishwanath and Bhuvaneshwari Devi, that the boy who was to become the greatest man of his age, whose influence was to shake the world, and who was to lay the foundation of a new order of things, was born.

BIRTH AND CHILDHOOD

Whoever knows the longing of a mother that a son should be born to her, enters into the world of Bhuvaneshwari, the wife of Vishwanath Datta. Though she had been blessed with motherhood at an early age, her first child, a son, and her second, a daughter, had died in their childhood. Her next three children were all daughters—Haramohini (also called Haramoni), Swarnamayi, and another who also died in child-hood. So, she longed for a son to carry on the family tradition, to be the link, forged out of the materials of love and suffering, between the past and the future. It has been the practice of Hindu women down the ages to place their wants and com-plaints before the household Deity, and to practise austerities while waiting to receive the blessings of the Lord. Thus, as Bhuvaneshwari went about her daily tasks, she prayed silently that her desire might be fulfilled. Now, it was customary in those days—and still is—for one in dire need, or anxious that some special event should come to pass, to make offerings and sacrifices to Shiva in Varanasi. Those who lived a long distance from that holy city could make their offerings through a relative or friend who might be resident there. Accordingly, Bhuvaneshwari Devi wrote to an old aunt of the Datta family in Varanasi, asking her to make the necessary offerings and prayers to Vireshwar Shiva that a son might be born to her. It was arranged that on Mondays the aunt would offer worship to Vireshwar Shiva, while Bhuvaneshwari would practise special austerities on those same days. It is said that by observing a vow of this sort for one year, one is blessed with a son. Thus Bhuvaneshwari was content to wait in perfect assurance that her prayers would be answered. She spent her days in practising Japa and meditation. She observed fasts and intensified her many other austerities, her whole soul given over to constant recollectedness, her heart fixed in love on the Lord Shiva. Often did her mind go to Varanasi, uniting in thought with the venerable aunt as the latter poured the sacred Ganga water on the symbol of Shiva, or worshipped Him with flowers and Mantras. One night Bhuvaneshwari had a vivid dream. She had spent the day in the shrine and, as evening deepened into night, she fell asleep. The household was hushed in silence and rest. Then in the highest heavens the hour struck—the time had come for the pious woman to receive the special grace of the Lord. In her dream she saw the Lord Shiva rouse Himself from His meditation and take the form of a male child who was to be her son. She awoke. Could this ocean of light in which she found herself bathed be but a dream? Shiva! Shiva! Thou fulfillest in various ways the prayers of Thy devotees! From the inmost soul of Bhuvaneshwari a joyous prayer welled up, for she was confident that her long months of supplication were over and that the vision was an announcement that her prayers were to be answered. Her faith was justified; for in due course a son was born to her.

The light of the world dawned for the first time upon the future Swami Vivekananda on Monday, January 12, 1863. It was the holy morning hour—33 minutes and 33 seconds after six, a few minutes before sunrise. At the time of his birth the constellation Sagittarius was rising in the east, the moon was in the constellation Virgo, the planet Jupiter was in the eleventh house, and Saturn was in the tenth from that of his birth. It was the seventh day of the new moon (Krishna Saptami) and, as chance would have it, the last day of the ninth Bengali month Poush, known as Makara Sankranti day—a great Hindu festival. The millions of men and women who were observing the festival unknowingly greeted the new-born babe with prayers and worship. They little knew that he had just been born, who was to usher in a new age of glory for his country, who was to reorganize the spiritual and national consciousness of India, and who was to become a great apostle—a St. Paul —preaching unto the world another gospel of redemption, namely the message of Vedanta. And only a few miles north

of Calcutta, in the garden of Dakshineshwar, a great seer was
waiting for the coming of this babe, who was to grow into
manhood to carry on his great work.

The household members were surprised at the features of the
new-born babe. They believed that they resembled in many ways
those of his grandfather, Durgaprasad, who had renounced
the world; and they wondered if the monk had been born
again. Thus when the time came for a name to be given to the
infant, there was much discussion. Some thought it should be
Durgaprasad. But when they asked the mother, she looked into
the depths of the child's eyes, as if she would see into his very
soul. There was a strange stillness for some moments; then she
turned to them and with much feeling said: "Let his name be
Vireshwar! So shall he be called." Those who heard this were
satisfied. They called him Bileh for short. Later he came to be
called Narendranath or Naren.

As Bhuvaneshwari would gaze unblinking at the face of the
lovely, healthy babe in her lap, her heart would fill with pride
and she would shed tears of joy; for she at last held in her arms
her much-longed-for darling of many prayers. But this was no
ordinary babe; in him was hidden a tremendous power, and
she was faced with the difficult problem of containing his
irrepressible restlessness. He was hardly three, but already
complaints against him for breach of peace were mounting.

Narendranath was a naughty child, subject to fits of restlessness during which he was beyond control. At such times he
would wear the family out. Bribes, threats, everything was
tried—nothing was of any avail. Finally, Bhuvaneshwari found
that if she poured cold water on the head of the screaming
child, chanting the name of Shiva in his ears at the same time,
or if she threatened him with "Shiva will not let you go to
Kailas if you do not behave," he would quiet down and become
his eager, joyous self again. It was after such scenes that the
mother used to say, "I prayed to Shiva for a son and He has
sent me one of His demons!" In her old age Bhuvaneshwari
once told this to a group of disciples whom her son had brought
from the West. There was laughter, and the mother smiled in

a reminiscent way. "Was he turbulent?" asked one of the Western disciples. "Well, I had to have two nurses for him constantly", she replied. But aside from these outbursts, he was a sunny-tempered, sweet and loving child, and would scamper to anyone who would take him on his lap. He was one of those children who trust all implicitly, and feel joy each moment of that period during which the world is a constant surprise.

Naren had a great fancy for wandering monks; whenever a sadhu came to the door, the boy was delighted and rushed towards him. One day a monk came and asked for alms. All that Naren had was a hand-embroidered dhoti wrapped round his waist. He was proud of his new cloth, for it was his first garment marking his passage out of infancy, but straightway he gave it to the sadhu, who tied it round his head and went away blessing the boy. When asked what had become of the cloth, the boy replied, "The sadhu begged for alms and I gave it to him." Many sadhus came to the house, knowing that they were always welcome there. Vishwanath Datta was very hospitable, and there was with him the memory of his own father, who had become a monk. But after the above incident, a close guard was kept on Naren. Whenever any sadhu put in an appearance, Naren was kept locked up until the wanderer had left. Still, that did not disconcert the child; he would throw out of the window to the caller anything the room contained, as an offering. He would have his way—and then he would dance with glee.

What a tease he was! There were his two elder sisters, whom he would tease, and tease, and tease! The sisters would be furious, and there would be a chase. He would fly to the open drain, where they could not follow. And from that refuge he would grin and make faces at them, and would further infuriate them with his triumphant challenge, "Catch me! Catch me!"

Naren had a number of pet animals, whom he loved playing with—a monkey, a goat, a peacock, pigeons, and two or three guinea-pigs. He was also especially fond of the family cow, and would join his sisters on the festive occasion when they adorned the "mother cow" with garlands, put a vermilion mark on her forehead, and bowed down to her. He would pat her with his little hands and talk to her sweetly.

Of the servants, the coachman was his special friend. The ambition of his childhood was to become a syce or groom. To him the syce with his turban, his grand livery, and his whip, which he flourished as the carriage rolled on, was a magnificent person. He was wont to make the stables his headquarters and to watch every turn of men's duties. And how he loved horses!

The first education is always at the knee of the mother, and immense was Bhuvaneshwari's eagerness to educate her son well. It was in her lap that Narendranath first became aware of the glory of the gods and goddesses, the greatness of the sages of India, and that of his ancestors, among whom was his grandfather, the sannyasi Durgaprasad. It was also from his mother that he first heard the tales of the *Ramayana* and *Mahabharata*. At the Datta home these epics were read every day at noon. One elderly lady—sometimes Bhuvaneshwari herself—would read aloud, and the ladies of the family, who for the time being had finished their duties, would sit round her. In this small congregation, turbulent Naren would be found sitting quietly throughout the reading and listening with rapt attention. There can be no doubt that the stories from the epics exerted a great influence on his mind.

Naren also learnt many things from his maternal grandmother and her mother. One of his younger brothers, Mahendranath, later wrote that their maternal grandmother's mother belonged to the Vaishnava sect and knew many teachings and anecdotes from the epics, the *Bhagavatam*, and from Vaishnava lore. The maternal grandmother told many anecdotes of the *Bhagavatam*. Indeed, most of the stories that Swami Vivekananda later told to his Western audiences he had heard in his childhood from these two elderly ladies.

Even the singers in the street contributed to young Naren's education. Fascinating are those singers. Sometimes they come in large parties—perhaps as a family in straitened circumstances; but they are always joyous. Some carry with them an image of the Divine Mother; or it may be that a father will come with his son dressed as Sri Krishna: the boy's silver anklets ringing as he dances, while the father sings in a deep basso, beating time on his tom-tom. From house to house the singers go, joyously singing of the Lord or telling sacred stories in song. Beggars though they are, in the ecstasy they arouse, they are givers, enhancing the spiritual sense of the people. Often they would come to Naren's house, and for her son's sake, his mother always made them welcome, for she realized that the more often and intimately a child is exposed to the national culture, the better and truer man does he become.

The first seed of spiritual life was sown during this period of Naren's early education. Again and again he had heard of Rama and Sita. He had listened enrapt to readings from the *Ramayana*, and had followed the long story of Rama's struggle and conquest with all the thrill of personal romantic adventure. He had, as well, observed the elder members of the family sitting in worship and meditation, and it occurred to him that he, too, should worship Rama. One day, he and a little Brahmin boy named Hari purchased a clay image of Sita-Rama, and when no one was about, they climbed the stairs that led to a room on the roof above the women's quarters. After securely closing the door, they installed the image, and sat down to meditate. Meanwhile, parents of both the boys noticed their prolonged absence, and an anxious search for them was begun. The hunt led at last to the little locked room on the roof. The searchers knocked and shouted, but there was no response. At last their strong blows smashed the latch, and the door flew open. Hari, his meditation disturbed at the first ominous signal, fled down the stairs. But Naren had not heard anything. He was seated before the flower-decked image, motionless in deep meditation. When he did not respond on being called by name, he was shaken out of his meditation; but he insisted on being left alone. So they let him remain, knowing not what to make of it all; for it seemed strange at his age.

Shortly after this, the all-knowing syce created a disturbance

in Naren's immature mind. One day when the boy was visiting
the stable, the talk drifted to marriage, which was something
intolerable to this man. With the memory of some bitter personal experience, he forcefully denounced married life, telling
his young listener of its difficulties, absurdities, and of the
terrible bondage it entails. Naren stood as if terror-struck—as
if the spectre of matrimony were already before him. And what
of his image of Sita-Rama? He had given all the love and
loyalty of his heart to these two very pure personages and
worshipped them with all devotion. He had learnt to respect
deeply their wonderful characters, had admired their loyalty
to one another. But the syce had thrown too dreadful a meaning
over the idea of marriage. And Rama and Sita were married
—that was enough!

The irreconcilable conflict between the words of the syce
and his regard for the image of Sita-Rama caused deep anguish
in his heart, which burst forth in tears. One of the golden
dreams of childhood was broken. Naren ran to the women's
quarters. The mother saw his tears and inquired what made
him sad. There was silence—then loud sobbing. "How can I
worship Sita-Rama? Was not Sita Rama's wife?" he asked.
Intuitively, Bhuvaneshwari understood the anguish of her son.
But how to console him? Then, as light bursts upon darkness,
the thought of Shiva came to her mind. She addressed her son
not as Naren but as Vireshwar, and said, "There is Shiva to
worship!" These words of the mother settled deeply in Naren's
heart.

Shortly afterwards Naren left the room and climbed the
stairs to the roof, unseen in the gloom of the evening. Overhead was the canopy of sparkling stars. He opened the door of
the room where he had installed the image of Sita-Rama. He
paused for a moment, then clasped the image and went to the
edge of the roof. The next moment, the image of Sita-Rama
was smashed on the pavement below.

On the following day Naren bought an image of Shiva with
the money given by his mother. At once he enthroned it on the
very spot from which Rama and Sita had been dethroned; and

Bhuvaneshvari Devi (1841-1911)

Vivekananda's Ancestral Home

he was soon seated before Shiva with eyes closed to all outer things, in the depth of meditation.

But what suffering this had entailed! Poorer than a man despoiled of his wealth is the mind of a child bereft of its illusion. And yet this incident not only shows the fearlessness and sincerity of the boy who gave up his cherished ideal when he found it did not match with his conception of the truth; but also makes evident the deep desire of his soul for freedom from the bondage of the senses, which he expressed later in these words: "Ever shall the soul be free! We must have freedom from bondage however sweet."

Nevertheless, his devotion to Sita-Rama was never destroyed, and the *Ramayana* had still a great fascination for him. Whenever it was read in the neighbourhood he was sure to be there, rapt in the thrilling episodes of Rama's life. Particularly was that matchless devotee, the great hero Hanuman, attractive to him. Once when the reader told of how Hanuman lived in banana-groves, Naren, who was anxious to meet the monkey chief, asked, "Shall I be able to see him if I go there?" "Yes, why not go and see!" said the reader rather sarcastically in reply to the boy's naive question. On his way back, the boy remembered a banana-grove near his home and made his way there, sat down under a banana-tree, and prayed to Hanuman to show himself. He sat and sat, but Hanuman did not come. He was bitterly disappointed. But they told him at home that Hanuman had more than likely gone forth on some urgent mission of Shri Rama, and that solaced him.

But it was Shiva, the god of renunciation, whom now he worshipped. Even in childhood he had the fancy of becoming a sannyasi. One day he was found moving about nude except for an ochre loin-cloth which he had put on in the manner of sadhus. "What is this?" asked his mother in alarm. "Why Naren, what are you up to?" "I am Shiva! Look, I am Shiva!" cried out Naren in triumph.

The elders of the household had told him, in fun, that if one meditated, one's hair would become as long and matted as the monks', and would gradually enter deep into the earth

2

like the roots of a banyan tree. So the simple child, seated in meditation, would once in a while open his eyes to see if his hair had grown long and matted. But when his expectations were not fulfilled, he ran in bewilderment to his mother, and asked, "I have meditated; but why has no matted hair grown?" His mother consoled him: "It is not grown in an hour or a day. It takes many many days, yes, many many months, before matted locks can be grown." Then the talk drifted to other things. It turned to the Shiva-image he had bought a few days before. He said that while he had sat before the image that morning, the thought of his mother's words—that he had been sent away from the real Shiva because he had been naughty —had come to him very forcibly. Reincarnation is accepted, unconsciously, as a fact by every Hindu child; so he added, "I think I have been a sadhu once. Will Shiva let me go back to Him if I am good?" The mother answered, "Yes." But her heart sank at the thought that perhaps he, like his grandfather, would renounce the world and return to Shiva. Then she banished the thought, thinking that there were many years yet before he could grow into that discrimination in which he would feel all the joys of the world as an intolerable burden, knowing joy only in the thought of God.

From this time on, the family often found little Naren playing at meditation. Though it was play, it awakened in him deep spiritual emotions. They would see him quietly sitting for a long time, absorbed. So deep was this absorption that sometimes he had to be shaken from it back to the normal condition of a child; and it grew more and more difficult sometimes to rouse him on such occasions. The boys of the neighbourhood sometimes joined him in this pastime. One evening when the crescent moon was in the sky and they had seated themselves in meditation posture in the worship-hall, one of the boys noticed a big cobra gliding along the stone-paved floor. With a shout he announced the newcomer. Others sprang to their feet in terror, but Naren remained lost in meditation. His friends shouted to him, but there was no response; so they ran to his parents, who came in haste. What horror was theirs when they saw a cobra with its hood spread, as if strangely fascinated! They were afraid to call out lest they disturb the snake and provoke it to strike. Then suddenly it glided away; and a moment later it was nowhere to be found. When his parents inquired why he did not run away, Naren said, "I knew nothing of the snake or of anything else; I was feeling inexpressible bliss."

Every night brought some strange vision to Naren. Singular was the manner in which he fell asleep. As soon as he closed his eyes, there would appear between his eyebrows a wonderful spot of light of changing hues, which would expand and burst and bathe his whole body in a flood of white radiance. As his mind became preoccupied with this phenomenon, his body would fall asleep. It was a daily occurrence which he would court by lying down on his chest; as soon as drowsiness overtook him, the light appeared. Thinking it to be a perfectly natural thing which happened to everybody, he did not mention it until long after, when he asked a schoolmate, "Do you see a light between your eyebrows at night when you go to sleep?" The friend said he did not. "I do", said Naren. "Try to remember. Do not fall into sleep as soon as you go to bed. Be on the alert for a while and you will see it."

In later years, there was to be someone who would put that very question to Naren himself: "Naren, my boy, do you see a light when you go to sleep?" This questioner was his spiritual teacher, Shri Ramakrishna; but of this later. The phenomenon remained with him until the end, although in the latter part of his life it was not so frequent or so intense. It told, assuredly, of a great spiritual past in which the soul had learnt so well to sink itself deep in meditation that the meditative state had become spontaneous with him.

At the age of six, Naren went to the Pathshala, the traditional-type Indian school. He was in a brand-new dhoti. He carried a mat under his arm, for each child had to bring his own to sit on; and from his waist dangled a little reed-pen held fast by a long string. He felt himself very superior, as do all boys on their first day of school.

Indeed, that day was an important one for him. Early in the morning, the priest of the family had called him for the ceremony that is performed when a boy first goes to school. All the family were present. After the recitation of a few prayers, and the dedication of the lad to Saraswati, the presiding goddess of learning, the priest took Naren's right hand, putting into it a kind of red-tinged writing chalk called Ramkhadi, and then, guiding it, wrote on the ground the Bengali alphabet saying, "This is *Ka*, this is *Kha*"; and Naren repeated after him, "This is *Ka*, this is *Kha*."

But schools are places where one is apt to meet with all sorts of comrades, and within a few days Naren had acquired a vocabulary which quite upset his family's sense of propriety. Never again, determined all the household, should he go to school. Instead, a private tutor was engaged, who conducted classes in the family worship-hall for Naren and other boys— some of whom were his cousins, and others the sons of his father's friends.

Soon Naren was noticed for his exceptional intelligence. He learned to read and write while other boys were wrestling with the alphabet. His memory was prodigious. He had a peculiar way of his own of closing his eyes and sitting motionless or lying down when attending the classes. The private tutor who had been engaged did not understand this peculiarity in his charge at first, and at last he became quite provoked. He caught hold of his pupil, shaking him rudely, to rouse him from his seeming sleepiness. Naren opened his eyes in wounded surprise. He listened to the angry words of the tutor. Then, in self-defence, he recited word-for-word the whole text that had been read in the preceding hour. Ever afterwards the tutor regarded this pupil with admiration; for in his long acquaintance with boys, never had he found such a remarkable memory.

Though Naren's schooling started in this way, his learning at his mother's knee did not stop. As to book-learning, he learned from his mother the Bengali alphabet and the *First Book of English* by Pyaricharan Sarkar. It was from his mother again that he learned how to hold aloft his moral standards, even while struggling in the eddies of the world, and how to take refuge at the feet of God, knowing Him to be the best support in life.

The mother also taught Naren; "Remain pure all your life; guard your own honour and never transgress the honour of others. Be very tranquil, but when necessary, harden your heart." Throughout his life Narendranath loved his mother with all his heart and remembered her precepts. He used to say, "He who cannot literally worship his mother can never become great." On many occasions he proudly declared, "I am indebted to my mother for the efflorescence of my knowledge."

Other members of the household also contributed to Naren's education. At night he slept under the protecting presence of an old relative—Nrisimha Datta, the father of Ramachandra Datta, who was to become a lay devotee of Shri Ramakrishna. This man, who was very learned in Sanskrit lore, thought that the best way of training a youth in mind and character was to get him to memorize difficult intellectual subjects. At night, therefore, he taught the boy the aphorisms of the Sanskrit grammar *Mugdhabodha*, the genealogy of his family, hymns to gods and goddesses, as well as passages of great length from the *Ramayana* and *Mahabharata*. Thus in a year's time Naren had acquired considerable grounding in Sanskrit, and certainly this training in early boyhood constituted one of the formative elements in that passion for Sanskrit learning which he possessed in later years.

On a certain occasion a party of wandering singers, who earned their livelihood by chanting the *Ramayana*, came to Naren's house. They made a number of mistakes in reciting the text. Naren stopped them and pointed out their errors, greatly surprising and pleasing them.

Naren's father also played a significant part in his son's education. It was he who insisted that the boy should study music, for he looked upon it as a source of much innocent joy. Perhaps the deep attraction of his family for music helped turn Narendranath into an accomplished singer.

In his attitude towards his children Vishwanath showed considerable wisdom. He believed in inspiring them to develop self-respect and politeness. If any of them misbehaved, he did not reprimand him, but in order to produce the required reform, exposed him to the ridicule of his friends. To cite an instance: One day Naren behaved very rudely to his mother. The father, instead of scolding the boy, wrote on the door of the room where Naren received his friends: Naren Babu said these words today to his mother—followed by the words actually said. Every time Naren or his friends entered that room they were confronted with this statement. It was not long before Naren showed signs of repentance.

Even at an early age Naren asserted himself as leader among his fellows. Whenever occasion offered, he put himself at their head. One such occasion came on the Makara Sankranti day, the last day of Poush (the Bengali month corresponding to December-January), and a holiday when boys worship Mother Ganga, and everyone thinks it most auspicious to bathe in the sacred waters. Naren had insisted that this festival should be celebrated, and obtained permission from his father, together with the necessary expenses. Then he gathered together a group of boys, and the father instructed the private tutor, or the Guru Mahashaya, as he was called, to teach them songs to Mother Ganga. On the appointed day the procession of little fellows headed by Naren set out from the Datta home. Marching with flying flags and garlands of flowers in their hands, they went through the streets to the Ganga, singing all the while. When they reached the river, they burst into that song which all Hindu children in Bengal know so well—"Worship the Mother Ganga"—and they then threw their garlands upon the flowing waters. That evening they again repaired to the river, and after improvising toy boats out of sheaths of banana stems, they fastened at their prows the lights of reverence. What a pretty sight! All along the river floated these toy boats. Naren's party was only one of many; for miles the Mother Ganga's waters were lighted by the love of the children.

Acknowledged as leader wherever he went in the course of

his life, peerless among his contemporaries, in early manhood the prince of the disciples who sat at the feet of his Master, unmatched in intellect, East or West, Naren was also king among his playmates. He was the all-in-all of their world. "I am the Samrat, the King of kings", Naren would shout as he scampered up the stairs that led from the ground floor of the courtyard to the veranda of the Puja-hall, and would sit himself down as the lord of men. Pointing to the steps below, he would tell two of his fellows to stand before him as prime minister and commander-in-chief. Lower on the stairs he bade five others stand as tributary princes. To his courtiers he gave the privilege of sitting one step lower than the princes. He would then formally open his durbar. One by one the princes, the higher officials of state and the courtiers would prostrate themselves in proper oriental fashion before the Imperial Presence, addressing him as Son of Solar Splendours, the Lord of Lands and Seas, and the Protector of Dharma. The ceremony over, the king would ask about the welfare of his realm and listen to the grievances of his subjects. A criminal was perhaps then brought before him, and the grave accusations against him being proved, His Majesty would exclaim, "Off with his head! Ho, guards!" and then ten guards would spring upon the offender. So went Naren's favourite game of "King and the Court", in which he administered justice with royal dignity and put down the slightest insubordination by a disapproving frown.

There used to come to Naren's house many of his father's clients. They would sit together chatting until their turn for consultation came. They were of various castes; there was even a Mohammedan, with whom Naren was particularly friendly, and each was provided with his own hookah. Caste was a mystery to the boy. Why should not a member of one caste eat with a member of another or smoke his hookah? What would happen if one did? Would the roof fall in on him? Would he suddenly die? He decided to see for himself. Boldly he went round the hookahs and took a whiff from each and every one. No, he was not dead! Just then his father entered. "What are you doing, my boy?" he questioned. "Oh, father! why, I was trying to see what would happen if I broke caste! Nothing has happened!" The father laughed heartily and with a knowing look on his face walked into his private study.

Naren's boyish exuberance expressed itself in all sorts of ways, naughty and otherwise. One day while romping with his comrades, he fell from the veranda of the worship-hall, striking his head against a stone. To his death he carried the scar of this on his forehead just above his right eye. The Sage who was his teacher in his later life once said: "Had Naren's powers not been checked by this accident, he would have shattered the world!" As it was, he raised the world.

We have already mentioned that Naren was the leader among his fellows. Indeed, leadership was innate in him, and very early in life he demonstrated the truth that leadership means self-sacrifice. One day when he was about six years old, he went with a younger relative to a Charhak fair at which Lord Shiva is worshipped. He purchased some doll-images of Shiva at the fair, and as the two boys were returning home in the dusk, they became slightly separated in the crowd. At that moment a carriage came dashing along. Naren, who thought his companion was immediately behind him, turned at the noise and to his horror saw that it was a question of life or death for the little lad, who stood terrified in the middle of the road about to be run over. Putting his dolls underneath his left arm Naren rushed to the lad's help, heedless of his own safety, and grabbing him with his right hand, pulled him almost from under the horses' hoofs. Those close by were wonderstruck. The danger had appeared so suddenly that there was little chance for another to have run to the small boy's assistance. Some patted Naren on the back, while others blessed him; and when, on his return home, his mother heard the story, she wept for happiness and said, "Always be a man, my son!"

There were those who saw marks of Naren's future greatness even at this time. In the year 1869, Kaliprasad, Naren's grand-uncle and once the head of the Datta house, lay on his death-bed. When he found that he was to live but a few hours more, he called in his whole family, and then asked any one of the children to read to him passages from the *Mahabharata*, so that his soul could pass on to another sphere with the thoughts contained in that great epic. All except Naren and one of his sisters felt too shy to read aloud to the dying elder. So Naren took up the heavy volume and placing it on his lap, turned page after page, while his voice, loud and clear, rang with the glories of the heroes and the Lord. As he was reading that particular portion where Garuda flew off with his mother Vinata on his shoulders, which symbolizes the soul's rising on the wings of knowledge to blessedness, the breathing of Kaliprasad became slower and slower. Then he spoke in an undertone—yet with all the burning certainty of vision that the dying sometimes show—"Child, you have a great future before you." Having uttered these words his soul passed out into higher spheres.

There is a saying, morning shows the day. Likewise by observing the sum total of qualities manifested in a child one can have a preview of the life that is yet to be. About Naren one can say that the morning of his life was auspicious indeed! With his well-shaped graceful form, fair complexion, large bright eyes, and face bearing the impress of budding genius, he naturally attracted everyone's love. His mind filled with a hundred soaring visions, heart soaked in affection, intellect razor-sharp, courage boundless, inventive genius astounding, working capacity unreckoned, and enthusiasm irrepressible —Naren was peerless even from childhood. Above all was his spontaneous inclination towards God. From his very childhood he was an adept in meditation, and had delight in worship, prayer, and search for God. When we have deeply studied his life, we shall find ourselves having to admit that the foregoing account of Narendranath is not only not exaggerated, but is rather a pale representation of the truth.

Those who are to change the thought of the world as did Plato and Aristotle, or alter its destinies as did Alexander and Caesar, are from their childhood conscious of their power; they are instinctively aware of the greatness which is to come.

Narendranath, too, felt the spirit of greatness within him; he saw things to which others of his age were blind, and he felt already, in the feeble and yet certain way of a child, the struggle which was to be his in giving expression to his vision.

EARLY EDUCATION AND GLIMPSES
OF SPIRITUALITY

In 1871, when Narendranath was eight years old, he entered the ninth class (equivalent to the present primary class two), in the English Department of Pandit Ishwarchandra Vidyasagar's Metropolitan Institution, then situated on Sukia Street. Vidyasagar's school was famous at the time, and so it was that boys of Naren's family used to be students there. During the first days of Naren's attendance at the Metropolitan Institution his father dressed him in trousers, but every day they got torn owing to his high spirits. He was unusual in his restlessness. At school he never really managed to sit at his desk. It was a sort of compromise between sitting and standing with frequent change of position. When he played, he played furiously. Among the games were marbles, jumping, running, boxing and cricket, at the last of which he had been proficient from his early youth. It was left to him to arrange the play-programme for the following day. Quarrels often arose as they do among boys; and it was to Naren that the others came for settlement. He disliked quarrelling; above all, he could not bear to witness a physical fight. If such a climax occurred he would rush between the contending parties, often at the risk of blows from both sides; but he was master of such situations, for he had learnt boxing even at this early age. He was the foremost boy amongst them all, in all things. His exceptional intelligence was at once recognized by both teachers and classmates. He was the first not only in play but in studies as well.

To those whom he loved among his fellows, he was kindness itself. Should anyone become hurt or ill in a party he had taken for a boyish excursion, he would give up the prospect of fun to attend on him. For instance, one day he went with twenty or more boys to see the Calcutta Fort. One of the party complained of pain, while others joined in a laugh at the sick boy's expense, and went ahead. Left alone, the boy sat down on the ground, his pain growing worse. Naren had gone with the party, but suddenly he turned and said, "It may be that he is seriously ill. You boys run on. One of us must go back to him; so I will go." He retraced his steps just in time. The boy had been overtaken with fever. Naren assisted him, half carrying him to a carriage nearby, and took him home.

Around this time he also saved a child and its mother from being run over by a carriage and seriously injured. Hastily snatching the child with one hand, he pulled the mother out of danger with the other.

It was this spirit of self-sacrifice in Naren that made him the idol of his fellows, and so deep was the impression he made upon most of them that later on in their college days they followed his lead in matters of grave importance.

The two traits, restlessness and kindness, were among the prevailing characteristics of Naren's family and of Naren himself. Naren's restlessness, so-called, was the visible expression, it seems, of an immense dynamism, an immense energy and aspiration. It took various forms: high spirits, adventurousness, ardour, thirst for knowledge and travel, and dissatisfaction with monotony and stagnation. It was this dynamism that later took him round India, and then round the world. It was this dynamism again that created in him a spiritual restlessness, the same restlessness that is at the back of the Hindu monk's struggle for complete liberation, and is only satisfied by the realization of the Infinite. Kindness also, as we have seen and shall see, was a quality of Naren's throughout his life.

Soon after his entrance into the Metropolitan Institution Naren was told he would have to learn the English language. But he was unwilling to do so. It was a foreign language, he said, so why should one learn it? Why should one not first of all become master of one's own tongue? He refused flatly and went home crying to his father and mother. But they, too, said it was necessary, and again he refused. Then his old relative,

Nrisimha Datta, of whom Naren was especially fond, heard of his obstinacy. He took Naren aside and talked quietly to him, at first to no purpose. Only after several months did he follow his advice and start to study English. But once started, he studied it with an earnestness that surprised everyone; and later became master of the language. And this was indeed imperative. His words in English have since become a new gospel. Through English he gave voice to his mission and expression to that which he himself was—the centre of a spiritual world impulse.

Many are the stories told of Narendranath's school-days, revealing him as full of force and vitality, fond of play and boyish delights. Like other lads he played pranks and called his friends by nicknames of his own devising, picking some from story books and fables, or various other sources.

Naren was still the devout admirer of mendicant monks. To see one was a moment of pleasure for him. If the meeting took place at his home, he would anticipate and fulfil the sadhu's needs as far as he could. And the monks always blessed him, for his eyes spoke volumes, and it is in the eyes that the monks see the soul reflected. The longing to be a monk himself was always in Naren. He often thought of the time when he would be free to follow that life. In his boyish fervour he would tell his friends what he would do, where he would go, and so on, enthusing his companions also. Often would he ask a newcomer to the Metropolitan Institution if there was an ancestor in the family, more particularly a grandfather, who had adopted the sannyasi's life. If the reply was positive, Naren would regard the new lad with special favour. Sometimes the boys would get together and in play try, by reading one another's palms, to foretell the future. Naren was the chief palmist of them all. He told them that he would be a monk: there was no mistake about it. "See!" he would say triumphantly, "there is the sure sign of a sannyasi." And he would point out certain lines on his hand which an old man had once told him were characteristic of the tendency to monkhood. Others were also eager to learn their fate in this respect. All of them wanted to be sannyasis because Naren wanted to be one. But as fate would have it, they were to be disappointed.

Even at this early age Naren evinced impatience with superstition and fear, no matter how hallowed by popular tradition. As he himself expressed it to a disciple in later years, "From my boyhood I have been a dare-devil; otherwise could I have attempted to make a tour round the world, almost without a penny in my pocket?" An incident that occurred around this time is illustrative of his "dare-devilry", which is to say, courage and independence of thought and action. To the house of a certain friend he would often have recourse as to a refuge from the monotonous moments that come even to boys. There was in their compound a favourite tree from which he loved to dangle head down. It was a Champaka (*Michelia Champaca*) tree, the flowers of which are said to be liked by Shiva, and which Hindu boys would go a long way to collect. It was the flowers of this tree that Naren also loved. One day as he was swinging from the tree, the old and nearly-blind grandfather of the house recognized his voice, which he knew and loved so well. The old man was afraid that the boy might fall, and that he himself might lose his Champaka flowers; he called Naren down and told him that he must not climb the tree again. Naren asked the reason. The old man answered, "Because a Brahmadaitya [a ghost of a Brahmin] lives in that tree, and at night he goes about dressed all in white, and he is terrible to look at." This was news to Naren, who wanted to know what else this ghost could do besides wander about. The old man rejoined, "And he breaks the necks of those who climb the tree."

Naren said nothing, and the old man went away smiling to himself in triumph. As soon as he had gone some distance Naren climbed the tree again just to spite the ghost of the Brahmin. His friend remonstrated, "The Brahmadaitya is sure to catch you and break your neck." Naren laughed heartily, and said, "What a silly fellow you are! Don't believe everything just because someone tells you! Why, my neck would have been broken long ago, if the old grandfather's story were true."

Only a boyish lark it was, true, but significant when viewed in the light of later developments: a forecast of the time when, as Swami Vivekananda, he was to say to large audiences, "Do not believe a thing because you read it in a book! Do not believe a thing because another has said it is so! Find out the truth for yourself! That is realization!"

The father of this friend of Naren's loved him very much and had great hopes for his future. On one occasion, finding him dangling from the "forbidden" tree, he called him into the house and asked, "Do you play all day, going from one house to another? Do you never read?" Naren answered, "Sir, I both read and play." Then he was put to the test. He was examined in Geography and Mathematics, and was made to recite poems. To the surprise of the strenuous examiner, he acquitted himself well. Then the questioner blessed him and asked, "Who is there to guide you, my son? Your father is in Lahore." Naren assured his friend's father that he read in the morning and that his mother guided him. The man, though he said little for fear of flattering Naren, saw the greatness of the boy's intellect at once. He watched Naren's career with keen interest and saw fulfilled what he had predicted when he gave his blessings: "My boy, you will be a man among men. I give you my blessings."

Naren could indeed both read and play. He manifested remarkable alacrity in preparing his daily lessons, one hour being sufficient for him to master them. He had a prodigious memory; he could read through a book very fast and in no time have it memorized. Small wonder, then, that he could be the foremost student in his class at school, and still have long hours left for fun! Only during two or three months before examinations did he apply himself strenuously to his studies. He showed proficiency in English, History, and Sanskrit, but had great distaste for Mathematics, and in this he was like his father who was wont to speak of Mathematics as "grocer's craft".

Although Naren generally kept good health, he suffered from chronic dyspepsia for some years during this time at the Metropolitan Institution. He became very thin, and felt a strong craving for certain foods that were specially harmful to him. This, however, in no way depressed his nature—neither his studies nor his vitality suffered. He was as energetic as ever, and as merry, as kind and as courageous.

Not all of Naren's recreation involved strenuous physical activity. In childhood he had a fine hand for drawing pictures. He also had a melodious voice and could pick up a song by listening to it once at a theatrical performance.

With his class fellows Naren mingled intimately. Whenever there was leisure at school he either played with them, told stories, sang songs, or made them laugh with his expert mimicry. Often he teased his friends or played pranks on them, but he never harmed anyone, and through it all he would draw everyone to him, making them his own. In five minutes he could win anyone over. He could outwit anyone in talk, and none could outwit him. He had wonderful presence of mind and seemingly endless capacity to extemporize. And never would Naren be morose. He knew very well how to make others laugh, and he kept all his class-mates charmed.

In him there was immense pent-up strength. In London, many years later, Swami Vivekananda told Mr. E. T. Sturdy (one of his English disciples): Well, Sturdy, in my childhood I used to observe an inexhaustible force arising in me, overflowing my body, as it were. I used to become restless and could not keep quiet. This was why I used to fidget all the time. If I had nothing to read, I would turn to making mischief. If I had been made to sit quietly for three or four days, I would have either become seriously ill or have gone mad. My insides would all the time vibrate, as it were, and make me restless to do something.

But even in the midst of extreme restlessness, he was occasionally noticed to have been overwhelmed by some inspiration, as though his mind had travelled far away from his body. He then appeared to be gazing at something in the air, and his face would turn so grave that, to the dismay of those watching him, all his laughter and fun would vanish. Sometimes, after keeping quiet for a while, he would speak out: "I shall become a king. I shall do this. I shall do that." Or he would go on prattling: "This has to be done that way. This will be done this time." It would seem that his words at those times had no relation to anything he had been saying or doing just before. Sometimes he would burst into loud soliloquy. At these times he would become a different boy, as it were. When that mood would pass, he would return to normal and stand blinking and wrinkling his face in embarrassment; and then he would become the same naughty Bileh again. Observing him behave like this now and then, his playmates, either out of affection or mockingly, would often call him "Pagla Bileh (crazy Bileh)". "Bileh is a very good boy", they would say; "he is great in laughter, fun and merry-making, but he is a bit crazy. Sometimes there is no knowing what he will say."

There were many trying experiences in Naren's boyhood, but none more so than that which he had one morning in the class-room. The incident shows the boy's innate fortitude and the difficulty of intimidating him. One of the teachers of the Institution was a man of very ugly temper and given to beating the boys severely when he thought that discipline was needed. One day, as he was severely castigating a boy, Naren began to laugh from sheer nervousness, so revolted was he by the exhibition of brutality. The teacher now turned his wrath on Naren, raining blows on him, and demanded that he promise never to laugh at him again. When Naren refused, the teacher not only resumed the beating, but seized him by the ears as well, even going as far as lifting the boy up from the bench by them and damaging one ear, so that it bled profusely. Still Naren refused to promise. Bursting into tears of rage, he cried out, "Do not pull my ears. Who are you to beat me? Take care not to touch me again."

Luckily, at this moment Pandit Ishwarchandra Vidyasagar came in. Naren, weeping bitterly, told him what had happened; then, taking his books, he declared that he was leaving the school for good. Vidyasagar took him to his office and consoled him. Later, an investigation was made of the disciplinary

3

measures obtaining in the school and steps were taken to prevent any repetition of such incidents. When Naren's mother, in whom he always confided, heard of it, she was greatly incensed. She begged the boy not to return to the school; but he went the following day as though nothing had happened. For a long time his ear did not heal.

Even as a boy Naren was strong-minded and fearless. Before the incident just mentioned, he had been assaulted by another teacher who thought he had made a mistake in geography. Naren insisted that he was in the right. Angered, the teacher ordered him to stretch out his hand. Naren did so and was struck on his palm time and again. He did not murmur. Shortly after, the teacher saw that it was he himself who had been in error. He apologized to the boy, and thenceforth held him in respect.

On this occasion as well Naren went to his mother, who consoled him and said, "If you are right, my boy, what does it matter? It may be unjust and unpleasant, but do what you think right, come what may." Many times he suffered, many times he was misunderstood even by those nearest and dearest to him when he adopted a course which to them seemed strange, but which to him was inevitable because, in his opinion, it was right. The maxim he had learned, and which he followed always in life was, "Stick to your guns, dead or alive!"

Since Naren hated monotony, every day he had to invent new pastimes. But he was so pure, and the training he had received in the family was so excellent, that he never took a false step. Truthfulness was the very backbone of his life, and his fun was always innocent. Further, as he grew older, his liking for meditation grew ever more intense and serious. He was beginning to meditate during the night and soon was blessed with some wonderful visions—and this even as his daytime activities and restlessness continued unabated.

For fun, Naren organized an amateur theatrical party, and presented plays in the worship-hall of his home. But after a few performances his uncle became annoyed and broke up the stage.

Next, Naren started a gymnasium in the courtyard of the house, where his friends used to do regular physical exercise. This venture flourished for some time, until one of his cousins broke his arm. Again the uncle showed lack of sympathy, this time destroying the equipment of the gymnasium. Thereupon Naren, along with his friends, joined the gymnasium of a neighbour, Shri Navagopal Mitra. Finding this suitable place, which was situated on Cornwallis Street, Naren applied himself earnestly to physical culture, and gradually attained proficiency in lathi-play (playing with long sticks), fencing, rowing, swimming, wrestling and other sports. Once, at a physical training show and handicrafts fair, he carried off first prize for boxing— a handsome silver butterfly. At the same fair one of his sisters won the first prize for needlework on velvet.

Naren had special enthusiasm for lathi-play. In this sport he took lessons from a number of Mohammedan experts, and acquired considerable mastery. When ten years old and a student of the Metropolitan Institution, he was present at a display of gymnastics. After some time, when lathi-play was going on and interest was sagging, Naren suddenly challenged anyone to cross lathis with him. The strongest of the participants took up his challenge and soon the lathis of the two were clashing. Naren's opponent was an older and stronger person, and so the outcome of the bout seemed to be a foregone conclusion. Yet, such was Naren's skill and courage that he won the enthusiastic applause of the audience. Unmindful of it, and deftly manoeuvring himself, Naren all on a sudden gave such a resounding blow that his opponent's staff broke in two and fell on the ground, signifying total defeat. Naren had graduated, so to say, in his training. He won the day, and there was no end to the rejoicing of the spectators.

Ever averse to passivity, Narendranath always led an active life. When he was not busy at the gymnasium, he would show magic-lantern pictures at home. Or he would go out in the evening on his pony, which his father had bought for him. Riding was one of his favourite pastimes, and gradually he mastered the art.

Besides his fondness for animals noted earlier, Naren also kept pigeons, white mice with tiny bells, and parrots. He also used to amuse himself in making toy gas-works and aerated waters, which had been newly introduced in Calcutta at that time. He even interested himself in manufacturing toy railways and all sorts of machinery. About the gas-works his younger brother writes as follows:

With old zinc tubes, earthen cooking-pots and straw he made his gas-works in the outer courtyard of the house. The straw when lighted gave out a peculiar smoke, but to his mind it was a miniature gas-works, which lighted the whole city of Calcutta. It was amusing to see his gas-works and himself as he stood with arms akimbo, gravely looking at his contrivance as the smoke issued forth. Sometimes, however, he would express disapproval by turning up his nose—a family peculiarity—and impatiently ordering his playmates to put more fuel on the fire, or to blow more fiercely whenever the smoke rose up too sluggishly.

At this time he conceived the idea of learning to cook. He induced his playmates to subscribe towards the project, he himself bearing the greater part of the expense. He was the chief cook and the others were his assistants. He cooked different sorts of Khichuri, meat curries and other good things. Although he was inclined to use too much chilli (cayenne-pepper), his cooking was excellent, and the group of gastronomists remained together for a long time, enjoying their art thoroughly.

With every family in the locality, of whatever caste or means, Naren established some sort of relationship, and they looked on him as their own. Did any boy nearby suffer bereavement, Naren would be there to console him. At other times he kept everybody amused, elders included, with his ready wit and merrymaking. His handsome appearance, his musical voice, his jolly temperament, his good taste and manners, endeared him to all. He was a sort of life-giving spirit to everyone of the locality.

Naturally, Naren was also greatly loved by his brothers and sisters, whom he in turn loved dearly. At night, before going to bed, they would pester him for stories. The stories which he had heard from his mother, maternal grandmother, and her mother, had become his own. And by this time he himself had become a fine story-teller and actor.

His little brothers and sister would also importune Naren for a hand-shadow show, and he would readily oblige. An earthen lamp on a brass stand used to be the light in their bedroom. By interlocking his thumbs and moving the other fingers against the light he would show on the wall a flying bat, a rider on a galloping horse, and the figures of deities like Durga, Kartika, Saraswati, Lakshmi and Ganesha. While Naren's talents for shadowgraphing were unquestionably bright, the little onlookers had also to use their imagination!

Often Naren took his friends to various interesting places in Calcutta. Sometimes it was a garden, another time the Ochterlony Monument, or again the Museum. One day, he set out with a party by way of the Ganga for the Nawab's Zoological Gardens at Metiabruz, a suburb of Calcutta. When they were returning, one of the boys became sick and vomited in the boat. The boatmen were annoyed and insisted that they should immediately clean up the boat. They refused to do so, offering instead to pay double. The offer was rejected. On reaching the ghat, the men would not allow the boys to land and threatened them. While the boatmen were abusing the boys, Naren jumped ashore and asked two British soldiers walking near by for help. In broken English he told his tale of woe. Slipping his small hands into theirs, he led them to the scene. The soldiers understood the situation, and ordered the boatmen to release the boys. Terrified at the sight of the soldiers, the boatmen set the boys free without a word. Fascinated with Naren, the soldiers invited him to go with them to the theatre. But he declined and took leave after thanking them for their kindness.

Another delightful story is told of him, when he was about eleven years old. A British man-of-war, the *Syrapis*, visited the Port of Calcutta when the Emperor Edward VII came to India as the Prince of Wales. Naren's friends urged him to try and secure a pass for them all to see the ship. For this it was necessary to see an English official. When Naren made his appearance, application in hand, the attendant at the door, thinking him too young, refused him entry. As Naren stood aside wondering what to do, he noticed that applicants who passed the porter proceeded to a room on the first floor. Realizing that that must be the room where permits were issued, he set about to find another entrance. In the rear was a staircase. Stealthily he made his way to the top, pushed aside a curtain, and found himself in the room. He took his place in the line and when his turn came the application was signed without question. As he passed the door-keeper on his way out, the latter said in amazement, "How did you get in?" "Oh, I am a magician", Naren answered.

As we have seen earlier, Naren and his friends were members of the gymnasium of Shri Navagopal Mitra, who had practically left its management in their hands. One day while they were trying to set up a very heavy trapeze, a crowd gathered to watch. Amongst them was an English sailor, whom Naren asked to help. But as the obliging sailor was lifting the trapeze to help the boys, it fell and knocked him unconscious. Nearly everyone but Naren and one or two of his friends disappeared from the scene, thinking the sailor had been killed. Immediately Naren tore a piece off his dhoti, bandaged the wound, sprinkled the sailor's face with water, and fanned him gently. When the sailor regained consciousness, Naren and his friends lifted him up and took him to a neighbouring schoolhouse. A doctor was sent for, and Navagopal Mitra was informed. After a week's nursing the sailor recovered, and Naren presented him with a modest purse, which he had collected from his friends.

Another occasion which revealed the boy as the man in the making was when Naren, about fourteen years of age, saved a theatrical performance from disruption. The drama was progressing nicely, when suddenly, right in the midst of the performance, a bailiff came onto the stage with a warrant to arrest one of the leading actors on some charge. He advanced to the actor, saying, "I arrest you in the name of the law!" That very moment a voice called out, "Get off the stage! Wait

until the end of the performance! What do you mean by disturbing the audience like this?" It was a shrill voice with an
unmistakable tone of command in it—and it was the voice of
Naren. Immediately a score of voices burst out in support:
"Get off the stage! Get off the stage!" And the bailiff retreated
in bewilderment. Those about Naren patted him on the back
saying, "Well done! Well done! We should not have had our
money's worth but for you."

Naren's bold, generous, compassionate nature shines out
from these and similar incidents, together with his presence of
mind, incredible energy, and love of fun and adventure—it
was such qualities as these that made him the leader of his
companions.

As Naren grew older a definite change in his temperament
was noticeable. He began to show a preference for intellectual
pursuits, to study books and newspapers, and to attend public
lectures regularly. He was able to repeat the substance of what
he had read or heard to his friends with such original criticism
that they were astonished, and he developed a power of
argumentation which none could withstand.

One day, hearing a friend singing like a professional, Naren
said, "Mere tune and keeping time are not all of music. It must
express an idea. Can anyone appreciate a song sung in a
drawling manner? The idea underlying the song must arouse
the feeling of the singer, the words should be articulated
distinctly, and proper attention be given to tune and timing.
The song that does not awaken a corresponding idea in the
mind of the singer is not music at all."

We have already seen that Naren's father used to travel to
various places in central and northern India in connection
with his professional work. In 1877, when Naren was fourteen
years old and a student of the third class (equivalent to the
present class eight), his father went to Raipur in the Central
Provinces. Knowing that he would have to live there for quite
a long time, his father, Vishwanath, had his family brought
there shortly afterwards. The place was not then connected by
railway; so one had to travel by bullock-cart for more than a

fortnight through dense forests full of beasts of prey. Naren was charged with taking the family there. Although he had to suffer many hardships, he did not feel them at all on account of the wonderful beauty of these forest regions of central India. His heart was charmed with the boundless power and endless love of Him who had adorned the earth with such incomparable robes and ornaments. He said later:

What I saw and felt when going through the forest has for ever remained firmly imprinted in my memory, particularly a certain event of one day. We had to travel by the foot of the Vindhya mountains that day. The peaks of the ranges on both sides of the road rose very high in the sky; various kinds of trees and creepers bending under the weight of fruits and flowers produced wonderful beauty on the mountainsides. Birds of various colours, flying from tree to tree, filled the quarters with sweet notes. I saw all these and felt an extraordinary peace in my mind. The slow-moving bullock-carts arrived at a place where two mountain peaks, coming forward as though in love, locked themselves in an embrace over the narrow forest path. Observing carefully below the meeting-points I saw that there was a very big cleft from the crest to the foot of the mountain on one side of the path; and filling that cleft, there was hanging in it an enormous honeycomb, the result of the bees' labour for ages. Filled with wonder, as I was pondering over the beginning and the end of that kingdom of bees, my mind became so much absorbed in the thought of the infinite power of God, the Controller of the three worlds, that I completely lost my consciousness of the external world for some time. I do not remember how long I was lying in the bullock-cart in that condition. When I regained normal consciousness, I found that we had crossed that place and come far away. As I was alone in the cart, no one could know anything about it.

This was perhaps the first time that, with the help of a strong power of imagination, Naren entered the region of deep meditation and was completely merged in it.

Another characteristic of his mind was described by him in these words:

From my very boyhood [Naren, as Swami Vivekananda, said later], whenever I came in contact with a particular object, man or place, it would sometimes appear to me as if I had been acquainted with it beforehand. But all my efforts to recollect were unsuccessful, and yet the impression persisted. I will give you an instance: One day I was discussing various topics with my friends at a particular place. Suddenly something was said, which at once reminded me that in some time past in this very house I had talked with these friends on that very subject and that the discussion had even taken the same turn. Later on I thought that it might be due to the law of transmigration. But soon I decided that such definite conclusions on the subject were not reasonable. Now I believe that before I was born I must have had visions somehow, of those subjects and people with whom I would have to come in contact in my present birth. Such memories have come every now and then throughout my life.

In those days there was no school in Raipur. This gave Naren the time and opportunity to become very intimate with his father—a great privilege, for his father had a noble mind. Vishwanath attracted the intellect of his son. He would hold long conversations with him upon topics that demanded depth, precision and soundness of thought. He gave the boy free intellectual rein, believing that education consists in stimulating, and not in superimposing ideas. To his father Naren owed his capacity for grasping the essentials of things, of seeing truth from the widest and the most synthetic standpoint, and of discovering and holding to the real issue under discussion.

Many noted scholars used to visit Vishwanath at Raipur. The boy would listen to their discussions, and occasionally join them, introducing his personal views. Sometimes the elders, astonished at his cleverness, would treat him on an equal footing —a sight which gladdened his father's heart. With one friend of his father, a great authority on Bengali literature, Naren joined in conversation and took the man by storm, quoting verse after verse and paragraph after paragraph from standard works. So impressed was the man that he said, "My lad, we shall hear of you some day." And the prediction has come true, for Narendranath, as Swami Vivekananda, became a significant writer in the Bengali language. His English writings have been praised as well, both in the East and in the West.

Even in his youth, Naren sought, nay demanded, intellectual equality with and recognition from everyone. So ambitious
was he in this respect that if his mental powers were not given
recognition, he would fly into a rage, not sparing even his
father's friends; and nothing short of an apology would quiet
him. Nachiketa of *Katha Upanishad* fame had also this sense of
self-respect, refusing to be belittled. "Among many I am the
first;" he said, "and among many others I am the middlemost.
(But certainly I am never the last.)" Of course, Vishwanath
could not tolerate such outbursts of Naren, especially against
elderly persons, even though they proceeded from a sense of
self-respect. So Naren was each time severely reprimanded;
but in his heart the father was glad that his son was so
spirited.

Indeed, during this period Naren had acquired a keen sense
of personal dignity, and when he returned to Calcutta from
Raipur, he was a changed boy. Even his physical appearance
was becoming manly. He had always been physically perfect,
but he was now acquiring that regal bearing which made him,
in after years, a notable figure wherever he went. Further, he
was beginning to discriminate in the choice of his friends,
accepting only his intellectual peers. But however his temperament might conflict with circumstances and with people, he was
consistently large-hearted and generous, for such was his nature
and heritage, and he was always loved.

In Raipur Naren learned the old Indian game of chess, and
often came out victorious in many hard contests. Again, it was
at Raipur that he was taught the secrets and mysteries of
the culinary art by his father; for Swami Vivekananda was,
like his father, an excellent cook.

We have already mentioned that Vishwanath was a lover
of music and used to sing himself. He also created in his house
an atmosphere suitable for the cultivation of music. As mentioned in a foregoing chapter, he had noticed Naren's love
of music and his musical potentialities from early in the boy's
life and had nurtured them carefully. He was of the opinion
that unless one received proper training in a traditional manner

under masters of music, one could not really earn competency in the art. He himself had given Naren his first training in music, and now while at Raipur, where he had more intimate contact with his son, he taught him many songs of various kinds. Later, after the family's return to Calcutta, he arranged for Naren's training in classical vocal and instrumental music under reputed masters like Beni Gupta (also known as Beni Ostad), and later under the latter's Mohammedan teacher, Ahmad Khan. (According to some researchers, Beni Ostad's real name was Beni Adhikari.) From Ahmad Khan, Narendranath learnt many Hindi, Urdu and Persian songs, most of them devotional. Ujir Khan, Senior and Junior Dunni Khan, Kanailal Dhendi and Jagannath Mishra are also named by some as his music teachers. We do not have conclusive information about his teachers in instrumental music. It has been said that Kasi Ghoshal, who used to play the Pakhawaj at the Adi Brahmo Samaj, taught him Pakhawaj and Tabla; but according to others Beni Ostad taught him these instruments. It is also said that he learnt Esraj from Jagannath Mishra. Though Naren learnt to play with mastery on Pakhawaj, Tabla, Esraj and Sitar, his forte was vocal music, in which he even excelled the masters who taught him singing. He was taught and trained until he became widely known as an accomplished singer of high calibre. He himself became infatuated with music and with song, and practised for hours in a small room on the first floor of his maternal grandmother's house, or at the house of a friend. His companions would often assemble to listen to his music. Naren's own family was charmed with his voice, and he often sang to his father, now seriously, now gaily, as the mood took him. Of all his earlier attainments, music must be counted as one of the most remarkable, because his musical attainments at this time were rather striking.

Naren's voice was so lively and sweet that whenever he rendered a tune in a song, the spirit of it became incarnate, as it were, in cadence and beauty. In fact, with Naren music became a wonderful instrument for the adoration of the Divine. It was through music that his first communion with Shri Ramakrishna took place. On listening to his singing, the latter would be deeply moved and go into Samadhi.

Besides training Naren in music, Vishwanath also taught him some lessons in manliness. On one occasion, Narendranath went to his father with the question: "What have you done for me?" Instantly came the reply, "Go, look at yourself in the mirror." And there was immediate understanding for the son. He knew that his father was a king amongst men, verily as the Vedas say, "a bull among the herd".

There was another time when Naren came to his father for instruction in the ways of the world, asking him what were the elements of real good manners. "Never show surprise!" said the father. Was it this laconic counsel, deeply understood and assimilated, that made it possible for Vivekananda in his later life to walk with equal dignity into the palaces of the East and West and into the huts and hovels of the poorest of India's poor?

When Vishwanath returned to Calcutta with his family in 1879, there was some difficulty about getting Naren into school, for he had been absent for nearly two years; but his teachers loved him and, remembering his ability, made an exception in his case. The boy then gave himself up to study, mastering three years' lessons in one, and passed the Entrance examination in the first division. He was the only student in the school to attain that distinction. His father gave him a watch as a reward.

While Naren was still a student at the Metropolitan Institution, a ceremony took place at which prizes were distributed to the outstanding, and honour was paid to one of the teachers who was about to retire. Naren's class wanted to give the teacher an address of thanks and appreciation. Mr. Surendranath Banerjee, the foremost national leader of the day, was to be in the chair. Since he was known as the greatest orator of the time, the students felt understandably diffident about speaking before such a distinguished man. They came to Naren in their quandary, and he promised that he would speak. When the time came, he rose in the gathering and spoke for almost half an hour, telling the retired teacher how the boys felt towards him and how they regretted his departure from the

Institution. When he sat down, Mr. Surendranath Banerjee rose and, in his speech, praised the young speaker. Later in life this gentleman, at a time when his reputation as an orator was at its height, referred to Swami Vivekananda as the greatest public speaker India had ever known.

By the time Naren had passed the Entrance examination, he had acquired extensive knowledge. While in the Entrance Class, he had mastered a great many standard works of English and Bengali literature. Besides mathematics in the usual school curriculum, he knew something of higher mathematics. He was well versed in Sanskrit for his age, and had studied with much success the history of his own land, especially the standard works on Indian history by such authors as Marshman and Elphinstone. As he paid little attention to textbooks, sometimes he had to work hard on the eve of the examinations. Once he said, "Just two or three days before the Entrance examination I found that I hardly knew anything of geometry. So I began to study the subject, keeping awake the whole night, and in twenty-four hours I mastered the four books of geometry."

At this time he acquired a special power of reading which he described as follows: "It so happened that I could understand an author without reading his book line by line. I could get the meaning by just reading the first and the last line of a paragraph. As this power developed I found it unnecessary to read even the paragraphs. I could follow by reading only the first and last lines of a page. Further, where the author introduced discussions to explain a matter and it took him four or five or even more pages to clear the subject, I could grasp the whole trend of his arguments by only reading the first few lines."

The playtime of boyhood with its joys and sorrows was over for Naren, and a new life with a more serious outlook dawned for him when, in 1879, at the age of sixteen, he passed the Entrance examination and entered the Presidency College early the next year. Hereafter one sees him as a student, intensely intellectual. A vast change in his personal life was in the offing as he stepped from boyhood to youth, and into a world of new ideas and experiences.

4

COLLEGE DAYS

Narendranath entered the first year Arts class of the general department of Presidency College in January 1880. He had just turned seventeen and had grown to manhood's stature. He was muscular, agile and inclined to stoutness. Since the college was run by the Government and the professors were for the most part Europeans, it was incumbent upon the students to attend in either European dress or in Indian Chapkan and trousers. They were also required to wear a wrist watch. Of these two, Narendranath preferred to dress himself in alpaca Chapkan (a kind of loose and long robe) and trousers, and wore a Swiss-made wrist watch.

He regularly attended the Presidency College for one year; but in the second year he contracted malaria, as a result of which his class attendance fell short, and he was not allowed to appear in the First Arts (F.A.) examination. But the General Assembly's Institution, founded by the Scottish General Missionary Board and now known as the Scottish Church College, accepted him, and sent him up for the F.A. examination.

Hard study on the eve of the Entrance examination together with his ascetic practices had already impaired his health to some extent. So before taking the F.A. examination Narendranath went to Gaya for a change to recover his health and returned to Calcutta only a few months before the examination. In 1881 he passed the First Arts examination in the second division, and continued to study in the same Institution until he passed his Bachelor of Arts examination in 1884. In connection with this Scottish Church College, it may be mentioned here that when Narendranath returned to Calcutta from the West in January 1897 as the famous Swami Vivekananda, it was the students of the College who stopped the carriage in which he was riding with some of his European and Indian admirers, unharnessed the horses, and drew the carriage themselves. The memory of Narendranath, as a student, is still with the Institution.

Narendranath's college days were marked by tremendous intellectual ferment and spiritual upheaval, which will reveal themselves as we review these years in more detail. The curriculum he had pursued for the F.A. examination was almost an extension of the subjects he had offered for the Entrance examination. In addition to English, Second language, History and Mathematics, he had offered Logic and Psychology for his F.A. examination. He had chosen the same subjects for his B.A. examination also only with the difference that Logic and Psychology had been replaced by Philosophy in the advanced course. He preferred these subjects for study because, with the guidance of his father, he believed that they, best of all, conduced to the development and refinement of the mind and sensibility. He was devoted to literature and made great headway in the arts of composition and rhetoric. He evinced keen interest in philosophy and logic and in some forms of higher mathematics. He grew more reserved while following these studies, discovering that his development lay along the lines of intense learning. He made great efforts to master the English language and more specially in the arts of conversation and debating, in which he excelled. Indeed, he became virtually the leader of the college in this regard.

Narendranath was not in the habit of limiting his studies to the university curriculum. During the first two years of college he acquired a thorough grasp of the masterpieces of Western logic, and in the third and fourth year he set himself to mastering Western philosophy as well as the ancient and modern history of different nations of Europe.

It was in November 1881, while Narendranath was in the second year of the F.A. classes, that he met for the first time Shri Ramakrishna Paramahamsa at the house of Shri Surendranath Mitra of Simulia. It will be interesting to note here how he first came to hear of the great saint. Professor William Hastie, the noted scholar, was at that time the Principal of the

General Assembly's Institution. One day during the absence of the professor of English he took over the literature class. He was explaining Wordsworth's *Excursion*, where the state of trance is referred to, and of which the poet had had a glimpse while contemplating the beauties of nature. But the students did not understand what he meant by trance. Professor Hastie then said, "Such an experience is the result of purity of mind and concentration on some particular object, and it is rare indeed, particularly in these days. I have seen only one person who has experienced that blessed state of mind, and he is Ramakrishna Paramahamsa of Dakshineshwar. You can understand if you go there and see for yourself." It was thus that Naren first heard of his future Master, and not through the Brahmo Samaj, of which he was a member.

Those who were Narendranath's friends and acquaintances at college remembered him as regal in his bearing, and self-confident, as though royally born. He attracted the attention of both Indian and English professors, who recognized his ambitious mind and the latent powers of his personality. About him Principal William Hastie said, "Narendranath is really a genius. I have travelled far and wide but I have never yet come across a lad of his talents and possibilities, even in German universities, amongst philosophical students. He is bound to make his mark in life!" After passing the F.A. examination Narendranath developed a remarkable originality in his intellectual pursuits. He would test everything by argument. Even in the hours of recreation he would continue discussions that had commenced in the hours of study. He would argue with those who challenged his point of view, and invariably argued with success. He was a lion among the students, defiant of conventional thought. He was vehement, of untiring energy, and his topics of conversation were endless.

During his college days he underwent a wonderful psychological transformation. His mind became intensely analytical, and it was in this becoming that he subordinated imagination to the demands of reason. He related himself, also, to the needs and spirit of his times, and subjected Hinduism to a severe analysis. It will be seen later on to what this led. He demanded that his own freedom of belief be respected, whatever the character of that belief, and he was literally voracious of information.

Furthermore, he was a born idealist and seeker of truth, not content with mere worldly enjoyments. He longed to pierce the veil of nature, but his reason had to be satisfied at the same time. Beneath the surface of his conscious mind ran the strong current of desire for Reality, which made him aware from his earliest years that his life was to be different from the rest of mankind.

Let it not be imagined, however, that Narendranath had grown unduly serious in other things. There was another side to him that relieved the seriousness of his intellectual temperament. He was as keen for adventure as ever; he was the wit among the students, and the first to see the humorous side of a situation. They were a cheerful lot that mixed with him in his college days; and, out for an excursion, there was no one jollier than he. Many were the times when they would pack themselves into a hackney-carriage and go singing through the streets. When the occasion was a religious festival, they would repair to the Ganga for a bath and swim, making religion a joyful matter. On other public festivals they would go out at night through the lighted streets, in eager pursuit of interesting sights and festivities. Naren was always the leader; he saw that they had full measure of fun and benefit from every occasion. The recreations in which they indulged were of the manly sort. During these days Narendranath unconsciously wove about himself the threads of many warm friendships which remained with him to the end.

One of his specialities during college life was a dislike of foppishness. He could not tolerate the dandy and would speak openly to the fellow who made it his sole business to dress well. He hated any tendency to effeminacy in manner or apparel.

A characteristic of Narendranath was his solicitude for others. For instance, it was customary in those days for the General Assembly's Institution to help those who, for lack of funds,

4

could not pay the required fees; there was also provision for
exemption from college dues in special cases. But the need of
an applicant for funds or for exemption had to be substantiated
before his name could be put on the free list. Rajkumar, a
senior clerk, was in charge of making decisions in such matters.
Now, it so happened that Haridas Chattopadhyaya, a class-
mate of Narendranath, was in great financial difficulty before
the examination. He could not pay the accumulated college
dues, nor was it easy for him to pay the examination fees.
Narendranath assured his friend that he would see what could
be done.

After one or two days, when a crowd of students had assembled at the counter in Rajkumar's office to deposit dues and
fees, Narendranath made his way through the crowd and said
to Rajkumar, "Sir, Haridas is incapable of paying his dues.
Will you kindly exempt him? If you send him up for the examination he will pass with credit; otherwise he will be undone."
"Your presumptuous recommendation is uncalled for", said
Rajkumar; "you had better 'oil your own machine'! I won't
send him up unless he pays his dues." Thus rebuffed Narendranath left the place, and his friend was naturally disappointed.
But Narendranath consoled him saying, "Why are you giving
way to despair? The old man is in the habit of giving such
rebuffs. I tell you, I shall find a way out for you; so be at rest."

After college hours, instead of returning home, Narendranath
searched out the opium-smoking den to which Rajkumar
usually resorted. As the darkness of the evening gathered, sure
enough, Rajkumar was espied stealthily advancing towards the
den. With surprising suddenness Narendranath presented himself before the old man and stood in his way. Rajkumar, though
puzzled at the sight of Narendranath at such a place and time,
kept his nerve and said as calmly as he could, "What's the
matter, Datta? You are here!" Narendranath again presented
his plea on behalf of Haridas, and added that, if the request
were ignored, he would publicize in the college Rajkumar's
frequenting the opium-smoking den. "Well, my dear, why are
you so angry?" said the old man: "What you want will be done.

Can I ever ignore your request?" And he conceded that the arrears of the college dues of Haridas would be remitted, but he would be required to pay the examination fees. Narendranath agreed to this and took leave of him.

Early next morning, before sunrise, Narendranath went to Haridas's house and after knocking at the door sang the song:

> In this pure pellucid dawn,
> Meditate on Brahman of incomparable glory.
> Behold the newly risen sun,
> The light of its lovely face
> Showing on the mountain top.
>
> The sweet breeze blowing on this auspicious day
> Pours nectar while singing His glory.
> Let us all go to the abode of God
> With offerings of love in our hearts.

Then he said to Haridas, "Come, be of good cheer, your work is done. You will not have to pay the college dues." And he narrated the incident of the previous evening with all his mimicry and dramatic skill and raised a storm of laughter.

A friend of Narendranath's refers to him in a manner that gives one an insight into the nature of the feelings that all his friends bore for him at this time:

It was delightful to listen to him. His voice was like music to us. We would often open a subject for discussion just for the pleasure of hearing him. He was so interesting and, above all, so original. We learned much from listening to him. Did anyone oppose him, however, he would fall upon him with all his power of thought and language, and would vanquish the opponent in no time. Even in those days he detested any sort of weakness. He was a great admirer of Napoleon and tried to impress upon us that the followers of any great cause must give the unquestioning obedience which Marshal Ney showed to his emperor. He was kindness itself to us. I remember one striking instance of this. Having heard that he was ill with fever, I repaired to his grandmother's house. I found him almost helpless, yet he insisted upon serving me. I was his guest, he said, and he was the host. I remonstrated but he persisted. He rose from the floor and busied himself preparing the hookah for me with his own hands. A servant of the family entered the room and was horrified to see Naren at this. The servant looked upon his master as a devotee looks upon a saint. To him Narendranath was everything, and he scolded his charge, urging him to rest.

Examinations are a trial to students in every country. In India, they are especially a trial because so much depends on them, as doors both to status and to a lucrative career. In preparation for them an extraordinary amount of energy is put forth. Yet Narendranath was ready to give only as much time to academic examinations as was unavoidable. The rest of his time and energy went, as we have seen, to meditation, to extra-curricular studies, to music, to exercise, to debates and discussions. Above all, the ever-blazing inner spiritual urges did not permit him to set great value on the worldly prosperity a university degree would afford him. Academic competition and high grades interested him not in the least. Only at the time of his examinations did he busy himself in assigned reading, and then only to pass. Indeed, his academic study was generally a last-minute affair and dependent upon his prodigious memory.

Up until a month before the B.A. examination he had not read a single page of Green's *Short History of the English People*, which was one of the textbooks prescribed. He did not even own a copy. So he procured one and vowed that he would not leave his room until he had mastered its contents. In three days he knew the book thoroughly. But there were other books to read and studies to master. Thus when the days for the Examination drew near, Narendranath retired to his maternal grandmother's home nearby, where there were less noise and fewer distractions. There he confined himself for days at a time, studying day and night. He took a vow to the effect that he would not leave the room until he had mastered the daily task which he had chalked out for himself. In later years he described his pre-examination trials as follows: "I sat in the room, book in hand, with a pot of strong tea or coffee by my side to keep the brain from getting overtired. When I felt inclined to sleep at night, I would tie a rope to my foot. Then, if I fell asleep and moved to make myself more comfortable, the rope would jerk me, and I would awake with a start."

In this room Naren often used to sing between his bouts of study. There was a young widow in the house opposite, across the lane. She often came and stood by her window, unknown to him, and listened to him singing. On one occasion she crossed over from her house, and in the dim light Narendranath saw her standing in the doorway of his room. She was young, and she had come. She had seen him often without his knowledge, and bore great love for him. She had heard him singing this night. To her it was romantic. Narendranath was amazed. He had never seen the girl before. He fell at her feet. "Mother! Mother!" he exclaimed, emphasizing the word; "why have you come? Let me regard you as I would my own mother." The girl understood. A moment later, and Naren was alone. The next day he changed his quarters and was never seen again in that room. Already his great renunciation was being foreshadowed.

On the morning before the B.A. examination we find Naren in a strange mood: "Fling away all books, for what shall learning be in the presence of the Lord!"—this was how he felt. The deeper self in him had risen and had asserted itself. We find him standing outside his college-mates' rooms, singing absorbedly, almost ecstatically, his face radiant. He began with the opening verse of the song: "We are like children, with little understanding. Shall we not rely upon Him, the Ocean of Wisdom!" Again, it was a song of praise:

> Sing ye, O mountains, O clouds, O great winds!
> Sing ye, sing ye, His Glory!
> Sing with joy all ye, the suns and moons and stars!
> Sing ye, sing ye, His Glory!

He sang and talked until nine o'clock. A friend intervened and reminded him of the examination. Narendranath paid no heed. Yet he appeared for the examination the next day—and passed.

Narendranath had become adept in music by this time. It

had indeed become second nature to him, and a source of joy and inspiration to his family, his friends, as well as to himself. Frequently the students at the General Assembly's Institution gathered round him to hear him sing. There would be perfect silence except for the singer's voice.

Not only was Narendranath a great musician, he was as well an authentic theoretician of music. This fact is proved by a treatise on music entitled *Sangita-Kalpataru*, in Bengali, published by Shri Chandicharan Basak in 1887. The book was mostly compiled by Narendranath, and later completed by Shri Vaishnavcharan Basak. In its elaborate Introduction various aspects of the science and art of vocal and instrumental Indian music are discussed with masterly knowledge and insight. The major part of the book named *Sangita-Sangraha* contains devotional and inspirational songs composed in various languages of India. In the appendix of the book biographical information is provided about the composers of the songs. Scholars are of the opinion that this learned Introduction was written by Narendranath. Though at the time Narendranath himself was struggling against poverty, he compiled this book solely to help the poor publisher.

On the creative side also, Naren was strong. Later in life he composed several songs and hymns that are now used in religious worship by the devotees of Ramakrishna-Vivekananda.

From ancient times in India the art of dancing has been considered an art of the gods, revealed by Brahma himself. And of the gods, Shiva, known in south India as Nataraja, King of Dancers, is the most dynamic dancer of all. It seems almost inevitable that Narendranath, devoted as he was to Shiva, would have learned this manly, nay, godly, art, as well as that of music. He had a strong, beautiful body, and more than that, a beautiful mind and a highly developed aesthetic sense. Thus, when he was dancing and simultaneously singing, every movement of his limbs scintillated beauty, and the eyes and ears of those who watched would be filled with a unique experience of gracefulness.

Those were days of the first stirrings of political awakening in India, and physical culture was considered to be a hall-mark of patriotism. Surendranath Banerjee and Ananda Mohan Basu were thundering from the "Students' Association" founded by them, that young Bengalis must be physically strong and aggressive. Narendranath, who was always quick to catch what was constructive in the time-spirit, joined Ambu Guha's gymnasium to practise wrestling. Many young men from respectable families used to throng the gymnasium, and Rakhal (later, Swami Brahmananda) was one of them.

Narendranath began now to interest himself in the issues of the day, especially in the views of the Brahmo Samaj. The activities of the Brahmo Samaj were dynamic and new in sharp contrast to the moribund state of Hindu society; and its leader, Keshabchandra Sen, the eloquent hero of a hundred platforms, was the idol of young Bengal. We shall state here very briefly the underlying principles of the Brahmo movement.

A nation's travail in passing through a new birth brings in its train movements of reform. A new vision seeks expression, while the established order wants to conserve its traditions. From the clash between these two come the reformers and the reactionaries. In brief, the Brahmo Samaj was the outward expression of an endeavour to liberalize and at the same time conserve the evolved traits of the Hindu race. Its coming into existence in the year 1828 was the result of the awakening inspired by the illustrious Raja Rammohan Roy, a man of gigantic intellect and inflexible will; and a man who had the courage and prestige necessary to lead an attack on the evils which threatened the very existence of the nation. He saw that if Hinduism were to survive, it would have to be at the cost of many religious and social customs. Later, Maharshi Devendranath Tagore and Keshabchandra Sen became his most powerful followers; indeed, it was owing to these two influential persons that the life of the movement was assured.

This movement protested against certain forms and tenets of orthodox Hinduism, such as polytheism, image worship, the doctrine of Divine Incarnations, and the need for a Guru. It offered a monotheistic religion which repudiated all these. On the social side, it demanded the eradication of the caste system, the recognition of the equality of man, the education and emancipation of women, with the raising of the marriageable age. It was a tremendous task which the Brahmo Samaj assigned itself, one requiring endless patience and wisdom. But it lacked the means to carry out these reforms; nor did it recognize that reforms must come from within, that imposing them from outside can have no lasting effect.

The movement, however, was progressive in its views, and it is not to be wondered at that it captured the imagination of young Bengal. In Narendranath it aroused a tumult of thought and feeling, and he came to regard the Samaj, whose meetings he often attended, as an ideal institution which might help to solve all life's problems, individual or national. He was imbued with the same ideas as the Brahmo leaders. He knew the burden of caste and had chafed under its rigidity; he had no sympathy with polytheism and image worship. He also felt that the women of his nation must be educated. Thus he espoused the cause of the Samaj with all earnestness, and it was his fervent hope that the strength of thought, depth of feeling, enthusiasm, and personal magnetism, which were characteristic of Keshab-chandra Sen, and through which he influenced his numerous followers, would one day be his.

In 1878 there was a split in the Brahmo Samaj, and a number of its members headed by Pandit Shivanath Shastri, and Vijay-krishna Goswami formed a new society on May 15, 1878, called the Sadharan Brahmo Samaj. Narendranath identified himself with the new organization, and his name can still be seen on the roll of the original members. He also joined at this time a movement for the education of the masses, irrespective of caste, creed or colour. His intense desire for freedom made him willing to identify himself with anything that promised liberation from obsolete methods and willing to cast aside what-ever might interfere with his gaining a larger vision. He was not content with passivity; he wanted to know the "why" and "how" of every phenomenon, mental or spiritual.

Indeed, it would appear that Narendranath's versatile mind

sought to encompass the entire range of the renaissance—religious, cultural and national—of his time. It is said that he also used to frequent the Hindu Mahamela of Navagopal Mitra, whose gymnasium has been mentioned in a foregoing chapter. The Hindu Mahamela was an organization devoted to the all-round welfare of Hindu life and of the Hindus as a nation.

The chief element of Narendranath's character was purity. He was inexorable in this respect. In youth, one is often open to many influences of a dubious nature; the opportunities for questionable adventures are many. But Narendranath's mother had made him understand that goodness was a matter of personal loyalty to herself and to the family. Then, too, something always "held him back", as he himself later remarked. Though a boy to the core of his heart, delighting in all that called forth the spirit of manliness, he stood as one of another world when it was suggested that he enter upon devious paths. In this connection, the testimony of a college-mate of Narendranath's may be cited. This person, who, in his youth, did not have a particularly fine moral sense, later on changed his ways and became a disciple of Swami Vivekananda. Speaking of college days, he said that even then Narendranath was a flame of spirituality. Though this person frequently made sport of his college-mate as being over-puritanical, yet, he said, there were times when he felt depressed beyond words in Narendranath's presence; for he would then feel his own moral deficiency in its fiercest colour and in all its degrading reality. He said that spirituality literally radiated from Narendranath as an overwhelming influence. He was not alone in saying so; other companions of Narendranath also said they perceived the same radiance of purity. All through his life this virtue continued to characterize him. It was the background of all his thought and feeling.

He always considered purity the cardinal virtue and made it so in his life. As he came to know the principles of the Vedanta philosophy, he believed that without chastity, or better said, without purity spiritual life is impossible. To him, in his manhood, purity was not a state of resistance to evil, but an over-

whelming passion for good, in each and every aspect. It was a
burning, radiant, spiritual force. It related itself to all forms of
life. It became the keynote of his message. It outgrew for him
its special definitions, developing far beyond the idea of sex
into the actual vision of divinity and truth. He realized the
truth of the great teaching of Jesus: "Blessed are the pure in
heart, for they shall see God!" Yes, he knew it was only they,
only the pure in heart, who see God.

The spirit of manliness—or was it something vaster, higher,
more profound?—ran through all the experiences of his youth.
One becomes conscious of him as a *power*. It was not through
weakness that he was good, but through strength. Brahmacharya (absolute continence) was his ideal for the student stage
of life—Brahmacharya viewed as hard intellectual labour
combined with and governed by a great personal purity. This
is the stage of preparation in mind and heart for the divine
vision which shall come, as the scriptures say, to those who lead
that life.

The boy Narendranath had become a Brahmacharin in spirit.
He had accustomed himself to regard every woman, as all
monks should, as "Mother". His purpose was fixed, so far as
intention and character went. But though he had entered into
a serious mood, he did not understand as yet the full purport of
life, and his enthusiasm, though deep and abiding, had not as
yet been tested by difficulties and doubts that were to come.
He had not yet known, nor could even begin to know, that
struggle of soul which inevitably comes with a tempest of
thought. He was all idealist; his spirit nourished itself upon
idealism and ideal things. He had not, even for a moment,
known the pang of disillusionment; the horizon was roseate for
him. Youth sees only the ideal as in a dream. It requires much
pressure of circumstance, much thought and much overcoming
of the sense of defeat to make the vision of the ideal an actuality
in the domain of the real.

The inward spiritual urge was becoming very strong now.
During his youth, two strikingly dissimilar visions of life would
come up before his mind's eye as he would go to sleep. One

was of a life of ease and luxury, the life of the senses, of the enjoyment of wealth, power, name and fame, and, along with all this, the love of a devoted wife and family; in short, the worldly life. The other picture was of the sannyasi, a wandering monk having no possessions, established in the consciousness of Divine Reality, drifting in the current of God's will, eating only such food as chance might bring, and resting at night with the sky for roof, in the forest or on the mountainside. He believed himself capable of realizing either of these ideals, and he often pictured himself in one or the other, for he felt these two were within him, two painters, one, the spirit of desire, the other the spirit of renunciation. But the more inward he became, the clearer became the picture of renunciation, while the worldly one began to fade until finally it disappeared. Thus the spiritual self of Narendranath gained mastery, choosing the renunciation of desire—the only way to the vision of God.

For a time the intellectual atmosphere of the Brahmo Samaj satisfied him; he felt uplifted during the prayers and devotional songs. True to his uncompromising nature, he strictly observed the Samaj's tenets. Indeed, it is said that when he came under the influence of the movement he took to vegetarianism. An interesting anecdote is told in this connection, which throws some light on the relationship between Narendranath and his father. One day Narendranath quarrelled with his sister Swarnamayi, charging her with serving him a fish curry from which the fish had been taken out. Vishwanath, who was bathing in the courtyard, overheard their altercation and angrily shouted, "His ancestors for fourteen generations lived on 'clams and snails'; now he has become a Brahmadaitya [lit. ghost of a Brahmin; here, a critical allusion to Brahmo influence on Narendranath] and will not eat fish!" But though Vishwanath said this, he never curbed the liberty of his son in this matter. In fact, the notable Brahmo leaders, Maharshi Devendranath, Pandit Shivanath Shastri and others, visited the Datta family at one time or another.

With the rest of the Brahmo Samaj, Narendranath believed in a formless God with attributes (as distinguished from the

Absolute of the Advaita Vedanta), but, unlike the others, he was convinced that if God really existed He would surely appear in answer to the sincere prayers of the devotees. He felt that there must be a way of realizing him, else life would be futile. And presently it began to dawn on him that if God was to be realized, he was no nearer the goal than before he had joined the Samaj.

In his longing to know the Truth Narendranath turned to Maharshi Devendranath Tagore, who was regarded by many as one of the best spiritual teachers of the time. He had been to see the Maharshi before, in company with some friends, and the latter had advised them to practise meditation with great intensity. Later, when the Maharshi was living in retirement in a boat on the Ganga, Narendranath went to him alone, burning with the desire to know God. His sudden appearance startled the venerable old man. Before he could say a word, Narendranath, tense with excitement, flung out the question: "Sir, have you seen God?" The Maharshi was unable to answer and contented himself with: "My boy, you have the Yogi's eyes." Narendranath came away disappointed. He went to the leaders of other religious sects, and not one of them could say that he had seen God. Where then should he go?

He then remembered Shri Ramakrishna, whom he had met for the first time in November of 1881, at the house of a devotee of his, named Surendranath Mitra. Narendranath had gone there to sing, and the Master, greatly attracted by his music, had made inquiries about him, and had even invited him to Dakshineshwar. So Narendranath decided now to go to Dakshineshwar and put this question to him.

This decision was reinforced by the following incident: When Narendranath had refused to marry, Ramachandra Datta and other relatives had tried in various ways—all in vain—to persuade him to bow to his father's wishes. But when Ramachandra, who had already been visiting Shri Ramakrishna at Dakshineshwar, came to know that Narendranath had declined to marry for the sake of pursuing spiritual enlightenment, he said to him, "If you have a real desire to realize God, then come to the Master at Dakshineshwar instead of visiting Brahmo Samaj and other places." Around this time, Surendranath Mitra, who was a neighbour, also invited him to accompany him to Dakshineshwar in his horse-drawn carriage. Narendranath accepted the invitation and in the company of two of his friends went for the first time to Dakshineshwar one day in December of 1881.

We shall see later what happened there and what was Shri Ramakrishna's answer to the question. This meeting was to open a new chapter in the spiritual life of Narendranath.

5

SHRI RAMAKRISHNA

Adjustment is the law of nature, whether in the domain of spirit or matter. Through an inscrutable law, East and West offer two fields of activity, one mainly in the domain of spirit and the other largely in the domain of matter, for the glorious consummation of the ideal to which all humanity has been moving through its science, philosophy, metaphysics and religion. The West has mostly devoted itself to researches in and discovery of the nature of material things; the East from time immemorial has experimented in religion in order to learn the laws that rule the realm of spirit. Both ideals are necessary for the progress of humanity, whose future rests on co-operation and mutual understanding between East and West.

In the last century one more adjustment on the spiritual plane was needed. Materialistic ideas were at the height of their glory and power. The rampant growth of materialism, uninspired by higher idealism, governed the world. While the West was running after worldly enjoyments, the East had fallen from its true ideals. Devoid of the spirit of renunciation, the Eternal religion of the Vedas was broken up into conflicting sects. The world was awaiting the birth of a divine Incarnation in whose mind, purified of all worldly taint, the great truths underlying all the religious systems of the world would be revealed once more—an Incarnation whose life would harmonize all the apparently contradictory religious ideals and the various national and social ideals of different races and countries, thus uniting humanity by the ties of love and toleration into a single brotherhood.

At this psychological moment of the world's history, the Lord, true to His promise that whenever virtue subsides and vice prevails He bodies Himself forth, incarnated Himself as Shri Ramakrishna, combining in a single personality the wonderful love and compassion of Buddha and Christ with the keen intellect of Shankara to demonstrate what true religion is.

On Wednesday, February 18, 1836, at Kamarpukur, a village of Bengal, a child was born of poor Brahmin parents. Both father and mother were venerated as living saints by the simple villagers. The child was named Gadadhar. He grew up amid the simplicities of a village—the cows, the fields and the typical rural life—yet he manifested even in his early boyhood remarkable traits. It is said that religious songs in praise of the gods or the discussing of religious topics would often send him into a trance. When the father passed away, the family fell into straitened circumstances. The eldest son, Ramkumar, came to Calcutta and opened a school. Soon Gadadhar joined his brother there.

Here for the first time Shri Ramakrishna—for that is the name by which Gadadhar has become famous all over the world—came in touch with modern ideas. His brother wanted him to have the education usual for a Brahmin boy in those days; but Ramakrishna, who was already beginning to realize that he was born for a definite purpose, asked himself, "Shall I attain piety, devotion and divine fervour by pursuing this education?" "No", was the emphatic reply of his mind. "Will it enable me to be as God-fearing and upright as my father?" "No", echoed his innate religious instinct. "Shall I be able to realize God through this education and escape from universal ignorance and the glamour of material enjoyments?" The same reply came from his heart. "Then what shall I do with this education which will not help me realize God or overcome the miseries of the world? I would rather remain ignorant all my life and follow the path of God, than throw away my cherished ideals", was his conclusion. To his brother's persuasion he emphatically replied, "Brother, what shall I do with a mere bread-winning education? I would rather acquire that wisdom which will illumine my heart, getting which one is satisfied for ever."

About this time the Kali temple at Dakshineshwar, some four miles to the north of Calcutta on the east bank of the Ganga, was founded by Rani Rasmani, a pious Hindu lady of great wealth and influence. Mathuranath Biswas, her son-in-law, was the manager of her estate. Ramkumar was invited to be the priest at the temple. He accepted; and so, with his brother Ramakrishna, came to live at Dakshineswar. In course of time Ramakrishna was appointed as a priest at the Kali temple. The proximity of the holy Ganga, the quietness and solitude of the temple-compound in contrast with the turmoil of the busy metropolis, and above all, the living presence of Kali, the Divine Mother of the Universe, filled the mind of Ramakrishna with a strong desire for the realization of God.

There came a great change in him. The boy became the devotee; the devotee became the ascetic; the ascetic became the saint; the saint became the man of realization; the man of realization became the prophet; the prophet often became merged in the Divine Nature which is God. And all this happened in the course of twelve years. It is impossible to give an idea of Ramakrishna's passionate yearning for realization, his utter renunciation of worldly enjoyments, his sincerity, his single-minded devotion, and the ecstasies of soul, which characterized the early period of his spiritual life. He was innocent of scriptures and the intricacies of religious practices. He hardly received any help from spiritual guides at this stage. All he possessed was the extreme eagerness of the child to see his mother, and a strong dispassion for worldly enjoyments. The day was spent in worship, prayer and song; in the twilight of the early morning and dusk he would stroll along the bank of the Ganga absorbed in the contemplation of the Divine Mother; the nights were spent in meditation. Thus while those about him were wasting time in all sorts of frivolity, he was burning day and night with this consuming thirst for God. The vision of the Divine Mother became the one passion of Ramakrishna; but he had not, as yet, realized Her. Days and months passed in this way, with no abatement of his zeal. The agony of longing for his Divine Mother was gradually increasing. In the evening on the bank of the Ganga he would cry aloud, "Another day is gone in vain, Mother, for I have not seen Thee. Another day

Shri Ramakrishna

The Dakshineswar Temple

The Western
Verandah of Shri
Ramakrishna's
Room

Mother
Bhavatarini at
Dakshineswar

of this short life has passed, and I have not realized the Truth." Then doubts would cross his mind, and he would say, "Art Thou real, Mother, or is it all fiction, mere poetry without any truth? If Thou dost exist, why can I not see Thee? Is religion just a phantasy, a mere castle in the air?" But this scepticism was only momentary; in a flash he would recall the lives and the struggles of those who had been blessed with the vision of God, and he would redouble his efforts.

One day the agony became unbearable. It was an excruciating pain. Feeling that life was useless without the vision of God, and determining to put an end to it, he seized the sword that was hanging in the Mother's temple. All on a sudden the Divine Mother, illuminating everything with Her effulgent splendour, revealed Herself to him. He fell unconscious to the floor. What happened after that he did not know, nor how that day or the next passed, for within him was a constant flow of ineffable bliss altogether new; and he felt the direct presence of the Divine Mother. After this vision Shri Ramakrishna became intoxicated with God. The period subsequent to this was replete with thrilling spiritual experiences. He was just stepping into a new, limitless realm. He had many and various visions, in trance and also in normal consciousness. It was as if he were living in another region where he held communion with strange beings. To people about him all this looked like madness.

Though the young priest had been blessed with the vision of the Divine Mother, he was not happy, for it was not continuous. He put fresh energy into his struggles and intensified his prayers. As his realizations deepened, his vision of the Mother began to be continuous; the image in the temple disappeared, and in its place there stood the living Mother Herself, smiling and blessing him. He even felt Her breath on his hand, and heard Her anklets tinkling as She went to the upper storey of the temple. The sense of separation from his Divine Mother gradually vanished, and he became Her child.

His whole mind and nervous system thus became attuned to the Highest Reality, unable to respond to any worldly stimulus. Sex consciousness was completely erased from his mind.

Mathuranath even contrived to tempt him secretly; but he passed through such trials quite unscathed, embodiment of purity and self-control that he was. He himself said that in his whole life not even in dream did he look upon a woman other than as the visible representation of the Divine Mother.

The strain of intense spiritual practices and austerities before the first vision of the Mother was so great that for a time his body became subject to various ailments. He went back to Kamarpukur at the request of his mother, and there his relatives, anxious on account of his health and in order to divert his mind to worldly affairs, arranged his marriage with a young girl from a neighbouring village. He readily agreed to the proposal, seeing it as the will of the Divine Mother. This stay at Kamarpukur did him much good; but soon he returned to Dakshineswar and was plunged once more into stormy struggles, forgetting his mother, wife and relations. Days, weeks and months passed in this search for Truth through other spiritual paths. At this time there came to Dakshineswar a nun who was an adept in the Path of Devotion as well as in the intricacies of the Tantrika Sadhana (spiritual practice according to the class of scriptures called Tantras). She was the first to diagnose the cause of Shri Ramakrishna's maladies and his so-called madness. She saw that he was in the state which is known in the Vaishnava scriptures as Maha-bhava and that his experiences were the result of his extreme love for God. Happy the man who had them! She was convinced that in his trances he had scaled the ultimate heights of spiritual realization. She came to the conclusion that Shri Ramakrishna was an Incarnation of God, and this she established before an assembly of pundits, giving the scriptures as her authority. Ramakrishna accepted her as his guru and practised under her guidance the devotional and Tantrika methods of Sadhana (spiritual practices), in which he attained perfection in an incredibly short time.

Later there came to Dakshineswar a Vaishnava saint, an itinerant monk and a devotee of Rama. Ramlala, or the Child Rama, was his favourite deity, and he had already had a vision of Him. He carried a metal image of Ramlala with him which

he showed to Shri Ramakrishna. But Ramakrishna saw the
living Rama in it, and soon established a loving relationship
with it. He saw Ramlala as vividly as he saw anyone else—now
dancing, now jumping up on his back or insisting on being taken
in his arms. The latter became so attached to Ramakrishna
that he refused to go with the monk, who was finally
obliged to leave him behind, glad to see him happy in
Ramakrishna's company.

Shri Ramakrishna next took up the highest form of Vaishnava
Sadhana, the Madhura Bhava, or intensest love of a woman
for her lover. All the Vaishnava disciplines centre on love. In
this particular one the closest union between worshipper and
worshipped is found. Not the grandeur of the Ideal but the
sweetness and closeness of the relationship is what counts here.
The most beautiful example of this form of worship is found in
Shri Radha's life; and the perfect devotee in this path is one
who looks only to the comfort of the Beloved, regardless of his
or her own personal pleasure or convenience. This discipline
roots out the sex idea. The soul has no sex; it is neither male
nor female. Sex is of the body. The man who desires to reach the
Spirit must get rid of sex distinctions. Shri Ramakrishna took
up this discipline with his usual zeal. He brought femininity
into everything. He dressed and spoke like women, and lived
with the women in Mathuranath's family. He made every
detail of their life his own till at last he found that the Truth
could be gained as a woman too.

About this time Totapuri, a sannyasi of the highest Vedantic
realization, came to Dakshineswar. Appreciating the spiritual
gifts of Shri Ramakrishna he asked if he might teach him the
secret of the Advaita (Non-dual) philosophy. Under his guidance Ramakrishna attained Nirvikalpa Samadhi, the state in
which the soul realizes its identity with Brahman, the Absolute
Truth. Shri Ramakrishna later said: "I was for six months in
that state from which ordinary mortals never return. Their
body lives for twenty-one days only and then falls like a dried
leaf from a tree; and the soul that was embodied realizes its
identity with Existence Absolute." It had taken Totapuri forty

years to attain this Supreme Consciousness; but Ramakrishna attained it in a single day!

A wandering monk who hitherto had never stayed at one place for more than three days, Totapuri remained at Dakshineswar for eleven months, imparting his knowledge to this wonderful disciple, setting him firmly on the lofty heights of Advaita. The disciple, in turn, became the guide of his teacher and enlightened him regarding the reality of the personal aspects of Truth which Totapuri had hitherto refused to recognize.

Shri Ramakrishna next sought to realize the ideals of religions other than Hinduism. He found from personal experience that they also led to the same goal which he had already attained through Hinduism. In his association with people of various sects, and in comparing their realizations with his own, he arrived at the conclusion that the ultimate aim of all religions was the realization in different aspects of one and the same Truth.

Meanwhile, strange stories that Shri Ramakrishna had gone mad were current in his native village. His wife Saradamani Devi resolved to learn the truth for herself. So she set out and walked to Dakshineswar, where she was very cordially received by her husband. He accommodated her in his own room for three or four days, and then made arrangements for her to live with his mother in the Nahabat (concert room) near by. When Saradamani saw how loving her husband was, the anxiety caused by the rumours was removed from her mind.

Whenever opportunity arose, Shri Ramakrishna used to teach Saradamani a variety of things, from housekeeping to the knowledge of Brahman. Once he told her, "Just as 'uncle' moon is the uncle of all children, so God is everybody's own. Whoever calls on Him will be blessed with His vision. If you call on him, you also will see Him." On another occasion he asked her, with the intention of testing her, "Did you come here to drag me into the world?" Saradamani, pure and noble soul that she was, at once understood and replied without hesitation, "No,

The Holy Mother, Shri Sarada Devi

why should I drag you into the world? I have come here to help you on your spiritual path."

One day during this period, Saradamani, while massaging Ramakrishna's feet, asked him, "How do you look on me?" He replied, "The Mother who is in the temple, the mother who gave birth to this body and now resides in the Nahabat—it is the same Mother who is now massaging my feet. Truly, I always look upon you as a form of the blissful Divine Mother."

On another occasion, seeing Saradamani asleep by his side, Ramakrishna addressed his own mind, discriminating: "This, O mind, is a female body. People look upon it as an object of great enjoyment, a thing to be highly prized, and they die for the sake of enjoying it. But if one goes after it, one has to remain confined in the body, and cannot realize God, who is Existence-Knowledge-Bliss. O mind, do not have one thought within and a contrary attitude without. Say in truth whether you want to have this or have God. If you want it, it is here before you; take it." Scarcely had he entertained the idea of touching the person of Saradamani than his mind recoiled. At once he was so deeply lost in Samadhi that he did not regain normal consciousness that night. He had to be brought back with great care the next morning by repeating the divine name in his ears.

Later on Shri Ramakrishna used to say, "Had she (Sarada-mani) not been so pure and, losing herself, assailed me, who knows that my self-control would not have broken down and body-consciousness arisen? I had importunately asked the Divine Mother after my marriage to keep her mind absolutely free from lust. After living with her at that time, I knew that the Divine Mother had really granted my prayer." Saradamani was thus endowed with rare spiritual fervour, and she became Ramakrishna's first disciple.

Some months after this, there arose in Shri Ramakrishna's mind a desire to worship Saradamani as a symbol of the Divine Mother Shodashi Mahavidya (a form of Kali), and to offer himself to her. This he did on the new-moon day of the month of Jyaishtha (May 25, 1873), when Phalaharini Kalika Devi is worshipped. While the worship was going on Saradamani went into Samadhi; and so did Ramakrishna after finishing the ritual. Priest and Goddess were joined in a transcendental union in the Self. When the Master recovered, he surrendered himself, the fruits of his lifelong spiritual practices, and his rosary, with appropriate Mantras, at the feet of Saradamani. It was the consummation of his spiritual disciplines. Everything now became to him a symbol of God.

Among the innumerable aspects of divinity which Shri Ramakrishna realized, the one that stands out most prominently is that of Kali, the Divine Mother whose emblem is death and destruction. She, as time, engulfs all things; as Death She destroys all. Therefore Her garland is a necklace of skulls, Her girdle is made of human arms, and in Her hand She holds a bleeding head. And yet Kali is Brahman; for does not the eternal Consciousness, the background of the mind, remain when all ideas, temporal and mortal, have been eliminated?

Shri Ramakrishna worshipped Kali both as the Mother and as Brahman; in Her terrible forms as well as in the blessedness and bliss of Brahman. The Personal Kali merged, in his realization, in the Impersonal. To Ramakrishna, She was also the giver of immortality. She puts down the mighty from their seats and exalts those of low degree; She fills the hungry with good things and the rich She sends empty away. To Her devotee the Mother reveals Herself as the Ocean of Reality: Her heart-throb is that of the Infinite Soul. For him, Kali held the scales of life and death, and the keys of wisdom and ignorance. At Her bidding the world begins the whirl of creation and at Her bidding it ends in destruction. Yet She is, also, ineffable Peace. Shri Ramakrishna saw the Mother in all things. He likewise realized Her as the indwelling Divinity in all souls. Though change, time, death and destruction are aspects of Her, She is the everlasting, unchanging Reality—Brahman. His ideas of Her took on their intrinsic reality as his conscious mind was transcended, and his soul shone forth as the Mother Herself. Lost in Samadhi, his whole body stiff, his hands automatically took the form of Varabhaya—offering boons with one hand and protection with the other. The vastness of nature was seen by Shri Ramakrishna as the living reality of the Mother. Of what was embodied, She was the embodiment; of what was ensouled, She was the soul. Beyond all and as all She dwelt incarnate as the active power of Supreme Reality. "Brahman and Shakti are one", Ramakrishna would say, "as fire and its heat, or milk and its whiteness, are one. When static the reality is Brahman; when active it is Shakti, the Mother." She is beyond speech and thought; verily, She is the Brahman of the Vedas and the Vedanta.

In the higher forms of Samadhi, Ramakrishna merged in the impersonal aspect of the Divine Mother. But for the fulfilment of the divine mission his mind had to be brought down, as if by force, to the phenomenal plane of consciousness. Then he regarded the world as the play of the Divine Mother. He, like a child, placed implicit trust in Her and, as will be seen, followed Her guidance in everything.

Living in intimate union with the Divine Mother Shri Rama-krishna had a number of intuitive experiences towards the close of his period of spiritual disciplines: some of them concerned himself, while others related to spiritual life in general. About himself Ramakrishna came to know that he was an Incarnation of God, a specially commissioned person, whose realizations were for the benefit of others, to usher in a new age of spirituality for mankind. Further, that he had always been a free soul, and so the aim of Mukti (freedom) had no meaning for him; at the same time he understood that he would not attain final libera-tion like an ordinary mortal, but would be born again and again to show humanity the way to freedom. Lastly, he foresaw the time of his own passing away and spoke of certain signs which would precede it. These signs were in due course seen and their import verified.

About spiritual matters in general, the following were his convictions: As the result of his realizations through all forms of discipline, he was firmly convinced that all religions were true, that every religious system was a path to God. Secondly, the three great systems of thought known as Dualism, Qualified Nondualism, and Nondualism—Dvaita, Vishishtadvaita, and Advaita—were not contradictory but complementary to one another; they were stages in man's progress towards the Goal. With regard to activity and inactivity he said, "A man whose mind is absolutely pure naturally goes beyond action. He cannot work even if he tries to; or the Lord does not allow him to work. But the ordinary man must do his duties unattached, depending on the Lord—like the maidservant in her master's house. She does everything for her master, but knows in her heart that her home is elsewhere." Thirdly, Ramakrishna realized that through him the Mother would found a new monastic Order, comprising those who would put into practice the doctrines of universality illustrated in his life. Lastly, his spiritual insight told him that those who were in their last incarnation—those who had sincerely prayed to the Lord at least once—must come to him. This statement may be taken in a universal or in a personal way, as one chooses.

Firmly established in the consciousness of God and totally unified with the Cosmic Will, Shri Ramakrishna was eager to disseminate the results of his realizations to all earnest seekers of Truth. He literally burned with that desire. He would say later: "There was no limit to the yearning I had then. In the day-time I managed somehow to control it. The ordinary talk of the worldly-minded was galling to me, and I would look wistfully to the day when my beloved, all-renouncing spiritual companions [his future apostles] would come. I hoped to find solace by telling them about my realizations, and so unburdening my mind. Every little incident would make me think of them. I used to arrange in my mind what I should say to one, give to another, and so on. But when the day came to a close, I could not curb my feelings. Another day had gone by and they had not come! When during the evening service the temple precincts rang with the sound of bells and conchs, I would climb to the roof of the building in the garden, and writhing in anguish of heart, cry at the top of my voice, 'Come, my boys! Oh, where are you all? I cannot bear to live without you!'

A mother never longed for her child so intensely, nor a friend for his companions, nor a lover for his sweetheart, as I did for them! Oh, it was indescribable! Shortly after this yearning the youngsters began to come."

To the fragrant full-blown lotus of the soul of Ramakrishna also came, like bees, Gauri Pandit, Padmalochan, Vaishnava-charan, Shashadhar Tarkachudamani and a host of other great pundits and aspirants; Keshabchandra Sen and Pratap-chandra Mazumdar, Vijaykrishna Goswami and the great Nag Mahashaya; Christians, Mohammedans, Sikhs and Hindus, hundreds of them. There came poets and thinkers, preachers and theologians, professors and leaders of public opinion, rich and poor, great devotees and fit disciples. It was at this time that Narendranath was pining for the vision of Truth. Un-consciously attracted by the wonderful aroma of Shri Rama-krishna's realizations, he also came to Dakshineshwar—he and that group of young men who were later to become the first monks of the Ramakrishna Order.

AT THE TOUCH OF THE MASTER

The Incarnations bear a special message for the world. Moved by compassion at the sight of the sorrows and miseries of humanity, the Lord, who is beyond the contamination of ignorance, incarnates Himself in this world, acknowledging a temporary allegiance, as it were, to all-powerful Maya, His own inscrutable Power. His is only a translucent veil, and he is aware, even from his very birth, of the special mission he has for the world. After intense spiritual practices of some years the veil is rent and his real self shines forth, a consummation which takes an ordinary mortal thousands of births to attain. Then his power becomes irresistible. He revolutionizes the world. His very presence radiates spirituality; his look and touch work miracles. But an Incarnation, constituted as he is of pure Sattva (light and wisdom), does not always have a widespread effect on humanity. Another personality is required, with more Rajas (activity), who is capable of giving the ideas of the Perfect One to the world. The inscrutable power which brings the Lord down from His high abode to take birth as an Incarnation also projects a portion of Him as a complementary being for the fulfilment of His mission. At the right time, the Incarnation seeks him out and makes him the conduit for his Gospel. The spiritual history of the world demonstrates the truth of this. Though having a number of disciples and devotees, Christ chose Peter as the rock on which to build his Church. Shri Krishna had Arjuna, Buddha had Ananda, Gauranga had Nityananda—all giving further evidence of this phenomenon. For Shri Ramakrishna, Narendranath played this complementary role.

At their first meeting Shri Ramakrishna instantly knew that Naren was the one who was to carry his message to the world. Through his Nirvikalpa Samadhi, Shri Ramakrishna had gained the power to identify himself with the Cosmic Mind in which this universe rises and disappears like a bubble in the ocean. Past, present and future held no secrets for him. It was thus that Shri Ramakrishna knew of the devoted souls who were born specially to assist him, and of the measure of help he would get from each.

Shri Ramakrishna represented traditional India, with its spiritual perspective, its asceticism and its realizations—the India of the Upanishads. To him came Naren with all the doubts and scepticism of the modern age, unwilling to accept even the highest truths of religion without verification, yet with a zeal for Truth burning within him. Naren had yet to learn that reason, though the best instrument in the relative world, could not carry one beyond relativity to the Absolute where the truth of religion abides. The result of this contact of Shri Ramakrishna with Narendranath was Swami Vivekananda— he who was to become the heart and mind of a New India, its ancient spiritual perspective heightened, widened, and strengthened to include modern learning. The intense activity of the West was to be combined with the deep meditation of the East. Asceticism and retirement were to be supplemented by work and service to others. From the merging of these two currents came the New Hinduism—the faith of a glorious Tomorrow, in which all should be fulfilment and nothing denial.

On the personal level the meeting was also extraordinary. Here is Shri Ramakrishna's own account of it:

Narendra entered this room by the western door. He seemed careless about his body and dress, and unlike other people, not mindful of the external world. His eyes bespoke an introspective mind, as if some part of it were always concentrated on something within. I was surprised to find such a spiritual soul coming from the material atmosphere of Calcutta. A mat was spread on the floor. He sat on it just near the place where you now see the big jar containing Ganga water. The friends with whom he had come appeared to be ordinary young men with the usual tendencies towards enjoyment. On inquiry, I came to know that he had learnt three or four Bengali songs only. I asked him to sing them. He began singing the Brahmo song which begins:

> O my mind, go to your own abode.
> In the foreign land of this world
> Why roam uselessly like a stranger!

He sang the song with his whole heart and put such pathos into it that I could not control myself, but fell into an ecstatic mood.

Then he took leave. But after that I felt such a constant agonizing desire to see him! At times the pain would be so excruciating that I felt as if my heart were being squeezed like a wet towel! Then I could no longer check myself. I ran to the northern quarter of the garden, a rather unfrequented place, and there cried at the top of my voice, "O my darling, come to me! I cannot live without seeing you!" After some time, I felt better. This state of things continued for six months. There were other boys who also came here; I felt greatly drawn to some of them, but nothing like the way I was attracted to Narendra.

Narendra too was profoundly moved on his first visit to the Master at Dakshineswar. He told some of his friends of it later, though with a touch of reserve:

Well, I sang the song; but shortly after, he suddenly rose and, taking me by the hand, led me to the northern veranda, shutting the door behind him. It was locked from the outside; so we were alone. I thought that he would give me some private instructions; but to my utter surprise he began to shed profuse tears of joy as he held my hand, and, addressing me most tenderly as one long familiar to him, said, "Ah, you come so late! How could you be so unkind as to keep me waiting so long! My ears are well-nigh burnt by listening to the profane talk of worldly people. Oh, how I yearn to unburden my mind to one who can appreciate my innermost experience!" Thus he went on amid sobs. The next moment he stood before me with folded hands and began to address me, "Lord, I know you are that ancient sage, Nara, the Incarnation of Narayana, born on earth to remove the miseries of mankind," and so on!

I was altogether taken aback by his conduct. "Who is this man whom I have come to see," I thought, "he must be stark mad! Why, I am just the son of Vishwanath Datta, and yet he dares to address me thus!" But I kept quiet, allowing him to go on. Presently he went back to his room, and bringing some sweets, sugar candy, and butter, began to feed me with his own hands. In vain did I say again and again, "Please give the sweets to me, I shall share them with my friends!" He simply said, "They may have some afterwards", and desisted only after I had eaten all. Then he seized me by the hand and said, "Promise that you will come alone to me at an early date." At his importunity I had to say "yes" and returned with him to my friends.

To the other devotees the Master said, "See! how Naren beams with the light of Saraswati [the Goddess of learning]!" Those who heard him say this looked upon Naren with wonder. Not only was it strange that the Master should speak thus, it was still more strange that he should have seen such profound spirituality in the boy. "Do you see a light before falling asleep?" asked Shri Ramakrishna. Narendra said, "Yes, sir." The Master cried, "Ah! everything is tallying. He is a Dhyana-Siddha [an adept in meditation] even from his very birth."

Regarding his conflicting thoughts about the strange words and conduct of Shri Ramakrishna, Narendranath used to say:

I sat and watched him. There was nothing wrong in his words, movements or behaviour towards others. Rather, from his spiritual words and ecstatic states he seemed to be a man of genuine renunciation; and there was a marked consistency between his words and life. He used the most simple language, and I thought, "Can this man be a great teacher?" I crept near him and asked him the question which I had asked so often: "Have you seen God, sir?" "Yes, I see Him just as I see you here, only in a much intenser sense." "God can be realized," he went on; "one can see and talk to Him as I am seeing and talking to you. But who cares? People shed torrents of tears for their wife and children, for wealth or property, but who does so for the sake of God? If one weeps sincerely for Him, He surely manifests Himself." That impressed me at once. For the first time I found a man who dared to say that he had seen God, that religion was a reality to be felt, to be sensed in an infinitely more intense way than we can sense the world. As I heard these things from his lips, I could not but believe that he was saying them not like an ordinary preacher, but from the depths of his own realizations. But I could not reconcile his words with his strange conduct with me. So I concluded that he must be a monomaniac. Yet I could not help acknowledging the magnitude of his renunciation. "He may be a madman," I thought, "but only the fortunate few can have such renunciation. Even if insane, this man is the holiest of the holy, a true saint, and for that alone he deserves the reverent homage of mankind!" With such conflicting thoughts I bowed before him and begged leave to return to Calcutta.

Though Naren considered Shri Ramakrishna to be a madman, he was at a loss to account for the strange feeling of blessedness that came over him as he sat near the Master. But it was all strange—the number of adoring devotees, the unaccountable religious ecstasy of the Master, his return from ecstasy, the atmosphere of intense blessedness, his words, the uplifting of his own soul—all these were bewildering to Naren. But in spite of the impression made on him, Naren was slow to accept the Master as a teacher. He allowed the various preoccupations of his daily life to prevent him from keeping his promise to repeat the visit; and it was not until nearly a month later that he set out alone on foot to the temple-garden of Dakshineswar. The following is the description of this meeting given by Narendra to some of his brother-disciples:

I did not realize then that the temple-garden of Dakshineswar was so far from Calcutta, since on the previous occasion I had gone there in a carriage. The road seemed to me so long as to be almost endless. However I reached the garden somehow and went straight to Shri Ramakrishna's room. I found him sitting alone on the small bedstead. He was glad to see me and, calling me affectionately to his side, made me sit beside him on the bed. But the next moment I found him overcome with a sort of emotion. Muttering something to himself, with his eyes fixed on me, he slowly drew near me. I thought he might do something queer as on the previous occasion. But in the twinkling of an eye he placed his right foot on my body. The touch at once gave rise to a novel experience within me. With my eyes open I saw that the walls, and everything in the room, whirled rapidly and vanished into naught, and the whole universe together with my individuality was about to merge in an all-encompassing mysterious void! I was terribly frightened and thought that I was facing death, for the loss of individuality meant nothing short of that. Unable to control myself I cried out, "What is it that you are doing to me! I have my parents at home!" He laughed aloud at this and stroking my chest said, "All right, let it rest now. Everything will come in time!" The wonder of it was that no sooner had he said this than that strange experience of mine vanished. I was myself again and found everything within and without the room as it had been before.

All this happened in less time than it takes me to narrate it; but it revolutionized my mind. Amazed, I wondered what it could possibly be. It came and went at the mere wish of this amazing man! I began to question whether it was mesmerism or hypnotism. But that was not likely, for these acted only on weak minds, and I prided myself on having just the reverse. I had not as yet surrendered myself to the stronger personality of the man. Rather I had taken him to be a monomaniac. So to what might this sudden transformation of mine be due? I could not come to any conclusion. It was an enigma, I thought, which I had better not attempt to solve. I was determined, however, to be on my guard and not to give him another chance to exert a similar influence over me.

The next moment I thought, how can a man who shatters to pieces a resolute and strong mind like mine be dismissed as a lunatic? Yet that was just the conclusion at which one would arrive from his effusiveness on our first meeting—unless he were an Incarnation of God, which was indeed a far cry. So I was in a dilemma about the real nature of my experience as well as about the truth of this wonderful man, who was obviously as pure and simple as a child. My rationalistic mind received an unpleasant rebuff at this failure in judging the true state of things. But I was determined to fathom the mystery somehow.

Thoughts like these occupied my mind during the whole of that day. But he became quite another man after that incident and, as on the previous occasion, treated me with great kindness and cordiality. His behaviour towards me was like that of a man who meets an old friend or relative after long separation. He seemed not to be satisfied with entertaining and taking all possible care of me. This remarkably loving treatment drew me all the more to him. At last, finding that the day was coming to a close, I asked leave to go. He seemed very dejected at this and gave me permission only after I had promised to come again at my earliest convenience.

A few days after the above experience, Narendranath paid his third visit to the Master at Dakshineswar. Though he was determined not to be overpowered this time, yet he fared no better than previously. Shri Ramakrishna took him that day to the adjacent garden of Jadunath Mallik. After a stroll they sat down in the parlour. Soon Shri Ramakrishna went into a trance and in that state touched Narendranath. In spite of his precautions Naren was totally overwhelmed and immediately lost all outward consciousness. When he came to himself after a while, he found the Master stroking his chest. Naren had no idea of what had happened during this period; but it was then that the Master learned many strange things about him.

Referring to this incident, Shri Ramakrishna later said: "I put several questions to him while he was in that state. I asked him about his antecedents and where he lived, his mission in this world and the duration of his mortal life. He dived deep into himself and gave fitting answers to my questions. They only confirmed what I had seen and inferred about him. Those things shall be a secret, but I came to know that he was a sage who had attained perfection, a past master in meditation, and that the day he knew his real nature, he would give up the body through Yoga, by an act of will."

These revelations did not come as a surprise to the Master; for wonderful things had been revealed to him about Naren even before this great disciple came to Dakshineswar. This is how Ramakrishna spoke of them:

One day I found that my mind was soaring high in Samadhi along a luminous path. It soon transcended the stellar universe and entered the subtler region of ideas. As it ascended higher and higher I found on both sides of the way ideal forms of gods and goddesses. The mind then reached the outer limits of that region, where a luminous barrier separated the sphere of relative existence from that of the Absolute. Crossing that barrier, the mind entered the transcendental realm where no corporeal being was visible. Even the gods dared not peep into that sublime realm, but had to be content to keep their seats far below. The next moment I found seven venerable sages seated there in Samadhi. It occurred to me that these sages must have surpassed not only men, but even the gods, in knowledge and holiness, in renunciation and love. Lost in admiration I was reflecting on their greatness, when I saw a portion of that undifferentiated luminous region condense into the form of a divine child. The child came to one of the sages, tenderly clasped his neck with his lovely little arms, and addressing him in a sweet voice attempted to drag his mind down from the state of Samadhi. The magic touch roused the sage from his super-conscious state, and he fixed his unmoving, half-open gaze upon that wonderful child. His beaming countenance showed that the child must have been the treasure of his heart. In great joy the strange child said to him, "I am going down. You too must go with me." The sage remained mute, but his tender look expressed his assent. As he kept gazing on the child, he was again immersed in Samadhi. I was surprised to find that a fragment of the sage's body and mind was descending on earth in the form of an effulgent light. No sooner had I seen Naren than I recognized him to be that sage. [Subsequent inquiry elicited from Shri Ramakrishna the admission that the divine child was none other than himself.]

On another occasion, Shri Ramakrishna saw in a vision a streak of light flash across the sky from Varanasi towards Calcutta. In great joy he exclaimed, "My prayer has been granted and *my man* must come to me one day."

It would seem that Naren's inability to discover what had happened during his trance was due to the will of the Master, who thought it best that his disciple should not know of the highest state too soon. He was not as yet prepared for it and would only have been terrified by it. And when Naren was in that state of Samadhi, the Master turned the subconscious currents of Naren's nature, by force, as it were, into the super-conscious channel, working a great transformation in his mind. So it was that, little by little, he began to regard Shri Rama-krishna not as a madman, but as the only sane man among the myriad lunatics of the world, who dwell in an asylum of selfishness and desire, bound down in a prison-house of lust and gold. Still, the strange words Shri Ramakrishna addressed to him during the first meeting at Dakshineswar were an anomaly to him. The full significance of the part he was to play with the Master dawned on him only later, after repeated tests and trials.

Naren was the Master's, from the moment the latter touched him. It was a possession, however, which meant the highest freedom for Naren's soul. He lost many of his cherished con-victions: for instance, that a Guru (spiritual teacher) was not

6

necessary. How could a man, he had reasoned, necessarily weak and short-visioned, be the unerring guide that the principle of implicit obedience implied! Now he realized that it was possible for such a man to exist and for his help and influence to be of inestimable value. His faith in asceticism and renunciation was strengthened by coming in contact with the Master. He devoted himself heart and soul to the endeavour of realizing God. After a searching analysis of the Master's realizations and mode of life, he accepted from him the advice and help which appealed to his (Naren's) reason.

Narendra was at that time a sceptic, with no faith in the Hindu gods. He laughed at many of the injunctions of the Hindu scriptures. Nor was he one to silence the questionings of his mind, or drive off a doubt with the lash of a fanatic creed. His soul was open to all that might come to it. At first came darkness, appalling darkness, intensified by anguish. Even here he tried to see; and, when the gloom was blackest and he was beginning to ask himself whether he might not be chasing phantoms, a faint light as of the dawning of Truth became apparent. This gave him hope to go on in the face of failures and persisting darkness. To allay his doubts he demanded direct vision. The more Naren struggled against doubt, the more insistently it arose within the silence of the soul. He was, however, a born sailor on the ocean of the struggle for Reality, and his sailor's instinct kept him afloat. He was confident that the beatific knowledge would come as a triumphant climax to all his struggles and sufferings.

Shri Ramakrishna understood and loved Naren the better for all this turmoil, for he himself had had to pass through upheavals which, though they were tempests of the soul rather than of the mind as in Naren's case, were similar in their cause and intensity. He saw that Naren's intellect, because of the very intensity of his desire for the Truth, would for long doubt; but he saw also that Naren would conquer in the end, that he would transcend all limitations and become a spiritual giant. So he continued to guide and instruct him with love and patience.

Hereafter Naren's life is that of the saint-in-the-making. It is no longer his mind to which one's attention is chiefly drawn, though that does indeed become more and more luminous as the years go on: it is his heart, his soul, his vision, that captures attention. A time was to come when the orb of his soul was to shine with the radiance and glory of the full moon. He was to attain to the highest possibilities of the mystical consciousness, wherein the soul and the Supreme Reality are revealed as a perfect and distinctionless Unity. In the imperious question asked by Naren of the Maharshi Devendranath—"Mahashaya [Venerable Sir], have you seen God?"—was the dawn of his spiritual life. Prior to that the intellect ruled and doubt was supreme; though even then were to be seen, if faintly, the streaks of an approaching dawn. These grew into the day of glorious vision in the effulgent presence of Shri Ramakrishna, the Sun of Truth.

7

GURU AND DISCIPLE

During his training with Shri Ramakrishna, the story of Naren's life is to be told in terms of ideas and realizations. Wonderful was the relationship between Guru and disciple, a full account of which can never be given. So close, so deep was their love and regard for each other, that their followers always think of them as one soul—Ramakrishna-Vivekananda—; for thought of the one involves awareness of the other. Theirs was a spiritual relationship without a touch of worldliness. From the moment Naren came to the Master and asked, "Sir, have you seen God?" began the spiritual growth of the disciple ending in his illumination. The climax was reached when the spirit of the Master, before he left the body, descended upon the disciple. This relationship served a great impersonal purpose—the revival of the religion of the Vedas and the preaching of a New Gospel suited to the needs of the modern world.

Great Teachers who have themselves realized the highest Truth, when they come in contact with a fit disciple, are eager to impart that Truth. Shri Ramakrishna recognized Naren's spiritual potentialities. Nevertheless Naren needed time to ripen, as we see from his terror of losing his individuality when the Master tried to put him into Nirvikalpa Samadhi. Referring humorously to this incident later on one occasion, Ramakrishna said to Naren: "A man died and became an evil spirit. Anxious to have a companion, whenever the spirit heard that someone had passed away it would at once go to that place hoping to get a companion; but every time it returned disappointed, because the soul had been liberated through some act or other of piety. Such is the case with me. As soon as I saw you I thought I had a friend, but you too said that you had your father and mother at home! I am therefore living alone without a companion, like the spirit in the story."

Shri Ramakrishna's love for Naren was so deep that if Naren failed to come to Dakshineswar for some days he would become disconsolate. He would weep and pray to the Divine Mother, begging Her to make him come, and refusing to be comforted in the meantime. The other devotees did not understand, nor did Naren. Sometimes he regarded Shri Ramakrishna as an old man subject to hallucinations; at other times he was overcome by the Master's affection and lovingly responded to it. It was really the Master's love which enabled Naren to hold on until he could appreciate him intellectually. Something "held" him, as it were. As Naren said at that time, "It is his love for me that binds me to him."

Once Narendra did not appear at Dakshineswar for several days and Shri Ramakrishna was much disturbed. One day during this period, two devotees, Ramdayal and Baburam (later Swami Premananda), came to see the Master. Shri Ramakrishna asked Ramdayal about Narendranath, and said, "Well, he has not come here for a long time. I long to see him. Will you please ask him to come here soon? You won't forget it?" The visitors remained there for the night. About 11 o'clock, when everyone had retired to bed, Shri Ramakrishna with his cloth under his arm suddenly came to them and said to Ramdayal, "Well, are you asleep?" "No, sir", replied Ramdayal, and both he and Baburam at once sat up. "Look here. Please tell Naren to come, I feel as if somebody were wringing my heart like a wet towel", said Shri Ramakrishna, twisting his cloth to give force to his words. Ramdayal, who was familiar with Shri Ramakrishna's childlike simplicity, consoled him in various ways and assured him that he would persuade Naren to come to Dakshineswar. The same scene was repeated several times during the night, and the two devotees could not but be astonished and puzzled by Ramakrishna's eagerness to see Narendra.

Another devotee of Shri Ramakrishna, Vaikunthanath Sanyal, once found the Master very restless on account of the prolonged absence of Narendranath. Vaikuntha said

later: "The Master was that day full of praise for Narendranath. Talking about him made him so desirous of seeing him
that he was completely overwhelmed, and could no longer
control himself; he hurried to the adjacent veranda and cried
out, 'Mother dear, I cannot live without seeing him.' When
he returned, he said to us, in a voice full of grief, 'I have wept
so much, and yet Narendra has not come. My heart is being
squeezed as it were, so excruciating is the pain at not seeing
him. But he does not care.' He left the room again, but soon
returned and said, 'An old man pining and weeping for the
boy! What will people think of me? You are my own people;
I do not feel ashamed to confess it before you. But how will
others take it? I cannot control myself.' But his joy was corre-
spondingly great when Naren came." At one time when the devotees were celebrating the Master's birthday at Dakshineswar,
and the beloved disciple did not come until noon, he asked
about him again and again. When Naren finally appeared and
bowed down before him, the Master leaned on his shoulder
and fell into deep Samadhi. When he returned to normal
consciousness, he fed and caressed Naren. Often, the mere
sight of Naren would send the Master into Samadhi. Once,
when he had not seen him for some time, he went to meet him
at the landing ghat at Dakshineswar. Touching the disciple's
face, he began to chant the most holy word of the Vedas, and
went into Samadhi.

During about five years of Narendra's discipleship he went
to see the Master once or twice a week. Sometimes he would
stay on for a few days. During the later years family troubles
prevented him from going to Dakshineswar as frequently as he
would have wished. Shri Ramakrishna consoled himself during
those days with the thought, "It is good that Naren does not
come, for I experience a commotion of feeling when I see him.
His coming is a great event here."

Shri Ramakrishna's greatest attractions in Naren's eyes
were his renunciation, purity and constant devotion to God;
whereas, in the disciple the Master respected the unbounded
self-reliance, manly spirit and single-minded devotion to

Truth. It is impossible to describe Shri Ramakrishna's faith in Naren. Ordinary people looked upon Naren's self-reliance as foolhardiness. His manliness appeared to them as obstinacy. His uncompromising regard for Truth was taken as evidence of an immature intellect. People could not understand his supreme disregard for praise or contumely, his childlike frankness and, above all, his spirit of freedom and fearlessness in thought, speech and action. But Shri Ramakrishna from the very outset knew the apparent vanity and obstinacy of Narendranath to be manifestations of self-reliance and consciousness of uncommon mental powers; his freedom in thought and action to be the outcome of self-control; and his indifference to praise or blame to be due to purity of heart. He foresaw that when the latent genius of Narendranath matured, the apparent pride and stubbornness would be transformed into love for the afflicted, his self-reliance would inspire the despondent with courage, and his love of freedom would show mankind the way to liberation.

He used to call Naren, Rakhal, Baburam, Yogen, Niranjan and Purna, Ishwara-Kotis, persons who assume bodies to aid God in His mission on earth. "What training they go through," he used to say, "they do not need for themselves; it is for the good of the world." Indeed the Master thought so highly of Naren that if anybody spoke disparagingly of him, he would remonstrate with the reviler saying, "What are you doing! You are committing Shiva-ninda!" meaning that to speak slightingly of Naren amounted to blasphemy against Shiva. He would also say, "Let no one judge Naren. No one will ever be able to understand him fully." Once when a devotee brought the news to him that Naren was falling into evil ways by mixing with persons of questionable character, Shri Ramakrishna took him sharply to task saying, "That is not true. Mother has told me that Naren can never fall into evil ways. If you talk to me in that strain any more, I shall never see your face again." Shri Ramakrishna never hesitated to praise Naren in front of his devotees. He knew well that such praise might give rise to pride and vanity in weaker minds, but he was convinced that Narendra was above such small-mindedness.

One day Shri Ramakrishna was seated in his room with Keshabchandra Sen, Vijaykrishna Goswami and other celebrated leaders of the Brahmo Samaj. Narendranath was also present. The Master, in an exalted mood, cast his eyes upon the Brahmos and then on Naren, and, as a picture of the latter's future greatness flashed before his mind, he was filled with tenderness for the disciple. After the meeting was over he said to some devotees, "Well, if Keshab is possessed of one sign of greatness which has made him famous, Naren has eighteen such signs. In Keshab and Vijay I saw the light of knowledge burning like a candle-flame, but in Narendra it was like a blazing sun, dispelling the last vestige of ignorance and delusion." An ordinary man would have become inflated at such compliments; but Naren was different. In comparison with Keshab and Vijay he thought himself very insignificant and he protested to the Master, "Sir, why do you say such things! People will think you mad. How can you compare the world-renowned Keshab and the saintly Vijay with an insignificant young student like me? Please do not do so again." At this Shri Ramakrishna was pleased and said, "I cannot help it. Do you think those were my words! The Divine Mother showed me certain things which I simply repeated. And She never reveals to me anything but the truth." This reference to divine revelation for support did not impress Narendranath. He doubted, saying frankly and boldly, "Who knows whether these are revelations from the Mother or mere fancies of your brain! If I were in your position I should attribute them to imagination, pure and simple. Western science and philosophy have demonstrated that we are often deceived by our senses, and the chances of deception are much more when it ministers to a personal predisposition. Since you love me and always wish to see me great, it is but natural that these fancies should come into your mind." When the Master's mind was on higher planes, he would take no notice of Naren's words; at other times Naren's apparently incontrovertible reasoning upset him. In his perplexity the

Master appealed to the Divine Mother, and was comforted when She replied, "Why do you care for what he says? In a few days he will admit every word of it to be true."

But the high opinion of Shri Ramakrishna was a source of strength and inspiration to Naren, especially in later years when, as the Swami Vivekananda, he was preaching his message to the world.

Once, when several days had elapsed since Naren's last visit to Dakshineswar, Shri Ramakrishna became very anxious and sent for him; but Naren did not come. Thereupon Shri Ramakrishna set out for Calcutta himself. Guessing that Naren would be at the evening service of the Sadharan Brahmo Samaj, he directed his steps there. He had often visited the Samaj and knew intimately many of its prominent members. The service was already in progress when Shri Ramakrishna in a semi-conscious state made his appearance. The preacher broke off his sermon, and the congregation stared at the newcomer. Shri Ramakrishna, unmindful of the commotion his presence was causing, advanced slowly to the pulpit, going into a superconscious state! This further heightened the curiosity of the assembly and the disorder increased. Some of the leading Brahmos present, connecting Shri Ramakrishna with a recent split in their camp because Keshab and Vijay had changed their views under his influence, considered this visit an intrusion. They turned off the lights in order to restore order. This only added to the confusion and everybody rushed towards the door. Naren, who was in the choir, guessed the reason for the Master's visit and went instantly to his rescue. He conducted him through the crowd to the backdoor and took him to Dakshineswar. Shri Ramakrishna paid no heed to Naren's expostulations on the wisdom of his action and was not in the least repentant. About this, Naren said later:

It is impossible to describe the pain I felt to see the Master thus ill-treated on my account that day. Ah, how much did I scold him for that action of his! But he? Neither did he feel hurt at the humiliation nor did he give ear to my words of reproach, supremely satisfied as he was at having me with him.

Seeing that the Master gave no thought to himself on account of me, I did not hesitate on occasion to use harsh words about his blind love for me. I used to warn him, saying that if he constantly thought of me, he would become like me, even as King Bharata of the old legend, who so doted upon his pet deer that even at the time of death he was unable to think of anything else, and, as a result, was born as a deer in his next life. At these words, the Master, so simple was he, became very nervous, and said, "What you say is quite true. What is to become of me, for I cannot bear to be separated from you?" Dejected, he went to the Kali temple. In a few minutes he returned smiling and said, "You rogue, I shall not listen to you any more. Mother says that I love you because I see the Lord in you, and the day I no longer do so, I shall not be able to bear even the sight of you." With this short but emphatic statement he dismissed once for all everything that I had ever said to him on the subject.

This was really the key to Shri Ramakrishna's overwhelming love for Naren and his other disciples: it was beyond any human or personal sentiment.

On another occasion, referring to his relationship with Naren and the other young boys, Shri Ramakrishna said: "Hazra took me to task because I was anxious to see the boys. He said, 'When do you think of God?' I felt uneasy and said to Mother, 'Hazra asks why I think so much of Naren and the other boys.' And Mother at once showed me that She Herself was in all human forms. She manifests Herself specially in pure bodies. When I came out of this Samadhi, I felt angry with Hazra. I said to myself, 'That rascal! how he unsettled my mind!' Then I thought, 'Why blame the poor fellow! How could he know!'"

The Master continued: "I regard these boys as embodied Narayana. When I saw Naren for the first time I noticed that he had no body-idea. As soon as I touched him in the region of the heart he lost outward consciousness. Gradually intense longing came over me to see him again and again, and it filled my heart with pain. Then I asked Bholanath [an officer of the Kali temple], 'How is it that I feel this, and that for a boy, a Kayastha by caste?' And Bholanath said, 'Sir, that is all right. It is explained in the *Mahabharata* that when the mind of a man of Samadhi comes down to the normal plane, it finds recreation only in the company of men of Sattva quality, men of the highest spirituality.' This comforted me."

Shri Ramakrishna himself explained on various occasions why Naren was so dear to him. Here is one recorded by Swami Saradananda: "Speaking with Ratan, the chief officer of the garden house of Jadunath Mallick, and pointing to us, the Master said, 'These boys are good. . . . But I have not seen another boy like Narendra. He is as proficient in music, vocal and instrumental, as in the acquisition of knowledge; as gifted in conversation as in religious matters. He loses normal consciousness in meditation for whole nights. My Narendra is a coin with no alloy whatever: it rings true. I see, other boys somehow pass two or three examinations after straining to their utmost: there it ends; they are a spent force. But Narendra is not like that; he does everything with ease; to pass an examination is a trifle for him. He goes to the Brahmo Samaj also and sings devotional songs there; but he is not like other Brahmos—he is a true knower of Brahman. He sees light when he sits for meditation. Is it for nothing that I love Narendra so much?"

On another occasion, while giving an eloquent description of Naren's qualities in comparison with those of others, he said:

Narendra belongs to a very high plane—the realm of the Absolute. He has a manly nature. So many devotees come here, but there is not one like him.

Every now and then I take stock of devotees. I find that some are like lotuses with ten petals, some like those with sixteen petals, some like those with a hundred petals; but among lotuses Narendra is a thousand-petalled one. Other devotees may be like pots or pitchers; but Narendra is a large water-barrel. Others may be like pools or tanks; but Narendra is a huge reservoir like the Haldarpukur. Among fish, Narendra is a huge red-eyed carp; others are like minnows or smelts or sardines. Tarak of Belgharia may be called a bass. Narendra is a very big receptacle, one that can hold many things. He is like a bamboo with a big hollow space inside.

Narendra is not under the control of anything. He is not under the control of attachment or sense pleasures. He is like a male pigeon.

If you hold a male pigeon by its beak, it breaks away from you; but the female pigeon keeps still. Narendra has the nature of a man; so he sits on the right side in a carriage. Bhavanath has a woman's nature; so I make him sit on the other side. I feel great strength when Narendra is with me at a gathering.

Once Naren was seated in his study with a few of his friends. He had not visited Dakshineswar for some time. During the conversation a voice was heard calling, "Naren! Naren!" All started to their feet. Naren hastened downstairs to receive Shri Ramakrishna, for it was he who had come. His eyes were filled with tears. "Naren, why do you not come to see me these days?" he asked. He was as simple as a child. He had brought some sweetmeats with which he fed Naren with his own hands. Ah! wonderful is the way of the Lord in pointing out the path of illumination to the struggling seeker! The Lord Himself comes to him who looks for Him, the Teacher to the disciple when the latter is prepared. "Come!" Shri Ramakrishna urged, "sing me one of your songs." Naren took the Tanpura and began a song to the Divine Mother. The others sat still. Soon Shri Ramakrishna became unconscious of all outward things.

On one of Naren's early visits to Dakshineswar, Shri Ramakrishna said to him, "Look! In you is Shiva! In me is Shakti! And these two are One!" Naren, of course, was not able to understand the meaning of such utterances then. In this connection it is noteworthy that Naren was rarely allowed to do any personal service for the Master, such as fanning and the like—services which it is customary for the disciple to render the Guru. Was it that Shri Ramakrishna saw Shiva—the Divine—so intensely in Naren, that to have accepted service from him would have been to accept it from one too exalted? Seva (service) is for the purification of heart; what need has he for Seva whose heart is already pure! Let it not be thought, however, that Naren did not feel this as a deprivation. He would insist on offering service in some way or other, for love of the Master and because of his own sense of humility; but the Master would seldom allow it, saying, "Your path is different!"

Shri Ramakrishna's relationship with Narendra differed a great deal from that with the other disciples. He expected them to observe restrictions as regards food, meditation, prayer, sleep and other affairs of daily life. There were no such restrictions for Naren. He would say, "Naren is a Nitya-siddha, perfect in realization even from his very birth; Naren is a Dhyana-siddha, an adept in meditation; the roaring fire of knowledge, always ablaze in Naren, burns to ashes whatever impure food he may take. Impurity of food can never tarnish his pure mind. He is always cutting to pieces the veils of Maya with the sword of knowledge. The inscrutable Maya can never bring him under Her control." When any admirer came to Dakshineswar with offerings of fruits and sweetmeats for the Master, they would be set aside, not to be eaten by himself or given to the disciples unless he were sure that the donor was pure in character and unselfish in motive. But he allowed Naren to take them. Nothing could affect him, he said, and sometimes, when Naren did not make his appearance, the Master would even send the delicacies to Naren's home. Sometimes after eating at a hotel Naren would say to the Master, "Sir, I have eaten today what is considered forbidden food." Shri Ramakrishna, realizing that Naren was not just speaking in a spirit of bravado, would say, "That will not affect you in the least. If one can keep one's mind steadily on God after eating beef or pork, these things are as good as Havishyanna [rice specially prepared and taken with clarified butter only]. But vegetables eaten by a man engrossed in worldliness are no better than beef or pork. That you have taken forbidden food does not make any difference to me. But if any of these [pointing to the other devotees] had done so, I could not bear to have them even touch me."

Narendra wondered at this discrimination exercised as to food and the receiving of presents from certain persons. He thought it was perhaps superstitious eccentricity or puritanical squeamishness. But Shri Ramakrishna insisted that when he refused to accept offerings it was because the giver was of questionable character. This interested Naren. Was it true?

He determined to find out for himself. He observed and studied the characters of those whose offerings the Master had rejected. He found that in every case Shri Ramakrishna had been right. Amazed, he said to himself, "What a wonderful man! His purity is past understanding. How he can read the minds of others!"

Shri Ramakrishna was delighted when Naren engaged in arguments with the other devotees. Naren would storm their minds, startling them with the profundity of his knowledge as he cited Eastern and Western philosophers. It was not mere learning that Naren revealed: it was the spirit of learning itself that seemed to be incarnate in him. The Master's delight knew no bounds when he found others much older than Naren unable to withstand Naren's reasoning power.

As a member of the Brahmo Samaj, Naren was committed to belief in a formless God with attributes. He had thus turned his back on the gods of Hinduism. In his enthusiasm he had persuaded Rakhal, another of Shri Ramakrishna's great disciples, to embrace the Brahmo creed. But Rakhal was really a devotee whose latent devotional fervour was roused when he came in contact with Shri Ramakrishna. When he went with the Master to the Kali temple, he bowed down before the images. This was against the Brahmo creed. One day Naren saw him doing so, and took him to task. Rakhal possessed a gentle nature, and rather than argue he avoided Naren. Shri Ramakrishna intervened, saying to Naren, "Please do not intimidate Rakhal. He is afraid of you. He believes now in God with forms. How are you going to change him? Everyone cannot realize the formless aspect of God at the very beginning." That was enough for Narendra, and he never interfered with Rakhal's attitude again.

Sometimes Naren revealed a tendency to fanaticism. Shri Ramakrishna would admonish him: "My boy, try to see the Truth from all angles and in every perspective." This tendency to bigotry disappeared when Naren realized the oneness of all spiritual endeavour and religious belief. But he continued to argue against image worship with Shri Ramakrishna. One day the Master, tired of trying to convince him that the images worshipped were the presentment of spiritual ideals, said, "Why do you come here if you won't acknowledge my Mother?" Naren, undismayed, replied, "Must I accept Her simply because I come here?" "All right," said the Master; "before long you will not only acknowledge my beloved Mother, but weep in Her name." Then to the other devotees he said, "This boy has no faith in the forms of God and tells me that my supersensuous experiences are hallucinations; but he is a fine boy of pure tendencies. He does not believe anything unless he gets direct proof. He has studied much and is possessed of great judgement and discrimination."

One of the bones of contention between the Master and Naren was the Radha-Krishna episode of the Hindu tradition. In the first place Narendra doubted its historicity, and in the second, he considered the relationship of Krishna with Radha immoral and objectionable. Unable to convince him, Shri Ramakrishna said one day, "Even if it is agreed that Radha was not a historical personality and that the episode is imagined by some lover of God, why not fix your mind on the intense yearning of Radha and the Gopis for the Supreme? Why dwell on the expression? This may appear human to you, but the yearning and vision you must take as divine."

However, the Master was glad at heart that Naren was a rebel, for without intellectual questioning and struggle no one can arrive at illumination; besides, Naren's own struggles would later on be a help to him in understanding and solving the difficulties of others. At the same time, the overcoming by Naren of his difficulties and his progressive realization of Truth, prove the rare quality of Shri Ramakrishna's teaching, and reveal him as the living Incarnation of Hinduism in this modern age.

From the first it was Shri Ramakrishna's idea to initiate Narendra into the truth of the Advaita Vedanta. With that end in mind he would ask Naren to read aloud passages from the *Ashtavakra Samhita* and other Advaita treatises in order to familiarize him with the teaching. To Narendra, a staunch adherent of the Brahmo Samaj, these writings seemed heretical. He would rebel saying, "It is blasphemous, for there is no difference between such philosophy and atheism. There is no greater sin in the world than to think of myself as identical with the Creator. I am God, you are God, these created things are God—what can be more absurd than this! The sages who wrote such things must have been insane." Shri Ramakrishna would be amused at this bluntness and would only remark, "You may not accept the views of these seers; but how can you abuse them or limit God's infinitude? Go on praying to the God of Truth and believe in any aspect of His which He reveals to you." But Naren did not surrender easily. Whatever did not tally with reason, he considered to be false, and it was his nature to stand against falsehood. Therefore he missed no opportunity to ridicule the Advaita philosophy.

But the Master knew that Narendra's was the path of Jnana (knowledge); for this reason he made it a point to continue to talk Advaita to him. One day he tried to bring home to him the identity of the individual soul with Brahman, but without success. Narendra left the room, and going to Pratapchandra Hazra said, "How can this be? This jug is God, this cup is God and we too are God: nothing can be more preposterous!" On hearing Naren's laughter, Shri Ramakrishna, who was in his room in a state of semi-consciousness, came out nude, with his cloth under his arm like a child. "Hullo! what are you talking about?" he said smiling. He touched Narendra and plunged into Samadhi. The effect of the touch Naren described as follows:

The magic touch of the Master that day immediately brought a wonderful change over my mind. I was astounded to find that really there was nothing in the universe but God! I saw it quite clearly, but kept silent to see whether the impression would last; but it did not abate in the course of the day. I returned home, but there too, everything I saw appeared to be Brahman. I sat down to take my meal, but found that everything—the food, the plate, the person who served, and even myself—was nothing but That. I ate a morsel or two and sat still. I was startled by my mother's words, "Why do

you sit still? Finish your meal", and then began to eat again. But all
the while, whether eating or lying down, or going to College, I had
the same experience and felt myself always in a sort of trance. While
walking in the streets, I noticed cabs plying, but I did not feel inclined to move out of the way. I felt that the cabs and myself were of
one stuff. There was no sensation in my limbs, which seemed to be
becoming paralysed. I did not relish eating, and felt as if somebody
else were eating. Sometimes I lay down during a meal; after a few
minutes I got up and again began to eat. The result would be that on
some days I would take too much, but it did no harm. My mother
became alarmed and said that there must be something wrong with
me. She was afraid that I might not live long. When there was a slight
change in this state, the world began to appear dream-like. While
walking in Cornwallis Square, I would strike my head against the
iron railings to see if they were real or only a dream. This state of
things continued for some days. When I became normal again, I
realized that I must have had a glimpse of the Advaita state. Then
it struck me that the words of the scriptures were not false. Thenceforth
I could not deny the conclusions of the Advaita philosophy.

Such was Shri Ramakrishna's teaching and such the training
of Naren. Little by little the disciple was led from doubt to
certitude, from darkness to light, from anguish of mind to the
peace of vision, from the seething vortex of the world to the
grand expanse of universal Oneness. He was taken, little by
little, and by the power of Shri Ramakrishna, from bondage to
spiritual freedom, from the pale of a little learning into that
omniscience which is the consciousness of Brahman. He was
lifted out of objective conceptions of the Godhead to awareness
of the beyond-subject-object nature of True Being—above
form, above sense, above thought, above all relative good
and evil, to the sameness and absoluteness of Brahman. Now
Naren's regard for the Master was increasing a thousandfold;
he was beginning to accept him as the highest ideal of spirituality. The scene of the young hero's highest realization was
to be the Cossipore garden; and the time: the immediate
future.

Again and again the Master told his disciples to test him and
his realizations. "Test me as the money-changers test their

7

coins. You must not accept me until you have tested me thoroughly." One day whilst the Master was absent in Calcutta, Naren came to Dakshineswar and found Shri Ramakrishna's room empty. The desire arose to test Shri Ramakrishna's renunciation of gold. So he hid a rupee under the Master's bed and then went to meditate under the Panchavati. Soon Shri Ramakrishna returned, and as usual sat on the bed. But no sooner did he touch it than he started up in great pain. Naren, who had returned by then, stood watching silently. An attendant at once examined the bed; as he pulled off the cover the coin fell to the ground. Naren left the room without a word. Shri Ramakrishna realized that he had been tested by Naren and rejoiced.

But the disciples were tested in their turn by Shri Ramakrishna. Even Naren had to go through many tests before the Master accepted him. One day, after examining Naren's body thoroughly, the latter remarked, "Your physical signs are good. The only fault I find is that you breathe rather heavily while asleep. Such a man, the Yogis say, is short-lived." On another occasion the Master said, "Your eyes show that you are not a dry Jnani [man of knowledge]. In you tender devotion and deep knowledge are blended." As a result of these investigations Shri Ramakrishna concluded that Naren possessed to a rare degree spirituality, boldness, restraint and the spirit of self-sacrifice; that never in the midst of the most adverse circumstances would his actions be ordinary.

At one time Shri Ramakrishna tested Naren severely for an extended period. We have already seen how his very presence at Dakshineswar filled the Master with intense joy. Even to see Naren at a distance would move him deeply. Sometimes he would go into Samadhi at the mere sight of him. A day came, however, when all this was changed: Ramakrishna began to treat Naren with utter indifference. Narendra came, saluted the Master, and sat down before him. He waited for a while but the Master did not speak. Thinking that perhaps he was absorbed, Naren left the room, went to Hazra, and began to chat and smoke with him. Then, when he heard the Master

talking with others, he went back, only to be met with worse
treatment; for not only did the Master not greet him, but he
deliberately turned his face away, towards the wall. When
Narendranath left for Calcutta there was no change in the
Master's attitude.

A week later, Naren came to Dakshineswar again to find the
Master's manner towards him as it was on the previous visit;
so he spent the day talking with Hazra and other devotees,
and returned home at nightfall. The third and the fourth time
it was the same; but Narendranath kept going to Dakshineswar,
and showed no resentment. Between these visits the Master
would sometimes send to Calcutta to enquire about Naren's
health, but without changing his demeanour in Naren's presence. At the end of a month, during which time there was no
reaction from Naren, the Master said to him, "Though I do
not exchange a single word with you, you still continue to
come! How is that?" Narendranath replied, "Do you think
that I come here only to listen to you? I love you and want to
see you. This is why I come to Dakshineswar." Shri Ramakrishna was highly pleased at the reply and said, "I was only
testing you to see if you would stay away when I did not show
love and attention. Only one of your calibre could have put up
with such neglect and indifference. Anyone else would have
left me long ago, never to come again."

On another occasion Shri Ramakrishna called him to the
Panchavati and said, "Through the practice of severe spiritual
discipline I have acquired supernatural powers. But of what
use are they to me? I cannot even keep my body properly
covered. Therefore, with the Mother's permission, I am thinking of transmitting them to you. She has made known to me
that you will have to do much work for Her. If I impart these
powers to you, you can use them when necessary. What do
you say?" Narendra knew that the Master possessed powers.
After a moment's thought he said, "Will these help me to
realize God?" "No," replied the Master, "they will not help
you to do that; but they will be very helpful to you when, after
realizing God, you will be engaged in doing His work." Naren

said, "I do not want them. Let me realize God first; maybe I
shall then know whether I need them or not. If I accept them
now, I may forget my ideal and, making use of them for some
selfish purpose, come to grief." We do not know whether
Shri Ramakrishna really wanted to impart his powers to Naren
or whether he was simply testing him; but we do know that
he was much pleased when Naren refused them.

It is not possible to give the reader an adequate idea of the
relationship between these two; of the love and liberty which
Naren enjoyed at the hands of the Master. Shri Ramakrishna
confided the secrets of his heart to Naren. He helped him
develop independence of thought, thus increasing a thousandfold Naren's self-reliance, regard for truth and innate spirituality. The Master's love for and faith in Naren acted as a
restraining force on the freedom-loving young disciple and
proved an unconscious protection from temptations.

8

THE MAN IN THE MAKING

The weaving of the web of a great personality is a wonderful and unique process. The days are the weavers and every experience a thread; intellect and heart with their variations are the warp and woof; and of these elements the pattern is made by the awakening soul. The spiritual stature of the person in question and his realizations of the Truth, however, depend entirely on his awareness that his real nature is spiritual; with that must go the will to renounce the whole world, if need be, to uncover that nature. Not less clearly does the mandate of renunciation ring from the mouth of the sage who walked the hills of Judea: "What doth it profit a man if he gain the whole world and lose his own soul?" than it does from the Indian sages centuries earlier: "All this is Maya—unreal. The real alone matters."

A survey of Naren's youth shows three main factors shaping his character and destiny: his innate spiritual tendency, or, in the terms used above, his awareness of his real nature; the influence of his family and of his studies; and thirdly, the guidance of his spiritual teacher Shri Ramakrishna, who raised him from the mire of unhappiness and scepticism to certainty and Peace. In the foregoing pages we have given an idea of his innate spiritual tendency, evident from his purity, his thirst to know God, his search for one who had seen Him, and his final surrender at the feet of the Master at Dakshineswar.

The influence of his family, exerted mainly through his parents, was far-reaching in its effects. It was his mother who imbued him with the ideals of feeling nobly, thinking highly and acting rightly. At her knee he gained his wide knowledge of the *Ramayana* and the *Mahabharata*, the two great Hindu epics, as she read them aloud to him in the twilight. To his father he owed his broadmindedness, manliness and respect for any genuine national tradition. His father's influence served to widen the scope of Naren's learning by directing his attention to the cultures of other lands. This was as it should be, for, as Swami Vivekananda in the making, he needed to develop a sympathetic understanding broad enough to include all cultures and all religions. So we find Naren desirous of encompassing all knowledge, Eastern and Western, in philosophy and history, in the arts and sciences, but especially in Western philosophy. He threw himself into these studies with his usual intensity, determined to discover and master their underlying principles and value.

He was aware that most philosophical systems are only intellectual diagrams, giving no place to the emotions of man, thereby stifling his creative and responsive faculties. Moreover, it requires as great an act of faith to believe in a speculative system of thought as to "believe without understanding" in theological dogmas. Naren did not want diagrams of Truth, no matter how clever: he wanted the Truth. True philosophy should be the mother of spiritual action, the fountain-head of creative energy, the highest and noblest stimulus to the will. Short of that, it was worthless.

The philosophy of Herbert Spencer interested him particularly, and later on he used the Spencerian mode of reasoning in his discussion of the doctrines of the Upanishads and the Vedanta. From such study Naren gained a power of thought, penetrating discrimination, and spirit of search for a scientific basis, that stood him in good stead when delivering his message in later years. The philosophy of Spencer is dangerous to traditional theological conceptions. It pulverizes the foundations of belief itself. Only an innate idealism, and the power of a poetic and imaginative temperament, could save any part of Naren's former outlook. It was his inherent capacity for the broader vision that saved him from becoming a fatalist and atheist. The mystic was latent in him, and his spirited soul could not stop its questionings at the agnostic's half-way house. He studied the systems of the German philosophers, particularly those of Kant and Schopenhauer. He studied also John

Stuart Mill and Auguste Comte, and delved into Aristotelian
analysis and speculations. For a time he found satisfaction in
the Positivist philosophy of Comte which embraces a wide
ethical outlook. But never did his enthusiasm for exploration
beguile him into accepting any newer and greater vision
of Truth without subjecting it to the same keen-eyed scrutiny
he had given his earlier beliefs, and comparing it with the
systems of his own land.

He now was in full rebellion against the Hindu social system.
He saw that the whole nation was in bondage to the priestly
caste. The net of caste and creed became intolerable to him.
With most persons, particularly those of a romantic temper,
this phase of revolt is critical, for there is the danger of a dulling
of the moral sense. When gods and religious duties, ascetic
and spiritual ideals, go, what is left to curb the senses? Truly
this was a period of conflict and perplexity for Naren, involving his whole personality; but wonderful was the inner
strength which bore him up. His mind was carried beyond the
perilous realm of the senses into the world of intellectuality, by
his subconscious determination to find a way out of the net of
ignorance entangling him—ignorance of his own real nature.
To find a way to God—if God existed—was for him the imperative need. To a mind of his mould agnosticism was only a
mood. The mystical temperament cannot stop at "I do not
know". The problem of life for such a one has to be solved;
the Truth has to be attained. His mind is swept by currents
peculiar to itself, which, if he is fortunate, carry him past
doubts and agnosticism to the haven of realization. Naren,
though for the time being lost in a maze of agnosticism, did
not lose heart. If philosophy could not help him, if it was not
the door to undistorted vision, he felt it would have to be
discarded as an abstraction which, interesting though it might
be, was not of ultimate worth.

Empirical science cannot enable one to transcend the realm
of the intellect and senses and realize that Eternal Reality
which is the foundation and cause of all phenomena. Naren was
in accord with the views of Western science and philosophy,

that what man knows of the world is the result of the interaction between physical objects and his senses, after the application to sense-data of the categories of the understanding, such as time and space. The external world as it is in itself, is thus unknown and unknowable. This last is also true of the internal nature of man. He can never truly know his inner reality, because it is "beyond" the categories of time and space. Narendranath was aware that the sense-organs, mind and intellect are incapable of enabling man to solve the riddle of the ultimate nature of the universe, because the sense-perceptions and still more the ideas which he forms from them, on which he bases his various speculations and theories, are not free from a large quota of subjectivity, and hence are unreliable as representing what is originally given in sense experience. Western savants have failed to establish the existence of the Self apart from objective consciousness and consequently have failed to come to a final conclusion regarding the ultimate Truth.

Nevertheless, Narendra had a great respect for Western material science and its analytical processes. He used them to test Shri Ramakrishna's various supernatural experiences and accepted only those which stood the test. Though he was literally pining for Truth, yet he would not accept anything through fear or because of outside pressure. He was even willing to become an honest atheist if that was to be the end of all reasoning. So eager was he to solve the mystery of the universe that he was willing to surrender all the pleasures of the world, nay, even life itself, for a vision of the Truth. In this frame of mind, he pursued his study of Western science and philosophy, accepting whatever was good in them. He did not pursue learning for the sake of material power, but because he desired to realize Truth. Rebelling against his inherited faith, he was forced into much wandering and intellectual struggle, only to return to it in his final illumination.

His researches were not confined to philosophy and physical science. He took a course in Western medicine to acquaint himself with the working of the nervous system—especially the brain and spinal cord. He had a passion for history, the story of the conditions under which human character and human events developed. History was, to him, the record of the aspirations and realizations of nations through the centuries.

Poetry, because it is the language of ideals, made a strong appeal to Naren. Wordsworth was the fixed star of his poetic firmament. He lived in a world of ideals, where history and philosophy, poetry and all the sciences, are recognized as phases of Reality. He possessed a prophetic vision of learning, wherein thought was seen as subservient to the real purpose of life, ideas and ideals being the fuel which the soul burned in its supreme effort to go beyond intellect, beyond thought.

With all his seriousness there was another side to Naren. He had a great love of fun and gave himself up to it whole-heartedly. Thoroughly human and interested in human ways, he was known in college as "a good fellow" because of his stories, wit and merry-making. He was the leader in all in-nocent revels, and no party was considered complete without him; but amusements were not allowed to interfere with studies. Often, after spending the day with friends, he would plunge late at night into the study of some historical or philo-sophical treatise, not giving over until he had mastered it. His brain was always clear, even when his health was impaired and he was physically weak. In the last days of a life in which he had often subjected his body to the utmost strain, he used to say, "Though my body is worn out, my brain is as clear as ever." Naren's was a personality made up of a variety of moods and qualities. In recreation a boy, in song an artist, in intellectual pursuits a scholar, and in his outlook on life a philosopher.

Naren did whatever was to be done because he saw and understood the fitness of the doing, and not because of some external pressure. Freedom, he was convinced, was the basis of all true self-development; but that freedom had to be supplemented, and its use guided, by a right and matured discrimination. Then one obeyed moral laws as a master, not as a slave. He possessed that qualification needed for the attainment of the spiritual consciousness—a passion for good. Though his mind plunged into agnosticism, he hated a materialistic outlook on life.

The monastic tendency was natural to him; yet he was a jubilant lover of life. He had the physical vitality of a child with the intellect and detachment of a spiritual genius. It is not strange, therefore, to find him rising from his study, when he was preparing for the B.L. examination and saying to a friend, "Yes, I must abandon the idea of appearing for the examination. What does it all mean! I must be free!" In early youth he recognized marriage to be a barrier to spirituality and said to this same friend, "You are married. You are under the bondage of the householder's life. I am free. Mine will be the monastic life, I am sure." He knew life to be a dream. His very agnosticism had impressed on him the meaninglessness of all things. Hence he looked on the monastic life as the only method of protest against the falseness of it all.

The great barrier to his final realization at this period was the intellect. But it had to be silenced, not by stunting its growth through the acceptance of some sort of belief, not by suppressing it as one would an evil thought or desire, but by developing it to its highest capacity. It had to have dealt successfully with all phases of uncertainty and to have won through to the perception of reality, before it would be able to join the emotions in the living of the spiritual life. How Naren arrived at this consummation is a mystery. How his intellect became illuminated, no one knows. It was perhaps due to his contact with his teacher Shri Ramakrishna, whose realization was the fulfilment and solution of all intellectual searches and doubts. Do not the scriptures say that when one knows God one knows the universe in its essence? Nature cannot withhold from such a one her secrets. But Naren had still to grope in darkness for some time to come. There were difficulties to be faced, doubts to be settled, before he could resign himself to a teacher and accept his teachings without question. He was to fight every inch of the way, accepting nothing until it was no longer rational to deny it. When any point was gained it became insight, illumination. Through all his struggles and sufferings of mind and heart he felt that victory was to be his. He was pure in heart, and such, we are taught, shall see God.

To gain a still clearer view of Naren's personality and the early stage of his mental development, it would be well to quote the observations of one of his fellow-students, Dr. Brajendranath Seal, a leading intellect of India in his day. In an article written for the *Prabuddha Bharata* (April 1907, and reproduced in the *Brahmavadin* the following month), he says:

When I first met Vivekananda in 1881, we were fellow-students of Principal William Hastie, scholar, metaphysician, and poet, at the General Assembly's College. He was my senior in age, though I was his senior in the College by one year. Undeniably a gifted youth, sociable, free and unconventional in manners, a sweet singer, the soul of social circles, a brilliant conversationalist, somewhat bitter and caustic, piercing with the shafts of a keen wit the shows and mummeries of the world, sitting in the scorner's chair but hiding the tenderest of hearts under that garb of cynicism; altogether an inspired Bohemian but possessing what Bohemians lack, an iron will; somewhat peremptory and absolute, speaking with accents of authority and withal possessing a strange power of the eye which could hold his listeners in thrall.

This was patent to all. But what was known to few was the inner man and his struggle—the *Sturm und Drang* of soul which expressed itself in his restless and Bohemian wanderings.

This was the beginning of a critical period in his mental history, during which he awoke to self-consciousness and laid the foundations of his future personality. John Stuart Mill's *Three Essays on Religion* had upset his first boyish theism and easy optimism which he had imbibed from the outer circles of the Brahmo Samaj. The arguments from causality and design were for him broken reeds to lean upon, and he was haunted by the problem of the Evil in Nature and Man which he, by no means, could reconcile with the goodness of an All-wise and All-powerful Creator. A friend introduced him to the study of Hume's scepticism and Herbert Spencer's doctrine of the Unknowable, and his unbelief gradually assumed the form of a settled philosophical scepticism.

His first emotional freshness and *naïveté* were worn out. A certain dryness and incapacity for the old prayerful devotions, an ennui which he concealed under a nonchalant air of habitual mocking and scoffing, troubled his spirit. But music still stirred him as nothing else could, and gave him a weird unearthly sense of unseen realities which brought tears to his eyes.

It was at this time that he came to me being brought by a common friend, the same who had introduced him to the study of Hume and Herbert Spencer. I had had a nodding acquaintance with him before, but now he opened himself to me and spoke of his harassing doubts and his despair of reaching certitude about the Ultimate Reality. He asked for a course of Theistic philosophic reading suited to a beginner in his situation. I named some authorities, but the stock arguments of the Intuitionists and the Scotch common-sense school only confirmed him in his unbelief. Besides, he did not appear to me to have sufficient patience for humdrum reading—his faculty was to imbibe not so much from books as from living communion and personal experience. With him it was life kindling life and thought kindling thought.

I felt deeply drawn towards him, for I now knew that he would grapple with difficulties in earnest.

I gave him a course of readings in Shelley. Shelley's Hymn to the Spirit of Intellectual Beauty, his pantheism of impersonal love and his vision of a glorified millennial humanity moved him as the arguments of the philosophers had failed to move him. The universe was no longer a mere lifeless, loveless mechanism. It contained a spiritual principle of unity.

I spoke to him now of a higher unity than Shelley had conceived, the unity of the Para Brahman as the Universal Reason. My own position at that time sought to fuse into one, three essential elements, the pure monism of the Vedanta, the dialectics of the Absolute idea of Hegel and the Gospel of Equality, Liberty and Fraternity of the French Revolution. The principle of individuation was with me the principle of Evil. The Universal Reason was all in all, Nature, life, history being the progressive unfolding of the Absolute idea. All ethical, social and political creeds and principles were to be tested by their conformity to Pure Reason. The element of feeling appeared to me merely pathological, a disturbance of sanity and order. How to overcome the resistance of matter, of individuality and of unreason, to the manifestation of the Pure Reason was the great prob-

lem of life and society, of education and legislation. I also held with
the ardour of a young inexperienced visionary that the deliverance
of the race from the bondage of unreason would come about through
a new revolutionary polity of which the watchwords were Equality,
Liberty and Fraternity.

The sovereignty of Universal Reason, and the negation of the
individual as the principle of morals, were ideas that soon came to
satisfy Vivekananda's intellect and gave him an assured conquest
over scepticism and materialism. What was more, they furnished
him with the card and compass of life, as it were. But this brought
him no peace. The conflict now entered deeper into his soul, for the
creed of Universal Reason called on him to suppress the yearnings
and susceptibilities of his artist nature and Bohemian temperament.
His senses were keen and acute, his natural cravings and passions
strong and imperious, his youthful susceptibilities tender, his conviviality free and merry. To suppress these was to kill his natural
spontaneity—almost to suppress his self. The struggle soon took a
seriously ethical turn—reason struggling for mastery with passion
and sense. The fascinations of the sense and the cravings of a youthful
nature now appeared to him as impure, as gross and carnal. This was
the hour of darkest trial for him. His musical gifts brought him asso-
ciates for whose manners and morals he had bitter and undisguised
contempt. But his convivial temperament proved too strong for him.
It was, therefore, some relief to him when I occasionally kept him
company of an evening when he went out for a musical soirée.

I saw and recognized in him a high, ardent and pure nature,
vibrant and resonant with impassioned sensibilities. He was certainly
no sour or cross-grained puritan, no normal hypochondriac; he would
indulge cynically in unconventional language except when he would
spare my innocence. He took an almost morbid delight in shocking
conventionality in its tabernacles, respectability in its booths; and
in the pursuit of his sport would appear other than he was, puzzling
and mystifying those outside his inner circle of friends. But in the
recesses of his soul he wrestled with the fierce and fell spirit of
Desire, the subtle and illusive spirit of Fancy.

To his repeated quest for some power which would deliver him
from bondage and unavailing struggle, I could only point to the
sovereignty of Pure Reason and the ineffable peace that comes of
identifying the self with the Reason in the Universe. Those were for
me days of a victorious Platonic transcendentalism. The experience of

a refractory flesh or rebellious temperament had not come to me. I had not sufficient patience for the mood or attitude of mind which surrenders the sovereign right of self-government to artificial props or outside help, such as grace or mediation. I felt no need of conciliating feeling and nature in the cult of Reason, nor had had any experience of a will divided in its allegiance to the Self. The experience of a discord between the Ideal and the Real, between Nature and Spirit, had indeed come to me already in an objective way as an outstanding reality and was to come afterwards in subjective fashion though in forms quite other than what obtained in Vivekananda's case. But at the time, his problems were not mine, nor were my difficulties his.

He confessed that though his intellect was conquered by the universal, his heart owned the allegiance of the individual Ego and complained that a pale bloodless reason, sovereign *de jure* but not *de facto*, could not hold out arms to save him in the hour of temptation. He wanted to know if my philosophy could satisfy his senses, could mediate bodily, as it were, for the soul's deliverance; in short, he wanted a flesh and blood reality visible in form and glory; above all, he cried out for a hand to save, to uplift, to protect, a Shakti or power outside himself which could cure him of his impotence and cover his nothingness with glory—a Guru or master who by embodying perfection in the flesh would still the commotion in his soul.

At the time, this appeared to me a weakness born of unreason, this demand for perfection in the flesh and for a power out of ourselves to save—this sacrifice of reason to sense. My young inexperienced self, confronted with this demand of a soul striving with itself, knew not wherewith to satisfy it, and Vivekananda soon after betook himself to the ministers and missionaries of the Brahmo Samaj, asking Brahmos with an unconscious Socratic Irony for an ideal made real to sense, for truth made visible, for a power unto deliverance. Here he had enough, he bitterly complained, of moral disquisitions, principles, intuitions for pabulum which to him appeared tasteless and insipid. He tried diverse teachers, creeds and cults, and it was this quest that brought him, though at first in a doubting spirit, to the Paramahamsa of Dakshineswar, who spoke to him with an authority as none had spoken before, and by his Shakti brought peace into his soul and healed the wounds of his spirit. But his rebellious intellect scarcely yet owned the Master. His mind misgave him and he doubted if the peace which would possess his soul in the presence of the Master was not illusory. It was only gradually that the doubts of that keen intellect were vanquished by the calm assurance that belongs to ocular demonstration.

I watched with intense interest the transformation that went on under my eyes. The attitude of a young and rampant Vedantist-*cum*-Hegelian-*cum*-Revolutionary like myself towards the cult of religious ecstasy and Kali-worship, may be easily imagined; and the spectacle of a born iconoclast and free-thinker like Vivekananda, a creative and dominating intelligence, a tamer of souls, himself caught in the meshes of what appeared to me an uncouth, supernatural mysticism, was a riddle which my philosophy of the Pure Reason could scarcely read at the time. But Vivekananda, "the loved and lost" was loved, and mourned most in what I could not but then regard as his defection; and it was personal feeling, after all, the hated pathological element of individual preference and individual relationship, which most impelled me, when at last I went on what to a home-keeping recluse like myself was an adventurous journey to Dakshineswar, to see and hear Vivekananda's Master, and spent the greater part of a long summer day in the shady and peaceful solitude of the Temple-garden, returning as the sun set amidst the whirl and rush and roar and the awful gloom of a blinding thunderstorm, with a sense of bewilderment as well moral as physical, and a lurking perception of the truth that the majesty of Law orders the apparently irregular and grotesque, that there may be self-mastery in apparent self-alienation, that sense even in its errors is only incipient Reason and that faith in a Saving Power *ab extra* is but the dim reflex of an original act of self-determination. And a significant confirmation of all this came in the subsequent life-history of Vivekananda who, after he had found the firm assurance he sought in the saving Grace and Power of his Master, went about preaching and teaching the creed of the Universal Man, and the absolute and inalienable sovereignty of the Self.

Naren yearned sincerely for knowledge, sure, real, permanent and satisfactory. He wanted to get out of the quagmire of doubt and uncertainty. To him the voice of agnosticism was the voice of anguish, causing him much mental tribulation and stress of soul. A feeling of emptiness and sadness obsessed him. Why, he could not explain. He entered that world in which every glance and every step is suffering, because it is the world of uncertainty in which man says, "I do not know the way". The ordinary philosopher says this with indifference; the saint-to-be, with a laden heart. The worldly man is heedless whether the world of idealism and tradition stands or falls; he is unaware of the suffering which disillusionment gives rise to.

In all this agnosticism and confusion of intellect Naren continued his spiritual exercises. He practised meditation. It gave him great mental peace, this effort to quiet the mind in meditation. And when silence and stillness came, he would sometimes pass into the innermost recesses of himself. There the doubting mind could not follow. During this period the visions he had had on the first few visits to Dakshineswar helped him keep his mind firm in the belief in an ultimate Reality. Shri Ramakrishna's words were comforting and steadying, no matter what the tumult of his mind: "God listens to the sincere prayer of the human mind. I swear that you can see Him more intensely than you see me. You can talk to Him more intimately than you talk to me. One can hear His words and feel His touch." Again: "You may not believe in various divine forms and may discard them as products of the human imagination. But if you believe in some ultimate Reality which is the regulator of the universe, you can pray thus: 'O God, I do not know Thee. Graciously reveal to me Thy real nature!'—He must listen to you if your prayer is sincere." These words of the Master encouraged Naren a great deal and helped turn his mind more and more to the practice of spiritual exercises. He had been impressed with the view of Hamilton that the human intellect can only gain hints of the truth of a God who regulates the universe. It is beyond the power of intellect to arrive at a correct knowledge of God. Here philosophy ends and religion begins. Naren would often refer to this. Though he was now giving much time and energy to spiritual practices, he did not throw away his philosophical books. Study, music and meditation wholly occupied his mind.

Naren took to a new method of meditation. Formerly he used to meditate on God, following the Brahmo belief, as formless but endowed with attributes. Now he prayed from the bottom of his heart, "O God, be gracious and reveal to me Thy real nature, which is the embodiment of Truth!" Then he would banish from his mind all other thoughts. After a while his mind would dive so deeply into his soul that he would lose consciousness of body and of time. He would meditate in this manner at night when everybody in the house had retired. He would feel an ineffable peace within; and afterwards, a sort of intoxication which made it difficult for him to leave his seat. On one such occasion as he was thus seated after meditation, he was blessed with the vision of the Buddha. This is how Swami Saradananda remembers him to have related what happened:

When I kept my mind still and devoid of all objects, there flowed in it a current of serene bliss. Under its influence, I felt a sort of intoxication for a long time even after the end of the meditation; so I did not feel inclined to leave my seat and get up immediately. One day when I was sitting in that condition at the end of the meditation, I saw the wonderful figure of a monk appear suddenly—from where I did not know—and stand before me at a little distance, filling the room with a divine effulgence. He was in ochre robes with a Kamandalu (water-pot) in his hand. His face bore such a calm and serene expression of inwardness born of indifference to all things, that I was amazed and felt much drawn to him. He walked towards me with a slow step, his eyes steadfastly fixed on me, as if he wanted to say something. But I was seized with fear and could not keep still. I got up from my seat, opened the door, and quickly left the room. The next moment I thought, "Why this foolish fear?" I became bold and went back into the room to listen to the monk, who, alas, was no longer there. I waited long in vain, feeling dejected and repenting that I had been so stupid as to flee without listening to him. I have seen many monks, but never have I seen such an extraordinary expression on any other face. That face has been indelibly printed on my heart. It may have been a hallucination; but very often I think that I had the good fortune of seeing Lord Buddha that day.

Time passed and the days were marked by various higher

8

experiences. The man was in the making, stern with himself in his search for Reality. All the passionate longing, which, in ordinary persons, is related to the senses, was in Naren directed to the understanding of life and its problems. Where there is such sincerity of effort realization must come. The result of his study in the wisdom of man brought him to the conclusion that all worldly knowledge and experience is vanity and vexation of spirit. He gradually became convinced, by an intellectual process, of the existence of an Ultimate Reality, conscious and indescribable, from which all phenomena have emanated. The gods might be false, thought Naren, but not God.

It must be remembered, however, that there were other factors as important as his power of thought and discrimination, in Naren's finding of this intellectual, or rather spiritual, position. He began to build, though slowly at first, an enlightened life, under the watchful eye of an ever-wakeful spiritual guide. It was a long way from the agnostic to the prayerful state; but prayer and contemplation were gradually awakened in Naren as he began to lead the life of the quieting of the senses and of renunciation, and to centre the strength and intensity of his thought upon these noble ideals. Indeed, was not such concentration of thought, in itself, prayer? There came a longing for divine vision, where thought has become direct perception. The idea that God exists must become the direct perception that God *is*. And when one has that perception, who can say to him, "This is true and this is not true"? Intellectual truth is debatable; spiritual Truth is beyond debate. To feel such a longing, even just to believe in such an exalted state of consciousness, is spirituality.

Naren pondered deeply on the idea of God. He would reflect day after day on the infinite consciousness. Meditation became a habit with him. The desire to see, to know, the Truth had become so intense that the thought-built walls of his intellect were being undermined and washed away, leaving the way open for the intuitive mind, the chief servant of the soul. In the dream consciousness he would see dimly things which were beyond mortal dreaming, or in the morning would wake up with a feeling of exaltation—experiences which could only be explained on the ground that his dream and sleep were not of the ordinary kind. The exaltations, the temporary glimpses of Reality, were daily happenings with him. Frequently at this time it seemed to him that he was separate from his body.

When he met the Master, his spiritual guide and companion, he felt that he had found a haven of peace and the end of all his struggles; but he was unable to accept the teacher in him *in toto*. As the Master tried to kindle the sleeping spirituality of his disciple, the latter brought his intellectual strength to bear. He opposed and he fretted. But the Master, to use his own expression, was not a harmless water-snake: he was a deadly cobra whose bite was fatal. Gradually Naren's opposition died away in complete surrender.

The inner history of Naren's conversion and illumination is too subtle to be described: the Guru brought about these in an inscrutable manner. Only the outer strife and intellectual struggle Naren's friends observed and knew. But the inner processes are a mystery, known only to the teacher and, perhaps, the disciple.

STRUGGLES AND HARDSHIPS

By this time, Narendranath's father, Vishwanath Datta, had made a name for himself in Calcutta society. Even as a lawyer he had earned such a reputation that he often had to spend months in various cities of northern India for professional purposes. He made a good living; but as he had to maintain a large joint-family, and also was in the habit of spending lavishly on musical soirées and entertaining friends, his expenses were proportionate. Moreover, his uncle Kaliprasad, who was head of the joint-family and had no income of his own, not only spent from the ancestral property, but used to claim from Vishwanath's earnings as well. Towards the end, Vishwanath was not able even to supervise his own firm of attorneys in Calcutta owing to his practice outside. Taking advantage of his long absence, his partners drew large loans in Vishwanath's name and spent the money on themselves. Therefore, even though outwardly Vishwanath's family lived in style, their actual financial position had so deteriorated that at any moment there was the risk of bankruptcy. The hope of the family naturally centred on Vishwanath's earnings and on a little ancestral property that was left in the hands of Kaliprasad. But this property also became the cause of quarrels later; and towards the end of Vishwanath's life, owing to disputes in the joint-family, he had to leave the ancestral house along with his wife and children, and make his own arrangements for living. During this period, he moved to a rented house at 7 Bhairava Biswas Lane. Narendranath was then preparing for his B.A. examination, commencing on December 31, 1883. As the rented house was near his maternal grandmother's, he used to live in a room all to himself on the first floor of her house, and pass his days in study and meditation. Often he went to Dakshineswar to see Shri Ramakrishna.

On January 30, 1884, the B.A. examination results were announced, and Narendranath learned that he had passed in the second division. Following this, at the instance of his father, whose ambition it was to see his son with a good position in the legal profession, Narendranath entered the firm of Nimaichandra Basu, attorney-at-law, as an articled-clerk, in order to qualify himself as an attorney. Recent research shows that in 1883, he had gained admission to the three-year Law course in the Metropolitan Institution (now Vidyasagar College). This was a year before his graduation, and was a regular practice in those days. It is said that Narendranath had a mind to go to England to complete his Law studies, and that his father had agreed to the proposal; but this did not materialize, since the father passed away suddenly.

For the sake of his future career Vishwanath made Narendranath become a Freemason, for by this time he had reached the minimum age-limit of 21 years. On February 19, 1884, he joined the Anchor and Hope Lodge, No. 234 (now the Grand Lodge of India No. 1). In those days, it was the fashion for educated Indians, mainly lawyers, judges, and government officials, to become Freemasons; and Vishwanath's friends, W. C. Banerjee, the most distinguished advocate at that time, and Nimaichandra Basu, the attorney-at-law, were active members of that Lodge. When Narendranath's uncle asked Vishwanath why he wanted Narendranath to be a Freemason, the father replied that it would help him in later life; and in fact it did help. For, when, as Swami Vivekananda, Narendranath was facing difficult days in America in 1894, Mr. G. C. Connor, the Freemason who had examined him in "the English work" at the Anchor and Hope Lodge, at Calcutta in 1884, gave letters of introduction to certain Freemasons in Chicago, so that the Swami would receive "cordial consideration", as he (Mr. Connor) had received in India. After joining the Masonic Lodge, Narendranath "passed" their test on April 5, 1884, and was raised to "the sublime degree of Master Mason" on May 20 of the same year. It is probable that he ceased to be a Freemason soon after, on account of financial difficulties and the change in his way of life.

Vishwanath wanted his son to marry. But strange to say, every time the subject of marriage came up some unforeseen difficulty would arise, or events would take a turn that made it necessary to abandon the matter for the time being. Shri Ramakrishna was greatly opposed to Naren's marriage. He prayed to the Mother that it might never take place. Holding, as he did, that Naren was not born for the love of any one person, or to rear a family, but for the saving of souls, he used to feel greatly relieved when such negotiations fell through. However, in spite of all this, Naren's father did manage to make an arrangement with an influential and wealthy Calcutta family who were ready to give a magnificent dowry and send Naren to England to take the Civil Service examination. But Naren rebelled; and the marriage also could not take place owing to the sudden demise of his father. Naren now became his own master. His determination to remain unmarried was inflexible. The ideal of celibacy became a principle with him as his passion for purity became stronger. And when the members of his family repeatedly urged him to marry, he said to them with vehemence, "What, are you going to drown me? Once married, it will be all over with me!"

Naren often spoke about the glory of the monastic life to his friends; they did not understand, and tried to induce him to turn his attention to worldly pursuits. "Why not settle down to definite plans, Naren? You have a fine career before you if you only look more to the prospects which the world holds out", said a friend. Naren met this remark with a shrug and said that he had often desired reputation, position and popularity, with wealth and power; but reflection had shown him that death came and engulfed all. Why then build up a greatness that can be destroyed by death? "The life of the monk is really great, for he seeks to push aside the power of death. He seeks a changeless reality, while the world deals with what changes and is conditioned by change." The friends were not convinced. "The trouble is", said one of them, "that Naren has met an old man who goes into trances and lives a monk's

life in the grounds of the Kali temple at Dakshineswar on the
banks of the Ganga. He is always meditating and talking about
God and knows nothing about the world. This man is upsetting
all Naren's ambitions. He is turning his mind from worldly
affairs and ruining his future. The name of this old man is
Ramakrishna Paramahamsa.—Naren, if you have any sense,
give up going to see him. It is hampering your studies, and it
will ruin your whole future if you continue. You have great
talents. You can attain anything if you set your will to it and
give up going to Dakshineswar." Naren replied gravely, "You
see, you do not understand. I myself do not understand. No,
even I do not understand, but I love that old man, that saint,
Shri Ramakrishna."

If Narendra did not go to Dakshineswar for several days,
the Master would go to his disciple in Calcutta and give him
counsel regarding meditation and other spiritual exercises.
He was afraid Naren, unable to bear the importunities of his
parents and relatives, would accept the bondage of married
life. He encouraged him to live the strict life of Brahmacharya.
One day he said, "A man develops a subtle power as a result of
the strict observance of celibacy for twelve years. Then he can
understand and grasp very subtle things which otherwise
elude his intellect. Through that understanding the aspirant
can have direct vision of God. That pure understanding alone
enables him to realize Truth."

The ladies of the family concluded that Naren was averse
to marriage as a result of his intimacy with Shri Ramakrishna.
Referring to this, Naren said later: "One day when the Master
came to my study and was instructing me in the observance
of lifelong celibacy, my grandmother overheard everything
and informed my parents accordingly. From that day they
began making great efforts to get me married lest I should
become a monk as a result of mixing with sadhus. But of what
avail was all that? All their efforts against the strong will of the
Master failed. Even when, as happened at times, everything
was settled, the marriage negotiations broke down on account
of differences between the two parties over trifling matters."

In the early part of 1884, Narendranath suddenly came
face to face with the grim reality of the world; his lighthearted-
ness and boyish spirits received a rude shock. On the afternoon
of February 25 he went to Baranagar, about two miles from
Calcutta, invited by his friends. He was occupied in singing
devotional songs till about eleven at night. He then lay down
in the same room after taking his meal with the friends, and
was talking on different topics. About 2 a.m. his friend Hemali
came with the news that Naren's father had died suddenly of
heart failure. Overwhelmed by the news, Narendranath
hastened to Calcutta at once. The body of his father lay
ready to be taken to the burning-ghat on a funeral cot. His
mother, two young brothers and sisters were weeping and
wailing. When Naren came, he was dazed. At first he could
neither weep nor speak; later, he burst into tears. Being the
eldest son, he performed the last rites for his father according
to the Hindu custom.

It is said that while engaged in professional activities outside Bengal, Vishwanath contracted a severe urinary disease.
A month before his death he had a heart attack and had to
rest in bed on the doctor's advice. On the day of his death he
had to go out for some work. Returning home, he told his
wife that a client had taken him to Alipore to show some docu-
ments; as a result he was feeling pain in the heart. After taking
his meal that night, he rubbed some medicament into his
chest and engaged himself in writing, taking a smoke the while.
About nine o'clock he vomited; at ten his heart stopped
functioning. He had planned to go next day to select a bride
for Narendranath; but that came to naught.

Vishwanath's sudden death placed the entire family in a
desperate condition, for he was the only earning member and,
moreover, always spent more than he earned. Soon the creditors
were knocking at the door. Though Narendra had no income
he had to maintain seven or eight people. Days of suffering
came. From comfort Naren was suddenly thrown into direst
poverty, at times facing virtual starvation. Later he tried
to forget those terrible days, but in vain—so dark were they,

so heavy the clouds of misery. Yet he is the real man who meets fate undaunted and with energy: he is the captain of his soul. This Naren did. He had passed his B.A. examination and was studying Law. In college he was the poorest of the poor. Even shoes became a luxury; his garments were of the coarsest cloth, and many times he went to classes without food. Often he became faint with hunger and weakness. His friends now and then invited him to their homes. He would chat happily with them for long hours, but when food was offered, the vision of the desolation at his home would come up in his mind and prevent him from eating. He would leave with the excuse that he had a pressing engagement elsewhere. On reaching home he would eat as little as possible in order that the others might have enough.

After the passing away of her son in 1902, Bhuvaneshwari told many stories of the sacrifices that Narendranath made for her at this time. Often he would refuse to eat on the plea that he had already eaten at the house of a friend, when the fact was, he did not eat at home for fear of depriving the others of a full meal. Such was the character of this young man! At the same time he tried to be his usual happy self and make light of his trials. Out of pride the Datta family concealed its misery. Naren's friends, sons of wealthy families of Calcutta, drove up in magnificent carriages to take him for drives and pleasure trips, never suspecting that his wasting away physically was due to any other cause than an exaggerated grief at the loss of his father.

To make matters worse, the relatives who had been indebted to Vishwanath in so many ways now turned into enemies. They even deprived the family of their ancestral house. On some far-fetched basis a case was made out against them, and the matter taken to court. Indeed, disputes had already started while Vishwanath was living, and his family had been staying in a rented house since then. After his father's death Narendranath continued to stay in the same rented house for some days. Later, he moved to his maternal grandmother's at 7 Ramtanu Bose Lane.

The litigation dragged on for a long time. It was a blow for Narendranath, and his mother was greatly dismayed that their family affairs were to be aired in public. She had tried to settle matters by compromise, but Kaliprasad's wife was not prepared to do so on reasonable terms. During this critical time, Vishwanath's friends, Nimaichandra Basu and W. C. Banerjee, the barrister, were of great help. In these affairs Narendranath himself showed legal talent, which the English lawyer of the opposite party appreciated whole-heartedly. The case was finally decided in favour of Narendranath's family, and they secured their legal share in the property. Later on, they returned to their ancestral house, but by that time Narendranath had renounced the world.

After the lawsuit was over, things became somewhat easier, but by no means comfortable. For several years it was a struggle for them to obtain the coarsest food and clothing. Yet they were happy when they remembered that the house was theirs and that they were together. Naren made every effort to make both ends meet. He had to give up the articled-clerkship in the attorney's office in order to go in search of a job to maintain the family. For quite some time he could not get employment. But recent research has revealed that some time in 1884, Narendranath served as a teacher for a few months in the main Metropolitan Institution, then situated in Sukea Street, Calcutta. (Later, in June 1886, he was appointed headmaster of the newly-opened branch of the same Institution in Siddheswar Chandra Lane, Champatala, Calcutta; but after working there for a few weeks he was compelled by circumstances to leave the post.) It was a hand-to-mouth existence for Naren and his family. There were moments when he despaired, but he was too brave to show it. In other trying times later, the memories of these struggles and hardships were to give him strength, for nothing could be worse than the evils through which he had already successfully passed.

The relationship between mother and son deepened a hundredfold through these tempestuous experiences and through them she came to see that Naren had a trait which she especially admired in his father—never, never to acknowledge defeat. This critical period showed what Bhuvaneshwari was made of too. About her, Swami Saradananda writes:

Fallen on bad days after her husband's death, she was put on her mettle and showed wonderful patience, calmness, frugality and adaptability to sudden change of circumstances. She who was used to spending a thousand rupees monthly to manage the household, had now only thirty rupees to maintain her sons, daughters, and herself. But never for a day was she seen dejected. She managed all her family's affairs with that meagre income in such a way that those who saw how things went on took her monthly expenditure to be much higher. One shudders indeed to think of the miserable condition into which Bhuvaneshwari fell at the sudden death of her husband. There was no certain income with which to meet the needs of her family; yet she had to maintain her old mother, her sons and daughters brought up in opulence, and meet the expenses of their education. Her relatives, who had lived well by her husband's generosity and influence, now found an opportunity to their liking and, far from helping her, were even determined to deprive her of her just possessions. Her eldest son, Narendranath, possessed of many good qualities, failed to find a job in spite of his best efforts in various ways; and losing all attraction for the world, he was getting ready to renounce it for ever. One naturally feels respect and reverence for Bhuvaneshwari Devi when one thinks of the manner in which she performed her duties even in these straitened circumstances.

Narendranath often related the experiences of this darkest period to his brother-monks. Swami Saradananda recalls him saying:

Even before the period of mourning was over I had to go about in search of a job. Starving and barefooted, I wandered from office to office under the scorching noonday sun with an application in hand, one or two intimate friends who sympathized with me in my misfortunes accompanying me sometimes. But everywhere the door was slammed in my face. This first contact with the reality of life convinced me that unselfish sympathy was a rarity in the world—there was no place in it for the weak, the poor and the destitute. I noticed that those who only a few days ago would have been proud to have helped me in any way, now turned their face against me, though they had enough and to spare. Seeing all this, the world sometimes seemed to me to be the handiwork of the devil. One day, weary and footsore, I sat down in the shade of the Ochterlony Monument [the present Shahid Minar] on the Maidan. A friend or two were with me that day or maybe met me there by chance. One of them, I remember distinctly, sang by way of consoling me: "Here blows the wind, the breath of Brahman, His grace palpable! . . . " It was like a terrible blow on my head. I remembered the helpless condition of my mother and brothers, and exclaimed in bitter anguish and de- spondency, "Will you please stop that song? Such fancies may be pleasing to those who are born with a silver spoon in their mouth and have no starving relatives at home. Yes, there was a time when I too thought like that. But today, before the hard facts of life, it sounds like grim mockery."

My friend must have been wounded. How could he fathom the dire misery that had forced these words out of my mouth? Sometimes when I found that there were not provisions enough for the family and my purse was empty, I would pretend to my mother that I had an invitation to dine out and remain practically without food. Out of self-respect I could not disclose the facts to others. My rich friends sometimes requested me to go to their homes or gardens and sing. I had to comply when I could not avoid doing so. I did not feel inclined to express my woes before them nor did they try, themselves, to find out my difficulties. A few among them, sometimes, used to ask me, "Why do you look so pale and weak today?" Only one of them came to know about my poverty, and now and then, unknown to me, sent anonymous help to my mother, by which act of kindness he has put me under a deep debt of gratitude.

Some of my old friends who earned their livelihood by unfair means, asked me to join them. A few among them, who had been compelled to follow this dubious way of life by sudden turns of fortune as in my case, really felt sympathy for me. There were other troubles also. Various temptations came my way. A rich woman sent me an ugly proposal to end my days of penury, which I sternly rejected with scorn. Another woman also made similar overtures to me. I said to her, "You have wasted your life seeking the pleasures of the flesh. The dark shadows of death are before you. Have you done anything to face that? Give up all these filthy desires and remember God!"

In spite of all these troubles, however, I never lost faith in the existence of God or in His divine mercy. Every morning, taking His name, I got up and went out in search of a job. One day my mother overheard me and said bitterly, "Hush, you fool! you have been crying yourself hoarse for God from your childhood, and what has He done for you?" I was stung to the quick. Doubt crossed my mind. "Does God really exist?" I thought, "And if so, does He really hear the fervent prayer of man? Then why is there no response to my passionate appeals? Why is there so much woe in His benign kingdom? Why does Satan rule in the realm of the Merciful God?" Pandit Ishwarchandra Vidyasagar's words—"If God is good and gracious, why then do millions of people die for want of a few morsels of food at times of famine?"—rang in my ears with bitter irony. I was exceedingly annoyed with God. That was also the most opportune moment for doubt to creep into my heart.

It was ever against my nature to do anything secretly. On the contrary it was a habit with me from my boyhood not to hide even my thoughts from others through fear or anything else. So it was quite natural for me now to proceed to prove to the world that God was a myth, or that, even if He existed, to call upon Him was fruitless. Soon the report gained currency that I was an atheist and did not scruple to drink or even frequent houses of ill fame. This unmerited calumny hardened my heart still more. I openly declared that in this miserable world there was nothing reprehensible in a man who, seeking for a brief respite, should resort to anything; not only that, but that if I was once convinced of the efficacy of such a course, I should not, through fear of anybody, shrink from following it.

A garbled report of the matter soon reached the ears of the Master and his devotees in Calcutta. Some of these came to me for first-hand knowledge of the situation and hinted that they believed some of the rumours at least. A sense of wounded pride filled my heart on finding that they could think me so low. In an exasperated mood I gave them to understand plainly that it was cowardice to believe in God through fear of hell and argued with them as to His existence or non-existence, quoting several Western philosophers in support. The result was that they took leave of me convinced that I was hopelessly lost—and I was glad. When I thought that perhaps Shri Ramakrishna also would believe that, I was deeply wounded at heart. "Never mind," I said to myself, "if the good or bad opinion of a man rests upon such flimsy foundations, I don't care." And I was amazed to hear later that the Master had, at first, received the report coldly, without expressing an opinion one way or the other. But when one of his favourite disciples, Bhavanath, said to him with tears in his eyes, "Sir, I could not even dream that Narendra could stoop so low", he was furious and said, "Hush, you fool! The Mother has told me that it can never be so. I shan't be able to look at you if you speak to me like that again."

But notwithstanding these forced atheistic views, the vivid memory of the divine visions I had experienced since my boyhood, and especially since my contact with Shri Ramakrishna, would lead me to think that God must exist and that there must be some way to realize Him. Otherwise life would be meaningless. In the midst of all these troubles and tribulations I must find that way. Days passed and the mind continued to waver between doubt and certainty. My pecuniary needs also remained just the same.

The summer was over, and the rains set in. The search for a job still went on. One evening, after a whole day's fast and exposure to rain I was returning home with tired limbs and a jaded mind; overpowered with exhaustion and unable to move a step forward, I sank down on the outer plinth of a house by the roadside. I can't say whether I was insensible for a time or not. Various thoughts crowded in on my mind, and I was too weak to drive them off and fix my attention on anything in particular. Suddenly I felt as if by some divine power the coverings of my soul were being removed one after another. All my former doubts regarding the coexistence of divine justice and mercy, and the presence of misery in the creation of a Blissful Providence, were automatically solved. By a deep introspection I found the meaning of it all and was satisfied. As I proceeded homewards I found there was no trace of fatigue in the body, and the mind was refreshed with wonderful strength and peace. The night was well-nigh over.

Thenceforth I became deaf to the praise and blame of worldly people. I was convinced that I was not born like ordinary people to earn money and maintain a family, much less strive for sense-pleasures. I began secretly to prepare myself to renounce the world like my grandfather. I fixed a day for the purpose and was glad to hear that the Master was to come to Calcutta that very day. "It is lucky", I thought; "I shall leave the world with the blessing of my Guru." As soon as I met the Master, he pressed me hard to spend that night with him at Dakshineswar. I made various excuses, but to no purpose. I had to accompany him. There was not much talk in the carriage. Reaching Dakshineswar I was seated for some time in his room along with others, when he went into a trance. Presently he drew near me and, touching me with great tenderness, began to sing a song, with tears in his eyes:

> I am afraid to speak
> And am afraid not to speak.
> The doubt arises in my mind
> Lest I should lose you
> (Ah! my Rai, lest I should lose you).

I had suppressed my feelings for so long, but now they overflowed in tears. The meaning of the Master's singing the song was apparent —he knew of my intentions. The audience marvelled at this exchange of feeling between us. When the Master regained his normal mood, some of them asked him the reason for it. He replied with a smile, "Oh, it was something between him and me." Then at night he dismissed the others and calling me to his side said, "I know you have come for the Mother's work, and won't be able to live a worldly life; but for my sake, stay in the world as long as I live." Saying this he burst into tears again. The next day, with his permission, I returned home. A thousand thoughts about the maintenance of the family assailed me. I began to look about again for a living. By working in an attorney's office and translating a few books, I got just enough to live on—from hand to mouth, not permanent. There was no fixed income to maintain my mother and brothers.

One day the idea struck me that God listened to Shri Ramakrishna's prayers; so why should I not ask him to pray for me for the removal of my pecuniary needs—a favour the Master would never deny me? I hurried to Dakshineswar and insisted on his making the appeal on behalf of my starving family. He said, "My boy, I can't make such demands. But why don't you go and ask the Mother yourself? All your sufferings are due to your disregard of Her." I said, "I do not know the Mother; you please speak to Her on my behalf. You must." He replied tenderly, "My dear boy, I have done so again and again. But you do not accept Her, so She does not grant my prayer. All right, it is Tuesday—go to the Kali temple tonight, prostrate yourself before the Mother, and ask of Her any boon you like. It shall be granted. She is Knowledge Absolute, the Inscrutable Power of Brahman. By Her mere will She has given birth to this world. Everything is in Her power to give." I believed every word and eagerly waited for the night. About 9 o'clock the Master asked me to go to the temple. As I went, I was filled with a divine intoxication. My feet were unsteady. My heart was leaping in anticipation of the joy of beholding the living Goddess and hearing Her words. I was full of the idea. Reaching the temple, as I cast my eyes on the image, I actually found that the Divine Mother was living and conscious, the perennial fountain of Divine Love and Beauty. I was caught in a surging wave of devotion and love. In an ecstasy of joy I prostrated myself again and again before the Mother and prayed, "Mother, give me discrimination! Give me renunciation! Give me knowledge and devotion! Grant that I may have the uninterrupted vision of Thee!" A serene peace reigned in my soul. The world was forgotten. Only the Divine Mother shone within my heart.

As soon as I returned, the Master asked me if I had prayed to the Mother for the removal of my worldly needs. I was startled at this question and said, "No sir, I forgot all about it. But is there any remedy now?" "Go again," said he, "and tell Her about your needs." I again set out for the temple, but at the sight of the Mother again forgot my mission, bowed to Her repeatedly and prayed only for love and devotion. The Master asked me if I had done it the second time. I told him what had happened. He said, "How thoughtless! Couldn't you restrain yourself enough to say those few words? Well, try once more and make that prayer to Her. Quick!" I went for the third time, but on entering the temple a terrible shame overpowered me. I thought, "What a trifle I have come to pray to the Mother about! It is like asking a gracious king for a few vegetables! What a fool I am!" In shame and remorse I bowed to Her respectfully and said, "Mother, I want nothing but knowledge and devotion." Coming out of the temple I understood that all this was due to the Master's will. Otherwise how could I fail in my object no less than three times? I came to him and said, "Sir, it is you who have cast a charm over my mind and made me forgetful. Now please grant me the boon that my people at home may no longer suffer the pinch of poverty." He said, "Such a prayer never comes to my lips. I asked you to pray for yourself; but you couldn't do it. It seems that you are not destined to enjoy worldly happiness. Well, I can't help it." But I wouldn't let him go. I insisted on his granting that prayer. At last he said, "All right, your people at home will never be in want of plain food and clothing."

The above incident is, no doubt, a landmark in Naren's life. Hitherto he had not realized the significance of the Motherhood of God. He had had nothing but contempt for image-worship. From now on, the meaning and purpose of the worship of God through images, and the concept of God as Mother were brought home to him, thus making his spiritual life richer and fuller. Shri Ramakrishna was delighted beyond measure at this transformation. The following account of Vaikunthanath Sanyal, another devotee of the Master, who visited Dakshineswar the next day, bears this out:

Arriving at Dakshineswar at noon I found the Master alone in his room and Narendra sleeping outside. Shri Ramakrishna was in a joyful mood, and as soon as I saluted him he said, pointing to Narendra, "Look here, that boy is exceptionally good. His name is Narendra. He would not accept the Divine Mother before, but did so yesterday. He is in straitened circumstances nowadays; so I advised him to pray to the Mother for riches; but he couldn't. He said he was put to shame. Returning from the temple he asked me to teach him a song to the Mother, which I did. The whole of last night he sang that song. So he is sleeping now." Then with unfeigned delight he said, "Isn't it wonderful that Narendra has accepted Mother?" I said, "Yes." After a brief pause he repeated the question, and thus it went on for some time.

About four in the afternoon Narendra came to Shri Ramakrishna before leaving for Calcutta. No sooner had the Master seen him than he went closer and closer to him and sitting almost on his lap said, pointing first to himself and then to Narendra, "Well, I see I am this [himself] and again that [Naren]. Really I feel no difference —just as a stick floating on the Ganga seems to divide the water, which in reality is one. Do you see the point? Well, what exists after all, but Mother? What do you say?" After talking a few minutes like this, he wished to smoke. I prepared tobacco and gave him the hookah. After one or two puffs at it he said he would smoke from the bowl [of the hookah]. Then he offered it to Naren saying, "Have a pull through my hands." Naren of course hesitated. How could he defile the hands of his Guru by touching them with his lips? But Shri Ramakrishna said, "What foolish ideas you have! Am I different from you? This is myself and that [Naren] too is myself." He again put his hands in front of the lips of Narendra, who had no

9

alternative but to comply with his request. Narendra took two or three puffs. Shri Ramakrishna was about to smoke when Narendra hurriedly interrupted saying, "Please wash your hands first, sir." But his protest was in vain. "What silly ideas of differentiation you have!" the Master said and smoked without washing his hands, talking all the while in an exalted mood. I was surprised to see Shri Ramakrishna, who could not take any food if a part of it had already been offered to somebody else, making this remarkable exception in the case of Narendranath. It gave me an idea of his love for Narendra and of his feeling of kinship with him. When, about eight at night, he was in his normal mood again, Narendra and I took leave of him and walked to Calcutta.

Afterwards Narendra often said: "Shri Ramakrishna was the only person who, ever since he met me, believed in me uniformly throughout—even my mother and brothers did not do so. It was his unflinching trust in me and love that bound me to him for ever. He alone knew how to love another. Worldly people only make a show of love for selfish ends."

DAYS OF ECSTASY AT DAKSHINESWAR AND SHYAMPUKUR

To be with Shri Ramakrishna was itself a kind of austerity and spiritual discipline. It was a rising beyond all ideas of the body, beyond the limitations of the senses. It required concentration and character of the highest order to follow the Master in his flights of thought. The whole soul of the devotee was stirred to realization and ecstatic fervour. He was called to enter the sphere of divine emotion. Shri Ramakrishna tried to depict this in words; but in it he often soared beyond all words to God. The company of Shri Ramakrishna was itself a compelling stimulus to spirituality. Spiritual emotion blazed there, and the very soul of things shone forth.

Only those who have sat at the feet of the Master can know the ocean of sweet intimacy and oneness with him in which the disciples were bathed. It was a tender, natural, human and easy relationship, free from the affectation, egoism and aloofness which tend to mark the atmosphere surrounding the Guru. The atmosphere was indeed divine; the presence of God was palpable; and yet there was much laughter and fun beneath the spreading trees of Dakshineswar and in the Master's room. The Master and the disciples would often sit under the trees in sweet and intimate talk. And every now and then some remark of the Master would change the human joy into divine blessedness.

Referring to those days Naren used to say:

It is impossible to give others any idea of the ineffable joy we derived from the presence of the Master. It is really beyond our understanding how he could train us, without our knowing it, through fun and play, and thus mould our spiritual life. As the master wrestler proceeds with great caution and restraint with the beginner, now overpowering him in the struggle with great difficulty as it were, again allowing himself to be defeated to strengthen the pupil's self-confidence—in exactly the same manner did Shri Rama-krishna handle us. Realizing that the Atman [Self], the source of infinite strength, exists in every individual, pigmy though he might be, he was able to see the potential giant in all. He could clearly discern the latent spiritual power which would in the fullness of time manifest itself. Holding up that bright picture to view, he would speak highly of us and encourage us. Again he would warn us lest we should obstruct this future consummation by becoming entangled in worldly desires, and moreover he would keep us under control by carefully observing even the minute details of our life. All this was done silently and unobtrusively. That was the secret of his training of the disciples and of his moulding of their lives. Once I felt that I could not practise deep concentration during meditation. I told him of it and sought his advice and direction. He told me his personal experiences in the matter and gave me instructions. I remember that as I sat down to meditate during the early hours of the morning, my mind would be disturbed and diverted by the shrill note of the whistle of a neighbouring jute mill. I told him about it, and he advised me to concentrate my mind on the sound of the whistle itself. I followed his advice and derived much benefit from it. On another occasion I felt difficulty in totally forgetting my body during meditation and concentrating the mind wholly on the ideal. I went to him for counsel, and he gave me the very instruction which he himself had received from Totapuri while practising Samadhi according to Vedantic disciplines. He sharply pressed between my eyebrows with his finger-nail and said, "Now concentrate your mind on this painful sensation!" I found I could concentrate easily on that sensation as long as I liked, and during that period I completely let go the consciousness of the other parts of my body, not to speak of their causing any distraction hindering my meditation. The solitude of the Panchavati, associated with the various spiritual realizations of the Master, was also the most suitable place for our meditation. Besides meditation and spiritual exercises, we used to spend a good deal of time there in sheer fun and merry-making. Shri Ramakrishna also joined in with us, and by taking part enhanced our innocent pleasure. We used to run and skip about, climb on the trees, swing from the creepers and at times hold merry picnics. On the first day that we picnicked the Master noticed that I myself had cooked the food, and he partook of it. I knew that he could not take food unless it was cooked by Brahmins, and therefore I had arranged for his meal at the Kali temple. But he said, "It won't be wrong for me to take food from such a pure soul as yourself." In spite of my repeated remonstrations, he enjoyed the food I had cooked that day.

Naren was in his element at Dakshineswar. All his boyish enthusiasm was let loose there. He was like a young lion sporting joyously in the presence of a strong but indulgent parent. All his pent-up energy of mind and heart which had brought on anguish and tempest when it had partially revealed itself before, was now free to express itself fully. It manifested as a torrent of spiritual energy. Shri Ramakrishna understood and was delighted beyond words. The flights of Naren's soul were visible to him. Like a king grown venerable in long years of spiritual experience, was the older man; and Naren was like a young prince and heir, full of fire and vigour because of his spiritual inheritance. The Master let Naren's mind work under the pressure of its intrinsic force; he allowed it to become its own Guru. He held that sincerity of heart brings on, of itself, the gradual illumination of the mind. He allowed Naren to doubt him, to sound him. He said, "Do not accept anything because I have said so; but test everything for yourself. It is not in assent or dissent that the goal is to be attained, but in actual and concrete realization." And this Naren did, though often it called for extraordinary patience on the part of the Master and involved him in much suffering.

It is true to say that only Narendranath, amongst the disciples, understood the greatness of Shri Ramakrishna. He alone dared to doubt. He alone had an ascertained conviction with regard to the Master, which came of having weighed the Master's words in the balance and transcended doubt. The others hung with rapt attention on every word that fell from his lips. They were Bhaktas (devotees), they loved the Master; theirs was the conviction which comes of love. They knew Shri Ramakrishna only through their burning love for him. But Naren would question him, would smile at his statements and criticize them. Naren, too, had love for the

Master, love such as no other disciple had, and it was this love which made him revere and adore him. But he was not satisfied until he had completely satisfied himself of the truth of Shri Ramakrishna's teachings, so far as the analytical intellect was capable of sanctioning the utterances of a saint and seer.

It was Naren's power, partly intellectual and partly spiritual, of searching out and arriving at truth, which filled the Master with respect for Naren. Yes, this was the "Shiva-nature" or the "Shiva-power" in Naren, as Shri Ramakrishna used to call it. On a certain occasion the Master said to the disciples present, pointing to Narendranath, "Behold! Here is Naren. See! See! Oh what power of insight he has! It is like the shoreless sea of radiant knowledge! The Mother, Maha-maya Herself, cannot approach within less than ten feet of him! She is barred by the very glory which She has imparted to him!" Then he prayed that the Mother might dim that radiance in order that Naren might be able to work. "O Mother," he prayed, "put a little of Thy Maya into Narendra!" For otherwise, by the natural tendency of his soul, he would be concerned only with the highest reaches of personal realization; he would be immersed in eternal meditation and be mindful only of the Supreme Reality. He would thus be lost to the world.

The other disciples accepted Shri Ramakrishna's valuation of Naren as indisputable. Had he not gauged the depths of their own natures also? Had he not, at first sight, had the vision of the special forms of Divinity to which their minds tended! Had he not told every one of them his hidden tendencies! By mere touch he had imparted powers and realizations to them! Who were they to doubt when he said of Naren, "He has eighteen extraordinary powers, one or two of which are sufficient to make a man famous in the world"; or "He is a burning, roaring fire consuming all impurities to ashes"; and added, "Even should Naren live on beef and pork, it could not harm in the least the great power of spirituality within him!"

Wonderful was Shri Ramakrishna's method of teaching. He

would seldom enter into the argument of his disciples. With a
word, a glance or a song, he would teach, and the teaching was
always: "Realization is the only goal. When realization comes
into the heart, all arguments cease and divine knowledge shines
forth." One day Naren and other disciples were engaged in a
heated argument: "Is God Personal or Impersonal? Does God
become incarnate or is divine Incarnation a myth?" On and
on the argument raged, until it covered all points of theological
inquiry. Naren was the victor. He had overwhelmed all their
positions. Shri Ramakrishna approached the gathering, and
they heard these opening notes of a song come from his lips:

> O my mind, what avail thy efforts to realize that Being!
> Groping about, as thou dost, like a madman in a dark room?

The song continued:

> Go to the six schools of philosophy:
> There that Being thou shalt not find;
> Neither in the Tantras, nor in the Vedas.
> That Being is fond of the sweet essence of love.

The disputatious disciples sat silent and ecstatic. Yes, here
was the answer to all their questionings. Indeed, Shri Ramakrishna was a teacher who spoke only in the language of
realization. He was not a metaphysician. He had seen; he
had actually seen the Truth. So, what need of splitting hairs
over questions that must remain for ever debatable to the
human mind? Like the Buddha of old, Shri Ramakrishna had
little use for logic. Spirituality is not the capacity to put fine
theories into words. It is realization. It is character. It is the
conquest of lust and gold. Shri Ramakrishna took the concern
with realization from the plane of discussion into the sphere
of personal striving, of austerities, and of a realistic endeavour
for vision. Whenever the discussion grew heated, he became
impatient of "much talk". Often he would compare the argumentative scholars who soared on the wings of discussion to
vultures which, whilst soaring high, kept their eyes on the
carrion beneath. The minds of these scholars were likewise
fixed on the carrion of name and fame, lust and gold.

The Master did not normally interfere, however high the matter discussed. He let them talk. They would learn better, he would say: and sometimes he enjoyed the discussion. By it he sensed the spiritual insight of his disciples. Truly the Master's company was a grand school for the soul. It was a stimulus to personal growth. Everyone was free to discover and realize his own potentialities. But there were certain occasions when Shri Ramakrishna did intervene: for example, when Naren's towering thought overwhelmed the limited vision of another. There was that instance when Naren attacked faith as a means to liberation. He spoke of "blind faith". The Master said, "Naren, what do you mean by 'blind faith'? Faith is always blind. Has faith an 'eye'? Why say 'blind faith'? Either simply say 'faith' or say 'Jnana' [knowledge]. What do you mean by classifying faith—one kind having an eye, the other being blind?"

Slowly but surely Naren came to understand that it was realization that was true religion: man must see God. Thinking of Reality was good, but better was the vision of it—to attain which took time and much loving patience. But in time Naren discovered that the silence of insight was Shri Ramakrishna's most eloquent teaching. Sometimes, during conversations, Shri Ramakrishna would hold forth in soul-stirring utterances. At other times he would leave the disciples to themselves and their argumentative moods. Discussion ended, they would find him in deep Samadhi. This, they came to know after a time, was his way of protesting against their heated discussion. His character and the spiritual radiance of his personal life were the power behind his teaching. The man who preached universal love and toleration lived it. Shri Ramakrishna did not attack any social custom. He did not preach against caste. Himself a Brahmin, he had love for the downtrodden millions who were lowest in the social scale. By performing the most menial of all services, which even the lowest of the outcastes would shrink from doing, he revealed his utter humility.

What were Shri Ramakrishna's answers to questions pertaining to God-vision and methods of realization? How to pray?

"Pray in any way," he would say, "for the Lord hears even the footfall of an ant." How to find God? "By the conquest of lust and gold." Sincerity was the main theme of his teaching. Without sincerity nothing was possible; with sincerity all was possible. He would say to Naren and others that if they carried out but one-sixteenth of what he had done to realize God, they would be blessed for ever. Is God Personal or Impersonal? "He is both," said Shri Ramakrishna, "and yet He is beyond both; beyond any intellectual or theological dogmas. He is manifest to the soul in its own inmost realization. He assumes any form for the pleasure of His devotee. He is inexpressible. . . . He is not to be found between the covers of a book or within the walls of a temple." Is image-worship right or wrong? Such a question, to Shri Ramakrishna, was an idle one. Worship of anything which helped one to see God was right. Intense longing was the one thing needful.

Shri Ramakrishna was intimately acquainted with the various spiritual paths that led to the realization of God. The all-comprehensive Hindu scriptures prescribe certain methods of worship suited to particular temperaments, which appear indecent to others. Once the conversation drifted to such modes of spiritual discipline. The Master said to Naren: "These people cannot rightly pursue their course of spiritual practices. Most of them satisfy their base passions in the name of religion. Well, Naren, you need not hear about these things. As for myself, I look upon all women as my Mother. This is a very pure attitude of mind. There is no risk or danger in it. To look upon a woman as one's sister is also not bad. But the other attitudes are very difficult and dangerous. It is almost impossible to keep to the purity of the ideal. There are various ways to reach God. Some of these are dirty like the scavenger's entrance to a house. It is really better to enter the house by the front door." Then in an exalted mood he said: "There are many opinions and many ways. I do not like these any more. The aspirants of different ways quarrel among themselves. You are my own people. There are no outsiders here. I tell you, I clearly find that He is the whole and I am a part of Him. He is the Lord and I am the servant. Again sometimes I think that He is I and I am He."

Shri Ramakrishna's manner of teaching charmed Narendranath. It modified the puritanical view of life which he as a Brahmo had. Shri Ramakrishna could not bear the word "sin"; he had no such phrase in his spiritual vocabulary as "born in sin". He admitted that man was born with limitations; but whereas others fixed their attention upon the limitations, he saw that the destiny of every soul was the conquest of all limitations. On one occasion when Naren was denouncing certain weaknesses of schoolboys, the Master chanced to overhear and said, "Why talk of these matters? Talk of the Lord and nothing else." Such was his method of teaching and its substance.

Among the disciples, Narendranath was unique in the way he was able to arrive at the true spirit of the Master's teachings. His soul was the best attuned to the spiritual vibrations of the Master's words. Where others read pages, he read volumes, of the Revelation which the life and gospel of Shri Ramakrishna were. For instance, one day in 1884, Shri Ramakrishna was seated in his room at Dakshineswar surrounded by his disciples, among whom was Naren. The conversation drifted to the Vaishnava religion. The Master gave the gist of the cult of Lord Gauranga and finished by saying: "This religion enjoins upon its followers the practice of three things: relish for the name of God, compassion for all living creatures, and the service of the Vaishnavas, the devotees of the Lord. The real meaning of these precepts is this: God is not different from His name; therefore one should always repeat His name. God and his devotee, Krishna and the Vaishnava, are not separate from one another; therefore one should show respect to all saints and devotees. Realizing that this world belongs to Shri Krishna, one should show compassion to all creatures." Hardly had he uttered the words "compassion to all creatures", when he went into Samadhi. After a while he came back to a semi-conscious state of mind and said to himself: "Compassion for creatures! Compassion for creatures! You fool! An insignificant worm crawling on earth, you to show compassion to others!

Who are you to show compassion? No, it cannot be. Not compassion for others, but rather the service of man, recognizing him to be a veritable manifestation of God."

Everyone present there, no doubt, heard those words uttered from the Master's inmost consciousness, but only Naren could gauge their meaning. When Naren left the room he said to the others:

What a wonderful light I have discovered in those words of the Master! How beautifully he has reconciled the ideal of Bhakti with the knowledge of the Vedanta, generally interpreted as dry, austere, and incompatible with human sentiments! What a grand, natural and sweet synthesis! The usual idea is that the practice of the knowledge of Vedanta demands a complete withdrawal from society and a rooting out of all such sentiments as love, devotion and compassion. Cherishing hatred of the world and of fellow creatures, thinking them impediments to spiritual attainment, the aspirant goes astray. But from those words of wisdom that the Master uttered in an ecstatic mood, I have understood that the ideal of Vedanta lived by the recluse outside the pale of society can be practised even at home and applied to all aspects of daily life. Whatever a man's vocation, let him understand and realize that it is God alone who has manifested Himself as the world and created beings. He is both immanent and transcendent. It is He who has become all the diverse beings, objects of our love, respect or compassion, and yet He is beyond all these. Such a realization of Divinity in humanity leaves no room for arrogance. By realizing it, a man cannot be jealous of, or have pity for, any other being. Serving man, knowing him to be the manifestation of God, purifies the heart; and in a short time the aspirant who does this realizes that he is a part of God—Existence-Knowledge-Bliss Absolute.

Those words of the Master throw an altogether new light upon the path of devotion. Real devotion is far off until the aspirant realizes the immanence of God. By realizing Him in and through all beings and by serving Him in them, the devotee acquires real devotion. Those following the paths of work and Yoga are similarly benefited by these words of the Master. The embodied being cannot remain even for a minute without activity. All his activities should be directed to the service of man, the manifestation of God upon earth, and this will accelerate his progress towards the goal. If it be the will of God, the day will soon come when I shall proclaim this grand truth to the world at large. I shall make it the common property of all, the wise and the fool, the rich and the poor, the Brahmin and the Pariah.

It must be constantly borne in mind that the Master's life and teaching were true to the essence of Hinduism: not to sectarian Hinduism, but to that deep and all-comprehending attitude of soul which has in a marked degree been the Hindu ideal at all times. On the surface, Hinduism may seem to be a rigid framework of rituals and a congeries of myths. But with the Advaita philosophy as background the whole setting and details are seen in a different light. Therefore when Naren came to Shri Ramakrishna he found in it a new theology. True, it was the same theology that he had been taught from his infancy, but he was now approaching it with understanding, whereas, as a child, he had imbibed it without question, as a matter of custom and heritage. Formerly when the intellect bestirred itself, doubt also arose; but now, in the light of the new outlook that had been opened up, the Master's own life revealed to him potentialities and realities in Hinduism that he had not dreamt of. The Hinduism of Shri Ramakrishna was a positive, practical and living realization. However much Naren might question the spiritual ideals and the existence of the gods in which Hinduism abounded, he could not doubt the earnestness of his Master, who laid bare the living spirit of Hinduism. It might be superstition, Naren at first thought; the Master himself might be a madman; but it could be no ordinary superstition that enabled this madman to transmit spirituality by just a touch! To Shri Ramakrishna, Hinduism was alive. How superior it was, thought Naren, to the spiritually-lifeless Brahmoism! Indeed, this was more a social reform movement, even though the members, considered individually, might be possessed of spiritual aspirations. And did not Keshabchandra Sen, the leading spirit of the Brahmo movement, come and sit at the feet of Shri Ramakrishna?

To Shri Ramakrishna Naren was indebted for his understanding of Hinduism. This understanding was gained by watching the Master engaged in worship, in teaching, and absorbed in ecstasy. It was communicated to Naren in spite of himself. The Master injected his own consciousness, his own personal realization of the Mother and of Hinduism, into the soul of Naren. How he did this is not known; it was a process too subtle to be explained. The doubting Naren was passing away; the devoted Naren, the spiritual Naren, was being born—Naren the Hindu and more than Hindu.

In those days Naren, in common with many Brahmos, was uneasy about the consequences of intense meditation and of inebriation resulting from divine love. Shri Ramakrishna reassured him on this point, saying, "God is like an ocean of syrup. Would you not dive into it? Suppose, my boy, there is a vessel with a wide mouth containing syrup, and suppose you are a fly anxious to sip the syrup. How would you like to do so?" Naren said that he would sit on the edge and sip, for, if he chanced to fall in, he would be sure to be drowned. Thereupon the Master said, "You forget, my boy, this is the Ocean of Sachchidananda (Existence-Knowledge-Bliss Absolute). There need be no fear of death; this is the Ocean of Immortality. Only fools say that one should not go to excess in one's love of God. Can anybody ever go to excess in divine love? Therefore I say to you, dive deep into the Ocean of God." This advice Naren followed in his life. Though his intellect may at times have questioned, his heart went straight to the goal.

At this time, strange experiences came to him. Many times he saw Shri Ramakrishna in meditation when he himself was at home and the Master in Dakshineswar. One night Naren dreamt that Shri Ramakrishna came to him and said, "Come! I will show you Gopi Radha!" Naren followed him. After going some distance the Master turned to him and said, "Where else will you go?" Saying this, Shri Ramakrishna transformed himself into the beautiful personality and exquisite form of Radha herself. This so affected the conscious mind of Naren that whereas formerly he had only sung the songs of the Brahmo Samaj relating to the Formless Brahman, he now sang songs on the intense spiritual love of Radha, the individual soul, for Shri Krishna, the indwelling Beloved One. When he narrated this dream to his brother-disciples, they were amazed. One asked him, "Do you believe in the significance of this?" Naren answered, "Surely I do."

Naren once longed to be lost, forgetful of all outer things, in Bhava (ecstasy). He saw how the devotees of the Master, such as Nityagopal and Manomohan, would fall to the ground seemingly lifeless at the chanting of the names of God. He was depressed that he was not able to enter these states himself, and complained about it to Shri Ramakrishna. The Master, regarding him with tenderness, replied: "My child, do not be disturbed. What does it matter? When a huge elephant runs into a pond, it sets up a great commotion there; but if it goes into the waters of a huge lake, little commotion is set up. These devotees are, as it were, small ponds. A little of this great power of Divine Love going into these small ponds lashes the water into a fury; but you are like the huge lake."

About this time Naren passed through a test which proved that he was a roaring fire of spirituality and renunciation. Some of his wealthy friends one day invited him for a drive to their garden in the suburbs of Calcutta. He consented joyfully, having no idea what sort of an evening drive it would be. They stopped in front of a house, and all alighted and entered the grounds where a garden party was being held. These people were merry-makers. Naren enjoyed their singing, and sang himself. After a time he grew tired and was told that he might rest comfortably in a room close by. His friends, seeing him alone, sent a dancing girl to amuse him. He was as simple as a child and talked to her like a brother. She told him many interesting things about her life, about her sorrows and misfortunes. Seeing that she had engaged all his interest and sympathy, she misinterpreted his feelings and sought to entice him. Instantly he remembered Shri Ramakrishna and thought of God. He became serious, started to his feet, and said to the girl, "Excuse me, I must be going now. I have a genuine sympathy for you and wish you well. If you know that it is a weakness to lead such a life, you will get over it some day."

They parted. The girl returned in bewilderment and said to Naren's friends sarcastically, "A nice trick you have played on me—sending me to tempt a sadhu?" Such was the influence Shri Ramakrishna had on Naren.

One cannot bask in the radiance of a great personality without one's inner powers and potentialities being aroused. This happened to Naren. The words of hope and strength which the Master spoke concerning him had an invigorating effect. He became conscious of his future greatness. Once he said to his friends, "What! At best you will be lawyers or doctors or judges. Wait, I will chalk out my own path." He felt sure of himself because the Master was so sure of him. He saw outstanding men—physicians, lawyers, scholars and religious teachers—coming to the Master, attracted by his personality. Physicians tested his trances. They observed that, even when outward consciousness had receded, the Master's body would recoil if it came in contact with metal. Scholars noted down his sayings and found them to give expression to the highest realizations. All were convinced of the spiritual greatness of Shri Ramakrishna, Naren included. That the Master had given him the foremost place among his disciples and devotees —though from a worldly point of view Naren knew that he was nothing when compared with many of these—enhanced Naren's faith in himself. The Master was not guided by worldly considerations in his estimation. To one who was enormously rich and had won the title of Raja, he said, "People call you Raja, but I cannot do so! That would be a lie on my part." To another, a self-styled philanthropist, he said, "You are a small-minded man, low born as you are."

Thus Naren's all-round development, physical, intellectual and spiritual, was fostered by Shri Ramakrishna. Physically, he had the graceful bearing and supple movements of a wild animal. He would walk along, now slowly, now briskly, his mind absorbed in thought. And yet there was a boyishness about him, and a spontaneity of manner, which were a delight to all who knew him. His appearance was that of a young man full of vigour and vitality, slightly above the average in height, and somewhat thickset in the shoulders. His chest was well developed. His head was broad towards the front, indicating mental power and development; and it was well shaped all over. Indeed, he was one of those few men of whom it can be said, without implying femininity, that he was graceful. His eyes were his most striking feature. They were shaped like lotus petals. Rather prominent, though not protruding, they varied in colour according to the feelings of the moment. They revealed a keen, alert mind. At the time of steady gaze they were luminous and deep; at other times they would sparkle with joy and vivacity. When he spoke, it was as if, for the time being, only the person spoken to existed; one could not but feel pleased. Some accused him of intellectual avarice—if such a term can be used. They said that his interest in anyone ceased when, to use their expression, "he had wrung him dry". But it was always true of him that he gave more than he received: it was an intellectual exchange.

Although he was muscular and athletic in build, and of striking carriage, one forgot all that in the interest of studying the face. He had a strong jaw, evidence of a resolute nature. To some he seemed a happy dreamer, to others an intense thinker, to others again, one who lived in a world rich with ideal love and beauty; but to all he seemed a young man of high breeding. His smile was benign and engaging. But when he grew serious, his face would strike awe in his companions. There were times when he seemed a child to his brother-disciples; and they loved him all the more when, in that mood, he was cantankerous or exacting or impetuous. When he became excited in discussion, his face and eyes would glow, revealing the tremendous power in him. But when he was absorbed in his own thoughts, he could surround himself with such a repelling reserve that no one would dare approach him. In fact intense aloofness was one of his striking traits.

His was the temperament of a genius. Various moods would come upon him: now a strange impatience with his environment; again a sweet and loving patience as of one who is indifferent to results, who has eternity at his back. And considering the difficulties under which he laboured and suffered, and the scant appreciation he received from those for whom he laboured and suffered, it was a wonder that his heart did not become like steel. But love and a gentle bearing remained with him throughout. He would say to himself, "Why should one expect to be understood? It is sufficient that they love me. After all, who am I? The Mother knows best. She can manage Her work. Who am I to think myself indispensable?"

The love which Shri Ramakrishna bore for Naren had this as one of its fruits, that a balance was struck between intellect and heart; for it was above all through the vehicle of love that Naren could be taught and influenced. By nature Naren was a philosopher: Shri Ramakrishna made him a devotee also. But lest it be thought that the Master developed only devotional fervour in his disciple, it should be remembered that the highest metaphysical realization which Naren ever came to experience was likewise owing to the Master. Intellectual insight, tempered and softened by spiritual love, was the nature of Naren's spirituality. Though in general appearance he was a philosopher, the Master used to say that only a Bhakta, a devotee of God, could have such amiable and pleasing features. "Jnanis are generally dry in their appearance; but Bhaktas are pleasing to look at." But perhaps Naren's own words are the best guide to discerning his true nature. As Swami Vivekananda, he once compared himself with the Master: "He was all Bhakti without; but within he was all Jnana. I am all Jnana without; but in my heart all is Bhakti." He meant that a mantle of love hid the spiritual intellect of the Master, and a mantle of intelligence covered the devotion within himself.

One side of Naren's character was nurtured by his afflictions and poverty, another by his associations. Shri Ramakrishna perfected these two sides of Naren's character and moulded him according to the ideal he had in view—the ideal which became incarnate in the Swami Vivekananda. Shri Ramakrishna said that had Naren been brought up in luxury he would have certainly drifted in some other direction. He might have become a great statesman or lawyer, or a great

10

orator or social reformer. But poverty had given Naren sympathy with the poor. And from his Master he had learned that there was a difference between intellectuality and spirituality. Not that he denounced intellect; he acclaimed it. But hereafter he made reason subordinate to spiritual realization; he made philosophy the handmaid of it. Prayer and meditation were the wings upon which Naren now rose to spiritual consciousness.

How wonderful was the Master's love! After the passing away of Naren's father, Shri Ramakrishna said to an influential devotee, "Naren's father is dead. They are starving at home. Now it will be good if his friends help him." When the gentleman had taken his departure, Naren said, rather piqued, "Sir! Why did you tell him that?" The Master, seeing that he had hurt his disciple's sense of family pride in having thus made mention of their misfortune, exclaimed with tears in his eyes, "O my Naren, do you not know that I would do anything for you; that for you I would even go about begging from door to door!" Naren was overpowered. This was love indeed—overwhelming and selfless love. As Naren said of his Master long afterwards, "He made me his slave by his great love for me!"

Shri Ramakrishna, as we have already noted, was much alarmed when Naren's relatives were planning for his marriage. His love for Naren, his desire to save him from worldly life, made the Master prostrate himself at the feet of the Divine Mother. He prayed to Her many times, "O Mother, do break up all these plans! May Naren not sink!" But however great the Master's love, he would be strict with Naren if at any time he associated with evil companions, even though he did not do so of set purpose. Did the slightest shadow of an unworthy thought cross Naren's mind, the Master at once detected it. When Naren came to him after having associated with some questionable person, the Master would not even look at him, still less eat from his hand.

Naren's illustrious future was always present to Shri Ramakrishna's vision. He knew that Naren's was the path of renunciation, and trained him to this end. In that light he scrutinized his disciple's every movement. Once he found that Naren was associating intimately with a devotee who had led a worldly life, and warned him; but Naren protested that the devotee had given up his questionable habits. The Master said:

However much you may wash the pot where garlic has been kept, still some smell will linger. The boys are pure. They are as yet un-contaminated by any idea of lust and gold. You have seen mangoes that have been pecked by crows. Such mangoes cannot be offered to God or eaten by man. The devotees who have tasted worldly pleasure belong to another group.

A group of monks was seated together thinking of God. Some women passed by. One of the monks opened his eyes wider and cast oblique glances at them: he had renounced the world after being the father of three children. You cannot expect figs from thistles. Worldly men have no leisure to think of God; but do you think I hate them? No, not at all. I find God has become all these. I look upon all women as my Mother. So I find no difference between a chaste woman and a girl of ill fame. . . . I find everyone seeks glass beads: no one wants diamonds. Man is enchanted by lust; he is caught by the glamour of riches; but to one who has seen God, these are worthless trifles. Some-one said to Ravana, "You go to Sita assuming all sorts of forms in order to intimidate or seduce her. Why don't you take the form of Rama so that she may take you for her husband?" Ravana replied, "If I meditate on Rama, even the most exquisite beauty of the world appears as mere straw."

Devotion to God is impossible without purity of heart. An impure man cannot have single-minded devotion. His mind is diverted to various things. You cannot expect anything when you are attached to lust and gold. It is extremely difficult for a worldly man to be perfectly unattached. He is a slave to his wife, slave to his money, and slave to his master.

Then looking at Naren, he said, "My dear boy, you will never attain your goal if you are attached to lust and gold." Verily as the sun is far above the earth, so was this Guru above other Gurus. The Master and Naren transcended all con-ventional ideas of Guru and disciple. It is not surprising that

Naren should have counted these days of ecstasy at Dakshineswar as days of blessedness.

Such was the teaching Shri Ramákrishna gave Naren during
the first four years of their relationship, and such was the
environment in which Naren grew beyond the confines of his
former spiritual hopes. It is difficult to say just when Naren
became the Master's disciple. From a mystical point of view he
had become the disciple when Shri Ramakrishna touched his
heart. It was then that the Master can be said to have taken
possession of him. But consciously Naren became the disciple
only when his intellect had been convinced—a process which
took some time. This process was part of his training. Had he
accepted the Master from the beginning, without question,
he would not have become Swami Vivekananda, possessed of
the power of convincing others because he himself had not
been easily convinced.

But when conviction had come, and Naren did become the
disciple, it was to him irrevocable. For five years he had living
contact with his Guru. Every time he visited Dakshineswar
it was a stirring event both for himself and for the Master,
serving to intensify their relationship and as an occasion for
the further absorption of ideas and ideals by the disciple. He
was becoming saturated with spirituality. The Master gave
him all that was to be given, all that he had. Shri Ramakrishna
was like one who had struggled hard against almost insuperable
difficulties to acquire a great treasure, and Naren was the son
and heir who was to inherit this treasure. Shri Ramakrishna
had won a spiritual empire by conquering the chief foes, lust
and gold; Naren was to extend this empire over the earth.
Shri Ramakrishna had dived deep into the ocean of Spirit;
Naren was to show the world the treasures the Master had
found there. Shri Ramakrishna was the realization and revelation, and Naren the utterance thereof.

Through Naren one is able to enter the group of devotees
first at Dakshineswar, later on at Shyampukur and Cossipore,
and witness the spiritual experiences and observe the Master's
methods of teaching. The training was directed to making the

disciples gradually aware that all religions are paths to God and that all are essentially in harmony.

Whether Shri Ramakrishna was in fact an Incarnation of God or not, did not at this time occupy Naren's attention. It was the character of the Master that he saw: that told a more complete tale in the way of revelation than all the theories put together. Naren's views at this time were broad, in fact too broad for the average understanding. He viewed Shri Rama-krishna in a larger perspective than most of those about him. He often grew impatient of their tendency to a partisan and exclusive acceptance of the Master. He held him in too high a reverence to appraise him only in terms of the Incarnation doctrine. He unconsciously accepted Shri Ramakrishna's life as the demonstration of means to all spiritual ends—not just to the spiritual ends of one religion or sect. He saw him as a spiritual path-finder. The Master's words were to him veracious utterances in regard to the highest possibilities of the spiritual life. He sensed, from his association with the Master, what he later understood from spiritual science, namely, that human personality can transcend its own bounds by the intensification of transpersonal ideals. All the efforts of the saints had been to this end. In Shri Ramakrishna Naren saw these efforts brought to their highest realization. He saw him as the preserver and rejuvenator of the Hindu Dharma. He saw in Shri Rama-krishna a new Chaitanya, a new Shankaracharya, a new Buddha; yes, and even more, for the difficulties which stood in the way of the rejuvenation of Hinduism were more numerous and serious in the nineteenth century than at any previous time. Intuitively Naren was aware of all this, and of the great-ness of Shri Ramakrishna. This understanding grew in him at Shyampukur, and came to maturity at the Cossipore garden-house.

In the summer of 1885, seeing the Master suffer from the excessive heat, the devotees requested him to take ice. Finding that it gave him relief many of them now began to bring ice for him when they came to Dakshineswar. He liked to take it with sugared drinks, which he enjoyed like a boy. But after a month or two a pain started in his throat. It was probably in April that he felt the pain for the first time.

More than a month elapsed, but the pain did not abate; and scarcely had the month of May come when the disease developed new symptoms. It increased when he spoke much or went into ecstasy. It was at first diagnosed as inflammation of the throat due to cold, and an ordinary plaster was prescribed. But finding it not efficacious after a few days' use, a devotee brought Dr. Rakhal of Bowbazar, who was known to be an expert in such diseases. The doctor diagnosed the disease and prescribed an unguent and medicine for application inside and on the outside of the throat. He asked those attending on the Master to see that as far as possible he did not talk much for some days and did not often go into ecstasy.

The thirteenth day of the bright fortnight of Jyaistha (May-June) was drawing near, when a fair of the Vaishnava community is held annually in the village of Panihati on the east bank of the Ganga, a few miles north of Calcutta. The Master went there, persuaded by the devotees, and spent the whole day singing and dancing, often going into Samadhi. The result was aggravation of the disease. The doctors now diagnosed it as "clergyman's throat". The Master followed the physician's instructions in all matters but two. Whenever there was occasion for spiritual converse, he would lose body-consciousness and go into ecstasy; and when afflicted people came to him for solace he would talk, no matter what it cost him. At the same time his communion with God intensified; he had no regular hours for food or drink; most of his time was spent in meditation and prayer, which with him meant Samadhi. Thus the last year of his life became a slow crucifixion.

The devotees naturally became anxious. Narendra realized the gravity of the situation. He remarked to a friend, "I am afraid the object of our love and adoration will not live for long. I have read the medical books and consulted some doctor-friends about his disease, and I am afraid his throat trouble has turned into cancer, the cure for which has not yet been discovered." Shri Ramakrishna readily agreed to moving to

Calcutta for systematic treatment. Accordingly a small house was rented at Durgacharan Mukherjee Street in Baghbazar, but the Master did not like it and straightaway left for Balaram Bose's place. Within a week he was moved to a better house at 55 Shyampukur Street in Shyampukur. Doctor Mahendralal Sarkar, the leading homoeopath of Calcutta, agreed to treat him. Naren organized the nursing; the Holy Mother came from Dakshineswar to do the cooking. Naren's love for the Master, his self-sacrifice and enthusiasm, influenced the other disciples, and they all resolved to devote themselves to the service of their spiritual guide and to the realization of God. They forgot studies and home. Their parents and guardians began to intervene; and, but for the zeal and encouragement of Naren, it would have been almost impossible for them to have continued the course they were intent on.

As none of the householder devotees was rich enough to bear the expenses single-handed, at times the faith of the boys wavered, and they wondered where the money to meet the expenses was to come from. They feared that they might even have to give way to their families and return home. Whenever this happened some fresh proof of Shri Ramakrishna's divinity would be given them. Then they would reproach themselves saying, "Why this baseless apprehension, this anxiety about funds? The Master himself will provide the means." The devotees were convinced that any service rendered to him would conduce to their spiritual welfare, and they looked on his illness as an opportunity to serve the Guru, each according to his capacity. So the householders resolved to spend money in the service of the Master, and the boys gave themselves in personal service. All were caught up in an enthusiasm which was stimulated and strengthened by Shri Ramakrishna's revelation of spirituality. Many who were unable to go to Dakshineswar to see him found the opportunity at Shyampukur.

Naturally, there was much speculation among the devotees as to the reason for the Master's illness. Some ascribed it to the will of the Divine Mother: they held that it was necessary

for the fulfilment of some unknown purpose. Others thought
that it was self-imposed, as the Master was a divine Incarnation, for the good of mankind. A third group concluded that
as birth, disease, decay and death are inevitable phases of
human life, the disease of the Master was a perfectly natural
phenomenon, and that it was foolish to seek a supernatural
explanation for it. At the same time these last were willing to
sacrifice everything in the Master's service and to mould their
lives in the light of the lofty spiritual ideal set before them
by him. It hardly needs saying that Narendranath was the
leader of the last group: it consisted mostly of young men
reading in schools and colleges. Though the various groups of
devotees regarded the Master differently—as an Incarnation
of God, or as a superman, or as a man of God—all of them were
convinced beyond doubt that the goal of life would be realized
if they could follow his example and render him service.

Naren was not a fanatic. Yet he had to admit that the
loving, suffering human person whom he saw before him, could
be, and often actually was, transformed the next moment
into a divine person. In Shri Ramakrishna the human and
the divine, he began to see, were inseparable. He came to see
religion as consisting in realistic efforts for the conquest of
human limitations and as the achievement of that conquest.
He saw this lived before him daily by Shri Ramakrishna. In
the face of it, belief was neither here nor there: attaining to the
same conquest and realization was the thing that mattered.
Sitting thus at the feet of the Master, Naren read in him the
essential meaning of the Vedas and the Upanishads.

Narendranath, however, did not look on Shri Ramakrishna
either as an Incarnation of God, or as an ordinary being.
One day (October 27, 1885) in reply to certain criticisms of
Dr. Mahendralal Sarkar, Narendranath said, "We think of
him [meaning the Master] as a person who is like God. Do
you know, sir, what it is like? There is a point between the
vegetable creation and the animal creation where it is very
difficult to determine whether a particular thing is a vegetable
or an animal. Likewise, there is a stage between the man-

world and the God-world where it is extremely hard to say whether a person is man or God." He concluded by saying, "I do not say that he is God. What I am saying is that he is a Godlike man. Hence we offer him worship."

The Master, knowing that he was approaching the end of his mortal existence, was all the more eager to kindle in his young disciples a burning desire for the realization of God. Since this can only be attained by reducing to ashes all attachment to lust and gold, his utterances at Shyampukur were replete with the spirit of renunciation. Besides spiritual teaching, Shri Ramakrishna also gave his disciples the strength to follow the teaching. His own life, the force of his utterances, his communion with divine realities, and the ease with which he passed into the highest Samadhi—all these were as a great Light drawing them on to a glorious spiritual consciousness. Coming at a time when Naren was being buffeted on all sides, the Master's teaching sank deep into his heart to remain there for ever, a beacon light to show him the way through the wilderness of illusion.

When Doctor Mahendralal Sarkar, the Master's attending physician, met Naren, he was delighted with his conversation and invited him to dinner. Later when the doctor heard Naren sing at Shyampukur, he was so pleased that he embraced and blessed him. He said to Shri Ramakrishna, "I am very glad to see that it is boys like him who come here for religious instruction. Naren is a real gem, fit to shine in any sphere of life." The Master replied, "They say that the fiery appeal of Advaita Goswami brought about the incarnation of Shri Gauranga at Nadia. Similarly everything that you see here [meaning his own advent] is on account of him [Narendranath]."

Of all the disciples of the Master, Naren, though young, possessed the most penetrating intellect, as was shown by his power of discrimination and comprehensive outlook on life. This was one of the qualities that made him their natural leader, competent to chide as well as to guide, as will be seen from what follows.

While association with Shri Ramakrishna and wholehearted service to him gave the devotees increased faith and devotion, they were unwittingly walking on a dangerous road. The emotions of the boys were stirred by the tragic picture unfolding before their eyes. To the more sentimental among them, these emotions were insidiously replacing the sterner ideals of renunciation and self-restraint which are the bed-rock of spirituality. Emotion is good in its place, but it is not the goal—and too much indulgence in it might even cause one to miss the object to be attained. Of course, there were some reasons for their taking this mistaken view of spirituality. The mind naturally seeks the line of least resistance, trying to make a compromise between God and the world, between renunciation and enjoyment. Few realize their contrary natures; most are satisfied with a partial success in spiritual matters. Shri Ramakrishna, knowing this, tested newcomers to see if their idea was of a comfortable religion, one that would not interfere with the satisfaction of their worldly desires. In such cases he never gave the entire spiritual truth but contented himself with imparting as much as they would find easy to accept and assimilate. This entailed individual training. Of course, his instruction to householders was different from that given to his young boys not yet contaminated by the world. His general instructions were still different. There we find him saying, "In this Kali-Yuga the only way to cultivate spirituality is by chanting the name of the Lord and following the path of devotion as marked out by the sage Narada." The devotees, however, did not realize the full significance of this, that Narada taught complete renunciation of the world by a gradual process, through love of God.

Another cause of the devotees' error seems to have been their lack of comprehension of the significance of Shri Ramakrishna's life. They would see the Master weep and dance before he became lost in Samadhi; but his emotion, unlike theirs, had as its background a life of austerity and renunciation, and was evidence of strength rather than weakness. The situation took a new turn when Girishchandra Ghose arrived on the scene. Girish openly proclaimed the Master to be an Incarnation of

God, and he tried to induce everyone to share his conviction. This proved nearly fatal to some of the disciples. Girish's case was unique; but there were others, with none of his sincerity, who went about declaring that, like Girish, they had given Shri Ramakrishna the "power of attorney" in spiritual matters and had therefore no need of any discipline. Girish was soon supported in his view by Ramchandra Datta, who declared the Master to be the Incarnation of Shri Krishna and Shri Gauranga. Encouraged by Girish's public announcement, Ramchandra busied himself with working out an Incarnation theory of his own, and even went so far as to assign to different devotees the roles they had—so he said—played with these Incarnations. Those who displayed the greatest amount of sentiment were, in his estimation, spiritually the highest.

Matters were brought to a head by Vijaykrishna Goswami, the noted Brahmo preacher, who, though not a disciple of the Master, had had a vision of him as he sat in meditation in his room in Dacca. He lost no time in going to see the Master (on October 25, 1885) to tell him, "I have travelled all over the country and met many spiritual persons; but I have found none like you. Here is the full amount[1] of sixteen annas, whereas at other places I have found but two, three or four annas at most. I saw you at Dacca in a vision and I have no doubt about you. People do not understand you because you are so easy of access. You live very near to Calcutta. The mere wish takes us to you; there is no difficulty of conveyance. Therefore we cannot properly estimate your value. But had you been seated on the summit of a high mountain, the journey to which would mean much trouble and hardship, then we should have regarded you in a different light. Now we think that if such a very spiritual man lives near us, how much greater must be the spirituality of those who live far off! That is why we roam hither and thither in quest of spirituality instead of coming to see you."

It is not surprising that Vijay's presence at Shyampukur should have caused the smouldering embers to burst into flame. Belief in the Master as a divine Incarnation spread among the

[1] In those days a rupee was the equivalent of sixteen annas.

devotees like wild fire. Some of them waited eagerly for miraculous manifestations of Shri Ramakrishna's power; others would fall into partial trances accompanied by convulsions on hearing devotional music or the like.

Narendranath was the first to realize the dangers of the path the devotees were taking. He tried to warn the young ones of the danger by saying: "The sentimentalism that does not produce a permanent change in human life, that makes man eager to realize God at one moment but does not give him power to desist from seeking lust and gold at the next, has no depth in it, and is therefore of little value in life. Though under its influence some may shed tears and experience horripilation and other bodily changes, or even a temporary withdrawal of normal consciousness, it is, I am perfectly convinced, the result of nervous weakness. A man should by all means eat nutritious food and take the help of a physician if he cannot suppress his feelings through the exercise of his will. There is much of artificiality in those bodily changes and absence of normal consciousness. As our control over ourselves grows firmer, our sentiments become deeper and more genuine. It is only in the lives of rare persons that spiritual sentiments become so powerful as to assume the form of tidal waves, overflowing even a firm dam of control, and become manifest as bodily changes and temporary cessation of normal consciousness. Foolish men cannot understand this and reverse the process: depth of spiritual sentiments, they think, is the result of those bodily changes and that loss of consciousness; so they make efforts to produce those effects in themselves. That intention and effort of theirs gradually develop into a habit and weaken their nerves increasingly as days pass by, so that in the course of time those changes come on them at the slightest experience of sentiment. In the end they become insane or afflicted with a chronic malady by indulging freely in them. In trying to practise religion, eighty per cent of people turn charlatans and about fifteen per cent become mad; only the remaining five attain the immediate knowledge of the infinite Truth, and are blessed. Hence beware!"

That Naren was right became evident when it transpired later that some of those emotional outbursts had been carefully rehearsed at home; others were simply imitation. More and better food, and sustained efforts at self-control, proved sufficient medicine in most cases. But where these methods failed, Naren would make that person the butt of ridicule. He hated the weakness that permitted the surrender of straightforwardness and discrimination. He placed positive ideals before the young disciples and appealed to their innate strength. He would gather them together and through songs of renunciation and devotion would help them keep their minds surcharged with the ideals of austerity and of dispassion for the things of the world. Or he would narrate in glowing colours soul-stirring incidents from the life of the Master to illustrate his profound love of God. Sometimes he revealed the Master's glory in a way that amazed the disciples. At other times he would quote passages from the *Imitation of Christ* and say, "The life of anybody who truly loves the Lord will be perfectly moulded in His pattern. Therefore, whether we truly love the Master or not will be proved by this fact." He reminded the devotees of the Master's saying, "First tie the nondual knowledge in the corner of your cloth; then do whatever you like." He explained to them that the Master's emotional intoxication had that knowledge as its basis, and exhorted them to make efforts to attain the nondual knowledge first.

While Naren was thus engaged in his own spiritual pursuit and in shaping the character of his young brother-disciples, the condition of the Master was going from bad to worse. Medicines proved of no avail. Dr. Mahendralal thought that it might be due to the foul air of Calcutta and advised removal to some garden-house in the suburbs. After a search the garden-house belonging to Gopalchandra Ghosh at Cossipore was hired at eighty rupees a month. On the afternoon of December 11, 1885, the Master was moved to the new place where he felt much refreshed on account of its pleasing surroundings, clean air, and seclusion.

COSSIPORE AND THE PASSING AWAY
OF THE MASTER

The move to Cossipore ushered in the last scene of the
Master's life. These were days of intense physical suffering
for him, yet days of bliss too, for he felt that he had fulfilled
his mission on earth and was leaving a number of youthful,
all-renouncing, determined disciples, who would make his
message known. His great hope lay in Narendranath, and
even on his deathbed he devoted himself to the task of moulding the lives of Naren and the other youngsters. Of his approaching end he gave ample hints: "I shall make the whole
thing public before I go"; "When people in large numbers
begin to whisper about the greatness of this body, then the
Mother will take it back"; "The devotees will be sifted into
inner and outer circles towards the end"; and so on.

Naren grew in spiritual power from day to day, while Shri
Ramakrishna grew physically worse, although in his mind
and heart the same divine flame burned, all the brighter for
his sufferings. The disciples nursed him faithfully, making
their service to the Guru an act of worship; but nothing could
stay the course of the disease. The Master was again ordered
by his physician not to strain his throat by talking; but he did
not resist the urge to transmit his knowledge to the many
religious seekers who flocked to him at all hours.

Day by day the Master's body grew weaker. The boys,
under the direction of Naren, gave all their time to nursing
him. This required them to stay day and night at the Cossipore
garden. It gave rise to strong opposition from their relatives.
Naren was at that time studying for the Law examination, and
then also there was the lawsuit with some of his relatives,
which, as we have mentioned, had been pending. This latter
made it imperative for him to be in Calcutta part of the time;

but he resolved to do his studying in the time left to him at Cossipore.

Shri Ramakrishna was now practically alone with these young men. Having left their homes for the time being at the instance of Naren, they were giving themselves in devoted service to the Master. Naren was a constant source of inspiration to them. During their leisure periods, he would gather them together, and the time would be spent in study, devotional singing, and discussions about the Master and other serious matters. The blazing fire of Naren's personality by its heat welded the heterogeneous elements to be found among the boys into a homogeneous whole of one body and one soul, as it were. They were twelve in number, every one of them a tower of strength in consecration and single-minded devotion. Their names were Narendra, Rakhal, Baburam, Niranjan, Yogin, Latu, Tarak, Gopal Senior, Kali, Shashi, Sharat and Gopal Junior. Sarada, owing to the opposition of his father, could come only now and then, and stay for a day or two. Harish stayed for only a few days, after which his brain became deranged and he went home. Hari and Gangadhar practised Tapasya at home and came from time to time.

As the end of the Master approached, Narendranath's hankering after the realization of God intensified. One night, after deciding to go home for a day or two to settle some family affairs, he went to bed, but could not sleep. Calling Sharat, Gopal Junior, and a few others to him, he said, "Come, let us have a walk in the garden." As they walked about Naren said, "The Master's disease is extremely serious. May he not intend to lay down his body! Strive your best for spiritual enlightenment through service to him and prayer and meditation, while there is yet time. After his passing away, there will be no end to your repentance. We are wasting our time in the foolish thought that we shall pray to God after finishing this or that piece of business. That is only fastening more chains of desire on us, and desire means death. We must root that out at once."

On that cold starry night they felt a great urge to meditate. A heap of straw and dry twigs was lying near. Naren said, "Set fire to it. It is at this hour that the monks light their Dhuni fires. Let us do the same and burn our desires." The fire was lighted and the boys sat round it, feeling that they were really making a bonfire of their desires and being purged of all impurities.

One day Shri Ramakrishna initiated Naren with the name of Rama, telling him that it was the Mantra which he had received from his own Guru. In consequence of this, Naren's emotions were tremendously stirred. Towards evening he began to circle the house, repeating the name of the Lord, "Rama! Rama!", in a loud and animated voice. Outward consciousness had apparently left him, and he was full of ecstatic fire. When the Master was informed of this, he simply said, "Let him be; he will come round in due course." The emotional storm subsided in a few hours, and Naren became his old self again.

According to another version, when Shri Ramakrishna came to know of Naren's ecstatic state, he said to someone: "Go and ask Naren to come here." But the messenger could not manage Naren alone, and sought help from others. When they brought Naren, the Master said, "Oh, why are you going on like this? What good will it do?" After a pause he said, "See, I passed twelve long years in the state you are experiencing now. What are you going to attain in a single night?"

The Cossipore garden-house became a temple and a university hall in one. At times philosophy held the floor, at others, devotion. Singing and chanting would go on when time could be snatched from nursing. Naren would say to the Master, "Sir, give me a medicine that will cure all the illness of my mind and heart." The Master would respond by sending him and the other disciples to meditate; or he would ask him to sing. While singing, waves of rapturous love for God would sweep over Naren, carrying him to realms of ecstasy.

On January 1, 1886, something remarkable happened. Dr. Rajendralal Datta, a well-known homoeopath of Calcutta, examined the Master carefully and administered Lycopodium 200. The medicine alleviated the symptoms to some extent. Feeling better, Shri Ramakrishna expressed the desire to have a stroll in the compound. This was in the afternoon about

3 o'clock. Most of the young disciples who served him, and who used to practise meditation at night, were resting in the hall on the ground floor. It being New Year's Day, there was a holiday, and many householder devotees had come to the Cossipore garden to see the Master. Girishchandra Ghosh, who had also come, was conversing with Ramachandra Datta and a few others under a mango tree. Accompanied by some devotees the Master slowly approached Girish and said, "Girish, what have you seen in me as a result of which you say publicly so many things [that I am an Incarnation, and so on] to one and all?"

Girish, who had wonderful faith in the Master's divinity, said to him with folded hands in a choking voice, "What can I say of Him, a fraction of whose glory even Vyasa and Valmiki failed miserably to express [in their epics]?" At Girish's words the Master's mind ascended to a high plane and he went into Samadhi. Girish cried out with joy, "Glory to Ramakrishna, glory to Ramakrishna!" and took the dust of the Master's feet again and again.

Meanwhile the Master came down to a semi-conscious state and said, smiling: "What more shall I say to you? May you all be spiritually awakened!" When the devotees heard these words of blessing, they cried out, "Glory to Ramakrishna!" Some of them saluted the Master, some offered him flowers, while others took the dust of his feet, one by one. The Master in turn touched the chest of each devotee who approached him, and said, "Be spiritually awakened!" That day, most of the householder devotees of the Master had spiritual experiences of some sort or other. The Master became, as it were, the fabled Wish-fulfilling Tree (Kalpataru) on this day, and granted them spiritual realizations according to their path and capacity. In memory of this incident, Kalpataru day is celebrated every year on January 1 at the Cossipore garden and elsewhere.

One day (January 4, 1886) the Master asked Naren, "Won't you continue your college studies?" With emotion the latter replied, "Sir, I shall feel greatly relieved if I find some medicine that will make me forget all I have studied."

Naren's frame of mind at this time is also seen from the

11

record of a conversation he had with Mahendranath Gupta in the evening of that day.

Narendra: "I was meditating here last Saturday [January 2, 1886], when suddenly I felt a peculiar sensation in my chest."

Mahendra: "It was the awakening of the Kundalini."

Narendra: "Probably it was. I clearly perceived the Ida and Pingala nerves. I asked Hazra to feel my chest. Yesterday I saw him [meaning the Master] upstairs and told him about it. I said to him: 'All the others had their realization [on the Kalpataru day]; please give me something. All have succeeded; shall I alone remain unsatisfied?' He said, 'Why don't you settle your family affairs and then come to me? You will get everything. What do you want?' I replied, 'It is my desire to remain absorbed in Samadhi continually for three or four days, only once in a while coming down to the sense plane to eat a little food.' Thereupon he said, 'You are a small-minded person. There is a state higher even than that. "All that exists art Thou": it is you who sing that song. Settle your family affairs and then come to me. You will attain a state higher than Samadhi.'

"I went home this morning. My people scolded me, saying: 'Why do you wander about like a vagabond? Your Law examination is near at hand and you are not paying any attention to your studies. You wander about aimlessly.' I went to my study at my grandmother's. As I tried to read I was seized with a great fear, as if studying were a terrible thing. My heart struggled within me. I burst into tears: I never wept so bitterly in my life. I left my books and ran away. I ran past a haystack and got hay all over me. I kept on running along the road here [Cossipore]."

About nine o'clock on the same evening Niranjan and Shashi were sitting near the Master. Every now and then he talked of Narendra: "How wonderful Narendra's state of mind is! You see, this very Narendra did not believe in the forms of God; and now you see how his soul is panting for God! You know that story of the man who asked his teacher how God could be realized. The teacher said to the disciple: 'Come with me. I shall show you how one can realize God.' Saying this he took the disciple to a lake and held his head under the water. After a short time the teacher released him and asked, 'How did you feel?' 'I was dying for a breath of air', said the disciple. When your soul longs and yearns for God like that, then you will know that you do not have to wait long for His vision. The rosy colour on the horizon shows that the sun will soon rise."

In this way Shri Ramakrishna gave a hint that Naren was soon to reach the goal. That very night Naren with some of his brother-disciples left for Dakshineswar to practise meditation.

There was nothing unnatural in Naren's entreaty for Sama-dhi. It is the heartfelt desire and ambition of every sincere Sadhaka of all ages and climes to be merged in God through Samadhi. But Naren was born for the fulfilment of a higher and greater purpose. He was to be not only a Siddha-purusha—a perfected soul—but a saviour of souls. He was not only to cross the ocean of Maya himself, but to help others do so. In this light, Naren's own liberation was of comparatively minor significance. That Shri Ramakrishna was fully aware of this was shown by his telling Naren that he would enable him to realize a higher and nobler state than Samadhi. He wanted Naren to be a Jnani and a Bhakta in one, to see God in His various forms as well as experience the Absolute.

At this time Naren was practising many austerities and meditating a great deal, spending night after night in the Panchavati before a Dhuni fire. The Master had initiated him into various paths of spiritual discipline, and in carrying out these instructions Naren attained remarkable results.

Shri Ramakrishna was quietly preparing him to be the leader of the group of youngsters who were to consecrate their lives in the near future to the carrying out of his mission. One day the Master expressly commissioned him to look after them, saying, "I leave them in your care. See that they practise spiritual exercises even after my passing away, and that they do not return home."

One day, in preparation for the monastic life, the Master instructed the boys to beg their food from door to door. They immediately complied with enthusiasm; and with the name of the Lord on their lips went forth to beg in the neighbourhood. They had various experiences: some were abused for neglecting their duties in the world; the sight of others caused mothers to shed tears. The food which they collected in this manner was cooked in the garden and offered to the Master, who was over-joyed. He took a grain of rice and said, "Well done! This food is very pure." He knew that soon these young boys would put on the ochre cloth of renunciation and go forth empty-handed in quest of God, begging from pious householders such food as was necessary.

Naren was looked up to by the other young disciples because of Shri Ramakrishna's estimate of his spiritual worth. Then, too, he was the most intellectual of them all. He combined reason and a wide range of knowledge with a devotional nature; and was, besides, more strongly fortified in his religious convictions. When the Master's teaching and the monastic tendencies of himself and his fellow disciples were challenged, his explanations were irresistible. In speaking for himself, he spoke for his fellow disciples. It was he who fired them with enthusiasm by the power of his personality. If any differences or difficulties arose, they would come to him for a solution.

Shri Ramakrishna encouraged this central position of Naren in innumerable ways. He told them that Naren was their leader, and made them feel that the spiritual understanding of his chief disciple should be their guide in days to come. They for the most part understood the Master the better through Naren. He explained that great life to them. His understanding of the Master became their understanding and strength.

In the midst of all his striving and hankering for the realization of Truth, Naren did not lose sight of the fact that it was through the grace of the Master that he was being prepared for the realization of God. The illness of the Master—his friend, philosopher and Guru—was constantly in his mind. One day, about this time, Pandit Shashadhar Tarkachudamani, a great scholar and a devotee of Ramakrishna, came to Cossipore. In the course of conversation the pandit said, "Sir, it is written in

the scriptures that perfect souls like you can cure any physical
malady by mere wish. If you will concentrate your mind on
the affected part, determined that it shall be cured, the cure
will take place. Why don't you try it, sir?" Shri Ramakrishna
replied without a moment's hesitation, "You are a scholar and
yet you make such a senseless proposal! I have given my mind
once for all to God. How is it possible for me to take it away
and concentrate it upon this cage of rotten flesh and blood?"
The pandit was silenced. After he had left, Naren and a few
disciples begged the Master to heal himself saying, "Sir, you
must get rid of this disease, at least for our sake."

Shri Ramakrishna: "Do you think that I undergo this suffering voluntarily? I should like to see it cured; but it is still
there. Everything depends on the sweet will of the Divine
Mother."

Naren: "Then please ask the Mother to cure you. She
cannot but listen to your prayer."

Shri Ramakrishna: "It is easy for you to talk like that; but
I can never ask for such things."

Naren: "That will not do. You must tell the Mother about
it, at least for our sake."

Shri Ramakrishna: "Very well. Let me see what can be
done."

After a few hours, Naren came back and said, "Did you
ask the Mother about it? What was Her reply?" The Master
said, "I said to Her, pointing to my throat, 'I cannot eat anything on account of sore here. Please see that I am able to eat a
little.' The Mother replied, pointing to you all, 'Why! are you
not eating through so many mouths?' I was so ashamed that
I could not utter another word."

Naren was startled at these words. What an absence of
body-consciousness! What a firm realization of the Truth of
Advaita! Naren knew then that the Master was unique in his
realizations.

The meditative mood was becoming more and more spontaneous with Naren, and was manifest in the power to plunge
into deep concentration on any subject. Sometimes, following

meditation, Naren would see his double. It would appear as someone just like himself, and he would wonder, "Who is this?" It would respond to all his actions like an image reflected in a mirror, and remain with him sometimes for more than an hour. He told Shri Ramakrishna of it, but the Master passed it over lightly, saying, "It is only an incident in the higher stages of meditation."

Naren was now becoming aware of the spiritual power within him. There were moments when he, as it were, touched divinity and became almost physically conscious of Reality by the spiritual transmutation of the internal faculties of sense. His thought became a sweeping power. On one occasion he displayed it. It was on Shivaratri (the Night of Shiva) in March 1886. Naren was seated with three or four brother-disciples in a room in the compound of the Cossipore garden-house. They had fasted the whole day and intended to spend the night in meditation, worship and prayer. A mild shower of rain fell in the evening and the starlit sky was in parts fleeced with clouds. After finishing the worship, Japa and meditation proper to the first quarter of the night, Naren was resting and conversing with others, sitting on the worshipper's seat. One of the brother-disciples went out to prepare a smoke for him and another went to the main residence on a piece of work. Just then a feeling of divine power came to Naren. He wanted to test it out that night, and said to Kali (later Swami Abhedananda) who was sitting close to him, "Just touch me after a while." When the brother-disciple who had gone to prepare tobacco entered the room, he saw Naren sitting motionless in meditation and Kali, with his eyes shut, touching Naren's right knee with his right hand. He noticed that Kali's hand was trembling. After a minute or two Naren opened his eyes and said, "That is enough. How did you feel?" Kali answered, "I felt a shock as though from an electric battery. My hand was shaking all the while." The brother-disciple asked Kali, "Was your hand trembling because you were touching Naren?" Kali answered, "Yes, I could not keep it steady, though I tried."

A little later the young men applied themselves to the worship and meditation proper to the second quarter of the night. Kali entered into deep meditation at that time. He was never seen to enter into such deep meditation before. His whole body became stiff, with his neck and head inclined slightly forward. Consciousness of the outer world seemed to have completely left him for some time. Everyone present thought that he was having such meditation as a result of having touched Naren a little while previously. Naren also noticed that state and indicated it to a companion by a sign.

After the last quarter's worship was over at four in the morning, Shashi came to the worship-room and said to Naren, "The Master wants you." Naren went upstairs with Shashi to the Master. No sooner had the Master seen Naren than he said, "What is this? Spending with hardly anything accumulated! Allow it first to accumulate sufficiently in yourself; then you will know where and how to spend it. Mother Herself will teach you. Don't you see what harm you have done to him by injecting your attitude of mind into him? He has been progressing till now with a particular mental attitude, the whole of which has now been destroyed, like a miscarriage during the sixth month of pregnancy. What's done is done. Don't act so thoughtlessly from now on. The boy, however, is lucky that greater harm has not befallen him." Naren said afterwards, "I was completely flabbergasted. The Master was able to know whatever we did at the time of worship. What else could I do but keep silent when he scolded me like that!"[1]

Shri Ramakrishna was sinking daily. The anxiety and grief of the devotees knew no bounds. They redoubled their efforts to serve him. The young men made the Cossipore garden-house

[1] Swami Abhedananda (Kali) narrates this same incident in his autobiography. The gist of his account is as follows: On the Shivaratri night, when Naren and I were meditating, Naren's body suddenly began to shake. He asked me to put my hand on his thigh and see if I felt anything. When I put my hand there, I felt as though I had touched an electric battery, and as though a magnetic current were causing a violent tremor in his body. Gradually this current became so strong that my hand too began to shake. Naren did not infuse any power into me on this occasion; he only thought that he could do so. In order to disabuse Narendra of this illusion the Master said to him later, "This is the time to gain power, not to spend it."

their home, much to the chagrin of their relatives. The house-holder disciples defrayed all expenses ungrudgingly. All felt that the chief support of their life was going to be taken away. The sight of the haemorrhage would send a thrill of horror through their hearts. But the Master, in the midst of the suffering, looked as cheerful as ever, for he recognized the benign hand of the Divine Mother in it all. When the pain became unbearable, he would whisper with a smile, "Let the body and the pain take care of each other: you, O mind, be always in bliss!" One night he whispered to Mahendra, "I am bearing all this because otherwise you would be weeping. If you all say that it is better that the body should go rather than suffer so, let it go." To other devotees he said, "The disease is naturally of the body. I see many forms of God, and this too [his own form] is one of them."

On March 15, 1886, about seven o'clock in the morning, Shri Ramakrishna felt a little better. He talked to the devotees, sometimes in a whisper, sometimes by signs. Narendra, Rakhal, Latu, Mahendra, Gopal Senior, and others were in the room. They sat speechless and looked grave, thinking of the Master's suffering of the previous night.

Shri Ramakrishna: "Do you know what I see right now? I see that it is God Himself who has become all this. It seems to me that men and other living beings are made of leather, and that it is God Himself who, dwelling inside these leather cases, moves the hands, the feet, the heads. I had a similar vision once before, when I saw houses, gardens, roads, men, cattle—all made of one Substance; it was as if they were all made of wax.

"I see that it is God Himself who has become the block, the executioner, and the victim for the sacrifice."

As he described this experience, in which he realized in full the identity of all in the One Being, he was overwhelmed with emotion and exclaimed, "Ah! what a vision!"

Immediately Shri Ramakrishna went into Samadhi. He completely forgot his body and the outer world. The devotees were bewildered. Not knowing what to do, they sat still. Presently he regained partial consciousness of the world and said:

"Now I have no pain at all. I am my old self again." He cast his glance on Latu and said: "There is Leto. He bends down his head, resting it on the palm of his hand. I see that it is God Himself who rests His head on His hand."

The Master looked at the devotees and his love for them welled up in a thousand streams. Like a mother showing tenderness to her children he touched the faces and chins of Rakhal and Narendra. A few minutes later, he said to Mahendra, "If the body were to be preserved a few days more, many people would have their spirituality awakened."

After a pause: "But this is not to be. This time the body will not be preserved." The devotees eagerly awaited the Master's next words:

"Such is not the will of God. This time the body will not be preserved lest, finding me guileless and foolish, people should take advantage of me, and lest I, guileless and foolish as I am, should give away everything to everybody. In this Kali Yuga, you see, people are averse to meditation and Japa."

Rakhal: "Please speak to God that he may preserve your body some time more."

Shri Ramakrishna: "That depends upon God's will."

Narendra: "Your will and God's will have become one."

Shri Ramakrishna remained silent, evidently thinking about something. Then he said: "And nothing will happen if I do speak to God. Now I see that I and the Mother have become one. . . ."

He paused. The devotees looked at him eagerly to hear what he would say next.

Shri Ramakrishna: "There are two persons in this. One, the Divine Mother. (Pause) Yes, one is She. And the other is Her devotee. It is the devotee who broke his arm, and it is the devotee who is now ill. Do you understand?"

The devotees sat without uttering a word.

Shri Ramakrishna: "Alas! to whom shall I say all this? Who will understand me? (Pausing a few moments) God becomes man, an Incarnation, and comes to earth with His devotees. And the devotees leave the world with Him."

Rakhal: "Therefore we pray that you may not go away and leave us behind."

Shri Ramakrishna smiled and said: "A band of minstrels suddenly appears, dances, and sings, and it departs in the same sudden manner. They come and they return, but none recognizes them."

The Master and the devotees smiled. After a few minutes he said: "Suffering is inevitable when one assumes a human body. Every now and then I say to myself, 'May I not have to come back to earth again!' But there is something else. After enjoying sumptuous feasts outside, one does not relish ordinary home cooking. Besides, this assuming of a human body is for the sake of the devotees."

Shri Ramakrishna looked at Naren very tenderly and said to him: "An outcast was carrying a load of meat. Shankaracharya, after bathing in the Ganga, was passing by. Suddenly the outcast touched him. Shankara said sharply: 'What! you touched me!' 'Revered sir,' replied the outcast, 'I have not touched you nor have you touched me. Reason with me: Are you the body, the mind, or the Buddhi? Analyse what you are. You are pure Atman, unattached, and free, unaffected by the three Gunas —Sattva, Rajas, and Tamas.'

"Do you know what Brahman is like? It is like air. Good and bad smells are carried by the air, but the air is unaffected."

Narendra: "Yes sir."

Shri Ramakrishna: "He is beyond the Gunas and Maya— beyond both the 'Maya of knowledge' and the 'Maya of ignorance'. Lust and lucre are the 'Maya of ignorance'. Knowledge, renunciation, devotion, and other spiritual qualities are the splendours of the 'Maya of knowledge'. Shankaracharya kept this 'Maya of knowledge'; and that you and these others feel concerned about me is also due to this 'Maya of knowledge'.

"Following the 'Maya of knowledge' step by step, one attains the Knowledge of Brahman. This 'Maya of knowledge' may be likened to the last few steps of the stairs. Next is the roof. Some, even after reaching the roof, go up and down the stairs; that is to say, some, even after realizing God, retain the 'ego of know-

ledge'. They retain this in order to teach others, to taste divine
bliss, and to sport with the devotees of God."

Narendra: "Some people get angry with me when I speak of
renunciation."

Shri Ramakrishna: "Renunciation is necessary. (*Pointing to
his limbs*) If one thing is placed upon another, you must remove
the one to get the other. Can you get the second thing without
removing the first?"

Narendra: "True sir."

Shri Ramakrishna: "Didn't I say just now: 'When one sees
everything filled with God alone, does one see anything else'?
Does one then see any such thing as the world?..."

The Master looked tenderly at Narendra and became filled
with love. Looking at the devotees, he said, "Grand!" With a
smile Narendra asked: "What is grand?"

Shri Ramakrishna: "I see that preparations are going on for
a grand renunciation."

Narendra and the devotees looked silently at the Master.
Rakhal said: "Narendra is now beginning to understand you
rather well."

Shri Ramakrishna laughed and said: "Yes, that is so. I see
that many others, too, are beginning to understand...."

A few moments later the Master said: "I see that all things
—everything that exists—have come from this."

He asked Narendra by a sign, "What did you understand?"

Narendra: "All created objects have come from you."

The Master's face beamed with joy. He said to Rakhal, "Did
you hear what he said?"

This remarkable conversation was illuminating to Naren in
a number of ways. He had come to the Master with many
doubts, regarding the very existence of God, the nature of God,
and the Incarnations of God. The Master at first tried to convince Naren through intellect. Therefore, he expounded to him
the Advaita Vedanta, which makes an irresistible appeal to
reason. Naren assimilated this teaching quickly; but he longed
for the direct experience of Brahman, beyond name and form
and all relativity. He wanted to realize the Self in Samadhi.

However, the Master promised to take him to a higher plane than that: to the realization that Brahman not only transcends the universe, but is also immanent in it; that all that exists is Brahman. The universe is then seen as the manifestation of truth, the relative as a phase of the Absolute. The man of highest realization passes easily from the plane of the relative to that of the Absolute, and back to the relative. Naren had now come to see that it is possible for the transcendental Truth to embody Itself in a human form; that to embrace the universe after transcending it is the ultimate goal. Naren had thus come to see Shri Ramakrishna in a new light; and further, that the paths of Devotion and Knowledge lead to the same goal, that Love is the consummation of Realization.

At one time (April 1885) the chief topic of discussion and meditation among the disciples had been the life and gospel of the Buddha, the Enlightened One. The main speaker and the inspirer had of course been Naren. He had saturated himself with Buddhist lore. For the time being he was a Buddhist in spirit. The towering intellect of the Enlightened One, the eminent sanity of his views, his uncompromising demand for Truth, his burning renunciation, his compassionate heart, his sweet, deep and luminous personality, his sublime morality, and the manner in which he struck the balance between metaphysics and human character—all these had aroused tremendous enthusiasm in Naren, and this had spread to the other disciples. They were all determined, like Buddha, to realize Truth even at the sacrifice of life itself. They inscribed in bold characters upon the wall of the meditation room, "Let this body dry up on its seat; let its flesh and bones dissolve: without attaining the Enlightenment which is difficult to achieve even in aeons, this body shall not rise from its seat." Not surprisingly Naren's mind had turned to Buddha Gaya, the place of the Tathagata's Illumination, where these words were uttered: he determined to go there and meditate under the sacred Bo-tree. Only to Tarak and Kali did he confide this.

It was about the beginning of April 1886 that Naren, with Tarak and Kali, crossed the Ganga for the railway station at

Bally. Tarak had arranged for their railway fare. Since they left no information about their destination, their friends became very anxious, thinking that they might have renounced the world to take up the life of the wandering monk and that they might never return. Subsequently it was learned that they had gone to Buddha Gaya, dressed in ochre cloth, to practise austerities.

The three friends alighted at Gaya and walked the seven miles to the place of the Buddha's Illumination. The solitude of the place and its wonderful associations gladdened their hearts beyond expectation. One evening when all was silent and hushed, they repaired to the stone seat under the sacred Bodhi Tree and sat in meditation. The serenity of the evening hour and the solemnity of his thought stirred Naren's nature to its depths. Suddenly he burst into tears and putting his arm about Tarak seated next to him, he embraced him with great tenderness. Startled, Tarak asked him the reason. Naren said that as he meditated, the sublime character of the Buddha, his wonderful compassion, his humane teachings, and the subsequent history of India transformed by the magic wand of Buddhism —all these presented themselves before his vision in such glowing colours that he could not control his feelings.

The other young disciples at Cossipore were so attracted to Naren that it was painful for them to be without him. When they heard that he had gone to Buddha Gaya, some of them even thought of following him there. When news of all this reached the Master, he said to them: "Why are you anxious? Where can he go? How long can he be away? You will see that he will come back very soon." Afterwards he said, "Though you may journey to the four corners of the world, you will find nothing anywhere. Whatever is there is also 'here' (*showing his body*)." The word "here", it seems, was used by the Master in two senses: Firstly, that spirituality was not at that time manifest anywhere else in the degree that it was in himself; and secondly, that God existed within everyone, and that if devotion to Him had not been awakened within, there was no benefit in seeking Him outside by travelling to various places. The dis-

ciples to whom the Master spoke these words took them in the
first sense, and were firmly convinced that spirituality was
nowhere manifest in the same degree as it was in the Master.

Shri Ramakrishna knew that Naren had perceived something in him (the Master) which he would not find elsewhere
and that that would suffice to ensure his speedy return. Indeed,
this escapade rejoiced the Master, for he knew that Naren would
appreciate him and his worth all the better for this experience.

Meanwhile, the uneasiness of Naren's brother-disciples at
Cossipore had reached such a pitch that they went to the
Master, praying that Naren might return. Drawing a circle on
the floor he said, "Farther than this Naren shall not go." The
disciples took this to mean that the Master's will would influence
events and the thoughts in Naren's mind. And it so happened
that Naren and his companions did return shortly afterwards.

For three or four days they stayed at Buddha Gaya as guests
of the Mahant (Abbot) of the temple. At the end of that time
they had a desire to see the Master again. Part of the return fare
was obtained from the Mahant. On reaching Gaya town,
Naren met an old acquaintance of his father, a practising lawyer
there, who invited the three young monks to a soirée at his
home. The invitation was accepted, and Naren added to the
enjoyment of the evening by singing a number of songs. The
remainder of their return fare was contributed by the kindly
host, and soon they were back at the Cossipore garden. The
Master was overjoyed to see his beloved Naren and made him
tell all that he had seen, heard, felt and thought at Buddha
Gaya. Naren was indelibly impressed with what he had seen
and realized there, and for some days could talk of nothing else.

On April 9, 1886, while Shri Ramakrishna was sitting on his
bed in the big hall upstairs with Mahendra and Latu, Narendra
entered and took his seat. Shashi, Rakhal, and some others also
came in. The Master asked Naren to stroke his feet.

Master (*smiling to Mahendra*): "He [Naren] went there [to
Buddha Gaya]."

Mahendra (*to Naren*): "What are the doctrines of the
Buddha?"

Narendra: "He could not express in words what he had realized by his spiritual practices; so people say he was an atheist."

Master: "Why atheist? He was not an atheist. He simply could not express his inner experiences in words. Do you know what 'Buddha' means? It is to become one with Bodha, Pure Consciousness. It is to become Pure Consciousness Itself."

Narendra: "Yes sir. There are three classes of Buddhas: Buddha, Arhat, and Bodhisattva."

Master: "This too is a sport of God Himself, a new Lila [sport] of God. Why should the Buddha be called an atheist? When one realizes one's own Real Nature, one attains a state that is something between existence and non-existence."

Narendra (to Mahendra): "It is a state in which contradictions meet. A combination of hydrogen and oxygen produces cool water; and the same hydrogen and oxygen are used in the oxyhydrogen blowpipe. In that state both activity and non-activity are possible; that is to say, one then performs unselfish action. Worldly people, who are engrossed in sense-objects, say that everything exists. But the Mayavadis [those who hold to the doctrine of Maya] say that nothing exists. The experience of a Buddha is beyond both 'existence' and 'non-existence'."

Master: "This 'existence' and 'non-existence' are attributes of Prakriti. The Reality is beyond both."

The devotees remained silent a few minutes.

Master (to Naren): "What did the Buddha preach?"

Narendra: "He did not discuss the existence or non-existence of God. But he showed compassion for others all his life. A hawk pounced upon a bird and was about to devour it. In order to save the bird, the Buddha gave the hawk his own flesh. How great his renunciation was! Born a prince, he renounced everything! If a man has nothing, no wealth at all, what does his renunciation amount to?

"After attaining Buddhahood and experiencing Nirvana, the Buddha once visited his home and exhorted his wife, his son, and many others of the royal household to embrace the life of renunciation. How intense his renunciation was! But look at

Vyasa's conduct. He forbade his son Shukadeva to give up the world, saying, 'My son, practise religion as a householder.'

"The Buddha did not care for Shakti [God as Power] or any such thing. He sought only Nirvana. Ah, how intense his dispassion was! When he sat down under the Bodhi-tree to meditate, he took this vow: 'Let my body wither away here if I do not attain Nirvana.' Such a firm resolve! This body, indeed, is a great enemy. Can anything be achieved without chastening it?"

Shashi: "But it is you who say that one develops Sattva [purity] by eating meat. You insist that one should eat meat."

Naren: "I eat meat, no doubt, but I can also live on rice, mere rice, even without salt."

A little afterwards the Master said to Naren: "Well, here you find everything—even ordinary red lentils and tamarind. Isn't that so?"

Naren: "After experiencing all those states, you are now dwelling on a lower plane."

Master: "Yes, someone seems to be holding me to a lower plane."

Saying this, Shri Ramakrishna took the fan from Mahendra's hand and said, "As I see this fan *directly* before me, in exactly the same manner I have seen God. And I have seen . . . that He and the one who dwells in my heart are one and the same Person."

Narendra: "Yes, yes, Soham—I am He."

Master: "But only a line divides the two—that I may enjoy divine bliss."

Narendra (*to Mahendra*): "Perfected souls, even after their own liberation, retain the ego and experience the pleasure and pain of the body that they may help others to attain liberation. It is like coolie work. We do coolie work under compulsion, but great souls do so of their own sweet pleasure."

The few days that were left to Shri Ramakrishna on this mortal plane were memorable ones for the disciples. One day in January 1886, Gopal Senior, one of the disciples, expressed his wish to distribute ochre cloths and Rudraksha beads to sadhus who would be passing through Calcutta to attend the annual festival at Gangasagar, where the Ganga meets the sea. When the Master came to know of it, he said to Gopal, "Here are boys [meaning his young disciples] full of renunciation. It is useless to search for purer souls outside. You will earn merit by distributing the things to these boys." Accordingly Gopal handed over twelve sets of ochre clothing and Rudraksha beads to the Master, who in turn distributed them amongst his eleven monastic disciples—Naren, Rakhal, Baburam, Niranjan, Yogindra, Tarak, Shashi, Sharat, Kali, Latu and Gopal Senior. These were to be the foundation of the Ramakrishna Order. After the ceremony they were permitted to take food from all, irrespective of caste and creed. The remaining set of ochre clothing was given to Girishchandra Ghosh, according to some; while according to others it was given to Gopal Junior. Thus the Master himself initiated these boys into monastic life, fulfilling their heart's desire; and by that act also the seed of the Ramakrishna Order was sown.

Now we come to the greatest moment of Naren's spiritual disciplines and the crest of his spiritual realizations. Ever since the Master had opened the door of the Advaita Vedanta to him, he had been pining for experience of the Absolute. He prayed to feel Divinity; to have the whole of Nature erased from the tablets of perception. To lose the 'I' in True Being, beyond thought—such was Naren's prayer to Shri Ramakrishna. Naren wanted to realize the central truth of the Upanishads and to be able to say from his own experience, "Aham Brahmasmi", "I am Brahman".

Naren had pestered the Master for this realization. One evening it came unexpectedly. He was meditating, when suddenly he felt a light at the back of his head, as though a torch-light were playing there. It became more and more brilliant, and larger and larger. Finally it seemed to burst. His mind became merged in it. What transpired then in his consciousness was beyond words, for that Absolute State is beyond description. Some time after this realization he wrote some verses, "The

12

Hymn of Samadhi", which hint at the nature of that exalted state.

All was still and quiet in the room where Naren and Gopal Senior were meditating. Suddenly Gopal heard Naren cry out, "Gopal-da, Gopal-da, where is my body?" In coming down from that state Naren was at first conscious only of his head; his body seemed lost. "Why, Naren, there it is. It is there", answered the startled Gopal as he looked at Naren's rigid body, lying prostrate. He then hastened for help to Shri Ramakrishna, whom he found in a state of intense calm, his countenance deeply serious as though he knew what was happening in the next room. In reply to Gopal's entreaty he said, "Let him stay in that state for a while. He has teased me long enough for it."

According to another version, it was Niranjan, one of the monastic disciples, who went to the Master on seeing Naren in Samadhi, and said, "Naren is dead. His body is ice-cold." At these words Shri Ramakrishna laughed.

About nine o'clock at night Naren began to show faint signs of returning consciousness. When he regained full consciousness of the physical world he found himself surrounded by his anxious brother-disciples. Memory came back. He felt as though he were bathed in ineffable peace. His heart was full to over-flowing with ecstasy. He realized that the Absolute of Vedanta alone could reconcile all philosophies. When he presented himself before the Master, the latter said, looking deep into his eyes, "Now then, the Mother has shown you everything. Just as a treasure is locked up in a box, so will this realization you have just had be locked up and the key shall remain with me. You have work to do. When you have finished my work, the treasure-box will be unlocked again; and you will know everything then, as you did just now." He warned him to be careful about his body for some time, and to exercise the utmost discretion in his choice of food and companions, accepting only the purest.

Afterwards Shri Ramakrishna said to the other disciples, "Naren will pass away only of his own will. The moment he realizes who he is, he will refuse to stay a moment longer in the body. The time will come when he will shake the world to its foundations through the strength of his intellectual and spiritual powers. I have prayed that the Divine Mother may keep this realization of the Absolute veiled from Naren. There is much work to be done by him. But this veil is *so* thin, *so very* thin that it may give way at any time."

It was Naren's intense desire to realize the absolute Brahman that decided Shri Ramakrishna to give it to him, but the Master had no intention of permitting him to stay there. As Naren's work was to be in the form of compassion and service to humanity, he could not remain in Nirvikalpa Samadhi if he was to do it. It is only a Ramakrishna who is able to merge in and come from the Absolute at will; and even he assured his return to ordinary consciousness by creating some desire of the simplest kind before going into Samadhi and repeating it so that nothing was left to chance. He would say, "I—I—I shall smoke", "I shall have water to drink."

This was not the only occasion on which Narendranath experienced Nirvikalpa Samadhi. At least three other occasions are well known when, as Swami Vivekananda, he experienced it during his first visit to America: at Chicago, on the shore of the Lake Michigan; at Camp Percy, in New Hampshire; and at the Thousand Island Park. As we have noted, Shri Ramakrishna had said, "But this veil [covering the realization of the Absolute] is so very thin that it may give way at any time." These are occasions when it is known to have given way. Being an Ishwarakoti, he could return from this state to serve the Divine Mission; or it may be that Shri Ramakrishna himself unlocked the treasure-box occasionally, when Naren's mind simply panted for that experience. Who knows how many more such occasions there may have been!

The days passed in devotion, in service, in sorrow, in ecstasy —Naren leading, the others following. Few were the days left before Shri Ramakrishna would pass into Mahasamadhi, when the light of that great life would leave the body. The disciples were untiring in their attention, despite sleepless nights and busy days. What did it matter if their own bodies succumbed in his service? In August of that year, 1886, people came and went by scores; it seemed as if everyone who had ever known the Master felt that the end was drawing near—and of them all, Naren felt this most. His sorrow at the approaching separation was mixed with a spiritual consciousness and sense of power springing from the knowledge that he had been made the particular heir to Shri Ramakrishna's spiritual inheritance.

Naren remembered that the Master had had to wait three or four years before he (Naren) would accept the Mother and could be made over to Her. Only after this could the Master give him (Naren) the whole treasure of his realizations and be free to depart. Naren used to say, later, "From the time that he gave me over to the Mother, he retained his vigour of body only six months. The rest of the time he suffered." Indeed, the power of the Master was being diverted into a new channel— into Naren who had been prepared for this by more than four years of spiritual training.

Naren, at this time, was meditating with great intensity. One day he and Girish Ghosh sat under a tree to meditate. There were mosquitoes without number, and Girish was so disturbed that he became restless. On opening his eyes he was amazed to see that Naren's body was covered as if with a dark blanket, such was the number of mosquitoes on him; but Naren was unconscious of them.

An unpleasant, but significant incident occurred at Cossipore which shows how much the Master loved and trusted Narendranath. Ramchandra Datta, Kalipada Ghosh, and Surendranath Mitra, householder disciples of the Master, were the chief contributors towards the expenses at Cossipore during the Master's illness; and the young boys used to spend the amount according to need. Gopal Junior was asked to keep the accounts, which Rambabu used to check from time to time. Once these householder devotees scolded the boys for extravagance. The situation took such a serious turn that Naren had to approach Shri Ramakrishna and report everything to him. The Master said to Naren: "Wherever you take me on your shoulders, there I shall stay." The conversation has been well depicted in the well-known Bengali poetical work, *Sri Sri Ramakrishna Punthi*:

Seeing Naren thus worried, the Master said:
"Come, I shall go wherever you take me.
In whatever condition you keep me, in that I shall live."
"On my shoulders I shall take you," said Naren,
"And begging from door to door I shall feed you."
Again and again the Master then said,
"No more from these devotees shall I take any money."

Hearing this resolve of the Master, the boys became worried. How were they to meet the expenses? Lakshminarayan Marwari, a rich businessman of Calcutta, came to know of this, and offered money; but the Master did not accept it. He called Girishchandra Ghosh and asked him to bear all the expenses alone. Directed thus, Girish was overwhelmed with emotion and said, "I shall sell, if necessary, my house and land to meet the expenses." After this the young disciples did not allow those three householder devotees to meet the Master; but later on the Master pacified them and the two parties were reconciled with one another.

Towards the end of July, the condition of the Master's throat had become so bad that he could speak only in a whisper, or else had to communicate by signs. The disciples were grief-stricken that he, their father, their guide, he who loved them all as a mother loves her children, who had borne patiently with them, was sinking daily. They loved every shade of his personality. Naren, speaking in later life of him, said frequently: "Why speak of refinement! I have not yet found anyone more refined than my Master. His manner of walking, talking, resting, sitting, seeing to the arrangement of things in his room, his practical common sense—all were beautiful and perfect." The young men had really made him their own; and the Master had made them his own. Often he would call them to his side, would caress them lovingly, and by means of signs indicate the love he bore them. His constant thought was, "What will become of them without me?" But there was Naren!

Now that the last days were approaching, the Master set himself with greater energy than ever to mould, in a calm and silent way, the spiritual life of these boys, particularly that of

Naren. Every evening he would call Naren to his room and for two or three hours at a time would impart final instructions to him on various spiritual practices, and would advise him on how to keep his brother-disciples together, how to guide and train them so that they would be able to live the life of renunciation.

A significant incident that took place at Cossipore during this period is known from a letter which J. J. Goodwin wrote to Mrs. Bull on May 23, 1897. Mr. Goodwin, as we shall see, was to play a vital role in Swami Vivekananda's life. He evidently learnt of the incident either from the Swami himself, or from one of the other direct disciples of Paramahamsa Ramakrishna. He wrote: "When the Paramahamsa was passing away he called in all his disciples but Swamiji [Naren] and gave them an express command that they were always to pay every attention to Swamiji, and never to leave anything undone that could add to his health or comfort. Then sending them out and calling in Swamiji [Naren] he committed all his other disciples into his charge."

About this time Naren was called to the side of the Master, now suffering intensely and scarcely able to speak. The Master wrote on a piece of paper, "Narendra will teach others." Naren hesitated and said, "I won't do that." But the Master replied, "You shall *have* to do it." Some time before he had told Naren, "My Siddhis [powers] will manifest through you in time", meaning that in later years as a teacher, Naren would turn many of the worldly-minded to spiritual life.

It was now only three or four days before the Master's Mahasamadhi. Shri Ramakrishna called Naren to him. Looking steadfastly at him he entered into deep meditation. Naren felt as though a subtle force, resembling an electric shock, were entering his body. He lost outer consciousness. When he came to, he found the Master weeping. Wondering, Naren asked him why he wept, and was told, "O Naren, today I have given you my all and have become a Fakir, a penniless beggar. By the force of the power transmitted by me, great things will be done by you; only after that will you go where you came from."

Naren had suddenly become the possessor of the spiritual wealth of his Guru, acquired by years of superhuman effort and by means of the sternest austerities. Shri Ramakrishna willingly deprived himself of his powers in order that Naren might be endowed with spiritual omnipotence. When that which was Ramakrishna had completed its task in its human manifestation, it gave itself wholly to Naren, for the good of the world.

A couple of days before the Master's passing away, when Narendra and a few others were standing by his bed at night, a curious thought flashed across Naren's mind: "The Master has said many a time that he is an Incarnation of God. If he *now* says in the midst of the throes of death, in this terrible moment of human anguish and physical pain, 'I am God Incarnate', then I will believe." No sooner had Naren thought this than the Master turned towards him and, summoning all his energy, said, "O my Naren, are you not yet convinced? He who was Rama, He who was Krishna, He Himself is now Ramakrishna in this body: not in your Vedantic sense [according to which each soul is potentially divine], but actually so."

Naren was dumbfounded. He was stricken with remorse and shame for having doubted his beloved teacher even for a moment, in spite of so many revelations he had had from him (the Master) in the past. By these words Shri Ramakrishna conveyed to his disciples the momentous truth that the personalities of all the divine Incarnations of the past were the same Personality (the Purushottama), revealing Itself variously in different human forms according to the needs of the time: nay more, that he himself (Shri Ramakrishna) was that Personality—which is called God.

The last two days were sad ones for the disciples. They knew that all would soon be over. Earlier that month the Master had asked a disciple to read out from the almanac the days of the Bengali calendar. When the disciple had reached the end of Shravan, which fell on August 15, the Master had asked him to stop. Now, on the evening of the 15th, when a Dr. Navin Pal came to see him, the Master said, "Today my suffering has become too intense. No medicine is proving of any use. The disease has become incurable." The doctor said, "Yes." The Master said, "I feel like eating barrels full of rice and dal [lentils]." The physician was unable to do anything to give him relief. A little before dusk the Master complained of difficulty in breathing. Suddenly he entered into Samadhi, which was of rather an unusual kind. Narendranath asked the disciples to chant "Hari Om Tat Sat". The chanting continued for a long time. After midnight, Shri Ramakrishna regained consciousness of the physical world and said he was hungry. He ate a small quantity of porridge and seemed better. Leaning against five or six pillows supported by Shashi he talked up to the last moment with Naren, and gave him his last counsel in a low voice. Then uttering the name of Kali thrice he lay back gently on the bed. Suddenly, at two minutes past one that night (August 16), a thrill passed through the Master's body, the hair stood on end, the eyes became fixed on the tip of the nose, a divine smile lit up the face, and the Master again entered into Samadhi.

The disciples thought the Master would regain normal consciousness as usual. Narendranath started chanting "Hari Om Tat Sat" in a loud voice, and the others joined in. The chanting continued throughout the night, hour after hour, but there was no sign of the regaining of physical consciousness. Shashi rubbed cow ghee over the backbone of the Master, but it proved useless. In the dead of night Ramlal, the Master's nephew, was called from Dakshineswar to see what had happened. He hastened to Cossipore immediately. After examining the Master, he said, "The top of the head is still warm. You had better send for the Captain Vishwanath Upadhyaya [a devotee of the Master]." The Captain came promptly in the morning in response to their call. He found that the Master's body had become rather stiff, that the hair all over it was standing on end, and that his eyes were fixed on the tip of his nose; but the backbone was still warm. The Captain asked them to apply cow ghee all over the body and to call Dr. Mahendralal Sarkar. The doctor came and, after examination, declared that the Master had left the body. The trance into which he had entered on the previous night thus proved to have been Mahasamadhi, from which there was no return.

The curtain had fallen on a great spiritual life. The immortal spirit, so long confined in a physical case, had burst through its limitations of name and form, and become one with the Infinite Spirit. The barriers of time and space had been broken down, and he who had been the light and guide of a few souls, had now become a spiritual beacon for the universe. Though the disciples knew all this, they were overwhelmed with grief. That smile would bewitch them no more; that radiant face would no longer inspire them, except as a memory; the lips which had spoken such words of wisdom and love were now sealed in death.

When the Holy Mother came upstairs to the bedside of the Master, she cried out, "O Mother Kali! Where have you gone?" Such a scene it was as to print itself for ever on the memories of the young disciples who witnessed it. After a time the Mother was helped back to her room downstairs. That evening, when she was removing her ornaments and the other signs of a married woman from her person, as is the custom of the Hindu widow, the Master appeared before her and forbade her, saying, "Where have I gone? I am just here. It is like passing from one room to another." On two subsequent occasions, when she tried to take away her ornaments, Shri Ramakrishna caught hold of her hands and forbade her to do so. Thus it was that to the last day of her life she wore bracelets on her wrists and a sari with a red border—though a border thinner than usual.

That morning (August 16), on being informed of the passing away of the Master, the devotees assembled at the garden-house. They decorated the body and the cot on which the Master lay, with flowers and garlands, and sang devotional songs. About five in the afternoon a procession was formed and, to the sound of devotional music it moved towards the Cossipore burning-ghat on the bank of the Ganga, a little distance away. All took turns in carrying the beloved burden. Some held flags in their hands, others the signs of various religions, such as Om, the Cross, the Crescent, and so on. At the cremation ground the Master's body was bathed with Ganga water, clad in new ochre clothes, and decorated and worshipped again with flowers and garlands. The body was tenderly laid on the pyre prepared for it. The pyre was lighted; clarified butter and incense were poured on it; and in a couple of hours everything was finished.

The ashes and other remains of the body were collected and put into an urn. Slowly and heavily they retraced their steps and entered the garden-house that night shouting "Jai Rama-krishna!"—"Glory to Ramakrishna!" The urn was placed on the bed of the Master in the room upstairs. The disciples spent the night in discussing the holy life of the Master and medita-tion. Narendranath occasionally soothed them by telling stories of Shri Ramakrishna's wonderful life. Thereafter the Master's relics were worshipped daily by the disciples in the garden-house until they were removed elsewhere.

A spirit of calm resignation settled on the hearts of the dis-ciples, and somewhat assuaged their grief. Had he really gone? He who had sacrificed his life for their welfare—could he have left them for ever? Was he not their Lord, the Soul of their souls, the same in death as in life? Had not he himself said that he had simply passed from one room to another? Bereavement was transformed into the ecstasy they had so often felt while the Master was alive.

After Shri Ramakrishna's Passing Away

(1) Mahendra or M. (3) Kali (5) Sarat (6) Mani Mallick (7) Gangadhar‡(8) Navagopal (11) Tarak (13) the elder Gopal (15) Vaikuntha (17) Manmohan (18) Harish (19) Narayan (21) Shashi (22) Latu (23) Bhavanath (24) Baburam (25) Niranjan (26) Narendra (27) Ramachandra Datta (28) Balaram Bose (29) Rakhal (30) Nityagopal (31) Jogindra (32) Debendranath Mazumdar

Baranagore Math

Group at Baranagore Ma

THE BARANAGORE MATH

The death of Mahapurushas (great souls), whilst an incident of sorrow, generates a great urge towards the attainment of the highest ideals. So it was after the passing away of Shri Ramakrishna. His disciples and devotees were inspired with a powerful desire to attain the most exalted consciousness, and they found themselves strengthened by a Presence which they knew to be that of their departed Master. His work, they knew, was not to end with the death of the body. It was to express itself in an eternal flow of spiritual life and knowledge. And the channels of this flow were to be the hearts of the devotees and the souls of these young men who at the touch of the Master had renounced the world in search of Truth. The young disciples were at first too bewildered to know what to do. The Mahasamadhi of the Master, though long expected, yet caught them unprepared. Their grief knew no bounds. Moreover there was hardly a fortnight left before the expiry of the agreement on the Cossipore garden-house. The rent had been paid to the end of August. All the young disciples wished to continue staying there and to pass their time in spiritual practices and the worship of the Master's relics. But who would pay the rent? Tarak, Latu and Gopal Senior had no place to lay their heads. The young disciples asked Rambabu and others who used to pay the rent where they would stay and where the Master's relics would be kept and worshipped. They replied, "You should all go back to your own homes." Rambabu also said that the holy ashes would be interred and worshipped at his retreat at Kankurgachi, a suburb of Calcutta.

Narendranath and the other young disciples were sorry to hear this. They wanted to build a place for the relics on the bank of the Ganga, as the Master had wished. A controversy arose, but it was then agreed that the ashes would be kept at the Cossipore garden-house until a place had been built on the bank of the Ganga. But this proposal had to be dropped for lack of money. The householders headed by Ramchandra Datta, Devendranath Mazumdar and Nitya-gopal then demanded the ashes in order to bury them at Kankurgachi.

However, the young disciples refused to hand them over, and the dispute took a serious turn, characterized by intense feeling and high words. Shashi and Niranjan had constituted themselves guardians of the Master's relics. They were giants, the one in resolution, and the other in appearance; and they held themselves ready to stand their ground at any cost. They were determined not to give the ashes to the house-holders, and they were supported by others. Narendranath was appealed to. "Brothers, be reasonable!" he said; "We should not quarrel like this; otherwise people will say that the disciples of Ramakrishna fought over his relics. More-over it is not certain where we shall be staying. Let them have the ashes. After all, Rambabu is going to dedicate the retreat in the name of Shri Ramakrishna. Is it not good? We can very well go there and worship the Master. Let us mould our lives according to our Master's teachings. If we are true to his ideals, if we live up to them, we shall have done more than merely worship the relics."

But the young men thought that certainly the householders should not have all of the Master's relics. With Narendra-nath's consent, they transferred more than half of the ashes and bones to another pot. Narendra and his brother-disciples each swallowed a minute portion of the ashes and as a result had deep meditation that night. The pot into which the ashes were transferred was sealed and sent to Balarambabu's house where they would be worshipped regularly. The young disciples resolved that some day they would build a place on the bank of the Ganga for the preservation of their portion of the Master's remains. Of what had taken place the house-holders were not told. Ultimately everyone agreed to Rambabu's proposal to install the ashes at Kankurgachi, and the birthday of Shri Krishna, that year falling on August 23, was fixed for the ceremony.

There was still a week before the ashes were to be taken to Rambabu's retreat. During this period, Latu, Tarak and Gopal Senior stayed at the Cossipore garden-house, while the other young disciples went to their homes. But they and the householder disciples used to come to the Cossipore garden-house[1] and spend their time in meditation, singing devotional songs, and conversation, the topic of which was one only— their Master. There in that very house he had lived. They recalled again and again his last days, and the former days at Dakshineswar. Narendra thrilled them by recounting incidents in the Master's life, and by speaking of his mission and teachings, until they were filled with ecstasy. The place throbbed with a wonderful vitality and power.

During this week Narendranath had a vision of Shri Ramakrishna, which he could never forget. He and a brother-disciple named Harish were one evening standing beside the pond of the garden-house of Cossipore, talking, probably, of the loss with which their hearts were then so occupied. It was about eight o'clock. Suddenly, as they stood there, Narendra saw a luminous figure covered with a cloth. It was coming slowly towards them up the drive from the gate. Could it be the Master? He kept quiet, fearing that he was the victim of a hallucination, when he heard his companion say in a hoarse whisper, "What is that? Naren, look! look!" At this, Narendra called out loudly, "Who is there?" Hearing his voice, others hurried from the house to see what was happening; but they were too late. When the apparition came to a thick jasmine bush within ten yards of where the two were standing, it vanished. Lanterns were brought, and every nook of the garden was searched, but nothing could be found. The vision left a profound impression on Narendranath.

When the birthday of Shri Krishna came, the monastic and

[1] It was later on acquired by the Ramakrishna Math, Belur; and a branch was established there in 1946.

householder disciples took part in the removal of the Master's ashes. The procession made its way to Kankurgachi, Narendranath leading. They all joined in in the singing of devotional songs. Shashi took the urn on his head; Rambabu and others followed. At the retreat the ashes were buried with due ceremony. Shashi's eyes were filled with tears when he saw earth and stones falling on the urn and being stamped down. Afterwards he said, "It seemed as though they were hammering and crushing the very heart out of us." Later an altar and temple were built on the spot, which came to be known as the Yogodyana.[2] On this day every year a celebration is held there in honour of Shri Ramakrishna.

Balarambabu had taken the Holy Mother from Cossipore to his house on August 21. He also arranged for her pilgrimage to Vrindavan. She started on August 30, accompanied by Kali, Latu, Yogen and some women devotees of the Master. Tarak joined them later. She took the urn containing the young disciples' share of the Master's ashes with her, daily doing her worship before it, and feeling therein the presence of the Master. Portions of the relics were sent to Hardwar and other sacred places to be consigned to the Ganga according to Hindu custom. A year later, on her return to Calcutta, she handed over the urn of relics to Narendranath.

Before leaving the Cossipore garden-house the young monks took to Balarambabu's house, besides the Master's relics, his bedding, clothing, furniture, and the utensils which had been used in serving him. In all their subsequent moves these valuable treasures have gone with them. To this day they are devotedly preserved by the monks of the Order at the Belur Math.

The Cossipore garden-house had to be vacated by the end of August. Some of the young monks had left for Vrindavan; others had gone home and resumed their college studies. The Master had already made them monks, and had entrusted them to the care of Narendranath. Naturally the question

---

[2] Acquired in 1943 by the Ramakrishna Math, Belur, and recognized as a branch centre.

arose, what was to become of them? Narendra was determined that they should lead the life of renunciation without delay; but some of the householders discouraged them from doing so, thinking: "How will they get on? We cannot leave them to wander about like ordinary sadhus. They are still boys with bright prospects before them. Let them stay in their homes; that is the wisest course. It will make them, as well as their relatives, happy." The young men had already clashed with the householders over the ashes, so most of the latter were not sympathetic. But a few, like Balaram, Surendra and Mahendra, clearly saw that it was impossible for those who had left their homes to go back to them, and for those who had gone back to resume their studies, to remain at home—imbued as they now were with Shri Ramakrishna's ideal of renunciation. But these householder devotees felt helpless to do anything for the boys.

Later, in 1895, remembering these critical days, Narendra-nath was to write to Swami Brahmananda: "Rakhal, you remember, I suppose, how, after the Master's passing away, all forsook us as so many worthless, ragged boys. Only people like Balaram, Suresh [Mitra], Master [Mahendra] and Chunibabu were our friends in that hour of need. And we shall never be able to repay our debts to them." And still later (January 27, 1900), while speaking at Pasadena (America) on "My Life and Mission", he was to say: "Then came the sad day when our old teacher [Shri Ramakrishna] died. . . . We had no friends. Who would listen to a few boys, with their crank notions? Nobody. . . . Just think of it—a dozen boys, telling people vast, big ideas, saying they are determined to work these ideas out in life. Why, everybody laughed. From laughter it became serious; it became persecution. . . . Who would sympathize with the imaginations of a boy—imaginations that caused so much suffering to others? Who would sympathize with me? None—except one. . . ." That one, as we shall see, was a woman—Shri Sarada Devi, the Holy Mother.

The leaders of the householders were not only unsympathetic; they differed from the monks in their understanding of Shri Ramakrishna's teaching. Some of them were of the opinion that he had not preached the ideal of Sannyasa (the monastic ideal), and that therefore it was of no use establishing a Math (monastery). Even among the young disciples there were differences of understanding. Not all of them then felt the need to spread the Master's message in the world, or to serve man regarding him as a manifestation of God. Some, among whom was the householder disciple Mahendra, who sympathized with the young monks, were of the view that they should realize God first, and then take up preaching and other works of service; but Narendra held that the monks should serve mankind in a spirit of worship for the purification of their hearts, and that this would ultimately lead to the realization of God.

Even though the devotees believed that the Master had come for the regeneration of mankind, very few had appreciated the originality of his message, and that this would usher in a new age. Very few had understood that this religion for the modern age preached by the Master, though based on and developed from the eternal religion of the Vedas, was by no means a repetition or imitation of that religion. They did not see that it would give rise to a new current of thought and culture in the world, which would act as a force for the unification of mankind as a whole. Of those few who had understood this, Narendranath was the leader; and they were ready to lay down their lives for their vision.

The Holy Mother had understood all this. She always stood behind the boys—her sons. At a later date—in 1890—, the contrast between the wealth of the monastery at Buddha Gaya and the living conditions of her boys was to wring this prayer to Shri Ramakrishna from her: "O Lord, You came in human form, sported with the devotees, and went away! Should everything end with that? What then was the need to come and undergo so much suffering? I saw in Varanasi and Vrindavan many sadhus who get their food by begging, and shift their residence from the shade of one tree to that of another. There is no dearth of sadhus of that type. I cannot any more bear to see my children, who have given up everything for your sake, going from door to door for food. I pray that those who renounce the world in your name may never be in need of at least coarse food and clothing. They will live together, taking your name and holding to your ideas and ideals; and people afflicted with the sufferings of the world will resort to them and get relief by hearing your teachings from them. Was this not what you really came for? I am greatly pained at heart to see them wandering about like this!"

The young men's prospect was dark at this critical time, and they became disheartened. But unknown to them, Shri Ramakrishna was making arrangements for the fulfilment of their aspiration. One day, when Surendranath Mitra, a devotee of the Master who used to bear a part of the expenses at the Cossipore garden-house, returned home from office and sat for meditation in his shrine, Shri Ramakrishna appeared before him and said: "Oh! what are you doing? My children are wandering in the streets. Look at their sad plight! Make some arrangement for them without delay." Hearing this command of the Master, Surendra hastened to Narendra's home, which was near by, and with tearful eyes told him what had happened. He said, "Brother, where will you go? Let us rent a house. You will live there and make it our Master's shrine; and we house-holders shall go there from time to time to share your bliss and pacify our hearts. . . . I used to spend a sum of money for the Master at Cossipore. I shall gladly give it now for your expenses." Narendra was overpowered with emotion on hearing this.

He started out in search of a house, and wrote to Taraknath to be ready to come and take charge of the new Math when he should receive a telegram. Tarak accordingly came to Varanasi from Vrindavan and awaited word from Narendra. After an energetic search a house was found at Baranagore, midway between Dakshineswar and Calcutta. It was a dreary, deserted place, sadly in need of repairs, very old, and with the reputation of being haunted. It had two storeys, the lower one the resort of snakes and lizards. The gateway had long since tumbled down. The veranda which ran along the front of the upper storey showed signs of decay. The main room where the monks

13

were to live was in a most dilapidated state; indeed, nobody else would have lived there. To the east of the house was another room which had been used as a shrine; to the west was a jungle-like garden overgrown with weeds and shrubs; at the back was a pond covered with green scum which was a breeding-place for mosquitoes. There was something weird about the place. It was chosen because of its cheapness and its nearness to the holy Ganga and the Cossipore burning-ghat where the body of the Master had been cremated. The monks were pleased with it, for it provided not only a retreat from the turmoil of city life, but a solitude where their meditation would have few or no interruptions. The house was taken at a monthly rent of Rs. 11/- inclusive of tax. A cook was engaged at Rs. 6/- per month.

Gradually the young disciples began to gather at the monastery. Taraknath came from Varanasi as soon as he received the telegram from Narendra, and began to stay there with Gopal Senior. Gopal Junior took the bedding and the other belongings of the Master there from Balarambabu's house. After a month, when he got news of the place in Baranagore, Kali returned from Vrindavan and began staying there. Thus the monastery came into existence within six weeks of the Master's passing away.

At this time Narendranath would go to the homes of those young brother-disciples who had resumed their studies and, in a whirlwind of enthusiasm, would try to induce them to join the monastery. He would argue with them for hours in his efforts to persuade them to go with him to Baranagore, not desisting until he had gained his point. Once at the monastery, they could not resist the spiritual exaltation of Narendra's songs and discourses. He would talk of their departed Master and his life of renunciation in such vivid language and with such intensity of spirit that none could withstand him.

The brother-disciples of Narendranath looked upon him as their leader, not only because the Master had taught them to do so and because his personality had become interwoven with their every thought and desire, but because he seemed to be the true mouthpiece of the Master; and yet Narendra was their brother and comrade. He was like a spiritual lion; and hence their love for him amounted almost to reverence. The Master's words about him were constantly in their minds. Did they in their zeal for realization disobey him and go to excess in the practice of austerities, all that he would say was, "Did not the Master himself give all of you into my charge?" They could not escape the magnetism of his personality. His eyes, his face, his speech, the manner in which he walked, the ways in which he showed his confidence in them and cheered and spurred them on, even his methods of admonishing them, made him seem the spirit of the Master incarnate.

When the Baranagore Math was in this initial stage, with Tarak, Gopal Senior and Kali as permanent inmates, an event occurred which clinched the determination of the boys to renounce the world. In the middle of December, Baburam's mother, Matangini Devi, invited the young monks to visit her native village, Antpur, during the Christmas vacation. At first it was decided that only Narendra, Baburam, and one or two more would go; but when the others came to know, they also joined the party. Narendra, Baburam, Sharat, Shashi, Tarak, Kali, Niranjan, Gangadhar and Sarada boarded the Tarakeswar train at Howrah Station. They had taken musical instruments with them; so as soon as the train moved off, Narendra started singing, and the others joined in. They got down at Haripal station, and went to Antpur in a carriage. Baburam's mother received them as warmly as though they were her own children.

In the calm and quiet of the village, the spiritual fire in the young monks blazed up into a conflagration. Narendra's enthusiasm fanned the flames. The spirit of the Master as it were spoke and worked through him. He was intensely possessed by the vision of the sannyasi's life and would cry out, "Let man-making be the goal of our lives! Let us make this our only spiritual discipline! Away with vain learning! Let not the glamour of the world captivate our minds even for a moment! Realization of God is the one and only thing in life! That is

what Shri Ramakrishna's life represented! We must realize
God!" Inspired by these thoughts and fired by a oneness of
purpose, the young men became aware of a sense of unity—a
feeling that they were all linked by some wonderful spiritual
power. During their stay at Antpur they seemed to grow into
one body, one mind and one soul. The days passed in sadhana.
Ramakrishna was in their minds; his name on their lips. Upon
all alike there seemed to descend a spirit of renunciation,
a desire to take the sannyasi's vow, each in the presence of the
others. The monastic spirit seemed to be intensified in their
hearts, both for their own liberation and for the good of the
world. Each disciple saw in his brother-disciples a world of
spiritual force; and that vision intensified the love among them.
This was as it should have been, for the Master's spirit was
destined to be perpetuated, not through one or several individual disciples having disciples of their own, which is what
happens usually, but in a definite organized form.

Thus at Antpur, in still hours, subtle things were happening,
knitting the brothers together. It all found expression one night
before a huge Dhuni (sacred fire) in the compound. Overhead
was the clear night sky, and all around was quiet. Meditation
lasted a long time. When a break was made Narendra began to
tell the story of Jesus, beginning with the mystery of his birth,
through to his death and resurrection. Through his eloquence,
the brother-disciples could catch something of the apostolic
fervour that had impelled Paul to spread the Christian gospel
far and wide in the face of adversities. Narendra charged them
to become Christs themselves, and so aid in the redemption of
the world; to realize God and to deny themselves as Jesus had
done. Standing there before the sacred fire, their faces lit up
by the flames, the crackling of the wood the sole disturbing
sound, they took the vows of renunciation before God and one
another. The very air was vibrant with their ecstatic fervour.
Strangely, the monks discovered afterwards that all this had
happened on Christmas-eve!

In later years, Swami Shivananda (Taraknath), recalling
these days, used to say: "As a matter of fact, our resolve to

become organized became firm at Antpur. The Master had already made us sannyasis. That attitude was strengthened at Antpur." After staying there for a week, they returned to Calcutta by way of Tarakeswar, where they worshipped Shiva, Lord of Monks, at the famous temple.

As a result of the Antpur forgathering, and soon after it, Shashi, Sharat, Sarada, Niranjan, Subodh and Baburam, one after the other, left their homes for good and came to live in the Baranagore Math. Rakhal was in Monghyr when the Math started. He seems to have returned by January 1887 and joined them. (According to another version, when Tarak arrived from Varanasi, Narendranath took Rakhal and Tarak in the same carriage from Balarambabu's house to the Math, where they thenceforth lived.) Gangadhar could not bear to be separated from Narendra; he used to come and stay at the Math occasionally, until he went on pilgrimage to Tibet, setting out from the Math in February 1887. He joined the Math permanently after his return on June 9, 1890. Latu returned from Vrindavan within six months of going there, and started living at the Math. Yogen joined after about a year, on his return from Vrindavan with the Holy Mother. Hari joined sometime in 1887. Hariprasanna came into the Order much later, in 1895, when the Math was at Alambazar. Another name which should be mentioned is that of Tulsi. He had seen the Master more than once, but had not associated with him intimately enough to be his disciple. At one period of his life he prided himself on being the first disciple of Swami Vivekananda; and the Swami's brother-disciples too looked upon him as such: but later on he claimed to be a disciple of the Master. He joined the Baranagore Math probably sometime in the summer of 1887.

This formation of the Ramakrishna Brotherhood was largely the work of Narendranath. Apart from short trips here and there, for the three years until he became a wandering monk Narendra was steadily guiding and inspiring them. He had to go home frequently in order to arrange his family affairs before finally taking to the monastic life in its outward forms also. A case was pending in the court involving his ancestral home, and

Narendra, as eldest of the family, had to be present at the hearings. But he spent most nights and much of the days at the monastery.

The monastery was in Baranagore from 1886 to 1892. From 1892 to 1897 it was in Alambazar, near Dakshineswar. From there it was moved to the garden-house of Nilambar Mukherjee at Belur, where it was until 1898. This garden-house is on the west bank of the Ganga, exactly opposite Cossipore on the east bank. From there the Math was moved a quarter of a mile northward to its present site, where the Belur Math has been established since December 1898. This spacious site on the west bank of the Ganga was secured by Swami Vivekananda himself, and, as we shall see, it was he who was to carry and install the Master's relics there.

In the shrine of the Baranagore Math the Master seemed to be alive, ever ready to bless his children. He was worshipped daily, and soul-stirring devotional songs were sung before him. Ritual worship was done, Mantras were recited, lights waved, incense burned, conchs blown, and gongs beaten, in joyous adoration. Offerings of flowers and pure food were made. In the evening twilight the monks united their voices in prayer and praise. As Shiva, the Supreme Monk, was one of their Ideals, they would at that hour chant before the picture of Shri Ramakrishna a certain inspiring verse. It was adapted from the hymn chanted in Varanasi at the Vishwanath temple, and runs as follows:

Jaya Shiva Omkara! Bhaja Shiva Omkara!
Brahma, Vishnu, Sadashiva! Hara, Hara, Hara, Mahadeva!

Sometime in January 1887, Narendranath sought the opinion of his brother-disciples on going through the scripturally-prescribed ritual for initiation into Sannyasa. They gladly agreed to his proposal that they should observe it. Kali had already obtained from a sannyasi of the Puri denomination information about the performance of the Viraja-homa, and other matters connected with the Sannyasa rite. That he should have this seemed to them nothing but the grace of the Master and a sign

of his will. A day was fixed in the third week of January. Early
in the morning of that day the young men bathed in the Ganga
and then assembled in the shrine-room of the Math, where the
Master's photograph and relics were being regularly worshipped. Shashi did the worship of the Master as usual, and
then the Viraja-homa was performed. Narendra asked Kali to
chant the Mantras prescribed for the occasion. The brothers
offered the oblations one by one to the fire as the Mantras were
chanted. At first Narendranath, and then Rakhal, Niranjan,
Sharat, Shashi, Sarada and others repeated the Mantras and
offered the oblations. Afterwards Kali did the same. Shri Ramakrishna had already given them ochre cloths at Cossipore,
making them monks: this ceremony was the ritual and traditional confirmation of that. It is probable that it was on this
occasion that Baburam also went through the ceremony.

Afterwards Narendranath gave to Rakhal, Baburam, Shashi,
Sharat, Niranjan, Kali and Sarada the names Swamis Brahmananda, Premananda, Ramakrishnananda, Saradananda, Niran-
janananda, Abhedananda, and Trigunatitananda (or Trigunatita). Tarak and Gopal Senior went through the rite a few days
later and were named Swamis Shivananda and Advaitananda.
On the Shivaratri day (February 21, 1887) Mahendra saw
them as sannyasis. Latu and Yogen went through the
ceremony later, at different times, after their return from
Vrindavan. They were named Swamis Adbhutananda and
Yogananda. Hari did so sometime in 1887, and was named
Swami Turiyananda. Gangadhar performed the rite in the first
week of July 1890, after his return from Tibet, and became
Swami Akhandananda. When Subodh was ritually initiated
into Sannyasa is not known, but he was named Swami
Subodhananda.

Narendranath wanted to take the name Ramakrishnananda
for himself; but seeing Shashi's devotion to Shri Ramakrishna,
he gave him that name, and, according to Swami Abhedananda, himself took the name Vividishananda, which he seldom
used. During his days as a wandering monk, Narendranath
changed his name twice—first to Vivekananda (February 1891–

October 1892) and then to Sachchidananda (October 1892 – May 1893)—to prevent his brother-disciples following him. But on the eve of his departure for the West in May 1893, he took back the name Vivekananda for good, perhaps at the request of the Maharaja of Khetri.

Even though the young boys had formally taken Sannyasa, they used to wear ochre clothes only in the monastery, and plain clothes outside. Nor did they use their monastic names in the early days. It may have been because of social hostility then prevalent in Bengal to the institution of Sannyasa. Moreover, the Sannyasa of the Dashanami tradition founded by Shri Shankaracharya was not current in Bengal in those days. In the case of Narendranath there was the additional reason that he had to attend the lawsuit which was pending. But in spirit and for all practical purposes they were true sannyasis.

The transformation of Naren the disciple into Swami Vivekananda the world-renowned teacher was not an easy one. Starvation had to be faced, and much physical and mental suffering endured. It was a gradual, not a miraculous process, this development of the disciple of Shri Ramakrishna who sought spiritual illumination into the Vivekananda who was himself a focus of contagious spirituality. The story is intensely human and of great interest to all seekers after Truth.

From now on we find ourselves in a world where the unlimited energy of the great soul whose life we are studying is manifest in a tremendous will, which builds and expands his life-work to proportions of far-reaching significance. We are brought into contact with a powerful, fiery and yet most human personality, whose presence is suggestive of the great peace beyond the strife of life. There is laughter and human sentiment too, for he enjoyed life and had a sense of humour and fun. At heart he was, in a way, ever the boy of Dakshineswar; but one never knew when some illumination, intellectual or spiritual, some sudden transition from fun to spiritual revelation, would come. And yet he was at all times the monk, the prophet, the teacher. His soul, it seemed, was constantly with God, and his thought and love always in the service of man.

In the life of the Baranagore Math, it was Shashi who spent himself in constant service of the Master. Treating Shri Ramakrishna as though he were physically present, he used to offer the purest and the choicest food that could be procured for the few pice which their poverty limited them to. Recalling those blessed days to a disciple many years later, Swami Vivekananda said: "After the passing away of the Master we underwent a lot of spiritual practices at the Baranagore Math. We used to get up at 3 a.m. and after washing our face etc.—some after bath, and others without it—we would sit in the worship-room and become absorbed in Japa and meditation. What a strong spirit of dispassion we had in those days! We had no thought even as to whether the world existed or not. Shashi busied himself day and night with the duties pertaining to the Master's worship and service, and occupied the same position in the Math as the mother of the house does in a family. It was he who would procure, mostly by begging, the articles needed for the Master's worship and our subsistence. There were days when Japa and meditation continued from morning till four or five in the afternoon. Shashi waited and waited with our meals ready, till at last he would come and snatch us from our meditation by sheer force. Oh, what a wonderful constancy of devotion we noticed in him!"

The young men faced dire poverty; but it had no terrors for them. So rapt were they in their desire to follow in the steps of their Master that, forgetting sleep, they spent the nights in spiritual practices. Unwilling to beg, they lived on what chance might bring. They vied with one another in doing the household tasks, even the most menial ones. Many were the days when there was nothing to eat; but the spiritual discourses, meditation and singing went on as though their bodies did not exist. Their only clothes were the Kaupin (loin cloth) and a few pieces of ochre cloth; a mat on the floor sufficed for their bed; their beads, a Tanpura (stringed musical instrument), and a few pictures of gods, goddesses, and saints, hung from the walls. Their entire library ran to about a hundred books in all. One piece of cloth, and a wrapper to be worn about the shoulders, were common property. These were hung on a line so that whoever had to leave the premises might have wherewith to be clothed respectably. Surendranath Mitra, or Sureshbabu as he was called by the community, was its ministering angel; he looked after the bodily needs of the monks. The small sum of Rs 30/- which he at first gave being insufficient, he increased it to Rs. 100/- per month. Not satisfied with this, he kept himself secretly informed of the conditions in the Math, and often sent extra money or provisions to alleviate their extreme poverty.

Sometimes, however, there were visitors of a different sort. These were the relatives of the young monks, who came hoping to induce them to return to life in the world. They would implore, weep, threaten, but to no avail; the monks were inexorable. Their renunciation was complete and final. Not even the thought of their mothers was allowed to stand in the way of their realization of God. They flatly refused to recognize parental authority and took refuge in silence. The relatives would then say, "Naren is at the root of all this evil. The boys had returned home and resumed their studies, but he came and upset all our plans."

If a householder asked what they were achieving by such a way of life, Narendranath would reply, "What! even if we do not see God, shall we return to the life of the senses? Shall we degrade our higher nature?" There were times when Naren would cry out: "Of what value are my realizations! I have seen the Mantra in letters of gold and shining with effulgence! Many times have I seen the form of Kali and of other aspects of the Personal God! But, where, oh where, is Peace! I am dissatisfied with everything. Everything, even talking to devotees, has become distasteful to me. It seems that there is no such thing as God. Let me starve to death if I cannot realize the Truth." Was the memory of his Nirvikalpa Samadhi in Cossipore the cause of this discontent? Had he not experienced the Formless? No wonder he was dissatisfied with Forms!

At Baranagore it was indeed a life of spiritual endeavour and fervour. Often Sankirtana (religious songs sung in chorus) would begin in the morning and continue till evening with no thought of food or rest. In their burning desire for God-vision, Prayopaveshana (uninterrupted meditation, and so ignoring the body that death ensues) did not seem to be out of the question.

The best description of those days comes from the lips of Narendranath himself. Years later, at Belur Math, a disciple asked him, "Maharaj, how did you maintain yourselves at that time?" As the Swami's mind travelled back, his face took on an expression sad yet triumphant. Of a sudden he turned on the disciple with: "What a silly question! We were sannyasis, don't you see? We never thought of the morrow. We used to live on what chance brought. Sureshbabu and Balarambabu have passed away. Were they alive they would dance with joy at the sight of this Math!" He continued, "You have heard of Sureshbabu's name, I dare say. Know him to be the source of this Math. It was he who helped to found the Baranagore Math. It was Suresh Mitra who supplied our needs. Who can equal him in devotion and faith?" Musing, he went on, "There were days at the Baranagore Math when we had nothing to eat. If there was rice, salt was lacking. Some days that was all we had, but nobody cared. Leaves of the Bimba [*Momordica monadelpha*] creeper boiled, salt and rice—this was our diet for months! Come what might, we were indifferent. We were being carried along on a strong tide of spiritual practices and meditation. Oh, what days! Demons would have run away at the sight of such austerities, to say nothing of men! Ask Rakhal, Shashi and others; they will tell you. The more circumstances are against you, the more manifest becomes your inner power. Do you understand?" It was only with his own disciples in whom he desired to kindle the same fire of devotion and renunciation that the Swami was so frank; with others he was reticent about those days.

Besides regular meditation, singing and study the young monks observed the religious festivals. The following account of how they celebrated Shivaratri for the first time at the Baranagore Math is mainly based on Mahendra's diary. He was present for the occasion, which fell that year—1887—on Monday, February 21.

Narendra, Rakhal, Niranjan, Sharat, Shashi, Kali, Baburam, Tarak, Gopal Senior, Sarada and Harish were present. The day began with a song in praise of Shiva. Tarak and Rakhal sang "Ta-thaiya, Ta-thaiya, dances Bhola", composed by Narendra, and danced to its tune. Shashi performed the worship of the Master. Then Sharat sang another song of Shiva. They fasted the whole day, and spent the time in meditation and worship.

In the afternoon, preparations were made for the night worship. Leaves of the Bilva tree were gathered and Bilva wood was chopped for the Homa (sacred fire ritual). In the evening Shashi burnt incense before the pictures of the various gods and goddesses. The worship of Shiva was to take place under a Bilva tree in the monastery compound. He was to be worshipped four times, once in each of the four watches of the night. About nine at night the brothers assembled under the tree. One of them was in charge of the worship. Kali was reading the *Gita*. Now and then he argued with Narendra: "I am everything. I create, preserve, and destroy." Narendra said: "How is it possible for me to create? Another power creates through me. Our various actions—even our thoughts—are caused by that power." Kali reflected in silence and then said, "The actions you are talking about are illusory. There is no such thing as thought. The very idea of these things makes me laugh." Narendra replied: "The 'I' that is implied in 'I am He' is not this ego. It is that which remains after one eliminates mind, body, and so on." After completing the recital of the *Gita*, Kali chanted "Shantih! Shantih! Shantih!"

Narendra and others, their bodies smeared with holy ashes, stood up and at intervals circled round the tree, singing and dancing. Now and then the classic chant rang out—"Shiva Guru! Shiva Guru! Hara! Hara! Vyom! Vyom!"—as they repeated it in chorus, clapping their hands at the same time. It was midnight, the fourteenth day of the dark fortnight of the moon. Pitch darkness filled all the quarters. Men, birds, and

animals were hushed in silence. The young monks were clad in
ochre robes. The words "Shiva Guru!" chanted in their full-
throated voices, rose into the starlit sky like the rumbling of
thunder clouds and disappeared in the Infinite Sachchidananda. At the close of the worship of the last quarter oblations
were offered into the sacred fire in the names of all gods, goddesses, and Incarnations of all peoples. The sun, about to rise,
was painting the eastern horizon crimson. In the sacred twilight hour the young monks bathed in the Ganga.

In the morning they all went to the shrine room of the Math
and prostrated before the Master; then they gradually assembled in the hall. Mahendra writes: "Narendra was clad in a
new ochre cloth. The bright orange colour of his apparel
blended with the celestial lustre of his face and body, every pore
of which radiated a divine light. His countenance was filled
with fiery brilliance and yet touched with the tenderness of
love. He appeared to all as a bubble that had risen up in the
Ocean of Absolute Existence and Bliss and assumed a human
body to help in the propagation of his Master's message.
Narendra was then just twenty-four." Balaram had sent fruit
and sweets to the monastery for the monks' breakfast. Narendra
and a few others partook of the refreshments saying: "Blessed
indeed is Balaram!" And blessed too were those monks who
occupied themselves day and night with God and His service.

There was an intense spiritual atmosphere at Baranagore in
those days. Everyone marvelled at the austere life of Narendranath and his brother-monks. Yet they themselves were not
satisfied with their spiritual progress. In their distress at not
realizing God, they would sigh, "Oh, wonderful were Shri
Ramakrishna's renunciation and longing for God! We are not
able to attain even one-sixteenth part of what he attained!"

Hours would be consumed in the study of philosophy. The
theories of Kant, Hegel, Mill, Spencer, and even those of the
atheists and materialists, were discussed. Religion, history,
sociology, literature, art and science received attention. One
day Narendra would prove that God was a myth; the next day
he would argue that God was the only reality. The Sankhya,

Yoga, Nyaya, Vaisheshika, Mimamsa and Vedanta—each in turn was matched against the others, and their points of agreement and difference were brought out with analytical acumen. The Vedanta was compared with Buddhist philosophy, and vice versa. Occasionally Christian missionaries would come to the Math to argue with the monks. After defeating them at every point Narendra would hold forth to them on the greatness of Christ. He would develop original lines of thought, bringing out the historical importance of Shri Ramakrishna's life and teachings, and their significance for present and future generations of Hindus. He would show how that life was destined to alter their theological outlook by giving them a truer understanding of Hindu ideals.

Though outwardly a man of Jnana, Narendra was full of Bhakti within. One day, he said to a young brother-disciple who was disturbed because of his failure to realize God: "Have you not read the *Gita*? God is residing in the hearts of all creatures. He is, as it were, revolving the wheel of life to which we are tied. You are more insignificant than even the crawling worm. Can you really know God? Try to think for a minute of the real nature of man. Of these innumerable stars, every one is a solar system. We see only one solar system and know only an infinitesimal fraction of that. The earth compared with the sun is like a little ball and man but an insect moving on its surface." Then he burst into a song, resigning himself to God and beseeching His aid in steering clear of the pitfalls and temptations of the world. Again he said to the brother-disciple: "Take refuge in God. Resign yourself completely at His feet. Don't you remember the words of Shri Ramakrishna? God is like a hill of sugar. You are an ant. One grain of sugar is sufficient for you. Yet you want to carry home the entire hill. Shukadeva was at most a bigger ant. Therefore I would say to Kali, 'Do you want to measure God by your foot-rule?' God is the infinite ocean of mercy! He will shower His grace on you. Pray to Him, 'Protect us always, O Lord, by Thy benign mercy. From the unreal lead us to the Real, from darkness lead us to Light, from death lead us to Immortality!'"

"How should one pray to God?" the brother-disciple asked. "Why," Narendranath replied, "you need only repeat His Name. That is what the Master told us." Then the young monk said, "You say now that God exists; and in another mood you tell us that according to Charvaka and other philosophers the world was not created by any extraneous agency, that it has evolved of itself." Narendra said, "But have you not read chemistry? Hydrogen and oxygen do unite to form water and so forth, but not without the intervention of the human hand or some intelligence. Everybody admits that there must be an Intelligent Force guiding all these combinations, an Omniscient Being directing this phenomenal universe." "But how can we know that He is merciful?" Narendra said, " 'Your benign face', the Vedas say. John Stuart Mill echoes this. He must be an ocean of mercy who has infused one little spark of mercy into the human heart. The Master used to say, 'Faith is the one essential thing.' God is very near us. You only require faith to realize this." Then the young disciple said good-humouredly, "Sometimes you say that God does not exist. Now you are telling us that He does. You cannot be true in your statement when you change your opinions so often." Narendra replied, "I shall never change *these* words: *We do not have faith in God so long as we are assailed by egotism and desire.* Some sort of desire always persists." Then, overwhelmed with emotion he began to sing: "He is the merciful Parent always giving shelter to those who take refuge in Him." The devotional fervour of the songs that followed was enhanced by the quality of Narendra's voice—a voice which was the delight of all who heard him. Had not the Master said: "As the snake remains spellbound with its hood up on hearing the sweet notes of the flute, so does He who is in the heart, the Antaryami, when Naren sings!"?

In those days all were filled with the spirit of the Master. His personality was felt as living among them. There was neither day nor night, neither hours nor moments, for them: they dwelt in an ecstasy of spiritual zeal; indeed they were mad, mad for God-vision. All sorts of spiritual experiences were theirs. Some would sit motionless for hours plunged in meditation, whilst others sang themselves into devotional rapture. The nights of some were spent at the burning-ghat deeply absorbed in meditation; others would tell their beads all day and all night, or sit night after night before a Dhuni, in their determination to realize God.

Narendra was as intense as the rest, but his sense of responsibility for them caused him to be watchful. When he found any of them practising austerities that were too severe, he would say, "Do you think you are all going to be Ramakrishna Paramahamsas? That will never be. A Ramakrishna Paramahamsa is born once in an age!"

Swami Sadananda, an early disciple of the Leader, speaking later of these days as they were lived by his Guru, said: "During these years Swamiji would work twenty-four hours at a time. He was like a lunatic in his activity. Early in the morning, whilst it was still dark, he would rise and call the others, singing, 'Awake! Arise, all ye who would drink of the divine nectar!' And long after midnight he and the other monks would still be sitting on the roof of the monastery building, singing hymns of praise. The neighbours expostulated, but to no avail. And the musical voice of Swamiji would lead the chanting of the names of 'Sita-Rama' or of 'Radha-Krishna'. Those were strenuous days. There was no time for rest. Outsiders came and went. Pandits argued and discussed. But he, the Swami, was never for one moment idle, never dull."

To the devotees of Shri Ramakrishna and Swami Vivekananda the name "Baranagore" is synonymous with "spiritual fervour". And all who came in contact with these young monks at Baranagore were caught up in their God-intoxication. Each one of these young monks, whom Shri Ramakrishna had made his own, represented a phase of the Master himself.

13

ITINERANT DAYS IN NORTHERN INDIA

Thus the monks lived the spiritual life; and the monastic Order of Ramakrishna was consolidated too. But even as the Order was twofold in its provision, blending the ideal of personal freedom that itinerant monkhood had insisted on, with that of a brotherhood bound by a shared love for the Master and organized to further his mission, so there was a corresponding twofold tendency in each member of the Baranagore Math. In Narendranath especially, these two tendencies were seen, and at times were at war with one another. At these times he was torn between loyalty to the Math and its mission, and loyalty to the traditional vision of the wandering monk. And it was the same with his brother-monks. Indeed, there were times when it seemed that the traditional ideal would draw them apart to the isolated sannyasi's life in spite of themselves. However, if we view what happened from the standpoint of the Order as a unity, it will be seen that it was consistent throughout, for there was always a group at the Math, constituting the Ramakrishna brotherhood, even when most of the monks were out in different places. Some of them were continuously at the monastery for several years, whilst others were almost constantly wandering. From July 1890, for nearly seven years, Narendranath was himself absent; but for some four years immediately following the passing away of Shri Ramakrishna he was most of the time with his monastic brothers, either at Baranagore, or on various short pilgrimages, which will be mentioned presently.

A love of pilgrimage characterizes the Hindu monk. As the proverb has it, "A wandering monk and flowing water do not become dirty": by not remaining in any one place for long the wandering monk remains free from blemish. Moreover, who does not aspire to visit the places of pilgrimage, made more

14

holy by the visits of saints and countless others, where God is
accepting the worship of his devotees and showering grace on
them? It is but natural for those who have renounced the world
with the aim of realizing God, to seek Him where He is especially present; and this was so with the monks of the newly-
established Baranagore Math. As we have seen, the itinerant
tendency was manifest in some of them even when the Master
was at Cossipore; and immediately after his passing away some
went with the Holy Mother to Vrindavan, where they stayed
for several months.

Towards the end of February 1887, Saradananda, Abhedananda and Premananda went to Puri; and Akhandananda left
for Tibet. In the first week of May, Trigunatita suddenly disappeared from the monastery, saying that he was going away
somewhere, but confiding his plans to no one. Narendranath,
on hearing of this when he returned to the Math from Calcutta
—where he had been for the day—became agitated; for he
knew that the young monk had no experience of the world and
might meet with some serious misfortune, or might foolishly go
to an extreme in his ascetic zeal. Narendra said to a brother-
disciple, "Why did Raja [Brahmananda] allow him to go? Let
Raja come back to the monastery! I shall scold him. Why did
he allow Prasanna [Trigunatita] to go away? Couldn't you
prevent his going away?" The brother-disciple replied, "Brother
Tarak asked him not to go, but still he went away." Narendra
said to Mahendra, who was present there, "You see what a lot
of trouble I am in! Here, too, I am involved in a world of Maya.
Who knows where this boy has gone?" When Brahmananda
returned from Dakshineswar, he handed over the note left by
Trigunatita on the eve of his departure. The note read: "I am
going to Vrindavan on foot. It is very risky for me to live here.
Here my mind is undergoing a change. Formerly I used to
dream about my parents and other relatives. Then I dreamt
of woman, the embodiment of Maya. I have suffered twice; I
had to go back to my relatives at home. Therefore I am going
far away from them. The Master once told me, 'Your people
at home are capable of doing anything; never trust them.'"

Brahmananda said, "These are the reasons for his going away. We have achieved nothing by staying here. The Master always exhorted us to realize God. Have we succeeded? Let us go to the Narmada." Narendranath said, "What will you achieve by wandering about? Can one ever attain the Knowledge, that you are talking about it so much?" A devotee said, "Then why have you renounced the world?" Narendra replied, "Must we live with Shyam because we have not seen Ram? Must we go on begetting children because we have not realized God? What are you talking about?" To everyone's surprise Trigunatita returned to the monastery within a day or two. He could not go far.

But as the days passed, Narendra also became restless for pilgrimage. He felt his attachment to the brother-disciples as a chain—a golden one no doubt, but still a chain—impeding his progress to the realization of God. Therefore he resolved to strike out into the unknown paths of the monk's life. Trigunatita's eagerness to respond to the call of the wandering life was as a small cloud on the horizon compared to the storm that the same call was to raise in Narendranath. At times the latter held forth to his brother-monks on the glory of that life. Concerning them his attitude was: "Let them have their own experiences. They must break free from the monastery and test their own strength. Their experiences of the new life will make men of them, absolutely fearless and invincible, and spiritually independent; thus they will become giants." And one by one all the brother-disciples were to go on pilgrimage, except Ramakrishnananda. About him Narendra used to say in later years: "I used to fire them [his brother-monks] to break it up and go about the world begging. But on no account could I make Shashi yield. He would hear of nothing of the kind. You must know him to be the backbone of our Math."

Until the middle of 1888, Narendranath did not leave the Baranagore Math except for short visits to near-by places. For instance, in January 1887 he went to Antpur again with Brahmananda, Premananda and Advaitananda. In the summer of 1887 he had fever owing to kidney trouble, and subsequently went to Simultala and Vaidyanath at the request of his brother-disciples. They felt that he needed a short rest from the strenuous life of the monastery, and a change of environment. These and the other expeditions of Narendra prior to mid-1890 turned out to be only temporary absences. He would sally forth on them, but for some reason or other would return soon, against his will. When he left he would say, "It will be for good and all this time", but something brought him back. In two instances it was the serious illness of certain of his brother-monks; in another it was the death of Balaram Bose, a lay devotee of the Master.

However, when he left the monastery in July of 1890, he did not come back until February 1897, after his triumphant return from the West. This time he made up his mind to break with the monastery in order to test his own strength, to gather experience of another way of life, to make himself fearless, and at the same time to force his brother-disciples to stand alone on their own feet, in self-reliance. It was a struggle for him to free himself: his mind for some time wavered between the desire for the wandering life and his sense of responsibility for the brotherhood.

As wandering monk, Narendranath's very appearance was striking; indeed, it was regal. His body and bodily movements were instinct with grace. His luminous eyes and imperious personality, together with the suggestion of greatness that there was about him, made him conspicuous wherever he went. Staff and monk's water-pot in hand, a copy of the *Gita* and of *The Imitation of Christ* in his bundle, and ochre-clothed, he journeyed on in silence, joyful at heart. These were glorious days in the life of Narendranath. He did not assume any fixed name during his wanderings in India. Hereafter we shall call him "the Swami".

There are some blanks in this part of the Swami's life-story, for he himself was indifferent about keeping a note of his journeys and doings, and afterwards spoke of them vaguely and casually. As to his spiritual experiences during this time, he held them too sacred to be discussed even with his brothers. Yet something is known of him as a wandering monk. Sometimes one or other of the monks accompanied him; and those lay people whom he met and initiated as disciples on his long tours through his motherland, kept records of his stay with them, and even of his conversations on some occasions. Then there are his letters written occasionally to his brother-disciples and his own disciples. Thus it is possible to reconstruct his life from 1887 to 1893 with some accuracy. Each of his brother-monks, excepting Ramakrishnananda and Adbhutananda, was with him on one or other of his travels up to the time when he broke off communication with the Baranagore Math, and these have given verbal accounts—particularly Akhandananda, who was with him longer than any of the others were, from the latter part of July 1890 until the latter part of the autumn that year.

At the beginning of 1891, he said goodbye to his brother-monks at Delhi, and resolved to wander alone. When his brother-disciples later met him accidentally on two or three occasions, he rebuked them and forbade them to do so. During these days, he would conceal his learning, and wander like an ordinary monk. No one could guess that he had a good command of English, unless he happened to express himself in that language. At times he determined not to beg from door to door, but to accept whatever chance might bring. He told someone that the longest time he had to go without food, under this austerity, was five days. Many times his abode was a jungle, a temple, or a ruined wayside rest-house. Many times he was alone under the stars, or on foot in rain or scorching heat. On these travels he took the vow of not touching money. Sometimes at a devotee's earnest request he would avail himself of a railway ticket; at other times he would go on foot.

The remarks just made relate to the Swami's wandering days in general. Coming now to such details as we have of his extended pilgrimages, the first of these was to Varanasi, the home of monks, the centre of learning, and the Seat of Shiva. He set out from the Baranagore Math, accompanied by Premananda and Fakirbabu, a lay devotee of the Master. The sacred Ganga, the praying votaries, the numerous temples, especially those of Vishwanath, Annapurna and Durga, the atmosphere of holiness, the thought that it was here that the Buddha and Shri Shankara had preached—all these made a vivid impression on him.

One day he went to Sarnath, close to Varanasi, where, in the Deer Park, the Buddha had preached the first of his Sermons. But in those days, when the Swami visited the place, the Stupa or Topa, and the ruins of the Buddhist monastery, were still overgrown with jungle.

One morning, after visiting the temple of Mother Durga, the Swami was passing through a place where there were a large tank of water on one side and a high wall on the other. Here he was surrounded by a troop of large monkeys. They were not willing to allow him to pass along that way. They howled and shrieked and clutched at his feet as he strode. As they pressed closer, he began to run; but the faster he ran, the faster came the monkeys, and they began to bite at him. When it seemed impossible for him to escape, he heard an old sannyasi calling out to him: "Face the brutes." The words brought him to his senses. He turned and boldly faced the irate monkeys. As soon as he did that, they fell back and fled. With reverence and gratitude he gave the traditional greeting to the sannyasi, who smilingly responded with the same, and walked away. In a New York lecture years later, the Swami referred to this incident and pointed to its moral: "That is a lesson for all life—face the terrible, face it boldly. Like the monkeys, the hardships of life fall back when we cease to flee before them. If we are ever to gain freedom, it must be by conquering nature, never by running away. Cowards never win victories. We have to fight fear and troubles and ignorance if we expect them to flee before us."

At Varanasi the Swami stayed at the Ashrama of Dwaraka-das, where he met many sannyasis and scholars. This gentleman introduced him to the celebrated pandit and Bengali writer, Bhudev Mukhopadhyaya. The Swami and the pandit held long conversations on the merits of various Hindu ideals. When they parted, the pandit said, "Wonderful! Such vast experience and insight at such an early age! I am sure he will be a great man."

The Swami also visited the great saint Trailanga Swami, who lived in a Shiva temple, lost to all outward activity, absorbed in the deepest meditation, eating only when anyone fed him. It was only in his later days that he sometimes came down from that state to answer in writing a question which had been put to him. Shri Ramakrishna had also visited him many years before, and had put the question whether Jiva and Brahman were one or two entities. Trailanga Swami had answered by sign that they were two so long as duality was seen, but that ultimately they were one.

The Swami next went to Swami Bhaskarananda, a celebrated ascetic of great learning, who lived almost nude in his Ashrama. The conversation between them drifted to the subject of the conquest of lust and gold. This was one of the main conditions insisted on by the Master for the realization of God. Bhaskarananda, speaking *ex cathedra* as it were, said, "No one can completely renounce lust and gold." The Swami replied, "What do you say, sir! There have been many who have done so, for this is the very basis of the sannyasi's life and aspiration. And I myself have seen at least one who had completely conquered lust and gold." Bhaskarananda smiled and declared, "You are but a child. What do you know!" Finding his Master's life, his own aspiration, and the basic principle and norm of the monk's life challenged, the Swami rose to the occasion in animated defence. Bhaskarananda and his disciples were struck by his fire and eloquence. Turning to those who were present the renowned monk said, "This man has Saraswati [the Goddess of Learning] on his tongue. His mind is like a great light." But the Swami, fuming, left the place.

After spending about a week in the holy atmosphere of Varanasi, he left the city; and those monks and devotees who had made his acquaintance wondered where the Swami Vividishananda—the name the Swami was then using—had gone. He had returned to the Baranagore Math, there to spend days with his brother-disciples in meditation, study and discussion. As his outlook widened as the result of his travels and his contacts with various people, so he desired that that of his brother-disciples also should. Sometimes a dim vision of the missionary life, of ministering to the poor and downtrodden at the urge of the inner self, would present itself to the Swami's mind. This idea of service of man as the manifestation of God engrossed him at times. What better way could there be of applying the ideas of Vedanta to practical life? And he strove to inspire his brother-disciples with this new idea of religion. Even in those early days he would urge them to go to the locality of the outcastes to preach; but the monks were quite averse to preaching. Their ideal was the realization of God, first and foremost; after that, their example would be the teacher even as their Master's had been; and the former urgings of the Swami had confirmed them in this. Now, though he continued to insist on the necessity of making oneself fit by realization for preaching, yet sometimes the spirit of the preacher would take hold of him. Once, when this mood was on him, he said to a brother-monk who was inveighing against lectures and sermons: "Everyone is preaching; what they do unconsciously I will do consciously. Ay, even if you, my brother-monks, stand in my way, I will go and preach among the Pariahs in the lowest slums. Preaching means expression. Because Trailanga Swami remains silent and never talks, do you think he does not preach? His very silence is a sermon! Even trees and plants are preaching!" And that is what happened later on: Swami Vivekananda preached consciously and with soul-stirring eloquence what the saints had hitherto done in silence. At Baranagore, this work commenced, and his first audience was the small group of monks and devotees there.

The Swami's stay this time at the Baranagore Math was a short one, for he was eager to take up again the meditative life of the sannyasi, avoiding society. He soon started on pilgrimage to holy places in northern India. His first halt was at Varanasi, where he met Babu Pramadadas Mitra, the noted Sanskrit scholar, who was acquainted with Akhandananda. Through Akhandananda, Pramadadas had learnt of the Swami. The two became close friends, and the Swami wrote Pramadadas a number of letters asking his advice on the interpretation of the Hindu scriptures.

Next he visited holy Ayodhya, which had at one time been the capital of the divine king Ramachandra. Since childhood the Swami had loved Rama and Sita, and been delighted by the chanting of the *Ramayana*. Now, in the same Ayodhya, he must have reconstructed, out of the materials of his learning and imagination, the scenes and events of long ago. From Ayodhya he went to Lucknow, where he was lost in admiration of the splendours bequeathed by the Nawabs of Oudh, and of the city's gardens and mosques. From Lucknow on to Agra, of Mogul memories and grandeur. The artistry and workmanship of the Indian artisans astounded him; the beauty of the Taj Mahal overpowered him. He visited it many times, seeing it from different angles, in every light, and above all in the perspective of his love for India. He used to say, "Every square inch of this wondrous edifice is worth a whole day's patient observation, and it requires at least six months to make a real study of it!" The magnificent fort of Agra stimulated his historical imagination. Walking through the streets of the city with its palaces and tombs, he saw the whole Mogul era unfold before him.

From Agra he went on to Vrindavan, reaching it during the early part of August 1888. The last thirty miles he did on foot. About two miles from Vrindavan, he saw a man contentedly smoking a pipe (Chillum) by the wayside. The Swami, weary, felt that a smoke would do him good; so he asked the man to allow him to have a pull or two at the pipe. The smoker shrank back and said diffidently, "It would defile you, sir. I am a Bhangi [a sweeper]". The Swami, conditioned by caste-consciousness, shrank back too, and went his way. After going a short distance, the thought struck him, "What! I have taken the sannyasi's vow and have given up all ideas of caste, family prestige and so forth: yet I fell back into caste ideas when the man told me that he was a sweeper! And I could not smoke the pipe which he had touched! That was due to ages of habit." The thought made him so restless that he turned back and found the man still seated there. Sitting down beside him, he said, "Brother, do prepare me a Chillum of tobacco." But the man humbly expostulated, "Sir, you are a holy man: I am an outcaste!" But the Swami would not listen to his objections and insisted on having a smoke from that pipe.

Many days later, when Girishchandra Ghosh heard of this incident, he said to the Swami, "You are addicted to hemp. That's why you could not avoid the temptation of smoking even from a sweeper's pipe." The Swami said in reply, "No, G. C., truly, I wanted to test myself. After taking Sannyasa, one should test oneself, whether one has gone beyond the limitations of caste and colour. It is very difficult to observe the vows of Sannyasa strictly: there should be no contradiction between word and deed."

In speaking of Sannyasa to a disciple later on, the Swami cited this incident and said, "Do you think the ideals of Sannyasa are easy to practise in life, my boy? There is no other path of life so arduous and difficult. Let your foot slip ever so little on the edge of a precipice, and you fall to the valley below. If one has taken the sannyasi's vow, one has to examine oneself every moment to see if one is free from the ideas of caste, colour and so forth. That incident taught me the great lesson that I should not despise anyone, but must think of all as children of the Lord."

Arrived at Vrindavan, the Swami stayed at Kalababu's Kunja, a temple erected by the ancestors of Balaram Bose. Here he felt as though the flood-gates of his heart were suddenly opened. The place's association with the lives of Shri Krishna and his divine consort Radha evoked in him intense feelings of devotion. The acts of Krishna came to life for him, and he resolved to visit the environs of Vrindavan, where many of them had taken place.

While going round the Govardhan Hill, the Swami vowed that he would not beg his food from anyone, that he would eat only what was offered to him without asking. During the first day he became exceedingly hungry at noon. To add to his discomfort, heavy rain began to fall. He grew faint with hunger and with much walking, but still went on and on, without asking for food. Suddenly he heard someone calling him from behind, but he did not answer. Nearer and nearer came the voice, that of a devotee, calling out that he had brought food for him. The Swami began to run as fast as he could, to test this apparent act of Providence. The man, running after him for nearly a mile, overtook him and insisted that he accept the food. The Swami accepted it, saying nothing. Shortly after, the man disappeared among the trees. Ecstatic with devotion at this miraculous act of the Lord, and with tears streaming from his eyes, the Swami cried out, "Glory to Shri Radha! Glory to Shri Krishna!" In the wilderness the Lord had taken care of His devotee.

From Govardhan the Swami went on to Radhakunda, sacred for its association with Shri Radha. At this time he was wearing only a Kaupin (narrow strip of cloth about the loins). Having no other to wear after his bath, he took it off, washed it, and left it on the side of the tank to dry whilst he was bathing. When he had bathed, he found the Kaupin missing. In his search he chanced to look up in a tree: there he saw a monkey sitting, the Kaupin in its hands. When the monkey refused to surrender it, the Swami was filled with anger against Shri Radha, the presiding deity of the place. He vowed that he would go into the recesses of the forest and starve himself to death. As he advanced into the jungle in pursuance of his plan, a man, who probably had seen the whole incident, came up with a new ochre cloth and some food, which the Swami accepted. The Swami was no doubt astounded; it seemed like a miracle. When he retraced his steps to the tank, to his surprise he found his Kaupin lying just where he had put it to dry. Such incidents convinced him that he was beloved of the Lord and protected by Him wherever he was.

After his pilgrimage to Vrindavan the Swami had a mind to go to Hardwar, and from there to Kedar-Badri in the Himalayas; but he remained at Vrindavan a few days more, since one of his brother-disciples (Advaitananda) was expected there.

Next, we find the Swami seated in a secluded corner of

Hathras railway station, on his way to Hardwar, evidently rather weary and in need of food. His figure caught the eye of the Assistant Station-master, Sharatchandra Gupta, as the latter was attending to his duties. Now this Sharatchandra was a remarkable person: a Bengali who had grown up among the Muslims of Jaunpur, and spoke Hindi and Urdu more fluently than his mother tongue. His character could be summed up in three words: sweetness, sincerity and manliness. At first sight he was attracted by the appearance of the young monk and could sense the aura of spirituality about him; so Sharat went up to him to find out whether he could be of service. After an exchange of greetings, Sharat asked, "Swamiji, are you hungry?" The Swami replied, "Yes, I am." "Then please come to my quarters", said Sharat. The Swami asked, with the simplicity of a boy, "But what will you give me to eat?" Promptly quoting from a Persian poem, Sharat replied, "O beloved, you have come to my house! I shall prepare the most delicious dish for you with the flesh of my heart." The Swami was delighted to hear this reply and accepted the invitation.

When the tasks of the day were over, Sharat spent the time with the Swami, whose eyes attracted him beyond measure. He begged him to stay in Hathras for some days. Sharat's first words, almost, were, "Sir, teach me wisdom." The Swami answered him with a Bengali song in which the loved one says to her lover, "If you wish to attain knowledge, go and cover your moon face with ashes; otherwise find your own way." Sharat immediately replied, "Swamiji, I am at your service. I am ready to renounce everything and follow you." Saying these words he disappeared, to return divested of his official clothes, with ashes on his face. Sharat's elder brother was already a sannyasi, so this was not something quite new for him.

Soon after his arrival at Hathras, the Swami learnt of one Brajenbabu, an old acquaintance of his. This gentleman lived close by. When the Swami went to his residence, Brajenbabu recognized him at once, greeted him heartily, and insisted on his staying with him for several days at least. The Swami agreed, promising to go and stay with Sharat shortly. Whilst at the house of Brajenbabu, the entire Bengali population of the town poured in to meet the Swami. Prior to his arrival, there had been some differences amongst the resident Bengalis; but these were laid aside in their longing to come and hear the Swami. He spoke to them of religion and of their motherland with such fervour that most of the visitors spent hours in the house of Brajenbabu. During these days the Swami often visited the quarters of Sharat and of his friend, Natakrishna. These two became more and more attached to him and earnestly begged him to be their guest. He consented and went to live with them later. In a letter recalling those days Natakrishna writes:

Thus we with others spent the most blessed days of our life in constant spiritual conversations with him. By the power of his holy company, the sectarian quarrels and ill-feeling amongst the different factions of the Bengalis vanished. Those who entertained pride of age or high position in society, used to come and sit like children before the young monk, forsaking their conceit of knowledge and position, and asking him questions on religious matters. The evening was generally spent in music, and all the gentlemen who assembled there were simply charmed with his sweet voice, and sat for hours as if spellbound. The more they heard him the more they thirsted in their souls to hear him.

One day Sharat asked the Swami, "Why do you look so sad?" After a pause the Swami replied, "My son, I have a great mission to fulfil and I am in despair at the smallness of my capacity. I have an injunction from my Guru to carry out this mission. It is nothing less than the regeneration of my motherland. Spirituality has fallen to a low ebb and starvation stalks the land. India must become dynamic and effect the conquest of the world through her spirituality." Sharat, spellbound at these words, said with all the ardour of his soul, "Here I am, Swamiji; what do you want me to do?" The monk demanded, "Are you prepared to take up the begging bowl and the Kamandalu and work for the great cause? Can you beg from door to door?" "Yes", was the bold reply. The Swami was greatly pleased to see the courage and determination of Sharat. He spent many days at Sharat's house, speaking to groups of devotees and admirers.

One morning the Swami decided to leave Hathras. He said to Sharat, "I cannot stay here longer. I am a sannyasi and should never remain long in any one place. Besides, I am feeling a sort of attachment for you all. This is also a bondage in spiritual life." To attempts to dissuade him, he only replied, "Don't press me." Sharat became grief-stricken: he had fallen in love with the Swami. "Swamiji, make me your disciple", was his entreaty. The Swami replied, "Why, do not think that everything in spiritual life will be gained by becoming my disciple. Remember that God is in everything; and then whatever you do will make for your progress. I shall come and be with you now and then. For the present I must be going to the Himalayas." Sharat repeated his entreaty time and again, until at length he spoke out: "Swamiji, say what you will, wherever you go I shall follow you." Seeing his determination and sincerity, the Swami said, "Can you really follow me? Then take my begging-bowl and go and beg our food from the porters of the station." No sooner was the order given than Sharat went to beg from his own subordinates. Having collected some food he brought it to the Swami, who in turn blessed him heartily, and accepted him as his disciple.

Sharat soon found a substitute to take over his duties, and accompanied the Swami to Hrishikesh; but the journey proved too much for the disciple. Accustomed to a good deal of comfort, he found that the sannyasi's life was one of constant spiritual discipline, and full of uncertainties and hardships. "Once in our wanderings in the outlying districts of the Himalayas," said Sharat much later, "I fainted with hunger and thirst. The Swami carried me and thus undoubtedly saved me from certain death. On another occasion, like a syce he led the horse, which someone had kindly lent us for the journey, across a mountain river which was very dangerous to ford because of its swiftness and slippery bottom. He risked his life several times for my sake. How can I describe him, friends, except by the word Love, Love, Love! When I was too ill to do anything but stagger along, he carried my personal belongings including my shoes." It is not strange, then, that in later life feeling forlorn once and asking the Swami whether he was going to give him (Sharat) up, the Swami should answer with a sweet severity, "Fool, do you not remember that I have carried even your shoes!"

Still another time, as the Swami and his disciple were moving through the jungle, they came across some bleached human bones, with pieces of rotting ochre cloth lying here and there. "See," said the Swami, "here a tiger has devoured a sannyasi! Are you afraid?" The disciple promptly replied, "Not with you, Swamiji!" Even in those early days when he was an unknown monk, the force of the Swami's character and his power to inspire others could be plainly seen.

At Hrishikesh the Swami and the disciple lived like other monks. The Swami was in his element here, where the very atmosphere breathed the monastic life. The foot-hills were about them, but they longed to ascend the distant peaks of the Himalayas. The murmuring of the sacred Ganga was a delight to hear. They lived there in the company of other sadhus, and passed their time in spiritual disciplines. After a few days' stay at Hrishikesh, the Swami became very eager to go to Kedar-Badri; but because of his disciple's health and his inability to stand the hardships he kept his desire suppressed. But on one occasion, as though the monk in him had become awakened, he said to Sharat, "You have become a sort of chain on my feet. I was wandering alone so long. You came and became a source of botheration to me. Now I am going my own way. I shall stay here no more." Taking his staff and water-pot, the Swami set out alone on pilgrimage. Sharat was then cooking Khichuri for both of them. He became remorseful and sat silently in one place. After three or four hours, the Swami returned and, standing behind Sharat, said, "O Sharat, can you give me something to eat? I am terribly hungry." Sharat was very happy to see him back, and said, "Yes, I shall give you something just now." The Swami: "Did you not take your meal?" Sharat: "When you were not here, how could I!" The Swami: "You have really become like a chain round my feet. I had gone a long way, but then I remembered that you were alone here and were such a fool. I could not be sure what you might do. Look, it was for you I had to return." Then the disciple served the Khichuri, and they both ate it with joy.

The Swami, as we have seen, was longing to go up into the Himalayas, but now Sharat fell seriously ill, and there was no other course but to take him back to Hathras. Back at Hathras, the Swami himself fell ill, having contracted malaria at Hrishikesh. Both master and disciple became very weak and had a difficult time. Somehow the news of the Swami's illness reached the brothers at the Baranagore Math and they requested him to return to Calcutta. Just at this time, Shivananda, on his way to some holy places in northern India, reached Hathras. Hearing of the illness of his brother-disciple, he gave up his intention and brought the Swami back to the Baranagore Math. Before leaving Hathras, the Swami told Sharat to follow him to Baranagore as soon as he felt all right. In due course Sharat gave up his job and joined the monastery, where he was received with open arms. He was subsequently initiated into Sannyasa and given the name Sadananda.

Most of the monks were away on pilgrimage when the Swami reached the Baranagore Math towards the end of 1888. But those who were there, and all the householder disciples of the Master who used to visit the Math, were delighted to have him with them. With the exception of two short visits to near-by places, he remained at the Baranagore Math for a whole year. The first of those visits was with the Holy Mother and a few of his brother-monks to the Master's native village of Kamarpukur. They went via Antpur, arriving there on February 5, 1889, and stayed about a week. On the way to Kamarpukur the Swami had fever and vomiting. He returned to Calcutta unwell, and had homoeopathic treatment. (According to another account he did not even reach Kamarpukur because of illness.)

In the summer of 1889, still feeling very weak, he made the second of these visits. It was to Simultala (near Vaidyanath), a place noted for its healthy climate, where the Swami went for his health and also to see his relatives. But as the summer advanced he had an attack of acute diarrhoea and returned to Calcutta.

The days at the Math passed in worship, prayer, meditation, devotional singing and strenuous study, especially of the Hindu scriptures. Through loving discipline the Swami infused into his brother-monks his own fire, together with a wider appreciation of the mission that was before them—the mission that had been entrusted to them by the Master. Most of the sublime ideas which he gave to the world in the time of his fame were not new, except in mode of expression, to his brother-monks, for they had heard them in these Baranagore days. He broadened their horizon and made them think of India as an indivisible unit. He initiated them into his vision of a living, integrated Hinduism capable of meeting the requirements of the best modern minds on the intellectual and all other sides. He made them capable of being defenders of the Faith against bigoted and ignorant criticism. And he read with them and expounded the sacred books of the Hindus.

Too poor to buy books, the Swami borrowed some Vedanta literature from his friend Babu Pramadadas Mitra of Varanasi, together with a copy of Panini's grammar, so that his brother-disciples might study the Vedas. On November 19, 1888, he wrote thus to Babu Pramadadas: "The Vedas may well be said to have fallen quite out of vogue in Bengal. Many here in the Math are quite conversant with Sanskrit and are able to master the Samhita portion of the Vedas. They are of opinion that what has to be done must be done to a finish. So believing that a full measure of proficiency in the Vedic language is impossible without first mastering Panini's grammar, which is the best available for the purpose, a copy of the latter is felt to be a necessity. This Math is not wanting in men of perseverance, talent and penetrative intellect. I can hope that by the grace of our Master, they will acquire in a short time Panini's system and thus succeed in restoring the Vedas to Bengal."

The Swami at this time was passing through a phase of enquiry into social customs and into the inconsistencies of many

15

scriptural passages. In his wanderings he saw for himself what a load and drag the social system was on the masses: even the scriptures forbade the study of the Vedas by Shudras. The caste system, which originally rested on individual merit and quali-fication, had now hopelessly degenerated into slavish insistence on birth and heredity. The Swami was convinced that the regeneration of India demanded the throwing open of the immortal truths of the Vedas and the Upanishads to the masses.

He voiced his doubts to Pramadadasbabu, who was a great Sanskrit scholar. He also asked many searching questions re-garding the nature of the highest realization, the authority of the Vedas, the law of Karma, the apparent contradictions to be found in various schools of Indian philosophy, the real import of certain apparently meaningless injunctions of the Smritis, and other matters. These doubts and questions reflect only the intellectual aspect of his reaching out towards the wisdom which was his in after years. His faith in the ideal of Truth and in the realizations of the ancient seers as recorded in the scriptures was unshaken: he was striving to understand their real significance. He wanted to reach a standpoint from which he could reconcile all contradictions and differences. "I have not lost", he wrote to Pramadadasbabu, "faith in a benign Providence—nor am I ever going to lose it—; my faith in the scriptures is unshaken. But by the will of God, the last six or seven years of my life have been full of constant struggles with hindrances and obstacles of all sorts. I have been vouchsafed the ideal Shastra; I have seen the ideal man; and yet I fail myself to get on with anything to the end—this is my profound misery."

But there were times when the Swami felt much "agitated and cramped" in mind. He was close to his mother and brothers who were living in abject poverty. The litigation over their ancestral property left them almost destitute. This seemed, sometimes, too much for the Swami to bear. "Living near Calcutta", he wrote in the same letter to his friend Pramadadas-babu, "I have to witness their adversity, and with the quality of Rajas prevailing; my egotism sometimes develops into a desire to plunge into action. In such moments, a fierce combat ensues in my mind, and so I wrote that my mind was terrible. Now the lawsuit is settled. So bless me that after staying in Calcutta for a few days more to settle matters, I may bid adieu to this place for ever. Bless me that my heart may wax strong with supreme strength divine and that all forms of Maya may drop from me for aye: 'We have taken up the Cross. Thou hast laid it upon us; and grant us strength that we bear it unto death. Amen.' "

At such times the Swami would feel the strong desire to go on pilgrimage, to pass his days in meditation and austerity. Often he would resolve to go to Varanasi and spend time in the sacred city of Vishwanath. The presence of Pramadadasbabu there was an added attraction, for with him he might discuss many intricate problems having to do with the scriptures. Life in Calcutta was becoming unbearable to him. Akhandananda was wandering in the Himalayas, and several times wrote of crossing over to Tibet. He gave interesting descriptions of the Tibetan people and their customs. Four other brother-monks were also in the Himalayas; and so the Swami was irresistibly drawn there.

In the last part of December 1889, the Swami left the monastery for Vaidyanath, on his way to places of pilgrimage in northern India. His mind was longing for Varanasi. "My idea", he wrote to Pramadadasbabu from Vaidyanath on December 26, "is to remain there [at Varanasi] for some time and to watch how Vishwanath and Annapurna deal it out to my lot. And my resolve is something like 'either to lay down my life or realize my ideal'—so help me, Lord of Kashi."

But Providence decreed otherwise. At Vaidyanath the Swami learnt that Yogananda, one of his brother-disciples, was down with chicken-pox at Allahabad. He at once started for Allahabad, but was relieved to find on arrival there that Yogananda had completely recovered, having been cared for by the local doctor and his Bengali friends. These were pious men devoted to the service of sadhus. Here too the Swami received marked attention from the Bengalis of the town; they were astounded at his learning and wonderful character. The conversation centred chiefly around social and spiritual matters. He vehemently criticized the social abuses and iniquities of the Hindus; but with no less fervour would he speak to them of the glory of the eternal religion of the Hindus. These Bengali gentlemen were charmed by the Swami's personality and pressed him to pass the month there.

At Allahabad he came across a Mohammedan saint, "every line and curve of whose face showed that he was a Paramahamsa". Here also, he heard of Pavhari Baba, the famous saint of Ghazipur, of whom he had learnt years earlier at Dakshineswar. He had a longing to see him, and so he left Allahabad for Ghazipur in the third week of January 1890.

At Ghazipur the Swami stayed with Babu Satishchandra Mukherjee and Rai Gaganchandra Roy Bahadur. Satishchandra was an old friend of the Swami's Calcutta days. At his house many people came to see and hear the young monk. The Swami was pained to find his countrymen fallen from the ideals of the Hindu seers to the level of materialistic Western life. "Everything here", he wrote on January 24, 1890, to Pramada-dasbabu at Varanasi, "appears good. The people are all gentlemen, but much westernized; it is a pity. I am thoroughly against the affectation of the West. Luckily my friend is not much inclined that way. What a frivolous civilization it is indeed that the foreigners have created! What a materialistic illusion have they brought with them! May Vishwanath save these weak-hearted!" In a postscript to the letter he adds, "Alas for the irony of fate, that in this land of Bhagavan Shuka's birth renunciation is looked down upon as madness and sin!" He asked the local social-reform champions to refrain from violent denunciation and to carry on their work of mass education with love and patience, so that growth might be natural, from within. He pitied those who had lost sight of the spiritual standards of the Hindu civilization.

But this was by the way. The Swami's main object was to see Pavhari Baba. Who was this Pavhari Baba? He was born of Brahmana parents at Premapur, a village near Jaunpur, and about thirty miles from Varanasi. In his boyhood he went to Ghazipur where, under the training of his uncle, a lifelong Brahmachari, he became versed in Vyakarana (grammar) and Nyaya (logic), and in the theology of the Ramanuja sect. On his uncle's death he resolved "to fill the gap with a vision that can never change". Determined to find Reality, he wandered throughout the land. At length he was initiated into the mysteries of Yoga on Mount Girnar in Kathiawar, holy both to Hindu and Jain devotees. From Girnar he journeyed to Varanasi, where he met a great sannyasi, who lived in a cave in the high bank of the Ganga. Here he mastered the Advaita Vedanta system, after which he travelled for many years, studying and leading a life of great austerity. Finally he came back to his old home, Ghazipur, where, emulating his teacher in Varanasi, he dug a hermitage in the ground, on the riverside. For many hours a day he remained in meditation; and the nights he spent on the other side of the river in ascetic and religious practices. His daily diet consisted of a handful of bitter Neem (margosa) leaves or of a few pods of red pepper. He held all work to be "worshipping the Lord"; and he would often give the food he had cooked, after offering it to his Chosen Deity, to the poor or to wandering monks, himself refusing to eat. So spare was his diet that he was called Pavhari Baba, "Air-eating Father". As days went on, he spent more and more time in his cave, often months on end, until people wondered how he lived, or whether he was dead. After a time, however, the Baba would emerge. When not absorbed in meditation he would receive visitors in a room above the entrance to his cave. Later he would see no one. Finally, one morning, smelling burning flesh and seeing smoke rising from his retreat, people found that he had made an offering of his body to the Lord, his spirit having soared into the blessedness of Samadhi. But this last happened much later. When the Swami went there, Pavhari Baba was well known, and people used to go to Ghazipur to meet him. No wonder, then, that the Swami was also anxious to do so. He later admitted that he owed a deep debt of gratitude to the saint, and spoke of him as one of the greatest masters he had ever loved and served.

It was very difficult to get an interview with Pavhari Baba. When willing to speak at all, he would come only to the door, speaking from inside. The Swami could not meet him for several days, but when he did he was greatly struck with the Babaji's personality. "Through supreme good fortune, I have obtained an interview with Babaji", the Swami wrote to Pramadababu on February 4, 1890; "A great sage indeed!—It is all very wonderful, and in this atheistic age: a towering representation of marvellous power born of Bhakti and Yoga! I have sought refuge in his grace; and he has given me hope—a thing very few may be fortunate enough to obtain. It is Babaji's wish that I stay on for some days here, and he would do me some good. So following this saint's bidding I shall remain here for some time."

The Swami moved to the garden-house of Gaganbabu in order to be nearer to Babaji's place, and began severe ascetic practices. In March 1890 he wrote to Akhandananda: "There is a beautiful bungalow in a small garden belonging to a gentleman here; I mean to stay there. The garden is quite close to Babaji's cottage. A brother of the Babaji stays there to look after the comforts of the sadhus, and I shall have my Bhiksha [alms] at his place." The Swami had been suffering from lumbago for the last two months, and therefore could not meet the Babaji sometimes, though he was staying so near him; but Babaji used to send someone to enquire about his health. To add to the Swami's trouble, he had an attack of diarrhoea, and could not digest the food which was given there as Bhiksha. However, because Babaji had given him hope, the Swami stayed on.

Pavhari Baba was a wonderful man, and full of humility. He never gave a direct reply to questions, saying only, "What does this servant know?" But fire would flash as the talk went on. If the Swami were too pressing the Babaji would say, "Favour me highly by staying here for some days." So he waited.

During these days the Swami met many persons, including

some European officials. Some had been known to him before, others not. Gaganbabu introduced him to Mr. Ross, a Government official, who asked him many penetrating questions about the Hindu festivals, particularly about Holi and the Ramlila. He wanted to know whether there was any scriptural sanction for the practices associated with them. He also asked about Hindu social customs. The preacher in the Swami was roused by these questions, and he spoke with power and luminous insight, showing the relationship between Nature-worship and hero-worship and religious growth. He also explained the spiritual ideas at the bottom of each social custom until the astonished European scholar was convinced of the wonder of the Sanatana Dharma, acknowledging in it a vastness of spiritual perspective hitherto undreamed of by him. He asked the Swami to write a paper on the Hindu festival of Holi, which the latter did. Mr. Ross introduced the Swami to Mr. Pennington, the District Judge. This gentleman positively drew the Swami out, making him pour forth what he had come to understand of the revival of Hinduism and the trend of the modern transition in India. He spoke on the scientific basis of Yoga, on the ascetic disciplines of the Hindu sannyasis, and on many other subjects. The minds of his hearers were led into analytical study of the powers of the human faculties as awakened and manifest in the yogis. He considered these in the light of modern psychology. Mr. Pennington was so impressed by the Swami's exposition of Hindu religion and social customs that he asked him to go to England to preach the ideas there.

The Swami was also introduced to Colonel Rivett-Carnac, with whom he had lengthy discussions on the Vedantic ideals and their practicality in daily life. The Swami here revealed his genius. His spirit of renunciation, his insight, his power and personality, became radiant. He was, as it were, Vedanta incarnate to the astonished Westerners.

At Ghazipur the Swami was in regular correspondence with Akhandananda, who was sending him interesting descriptions of the Tibetans; and in February 1890 he wrote to Akhandananda explaining the Buddhist doctrines and the philosophy behind the Tantric rites. Being an admirer of the Buddha, he would have liked to go to Tibet to study the Buddhist scriptures. Although a little earlier he had asked Akhandananda to cease wandering and either to settle down at some place of his choice, or to return to the Math, he now, in March, suggested that Akhandananda should come to Ghazipur, and that from there they would set out together for Tibet via Nepal, where one of his friends was private tutor to the Maharaja. Entry into Tibet was very restricted. But with the help of this friend, the Swami wrote, it would be easy for them to enter Tibet with the Nepal Government officers who went annually to China via Lhasa. They might even be able to visit the holy seat of Tara Devi in China. But for one reason or another the Swami was never able to visit Nepal, Tibet, or that part of China.

Let us turn now to the inner workings of the Swami's mind. Daily he went to Pavhari Baba, when his health allowed. His spiritual dissatisfaction and restlessness were unremitting. He was always seeking, always striving, always analysing. It was in this spirit that he had retired to Gaganbabu's solitary garden-house, though it was said to be haunted. (There were numerous lemon-trees here, loaded with fruit, and the Swami, then suffering from diarrhoea, took plenty of lemons to increase his digestive power.) In spite of ill health he practised hard spiritual discipline, and made every effort to plunge his soul into the highest Reality.

The Swami suffered at this time from various mental and physical agonies. The lumbago was giving him a good deal of trouble, sometimes making him frantic with pain. "I know not", he wrote, "how I shall climb up the hills. I find that the Babaji has wonderful endurance, and that is why I go to him." He was greatly upset to learn from Akhandananda, in the third week of February, that Abhedananda, his brother-disciple, was suffering from repeated attacks of malaria at Hrishikesh. The Swami sent a wire from Ghazipur to ask whether he was needed. On February 19, 1890, he wrote to Pramadababu: "Well, you may smile, sir, to see me weaving this web of Maya,—and that is, no doubt, a fact. But then there is the chain of iron and there is the chain of gold. Much good comes of the latter, and it drops off by itself when all the good is reaped. The sons of my Master are indeed the great objects of my service, and here alone I feel I have some duty left for me." But a few days later he writes to Pramadababu again: "You know not, sir, I am a very soft-natured man in spite of the stern Vedantic views I hold. And this proves to be my undoing. At the slightest touch I give way. For however much I may try to think only of my own good, I begin, in spite of myself, to think of other people's interests." He had set out from the Math this time with the resolve to carry out his own plans, but he had had to give them up because of Yogananda's illness at Allahabad. Now there was this news from Hrishikesh. No reply to his telegram had come as yet from there. He was in a quandary, caught between monastic detach-ment and loving sense of responsibility for his brother-disciples. What form of Yoga would best enable him to remain serene amid these disturbing phenomena and to concentrate on Brahman? That was what he kept asking himself. It was to learn this Yoga that he had come to the Babaji.

But the Babaji was proving difficult and showed no inclina-tion to pass on to the Swami the knowledge he craved. This is how, later on, the Swami described the struggle that was going on in his mind at that time: "Associating with Pavhari Baba, I got to like him very much; and he also came to love me deeply. One day I reflected that I had not learnt any art for making this weak body strong, even though I had lived with Shri Ramakrishna for so many years. I had heard that Pavhari Baba knew the science of Hatha Yoga; so I thought that I would learn the practices of Hatha Yoga from him, and through them strengthen the body. You know, I have a dogged resolu-tion, and whatever I set my heart on, I always carry out. On the eve of the day on which I was to take initiation, I was lying on a cot thinking; and just then I saw the form of Shri Rama-krishna standing on my right, looking steadfastly at me, as if very much grieved. I had dedicated myself to him, and at the thought that I was taking another Guru I felt much ashamed and kept looking at him. Thus perhaps two or three hours passed, but no words escaped my mouth: then he disappeared all on a sudden. Seeing Shri Ramakrishna that night my mind became upset, so I postponed the idea of initiation from Pavhari Baba for the day. After a day or two, again the idea of initiation from Pavhari Baba arose in the mind—and again at night Shri Ramakrishna appeared, as on the previous occasion. So when, for several nights in succession, I had the vision of Shri Rama-krishna, I gave up the idea of initiation altogether, thinking that since every time I resolved on it, I was having such a vision, no good, but only harm, would come of it."

Thus it was Shri Ramakrishna who in the end triumphed. Long afterwards, the Swami composed a song in Bengali entitled "A Song I Sing to Thee" in which one finds a glimpse of this experience. It reads in part:

Like to the playing of a little child
Is every attitude of mine to Thee.
Even at times I dare be angered with Thee;
Even at times I'd wander far away;
Yet there, in greyest gloom of darkest night,
Yet there, with speechless mouth and tearful eyes,
Thou standest fronting me, and Thy sweet Face
Stoops down with loving look on face of mine.
Then, instantly, I turn myself to Thee,
And at Thy Feet I fall on bended knee.
I crave no pardon at Thy gentle hands,
For Thou art never angry with Thy son.
Who else with all my foolish freaks would bear!
Thou art my Master. Thou my soul's real mate.
Many a time I see Thee—I *am* Thee!
Ay! I am Thou, and Thou, my Lord, art I!

The impact of this vision of Shri Ramakrishna on the Swami's mind was profound. After this he understood the Master better. He clearly saw that Shri Ramakrishna was the fulfilment of spirituality; that one who had sat at his feet and been blessed by him, stood in need of no other spiritual help. On March 3, 1890, he wrote to Pramadababu, referring to Pavhari Baba:

But now I see the whole matter is the opposite of what was expected!

While I myself have come, a beggar, at his door, he turns round and wants to learn of me! This saint perhaps is not yet perfected—too much of rites, vows, observances, and too much of self-concealment. The ocean in its fullness cannot be contained within its shores, I am sure. So it is not good, I have decided, to disturb this sadhu for nothing, and very soon I shall ask leave of him to go. . . .

To no big person am I going any longer—"Remain, O mind, within yourself, go not to anybody else's door; whatever you seek, you shall obtain sitting at your ease, only seek for it in the privacy of your heart. There is the supreme Treasure, the philosophers' stone, and He can give whatever you ask for; for countless gems, O mind, lie strewn about the portals of His abode. He is the wishing-stone that confers boons at the mere thought." Thus says the poet Kamalakanta.

So now the great conclusion is that Ramakrishna has no peer; nowhere else in this world exists that unprecedented perfection, that wonderful kindness for all that does not stop to justify itself, such intense sympathy for man in bondage. Either he must be the Avatara [Incarnation] as he himself used to say, or else the ever-perfect divine man, whom the Vedanta speaks of as the free one, who assumes a body for the good of humanity. This is my conviction sure and certain; and the worship of such a divine man has been referred to by Patanjali in the aphorism, "Or the goal may be attained by meditating on the pure heart of a saint".

Never during his life did he refuse a single prayer of mine. Millions of offences has he forgiven me. Such great love even my parents never had for me. There is no poetry, no exaggeration in all this. It is the bare truth and every disciple of his knows it. In times of great danger, great temptation, I have wept in extreme agony with the prayer, "O God, save me", and no response has come; but this wonderful saint, or Avatara or whatever you may wish to call him, knew, through his power of insight into the human heart, of all my afflictions and removed them, in spite of myself, by bringing me to him.

The Swami was satisfied; no more was his mind distracted; and soon he was able to give himself over to single-minded meditation. Not that any of this indicates loss of faith in his Master: rather, it shows his aptitude for many-sided knowledge —an aptitude often viewed askance by his brother-monks. His position is clear from a letter to Akhandananda from Ghazipur in March 1890: "My motto is to learn to recognize good, no matter where I may come across it. This leads my Baranagore brothers to think that I may lose my devotion to the Guru [Shri Ramakrishna]. These are ideas of lunatics and bigots; for all Gurus are one, fragments and radiations of God, the Universal Guru." That the Swami's idea was only to learn Raja-Yoga from Pavhari Baba is clear from an earlier portion of the same letter. He writes, "Our Bengal is the land of Bhakti and Jnana. Yoga is scarcely mentioned there. What little there is, is but the queer breathing exercises of the Hatha-Yoga—which is nothing but a kind of gymnastics. Therefore I am staying with this wonderful Raja-Yogi—and he has given me some hope, too."

Premananda was one of those who mistook the Swami's devotion to Pavhari Baba for disloyalty to Shri Ramakrishna. He came to Ghazipur towards the middle of March, to persuade the Swami to go to Varanasi; moreover, he had set out in bad health. The Swami reproved him and sent him to Varanasi to look after Abhedananda. On March 31, he wrote to Pramadababu: "Another brother of mine [Premananda] has been with me, but has left for Abhedananda's place [at Varanasi]. The news of his arrival has not yet been received, and, his health being bad, I am rather anxious for his sake. I have behaved very cruelly towards him—that is, I have harassed him much to make him leave my company. There's no help, you see; I am so very weak-hearted, so much over-mastered by the distractions of love! Bless me that I may harden. What shall I say to you about the condition of my mind! Oh, it is as if hell-fire were burning there day and night! Nothing, nothing could I do yet! And this life seems muddled away in vain. I feel quite helpless as to what to do. The Babaji throws out honeyed words and keeps me from leaving. My brother-disciples must be thinking me very cruel and selfish. Oh, what can I do? Who will see deep down into my mind? Who will know how much I am suffering day and night?" The Swami was determined not to be overpowered any more by love for his monastic brothers. He had written to Akhandananda not to tell anyone at Baranagore that he was at Ghazipur.

The Swami, we have seen, was very anxious about Abheda-

nanda, who was ill at Hrishikesh. As soon as he had mentioned
the matter to his host, Gaganbabu, that gentleman had sent
Abhedananda his fare to enable him to come down to Varanasi.
The Swami had also asked Pramadababu to look after Abhedananda if he came down.

Ill and weak though he was, Abhedananda came alone to
Varanasi towards the end of March. But rumours of his illness
persisted, and so the Swami felt compelled to go to Varanasi
himself in the first week of April. This fitted in with his plans,
because he had had for some time the secret desire to practise
spiritual disciplines in the holy city. He hastened to Varanasi as
the guest of Pramadababu. After making every arrangement
for the care of Abhedananda, he settled himself in Pramadababu's garden and devoted his entire time to spiritual practices.
But soon he too fell ill, with influenza. Thanks to the care of
Pramadababu and the ailing Abhedananda, he recovered in a
couple of days. Then he served Abhedananda, who had a
severe relapse of fever for the second time.

While at Varanasi the Swami received news of the passing
away, on April 13, 1890, of Balaram Bose, the great devotee of
the Master. He was deeply grieved to hear it. The memories of
innumerable days of sweet companionship and of staunch
friendship crowded in on him and made him lament the more.
Pramadababu was struck to see a monk, a strict Vedantin, so
upset by death. But the Swami said, "Please do not talk that
way. We are not dry monks. What! do you think that because
a man is a sannyasi he has no heart!" And with the intention of
bringing solace to the bereaved family, who were all devotees of
the Master, and also to inquire into the affairs of the Math, the
Swami left Varanasi for Calcutta some time in the second week
of April.

Back at the Baranagore Math, the Swami was, as ever, the
guide and leader of the band of monks so dear to his heart. He
set their souls afire with the memory of the Master's words and
with rousing stories of his own life as a wanderer. His extensive
learning went to the intellectual development of his monastic
brothers. In giving up their university studies, they had lost

nothing of importance. Indeed, they were now admitted to a richer intellectual life, for the Swami was in himself an encyclo-paedia. Not that he set himself up as a teacher : he would simply talk for hours, sometimes continuing the same subject for days, as the others sat round him. There were no formal classes : he was just expressing himself.

The Swami's presence was sorely needed at the Math. Chiefly on his shoulders lay the responsibility of furthering his Master's mission; but circumstances were by no means favourable. There was not only the opposition of the social tradition, but the brotherhood was financially in a crisis. At times there was scarcity of food, and especially after the passing away of Balarambabu in April 1890, and of Surendranath Mitra on May 25 of the same year. Who was to bear the expenses? Where would the monks live? And where would the sacred relics of the Master be preserved? The Swami sought help from Girishbabu, Mahendranath, and others. They readily gave a helping hand; but they were not so rich. Moreover, at this time he was assailed by the thought that something should be done to perpetuate the memory of Shri Ramakrishna in Bengal, the land of his birth : for instance, a temple in his name built on the bank of the Ganga.

Caught in a vortex of untoward circumstances, and in great agitation of mind, the Swami sought the advice of Pramada-babu on May 26 in a long and appealing letter. It reads in part:

I have already told you at the outset that I am Ramakrishna's slave. Having laid my body at his feet, . . . I cannot disregard his behest. ..Now his behest to me was that I should devote myself to the service of the order of all-renouncing devotees founded by him, and in this I have to persevere, come what may, being ready to take heaven, hell, salvation, or anything that may happen to me.

His command was that his all-renouncing devotees should group themselves together, and I am entrusted with seeing to this. Of course, it matters not if any one of us goes out on visits to this place or that, but these shall be only visits. His own opinion was that absolute home-less wandering suited him alone who was perfected in the highest degree: before that state was reached, it was proper to settle some-where to dive down into practice. . . . So in pursuance of this his commandment, his group of sannyasins are now assembled in a dilapidated house at Baranagore, and two of his lay disciples, Babu Sureshchandra Mitra and Babu Balaram Bose, so long provided for their food and house-rent.

For various reasons, the body of Shri Ramakrishna had to be consigned to fire. There is no doubt that this act was very blame-worthy. His ashes, however, have been preserved, and if they be now properly enshrined somewhere on the bank of the Ganga I presume we shall be able, in some measure, to expiate the sin lying on our heads. These sacred remains, his seat, and his picture are every day worshipped in our Math in proper form; and it is known to you that a brother-disciple of mine, of Brahmin parentage, is occupied day and night with the task. The expenses of the worship used also to be borne by the two great souls mentioned above.

What greater regret can there be than this, that no memorial could yet be raised in this land of Bengal in the neighbourhood of the place where he lived his life of spiritual striving?—he by whose birth the race of the Bengalis has been sanctified and the land of Bengal hal-lowed; he who came on earth to save Indians from the worldly glamour of Western culture, and who therefore chose most of his all-renouncing monks from university men.

The two gentlemen mentioned above had a strong desire to have some land purchased on the banks of the Ganga and to see the sacred remains enshrined on it, with the disciples living there together; and Sureshbabu had offered a sum of Rs. 1,000 for the purpose, promising to give more; but for some inscrutable purpose of God he left this world last night! And the news of Balarambabu's death is already known to you.

Now there is no knowing where his disciples will go with his sacred remains and his seat (you know well people here in Bengal are profuse in their professions, but do not stir out an inch in practice). The disciples are sannyasins and are ready to depart forthwith anywhere their way may lie. But I, their servant, am in agony, and my heart is breaking to think that a small piece of land could not be had on which to install the remains of Bhagavan Ramakrishna.

It is impossible with a sum of Rs. 1,000 to secure land and raise a temple near Calcutta. Such a piece of land would cost at least from five to seven thousand.

You remain now the only friend and patron of Shri Ramakrishna's disciples. In the North-Western Province great indeed is your fame, your position, and your circle of acquaintance. I request you to consider, if you feel like it, the propriety of your seeing the matter through by raising subscriptions from well-to-do pious men known to you in your province. If you deem it proper to have some shelter erected on the banks of the Ganga in Bengal for Bhagavan Ramakrishna's sacred remains and for his disciples, I shall, with your leave, report myself to you; and I have not the slightest qualm about begging from door to door for this noble cause, for the sake of my Lord and his children.

If you ask: "You are a sannyasin, so why do you trouble over these desires?" I would then reply, I am Ramakrishna's servant, and I am willing even to steal and rob, if by doing so I can perpetuate his name in the land of his birth and spiritual struggle, and help even a little his disciples to practise his great ideals. . . . It would be the greatest pity if the memorial shrine could not be raised in the land of his birth and spiritual struggle. The condition of Bengal is pitiable. The people here cannot even dream what renunciation truly means—luxury and sensuality have so much eaten into the vitals of the race. May God send renunciation and unworldliness into this land! . . .

We can take it for granted that this letter did not bear fruit as expected. This is evident from the Swami's letter of June 4 to Pramadababu: "There is no doubt that your advice is very wise. It is quite true that the Lord's will will prevail. We also are spreading out here and there in small groups of two or three." The last remark refers to the monks' decision to lead a wandering life. With the passing away of the two chief financial supporters of the Math, it had become very difficult to meet the expenses.

Though Pramadababu's coldness must have been something of a disappointment to the Swami, we find him writing on July 6, 1890, to Saradananda, who was living with a brother-disciple at Almora: "Girishchandra Ghosh is bearing the expenses of the Math, and for the present the daily maintenance is being managed nicely." The buoyant tone of this letter is partly accounted for by this fact, partly by the Swami's now-improved health, and partly because a certain buoyancy was natural to him. In another letter to Saradananda, on July 15, he is holding out a definite hope: "The best thing is for you both to come down and live here. The widow of Mohindra Mookherjey is trying head and heart to build a *Math* for you, and S. [Surendranath] Mitra has left another thousand; so that you are very likely to have a beautiful place on the river soon." But nothing came of this.

However, even in the midst of training his brother-disciples and planning to raise a memorial to the Master, the wandering spirit seized the Swami anew. He was "longing for a flight to the Himalayas". Day by day he found himself being more and more drawn into a web of relationships and responsibilities, and calls on his time and attention were coming from all sides. All this was interfering with his following the life of the itinerant monk, and through just that way of life becoming more confident of himself and of the message he was to give. He hoped to find some place in Garhwal, on the Ganga, where he could give himself up to contemplation. He must solve the problems of the soul, and of the land he was born in. "I am longing for a flight to the Himalayas", he wrote in the July 6 letter cited above; "This time I shall not go to Pavhari Baba or any other saint—they divert one from his highest purpose. Straight up!" And in the July 15 letter, also cited, he wrote: "I leave this place before the letter reaches you . . . I have my own plans for the future and they shall be a secret."

After a three months' stay in the monastery, the Swami set out, in the third week of July 1890, with the same old determination—not to return until he had achieved his spiritual goal. This time he was to be away from the Math and his brother-disciples for years. He had brought Akhandananda down from Kashmir to accompany him. "You are my man!" he said to Akhandananda: "You have faith! Come, let us be off together."

To his brother-disciples the Swami said, "I shall not return until I acquire such realization that my very touch will transform a man." Before leaving Calcutta he went with Akhandananda to Ghusuree, a village across the Ganga, where he sought

16

out the Holy Mother to receive her blessings. He told her, "Mother, I shall not return until I have attained the highest Jnana." The Holy Mother blessed him in the name of the Master. She said, "My son, will you not see your own mother at home before leaving?" "Mother," he answered, "you alone are my mother." Seeing his spirit, the Holy Mother again blessed him. She blessed Akhandananda also, saying "My son, I am leaving my all [meaning the Swami] in your hands. You are familiar with life in the mountains: see that Naren has not to suffer for food."

On returning to the Math the Swami said to Akhandananda (whom he used to address out of affection as "Ganges"), "Look, Ganges, we shall not get down anywhere. We go straight to the North-West Province."

WANDERINGS IN THE HIMALAYAS

With his heart rid of attachment, and intent on his purpose,
the Swami was glad to be off once again to the Himalayas, in
the middle of July 1890. He planned to travel on foot along the
Ganga, to beg his food as an ordinary monk, and thus to make
the journey a spiritual exercise and adventure. From the
moment he left Calcutta he was happy. The solitude, the
country air, the seeing of new places, the meeting of new people,
and the abandoning of old impressions and worries delighted
him.

The first place at which he and Akhandananda halted was
Bhagalpur, which they reached in the first week of August. On
arrival there they betook themselves to the bank of the Ganga,
near the palace of Raja Shivachandra. They looked tired, but
their faces glowed with the fire of dispassion. The attention of
Kumar Nityananda Singh, one of the most prominent people
there, was at once drawn to them. He could see that they were
out of the ordinary; and a short conversation with them convinced him that this was so. Then they went to the house of
Babu Manmathanath Chowdhury. This gentleman was much
impressed by the Swami. It happened that one Mathuranath
Sinha, a pleader, was a guest in the same house, and so had an
opportunity of meeting and talking with the Swami. At a later
date both of these gentlemen wrote their reminiscences of the
Swami's visit at the request of one of his disciples. In his letter
of August 11, 1905, Mathuranath wrote:

About fifteen years ago I was at Bhagalpur, as the guest of Babu
Manmathanath Chowdhury. One morning I heard of a stir caused by
the arrival of two sannyasins. They were seen by Kumar Nityananda
Singh. Something led the Kumar to suppose that they were not of the
ordinary type of sadhu; and a short conversation confirmed his view
and disclosed the fact that they were highly educated and that one of

them, who was later known as Swami Vivekananda, was marvellously gifted. The very sight of them prepossessed me in their favour. I remembered to have seen one of them in my college days at Calcutta, as often leading the choir at the Sadharan Brahmo Samaj. My conversation with him covered much ground, including literature, philosophy and religion. The main topics were the last two. It seemed that learning and spirituality were the very air he breathed. I discovered that the soul of his teaching was an intense and unselfish patriotism with which he invested and vivified his subjects. This was an abiding characteristic with him. When I read the glowing descriptions of the success he had won at the Chicago Parliament of Religions, I felt that in him India had found her man.

Manmathababu, the Swami's host, was a staunch Brahmo, but became re-Hinduized by the Swami's eloquence and spiritual genius. The Swami explained to him the various aspects of Hindu religion and impressed him by his interpretations of the different episodes of Shri Krishna's life. In June 1906, Manmathababu wrote to a disciple of the Swami:

One morning in August of the year 1890, Swami Vivekananda with Swami Akhandananda came unexpectedly to my house. Thinking them to be ordinary sadhus, I did not pay much attention to them. We were sitting together after our noonday meal; and believing them to be ignorant, I did not enter into conversation with them, but began to read an English translation of a work on Buddhism. After a while, Swamiji asked me what book I was reading. In reply, I told him the title of the book and asked, "Do you know English?" He replied, "Yes, a little." Then I conversed with him on Buddhism, but after a short time I found out that he was a thousand times more learned than I. He quoted from many English works, and Babu Mathuranath Sinha of Danapur and myself were astonished at his learning and listened to him with rapt attention. . . .

One day Swamiji asked me if I practised any special Sadhanas, and we conversed on the practice of Yoga for a long time. From this I was convinced that he was not a common man, since what he said of Yoga was exactly the same as that which I had heard from the Swami Dayananda Sarasvati. Besides, he gave out many other important things on the subject which I had not heard before.

Then, to test his knowledge of Sanskrit, I brought out all the Upanishads that I had with me and questioned him on many abstruse passages from them. By his illuminating replies I found that his mastery of the scriptures was of an extraordinary kind. And the way in which he recited from the Upanishads was charming. Thus, being firmly convinced of his wonderful knowledge equally in English, Sanskrit and in Yoga, I was greatly drawn towards him. Though he stayed in my house for only seven days, I became so devoted to him that I resolved in my mind that by no means whatever would I let him go elsewhere. So I strongly urged him to live always at Bhagalpur.

Once I noticed him humming a tune to himself. So I asked him if he could sing. He replied, "Very little." Being pressed hard by us he sang, and what was my surprise to see that as in learning so in music he was wonderfully accomplished! Next day I asked him if he were willing that I invite some singers and musicians; he consented, and I asked many musicians, several of whom were *ostads*, or adepts in the art, to come. Believing that the music would end by nine or ten at the latest, I did not arrange supper for the guests. Swamiji sang without ceasing till two or three o'clock in the morning. All without exception were so charmed that they forgot hunger and thirst and all idea of time! None moved from his seat or thought of going home. Kailash-babu, who was accompanying the Swami [on Tabla?] in his songs, was forced to give up finally, for his fingers had become stiff and had lost all sensation. Such superhuman power I have never seen in anybody, nor do I expect to see it again. The next evening, all the guests of the previous night, and many others, presented themselves without any invitation. The player on the instrument also came, but Swamiji did not sing that evening; so everyone was disappointed.

Another day I proposed that I introduce him to all the rich men of Bhagalpur, and that I myself should take him to them in my carriage so that it would not be any trouble to him. But he declined and said, "It is not the sannyasi's Dharma to visit the rich!" His fiery renunciation made a deep impression on me. Indeed, in his company I was taught many lessons which have always remained with me as spiritual ideals.

From my boyhood, I was inclined to live in some solitary place and engage in spiritual practices. When I met Swamiji, this desire grew strong. I often told him, "Let us both go to Vrindavan, and depositing three hundred rupees for each of us in the temple of Shri Govindaji we shall have Govindaji's Prasad for the rest of our lives as food. Thus, without being a burden to anyone, we shall practise devotion day and night in a sequestered spot on the banks of the holy Jamuna!" In reply to this he said, "Yes, for a special temperament or nature, this scheme is no doubt good, but not for all", meaning not for himself, who had renounced everything. Amongst his many new ideas, the two most impressive to me were:

"Whatever of the ancient Aryan knowledge, intellect and genius is still left can be mostly found in those parts which lie near the banks of the Ganga. The further one goes from the Ganga, the less one sees them. This convinces one of the greatness of the Ganga as sung in our scriptures.

"The epithet mild Hindu, instead of being a word of reproach, ought really to point to our glory, as expressing greatness of character. For see how much moral and spiritual advancement, and how much development of the qualities of love and compassion, have to be acquired before one can get rid of the brutish force of one's nature, which actuates the ruining and the slaughter of one's brother-men for self-aggrandizement!"

Swamiji visited only two places while staying at Bhagalpur. The first occasion was when we went to see the holy man of Barari, the late Parvaticharan Mukhopadhyaya; the second was when we paid a visit to the Temple of Nathanagar, one of the holy places of the Jaina community; and there Swamiji talked with the Jaina Acharyas on their religion. He was much pleased with his visits, and was also delighted to see the beauty of the scenery on the banks of the Ganga. He remarked, "These spots are very suitable for spiritual practices."

It used to pain me very much when certain detractors criticized him for taking Sannyasa, because he had been born a Kayastha and not a Brahmana. They little knew what he was, and that birth had very little to do with the making of a saint. Of course, one has to look to the caste of a sadhu when his only qualification is the garb he wears; otherwise how can the Brahmanas reconcile themselves to offering worship to such a person, unless they have at least the consolation of knowing that the object of their veneration is a Brahmana by birth? The Swami was born with the Brahmanical consciousness, and thus is ten times more a Brahmana than he whose sole claim to Brahmana-hood is the fact that he was born of Brahmana parents. And after all, who can resist worshipping what is of true worth and saintliness!

Swamiji well knew in his heart that I would not willingly or easily let him depart from Bhagalpur. So, one day when I was away on some important business, he grasped this opportunity of leaving, after

taking farewell of those at home. When I came back I made a strenuous search for him, but could discover no clue of him anywhere. And
yet, why should I have thought that my will should prevail? Why
should Swamiji be like a frog in the well, when his field of work was
the whole wide world?

He had expressed to me his intention of going to Badrikashrama.
Therefore, after he had left Bhagalpur, I even went up to Almora in
the Himalayas in search of him. There Lala Badri Sah told me that
he had left Almora some time before; and knowing that he must have
already journeyed a long way in the direction of the Northern Tirtha,
I was compelled to give up my idea of following him.

It was my heart's desire to bring him once more to Bhagalpur after
his return from America, but he could not come, having then, perhaps,
very little leisure or opportunity to do so.

The reconversion of Manmathababu to the Hindu faith gives
a hint, by implication, of the powerful influence the Swami's
words and personality were capable of exerting. Before leaving
Bhagalpur he had discussions with the Jaina teachers concerning
religious beliefs. He regarded the Jaina religion as a part of the
Sanatana Dharma itself, and saw its kinship with Buddhist
philosophy.

Manmathababu enjoyed the company of the Swamis, and
pressed them to stay on, but after spending about a week in this
manner, they suddenly left Bhagalpur. Their next halt was at
Vaidyanath, where Akhandananda had not gone before. It
was his wish that they should go there to visit the shrine of
Vaidyanath Shiva. Here the Swami met Babu Rajnarayan
Bose, the venerable old Brahmo preacher, veteran social reformer, and national leader. Born in 1826, this fiery old man
had, in his youth, been enamoured of Western culture, and had
started to hate everything Indian. But after the death of his
parents, his faith in religion was restored, and he embraced
Brahmoism, which he did not regard as separate from Hinduism. When in his mid-thirties, he started a movement in Bengal
to promote national feeling among the educated. He preached
that Indians should speak and write in their mother tongue,
wear their national dress, and eat the food of their own country.
In his Society he did not tolerate the use of the English lan-

guage, English dress, or English food. His hatred of the English language had gone so far that he would fine any member one pice for the inadvertent use of one English word.

The Swami must have known of the old man's eccentricities, for he had instructed Akhandananda beforehand not to let it be known that he (the Swami) knew English. He spoke eloquently in Bengali, and with a brilliance of thought which charmed Rajnarayanbabu. In the course of conversation, many ideas arose that required the use of English words, as for example "plus"; but the Swami got over the difficulty, making the plus sign by crossing his fingers. According to another version, it was Rajnarayanbabu who used the word "plus" by mistake, and thinking that the Swami might not have understood the meaning, made the sign by crossing his fingers. The Swamis were much amused at the behaviour of this old man, but suppressed their laughter until the visit was over. Not once did Rajnarayanbabu dream that the monk before him was as fluent in the foreign tongue as in his mother tongue; and was a graduate of Calcutta University.

Akhandananda had a hard time refraining from letting out the secret, for he delighted to extol the Swami. Much later when the latter had become famous throughout India, Rajnarayanbabu came to know who it was that had visited him years ago. Recalling his meeting with the Swami, he exclaimed, "What! not for an instant did I imagine, when he talked with me, that he knew English. He must indeed be a wonderful man." After spending the night with him, the monks left Vaidyanath.

They next went to Ghazipur, and from there to Varanasi, where they stayed with Pramadababu for a few days. The Swami spent hours in discussion of scriptural topics with this friend of his; but, being impatient to see the snow-capped Himalayas, he did not stay for long. On the eve of his departure he said to Pramadababu, in the presence of many others, "I am now leaving Kashi, and shall not return until I have burst on society like a bomb-shell; and it will follow me like a dog." And it is true, he did not return to that city until he had stirred the world with new modes of thought and had resurrected the spirit of the Indian sages.

Despite the Swami's eagerness to go straight to the Himalayas, Akhandananda said to him, "Swamiji, you must see the Mahant, Janakibar Saran of Ayodhya. You will find him a great man. He is full of Bhakti." The Swami answered, "What do I care for all this nonsense! I am through now. It will only mean more and more delay. Let me go to the Himalayas." However, Akhandananda bought two tickets for Ayodhya, and they both boarded the train for that place. The Swami did not speak a word; from which Akhandananda understood that the Swami was not pleased with the detour. Nevertheless, at Ayodhya, he took him next day and introduced him to the Mahant—a Vaishnava of great renunciation and devotion. The Mahant was also a Sanskrit and Persian scholar, and had charge of a temple there with large estates. He cordially welcomed the monks to his Ashrama, and they talked a great deal on Bhakti. The Swami was much impressed with the Mahant's learning and spiritual fervour, and said to his brother-monk, "I am glad you brought me here. I have seen a man, a real holy man."

Next, one sees the Swami and his brother-disciple as guests of Babu Ramaprasanna Bhattacharya in Naini Tal, which they had reached by walking through the foothills. They were there for six days. Then they started for Almora, on their way to Badrikashrama. They determined to do the whole distance on foot, without a pice, "eating what chance might bring". While on the way, the Swami asked Akhandananda to go by the foot-path, and said that he would go by a short-cut through the forest alone, and meet him later. On the third day they stopped for the night under an old peepul tree, where the Koshi met another mountain river named Suial. This place, known as Kakrighat, is about fourteen and a half miles from Almora by road. The Swami said to his companion, "This place is charming. What a wonderful spot for meditation!" After bathing in the river, the Swami sat under the tree, absorbed in deep meditation for a long time. Later, returning to normal consciousness, he said to Akhandananda: "Oh, Gangadhar! I have just passed through one of the greatest moments of my life. Here under this peepul tree one of the greatest problems of my life has been solved. I have found the oneness of the macrocosm with the microcosm. In this microcosm of the body everything that is there [in the macrocosm], exists. I have seen the whole universe within an atom." For that whole day the Swami was in a high state of mind and discussed his realization with his companion. The fragments he wrote in Bengali in his notebook then, read:

In the beginning was the Word etc.

The microcosm and the macrocosm are built on the same plan. Just as the individual soul is encased in the living body, so is the universal Soul in the Living Prakriti [Nature]—the objective universe. Shivā [i.e. Kali] is embracing Shiva: this is not a fancy. This covering of the one [Soul] by the other [Nature] is analogous to the relation between an idea and the word expressing it: they are one and the same; and it is only by a mental abstraction that one can distinguish them. Thought is impossible without words. Therefore, in the beginning was the Word etc.

This dual aspect of the Universal Soul is eternal. So what we perceive or feel is this combination of the Eternally Formed and the Eternally Formless.

This realization of his seems to be reflected in the lectures he later on gave in the West under the title, "Cosmos—the Macrocosm and the Microcosm".

When the monks were about two miles from Almora, having gone for many hours without food, they sat down on the roadside opposite a Muslim cemetery. The Swami almost fainted with hunger, and sank to the ground from sheer exhaustion. Akhandananda went to fetch water at a distance. The keeper of the cemetery, a fakir named Zulfikar Ali, lived in a hut near by. Happening to see the plight of the Swami, he offered him a cucumber, which was the only thing in the shape of food that he could provide. The Swami asked the fakir to put the cucumber into his mouth, saying that he was too weak to do so himself. The man remonstrated, saying, "Holy sir, I am a

Muslim!" "That does not matter at all," said the Swami with a smile; "are we not all brothers?" After having been fed by the fakir, the Swami felt refreshed. Speaking of this incident, he used to say, "The man really saved my life: I had never felt so exhausted."[1]

Seven years later, when he visited Almora again as the world-famous Swami Vivekananda, he was given a grand reception, and taken in procession through the town. As this was going on, the Swami happened to see the fakir peering at him from the crowd. The fakir had forgotten the Swami, but the latter recognized him at once. Telling those who were with him of the above incident when the man had practically saved his life, the Swami gave him some money in token of his grateful remembrance.

The long journey from the plains to Almora had been more than interesting. Amid the stillness and beauty of the hills the Swami found a quietude of heart and mind that he had rarely known before. The mountain air invigorated him; and in spite of physical weariness caused by the long trek and the want of food, this first part of his tour in the Himalayas was for him the acme of happiness.

The two monks arrived in Almora just before the end of August 1890. Akhandananda took the Swami to the garden of Amba Dutt, and went to inform Saradananda and Kripananda (Vaikunthanath Sannyal, a lay disciple of the Master) of their arrival. These two brother-disciples had been in the Himalayas for some time, and the Swami had written to them in July from Calcutta. When they learnt of the Swami's arrival, they, along with their host Lala Badri Sah, hastened to Amba Dutt's garden. They were half-way to the place when they met the Swami himself coming to see them. Lala Badri Sah welcomed the Swami, and took him to his house.

Here the Swami had a long discussion with one Shri Krishna Joshi, the Sheristadar (a Government official), on the need of

[1] In July 1971, a Vivekananda Resting Hall was built by the efforts of Mr. and Mrs. Boshi Sen of Almora, on the place where the fakir had fed the Swami with the cucumber.

becoming a sannyasi. He spoke of the glory of the life of renunciation, which to his mind was the ideal of all religions. He presented his arguments eloquently, backed up by reference to his personal experience. The gentleman was struck with the young monk's learning, and bowed down before him. During this visit, at the persistent request of the local people, the Swami relieved a man possessed by a demi-god.

The Swami lived for a few days at the house of Lala Badri Sah, and then left his devoted host and beloved fellow monks. Finding a solitary cave above a mountain village, he entered it to perform the most severe forms of spiritual practice day and night. He determined to find Truth. And there in the silence, with no one to disturb his meditation, he had higher and higher spiritual illuminations until his face shone with a celestial fire. And then, at the very climax of all his spiritual exercises, instead of abiding in the ultimate of personal bliss which he expected to do, he felt the impetus to work, and this, as it were, forced him out from his spiritual practice. About this strange period through which the Swami passed, Akhandananda said in later years: "It seemed as though every time the Swami desired to retire into the life of silence and pure monasticism, he was compelled to give it up by the pressure of circumstances. He had a mission to fulfil, and the very essence of his nature would force him into the realization of this line of work."

After spending some days in this manner, the Swami returned to Badri Sah's house, where tragic news awaited him. A telegram had come from his brother telling of the suicide of one of his sisters. A letter which followed gave the details. This caused the Swami great anguish of heart; yet even in this grief he saw other realities. Through this perspective of personal woe he seems to have been rudely awakened to the great problems of Indian womanhood.

The Swami was much impressed with Badri Sah's devotion and hospitality, and remarked that he had rarely seen a devotee like him. After staying at his house for a few days, the Swami longed to go into Garhwal, which would be wilder country and further into the Himalayas, in order to practise spiritual disciplines. His inner predicament was a peculiar one: a mingling of the domestic and the monastic consciousness: but the latter prevailed. He left Almora for Garhwal on September 5, with Saradananda, Akhandananda, Kripananda and a coolie to carry their load. On the way to Badrikashrama the party reached Karnaprayag, where they were nicely entertained by a doctor of the Government hospital. Saradananda and Kripananda had severe stomach trouble, but fortunately it was soon put right with the help of the doctor.

After leaving Karnaprayag, the Swami and Akhandananda fell ill, and they were all compelled to halt in a roadside rest-house for about a week. They came to know that the road leading to Badrikashrama and Kedarnath had been closed by the Government on account of famine in that part. This made the Swami cancel his plan of going to Badrikashrama, and the party proceeded towards Srinagar in Garhwal State. The waterfalls, streams, wild forests, and the peace and solitude of these parts, with occasional glimpses of the eternal snows, gladdened the Swami's heart.

At Rudraprayag, on their way, they met a Bengali monk, Purnananda by name, with whom they spent the night. Here the Swami and Akhandananda again had an attack of fever, this time worse than before; but fortunately, they met the Sadar Amin (a Government official), named Badri Dutt Joshi, who was on tour and had camped there. Seeing the suffering of the two monks he gave them some Ayurvedic medicines, and when they were sufficiently improved, sent them by Dandi (a chair-like device carried on the shoulders of coolies) to Srinagar, nine miles off, where they gradually recovered. Begging their food, meditating, having religious discussions, and in spite of recurring illness, they had yet covered the 120 miles from Almora in a little over two weeks.

At Srinagar the monks dismissed the coolies and took up their abode in a lonely hut on the banks of the Alakananda river, in which Swami Turiyananda had once lived. Here they stayed about a month and a half, living on Madhukari (food procured by begging from house to house, rather as a bee collects honey from different flowers). During these travels and specially here, the Swami instructed his brother-disciples in the Upanishads. The days passed happily in prayer, meditation and scriptural study. At Srinagar the Swami met a schoolmaster, a Vaishya by caste, who was a recent convert to Christianity. So eloquently did the Swami speak to him of the glories of Hinduism that he longed to return to the Hindu fold. He became greatly attached to the monks and often entertained them in his house.

From Srinagar they moved to Tehri. As they went they reached a village when it was quite dark. They were hungry and thoroughly exhausted, since they had not been able to get anything on the way. They took shelter in a dilapidated rest-house, and went into the village in search of food; but the villagers did not respond in spite of repeated calls. There is a saying: "There's no giver like a Garhwali (a resident of Garhwal); but he does not give anything unless he is threatened with a stick." Akhandananda remembered this; so, waving their staffs and shouting at the top of their voices, they threatened the villagers until food was brought. The monks had begged mildly at first, but that had not worked. Now the villagers meekly came forward with foodstuffs and placed them before the monks.

At Tehri they found two rooms specially built for wandering monks, in a deserted garden. Here on the bank of the Ganga they lived by begging, and spent most of their time in spiritual practices. They became acquainted with Babu Raghunath Bhattacharya, the Dewan of the Tehri State and an elder brother of Pandit Haraprasad Shastri of Calcutta. At his request the Swami stayed with him for a few days. The Swami was very eager to find a suitable place for meditation on the bank of the Ganga. The Dewan offered to help, and had a hut built for them at Ganeshprayag, at the confluence of the Ganga and Vilangana rivers. But Akhandananda had a severe relapse of bronchitis. The local physician examined him and advised him to go to the plains, since the mountain air was not suiting his health and winter was approaching. Though everything was settled for going to Ganeshprayag, the Swami immediately

changed his plans and went at once to the Dewan to explain
the reason for the change. He said that he would avail himself
of the latter's kindness sometime in the future. The Dewan gave
him a letter of introduction to the Civil Surgeon of Dehra Dun,
and provided two ponies to take the Swami and Akhandananda
to Mussoorie, and money for their expenses on the way. So,
for the sake of his brother-disciple, whom Shri Ramakrishna
had entrusted to his care, the Swami set out for Dehra Dun
with his three brother-disciples, after some 15 or 20 days' stay
at Tehri.

Leaving Tehri, the monks went to Rajpur via Mussoorie.
Near Rajpur, some six miles from the broad valley, they were
surprised to see a sannyasi walking near them. He looked like
Turiyananda. When they went closer they cried out together,
"Yes, it is Hari." There was great rejoicing at this unexpected
meeting with their beloved brother-disciple. They all went
down to Dehra Dun, where Akhandananda was taken to have
his chest examined by Dr. Maclaren, the Civil Surgeon, to
whom the Swami had brought the letter of introduction. The
patient was found to be suffering from a slight attack of bronchitis. The doctor advised him not to return to the hills, but to
live in the plains, taking precautions and having medical
treatment.

Some sort of shelter had therefore to be found out for
Akhandananda in Dehra Dun. The Swami went from house
to house to ask for shelter, but no one was prepared to take
them in. Ultimately, after much effort, they found shelter in the
newly-built, but incomplete, house of a businessman. They
somehow accommodated themselves there, but it was not good
for the patient to be in that damp house. While they were
searching for another place, they fortunately met one Hridaybabu, a class-mate of the Swami in the General Assembly's
Institution in Calcutta. He was a Christian convert, and employed as a school-teacher. He willingly agreed to accommodate
Akhandananda in his house; but Akhandananda, so long accustomed to Hindu modes of life, revolted against the Christian
ways in this friend's house. He therefore returned to the pre-

vious house to live with his brother-monks. The Swami again went about the town in search of a suitable place, enquiring at many houses and saying, "My brother-disciple is ill. Can you give him a little space in your house and arrange for suitable diet for him?" He received cold replies and excuses. At last Pandit Ananda Narayan, a Kashmiri Brahmin and a pleader of the town, took charge of the sick monk. He rented a small house for him and provided suitable diet and warm clothing.

At Hridaybabu's house, the Swami once had a hot discussion with some Christian preachers. The Swami spoke to them of the higher criticism of the Bible, something they had never heard of. The Christian missionaries could not withstand the force of his arguments and left the place. The Swami afterwards begged his Christian friend to excuse him for conducting such a discussion in his house against the Christian faith.

The Swami remained in Dehra Dun for about three weeks, and then, advising Akhandananda to go to a friend's house at Allahabad, and leaving Kripananda to look after him, left for Hrishikesh with the others. Kripananda joined them later, when Akhandananda left for Saharanpur on his way to Allahabad. At Saharanpur Akhandananda's host Bankubihari Chatterjee, a pleader, advised him to go to Meerut instead of Allahabad, to the house of his friend, Dr. Trailokyanath Ghosh, the Assistant Civil Surgeon. Akhandananda accordingly went with a letter of introduction to Meerut and was under this doctor's treatment for a month and a half.

Hrishikesh, where the Swami now found himself again, is a place hallowed by Hindu legend and story. It is a picturesque spot—and was then a secluded one—, situated at the foot of the Himalayas, in a valley surrounded by hills and half-circled by the Ganga. The whole place is monastic; the very air is pure and holy. Thousands of Yogis and sannyasis of diverse sects assemble there every year to spend the winter in reading the scriptures and practising Yoga and meditation. In those days it was almost a jungle. Here and there were thatched cottages put up by the sadhus to live in.

The Swami and his brother-disciples lived for some time in a hut erected by themselves, near the temple of Chandeshwar Mahadev. They lived by begging. Again the Swami wanted to engage in severe spiritual practices, but before he could plunge into them he fell ill. One day his brother-disciples had gone into the jungle to cut bamboo, in order to enlarge their hut. When they returned they found that the Swami had high fever and diphtheria. He grew worse and worse until his brethren became extremely fearful. His pulse sank low as time went on, and his body became cold. Then his pulse seemed to have stopped: it appeared that his last moments had come. He lay unconscious on a couple of rough blankets laid on the ground. His brothers, overwhelmed with grief and anxiety, did not know what to do. They lost all hope and started to weep. In those days no medical attention could be had there. Turiyananda chanted some hymns. While they were in this predicament, a sadhu, clad in a woollen blanket, came from somewhere near and said, "Why are you all weeping?" He took from his wallet some honey and some powdered peepul, and mixing them together, forced the medicine into the Swami's mouth. This seemed to be the one remedy, a godsend to be sure. Soon after, the Swami regained consciousness and his body became warm.

After a while he opened his eyes and attempted to speak. One of the brother-disciples put his ear near the Swami's mouth and heard the words: "Cheer up, my boys. I shall not die." Gradually he recovered. Later he told them that, during that apparently unconscious state, he had seen that he had a particular mission in the world to fulfil, and that until he had accomplished that mission, he would have no rest. Indeed, his brother-disciples noticed such a superabundant spiritual energy welling up in him that it seemed that he could hardly contain it. He was restless to find a proper field for its expression.

The experience that the brother-disciples went through on his occasion made them realize what the Swami was to them. The Master had left them: if he also should die, what would become of the Order? Where would they be? Without him,

17

they would be alone in the world, and the world would be a wilderness.

In the meantime, Babu Raghunath Bhattacharya, the Dewan of Tehri State, along with the Maharaja of Tehri, passed through Hrishikesh on his way to Ajmer. He learnt of the illness of a Bengali Swami. Guessing that this must be the sadhu who had recently been his guest at Tehri, the Dewan went to see him. He advised the Swami to go to a particular Hakim (Mohammedan doctor) in Delhi, and gave him a letter of introduction. He also gave the party some money for the repair of their hut.

From Hrishikesh the Swami went alone to Hardwar for hard spiritual practice. Brahmananda was at this time engaged in spiritual practices at Kankhal. Hearing of the arrival of the Swami, he came to see him at Hardwar. Later on the other brother-disciples at Hrishikesh joined them at Hardwar. Then they went together to Saharanpur, and stayed at the house of Bankubihari Chatterjee. Here they learnt that Akhandananda had gone to Meerut; so they immediately set out for that place.

At Meerut they found Akhandananda at the house of Dr. Trailokyanath Ghosh. This was about the second week of November, that is, after the time of year when Mother Kali is offered special worship. (According to another view, based on Swami Akhandananda's letters of November 20 and December 5, 1890, Swamiji and party did not reach Meerut earlier than the first week of December. In the former letter Akhandananda had written to Shivananda about Swamiji and his party: "I came alone from Dehra Dun; since then I don't know anything about them, nor do they know anything about me." Even in Akhandananda's letter of December 5, there is no news of the party's arrival at Meerut.)

Akhandananda was very happy to see the Swami, and the other brother-monks; but he was dismayed to see the ravages that illness had made on their leader. "I had never seen him thinner," Akhandananda said; "he was worn to a shadow. It seemed that he had not as yet recovered from his terrible illness at Hrishikesh." The Swami stayed at the house of the doctor with Swami Akhandananda, while the others went to stay with one Yajneshwarbabu, who later on embraced the monastic life and became Swami Jnanananda, the well-known leader of the Bharat Dharma Mahamandal. After staying at the doctor's house for about a fortnight, the Swami and Akhandananda went to stay at a Shethji's garden-house, where the other brother-disciples also joined them. The Shethji was a friend of Yajneshwarbabu, and gave them everything they needed. The monks cooked their own food, and spent their time in spiritual practices. The Swami was still taking medicine to help him recuperate from the recent illness, and the frequent relapses of fever that he had had since leaving Almora. The austere life he had led during his wanderings, and the haphazard eating, had weakened him greatly; but here he was growing stronger.

At this time Advaitananda, also on pilgrimage, came to Meerut; and the Shethji's garden was transformed into a second Baranagore Math, with the Swami, Brahmananda, Saradananda, Turiyananda, Akhandananda, Advaitananda and Kripananda living there. They passed their time in meditation, prayer, singing devotional songs, and study of the scriptures and other literature in Sanskrit and English. In the evening they used to go for a walk, and watch the sports and games of the troops on the parade ground. At the Swami's bidding, Akhandananda used to bring books for him from the local library. Once the Swami asked him to bring the works of Sir John Lubbock. Accordingly Akhandananda brought them, one volume each day. The Swami would finish a volume in a day and return it the next day, saying that he had read it. The librarian argued with Akhandananda that the Swami had surely returned the volume without reading it, and remarked that the latter was only making a show of reading. Hearing of this, the Swami himself went to the librarian and said, "Sir, I have mastered all those volumes: if you have any doubt, you may put any question to me about them." The librarian then examined the monk, and by doing so became fully satisfied. Great was his astonishment. Later Akhandananda asked Swamiji how he could do it. The Swami replied, "I never read a book word by word. I read sentence by sentence, sometimes even paragraph by paragraph, in a sort of kaleidoscopic form."

While in the Shethji's garden-house, Akhandananda brought to the Swami an Afghan gentleman who was a refugee Sardar and a relative of the Amir Abdar Rahaman of Afghanistan. In coming to see the Swami this gentleman took the same care as Hindus themselves do when approaching a sadhu. He had performed his ablutions, and then came with a basket of sweet-meats in his hand, to present to the Swami. During his talk he referred to a well-known Muslim fakir of Swat. Many Bengali gentlemen and others also came to the garden to hear religious discourse from the Swami's lips.

After staying for some weeks at Meerut the Swami again grew restless. He remembered the free, stern life of the ascetics in the Hardwar and Hrishikesh areas. "I saw many great men in Hrishikesh", said the Swami in later life: "One that I remember was a man who seemed to be mad. He was coming nude down the street, with boys pursuing him and throwing stones at him. The whole man was bubbling over with laughter, while blood was streaming down his face and neck. I took him and bathed his wound, putting ashes (made by burning a piece of cotton cloth) on it to stop the bleeding. And all the time, with peals of laughter, he told me of the fun the boys and he had been having, throwing the stones. 'So the Father plays', he said. Many of these holy men hide in order to guard themselves against intrusion. People are a trouble to them. One had human bones strewn about his cave and gave it out that he lived on corpses. Another threw stones, and so on." The Swami continued, "The sannyasi needs no longer to worship or to go on pilgrimage or perform austerities. What, then, is the motive of all this going from pilgrimage to pilgrimage, shrine to shrine, and austerity to austerity? He is acquiring merit, and giving it to the world!"

Such a life was calling the Swami, if not in all the severity of its outward form, at least in its spirit, and in its desire for realization and for solitude. His longing for Self-realization became so great that his brother-disciples were struck with awe.

At Meerut the Swami told them that he had decided on the immediate course he was going to follow, and that he already knew his mission. He had received the command of God regarding his future, and was going to leave them in order to become a solitary monk.

On the eve of the Swami's departure, Akhandananda said to him, "It was for you that I cancelled my plan of going to Central Asia, and came to Baranagore Math; and now you are going away leaving me here!" The Swami replied, "The company of the brother-disciple is a great hindrance to spiritual practices. Just see, it was because of your illness that I could not practise any spiritual disciplines at Tehri. It is not possible to perform any spiritual disciplines, unless the Maya [bondage] of the brother-disciples is given up. Whenever I plan to practise disciplines, the Master puts some obstacle in my way. Now I shall go alone. I shall not tell anyone where I am staying." Akhandananda said, "Even if you go to Patal [the nether regions], I shall hunt you out."

And so, one morning in the latter part of January 1891, the Swami left his devoted brethren and journeyed on to Delhi by himself.

15

IN HISTORIC RAJPUTANA

The Swami, with his scanty belongings and regal bearing, came to Delhi, for ages the capital of India under Hindu and Mogul dynasties, and the scene of numerous historic events. The royal sepulchres and palaces, the sites of deserted capitals, the ruins of imperial greatness, make Delhi the ancient Rome of India. Its very atmosphere is imperial. The crisp winter air, the grandeur of the place, its noble history, filled him with physical and spiritual elation. He put up at the residence of Seth Shyamaldas, where he was received with open arms.

Here in Delhi he went everywhere and saw everything. The ruins of royal and imperial greatness impressed on the young monk the ephemeral nature of all human glory and the permanence of the spirit, which neither comes nor goes. At the same time, the historian in him found in Delhi the symbol of the immortal glory of the Indian people, with its grand, composite culture.

After about ten days, the other brother-disciples at Meerut left for Delhi, where they inadvertently met the Swami again. The brethren were no doubt happy to meet him, but the Swami was not pleased. He said to them, "Brothers, I told you that I wanted to be left alone. I said that I had work to do. I asked you not to follow me. Now I insist that you obey me. I do not want to be followed. With this I leave Delhi. And he who follows me, does so at his peril; for I am going to lose myself to all old associations. Where the Spirit leads, there I shall wander, no matter whether it is a forest or a desert waste, a mountain region or a densely populated city. I am off." The brother-disciples, stunned by his resolve, said, "We did not know that you were staying here. We have come to Delhi to see the old imperial capital. Here we heard of a Swami Vividisha-nanda, an English-speaking monk, and we were curious to see him. It is by accident that we have met you."

It appears that the Swami had introduced himself in Delhi as Swami Vividishananda, which, as we have seen, was the name taken at the time of his formal initiation into Sannyasa. But his brother-disciples seem to have almost forgotten the name. To them he was always their beloved "Naren". Nor, to their knowledge, had the Swami used the name openly before. Thus it was that when they went to meet Vividishananda, they found to their surprise that he was none other than the Swami. Even after this parting from his brothers, the Swami lingered on in Delhi for a few days more. Though they lived apart, they gathered at the Sethji's house to take their food.

One day Dr. Hemchandra Sen, a well-known Bengali physician of Delhi, spoke slightingly about the Swami to Akhandananda. A few days earlier, when the Swami had consulted him about his tonsils, the doctor's attitude had been distinctly antagonistic. The doctor now, however, expressed to Akhandananda a desire to meet the Swami again. One evening many professors of the local college assembled at the doctor's house, where the Swami and his two brother-disciples had also been invited. A great discussion ensued. Many questions were asked, and the Swami with his erudition impressed them all. As a result, Dr. Sen was attracted to the small group of monks. The following day he invited them to a feast at his house.

Shortly afterwards the brother-disciples left Delhi one after another. Saradananda went to Etawah; and because he was ill, Kripananda went with him. Brahmananda and Turiyananda left for the Punjab; Akhandananda made for Vrindavan; and the Swami set out for Rajputana (now Rajasthan). His brothers knew in which direction their Leader had gone, but they dared not follow him. They knew that his soul was in the grip of a great restlessness to fulfil the mission for which he had been born; they knew that it was under the guidance of the Master, by the will of the Mother, that he wanted to be left alone. So, with moist eyes and anguish in their hearts, they had bidden him farewell and sought his blessings. But the Swami himself was glad to cut this last attachment of his soul—his love for his brother-disciples. He remembered the words of the *Dhamma-pada*:

> Go forward without a path!
> Fearing nothing, caring for nothing,
> Wander alone, like the rhinoceros!
> Even as the lion, not trembling at noises,
> Even as the wind, not caught in the net,
> Even as the lotus leaf, unstained by the water,
> Do thou wander alone, like the rhinoceros!

These words upheld and inspired him. Renouncing all ties, loosing all bonds, breaking down all limitations, destroying all sense of fear, the Swami went forth, even as the rhinoceros— towards Alwar, in the beautiful and historic land of Rajputana.

Rajputana! What memories of heroes and chivalry the very name awakens! The Indian heart throbs at the mention of it. In Rajputana, Indian history is condensed, as it were. Here reigned dynasty upon dynasty of those Rajput princes who defied even Akbar; here were women each of whom was as a queen. And Alwar is the pearl of Rajputana: surrounded by hills, and with a back-drop of rugged peaks in the distant west, it is lovely to look on. The palaces are of marble; the land is fertile; and the landscape pleasing.

One morning at the beginning of February 1891, the Swami alighted at Alwar railway station. Walking along the road, fringed with gardens and verdant fields, and passing a row of fine houses, he arrived at the State dispensary. A Bengali gentleman, Gurucharan Laskar, was standing there: he proved to be the doctor in charge. The Swami enquired in Bengali whether there was a place where sannyasis could put up. The doctor, impressed by the remarkable appearance of the monk, bowed low before him, and joyfully accompanied him to the bazaar where he showed him a room above one of the shops. "This is for sannyasis, sir," he said: "Will you make yourself comfortable here for the present?"... "Gladly!" responded the Swami. After seeing to the Swami's immediate needs, the doctor hastened to the house of a Muslim friend, a teacher of Urdu and Persian in the High School, and said, "O Moulavi Sahib!

A Bengali dervish [wandering sadhu] has just arrived. Come immediately and see him. I have never seen such a Mahatma [great soul] before! Please talk with him while I finish my work, and I shall join you presently." Both hurried to the bazaar. Taking their shoes off, they entered the bare room in which the Swami had arranged his belongings, consisting of a few books tied up in a blanket, a piece of yellow cloth, a Kamandalu, and a staff. They saluted him with reverence.

The Swami called the Moulavi Sahib to his side and discoursed with much love on religious matters. Of the Koran, he said, "There is one thing very remarkable about the Koran. Even to this day, it exists as it was found eleven hundred years ago. It retains its pristine purity and is free from interpolations."

Gurucharan, on returning to his dispensary, spoke to everyone of the "great monk" who had come. The Moulavi likewise informed his Muslim friends. Soon a concourse of people had gathered. The Swami's room and the verandas were crowded. His discourse was interspersed with Urdu songs, Hindi Bhajana, Bengali Kirtana, and with songs of those great devotees, Vidyapati, Chandidas and Ramprasad. Sometimes he recited from the Vedas and Upanishads, or from the Bible, or from the Puranas. He illustrated his teaching of the scriptures with inspiring stories from the lives of Buddha, Shankara, Ramanuja, Guru Nanak, Chaitanya, Tulsidas, Kabir, Ramakrishna and others.

In a few days the number of devotees and admirers had become so great that it was arranged for him to stay at the house of Pandit Shambhunathji, a retired engineer of Alwar State. Here the Swami was able to regulate his life. He remained alone in meditation from early morning until nine, when he emerged from his room to find some twenty or thirty people of all castes, creeds and classes awaiting him. Some were Sunnis and Shiahs of the Muslim fold, some were Shaivites and Vaishnavites; some were men of wealth and position and learning, while others were illiterate and poor. The Swami treated them all alike and answered their questions until noon. They were free to ask him what they liked. If one of them asked an irrelevant question, such as "Maharaj, to what caste does your body belong?", even while he was explaining a metaphysical point, he would immediately reply without vexation, "It is Kayastha!" Some monks would have evaded a direct reply, hoping to be taken for a Brahmin; but the Swami was above all thought of caste. Or another would ask him, "Sir, why do you wear Gerua [ochre cloth]?" He would reply, "Because it is the garb of beggars. Poor people would ask me for alms if I were to wear white clothes. Being a beggar myself, most times I do not have even a single pice to give them. It causes me pain to have to refuse one who begs of me. But seeing my ochre cloth, they understand that I also am a beggar. They would not think of begging from a beggar." This is an original and touching reason for wearing the sannyasi's robe. The popular explanation is, "Without Bhek [distinguishing garb of renunciation], no Bhiksha [alms] is to be had."

Sometimes, when the talk centred on Mother-worship, he would be so overwhelmed that he could say nothing but "Mother! Mother!" His chanting of the Mother's name, in a voice at first loud and full, would gradually become softer and softer as though it were travelling with his soul—far, far off. Finally it would die away, and the Swami with eyes closed would shed tears of joy, showing how close his communion with the Mother was. The devotees would share in his ecstasy and, with tears of joy, would cry out, "Jai Ma Kali! Jai Ma Kali!" Then the Swami would begin to sing, and it seemed as though a spring of divine love were welling up within his heart, carrying the devotees in its flow. In the afternoon, and particularly in the evening, the same transports would attend the song and prayer and conversation. Often many of those present would join the Swami in devotional singing. Sometimes, to ease the strain occasioned by metaphysical discourse and religious fervour, he would speak on the history of different countries, and also on the manners and customs peculiar to them in a way that would send his audience into roars of laughter.

On some days the Swami would sing of Shri Krishna's Vrindavan life. As he sang, tears would flow down the cheeks

of both the Swami and the audience. Some of those present
would feel: "Oh, he [the Swami] is enjoying the vision of Shri
Krishna! Oh, how his singing carries away our hearts!" Finally
the Swami's voice would become choked with intensity of
feeling and his body motionless; his face would evince an unspeakable sweetness, radiant with the love of God. Someone
present once remarked, "His face looked like that of a Gopi,
ecstatic with love for Krishna." Before singing a Bengali song,
the Swami would explain its meaning to them, and dictate the
words so that these could be taken down in Devanagari script
and committed to memory. The Rajasthanis are mostly devotees of Shri Krishna; hence his singing of Krishna to them.

Days slipped by in this manner: sense of time was almost
lost. Sometimes the meetings would continue until midnight.
Everyone became attached to the Swami, and each thought
himself the Swami's favourite. He initiated some, giving them
Mantras.

Of his new friends the Moulavi Sahib was one of the most
devoted. He had a strong desire to invite the Swami to his
house and feed him. He thought, "Swamiji is a great sadhu
with no sense of caste; but then Panditji, with whom he is staying, may object." Nevertheless he went to the Panditji one
evening and, with folded hands before all present, said, "Do
allow me to have the Swamiji in my house for his meal tomorrow. To satisfy you all I shall have all the furniture in my
sitting-room washed by Brahmins. The food offered to Swamiji
will be bought and cooked by Brahmins in vessels brought from
their homes." He added, "This Yavana [barbarian] will be
more than compensated if he can but see the Swami, at a distance, eating his food." The Moulavi spoke these words with
such sincere humility that all present were impressed. The
Panditji clasped his hands in friendship saying, "My friend,
Swamiji is a sadhu. What is caste to him! There is no need to
take such trouble. I, for my part, have no objection. Any
arrangement you may make will satisfy us. Indeed, under such
conditions as you propose, I myself can have no qualms of
conscience in eating at your house, to say nothing of Swamiji,

who is a liberated soul." And so it happened that the Moulavi Sahib entertained the Swami in his own house and felt himself blessed. Many other devout Muslims followed the Moulavi's example and cordially invited the Swami to their homes also.

Some time later Major Ramchandraji, the Dewan to the Maharaja of Alwar, chanced to hear of the Swami's presence in the city, and invited him to his house. On better acquaintance he came to feel that the Swami would be a good influence on the Maharaja, Mangal Singhji, who had become much anglicized in thought and manners. He wrote to the Maharaja, who was at that time living in a palace two or three miles away, saying, "A great sadhu with a stupendous knowledge of English is here." The very next day the Maharaja came to the Dewan's house, where he met the Swami and bowed down before him, at the same time urging him to be seated. This was according to the Hindu tradition, which requires even princes to show respect to the sannyasi.

The Maharaja opened the conversation by saying, "Well, Swamiji Maharaj, I hear that you are a great scholar. You can easily earn a handsome sum of money every month. Why then do you go about begging?" The Swami replied with a home thrust: "Maharaja, tell me why you spend your time constantly in the company of Westerners, go on shooting excursions, and neglect your duties to the State?" Those present were taken aback. "What a bold sadhu! He will repent of this", they thought. But the Maharaja took it calmly; and after a little thought replied, "I cannot say why, but no doubt because I like to." "Well, for the same reason I wander about as a beggar", rejoined the Swami.

The next question the Maharaja asked was, "Well, Swamiji Maharaj, I have no faith in idol-worship. What is going to be my fate?" He smiled as he spoke. The Swami seemed slightly annoyed and exclaimed, "Surely you are joking." "No, Swamiji, not at all. You see, I really cannot worship wood, earth, stone or metal, like other people. Does this mean that I shall fare worse in the life hereafter?" The Swami answered, "Well, I suppose every man should follow the religious ideal according to his own faith." The devotees of the Swami were perplexed at this reply, for they knew that the Swami sanctioned image-worship. But the Swami had not finished; his eyes lighted on a picture of the Maharaja which was hanging on the wall. At his desire it was passed to him. Holding it in his hand he asked, "Whose picture is this?" The Dewan answered, "It is the likeness of our Maharaja." A moment later they trembled with fear when they heard the Swami commanding the Dewan: "Spit on it." He continued: "Any one of you may spit on it. What is it but a piece of paper? What objection can you have against doing so?"

The Dewan was thunderstruck, and all eyes glanced in fear and awe from Prince to monk, from monk to Prince. But the Swami continued to insist, "Spit on it, I say. Spit on it." The Dewan cried out, "What, Swamiji! What are you asking me to do? This is the likeness of our Maharaja! How can I do such a thing?" "Be it so," said the Swami; "but the Maharaja is not bodily present in this photograph. This is only a piece of paper. It does not contain his bones and flesh and blood. It does not speak or behave or move in any way as the Maharaja does; yet all of you refuse to spit on it, because you see in this photo the shadow of the Maharaja. Indeed, in spitting on the photo, you feel that you insult your master, the Prince himself." Turning to the Maharaja he continued, "See, Your Highness; though this is not you in one sense, in another sense it is you. That was why your devoted servants were so perplexed when I asked them to spit on it. It is a shadow of you; it brings you into their minds. One glance at it makes them see you in it; therefore they look at it with as much respect as they would have in looking at your own person. Thus it also is with the devotees who worship stone and metal images of gods and goddesses. It is because an image brings to their minds their Ishta, or some special form and attributes of the Divinity, and helps them to concentrate, that the devotees worship God in an image. They do not worship the stone or the metal as such. I have travelled in many places, but nowhere have I found a single Hindu worshipping an image, saying, 'O Stone, I worship Thee.

O Metal, be merciful to me.' Everyone, Maharaja, is worshipping the same one God who is the Supreme Spirit, the Soul of Pure Knowledge. And God appears to all according to their understanding and their representation of Him. Prince, I speak for myself. Of course, I cannot speak for you."

Mangal Singh, who had been listening attentively all this time, said, with folded hands, "Swamiji, I must admit that, looking at image-worship in the light you have thrown on it, I have never yet met anyone who worshipped stone, or wood, or metal. Before this I did not understand its meaning. You have opened my eyes. But what will be my fate? Have mercy on me." The Swami answered, "O Prince, none but God can be merciful to anyone; and He is ever-merciful! Pray to Him. He will show His mercy to you."

After the Swami had taken leave, Mangal Singh remained thoughtful for a while, and then said, "Dewanji, never have I come across such a great soul! Make him stay with you for some time." The Dewan promised to do so, adding, "I shall try my best; but I do not know whether I shall succeed. He is a man of fiery and independent character." After many entreaties the Swami consented to live with the Dewan, but only under one condition, that all those poor and illiterate people who often came to him should have the right to see him freely whenever they desired, even as the rich and those of higher positions had. The Dewan readily agreed, and so the Swami consented to stay with him.

Many of those who visited the Swami found their lives completely changed as a result of their contact with him. Daily an old man would come, who constantly asked for his blessings and mercy. Accordingly the Swami instructed him in certain practices; but the old man would not follow them. Finally, the Swami became impatient with him. One day, seeing the man coming at a distance, and wishing to be rid of him, he assumed an attitude of extreme reserve. He did not answer any of the old man's questions; nor did he respond to any of the greetings of the many friends gathered there. They could not understand what was the matter with him. An hour and a half passed in

this way, and still the Swami sat like a statue. The old man
became angry and left, swearing to himself. The Swami then
burst into boyish laughter, in which those present joined. A
young man asked, "Swamiji, why were you so hard on that old
man?" The Swami replied lovingly," Dear sons, I am ready to
sacrifice my life for you, for you are willing to follow my advice
and have the power to do so. But here is an old man who has
spent nine-tenths of his life in running after the pleasures of the
senses; now he is unfit for both spiritual and worldly life, and
thinks he can have God's mercy for the mere asking! What is
needed to attain Truth is personal exertion. How can God have
mercy on one who is devoid of such exertion? He who is wanting in manliness is full of Tamas [inertia]. It was because
Arjuna, the bravest of warriors, was going to lose this manliness that Shri Krishna commanded him to follow the course of
life and duty proper to him, so that by fulfilling his duties
without attachment to results, he might acquire the Sattvic
qualities—purity of heart, renunciation of work, and self-
surrender. Be strong. Be manly. I have respect even for a wicked
person so long as he is manly and strong, for his strength will
some day make him give up his wickedness, and even renounce
all work for selfish ends. It will thus eventually bring him to the
Truth."

Following the Swami's advice, many young men of Alwar
applied themselves to the study of Sanskrit. At times the Swami
acted as teacher. He told them, "Study Sanskrit, but along
with it study Western science as well. Learn accuracy, my boys.
Study and labour, so that the time will come when you can
put our history on a scientific basis. Now, Indian history is
disorganized. It has no chronological accuracy. The histories
of our country written by English writers cannot but be weaken-
ing to our minds, for they tell only of our downfall. How can
foreigners, who understand very little of our manners and
customs, or of our religion and philosophy, write faithful and
unbiased histories of India? Naturally, many false notions and
wrong inferences have found their way into them. Nevertheless
the Europeans have shown us how to proceed in making re-

searches into our ancient history. Now it is for us to strike out
an independent path of historical research for ourselves; to
study the Vedas and the Puranas and the ancient annals of
India; and from this to make it our life-work and discipline to
write accurate, sympathetic and soul-inspiring histories of the
land. *It is for Indians to write Indian history.* Therefore set yourselves to the task of rescuing our lost and hidden treasures from
oblivion. Even as one whose child has been lost does not rest
until he has found it, so do you never cease to labour until you
have revived the glorious past of India in the consciousness of
the people. That will be the true national education, and with
its advancement a true national spirit will be awakened."

The Swami's personality endeared him to everyone. There
was a Brahmin boy who often came to him and who loved him
as a disciple loves his master. He was of the age when he should
have been invested with the sacred thread, but he lacked the
means. When the Swami heard of this he could not rest. He
spoke to the well-to-do among his devotees, "I have one thing
to beg of you. Here is a Brahmin boy who is too poor to meet
the expenses of his Upanayana [sacred thread ceremony]. As
householders it is your duty to help him. Try to raise a subscription on his behalf. It is not proper for a Brahmin boy of
his age not to know the obligatory religious duties of his caste.
Moreover, it will be very good of you if you can provide for his
education also." The devotees hastened to raise the necessary
money. The Swami left shortly after this, but one can see from
the letter which he wrote from Mount Abu on April 30, 1891,
to his disciple Govinda Sahay at Alwar, that he did not forget
the matter. The letter runs:

Have you done the Upanayana [thread-ceremony] of that Brahmin
boy? Are you studying Sanskrit? How far have you advanced? I
think you must have finished the first part. . . . Are you diligent in
your Shiva Puja? If not, try to be so. "Seek ye first the kingdom of
God and all good things will be added unto you." Follow God and
you shall have whatever you desire. . . . My children, the secret of
religion lies not in theories but in practice. To be good and to do good
—that is the whole of religion. "Not he that crieth 'Lord', 'Lord', but

he that doeth the will of the Father". You are a nice band of young men, you Alwaris, and I hope in no distant future many of you will be ornaments of the society and blessings to the country you are born in.

Yours with blessings
Vivekananda.

One day the Swami asked the devotees whether there were any sadhus (holy men) in the neighbourhood. On being informed of an old Brahmachari who lived at some distance, he went to see him in the company of some admirers. But this old man was a Vaishnava with a violent dislike of monks of the Vedantic school; for as soon as the Swami entered, he began, in a fanatical outburst, to criticize the sannyasi life and the wearing of the ochre cloth. The Swami did not react, but simply asked to be taught something about God and religion. The Brahmachari, finding his purpose defeated, said, "Well, let that go. I have no anger against you. Have something to eat." The Swami respectfully declined, saying that he had had his food just before coming. The old man again grew furious and cried out, "Get away." The Swami bowed down before him and took leave. Emerging from the Brahmachari's Ashrama, the Swami laughed, saying, "Oh! what a peculiar saint you have shown me! What a grumpy old man!" He laughed more and more, imitating the old man's way of speaking; and the Swami's companions joined in the fun.

Once a disciple invited the Swami to take food at his house. When the Swami went, the disciple was rubbing oil into his body before taking a bath. He welcomed the Swami and asked, "Swamiji, is there any advantage in rubbing in oil before taking a bath?" The Swami replied, "Yes, one-sixteenth seer of oil rubbed into the body serves the purpose of eating one-fourth seer of ghee."

After finishing food the disciple said, "Swamiji, you teach us about truthfulness, honesty, courage, purity, selfless work and so on; but it is not possible for one who is in service to follow these teachings strictly. Since we are working in order to earn money, how can we call it selfless service? Service is after all a sort of slavery. Moreover, business life, these days, is such that

18

truth and simplicity are almost impossible for a businessman. Swamiji, it is not possible to keep the moral side sound, if we have to work in this world."

The Swami said: "I, too, have thought about this matter a lot, and have at last come to the conclusion that no one really wants to earn money by keeping his character intact. No one even cares to think about the matter or feels it to be a problem, as you do. It is the fault of our present system of education. Personally, I feel that there is no harm if anyone makes agriculture his profession; but if you advise anyone to do so, he retorts, 'Then why have I gone in for so much education? Is it necessary for everyone in the country to be farmers? The nation is already full of them; that is why it has come to such ruin.' But this is not so. Read the *Mahabharata*. The sage Janaka held the plough in one hand and studied the Vedas using the other. Our sages of old were farmers. Not only that: look how America has become so advanced by developing agriculture. I do not mean that we should follow this profession as the ignorant farmers of our country do. We have to learn the science of it, and apply that knowledge to the development of our agriculture. We have to work like intelligent people, after acquiring the necessary knowledge. But these days, no sooner do the village boys read a book or two of English than they run to the cities. In the village they may have plenty of land, but they do not feel satisfied. They want to enjoy city-life and enter service. That is why the Hindus have not progressed like other races. Our death-rate is very high; and if it continues the same, our nation is bound to meet its doom in no time. The main cause of all this is that our agricultural production is not enough. The inclination to go to the cities is noticeable among the villagers. A farmer's son, after getting a little education, leaves his ancestral profession, goes to the city, and takes a job under the white men. Longevity increases by staying in the villages; and disease is almost unknown there. If educated men go to live in the villages, even small villages will become developed; and if agriculture is carried on scientifically, then the yield will be more. In that way the farmers will be awakened to their duty;

their intellectual faculties will develop; they will be able to learn more and better things; and *that*, which is very necessary for our nation, will be achieved."

The disciple asked, "What is *that*, Swamiji?"

The Swami replied, "What else but a sort of brotherly feeling developing between the higher and the lower castes. If educated men like you go to the villages, take up agriculture, mix with the village folk and treat them as your own, without hostility, then you will see, they will be so overwhelmed that they will sacrifice even their lives for you. And what is essential for us today—the education of the masses, the teaching of higher truths to people of the lower castes, and mutual sympathy and love—that also will be achieved."

The disciple asked, "How will that happen, Swamiji?"

The Swami replied, "Why! don't you see? If anyone mixes with the villagers, how eager they are for the company of the educated! Thirst for knowledge is in everybody. That is why, when they get the company of an educated man, they sit round him and listen with rapt attention to whatever he says. If educated people take advantage of this tendency of the villagers, invite a group of them to their homes each evening, and teach them with the help of stories and parables, then by means of such a national movement we shall be able to achieve a hundred times more in ten years than we could otherwise achieve in a thousand years."

So days grew into weeks. When seven weeks had passed in this manner, the Swami again felt the urge for the wandering life. In Alwar he had stayed so long because he had been pressed to do so by his disciples and admirers; but now he said to them, "I must be going. A sannyasi must always be on the move." So on March 28, 1891, he left, bidding them farewell. They could not bear the thought of parting from him. He also was affected, especially when they fell at his feet with tears in their eyes while he was taking leave of them. But he, the Teacher, had always to be wandering—teaching, preaching and helping mankind everywhere, with the Spirit of the Lord in his heart. His friends insisted that he travel by covered bullock-cart at least as far as Pandupol, some eighteen miles from Alwar, so as to avoid the heat and traverse the uninhabited areas. Several of his disciples begged to be allowed to accompany him for the first fifty or sixty miles; at first he objected, but was finally overcome by their pleading and gave way.

At Pandupol there is a well-known temple dedicated to Hanumanji. The Swami went straight there and slept the night in the temple-compound. On the following morning he abandoned the bullock-cart, and he and his party went on foot some sixteen miles through a mountainous region, infested with wild beasts, to a village called Tahla. But the members of the party were so occupied with the stories, now amusing, now serious, with which the Swami entertained them, and they felt so blessed in his presence, that they had no thought of danger. In this village they spent the night in a temple dedicated to Nilakantha Mahadeva.

The story of Shiva as Nilakantha Mahadeva runs thus. When the gods and demons churned the ocean, many wonderful things issued from out of the seething mass: for instance, a magnificent elephant, a stately chariot, a great horse, a beautiful maiden, a priceless jewel. Both gods and demons seized what they could. Then a poison, Halahala, whose very odour was fatal to life, came out. The gods and demons were faced with the problem of getting rid of it, in order to save their lives. They were directed by Vishnu to appeal to Mahadeva, who had all along remained indifferent to the prizes that the churning had produced, sitting far away in His abode, absorbed in meditation. On hearing their cries for help He arose, and, scooping up the poison in His hands, swallowed all of it. As a result His throat (Kantha) became blue (Nila). For this reason He is called Nilakantha Mahadeva—the Great God with the Blue Throat.

To this well-known story the Swami gave his own interpretation. All beings, he said, who dwell within the folds of earthly consciousness, churn the ocean of Maya, that is, human life, and obtain treasures that are pleasing to the senses; but soon the poison, death, must come to end the show. The monk, however, stands apart. Absorbed in the Self, he desires none of the enticing gifts which Maya offers; but like Mahadeva, he is ready to come to the assistance of those who lust after sense-pleasures, when, in the presence of death, they come to him (the monk) to save their souls. Then he destroys their Maya— their ignorance—and releases them from the fear of death. He also shows by this that the man of Realization has no fear of death.

Next morning the Swami and his companions walked some eighteen miles farther on, to the village of Narayani, where the Mother in one of Her many forms is worshipped. Every year a great Mela (fair) is held here, and from all parts of Rajputana people come to worship Her. The Swami now left the others and went on by himself to the next village, Baswa, some sixteen miles distant where he took the train for the city of Jaipur. He had been pressed to go there by a devotee who had met him at Alwar. This devotee had come from Jaipur to receive the Swami. He boarded the train at Bandikui and accompanied him for the rest of the journey to Jaipur. At Jaipur the disciple insisted on the Swami's posing for a photograph. The Swami, much against his wishes, finally consented. This was the first time that a photo of him as a wandering monk was taken.

The Swami remained at Jaipur for two weeks, during which time he met a noted Sanskrit grammarian. He decided to study grammar (Panini's *Ashtadhyayi*) with him. But the pandit, though very learned, had not the gift of teaching. For three days he tried to explain the commentary on the first Sutra (aphorism), but without success. On the fourth day, the pandit said, "Swamiji, I am afraid you are not deriving much benefit from studying with me, for in three days I have not been able to make you grasp the meaning of the Sutra." The Swami resolved to master the commentary by himself. In three hours he accomplished what the pandit could not do in three days. Shortly after, he went to the pandit and in a casual way explained the commentary and its purport. The pandit was amazed. After this the Swami proceeded to master Sutra after Sutra and chapter after chapter. Later he said, speaking of this experience, "If the mind is intensely eager, everything can be accomplished—even mountains can be crumbled into atoms."

At Jaipur the Swami became very intimate with Sardar Hari Singh, the Commander-in-Chief of the State. He passed some days in his home discussing spiritual and scriptural matters. One day the subject was image-worship. A strong believer in the doctrines of the Vedanta, Hari Singh did not believe in the value of images, and even after hours of discussion with the Swami he remained unconvinced. In the evening they went out for a walk. As they were going along the footpath they came on some devotees carrying the image of Shri Krishna and singing devotional songs as they went. The Swami and the Sardar watched the procession for a while. Suddenly the Swami touched Hari Singh and said, "Look there, see the living God!" The eyes of the Sardar fell on the image of the Lord Krishna, and he stood there transfixed, with tears of ecstasy trickling down his cheeks. When he returned to ordinary consciousness, he exclaimed, "Well, Swamiji, that was a revelation to me. What I could not understand after hours of discussion, was easily comprehended through your touch. Truly I saw the Lord in the image of Krishna!"

Another day the Swami was seated with a number of followers, giving them spiritual instructions, when a learned Sardar, Pandit Suraj Narain, honoured throughout the province for his erudition, came to see him. He caught the thread of the Swami's conversation and said, "Swamiji, I am a Vedantist. I do not believe in the special divinity of Incarnations—the Avataras of the Hindu mythology. We are all Brahman. What is the difference between me and an Avatara?" The Swami replied, "Yes, that is quite true. The Hindus count a fish, a tortoise and a boar as Avataras. You say that you are also an Avatara; but with which of these do you feel yourself one?" There was a peal of laughter at this, and the Sardar was silenced.

Desirous of moving on, the Swami next went to Ajmer, replete with memories of the magnificence of its Hindu and Mogul rulers. The Swami visited the palace of Akbar and the famous Dargah, sacred alike to Hindus and Muslims, being the burial-place of the renowned Muslim saint, Mainuddin Chisti. Here he also visited the temple dedicated to the creator, Brahma. It is the only one of its kind in India.

On April 14 the Swami left Ajmer for Mount Abu, a celebrated hill-resort of western India and Rajputana, where there is one of the most wonderful temples in India. For the delicacy and beauty of its sculpture it is almost unrivalled in the land. It is a Jaina temple, known as the Dilwara Temple. It was built in the early part of the thirteenth century by two pious brothers, merchant princes, and is said to have taken fourteen years to build. The Swami spent days examining the glories of this temple. He would also stroll by the lake—the treasure of Mount Abu. By the lake are rocks of strange shape, one like a praying nun, and another like a toad about to spring into the waters, and so on.

The Swami soon gathered round him some devoted followers with whom he used to walk in the evening. One day they were going along Bailey's Walk, which commands a fine view of the hill-station. Below them stretched the lake of Mount Abu. The Swami with his friends left the Walk and sat down among the rocks. He began to sing, and his song went on for hours. Some Europeans, also taking an evening stroll, were charmed with the sweet music, and waited long for a glimpse of the singer. At last he came down, and they congratulated him on his sweet voice and ecstatic song.

It was here at Mount Abu that destiny put the Raja of Khetri in his path. The Swami was then living in an abandoned cave, where he was engaged in spiritual practices. His sole belongings were one or two blankets, a water-pot, and a few books. One day a Muslim, the Vakil (pleader) of the Prince of a Native State, happened to pass by, and saw the Swami. Struck with his appearance, the Vakil decided to speak to him. A few minutes' conversation impressed him with the learning of the recluse, to whom he became much attached and whom he visited quite often. One day the Vakil asked the Swami if he could be of any service to him. The Swami said, "Look here,

Vakil Saheb, the rainy season is fast approaching. There are no doors to this cave. You can make me a pair of doors, if you please." Gratified, the Vakil said, "This cave is a wretched one. If you will allow me, I shall make a suggestion. I live here alone in a nice bungalow. If you would condescend to come and live with me, I should feel greatly blessed." When the Swami agreed to the proposal, the Vakil said, "But I am a Muslim. I shall, of course, make separate arrangements for your food." The Swami brushed this aside and moved to the bungalow. Through the Vakil and his brother-officers of other States, the Swami made many friends in Mount Abu, including the Vakil of the Maharao of Kotah, and Thakur Fateh Singh, the Minister of that Prince. After a few days the Muslim Vakil invited Munshi Jagmohanlal, Private Secretary to the Raja of Khetri, to meet his guest. As it happened, the Swami was resting at the time, having on only a loin-cloth and piece of ochre cloth. When the visitor saw the sleeping monk, he thought, "Oh! here is one of those common monks who are no better than thieves and rogues!" Presently the Swami awoke. Almost the first thing that Jagmohanlal said to him was, "Well, Swamiji, you are a Hindu monk. How is it that you are living with a Muslim? Your food may now and then be touched by him." At this question the Swami flared up. He said, "Sir, what do you mean? I am a sannyasi. I am above all your social conventions. I can dine even with a Bhangi [sweeper]. I am not afraid of God, for He sanctions it; I am not afraid of the scriptures, for they allow it: but I am afraid of you people and your society. You know nothing of God and the scriptures. I see Brahman everywhere, manifested even in the meanest creature. For me there is nothing high or low. Shiva, Shiva!" A sort of divine fire shone about him. Jagmohanlal was silenced; but he wished the Raja to make the acquaintance of such a monk. "Swamiji," he said, "do come with me to the palace to meet the Raja Saheb." The monk replied, "Very well, I shall go the day after tomorrow."

Jagmohanlal told the Raja of what had happened. The Raja became so eager to meet the Swami that he said, "I will go myself to see him." When the Swami heard this he went instantly to the palace, where His Highness warmly welcomed him. After the usual formalities the Raja asked him, "Swamiji, what is life?" The Swami replied, "Life is the unfoldment and development of a being under circumstances tending to press it down." The Swami's own life of hardship and renunciation caused a world of feeling to appear in his words. Impressed, the Raja next asked, "Well, Swamiji, what then is education?" The response was, "I should say, education is the nervous association of certain ideas." And he went on to explain this statement, saying that not until ideas had been made instincts could they be reckoned as real and vital possessions of consciousness. Then he told of the life of Shri Ramakrishna. The Raja listened attentively, his soul rapt in a burning passion for Truth, as words of spiritual nectar fell from the Swami's lips.

From the Waqyat Register (State Diary) of Khetri State, the Swami's activities at this time are known in some detail. His first meeting with Raja Ajit Singhji of Khetri took place at the summer palace at Mount Abu, on the evening of June 4, 1891. On this occasion the Raja talked with the Swami on various subjects, and Hardayal Singhji of Jodhpur was also present. After taking dinner at the palace, the Swami left. On June 6, 11, 15, 22, and 23 he lunched and had discussions with the Raja, chiefly on education, religion and philosophy, usually in English and sometimes in Sanskrit. On some days the Swami sang. On June 24 the Swami reached the palace about 9.30 a.m. and had discussions with the Raja until lunch-time. About 5 p.m. they were joined by Thakur Mukund Singhji of Jaleswar (near Aligarh), and Har Bilas Sarda, President of the Arya Samaj at Ajmer. On June 27 the Swami lunched and talked with the Raja, and afterwards he sang while the Raja accompanied him on the harmonium. More or less the same routine was followed on July 4, 6, 8, 9, 11, 14, and 17. On July 18 the Raja invited some honoured guests for dinner. Besides the Swami were Thakur Fateh Singhji Rathor, Thakur Mukund Singhji Chouhan of Jaleswar, and Man Singhji of Jamnagar.

They listened to the playing of the Sitar by one Choubeyji. Afterwards they took dinner about midnight.

Har Bilas Sarda, mentioned above, met the Swami more than once at Mount Abu, and again at Ajmer. He later distinguished himself as a historian of Rajputana, and as the member of the Central Legislative Assembly of India who championed the Child Marriage Restraint Act, popularly known as the 'Sarda Act'. He writes of these days at Mount Abu as follows:

> ... I met Swami Vivekananda four times. The first time I met him was at Mount Abu. It was sometime in the year 1889 or 1890 [June 1891] in the month of May or June (I do not recollect which). I went to Mount Abu to stay with my friend T. [Thakur] Mukund Singh of Chhalasar [Jaleswar], Aligarh district, who was staying at Mount Abu for the hot season. When I reached there, I found Swami Vivekananda staying with T. Mukund Singh. T. Mukund Singh was an Arya Samajist and a follower of Swami Dayananda Saraswati. I stopped with my friend for about ten days and we, Swamiji and I, were together there and talked on various subjects. I was about 21 years old then and was impressed by Swami Vivekananda's personality. He was a most delightful talker and was very well informed. We used to go out for our afternoon walks. After dinner the first day, Swami Vivekananda gave a song at Thakur Sahib's request. He sang in a most melodious tone, which gave me a great delight. I was charmed by his songs, and every day I begged him to give one or two songs. His musical voice and his manner have left a lasting impression on me. We sometimes talked about Vedanta, with which I had some acquaintance. ... Swami Vivekananda's talks on Vedanta greatly interested me. His views on various subjects were most welcome to me, as they were very patriotic. He was full of love of motherland and of Hindu culture. The time I passed in his company was one of the most pleasant times I have passed in my life. His independence of character particularly impressed me.

For days Raja Ajit Singhji of Khetri listened to the monk's words of wisdom. So devoted to him did he become that one day he said, "Swamiji, do come with me to my State. You will live with me there, and I shall serve you with my whole heart." The Swami, after reflecting for a moment, said, "Very well, Your Highness, I shall be glad to accompany you." Accordingly, when the Raja and his retinue left Mount Abu on July 24, the Swami went with him. Next morning they reached Jaipur, where they stayed at Khetri House. They were there for about ten days spending much of their time, as before, in talking on various subjects. On August 3 they left Jaipur for Khetri by train, halting at Khairthal for the night. Next day, in the Raja's state carriage, they started for Kot, where the party stayed for a day. On August 5 they left Kot for Khetri, which they reached on the 7th morning. On the way the Raja spent his time in the company of the Swami, asking him questions, and listening to his answers.

One day he asked, "Swamiji, what is Truth?" The Swami replied, "Truth, Your Highness, is One and Absolute. Man travels constantly towards it, from truth to truth, and not from error to truth." Then he went on amplifying his meaning, pointing out how all forms of knowledge and experience and all forms of worship and thought are paths to the same Truth. He showed how true monk and true householder could attain the same Truth by different paths. At Khetri, after some days, the Swami gave the Raja spiritual initiation. And what a wonderful disciple the Raja became! Memories still live of him kneeling in reverence before the Swami. The monk in his turn, knowing the depth and sincerity of the man, loved him dearly and expected much of him in the way of advancing the well-being of the country. Later, when in America, he kept the Raja informed of his progress and made him one of those who were privileged to receive letters from him. An idea of the Swami's regard for the Raja is given in a letter he wrote to Mrs. Ole Bull in 1895: "In India Raja Ajit Singh of Khetri and in America Mrs. Ole Bull—these are the two persons upon whom I can depend at any time. Of all the friends I have in the world you two show such wonderful steadiness of purpose and both are so calm and silent."

The Waqyat Register shows that the Swami stayed at Khetri from August 7 until October 27. He spent his time with the Raja and his royal guests, with the pandits and State officers, and with visiting sadhus and others: discussing scriptures, singing songs, studying books and teaching people. He showed great interest in science, and at his suggestion the Raja started a small laboratory on the top floor of his palace, equipped with a telescope and a microscope. The Swami and his disciple put these instruments to good use. It was from the Swami that the Raja learnt the fundamental principles of physics, chemistry and astronomy.

On October 4, which was the eve of the Navaratra festival, the Swami went with the Raja on horseback to visit the temple of Jin Mata (a well-known deity of Rajputana, in Sikar State). On the way they visited the Shiva temple sited on a hill at Gudha, and reached Signor the same day in the evening. They reached Sikar on the 6th, and from there went to visit the temple of Jin Mata, accompanied by the Maharaja Madho Singhji of Sikar. On the 10th they started back, and reached Khetri the next day. October 12 was Dasera. Special worship, a state procession, and state dinner were arranged by the Raja. His monastic guest took part in the celebrations.

At the Khetri palace the Swami became acquainted with Pandit Narayandas, the foremost Sanskrit grammarian of his time in Rajputana. Believing this to be a great opportunity, he decided to resume his study of the *Mahabhashya* (Patanjali's great commentary) on the Sutras of Panini, which he had begun at Jaipur. The pandit was pleased to have him as a pupil. At the end of the first day he remarked, "Swamiji, it is not often one meets a student like you!" One day the pandit questioned the Swami on a very long lesson given the day before. To his surprise the monk repeated it verbatim, adding his own comments. After a time the pandit, noting that his pupil was often forced to find the answer to his own questions in default of an answer from himself (the pandit), said, "Swamiji, there is nothing more to teach you. I have taught you all that I know, and you have absorbed it." And so the Swami, saluting the pandit respectfully, thanked him for his kindness, and became in many respects the teacher of the pandit.

On one occasion the Raja asked, "Swamiji, what is law?" Without a moment's hesitation the Swami replied, "Law is altogether internal. It does not exist outside; it is a phenomenon of intelligence and experience. It is the mind which classifies sense-observations and moulds them into laws. The order of experience is always internal. Apart from the impression received through the sense-organs and the reaction of intelligence upon these, in an orderly and consecutive manner, there is no law. The scientists say that it is all homogeneous substance and homogeneous vibration. Experience and its classification are internal phenomena. Thus law itself is intelligent and is born in absolute intelligence." Then the Swami spoke of the Sankhya philosophy and showed how modern science corroborated its conclusions.

Such was the devotion and reverence of the Raja for his spiritual teacher that he would serve him in various ways, even rubbing the Swami's feet gently while he slept, and, in the daytime, even doing acts of service before others; but the Swami forbade this last, saying that it would lower the dignity of the Raja in the eyes of his subjects.

One day the Raja expressed sorrow to the Swami for not having been blessed with a son and heir. "Swamiji," he said, "bless me that a son may be born to me. If you will only do so, there is no doubt that my prayer will be granted." Seeing his anxious longing, the Swami blessed him.

But the Swami did not spend all his time in the palace. He was often at the houses of his poorer devotees, and frequently ate at the house of Pandit Shankarlal, a poor Brahmin. The whole town of Khetri was enamoured of the Swami, and he treated the least of his admirers with the same love and affection as he bestowed on the Raja.

At Khetri an incident occurred which proved an eye-opener to the Swami. One evening the Raja was being entertained with music by a nautch-girl. The Swami was in his own tent when the music commenced. The Raja sent a message to the Swami asking him to come and join the party. The Swami sent word in return that as a sannyasi he could not come. The singer was deeply grieved when she heard this, and sang, as it were in reply, a song of Surdas, the Vaishnava saint. Through the still evening air, to the accompaniment of music, the girl's melodious voice reached the ears of the Swami.

> O Lord, look not upon my evil qualities.
> Thy Name, O Lord, is Same-sighted.
> One piece of iron is in the image in the temple,
> And another, the knife in the hand of the butcher;
> But when they touch the philosophers' stone,
> Both alike turn to gold.
> So, Lord, look not upon my evil qualities, etc.

The Swami was deeply touched. The woman and her song told him something he was forgetting, that all is Brahman, that the same Divinity is back of all beings—ay, even of this woman whom he had despised. He forthwith went to the hall of audience and joined the party. Speaking of this incident later, the Swami said, "Hearing the song I thought, 'Is this my Sannyasa? I am a sannyasi, and yet I have in me the sense of distinction between myself and this woman!' That incident removed the scales from my eyes. Seeing that all are indeed the manifestation of the One, I could no longer condemn anybody."

After a little over two and a half months at Khetri, the Swami felt that he must go forth into the wide world again, unattached. He left Khetri towards the end of October, and made for Ajmer, where he stayed for about three weeks. First he stayed for three or four days with Har Bilas Sarda; and later with Sarda's friend, Shyamji Krishna Varma. Mr. Sarda's reminiscences, relating to the Swami's visit to Ajmer in November and December 1891, run as follows:

The next time I met him [the Swami] was at Ajmer. . . . He was my guest, so far as I remember, for two or three days or four: I remember asking him what his name was before he became a sannyasi. He gave it to me. . . . He left me and went away to Beawar. Mr. Shyamji Krishna Varma, one of the most learned of men I have met, lived in Ajmer in those days, but had gone to Bombay, when the Swami was with me. On his return, I spoke to him about Swami Vivekananda's learning, eloquence and patriotism, and told him that he had left only two or three days ago and was in Beawar. P. Shyamji Krishna Varma had to go to Beawar the next day and promised to bring Swamiji with him back to Ajmer. The next day he returned to Ajmer with Swami Vivekananda. Swami Vivekananda was his guest for about fourteen or fifteen days and I met him every day at Mr. Shyamji's bungalow. We three used to go out together for our evening walk. I had the happiest time in the company of these two learned men. . . . I remember well that we had most interesting talks with Swami Vivekananda. His eloquence, his nationalistic attitude of mind and pleasant manner greatly impressed and delighted me. Very often I was a listener, when Mr. Shyamji and Swami Vivekananda discussed some Sanskrit literary or philosophic matters. . . .

He [the Swami] had large luminous eyes and discoursed eloquently on religious and philosophical subjects. I was charmed by Vivekananda's songs and admired his eloquence and patriotism. We had long conversations and talks on various subjects during the day and during our afternoon walks. . . . But what delighted me was Vivekananda's singing. He had a musical and melodious voice and I was entranced by his songs. [And in his diary Mr. Sarda wrote of the Swami:] His discourses are most interesting to me. I greatly like him. He is a most pleasant companion. He will be something in the world if I err not greatly.

After spending about two weeks in this manner at Ajmer, the Swami seems to have proceeded towards what was then the Bombay Presidency (now Gujarat and Maharashtra).

16

IN WESTERN INDIA

In the historic city of Ahmedabad the Swami wandered about for several days, living on alms. He was finally received as a guest by Lal Shankar Umia Shankar, a sub-judge of Ahmedabad District. During his stay here, he visited many places of historic interest, both in the city and in its environs. Previously known as Karnavati, it used to be the capital of the Sultans of Gujarat, and one of the handsomest cities in India. The Swami was fascinated by the Jaina temples, and by the splendour of Muslim culture as manifest in the mosques and tombs. Here he was able to add to his knowledge of Jainism, for Jaina scholars were in plenty.

After staying for a few days in Ahmedabad, he journeyed on to Wadhwan in Kathiawar, where he visited the old temple of Ranik Devi. The story behind the building of this temple runs thus: Ranik Devi was a beautiful girl born in the Junagadh territory, when Raja Sidh was ruling Patan State. She was betrothed to him, but the ruler of Junagadh, Ra Khengar, was in love with her. He abducted and married her. This caused a deadly feud between the two chieftains. In time Raja Sidh invaded Junagadh and slew Ra Khengar. When Ranik Devi heard of the death of her husband, and of the invader's wish to marry her, she performed *sati*; that is, to protect her chastity she offered herself into fire at the cremation of her beloved husband. In her memory the broken-hearted conqueror raised the temple. Visiting it, and knowing how it came to be built, the Swami could not but ponder on the sanctity of the marriage relationship as viewed in the Hindu tradition.

After spending some days at Wadhwan, the Swami went on to Limbdi, the chief town of the cotton-producing State of that name. As he went, he begged his food from door to door, slept where he could find shelter, and lived as chance dictated. On arriving at Limbdi itself, he learned that there was a place where sadhus lived. It was somewhat isolated, but the sadhus welcomed him warmly and urged him to stay with them as long as he wished. Tired and hungry after his long marches, he accepted the invitation. He had no idea of the character of the place. What was his horror to find, after he had been in the house for a few days, that the inmates belonged to a degenerate group of sex-worshippers. He could hear the prayers and incantations of women as well as of men in the adjoining room. His first thought was to leave the place at once; but to his bewilderment he found that he was locked in, and that a guard had been set to prevent his escape. The high-priest of the sect summoned him and said, "You are a sadhu with a magnetic personality. Evidently you have practised Brahmacharya [celibacy] for years. Now you must give us the fruit of your long austerity. We shall break your Brahmacharya in order to perform a special type of spiritual practice, and thereby acquire for ourselves certain psychic powers."

The Swami was shaken; but he kept his presence of mind, showed no sign of anxiety, and seemingly took the matter lightly. Among the Swami's devotees was a boy who used to come frequently to see him. Through him the Swami sent a note to the Thakore Saheb, the Prince of the State, explaining his predicament and asking for help. The boy hurried to the palace and managed to deliver the note to the Thakore Saheb himself. The latter immediately sent some of his guards to the Swami's rescue. Afterwards, on the Prince's invitation, the Swami took up his residence in the palace. While in Limbdi, he held many discussions in Sanskrit with the local pandits. His Holiness the Shankaracharya of the Govardhan Math, Puri, bore witness to this. He was astonished at the young monk's learning, and at his breadth of understanding and sympathy.

The life of the Thakore Saheb Jaswant Singhji of Limbdi, written in Gujarati and published in 1896, reveals that it was from the Thakore Saheb that the Swami first got the idea of going to the West in order to preach Vedanta. The Thakore Saheb, a strong upholder of the Sanatana Dharma and at the

19

same time a man of progressive views, had himself been to England and America a few years earlier. He was thrilled to hear the Swami's religious discourses and to have discussions with him on various matters.

After a short stay at Limbdi, the Swami left for Junagadh with letters of introduction from the Thakore Saheb to his friends there and elsewhere. The Prince entreated him to be cautious on his solitary wanderings, and the Swami too, after his experience at Limbdi, resolved to be more circumspect in accepting offers of lodging, and to be more discriminating as to the people with whom he came in contact. On his way to Junagadh he visited Bhavnagar and Sihor. At Junagadh he was the guest of Haridas Viharidas Desai, the Dewan of the State, who was so charmed with his company that every evening he, with all the State officials, used to meet the Swami and converse with him until late at night. The manager of the Dewan's office was one C. H. Pandya. He became the Swami's staunch admirer, and in his house the Swami stayed for a time. This is what he had to say:

The Swami's simplicity of life, his unostentatiousness, his profound knowledge of various arts and sciences, his catholicity of views and his devotion to religion, his stirring eloquence and his magnetic powers and extraordinary personality, influenced all of us in Junagadh. Added to these qualities he possessed a great proficiency in music and was conversant with all forms of Indian art. Ay, withal he was even an artist of the cuisine and could prepare excellent rasogollas. We were devoted to him.

In his talks at Junagadh the Swami spoke much of Jesus Christ. He said that he had long since come to understand the influence of Christ in regenerating the ethics of the Western world. Becoming fervent in his eloquence, he went on to relate how all the medieval greatness of Europe—the paintings of Raphael, the devotion of Saint Francis of Assisi, the Gothic cathedrals, the Crusades, the political systems of the West, its monastic orders and its religious life—all were interwoven in one way or another with the teachings of the sannyasi Christ. From this he went on to narrate the excellences of the

Sanatana Dharma, illuminating and enlarging his listeners'
understanding of it. And then, in a patriotic spirit, the Swami
made clear to them the nature and extent of the influence
exerted by Hinduism on the Western religious imagination, and
showed how Central and Western Asia was the scene of this
interracial exchange of ideas. He brought out the values for
which their own culture stood, and the essential worth of the
Hindu experience in the development of spiritual ideals
throughout the world. He told them also about the life and
teaching of the Saint of Dakshineswar; and thus Shri Ramakrishna came to be known and appreciated in those distant
parts. At Junagadh, too, he had long discussions with many
orthodox Hindu pandits.

Interested as he was in ancient monuments and ruins, the
Swami found ample scope for study at Junagadh. Here, there
are the old fortress called Uparkot, an old Rajput palace, two
ancient wells, and the Khapra Khodia caves dating back to the
Buddhist period and perhaps used as monasteries; but of chief
interest is the Ashoka Stone. It is a huge rock just outside the
town, in which the Edicts of the Emperor Ashoka and of two
other emperors are cut.

Girnar, about two miles from Junagadh, is a place of pilgrimage, sacred to Buddhists, Jainas and Hindus because
of its association with the traditions of all three religions. It
is a group of some ten hills, the highest of which, known as
Gorakhnath, is about 3,600 feet. Climbing starts from Girnar
Taleti. There are 10,000 or more steps cut in the rock, leading
to the many Jaina and Hindu temples built on the different
hills. After the first half of the climb the way becomes very
narrow, and at times turns on the edge of a great precipice.
Used to mountain paths, the Swami made the ascent with ease.
How many of the hills he climbed is not known; but his pilgrimage to the place brought on a yearning to be absorbed in
spiritual practices; for he soon sought out a solitary cave, where
he practised meditation for a few days. While he was there, the
Dewan took all possible care of him. This is known from the
letter the Swami wrote to him from Girnar:

Very kind of you to send up a man inquiring about my health and comfort. But that's quite of a piece with your fatherly character. I am all right here. Your kindness has left nothing more to be desired here. I hope soon to see you in a few days. I don't require any conveyance while going down. Descent is very bad, and the ascent is the worst part of the job, that's the same in everything in the world. My heartfelt gratitude to you. Yours faithfully, Bibekananda.

After a few days at Girnar the Swami, refreshed in mind, returned to his friends at Junagadh. From the signature to the letter just cited, it is evident that at Junagadh he gave his name as "Vivekananda". This is confirmed by Akhandananda who, as will be seen presently, was tracking the Swami down. At Wadhwan Akhandananda met someone recently arrived from Junagadh. This person said that at Junagadh he had met a learned monk named Vivekananda. The description of the monk tallied with that of Akhandananda's beloved "Naren".

Abhedananda was also wandering in Gujarat at this time. He happened to meet the Swami at Junagadh. This is the account that he gives in his autobiography of their meeting:

On arrival at Junagadh, I came to hear from people that a Bengali sannyasin with high English education was staying for some days at the house of Mansukhram Suryaram Tripathi, a Gujarati Brahmin, who was the Private Secretary of the local Nawab. . . . Elated with joy I reached the house of Mansukhram . . . by enquiry and immediately found that my conjecture was true. Narendranath brightened up with joy to see me unexpectedly. I too could not check my tears to meet him after a long time. Fortunately when I arrived there Narendranath was discussing some topic of non-dualistic Vedanta with Mr. Tripathi. . . . Mr. Tripathi requested me with courtesy to take rest and sent an order in his house for arranging food for me along with Narendranath. . . . I gladly stayed in his house for three or four days in the company of Narendranath, and then I got ready to start for Dwarka.

The Swami, we have noticed and shall be noticing, spent much of his time in the palaces of the Princes of India or with their Dewans. Many severely criticized him for doing so; others asked him why he did so. The Swami replied that his intention was to influence the princes, and by turning their attention to the religious life, thus to ensure that they were true to their Swadharma (own duty), that is, government for the good of the people whose custodians they were. Upon these princes depended not only the present welfare, but the future advancement also, of the governed. They alone could inaugurate reforms, improve methods of education, and establish and foster charitable institutions in their territories. "If I can win over to my cause those in whose power are wealth and the administration of the affairs of thousands, my mission will be accomplished all the sooner; by influencing one Maharaja alone I can indirectly benefit thousands of people." With this intention he consented on occasion to reside in a palace. One day would find him strolling in the gardens of some prince, or driving with him in his carriage; the next, perhaps alone and afoot on the dusty road making for some poor devotee's house.

Soon after returning from Girnar to Junagadh, the Swami felt that he must be on the move. He therefore took leave of his friends, and with letters of introduction to officials at Bhuj, went on to that place. There he stayed with the Dewan, with whom he had long discussions, as he had had with the Dewan of Junagadh, on the industrial, agricultural and other economic problems of the country, and on the need for the spread of education among the masses. When the Dewan of Kutch was visited by a disciple of the Swami several years later, he (the Dewan) recalled the Swami's prodigious intellect, his gracious personality, and his power of presenting abstruse thought in such a simple way that all who met him were fascinated. The Swami was introduced to the Maharaja of Kutch by the Dewan. The long talks which the Swami had with the Maharaja made a great impression on the latter.

As usual, the Swami visited the places of pilgrimage in the vicinity, mingling with the pilgrims and sannyasis, and so gaining in knowledge and experience. From Bhuj he returned to Junagadh, rested there for a few days, and then was off to Veraval and Patan Somnath, popularly known as Prabhas. Veraval's title to fame is its antiquity; Patan Somnath's lies in its great ruined temple. Three times it was destroyed, and three times rebuilt. It is said that in olden times ten thousand villages were held by the temple as endowment, and that three hundred musicians were attached to it. The Swami paused by this great ruin and pondered over the greatness that had been India's in the past. The very dust for miles about is sacred to the devout Hindu, for, as the story goes, it was here that the Yadavas—the clan to which Shri Krishna belonged—slew one another, and thus their extensive kingdom was brought to ruin by Shri Krishna's divine will. After this, knowing that his time was come, Krishna sat in Yoga under the spreading branches of an ancient tree. He left his body as the arrow of an aboriginal, who mistook him for a deer, struck him.

The Swami visited the Somnath temple, the Suraj Mandir, and the new temple of Somnath built by Rani Ahalyabai of Indore; and he bathed at the confluence of the three rivers. At Prabhas he again met the Maharaja of Kutch and had many long conversations with him. The prince was deeply impressed by the monk's magnetic personality and was astonished at his vast knowledge. He used to say, "Swamiji, as after reading many books the head becomes dazed, even so after hearing your discourses my brain becomes dizzy. How will you utilize all this talent? You will never rest until you have done wonderful things!"

After a short time the Swami returned to Junagadh. This place seems to have been a centre from which he made a number of side trips through Kathiawar and to Kutch. Leaving Junagadh a third time, he now went to Porbandar with a letter of introduction to the Dewan. Porbandar is held to be the site of the ancient city of Sudamapuri, known to readers of the *Bhagavata*. Here the Swami visited the ancient temple of Sudama. He was cordially welcomed by the Dewan, Pandit Shankar Pandurang, who was the administrator of the State during the minority of the Prince. The Dewan was a great Vedic scholar and was at that time translating the Vedas. Struck with the Swami's scholarship, he often asked his help to explain some of the more abstruse passages of the Vedas, which the Swami did with his usual lucidity. At the request of the Dewan he stayed at Porbandar for some days to help him with his book. Both kept at the work constantly, the Swami becoming more and more engrossed in it as his perception of the greatness of Vedic thought grew still keener. He finished his reading of Panini's *Mahabhashya*, and took up the study of French at the instance of the Dewan, who said, "It will be of use to you, Swamiji."

As he came to appreciate better the breadth and originality of the Swami's ideas, Pandit Shankar Pandurang said, "Swamiji, I am afraid you cannot do much in this country. Few will appreciate you here. You ought to go to the West where people will understand you and your worth. Surely you can throw a great light upon Western culture by preaching the Sanatana Dharma!" The Swami was glad to hear these words, for they coincided with his own thoughts, which, as yet vague, he had expressed to C. H. Pandya at Junagadh.

During this period the Swami was exceedingly restless. He was beginning to feel the truth of the Master's words, that he had power enough in him to revolutionize the world. Wherever he travelled and at all the courts he visited, the princes and pandits noticed in him the same "terrible restlessness" to do something for his country. The idea uppermost in his mind was the spiritual regeneration of India. He saw the limitations of orthodoxy, and those of the reformers too. Everywhere he found petty jealousies, animosity, and lack of harmony. He saw India, potentially supreme, glorious beyond words, and rich with its own ancient culture, being degraded by the stupid activities of the so-called "leaders"—demagogues who preached reforms which they were unable to incorporate into their own lives, and who, blinded by the glare of a foreign culture and its ephemeral power, were trying to throw overboard the experience of the race. He confided to those who loved and admired him that the time had come for a new order of things. To the Indian Princes and their Prime Ministers he announced this message. And they, recognizing that he was a genius, and a man of realization gifted with an irresistible personality, listened to his words. He felt that to enable the civilized world to have a truer estimation of India, he must first preach the glories of the Sanatana Dharma to the West. The more he studied the Vedas and pondered over the philosophies which the Aryan Rishis had thought out, the surer he was that India was truly the Mother of Religions, the fountain-head of spirituality, and the cradle of civilization.

When the Swami was at Porbandar a curious thing happened. Swami Trigunatita had been for some time making the round of pilgrimages on foot. He had just then come from Gujarat to Porbandar, and was staying with some other wandering sannyasis. They wanted to make the pilgrimage to Hinglaj, but it was an arduous journey of many miles, and they were weary and footsore; so they thought of travelling to Karachi by steamer and thence to Hinglaj by camel. But they had no money. They were at a loss what to do, when one of the group said, "There is a learned Paramahamsa stopping with the Dewan of Porbandar. He speaks English fluently and is accounted a great scholar. Let Swami Trigunatita go and interview him. Perhaps the Mahatma [great soul] will intercede with the Dewan for us so that our expenses may be paid."

Trigunatita set out for the palace at the head of the group. It so happened that at that time the Swami was pacing the parapeted roof of the palace and saw at a distance the sadhus on their way to the palace. He was surprised to see Trigunatita among them, but assuming an air of indifference, he went to the ground floor to receive him. Trigunatita was exceedingly glad to meet the beloved Leader so unexpectedly; but the latter sternly rebuked him for following him (the Swami) about. Trigunatita protested that he had not had the slightest idea that the Swami was in Porbandar; that he and his friends had come to the palace solely to beg the passage money to Hinglaj. The Swami was able to arrange this, and then dismissed Trigunatita with a warning never to seek him again.

A little more information about the Swami in Porbandar has recently been gathered from a centenarian named Acharya Revashankar Anupama Dave, who vividly remembers the happenings of this period. He had the opportunity of observing and talking with the Swami when the latter was the guest of the Dewan Shankar Pandurang Pandit. Mr. Dave was then a young boy of sixteen. He used to frequent the Dewan's house and the guest-house with his friend Madhav, who had free access there. Mr. Dave says that the Swami used to stay in the Bhojeshwar Bungalow. His room was in the north-west corner of the building and was reached by turning right at the main staircase. He remembers that the Swami talked mostly in Hindi, but at times many Bengali and Sanskrit words used to creep in. On one occasion, at the request of the Swami, the students of the Sanskrit school were brought to him, among whom were Revashankar, Govindaji, and others. The Swami asked Govindaji, "How far have you studied?" Govindaji replied, "I went to Benares and have studied the *Sama-Veda*. I have learnt six Mantras [Shastras?]." The Swami asked him, "Why did you not study further? Why did you come back?" Govindaji replied, "I happened to have Karelu; so I had to come back." On hearing the word "Karelu" the Swami had a hearty laugh, and the place seemed to vibrate with it. "Karelu" means bitter gourd, but the boy had meant that he had had an attack of cholera. Then the Swami asked him to recite some Shlokas (verses), which he did. Next, he asked Revashankar, "What are you studying?" Revashankar replied, "*Panchatantra* and *Aesop's Niti Katha* [Fables]", and recited a verse from each. Swamiji smiled and seemed to be pleased with him. Then the Swami went for a walk. Revashankar remembers that he used to go for walks in the desert of Bhojeshwar with the Dewan. The Swami always had his staff with him, and the Dewan a spear.

The Swami now left Porbandar and went as a wandering monk to Dwarka, holy with memories and legends of Shri Krishna. Of its glories nothing visible remains today. The ocean roars in tumult where once stood the mighty city of Shri Krishna the King-maker. Gazing out over the ocean, waves of agony rose in the Swami's mind at the thought that nothing but ruins remained of that Great India. He sat on the shore and yearned ardently to fathom the contents of the future. Then rising as from a dream, he betook himself to the monastery founded by Shri Shankaracharya, known as the Sarada Math, where he was received by the Mahant (the head monk), and assigned a room. There, in the silence of his cell, on the ruins of that city of the Yadavas, he saw a great light—the resplendent Future of India.

It will be remembered that, on the eve of the Swami's departure from Delhi, Akhandananda had said to him, "Even if you go to the nether world, I shall hunt you out." And indeed he did follow the Swami. The story of that hunt has thrown light on the Swami's route. At Jaipur, Akhandananda learnt that the Swami had gone to Ajmer, after staying for some months at Khetri. When he reached Ajmer, he learnt that the Swami had gone in the direction of Ahmedabad. On his way Akhandananda passed through Beawar, where he learnt that the Swami had been there, but had returned to Ajmer some time before. However, Akhandananda went on to Ahmedabad, thinking that the Swami would be going there; but there he learnt that the Swami had left for Wadhwan. At Wadhwan he came to know that the Swami was at Junagadh as the guest of the Dewan. On reaching Junagadh he had the news that the Swami had left four days previously for Dwarka via Porbandar. At Dwarka he was told that the Swami had left for Beyt Dwarka. Akhandananda halted for the night at Dwarka, and next day went to Beyt Dwarka, where he learnt that the Swami had left for Mandvi in Kutch, on invitation from the Maharaja. At Mandvi, he heard that the Swami had gone to Narayan Sarovar. The way to Narayan Sarovar was infested with dacoits; but this did not deter Akhandananda. For the sake of meeting the Swami, he set out for that place. On the way he was beaten and robbed by dacoits. When he reached Narayan Sarovar, he fell ill; but he was cordially received by the Mahant there. He was told that the Swami had gone to Ashapuri, a place of pilgrimage. The Mahant gave him a horse and a guide for going to Ashapuri, which he reached with great difficulty, only to learn that the Swami had gone towards Mandvi. Next day Akhandananda went to Mandvi. He learnt that the Swami was staying at the house of a Bhatia gentleman.

On reaching the Bhatia's house, Akhandananda was overwhelmed with joy to meet the Swami at last. He was also surprised to see a change in the Swami's face, which had a sublime radiance. The Swami was astonished to see his beloved brother-disciple after a long time. He heard with amazement the story of the chase. Noting the trouble that Akhandananda had taken to find him out, the Swami was afraid that this monastic brother would not leave him alone. He said to Akhandananda, "You see, I have a mission; and if you remain with me, I shall not be able to fulfil it." At first Akhandananda was adamant: he would not leave the Swami alone. It may have been because the Holy Mother had told him on the eve of their departure from Calcutta, "I am leaving my all [the Swami] in your hands. See that Naren does not suffer on the way for want of food."

The Swami then said to his brother-monk, "Look, I have become a spoiled man. You leave me." Akhandananda replied, "What would it matter to me even if you had lost your character? I love you, and that is not in any way affected by your good or bad character. But I do not wish to be in your way. I had a great longing to see you, and now I am satisfied. Now you can go alone." The Swami was happy to hear this from him, and next day left for Bhuj, which Akhandananda reached a day later.

At Bhuj, the Swami said to Akhandananda, "We should not stay here for long. The way in which the Raja is entertaining us will result in making us cankers in the eyes of his people. Let us leave this place tomorrow." Accordingly both of them returned to Mandvi, where they halted for a fortnight, and where the Swami made many friends. From there the Swami went to Porbandar. After about a week Akhandananda joined him. They stayed at the house of the Dewan Shankar Pandurang, with whom the Swami practised speaking in Sanskrit, and in that way increased his mastery of the language. From Porbandar the Swami went to Junagadh again. Akhandananda remained in Kathiawar, leaving the Swami to move on alone.

The Swami is next found at Palitana in Gujarat, where the holy mountain Shatrunjaya, sacred to the Jainas, is situated. Palitana is a city of temples, many of which date back to the eleventh century. High up on Shatrunjaya is a temple dedicated to Hanuman, and a Muslim shrine dedicated to Hengar, a Muslim saint. The Swami climbed to the top of the mountain to enjoy the view, which is magnificent. At Palitana he drew the attention of people because of his mastery of singing and playing on musical instruments. This was the last place in Kathiawar where he is known to have halted.

It appears from the Swami's letter of April 26, 1892, written from Baroda to Dewan Haridas Viharidas Desai, that his first stop after Palitana was Nadiad, where he stayed at the Dewanji's house. He wrote: "I had not the least difficulty in reaching your house from the station of Nadiad. And your brothers, they are what they should be, *your brothers*. May the Lord shower his choicest blessings on your family. I have never found such a glorious one in all my travels. . . . I have seen the Library and the pictures of Ravi Varma, and that is about all worth seeing here. So I am going off this evening to Bombay. . . . More from Bombay."

The Swami next went to Baroda, the capital of the Gaekwad of Baroda. He stayed for a short time with Bahadur Manibhai J., one of the ministers of the State and a man of piety and noble character. Then, on hearing that the Thakore Saheb of Limbdi was at Mahabaleshwar, he went there to see that prince. V. R. Joshi, in his life of the Thakore Saheb, writes: "On 24 April 1892, Namdar Thakore Saheb Sri Jasvanta Singhji visited Mahabaleshwar. There he stayed for about three months. During this period he had the company of Swami Sri Vivekananda and on several occasions he discussed the subject of philosophy and self-knowledge." From the personal diary (Nondh-Pothi) of the Thakore Saheb, which is published in the same life, it seems that the Swami reached Mahabaleshwar at the end of April or beginning of May 1892, and that he remained there until the middle of June. The relevant entries in the Thakore Saheb's diary run as follows:

4 and 5 May 1892: I have deeply pondered over the discussion which took place four days ago on reincarnation, and have also referred to several books on that subject. *9–11th May*: I am pleasantly surprised at Swami Sri Vivekananda's deep knowledge of the Shastras. Whatever knowledge of the Shastras I had, has been much increased through discussions with him. *12 May*: At the end of yesterday's discussion it was proved that in ancient times the caste system was based only upon Guna and Karma. . . . *18th May*: There was a considerable discussion on Adharma or sin. Any action contrary to the ten characteristics (Lakshanas) of Dharma is to be considered as Adharma, that is, sin. Such actions are of three kinds—Bodily, oral and mental. *23 May*: Different dispositions of men are caused due to the effect of Sattva, Rajas and Tamas. . . . *25 May*: Swami Sri Dayananda has stated that Jivas, Ishvara and Maya are beginningless (Anadi), but according to Vivekananda, Prakriti and Purusha are beginningless and the effect caused by their combination is the Jiva; I believe his opinion to be better.

Apart from his discussions with the Thakore Saheb, the Swami created a sensation at Mahabaleshwar. Narashimha Chintaman Kelkar, some time editor of the *Maratha* of Poona, calls to mind the Swami's visit in these words:

In 1892, he [the Swami] had come to our Bombay-Poona side; but he had not become well known then. I was at that time preparing for my LL. B. examination. In summer some pleaders had gone to Mahabaleshwar. On their return they said that they had had an opportunity to see a brilliant Bengali sannyasin there. His command of the English language was wonderful, which used to spellbind the hearers, and his philosophical interpretations were very lofty befitting a genius. They also said that they had invited the Swami to Satara, but till the end he could not go there, and I also could not see him then.

While the Swami was at Mahabaleshwar, he was again encountered by Abhedananda, who went there from Bombay. The latter writes in his autobiography:

After having seen Bombay, I went from there to Mahabaleshwar. I heard that Narottam Morarji Gokuldas was a hospitable gentleman in Mahabaleshwar. I went to Gokuldas's house by enquiry and on arrival there I found that Narendranath had already arrived there. ... Seeing me Narendranath said with laughter, "Brother, why are you on my trail for nothing? Both of us have come out with the name of the Master. We had better travel independently." At this I said, "Why should I pursue you? I have come here, as you too have, in course of my wanderings. Through the will of the Master we have met again. I assure you that I am not deliberately after you." Narendranath reacted with loud laughter. ... At the request of Gokuldasji, however, I spent three days at his house with Narendranath and on the fourth day I resolved to set out for Poona.

Describing the Swami at this last meeting before his (the Swami's) departure for America, Abhedananda spoke of him as a soul on fire. He found him tortured with emotions and seething with ideas relating to the spiritual regeneration of the Hindus. The Swami's restlessness frightened Abhedananda. He was like a hurricane. The Swami told his brother-disciple, "I feel such a tremendous power and energy, it is as though I should burst."

After about two and a half months at Mahabaleshwar, the Swami went to Poona. In his letter of June 15, to Haridasbhai, the Dewan of Junagadh, he wrote, "I came down with the Thakore Saheb from Mahabaleshwar, and am living with him. I would remain here a week or two more and then proceed to Rameswaram via Hyderabad." From the address on this letter, it appears that at Poona he stayed at Ellapa Balaram's house in the Neutral Line, where the Thakore Saheb had accommodation. The Thakore Saheb, who had been initiated by the Swami, made this request: "Swamiji, do come with me to Limbdi and remain there for good." But the Swami replied, "Not now, Your Highness. For I have work to do. I cannot rest now. But if ever I live the life of retirement it shall be with you." However, he could not carry out this intention, for he passed away in the midst of his work.

From the Swami's letters it is found that instead of going to Rameswaram via Hyderabad, he went to Khandwa in the Central Provinces, sometime in the later part of June 1892.

Walking through that town, he came across the residence of Babu Haridas Chatterji, a pleader. This gentleman found the Swami standing at his door when he returned from court. At first he took him to be an ordinary sadhu; but he found, to his surprise, that this monk was the most learned man that he had ever met. He invited him to stay at his house, and treated him as a member of the family. The Swami was there for about three weeks. During this time he went on a brief visit to Indore, about forty miles north of Khandwa.

At Indore he stayed with a friend of the Dewan of Junagadh, who perhaps treated him coldly; for on August 22 the Swami wrote to the Dewan from Bombay, "About the kindness and gentlemanliness of your friend Mr. Bederkar of Indore . . . the less said the better." Here he saw the celebrated Chhattri (umbrella), a monument to Ahalyabai, the famous queen of Indore State, who had been one of the greatest administrators India had ever known. It is said, "Her charitable foundations extended all over India, from the Himalayas to Cape Comorin, and from Somnath to the Temple of Jagannath."

When he returned to Khandwa, many prominent people, including members of the Bengali community, met him. All were impressed with his knowledge of the scriptures and English literature. Here the Swami became acquainted with Babu Akshaya Kumar Ghose, whose family in Calcutta he had long known. (This young man later became an adopted son of one Miss Müller of England, and on her behalf he invited the Swami to England in October 1894, when the latter was in America.) Describing the Swami's manner, his host, Haridasbabu, said later: "There was not the least trace of affectation in his conversation. His elevated thought and noble sentiments flowed in the choicest language in an easy and natural way. He had an earnestness about him which made him look as one inspired."

Once Haridasbabu asked the Swami to give a public lecture, but the Swami said he felt that personal teaching, as found in the traditional guru-disciple system, was best; for in that way the disciple was fortunate enough to meet the teacher in an affectionate and personal relationship, like that between father and son. On being pressed by his host, however, he became half-inclined to deliver a lecture, but said that he had never before given a public lecture and had no experience of how to modulate his voice on the platform; nevertheless, he did not mind trying if a gathering of earnest and sympathetic listeners could be convened; for this would help create the atmosphere necessary to arouse the latent powers of a speaker. "But as the conditions proposed", writes the host, "were not practicable in a backward place like Khandwa, the idea had to be abandoned."

During his stay there, Babu Madhavchandra Banerjee, the Civil Judge, gave a dinner for the Bengali residents in honour of the Swami. The Swami took with him some of the Upanishads, intending to expound them before and after the dinner. When the guests arrived, he read out some abstruse passages and then explained them in such a way that a child could understand. Among the guests was Babu Pyarilal Ganguly, a pleader and a Sanskrit scholar, who was inclined to play the role of critic; but when he heard the replies and comments of the Swami, he was completely disarmed. Afterwards he told Haridasbabu that the Swami's very appearance showed greatness.

At Khandwa one gets the first hint of the Swami's serious intention to be present at the World Parliament of Religions at Chicago. It was in Kathiawar that he had heard of this great religious convention which was to be held the following year. He now said to Haridasbabu, "If someone can help me with the passage money, all will be well, and I shall go."

Haridasbabu entreated the Swami to stay longer at Khandwa. The reply was: "I wish I could do so. Everyone is so kind, but I must be on my way to Rameswaram, to do the pilgrimage I have in mind. But if I go on in this way, halting for weeks in each town, it will never be done." Seeing that he was determined to leave, his host gave him a letter of introduction to his brother in Bombay, and said, "He will introduce you to Seth Ramdas Chhabildas, a noted barrister of Bombay [who later travelled with the Swami to Chicago from Yokohama]. Perhaps he will be able to help you. Really, Swamiji, you have a great future before you." "Well," the Swami replied, "I myself do not know; but my Master used to predict many things concerning me." Leaving many friends and admirers in Khandwa, and promising to return one day, he left for Bombay by train. His host had asked him to go by train and had bought him a ticket. He reached Bombay in the last week of July 1892.

In Bombay the Swami met Ramdas Chhabildas, to whom he was introduced by the brother of Haridas Chatterji of Khandwa. This gentleman received him cordially and asked him to be his guest. The Swami agreed. He used to spend most of his time there in further study of the Vedas. On August 22, 1892, he wrote to the Dewan of Junagadh: ". . . I have got here some Sanskrit books and help, too, to read, which I do not hope to get elsewhere, and am anxious to finish them. Yesterday I saw your friend Mr. Manahashukharam who has lodged a sannyasin friend with him. He is very kind to me and so is his son. After remaining here for 15 to 20 days I would proceed toward Rameswaram, and on my return would surely come to you."

One day the Swami went to see a noted politician of Bombay, who showed him a Calcutta newspaper containing an account of the controversy over the Age of Consent Bill. The Swami hung his head in shame when he read that the bill was opposed by the educated section of the Bengali community, and bitterly criticized the iniquitous practice of early marriage.

From the hitherto unpublished "Memoirs" of Sister Christine (an American disciple of Swamiji) we understand that sometime during his stay at Bombay, the Swami visited Kanheri Caves, about twenty miles north of the city, on the island of Salsette, which is, as a matter of fact, part of the mainland, but separated by a small stream. The ocean surrounds it on three sides. There are in all 109 caves, which were inhabited by Buddhist monks in the early years of the Buddhist era. It is said that Buddhaghosha lived here with his disciples for some time and later on went to Ceylon and Burma. About Swamiji's visit to these caves Swami Sadananda (Swamiji's first sannyasi disciple) told Sister Christine: "Swamiji in his wanderings in western India before he went to America, found these caves. The place stirred him deeply, for it seems that he had a memory of a previous life in which he lived there. At that time, the place was unknown and forgotten. He hoped that some day he might acquire it and make it one of the centres for the work which he was planning for the future."

Sister Christine's Memoirs continue: "While he [Swami Vivekananda] was at Thousand Islands [in New York State, U.S.A.] he made plans for the future, not only for his disciples in India and work there, but for those of his followers in America who were hoping sometime to go to India. At that time we thought these plans only day-dreams. One day he said: 'We shall have a beautiful place in India on an island with ocean on three sides. There will be small caves which will accommodate two each, and between each cave there will be a pool of water for bathing, and pipes carrying drinking water will run up to each one. There will be a great hall with carved pillars for the Assembly Hall, and a more elaborate Chaitya Hall for worship. Oh! it will be luxury.' " According to Sister Christine, the Swami said this with reference to the Kanheri Caves.

The Swami remained in Bombay for about two months, and then went to Poona, again on his way to South India. At the station, when the Swami was leaving Bombay, he was introduced to Lokmanya Bal Gangadhar Tilak, the renowned scholar and patriot, who happened to be his fellow passenger. Later, in his reminiscences, Mr. Tilak wrote:

About the year 1892, that is, before the famous Parliament of Religions in the World's Fair at Chicago, I was once returning from Bombay to Poona. At the Victoria Terminus [Bombay] a sannyasin entered the carriage I was in. A few Gujarathi gentlemen were there to see him off. They made the formal introduction and asked the sannyasin to reside at my house during his stay at Poona. We reached Poona, and the sannyasin remained with me for eight or ten days. When asked about his name he only said he was a sannyasin. He made no public speeches here. At home he would often talk about Advaita philosophy and Vedanta. The Swami avoided mixing with society. There was absolutely no money with him. A deerskin, one or two cloths and a Kamandalu were his only possessions. In his travels someone would provide a railway ticket for the desired station. . . .

I was at that time a member of the Deccan Club in the Hirabag [Poona] which used to hold weekly meetings. At one of these meetings the Swami accompanied me. That evening the late Kashinath Govind Nath [Natu] made a fine speech on a philosophical subject. No one had to say anything. But the Swami rose and spoke in fluent English presenting the other aspect of the subject very lucidly. Everyone there was thus convinced of his high abilities. The Swami left Poona very soon after this.

On another occasion Mr. Tilak wrote:

After this incident [the Swami's discourse at the Deccan Club] many people of the city started flocking around the Swami. The Swami used to talk to them on the *Gita* and the *Upanishads*. But the Swami never told his name. . . . When people started coming to him in large numbers, he said to me one day, "I am leaving tomorrow"; and really he went next morning, before anyone in the house had woken up.

Bal Gangadhar Tilak had publicly and strongly opposed the Age of Consent Bill, which, as we have already noted, the Swami had strongly approved of: hence it is sure that these two discussed other matters besides religion and philosophy. Mr. Tilak met the Swami again, at the Belur Math, when he went to Calcutta to attend a session of the Indian National Congress, in December 1901.

The Swami next visited the Maharaja of Kolhapur, to whom he had a note from the Maharaja of Bhavnagar. The Maharani of Kolhapur became greatly devoted to the Swami and was able to persuade him to accept a new ochre cloth. One Mr. Vijapurkar, in his reminiscences, has written of the Swami's visit to Kolhapur as follows:

In 1892, when he [the Swami] visited our holy place, each of us felt at the time that he would be a great orator in the future. Not only was he well read, but he had mastered the art of putting his subject in

such a manner that it would impress the mind of the hearer. We had
invited him to speak in our Rajaramiya Parishad. Had I not had the
good fortune of spending about an hour and a half in his company, I
should not have understood his power of fascinating his hearers.
Before he spoke, we asked him whether he would need any help from
our side. He did not take any notes for his lecture. We no doubt knew
in general what he said, but when it came through his mouth, it had
a unique power of attraction.

Raosaheb Lakshmanrao Golwalkar was the Private Secretary of
the Maharaja. He had arranged for the Swami's stay at the Khasbag.
We had learnt that a great sannyasi had come, and that he could
speak English. On the way back from our evening walk, we went to
see him. When we heard his voice from a distance, we could understand that he had a wonderful personality. When we approached and
saluted him, he did not bless us by saying "Narayana" or anything
else. He continued his talk without stopping. He would reply promptly
when anyone asked a question. We then invited him to come to our
Rajaramiya Parishad the next day. There also I witnessed the same
thing. . . . I remember two sentences which he spoke on that occasion.
He said, "My religion is that of which Buddhism is a rebel child, and
Christianity but a far-fetched imitation. . . . How will the Europeans
understand religion? They are running after luxury." Someone interrupted, saying, "How can flesh-eaters understand religion?" The
Swami immediately reacted saying, "No, no; your ancient sages were
flesh-eaters. Have you not read that in your *Uttara Ramcharita*?" Then
he quoted some verses from that epic, in which there are clear references to flesh-eating. After hearing this statement, some doubted his
caste; but who would dare to ask him about it?

After a short stay at Kolhapur, the Swami went south,
reaching Belgaum about October 15, 1892. Here he was the
guest of a Maharashtrian gentleman, whose son, Prof. G. S.
Bhate, has left a record of those days. It reads in part:

The Swami came to Belgaum from Kolhapur with a note from Mr.
Golvalkar, the Khajgi Karbhari [Private Secretary] of the Maharaja.
. . . I remember him appearing one morning about six o'clock with a
note from Mr. Golvalkar, who was a great friend of my father's. The
Swami was rather striking in appearance and appeared to be even at
first sight somewhat out of the common run of men. But neither my
father nor anyone else in the family or even in our small town was

prepared to find in our guest the remarkable man that he turned out to be.

From the very first day of the Swami's stay occurred little incidents which led us to revise our ideas about him. In the first place, though he wore clothes of the familiar sannyasi's colour, he appeared to be dressed somewhat differently from his brother sannyasis. He used to wear a banyan [thin, sleeveless vest]. Instead of the Danda [sannyasi's staff] he carried a long stick, resembling a walking-stick. His kit consisted of the usual gourd [for water], a pocket copy of the *Gita* and one or two [other] books. . . . We were not accustomed to a sannyasi using the English language as a medium of conversation, wearing a banyan instead of sitting bare-bodied, and showing a versatility of intellect and variety of information which would have done credit to an accomplished man of the world. . . . The first day after the meal the Swami asked for betel-nut and Pan [betel-leaf]. Then, either the same day or the day after, he wanted some chewing tobacco. One can imagine the horror which such demands from a sannyasi, who is supposed to have gone beyond these small creature comforts, would inspire. From his own admission we learned that he was not a Brahmin and yet he was a sannyasi; that he was a sannyasi and yet craved for things which only householders are supposed to want. This was really very upsetting to our preconceived notions, and yet he succeeded in making us accept the situation and to see that there was really nothing wrong in a sannyasi wanting Pan and Supari [betel-nut], or chewing tobacco. The explanation he gave of his craving disarmed us completely. He said that he had been a gay young man, a graduate of the Calcutta University, and that his life before he met Ramakrishna Paramahamsa had been very worldly. As a result of the teaching of his Guru he had changed his outlook on life, but some things he found impossible to get rid of, and he let them remain as being of no great consequence. When he was asked whether he was a vegetarian or meat-eater, he said that as he belonged not to the ordinary order of sannyasis but to the order of the Paramahamsas, he had no option in the matter. The Paramahamsa, by the rules of that order, was bound to eat whatever was offered. When there was no offering he had to go without food. Further a Paramahamsa was not precluded from accepting food from anyone because of that person's religious beliefs. When asked whether he would accept food from non-Hindus, he told us that he had often taken food from Muslims.

The Swami appeared to be very well grounded in the old pandit method of studying Sanskrit. At the time of his arrival, I was learning the *Ashtadhyayi* (of Panini) by rote, and to my great surprise, his memory, even in quoting from the portions of the *Ashtadhyayi* which I had been painfully trying to remember, was much superior to mine. If I remember aright, when my father wanted me to repeat the portions that I had been preparing, I made some slips, which to my confusion the Swami, smiling, corrected. The effect of this was almost overwhelming as far as my feelings towards him were concerned. . . .

For a day or two after his arrival my father was busy trying to take the measure of his guest. Soon he came to the conclusion that the guest was not only above the ordinary, but was an extraordinary personality. He gathered a few of his personal friends together, to see what their opinion would be. They agreed that it was worth while to gather together the local leaders and learned men to meet and argue with the Swami. What struck us most in the crowded gatherings which began to be held every day after the presence of the Swami became known in Belgaum, was the unfailing good humour which the Swami preserved even in heated arguments. He was quick enough at retort, but there was never any sting in it. One day we had a rather amusing illustration of the Swami's coolness in debate. There was at that time in Belgaum an Executive Engineer who was the best informed man in our town. He was one of the not uncommon type of Hindu whose external life was most orthodox but who was at heart a sceptic with a strong leaning towards science. He felt that religion or belief in religion was a custom which had gained sanction only through practice through the ages. With these views he found the Swami rather a formidable opponent, armed with larger experience, more philosophy, and more science, than he could muster. Naturally, he lost his temper in argument and was discourteous, if not positively rude, to the Swami. My father protested, but the Swami smilingly intervened, saying that he did not mind. . . . Though the Swami soon got the best of the argument with all, his aim was not so much to be victorious as to create the feeling that the time had come to demonstrate to the country and to the whole world that the Hindu religion was not dying and to preach to the world the priceless truth contained in the Vedanta. . . . He complained that the Vedanta had been treated as the possession of a sect rather than as the perennial source of universal inspiration that it really was.

The diary of the Subdivisional Forest Officer, Haripada

Mitra, with whom, for nine days, the Swami also stayed at Belgaum, has these impressions:

It is the late evening of Tuesday, the 18th of October 1892. A stout young sannyasi of cheerful countenance came to see me with a friend of mine, a lawyer. Looking at him, I saw a calm figure, with eyes flashing like lightning, clean-shaven, garbed in a Gerua Alkhalla [a kind of ochre-dyed garment], with an ochre turban on the head, and Mahratta sandals on the feet. He was most prepossessing. I was at once attracted to him. At that time I believed every sannyasi to be a cheat, and was a sceptic in matters of religion and God. My first thought was that this man must have come to beg something or to ask me to take him into my house because it did not suit him to live with a Maharashtrian. When I entered into conversation with him, I was surprised to find that he was a thousand times superior to me in every respect, and that he asked for nothing! I begged him to come to live with me, but he said, "I am quite happy with the Maharashtrian; if I should leave after seeing a Bengali, he might be hurt. Besides, the whole family treats me with great love. But I will think about it and let you know later on." However, he promised to take breakfast with me the next morning.

Next morning Haripadababu waited for a long time. Eventually, since the Swami did not come, he went to Mr. Bhate's house to bring him. There he was surprised to find a large gathering of pleaders, pandits and prominent citizens asking the Swami questions. Saluting the Swami, Haripadababu took his seat among them. He was amazed at the ready replies which the Swami gave, without pausing, in English, Hindi, Bengali, or Sanskrit.

When the visitors left, the Swami said to Haripadababu, "I hope you will excuse me for not keeping the appointment. You see, I could not go without hurting many people's feelings." On again being pressed to go and live in Haripadababu's house, the Swami said, "I shall go if you can make my host agree to your proposal." After much persuasion Mr. Bhate agreed. Among the Swami's few belongings at this time was a book on French music which he was studying.

In Haripadababu's house three days passed in constant discussion of religious matters with many educated people of the town; and doubts which had obsessed the host's mind for years were dispelled. On the fourth day the Swami said that it was high time for him to be on the move again. "Sannyasis", he remarked, "should not stay more than three days in a city, and one day in a village. If one stays for long in one place, attachment grows. We sannyasis should keep at a distance all the things that bind us to Maya." But the host protested, and the Swami consented to stay a few days more.

One day the Swami related to his host many incidents of his wandering life after he had taken the vow not to touch money. As the tale unfolded Haripadababu thought, "What pain and trouble and hardship have been his!" But the Swami regarded them lightly, as of no importance. He related how in one place he was very hungry and was given some food so hot with chillis that the burning sensation in the mouth and stomach did not subside for a long time; how he had been driven away with the remark that there was no place for sadhus and thieves; how for a time his movements were watched by detectives. To him these were laughing matters—"the play of the Mother", as he called them.

Haripadababu found the Swami well read not only in religion and philosophy, but in secular matters as well. To his surprise the Swami quoted at considerable length from *The Pickwick Papers*. Thinking it strange that a sadhu should be so familiar with profane literature, he asked the Swami how often he had read the book, and was astonished to learn that he had read it only twice. When asked how he could have memorized it in only two readings, the Swami answered that when he read anything he concentrated his entire attention upon it. "Power of mind arises from control of the forces of the body. The idea is to conserve and transform the physical energy into mental and spiritual energy. The great danger lies in spending the forces of the body in wanton and reckless pleasures, and thus losing the retentive faculties of the mind." "Whatever you do, devote your whole mind, heart and soul to it. I once met a great sannyasi who would clean his brass cooking vessels,

Vivekananda as a Wandering Monk

At Belgaum

making them shine like gold, with as much care and attention as he bestowed on his worship and meditation." Haripada Mitra continues:

Swamiji was a real teacher. Sitting before him was not like doing so before an austere schoolmaster. He was often merry in conversation, full of gaiety, fun and laughter, even while imparting the highest instruction. The next moment he would solve abstruse questions with such seriousness and gravity that he filled everyone with awe. Persons of various natures came to see him, some on account of his great intellect, some to test his learning, some from personal motives, others for instruction, still others because he himself was so interesting. Others, again, came because they desired to spend the time free from the troubles and vexations of worldly life. Everyone had free access to him and was cordially received. It was wonderful to see the Swamiji grasp the intentions and fathom the characters of those who came. No one could conceal anything from his penetrating eye. He seemed to read their inmost thoughts. There was a young man who often came to him thinking of becoming a sadhu, so that he might escape the trouble of preparing himself for his university examination. But on seeing the boy, Swamiji at once understood him and said with a smile, "Come for the monastic life after you have got the M.A. degree. It is easier to get an M.A. than to lead the life of the sannyasi." It was simply wonderful how Swamiji charmed our hearts. I shall never forget the lessons which he imparted while sitting under a sandal-tree in the courtyard of my house.

At this time Haripadababu was given to dosing himself with various medicines. The Swami advised him against it, saying that most diseases were purely of a nervous character and could be eradicated by vigorous and radically different states of mind. "And what is the use of thinking of disease always?" added the Swami. "Live a righteous life; think elevating thoughts; be cheerful, but never indulge in pleasures which tax the body or which cause you to repent; then all will be well. And as regards death, what does it matter if people like you and me die? That will not make the earth deviate from its axis! We should never consider ourselves so important as to think that the world cannot go on without us!" From that day Haripadababu gave up the habit.

Haripadababu had a coveted position and was drawing a handsome salary; but he used to get irritated when reprimanded at the office by his superiors, who were English. When the Swami heard this he said: "You have yourself taken this service for the sake of money and are duly paid for it. Why should you trouble your mind about such small things and add to your miseries by continually thinking, 'Oh, in what bondage am I placed!'? No one is keeping you in bondage. You are quite at liberty to resign if you choose. Why should you constantly carp at your superiors? If you feel your present position helpless, do not blame them, blame yourself. Do you think they care a straw whether you resign or not? There are hundreds of others to take your place. Your business is to concern yourself solely with your duties and responsibilities. Be good yourself and the whole world will appear good to you. You will then see only the good in others. We see in the external world the image that we carry in our hearts. Give up the habit of fault-finding, and you will be surprised to find how those against whom you have a grudge will gradually change their entire attitude towards you. All our mental states are reflected in the conduct of others towards us." These words of the Swami made an indelible impression on the listener, and he turned over a new leaf.

Haripadababu had been studying the *Bhagavad-Gita* by himself, but had been unable to comprehend its teachings, and so gave up the study, thinking that there was no practical value in it. However, when the Swami read and explained some portions of it to him, he realized what a wonderful book the *Gita* is. He was now able to grasp its spirit and its relevance to daily life. Under the Swami's instruction he also came to appreciate the works of Thomas Carlyle and the novels of Jules Verne. Haripadababu's account continues:

I had never found in anybody such intense patriotism as his. One evening, reading in a newspaper that a man had died in Calcutta from starvation, the Swami was overcome with sorrow. On asking the cause of his grief, he told me what he had read, and said, "It is not surprising that in Western countries, in spite of their organized charitable institutions and charity funds, many people die every year from the same cause—the neglect of society. But in our country, where righteousness has always been upheld, every beggar receives something, if only a handful of rice; and so we do not often have people dying of starvation, except when there is a famine. This is the first time I ever heard of anyone dying of starvation." "But, Swamiji," I rejoined, "is it not a waste of money to give alms to beggars? My English education leads me to believe that instead of really benefiting them it only degrades their nature, for with the pice given to them they get the means to indulge in such bad habits as smoking Ganja [hemp] and so on. Instead, it is far better to contribute something towards organized charity." Then the Swami said with great intensity, "Why should you worry your head about what a beggar does with the pice or two you give him? Is it not better for persons like you who can afford it, to give him something than to drive him to steal? Suppose he spends the trifle on hemp, that affects only him; but when he resorts to stealing or something worse it affects the whole of society."

In his talks with Haripada Mitra the Swami anticipated those mature views on life which he expressed publicly later on. Even at that time one finds him advocating reform with regard to early marriage, advising all, especially young men, to take a bold stand against this custom, which was enervating Hindu society. Haripadababu writes in his diary:

Speaking of the Sannyasa Ashrama [stage and way of life], he remarked that it was best for a man to practise the control of his mind during his life as a student or as a householder before taking to the life of a wandering monk. "Otherwise," he said, "when the first glow of enthusiasm fades out, the man is likely to consort with those hemp-smoking, idle vagabonds who in the guise of sadhus parade the country.". . . I said to him, "Swamiji, if according to your advice I give up anger and pride and look upon all with an equal eye, then my servants and subordinates will be rude and disobedient to me, and even my relatives will not let me live in peace!" He replied, "Be like the snake of Shri Ramakrishna's parable. At first the terror of the village, the snake met a sadhu who spoke to him of his evil ways. The snake repented and the sadhu gave him a certain Mantra to meditate upon and advised him to practise non-violence. The snake retired to a solitary nook and did as he was told. It so happened that the sannyasi, in his wanderings, passed through this same village some time later. What was his surprise when he saw the snake half-dead, as the result of violent beatings and maltreatment! He asked the snake how he had come to such a pass. He was met with the reply that by following the religious life he [the snake] had become harmless, and that those who had formerly feared him now pelted him with stones and beat him mercilessly. Then the Guru said, 'My child, I asked you not to harm anyone, but I did not forbid you to hiss.' So the snake did as he was bid, and ever afterwards, though he injured none, none dared injure him." And applying this parable the Swami told me that, though it is necessary to appear worldly before worldly people, one's heart should always be given over to the Lord and the mind kept under firm control.

The Swami used to say, "Religion results from direct perception. Put in a homely way, the proof of the pudding is in the eating. Try to realize religion, otherwise you will gain nothing." Quoting the Lord Buddha he said, "Argument is as a desert and wilderness where one loses one's way and comes to grief. Realization is everything." It was not his habit to answer the same question in the same manner, citing the same illustration. Whenever the same question arose he made of it a new subject, as it were. One never felt bored by hearing him, but always wished to hear more and more.

All those who heard the Swami speak at Belgaum were struck with his knowledge of the physical sciences. It was that knowledge which he used so as to furnish his discourses with scientific parallels. He also showed that the aim of religion and of science was the same—the attainment of Truth, which is always one. From religion he would go on to discuss social questions, telling, with sorrow in his voice, of the sad condition of the villagers who, not knowing the principles of hygiene, used the same ponds for drinking, bathing and cleaning purposes. "What brains can you expect of such people!" the Swami would exclaim in despair.

During the discussions in Belgaum he often became impatient with those who were fanatical and did not care to follow the drift of his thought. Sometimes they were obstreperous, and then he would blaze away at them. He was like a thunderbolt: he spoke the truth; he spoke boldly; he did not mince matters.

Regarding those who held to their own views obstinately and against all reason, the Swami told the following story: "There was once a king who hearing that the prince of a neighbouring territory was advancing upon his capital to lay siege to it, held a council, calling all the people for advice as to how to defend the country from the enemy. The engineers advised the building of a high earthen mound with a huge trench all around the capital; the carpenters proposed the construction of a wooden wall; the shoe-makers suggested that the same wall be built of leather, for 'there is nothing like leather', they said. But the blacksmiths shouted out that they were all wrong and that the wall should be built of iron. And then came in the lawyers with the argument that the best way to defend the State was to tell the enemy in a legal way that they were in the wrong and out of court in attempting to confiscate another's property. Finally came the priests, who laughed them all to scorn, saying, 'You are all talking like lunatics! First of all the gods must be propitiated with sacrifices, and then only can we be invincible.' Instead of defending their kindgom they argued and fought among themselves. Meanwhile the enemy advanced, stormed and sacked the city. Even so are men."

One day, when they were alone, the Swami told his host that he intended to sail for America to attend the Parliament of Religions to be held at Chicago. He spoke so fervently that his soul became aglow with the fire of the Rishis, and prophecy was in his words. His host, carried away with enthusiasm, proposed then and there that he raise a subscription in Belgaum for the purpose; but the Swami did not agree to the proposal. He said, "Not yet, my son; not yet. Now I must be off for Rameswaram. I have made a vow to visit that holy place."

Some time before the Swami arrived at Belgaum, Haripadababu's wife had expressed the desire to be initiated by a Guru. Her husband had replied, "You should choose one whom I can venerate also, otherwise you will neither be happy nor reap any benefit. If we meet any really holy man, both you and I will take initiation from him." The wife had agreed to this. Now

Haripadababu asked her whether she would like to be the Swami's disciple. This she had thought of many times, but had been afraid that the Swami would not accept her. She replied that she would consider herself blessed if the Swami would agree. Haripadababu said, "We must try anyway. If we let this opportunity pass, we may never find the like of him again." When Haripadababu spoke about the matter, the Swami protested, "It is very difficult to be a guru. A guru has to take on himself the sins of his disciple. Besides, I am a sannyasi. I want to free myself of all bonds and not to add new ones. Moreover, the disciple should see the guru at least three times before initiation." But Haripadababu was not to be put off. Finding them determined, the Swami finally initiated them.

On October 27, the Swami said to his host, "Now my son, I must be going. I must go to Rameswaram. If I proceed in this way I shall never reach there." Haripadababu entreated him to remain for a few more days, but the Swami was resolved to leave; so he prevailed on him to travel by train, and bought a ticket for him. On putting his guru into a railway compartment, the disciple fell at his feet and said, "Never before have I saluted anyone with heartfelt devotion and veneration. By saluting you I feel myself more than blessed." The Swami stretched out his hands and blessed his disciple.

Next we find the Swami at Margao, in Goa. This was then a Portuguese coastal colony. In his letter written during his stay at Margao (but wrongly dated 1893), he wrote to Haripada Mitra:

I have just now received a letter from you. I reached here safe. I went to visit Panjim and a few other villages and temples near by. I returned just today. I have not given up the intention of visiting Gokarna, Mahabaleshwar [different from the previous Mahabaleshwar, where the Swami had been that summer], and other places. I start for Dharwar by the morning train tomorrow. I have taken the walking-stick with me. Doctor Yagdekar's friend was very hospitable to me. Please give my compliments to Mr. Bhate and all others there. May the Lord shower His blessings on you and your wife. The town of Panjim is very neat and clean. Most of the Christians here are literate. The Hindus are mostly uneducated. Yours affectionately, Sacchidananda.

This is the first letter which the Swami is known to have signed "Sacchidananda". Evidently, during this period he changed to this name from "Vivekananda", which he had used in Rajasthan and Gujarat.

Something of the Swami's visit to Goa is also known from an article published in the *Hindu* of January 19, 1964. The author, Shri V. S. Sukhthanker, writes:

Swami Vivekananda, during his peregrination in India, happened to stop at Belgaum, where he expressed a desire to visit Goa to Dr. V. V. Shirgaonker, a prominent citizen of the city with whom he came into close contact. This was no ordinary visit, for he had a special purpose in mind. Dr. Shirgaonker wrote to Subrai Naik, his learned friend in Margao-Goa, to kindly be at the service of Swamiji.

The day on which Swamiji alighted at the railway station of Margao, he was received by hundreds of people who had come to accord him welcome. Seated in a horse carriage, he was taken in procession to the house of his host Subrai Naik.

Subrai Naik who was a scholar in Sanskrit and well versed in Hindu scriptures was naturally charmed by Swamiji's extraordinary intellect and the depth of his religious knowledge. Having come to know that the main object of his distinguished guest in visiting Goa was to study Christian theology from old Latin texts and manuscripts which were unavailable elsewhere in India, Subrai Naik invited a learned Christian friend, J. P. Alvares, and introduced him to Swamiji who had a talk with him on this subject in Latin [?]. Alvares who was greatly impressed by Swamiji's erudition, immediately made special arrangements for him to stay at the Rachol Seminary, the oldest convent-college of theology in Goa, four miles away from Margao, where rare religious literature in manuscripts and printed works in Latin [are] preserved.

Swamiji spent three days in this seminary assiduously perusing all the important theological works that he found there. His gigantic intellect and original views about Christianity based on sound knowledge were indeed a marvel to the Father Superior and to other Padres and also to all students of this Seminary.

On his return to Margao, visits to Swamiji from Padres even from distant places became a regular occurrence and they even took part enthusiastically in the farewell meeting organized by the Hindus in the town to honour this Hindu monk on the eve of his departure.

The Swami's host in Margao, Shri Subrai Naik, besides being a Sanskrit scholar, was a well-known Ayurveda physician. The guest was put up in a room adjoining the temple of Damodarji, the family deity. The room, together with whatever the Swami used, has been preserved to this day as a memorial of his visit. One day, it is said, the Swami sang some devotional songs and was accompanied on the Tabla by a reputed Tabla-player named Kharupji. After the singing was over, the Swami spoke to Kharupji of his habit of distorting his face while playing on the Tabla. He said that one could play on the Tabla without making faces; but Kharupji said that that was impossible. Then the Swami himself played on the Tabla and showed that it is possible.

On the eve of the guest's departure Mr. Naik asked the Swami for a photograph of himself, to keep alive the memory of his visit. The photograph given by the Swami is still preserved by the descendants of Mr. Naik. Later, this gentleman took Sannyasa and became Swami Subramanyananda Tirtha. He passed away in the same room that had been occupied by the Swami.

17

THROUGH SOUTH INDIA

From Margao the Swami went by train to Dharwar, and from there direct to Bangalore, in Mysore State. He was taken in as a guest by Dr. P. Palpu, the Municipal Medical Officer of Bangalore. Dr. Palpu belonged to the Ezhava community of Kerala,[1] and as a result had had to suffer at the hands of the higher-caste Hindus. Though having the necessary qualification, he had not been able to get a Government post in Travancore State, because of the caste prejudice prevalent there. Subsequently he obtained a post in the Mysore State service. At a later date, Dr. Palpu's son, Shri Gangadharan, recounted to a Swami of the Ramakrishna Order how his father had told Swamiji about the tyranny of the higher castes over the lower-caste people in his native State. Then Swamiji had said to him, "Why do you go after the Brahmins? Find out some good noble person from among your own people and follow him." Dr. Palpu took Swamiji's advice seriously and discovered such a person in Shri Narayan Guru, who became well known as the guide and the leader of the Ezhava community. Dr. Palpu devoted most of his spare time and the greater part of his salary to the cause of his community.

It was not long before the Swami became acquainted with Sir K. Seshadri Iyer, the Dewan of Mysore State. A few minutes' conversation was sufficient to impress this great statesman with the fact that the young sannyasi before him possessed "a magnetic personality and a divine force which were destined to leave their mark on the history of his country". It is not known where the Swami first met the Dewan, but recent findings show that he was the Dewan's guest for three or four weeks, at his house in Mysore City. There the Swami

[1] Kerala was then a common name for Cochin and Travancore States and some neighbouring districts, which comprise the present Kerala State.

met officials and noblemen of the Court of Mysore. Later he stayed at the palace as guest of the Maharaja of Mysore.

Wherever the Swami went he was sought after not only by Hindus, but by people of other faiths as well. For instance, one Abdul Rahman Saheb, a Muslim Councillor of the State, found, to his surprise, that the Hindu sannyasi was well acquainted with the Muslim scriptures: he did not know that the Swami had made the Koran an intellectual and spiritual possession some years earlier. This Muslim came to have some doubts concerning the Koran cleared.

Sir Seshadri Iyer was delighted with "this learned sadhu" and said on one occasion, "Many of us have studied much about religion; and yet what has it availed us? Here is this young man whose insight exceeds that of anyone I have ever known. It is simply wonderful. He must have been born a knower of religion, otherwise how could he at such a comparatively young age have gained all this knowledge and insight?" Thinking that the Maharaja of Mysore might be interested in this "young Acharya", Sir Seshadri Iyer introduced the Swami to him. The Swami, clad in ochre robe, himself princely in bearing, entered the audience-room of the Maharaja, Shri Chamarajendra Wadiyar. The latter was delighted with him. "Such brilliancy of thought, such charm of personality, such wide learning and such penetrating religious insight" quite won him over. The Swami was then made a State guest and given an apartment in the palace itself. Often he was closeted with the Maharaja, who discoursed with him and sought his advice on many important matters.

One day, in the presence of his courtiers, the Maharaja asked, "Swamiji, what do you think of my courtiers?" "Well, I think Your Highness has a very good heart, but you are unfortunately surrounded by courtiers, and courtiers are courtiers everywhere!" came the bold answer. "No, no, Swamiji," the Maharaja protested, "my Dewan at least is not such. He is intelligent and trustworthy." "But, Your Highness," said the Swami, "a Dewan is one who robs the Maharaja and pays the Political Agent." The Prince changed the subject.

Afterwards he called the Swami to his private apartments, and said, "My dear Swami, too much frankness is not always safe. If you continue to speak as you did in the presence of my courtiers, I am afraid you will be poisoned by someone." The Swami burst out, "What! do you think an honest sannyasi is afraid of speaking the truth, even though it costs him his very life? Suppose, Your Highness, your son should ask me tomorrow, 'Swamiji, what do you think of my father?' Am I to attribute to you all sorts of virtues which I am quite aware that you do not possess? Shall I speak falsely? Never!" But with what love and regard he spoke of this Maharaja in his absence! It was the Swami's habit to take a man to task for his weaknesses; but behind that man's back he would have nothing but praise for his virtues, while his defects would be disregarded.

During his stay at the palace, the Swami was introduced to a noted Austrian musician with whom he had a discussion on European music. All were amazed at the Swami's knowledge of Western music. Another day he met an electrician who was engaged in the installation of electricity in the palace. Casually the talk turned to the subject of electricity; and here also the Swami proved himself more informed than the electrician.

During his stay at Bangalore an assembly of pandits was held in the palace-hall. The Prime Minister was in the chair, and the Swami was invited to be present. The topic was Vedanta. The pandits discussed the various theories relating to different aspects of it, but without coming to any agreement. Then the Swami was asked to express his views. He rose, and in that assembly gave out some of those grand ideas about the Vedanta which he was often to express later, in his lectures in the West and in India. His hearers were startled with the originality of his perception and treatment, and in one voice applauded him.

Pleased beyond measure with the Swami, the Prime Minister one day requested him to accept some presents. He ordered one of his secretaries to take him to the best shop in the bazaar and to buy for him anything that he might like to have. To gratify his host the Swami went with the secretary, who took a cheque-book with him, and was ready to write a cheque for a thousand rupees if need be. The Swami was like a child: he looked at everything, admired many things, and in the end said, "My friend, if the Dewan wishes me to have anything I desire, let me have the very best cigar in the place." Emerging from the store, the Swami lighted the cigar, which had cost about a rupee only. He was driven to the palace, eminently satisfied with the purchase.

One day the Swami was called to the apartment of the Maharaja, and the Prime Minister went with him. The Maharaja asked, "Swamiji, what can I do for you?" Evading a direct reply, the Swami burst forth with an account of his mission, which went on for more than an hour. He dwelt on the condition of India. Its great possessions, he said, were philosophical and spiritual: its great needs were of modern scientific ideas and a thorough organic reform. The Maharaja was spell-bound. It was for India, the Swami continued, to give the treasure she possessed to the peoples of the West. He intended going to America himself to preach the gospel of Vedanta. "And what I want", he added, "is that the West should help us in improving our material condition by providing us with the means of educating our peoples in modern agriculture, industries and other technical sciences." The Maharaja promised, then and there, the necessary money to defray his travelling expenses; but for reasons best known to himself—one perhaps being his vow to visit Rameswaram first—, the Swami declined the Maharaja's offer for the present. But from that day the Maharaja and his Prime Minister regarded him as "the man born for the regeneration of India".

The longer the Swami remained with the Maharaja, the greater became the latter's attachment to him. When the Swami spoke of departing, the Maharaja was visibly distressed and requested him to stay a few days more. He added, "Swamiji, I must have something with me as a remembrance of your personality. So, allow me to take a phonographic record of your voice." This the Swami consented to, and even now the record is preserved in the palace, though it has long since become indistinct. So great was the ruler's admiration for the Swami that he proposed to worship his feet, even as one worships those of one's guru; but the Swami did not allow it.

Some days later the Swami said that it was high time for him to depart. Hearing this, the Maharaja wanted to load him with costly presents. The Swami was not willing to accept anything; but the Maharaja insisted. At last the Swami said, "Well, Your Highness, if you persist in offering me something, then please give me a non-metallic hookah. That will be of some use to me." With that he was presented with a rosewood pipe, delicately carved. When the Swami took leave, the Maharaja bowed at his feet; and the Prime Minister made unsuccessful attempts to thrust a roll of currency notes into his pocket. The Swami finally said, "If you desire to do anything for me, please buy me a railway ticket." Realizing that the Swami would not allow him to do more, the Prime Minister bought a second-class ticket and gave him a letter of introduction to Shri Shankariah, the acting Dewan of Cochin.

The next place the Swami is known to have visited was Trichur. In those days there was no railway in Cochin and Travancore States; and the nearest railway station for Trichur was Shoranur; so he travelled the twenty-one miles from Shoranur to Trichur by bullock-cart. It is said that when the bullock-cart passed in front of the house of one D. A. Subramanya Iyer, an officer in the Education Department of Cochin State, Swamiji got down and asked Shri Iyer, who was standing at the door, whether there was any suitable place for bathing. Impressed by the Swami's personality, this gentleman provided him with facilities for a bath and then entertained him as a guest in an annexe to his house. Afterwards, Subramanya Iyer took him to the District Hospital run by the Government, where a Dr. De Souza treated him for sore throat.

At Trichur the Swami stayed only a few days. He next went to Cranganore (also called Kodungalloor), a place famous as a seat of learning and for its Kali temple. At Cranganore people saw him sitting, early one morning, under a banyan tree near the Kali temple. The Swami tried to enter the temple to offer worship to the deity; but the temple guards prevented him. Without getting annoyed, he returned to the tree after bowing down to the Devi from outside. His ochre robes and brilliant eyes attracted the attention of a young man, who approached him with the intention of having some fun; but the young man came away disappointed when he found that the Swami was not as he had thought him to be. Just then two princes of the Cranganore palace, Kochunni Thampuran and Bhattan Thampuran, came to the temple, and the young man just mentioned brought them to the Swami sitting under the banyan tree. The two princes were well versed in the scriptures. They could see from the Swami's features that he was not an ordinary person. When they approached him, he asked them why he was not allowed to enter the temple. They replied that it was difficult to know the caste of people, especially of those who came from outside Kerala, and therefore there was this custom. They had an argument in Sanskrit over the issue. The Swami, however, did not want to interfere with their local tradition, even though the princes were later prepared to allow a person of his calibre to enter the temple.

They argued with the Swami for two days, and were defeated. On the third day they approached the Swami with the desire to have his holy company. When they reached the place where he was, they found him meditating. They waited until he had finished. The glowing, calm appearance of the Swami reminded them of what the scriptures say about the man of meditation. After the Swami had come back to normal consciousness, he conversed with the princes in Sanskrit. When they took their leave, they made obeisance at his feet.

Then some of the learned women of the royal family came to meet the Swami and spoke with him in chaste Sanskrit.

The Swami was surprised to find women speaking Sanskrit so fluently. In no other part of India had he come across this. No doubt he was delighted to do so now.

On the fourth day the princes again went to the temple; but they were disappointed when they did not find the Swami under the banyan tree. He had left the town and gone towards Cochin. Some months later, when they saw the picture of Swami Vivekananda in the papers and read about his success in the Parliament of Religions at Chicago, they recognized him to be the monk with whom they had spoken under the banyan tree. Only then did they come to know his name.

Recent research discloses that at Ernakulam, in Cochin State, where the Swami is next found, he met Shri Chattambi Swami, the guru of the well-known Narayan Guru of Kerala. This meeting took place during December 1892. In 1971 Mr. Bodhasharan, who knew Chattambi Swami intimately, gave these reminiscences to Shri Shankari Prasad Basu:

I was very intimately connected with the Chattambi Swami. I have often heard from him about his meeting with the Swami.

It may have been before or after Swamiji's visit to Kanyakumari. At Ernakulam, one Mr. [Chandu] Lal and a Brahmin [Shri Ramaiya] used to go for a walk every morning and evening. One day, when they had been for a walk to the seaside as usual, they saw a boat coming. A sannyasi clad in ochre robes, and with staff in hand, got out of it. On seeing him they thought that he must be a great man, and a genuine sannyasi, so they must not miss meeting him. They went forward and approached the monk, who spoke with them in Hindi. One of them took the Swami to his house. They asked him, "Do you know English?" In broken Hindi the Swami replied, "I know a little." But later it was revealed that he was a master of the language. The news soon spread. Many people of Ernakulam flocked round him. At this time Chattambi Swami was also in Ernakulam. Once he came to meet the Swami, but on finding a crowd round him, he left, after seeing him from a distance. The local people told the Swami many things about Chattambi Swami; and some of them promised to bring Chattambi Swami to him so that they could be introduced to each other. At this the Swami said, "If he is really a great man, as you tell me he is, why should he come to

me? I shall go to see him." Chattambi Swami was then living at
Shankar Menon's house. The Swami went to see him there. They
talked in Sanskrit, since Chattambi Swami did not know Hindi.
Chattambi took the Swami under a tree so that they could talk
together in a secluded place. On the tree was a monkey, which had
been reared by the host. When they were talking, the monkey
became restless and started shaking the tree. The Swami looked up
at the restless monkey and said, "Just like my mind." Chattambi
Swami said, "Only a great person like you can say such a thing."
Then both of them talked about "Chinmudra". The Swami asked,
"Why is the Chinmudra like this?" Chattambi Swami was a scholar
learned in Tamil literature; so he gave a proper reply. The Swami
was very pleased with it. Catching hold of Chattambi Swami's
hands, and bending his own head down, he said in Hindi, "Very
good." Some may interpret this by saying that the Swami placed
Chattambi Swami's hands on his [the Swami's] head; but Chattambi
Swami said, "That [interpretation] is not right. It was a way of
showing gratitude."

Whenever Chattambi Swami saw me, he used to talk of the
Swami. He was charmed by the Swami's voice. He used to say,
"When the Swami used to sing, it was just like the sound of a golden
pot. Oh, how sweet a voice!" He used to praise the eyes of the Swami
too.

Once when the Swami and Chattambi Swami were talking in
Sanskrit, a Sanskrit scholar happened to be present. He pointed out
a grammatical mistake in the Swami's language. The Swami immediately reacted: "I need not follow grammar; the grammar will
follow me."

Chattambi Swami and Narayan Guru did not approve of the
Swami's meat-eating. They used to say, "But for that, he was a
divinely-inspired person."

According to K. P. K. Menon, author of the short biography *Chattambi Swamigal*, the Swami's meeting with Chattambi Swami took place at the house of Rama Iyer, the
Dewan's Secretary, who was a great admirer of the latter.

Research into the Swami's visit to Kerala has been done
by Shri P. Seshadri. In the "Vivekananda Centenary
Souvenir", published by the Vivekananda Centenary Central
Committee of Trichur in 1963, he writes:

It is said that Swamiji met the great Chattambi Swami at Ernakulam. Both were impressed with each other and Swamiji asked
Shri Chattambi Swami to go over to him alone. He did so and they
were talking together one whole night. It is said that one of the
topics they discussed was the Chinmudra. It is also said that Swamiji
wrote down the name and address of Shri Chattambi Swami in
his diary and told him, "I am writing that I have met a real man
in Malabar [Kerala]." Shri Chattambi Swami often used to speak
of Swamiji with great admiration. In a letter he wrote, with his
characteristic modesty: "I doubt whether the difference between
Vivekananda Swami and me is merely that between Garuda [the
King of Birds] and a mosquito!"

Why did the Swami, so eager to visit Rameswaram, deviate
from his direct route and go into Kerala at all? One Shri
V. M. Korath, writing in the light of the researches of
P. Seshadri in the Malayalam "Vivekananda Sataka Prasasti" (Vivekananda Centenary Souvenir), published in 1963
by the Ramakrishna Ashrama, Trichur, suggests a likely
reason. We noted that in Bangalore the Swami was the guest
of Dr. Palpu, and that this doctor had told him of the miserable
condition of the lower classes in Cochin and Travancore
States. Seshadri thinks that the Swami, moved by what he
had been told, made a detour through these States to see for
himself the condition of the people. It should be added,
however, that even if the Swami had never been given this
account of caste-tyranny in Cochin and Travancore States,
there was sufficient reason for him to go there. It was his
intention to gain first-hand acquaintance with as much of
India as he conveniently could in the course of this pilgrimage.
Since these States had made substantial and distinctive contributions to the civilization and culture of his motherland,
it is not surprising that he took this circuitous route for
Rameswaram.

Some are of opinion that the Swami's inspiration was
behind the silent social revolution in Kerala, organized under
the leadership of Narayan Guru, the disciple of Chattambi
Swami. They say that the Swami inspired the lower classes

of Kerala to improve their condition through education and other means. And when we remember the Swami's rousing call to all classes of the Indian people, made in South India and elsewhere on his return from the West in 1897, this opinion would seem to have substance.

From Ernakulam, the capital of Cochin State, the Swami went south into Travancore. The scenery there enchanted him. It is about 140 miles from Ernakulam to Trivandrum, and in those days the journey took about a week, whether one went by road or waterway. Now we know that he reached Trivandrum on December 13, since he stayed there nine days and left on December 22: therefore the date of his leaving Ernakulam must have been about December 6. In Trivandrum, the capital of Travancore, he stayed with Prof. Sundararama Iyer, who was tutor to the First Prince, the nephew of the Maharaja of Travancore. This gentleman writes of the Swami's nine days' stay with him as follows:

I met Swami Vivekananda for the first time at Trivandrum in December 1892, and was privileged to see and know a good deal of him. . . . He came to me accompanied by his Mohammedan guide. My second son, a little boy of twelve, took him for, and announced him to me as, a Mohammedan too, as he well might from the Swami's costume, which was quite unusual for a Hindu sannyasin of Southern India. . . . Almost the first thing he asked me to do was to arrange for his Mohammedan attendant's meal. This companion was a peon in the Cochin State service and had been detailed to accompany him to Trivandrum by the Secretary to the Dewan, Mr. W. Ramaiya. . . . The Swami had taken almost nothing but a little milk during the two previous days; but it was only after his Mohammedan peon had been provided with food and had taken his leave that he gave any thought to his own needs.

After a few minutes' conversation I found that the Swami was a mighty man. Having ascertained from him that since leaving Ernakulam he had taken almost nothing, I asked him what food he was accustomed to. He replied, "Anything you like; we sannyasis have no tastes." We had some little conversation, as there was yet an interval of a few minutes for dinner. On learning that the Swami was a Bengali, I made the observation that the Bengali nation had

produced many great men and, foremost of them all, the Brahmo
preacher, Keshabchandra Sen. It was then that the Swami mentioned
to me the name, and spoke briefly about the eminent spiritual
endowments, of his Guru, Shri Ramakrishna, and took my breath
completely away by the remark that Keshab was a mere child when
compared with Shri Ramakrishna; that not only he, but many
other eminent Bengalis of a generation past, had been influenced
by the sage; that Keshab had in later life received the benefit of
his inspiration and had undergone considerable change for the
better in his religious views; that many Europeans had sought the
acquaintance of Shri Ramakrishna and regarded him as a semi-divine
personage; and that no less a man than the former Director of Public
Instruction in Bengal, Mr. C. H. Tawney, had written a paper on
the character, genius, catholicity and inspiring power of the great
sage.

   ... The Swami's presence, his voice, the glitter of his eye and
the flow of his words and ideas were so inspiring that I excused myself
that day from attending at the Palace of the late Martanda Varma,
the First Prince of Travancore, who was studying for his M.A. degree
under my tuition. . . . In the evening we went to the house of Prof.
Rangacharya, Professor of Chemistry in the Trivandrum College,
. . . who was even then at the height of his reputation as a scholar
and man of science throughout Southern India. Not finding him at
home, we drove to the Trivandrum Club. There I introduced the
Swami to various gentlemen present, and to Prof. Rangacharya
when he came in later on; [also] to the late Prof. Sundaram Pillai,
and others, among whom I distinctly remember a former Brahmana
Dewan Peshkar and my friend Narayana Menon. . . . [An incident
occurred] which, however trifling in itself, brought out a prominent
characteristic of the Swami, how he noted closely all that was passing
around him, how he combined with his rare gentleness and sweetness
of temper, the presence of mind and the power of retort which
could quickly silence an opponent. Mr. Narayana Menon had,
while leaving the Club earlier in the evening, saluted the Brahmana
Dewan Peshkar, and the latter had returned it in the time-honoured
fashion in which Brahmanas who maintain old forms of etiquette
return the salute of Shudras, that is, by raising the left hand a little
higher than the right. . . . As we were dispersing, the Dewan Peshkar
made his obeisance to the Swami, which the latter returned in the
manner usual with Hindu monks by simply uttering the name of

Narayana. This roused the Peshkar's ire, for he wanted the Swami's obeisance in the fashion in which he had made his own. The Swami turned on him and said, "If you can exercise your customary form of etiquette in returning Narayana Menon's greeting, why should you resent my own adoption of the sannyasin's customary mode in acknowledging your obeisance to me?" This reply had the desired effect, and next day the gentleman's brother came to us to convey an apology for the awkward incident of the previous night. Short as his stay had been at the Club premises, the Swami's personality had made an impression on all. . . .

The Swami paid a visit the next day to Prince Martanda Varma, who had, when informed by me of the remarkable intellectual and imposing presence of my visitor, expressed a desire for an interview. Of course, I accompanied the Swami and was present at the ensuing conversation. The Swami happened to mention his visits to various native princes and courts during his travels. This greatly interested the Prince, who interrogated him regarding his impressions. The Swami then told him that, of all the Hindu ruling princes he had met, he had been most impressed with the capacity, patriotism, energy and foresight of H. H. the Gaekwar of Baroda, that he had also known and greatly admired the high qualities of the small Rajput Chief of Khetri, and that, as he came further south, he had found a growing deterioration in the character and capacity of Indian princes and chiefs. The Prince then asked him if he had seen his uncle, the ruler of Travancore. The Swami had not yet had time to arrange for a visit to His Highness. I may here mention that a visit was arranged for two days later through the good offices of the Dewan, Mr. Shankara Subbier. The Maharaja received the Swami, inquired after his welfare, and told him that the Dewan would provide him with every convenience during his stay both in Trivandrum and elsewhere within the State. The visit lasted only for two or three minutes, and so the Swami returned a little disappointed. . . .

To return to the Swami's conversation with the Prince. . . . The Swami then made an earnest inquiry regarding Prince Martanda Varma's studies, and his aims in life. The Prince replied that he was taking an interest in the doings of the people of Travancore, and that he had resolved to do what he could, as a leading and loyal subject of the Maharaja and as a member of the ruling family, to advance their welfare. The Prince was struck, like all others who

had come in contact with him, with the Swami's striking figure
and attractive features; and, being an amateur photographer, asked
the Swami for a sitting and took a fine photograph which he skilfully
developed into an impressive picture and later on sent as an exhibit
to the next Fine Arts Exhibition held in Madras Museum.

. . . The Swami found me much inclined to orthodox Hindu modes
of life and belief. Perhaps that was why he spoke a good deal in the
vein suited to my tastes and views, though occasionally he burst
out into spirited denunciation of the observance of mere Deshachara,
or local usage. . . .

The Swami once made a spirited attack on the extravagant claims
put forth by science on men's allegiance. "If religion has its superstitions," the Swami remarked, "science has its superstitions too. Both
the mechanical and evolutionary theories are, on examination,
found inadequate and unsatisfying, and still there are large numbers
of men who speak of the entire universe as an open secret. Agnosticism
has also bulked large in men's esteem, but has only betrayed its
ignorance and arrogance by ignoring the laws and truths of the
Indian science of thought-control. Western psychology has miserably
failed to cope with the superconscious aspects and laws of human
nature. Where European science has stopped short, Indian psychology
comes in and explains, illustrates and teaches how to render real the
laws appertaining to higher states of existence and experience.
Religion alone—and especially the religion of the Indian sages—
can understand the subtle and secret workings of the human mind
and conquer its unspiritual cravings so as to realize the one Existence
and comprehend all else as its limitation and manifestation when
under the bondage of matter." Another subject on which the Swami
spoke was the distinction between the world of gross matter (Laukika)
and the world of fine matter (Alaukika). The Swami explained how
both kept man within the bondage of the senses, and only he who
rose superior to them could attain the freedom which is the aim of
all life and raise himself above the petty vanities of the world, whether
of men or gods. The Swami spoke to me of the institution of caste,
and held that the Brahmana would continue to live as long as he
found unselfish work to do and freely gave of his knowledge and all
to the rest of the population. In the actual words of the Swami
which are still ringing in my ears, "The Brahmana has done great
things for India; he is destined to do greater things for India in the
future." The Swami also declared himself sternly against all inter-

ference with the scriptural usages and injunctions in regard to the status and marriage of women. Women, like the lower classes and castes, must receive a Sanskrit education, imbibe the ancient spiritual culture, and realize in practice all the spiritual ideals of the Rishis; and then they would take into their hands all questions affecting their status and solve them in the light thrown on them by their knowledge of the truths of religion and by the enlightened perception of their needs and requirements. . . .

On the third and fourth day of the Swami's stay with me, I sent information to a valued friend of mine in Trivandrum, . . . M. R. Ry. S. Rama Rao, Director of Vernacular Instruction in Travancore. . . . I remember vividly how once Mr. Rama Rao wished the Swami to explain Indriya-nigraha, the restraint of the senses. The Swami launched forth into a vivid story very much like what is usually told of Lila-Shuka, the famous singer of *Krishna-Karnamritam*. The picture he gave of the last stage in which the hero is taken to Vrindavan and puts out his own eyes in repentance for his amorous pursuit of a Sett's daughter, and of his resolve to end his days in unswerving meditation on the divine Shri Krishna at the place of His childhood on earth, remains with me, even after the lapse of twenty-one years, with somewhat of the effect of those irresistibly charming and undying notes on the flute by the late miraculous musician, Sarabha Sastriar, of Kumbakonam. The Swami's concluding words were, "Even this extreme step [of putting out the eyes] must, if necessary, be taken as a preliminary. to the restraint of the wandering and unsubjugated senses and the consequent turning of the mind towards the Lord."

On the third or fourth day of his stay, I made enquiries, at the Swami's request, regarding the whereabouts of Mr. Manmathanath Bhattacharya, who was then Assistant to the Accountant-General, Madras, and who had come down to Trivandrum on official duty in connection with some defalcations alleged to have taken place at the Resident's Treasury. From that time on the Swami used to spend his mornings with Mr. Bhattacharya and stay for dinner. One day, however, when I complained that he was giving all his time to Mr. Bhattacharya, the Swami made a characteristic reply: "We Bengalis are a clannish people." He said also that Mr. Bhatta-charya had been his school or college mate, and that he had an additional claim for consideration as he was the son of the late world-renowned scholar, Pandit Maheshchandra Nyayaratna, for-merly the Principal of the Calcutta Sanskrit College. The Swami

also told me that he had long eaten no fish, as the South Indian
Brahmanas, whose guest he had been throughout his South Indian
tour, were forbidden both fish and flesh, and would fain avail himself
of this opportunity to have his accustomed fare. I at once expressed
my loathing for fish or flesh as food. The Swami said in reply that
the ancient Brahmanas of India were accustomed to take meat
and even beef and were called upon to kill cows and other animals
in Yajnas or for giving Madhuparka [prepared with honey and
meat etc.] to guests. He also held that the introduction and spread
of Buddhism had led to the gradual discontinuance of flesh as food,
though the Hindu scriptures had always expressed a theoretical
preference for those who avoided the use of flesh-foods, and that
the disfavour into which flesh had fallen was one of the chief causes
of the gradual decline of the national strength, and of the final
overthrow of the national independence of the united ancient Hindu
races and states of India. . . . The Swami's opinion, at least as expressed in conversation with me, was that the Hindus must freely
take to the use of animal food if India was at all to cope with the
rest of the world in the present race for power and predominance
among the world's communities, whether within the British Empire,
or beyond its limits. . . .

Once a visitor, the Assistant Dewan or Peshkar in the Huzoor
Office, Trivandrum, Mr. Piravi Perumal Pillai, detained the Swami
from his usual visit to his Bengali countryman, Mr. Bhattacharya.
He came to ascertain what the Swami knew of the various cults
and religions in India and elsewhere, and began by voicing objections to the Advaita Vedanta. He soon found that the Swami was
a master from whose stores it was more important to draw what one
could for inspiration without loss of time than to examine what
were the depths and heights in which his mind could range. I saw
the Swami exhibit on this occasion . . . his rare power of gauging in
a moment the mental reach of a self-confident visitor, and then
turning him unconsciously to suitable ground and giving him the
benefit of his guidance and inspiration. On the present occasion,
the Swami happened to quote from *Lalita Vistara* some verses descriptive of Buddha's Vairagya (dispassion), and in such an entranc-
ingly melodious voice that the visitor's heart quite melted; and the
Swami skilfully utilized his listener's passive mood to make a lasting
impression of Buddha's great renunciation, his unflinching search
after truth, his final discovery of it, and his unwearied ministry of

forty-five years among men and women of all castes, ranks and conditions of life. The discourse occupied nearly an hour, and at its close the Swami's visitor was so visibly affected and acknowledged himself as feeling so much raised for the time being above the sordid realities and vanities of life, that he made many devout prostrations at the Swami's feet and declared, when leaving, that he had never seen his like and would never forget the discourse.

... Once I happened to ask him [the Swami] to deliver a public lecture. The Swami said that he had never before spoken in public and would surely prove a lamentable and ludicrous failure. Upon this I inquired how, if this were true, he could face the august assembly of the Parliament of Religions at Chicago at which he told me he had been asked by the Maharaja of Mysore to be present as the representative of Hinduism. The Swami gave me a reply which at the time seemed to me decidedly evasive, namely, that if it was the will of the Supreme that he should be made His mouthpiece and do a great service to the cause of truth and holy living, He surely would endow him with the gifts and qualities needed for it. I said I was incredulous as to the probability or possibility of a special intervention of this kind. . . . He at once came down on me like a sledge-hammer, denouncing me as one who, in spite of my apparent Hindu orthodoxy so far as my daily observances and verbal professions went, was at heart a sceptic, because I seemed to him prepared to set limits to the extent of the Lord's power of beneficent interposition in the affairs of the universe.

On another occasion, too, some difference of opinion existed in regard to a question of much importance in Indian ethnology. The Swami held that wherever a Brahmana was found with a dark skin, it was clearly a case of atavism, due to Dravidian admixture. To this I replied that colour was essentially a changeable feature in man and largely dependent on such conditions as climate, food, the nature of the occupation as entailing an outdoor or indoor life, and so on. The Swami combated my view and maintained that the Brahmanas were as much a mixed race as the rest of mankind, and that their belief in their racial purity was largely founded on fiction. I quoted high authority—C. L. Brace and others—against him in regard to the purity of Indian races, but the Swami was obdurate and maintained his own view.

During all the time he stayed, he took captive every heart within the home. To every one of us he was all sweetness, all tenderness, all grace. My sons were frequently in his company, and one of them still swears by him and has the most vivid and endearing recollections of his visit and of his striking personality. The Swami learned a number of Tamil words and took delight in conversing in Tamil with the Brahmana cook in our home. . . . When he left, it seemed for a time as if the light had gone out of our home.

Just as he was about to leave, accompanied by his Bengali companion, Mr. Bhattacharya—it was the 22nd December 1892—an incident happened which is worth recording. Pandit Vanchisvara Shastri—a master of that most difficult branch of learning, Sanskrit grammar, and highly honoured by all who knew him for his piety, learning and modesty—was a dependant of the First Prince. . . . During all these days of the Swami's stay he never once came to my house. As the Swami was leaving, he made his appearance and implored me to arrange for an interview, however short . . . . The Swami and Mr. Bhattacharya were just then descending the stairs to get into their carriage and drive away. The Pandit entreated me in the most pressing manner to ask the Swami for at least a few minutes' delay. On being informed of this, the Swami entered into a brief conversation with him in Sanskrit, which lasted seven or eight minutes only. . . . The Pandit told me that it related to some knotty and controverted point in Vyakarana (grammar) and that even during that brief conversation, the Swami showed that he could display his accurate knowledge of Sanskrit grammar and his perfect mastery of the Sanskrit language.

With this the Swami's stay of nine days had come to a close. In my recollection of today, it seems to be somewhat of a nine days' wonder; the impression is one which can never be effaced. . . .

On the day of the Swami's arrival at Trivandrum, as we have seen, Prof. Sundararama Iyer introduced him to Prof. Rangacharya. This is how Shri S. K. Nair, of Travancore, wrote of these professors' association with the Swami and of the impression the latter made:

Both these gentlemen, who were themselves erudite scholars in English and Sanskrit, found great pleasure and derived much benefit by constant conversation with the Swami. Anyone who became acquainted with him could not but be struck with his powerful personality and be drawn to him. He had the wonderful faculty of

22

answering many men on many questions at one and the same time. It might be a talk on Spencer, or some thought of Shakespeare or Kalidasa, Darwin's Theory of Evolution, the Jewish history, the growth of Aryan civilization, the Vedas, Islam or Christianity— whatever the question, the Swami was ready with an appropriate answer.... Sublimity and simplicity were written boldly on his features. A clean heart, a pure and austere life, an open mind, a liberal spirit, a wide outlook and broad sympathy were the redeeming characteristics of the Swami.

Shri K. S. Ramaswami Shastri, the son of Prof. Sundararama Iyer whose reminiscences have just been quoted, was a college student when the Swami stayed in his home. He writes:

It was given to me to meet Swami Vivekananda and spend many days with him at Trivandrum towards the close of 1892 ... Swamiji stayed in our house for nine days. . . .

[One day] he said to me and my father: "Practical patriotism means not a mere sentiment or even emotion of love of the motherland but a passion to serve our fellow-countrymen. I have gone all over India on foot and have seen with my own eyes the ignorance, misery and squalor of our people. My whole soul is afire and I am burning with a fierce desire to change such evil conditions. Let no one talk of Karma. If it was their Karma to suffer, it is our Karma to relieve the suffering. If you want to find God, serve man. To reach Narayana you must serve the Daridra Narayanas—the starving millions of India."...

Although Shri Ramaswami Shastri does not say so here, it is known that at Trivandrum the Swami taught in private the necessity of many reforms affecting the whole Indian nation, with special reference to improving the condition of the poor. But to continue with the reminiscence being cited:

On yet another day, Swamiji told me: "You are still a young boy. I hope and wish that some day you will reverentially study the Upanishads, the *Brahma-Sutras* and the *Bhagavad-Gita* which are known as the Prasthana-traya, as also the Itihasas, the Puranas and the Agamas. You will not find the like of all these anywhere else in the world. Man alone, out of all living beings, has a hunger in his heart to know the whence and whither, the whys and wherefores of things. . . ."

Swami Vivekananda went from Trivandrum to Kanyakumari (Cape Comorin) towards the close of 1892. . . . From Cape Comorin Swamiji went walking to Ramnad and thence to Pondicherry and finally reached Madras. . . .

It was formerly thought that the Swami went from Trivandrum to Rameswaram, and from there to Kanyakumari. The above memoirs of K. S. Ramaswami Shastri, published in 1953, controvert that view. That the Swami went to Kanyakumari direct from Trivandrum was also confirmed by Ramaswami Shastri in his letter of January 19, 1965, to the General Secretary of the Ramakrishna Math, in which he wrote: "On the eve of departure from our house in 1893 [1892] Swamiji Maharaj said that he was going to Kanyakumari. . . . When he came to Madras in January 1897, I met him. He told me that he stayed on the rock overnight." This testimony fits in with what G. G. Narasimhacharya, one of the Swami's disciples, said on July 27, 1902, in his speech at the memorial meeting of the Vedanta Society of Bangalore: "He [the Swami] . . . reached Trivandrum. Mr. Sundararama Iyer . . . and Mr. Rangachariar . . . met him; the Swami was with them for some time and then joined the party of Mr. Bhattacharya, Assistant to the Accountant-General, who then happened to be there. Both of them being Bengalis, they travelled together, visited Rameswaram, and reached Madras via Pondicherry."

There is no mention here of the Swami's having reached Madras via Kanyakumari, but of his having done so via Pondicherry, which was on the direct route from Rameswaram to Madras. That the shortest route from Trivandrum to Rameswaram is via Nagercoil and Madurai is further evidence in favour of the Swami's having gone first to Kanyakumari, since Nagercoil is so close to Kanyakumari. If it were sure that the Swami was meditating on the rock at Kanyakumari on Christmas Eve or Christmas Day, 1892, then the Swami's route is certain. He is known to have left Trivandrum on December 22; and only by going directly could he have reached Kanyakumari by Christmas; but the dates when he was at the Cape are not known for certain. However, as already noted, the greater weight of the evidence, apart from any consideration of dates, leads us to think that the Swami travelled the fifty-five miles to Kanyakumari with Manmatha-babu and party. It is said that there he worshipped the Mother of the Universe in the form of Manmathababu's little daughter.

This view is supported by the article "Srimat Swami Vive-kanandante Kerala Darshanam (Swami Vivekananda's Visit to Kerala)" published in 1918 in the Malayalam journal *Prabuddha Keralam* (pp. 101–9). The relevant portion reads: "On 22nd December 1892 Swami Vivekananda left Travancore for Nagercoil. Mr. Bhattacharya also accompanied Swamiji. Swamiji's next stay was at Nagercoil. Shri Ratnaswami Iyer was then the Collector of Salt at Nagercoil. Swamiji stayed there as the guest of Shri Ratnaswami Iyer. . . . From Nagercoil Swamiji went to Kanyakumari on foot. . . . From there he went to Madurai *en route* to Rameswaram."

Kanyakumari is about twelve miles from Nagercoil. It is the southern extremity of India, the meeting-place of three seas, and a place of pilgrimage for Hindus. "Kanyakumari" means virgin girl. The famous temple there is dedicated to the Divine Mother manifest as a virgin girl. Eager as a child is to be back with its mother, so was the Swami to see the Mother in that seashore temple. Reaching the shrine he fell prostrate in ecstasy before Her image.

Some two furlongs out in the ocean from the tip of the mainland, where the Mother's temple is, are two rocks, known for the last few decades as the Vivekananda Rocks. According to the Puranas, the larger and farther of these two is the one that has been sanctified by the blessed feet (Shripada) of the Divine Mother; for it was here that, as Devi Kanya, She did Tapasya (disciplines and austerities) to win the hand of the Great God, Shiva. Hence the rock has long been considered by Shaktas a place highly favourable for spiritual practices. After worshipping the Mother in the temple, it was to this holy rock that the Swami wanted to go for meditation. But how could he go? He had not a single pice for the boatman.

Without more ado he plunged into those shark-infested waters and swam across. About him the ocean tossed, but in his mind was greater turbulence.

There, sitting on the last stone of India, he passed into a deep meditation on the present and future of his country. He sought for the root of her downfall. With the vision of a seer he understood why India had been thrown from the pinnacle of glory to the depths of degradation. Where only wind and surf were to be heard, he reflected on the purpose and achievement of the Indian world. He thought not of Bengal, or of Maharashtra, or of the Punjab, but of India and the life of India. The centuries were laid out before him. He perceived the realities and potentialities of Indian culture. He saw India organically and synthetically, as a master-builder might visualize in the concrete an architect's plans. He saw religion to be the life-blood of India's millions. "India", he realized in the silence of his heart, "shall rise only through a renewal and restoration of that highest spiritual consciousness that has made her, at all times, the cradle of the nations and cradle of the Faith." He saw her greatness: he saw her weaknesses as well—the central one of which was that the nation had lost its individuality. To his mind, the only hope lay in a restatement of the culture of the Rishis. Religion was not the cause of India's downfall; but the fact that true religion was nowhere followed: for religion, when lived, was the most potent of all forces.

The single-minded monk had become transformed into a reformer, a nation-builder, a world-architect. His soul brooded with tenderness and anguish over India's poverty. What use is a religion, he thought, from which the masses are excluded? Everywhere and at all times he saw that the poor had been oppressed by whatever power the changes of fortune had set over them. The dominance of the priesthood, the despotism of caste, the merciless divisions which these created in the social body, making outcasts of religion the majority of its followers—these the Swami saw as almost insurmountable barriers to the progress of the Indian nation. His heart throbbed for the masses, great in their endurance. He seemed to enter, in some high mode of feeling, their world. In their sufferings he found himself sharing; by their degradation he found himself humiliated. He longed to throw in his lot with theirs. Agony was in his soul when he thought how those who prided themselves on being the custodians of religion had held down the masses through the ages. In his letter of March 19, 1894, to Swami Ramakrishnananda, written from Chicago, one catches something of the ardour of the Swami's meditation on the rock:

In view of all this, specially of the poverty and ignorance, I got no sleep. At Cape Comorin, sitting in Mother Kumari's temple, sitting on the last bit of Indian rock, I hit upon a plan: We are so many sannyasis wandering about, and teaching the people metaphysics—it is all madness. Did not our Master use to say, "An empty stomach is no good for religion"? That those poor people are leading the life of brutes, is simply due to ignorance. We have for all ages been sucking their blood and trampling them underfoot.

But what was the remedy? The clear-eyed Swami saw that renunciation and service must be the twin ideals of India. If the national life could be intensified in these channels, everything else would be taken care of. Renunciation alone had always been the great dynamo of strength in India. So at this critical time he looked to the men of renunciation to uphold the cause of India's downtrodden masses. The plan he hit upon was this—to continue the same letter:

Suppose some disinterested sannyasis, bent on doing good to others, go from village to village, disseminating education and seeking in various ways to better the condition of all down to the Chandala [outcaste], through oral teaching, and by means of maps, cameras, globes, and such other accessories—can't that bring forth good in time? All these plans I cannot write out in this short letter. The long and short of it is—if the mountain does not come to Mohammed, Mohammed must go to the mountain. The poor are too poor to come to schools and Pathashalas; and they will gain nothing by reading poetry and all that sort of thing. We as a nation have lost our individuality, and that is the cause of all mischief in India. We have to give back to the nation its lost individuality and *raise the masses*. The Hindu, the Mohammedan, the Christian, all have trampled them underfoot. Again the force to raise them must come from inside, that is, from the orthodox Hindus. In every country the evils exist not with, but against, religion. Religion, therefore, is not to blame, but men.

What could he do, a penniless sannyasi? In the midst of despair, inspiration came to him. He had travelled the length and breadth of India: he was sure that in every town he could find at least a dozen young men who would help him in the service of the masses. But where was the money to come from? He asked for help: he got only lip sympathy. "Selfishness personified—are they to spend anything!" the Swami exclaimed. In his anguish he looked out over the ocean. A ray of light shot across his vision. Yes, he would go to America in the name of India's millions. There he would earn money by the power of his brain. Returning to India, he would devote himself to the regeneration of his countrymen—or die in the attempt. Shri Ramakrishna would show him the way, even if nobody in the world would help the work.

Here, then, at Kanyakumari was the culmination of days and months of thought on the problems of the Indian masses; here the longing to find a way by which the wrongs inflicted on them could be righted, was fulfilled. He gazed over the waters through a mist of tears. His heart went out to the Master and to the Mother in prayer. From this moment his life was consecrated to the service of India, but particularly to the service of her outcast Narayanas, her starving Narayanas, her millions of oppressed Narayanas. To him, in this hour, even the direct experience of Brahman in the Nirvikalpa Samadhi, and the bliss attending it, became subservient to the overwhelming desire to give himself utterly for the good of the Indian people. His soul was caught up in the vision of Narayana Himself, the Lord of the Universe, transcendent, yet immanent in all beings—whose boundless love makes no distinction between high and low, pure and vile, rich and poor. To him religion was no longer a special province of human endeavour: it embraced the whole scheme of things—the Vedas, the sages, asceticism and meditation, the Supreme Vision, *and* the people, their lives, their hopes, their misery and poverty and sorrows. He saw that religion, without concern for the poor and suffering, was so much dry straw. Yes indeed, at Kanyakumari[2] the Swami became the patriot and prophet in one!

And so his meditation confirmed him in his intention of going to the West. He would make that individualized and aggressively self-conscious West bow down to the Oriental experience as embodied in India's message to the world. That on which the monks of India concentrate as the ideal of their race and as the consummation of their lives—that in its entirety he would preach to the West. In the wake of that preaching, by him and by others to come, India would rise— a great light illuminating the whole world. He would renounce even the bliss of the Nirvikalpa Samadhi for the liberation of his fellow-men in India and abroad! Thus was the spirit of Shri Ramakrishna revealed to him in one of the most profound experiences of his life. No wonder he later spoke of himself as "a condensed India".

It would seem that the Swami meditated on the rock at Kanyakumari for three days. This view is supported by the evidence of two eye-witnesses. One of these was Shri Ramasubba Iyer. In 1919, when Swami Virajananda, a disciple of the Swami and a monk who came to be widely known and respected, went on pilgrimage to Kanyakumari, Shri Iyer told him that he had himself seen the Swami meditating on the rock for hours together, for three days consecutively. This came as a surprise to Swami Virajananda. In 1914, when he published Volume II of the first edition (in four volumes) of the present *Life of Swami Vivekananda*, he had not known it; hence he had there been unable to give definite information about the length of time the Swami was on the rock.

[2] In September 1970, the Vivekananda Mandapam, built as a memorial on the rock on which the Swami meditated, was consecrated and opened. The work was put through by the Vivekananda Rock Memorial Committee, Madras.

Vivekananda Rock, Kanyakumari

At Hyderabad

Years later, another eye-witness, Shri Sadashivam Pillai, told an admirer of Swami Vivekananda that the Swami had remained on the rock for three nights. The Swami had come to Kanyakumari on foot. Being impressed by the monk's personality, Shri Pillai had watched his movements. He had seen him swim over to the rock. When the Swami did not return in the evening, he became anxious. Next morning Shri Pillai went to the rock with food for the Swami. There he found him meditating; and when Shri Pillai asked him to return to the mainland, he refused. When he offered food to the Swami, the latter asked him not to disturb him. If Shri Pillai wished to give him some food, he could leave some fruit and milk in a hollow of the rock, so that he, the Swami, could take it at will. Shri Pillai was sure that the Swami spent three nights on the rock. Leaving Trivandrum on December 22, then, and in all probability going straight to Kanyakumari, the Swami was perhaps on the rock from December 24 to 26.

The Swami next made for Rameswaram, to the north. Going on foot, he stopped on the way at Madurai, where he met the Raja of Ramnad, Bhaskara Setupati, to whom he had a letter of introduction. This devout Prince, one of the most enlightened of Indian rulers, became an admirer and disciple of the Swami. To him the Swami expressed many of his ideas about the education of the poor, the improvement of agriculture, and about the problems and potentialities of India. The Raja persistently urged the Swami to go to the coming Parliament of Religions at Chicago, saying that that would be a most favourable opportunity for drawing the attention of the world to Indian spiritual thought, and also for laying the foundation of his future work in India. The Raja encouraged him and promised to help. Being eager to visit Rameswaram, the Swami took his leave, telling the Raja that he would let him know his decision about going to America in the near future.

Rameswaram is immortalized in the *Ramayana*. From Dhanushkodi, just close to it, Hanuman and his army bridged the strait between India and Lanka (now Sri Lanka), where Sita was held captive by Ravana. After Rama had recovered

Sita, and on his return to the mainland, he is said to have set up with due ceremony a Shiva-lingam at Rameswaram. It is around this symbol of Shiva that the great temple of Rameswaram is built; and to it pilgrimage is made from all parts of India. The Rajas of Ramnad have from ancient times had dominion over Rameswaram and Dhanushkodi. To this fact they owe the title "Setupati", or Lord of the Bridge; meaning that they control the approach to Rama's bridge, or more correctly, causeway, which, as mentioned, extended from Dhanushkodi to Lanka.

The pilgrimage to Rameswaram was the fulfilment of a cherished desire of the Swami. It was also the completion of his pilgrim journey through India, or, as we might say, of his pilgrimage to India herself. He had gone up into the Himalayas; had gone west to Dwarka; and now had come to Rameswaram, the southern of the four Dhamas (sacred places at the four "corners" of India). He had not in fact reached Badrinath in the far north; and though he had started out east of Puri, he had not gone there: but what he had not traversed physically he had traversed in spirit by his self-identification with the past and present conditions of India and her people, and by his self-surrender to the cause of her future progress.

18

FURTHER GLIMPSES OF PARIVRAJAKA LIFE

The life of a Parivrajaka, or wandering monk, is a chequered one. Though we have endeavoured to follow the Swami's journeying consecutively, there are a number of incidents, in those sections of it about which something is known, that have not been narrated so far. It was not the Swami's habit to speak about the adventures and experiences of his wandering days, unless asked to: hence the gaps in our knowledge; hence also the uncertainty as to the exact when or where of some of them. Before the account of his visit to Madras and of his doings afterwards is taken up, some of these disconnected incidents will be related. They further reveal the mind and inner stuff of the man.

Once he had a strange vision. He saw an old man standing on the banks of the Indus, and chanting Vedic hymns, in a way distinctly different from that which is normal in modern times. The passage that he heard was:

आयाहि वरदे देवि त्र्यक्षरे ब्रह्मवादिनि ।
गायत्रि छन्दसां मातर्ब्रह्मयोनि नमोऽस्तु ते ॥

"Oh come, Thou Effulgent One, Thou Bestower of Blessings, Signifier of Brahman in three letters! Salutation be to Thee, O Gayatri, Mother of Vedic Mantras, Thou who hast sprung from Brahman!" The Swami believed that through this vision he had recovered the musical cadences of the early Aryans. He also found some remarkable similarity to these cadences in the poetry of Shankaracharya.

There is next the incident that took place at Tari Ghat, now in Uttar Pradesh, which was then a railway station for Ghazipur where, as we have seen, the Swami met Pavhari Baba. The incident is related by a disciple of the Swami, who perhaps heard it from the Swami himself:

It was one of those scorching summer noons, when the Swami alighted from the train at Tari Ghat station. A cloak dyed in the usual ochre colour, and a third-class ticket for a station some distance away, which someone had given him, were about his only belongings. He did not possess even a water-pot. He was not allowed by the porter to stay within the station-shed; so he sat down on the ground, leaning against a post of the waiting-shed for the third-class passengers.

Of the motley crowd assembled there, we need mention only a middle-aged man of the North India trading-caste, a Baniya, who sat on a cotton mat a little way off under the shelter of the shed, almost opposite the Swami. Recognizing the Swami's starving condition, he had made merry at his expense as they journeyed in the same compartment the previous night. And when they stopped at different stations and the Swami, who was suffering intensely from thirst, was unable to obtain water from the water-bearers because he had no money to pay for it, the Baniya bought water to satisfy his own thirst and, as he drank it, taunted the Swami, saying, "See here, my good man, what nice water this is! You being a sannyasi, and having renounced money, cannot purchase it, and so you have the pleasure of going without it. Why don't you earn money as I do, and have a good time of it?" He did not approve of Sannyasa; no, he did not believe in giving up the world and money-making for an idea. In his opinion it was only right that the sannyasi should starve, and so, when they both alighted at Tari Ghat, he took considerable pains to make it clear to the Swami, by means of arguments, illustrations and taunts, that he [the Swami] was getting just what he deserved; for the Swami was in the burning sun whilst the Baniya had seated himself in the shade. "Look here," he began again with a derisive smile curling his lips, "what nice Puris and Laddus I am eating! You do not care to earn money, so you have to rest content with a parched throat and empty stomach, and the bare ground to sit on!" The Swami looked on calmly, not a muscle of his face moved.

Presently there appeared one of the local inhabitants carrying a bundle and a tumbler in his right hand, a mat under his left arm, and an earthen jug of water in his left hand. He hurriedly spread the mat in a clean spot, put on it the things he was carrying, and called to the Swami, "Do come, Babaji, and take the food I have brought for you." The Swami was surprised beyond words. What did this mean? Who was this newcomer? The jeering Baniya's look was changed to one of blank amazement. The newcomer kept on insisting, "Come on, Babaji, you must come and eat the food." "I am afraid you are making a mistake, my friend", said the Swami: "perhaps you are taking me for somebody else. I do not remember having ever met you." But the other cried out, "No, no, you are the very Babaji I have seen." "What do you mean?" asked the Swami, his curiosity fully aroused, while his jeering companion sat gaping at the scene. "Where have you seen me?" The man replied, "Why, I am a sweetmeat vendor and was having my usual nap after my noon meal. And I dreamt that Shri Ramji was pointing you out to me and telling me that He was pained to see you without food from the day before, and that I should get up instantly, prepare some Puris and curry, and bring them to you at the railway station, with some sweetmeats, nice cold water, and a mat for you to sit on. I woke up, but thinking it was only a dream I turned on my side and slept again. But Shri Ramji, in His infinite graciousness, came to me again and actually pushed me to make me get up and do as He had said. I quickly prepared some Puris and curry, and, taking some sweets which I had prepared this morning, some cold water and a mat from my shop, I ran here direct and recognized you at once from a distance. Now do come and have your meal while it is fresh. You must be very hungry." One can imagine the Swami's feelings at this time. With all his heart the Swami thanked his simple host, while tears of love flowed from his eyes; but the kind man protested saying, "No, no, Babaji! Do not thank me. It is all the will of Shri Ramji." The jeering Baniya was quite taken aback. Begging the Swami's pardon for the ill words he had used towards him, he took the dust of his feet.

This is one of many incidents in the Swami's life clearly revealing Divine Providence at work. And now to relate an incident of a different kind which occurred in Rajputana. Once when he was passing through that province, he travelled with two Englishmen in the same railway compartment. They took him to be an ignorant monk and made jokes in English at his expense. The Swami sat as though he did not understand one word. When the train stopped at a station further on he asked the station-master in English for a glass of water. When his companions discovered that he knew English and had understood all that they had said, they were much embarrassed by their conduct and asked him why it was that he had not shown any sign of resentment. He replied, "My friends, this is not the first time that I have seen fools!" The men showed fight, but seeing the Swami's strongly-built frame and undaunted spirit, they thought better of it and apologized to him.

During one of his long railway journeys the Swami had as fellow-passenger a learned occultist, who besieged him with all sorts of questions. Had he been in the Himalayas? Had he met any Mahatmas there, possessed of supernormal powers? And so forth. The Swami, wishing to disabuse the man, encouraged him to talk. Then he himself gave such a spell-binding description of the miracles of the Mahatmas that his listener gaped in amazement. Had they told him anything about the duration of the present cycle?—the listener asked. Yes, the Swami said, he had had a long talk on that with the Mahatmas: they had spoken to him about the coming end of the cycle, and about the part that they would play in the regeneration of mankind and the re-establishment of the Satya-yuga [Golden Age]; and so on and so forth. The man credulously hung on every word that fell from the Swami's lips. Gratified by the acquisition of so much new knowledge, he invited the Swami to have some food, which he readily consented to do, since he had not eaten anything for a whole day. His admirers had bought him a second-class ticket, but they had not been able to persuade him to take either money or food with him, for he was then living by the ideal of taking no thought for the morrow.

The Swami saw that the man had a good heart, but because of his credulous nature he had become entangled in pseudo-mysticism. When the meal was over, therefore, he spoke to him frankly and sternly: "You who boast so much of your learning and enlightenment, how could you unhesitatingly swallow such wild, fantastic tales?" The man hung his head at this reproof and said not a word. The Swami continued: "My friend, you look intelligent. It befits a person of your type to exercise your own discrimination. Spirituality has nothing to do with the display of psychical powers, which, when analysed, show that the man who occupies himself with them is a slave of desire and a most egotistical person. Spirituality involves the acquisition of that true power which is character. It is the vanquishing of passion and the rooting out of desire. All this chasing after psychical illusions, which means nothing in the solution of the great problems of our life, is a terrible waste of energy, the most intense form of selfishness, and leads to degeneracy of mind. It is this nonsense which is demoralizing our nation. What we need now is strong common sense, a public spirit, and a philosophy and religion which will make us *men*." On hearing this the man was overcome with shame, and understood the rightness of the Swami's attitude. He promised to follow his advice in future.

Speaking to Girish Ghosh about his wandering days, the Swami told of an event which happened at Khetri:

In the course of my wanderings I was in a certain place where people came to me in crowds and asked for instruction. Though it seems almost unbelievable, people came and made me talk for three days and nights without giving me a moment's rest. They did not even ask me whether I had eaten. On the third night, when all the visitors had left, a low-caste poor man came up to me and said, "Swamiji, I am much pained to see that you have not had any food these three days. You must be very tired and hungry. Indeed, I have noticed that you have not even taken a glass of water." I thought that the Lord Himself had come in the form of this low-caste man to test me. I asked him, "Can you give me something to eat?" The man said, "Swamiji, my heart is yearning to give you food, but how can you eat Chapatis baked with my hands! If you allow me I shall be most glad to bring flour, lentils and other things, and you may cook them yourself." At that time, according to the monastic rules, I did not touch fire; so I said to him, "You had better give me the Chapatis cooked by you. I shall gladly take them." Hearing this, the man shrank in fear; he was a subject of the Maharaja of Khetri and was afraid that if the latter came to hear that he, a cobbler, had given Chapatis to a sannyasi, he would be severely dealt with and possibly banished from the State. I told him, however, that he need not fear, that the Maharaja would not punish him. He did not believe me; but out of the kindness of his heart, even though he feared the consequences, he brought me the cooked food. I doubted just then whether it would have been more palatable even if Indra himself, King of the Devas, had held a cup of nectar in a golden basin before me. I shed tears of love and gratitude, and thought, "Thousands of such large-hearted men live in lowly huts, and we despise them as low-castes and untouchables!" When I became well acquainted with the Maharaja, I told him of the noble act of this man. Accordingly, within a few days the latter was called to the presence of the Prince. Frightened beyond words, the man came shaking all over, thinking that some dire punishment was to be inflicted upon him. But the Maharaja praised him and put him beyond all want.

Once it occurred to the Swami that going from place to place and begging for food from door to door was after all not the aim for the realization of which he had renounced his home. In a letter written about this time to one of his brother-disciples he says dejectedly, "I am going about taking food at others' houses shamelessly and without the least compunction, like a crow." On the occasion in question, the thought came to him: "Let me beg no longer! What benefit is it to the poor to feed me? If they can save a handful of rice, they can feed their own children with it. Anyway, what is the use of sustaining this body if I cannot realize God?" A desperate spiritual dissatisfaction and ascetic mood came upon him, as sometimes happens with great souls. In this moment of despair he determined to plunge into a forest and, like some Rishi of old, let the body drop from starvation and exhaustion. Without more ado he entered a thick forest that stretched for miles before him, and walked the whole day without food. Evening approached. Faint with fatigue, he sank to the ground beneath a tree, fixing his mind on the Lord, and looking vacantly into the distance.

After some time he saw a tiger approaching. Nearer and nearer it came. Then it sat down at some distance from him. The Swami thought, "Ah! this is right; both of us are hungry. After all, this body has not been the means of the absolute realization. Therefore by it no good to the world will possibly be done. It is well and desirable that it should be of service at least to this hungry beast." He was reclining there all the while, calm and motionless, waiting for the tiger to pounce on him at any moment; but for some reason or other the animal made off of its own accord. The Swami thought that it might yet return, and waited; but it did not. He spent the night in the jungle, communing with his own soul. As dawn approached, a sense of great power came upon him. The content of this experience was known only to himself.

On another occasion also, he became dizzy from exhaustion and could walk no farther. The sun was intolerably hot. Managing to reach a tree near by, he sat down beneath it. A sense of unutterable fatigue came over his limbs. Then, as a light shines in the darkness, the thought came to him, "Is it not true that within the Soul resides all power? How can it be dominated by the senses and the body? How can I be weak?" With that there was a surge of energy through his body. His mind was flooded with light; his senses revived. He rose and journeyed on, determined that he would never again yield to weakness. Many times he was in a similar condition during his wandering life; but he asserted his higher nature, and strength flowed back to him. Later, in one of his lectures in California, the Swami said:

Many times I have been in the jaws of death, starving, footsore, and weary; for days and days I had had no food, and often could walk no farther; I would sink down under a tree, and life would seem to be ebbing away. I could not speak, I could scarcely think, but at last the mind reverted to the idea: "I have no fear nor death; never was I born, never did I die; I never hunger or thirst. I am It! I am It! The whole of nature cannot crush me; it is my servant. Assert thy strength, thou Lord of lords and God of gods! Regain thy lost empire! Arise and walk and stop not!" And I would rise up, reinvigorated; and here I am today, living! Thus, whenever darkness comes, assert the reality, and everything adverse must vanish. For, after all, it is but a dream. Mountain-high though the difficulties appear, terrible and gloomy though all things seem, they are but Maya. Fear not, and it is banished. Crush it, and it vanishes. Stamp upon it, and it dies.

23

At another time, while travelling on foot in Kutch, he was passing through a desert. The sun scorched him; his throat was parched; and no human dwelling was to be seen. On and on he went, until he saw a village with inviting pools of water. He was happy at the prospect of finding food, drink and shelter there. He hastened forward, thinking that he would soon be there. After walking on for a long time he found the village as far off as ever. In despair, he sat down on the sands and looked about him. Where was the village? Where had it gone? Then he knew—it had been only a mirage! "Such is life!" he thought: "Such is the deceptiveness of Maya!" He rose and journeyed on; and though he saw the mirage again, he was no more deceived, for he now knew it for what it was. When he gave a series of lectures in the West on Maya, he compared it to a mirage, using this experience for illustration.

Once he said in the presence of a disciple, as if speaking to himself: "Oh, the days of suffering I passed through! Once, after eating nothing for three days, I fell down senseless on the road. I do not know how long I was in that state. When I regained consciousness I found my clothing wet through from a shower of rain. Drenched, I felt somewhat refreshed. I arose and, after trudging along some distance, I reached a monastery. My life was saved by the food that I received there."

Many were the times when the Swami faced danger, hardship and want in solitude—with nothing in his possession save perhaps a photograph of Shri Ramakrishna and a copy of the *Gita*. In central India he had many trying experiences because people refused to give him food and shelter. It was in that period that he lived with a family of the sweeper caste and saw the priceless worth and potentialities that could be found among those whom society rejected. It must have been contacts and experiences like this that made him realize the distressing condition of his country, and turned him into the champion of her depressed millions. Poverty and misery he saw on every side, and his heart was overwhelmed with compassion.

With all this he was in his heart of hearts the monk. As

days went by, he came to see more and more that the fundamental requirements of the modern renaissance were spiritual.
So, in his own life, he concentrated all the energies of his
personality on following the monastic ideal. It is not surprising,
then, that the monks who met him were impressed by him and
loved him. How often did he not do them a service, regarding
them as bearers of India's highest ideal! It is told that in the
Himalayas he chanced to meet an old monk suffering from the
extreme cold. He was one of those monks who wander about
like lions, scorning any protection over their heads; but he was
ill and miserably cold. The Swami was passing by and saw
his plight. At once he took off the only blanket that he had to
cover himself with and put it over the monk. The latter looked
up, and, with a smile of gratitude, uttered the words, "May
Narayana bless you!"

Sometimes the monks would confide to the Swami their past
life and express their repentance. For instance, when he was
at Hrishikesh, he met a sannyasi of luminous realization. In
the course of conversation this monk's voice became choked
with feeling. He told the Swami the story of his life; and an
amazing story it was. "Yes, I know Pavhari Baba", said the
Swami in answer to the other's question. "I suppose", continued the monk, "you have heard of the thief who visited
his Ashrama to rob him of his few belongings; how the Babaji
ran after the fleeing robber, who dropped the stolen goods in
haste; and how the Babaji picked them up and, catching up
with the fugitive, implored him to take them as rightfully
belonging to him, saying, 'All these are yours, Narayana.'"
"Oh yes," said the Swami, "I remember the story well. Wonderful indeed is Pavhari Baba." "Well," said the monk, overcome with feeling, "*I* was that thief!" The Swami was speechless
with wonder. "I saw my wickedness," went on the monk,
"and repenting of my ways, I adopted this life in order to
gain that most priceless of all possessions, the Lord Himself."
For hours their conversation continued, the monk pouring
forth all the knowledge of spiritual life that he had acquired
since becoming a sadhu. It was late at night when the two

356 LIFE OF SWAMI VIVEKANANDA

days over their meeting. When, later in America, he spoke
of sinners as potential saints, he must have had in mind this
thief who had gained realization.

At a place of pilgrimage in northern India the Swami was
for a time the guest of a police inspector. This man was of a
devout nature, and used to read the scriptures every day. He
took a fancy to the Swami. His salary was a hundred and
twenty-five rupees a month; but the Swami found that with
his way of living he must have been spending not less than
double his pay. When he became well acquainted with his
host, he asked him how he could manage all that expenditure.
The host smiled, and said in a confidential tone, "Swamiji,
it is you sadhus who really help me." "What do you mean?"
asked the Swami. "You see," said the police officer, "many
sadhus come to visit this place of pilgrimage, and most of
them are not so good as you. Those who give cause for suspicion, I search. Sometimes a good deal of money is found on
their persons, hidden in all sorts of strange ways. I put pressure
only on those whom I suspect to possess it by unlawful means.
They are thankful to me for letting them go, and leave behind
them all their money." "But Swamiji," proudly added this
custodian of the law, "I swear to you, I do not take bribes in
any other way."

At one time, during his wanderings in the Himalayas, the
Swami lived with a family of Tibetans, among whom polyandry
prevails. The family consisted of six brothers with but one
common wife. When the Swami came to know them well
enough, he argued with them about polyandry, becoming
fervent in his denunciation of it. One of the men became
vexed with the Swami and asked him, "How can you, a monk,
bring yourself to teach others to be selfish! 'This is a thing
which only I should possess, to the exclusion of anyone else'—
is not such an idea wrong? Why should we be so selfish as to
have each a wife for himself? Brothers should share everything among themselves, even their wives." Though the
argument may have had its weaknesses, the Swami was

astonished at this reply from simple-minded hill people. It was such encounters as these that caused him to think deeply over the differences in the customs and manners of the various peoples that he came across in his travels through India. His perspective broadened, and he developed the ability to see the ethical and social standards of the races of the world through the eyes of those to whom the standards belonged.

Before closing this chapter it will be in place to note some of the changes that the Swami's outlook had undergone since he had started out from Baranagore. Before then, he had not seen much of the outside world. The wandering life was of great educational value to him. It gave him opportunities for first-hand observation and original thought: it also opened up to him a situation where the synthetic ideas absorbed at Dakshineswar were relevant and needed putting into practice. As one of his brother-disciples said of him, "He was constantly on the look-out for new experiences at this time, constantly gathering ideas, making contrasts and comparisons, saturating his mind with the religious and social ideas of every province, studying various systems of theology and philosophy, and finding out the inherent worth of all the varied Indian peoples whose life he closely observed."

The Swami was tirelessly in search of unity in the world of Indian ideals. He finally came to see that underlying all the diversity of customs and traditions was the oneness of the spiritual vision. The differences between the Muslim and Hindu worlds he found to be more apparent than real; for the Muslims as a race were as generous and human, and at heart as Indian, as the Hindus. The enlightened among them appreciated Hindu culture, and were aware that there was an affinity between Sufism and Advaita Vedanta. To him Muslims and Hindus were Indians first; hence the distinction between them by reason of their different beliefs was subordinate to their identity as compatriots.

The Swami's horizon had now so widened that he saw the intrinsic perfection, and could sympathize with the aspirations, of all forms of religion. He saw that, given a spirit of brotherhood, the peoples and sects and castes of India could unite in an organized civic life, especially if a feeling of responsibility to the poor were cultivated by the educated classes. He felt that the choice of religious ideal, and the practice of it, should be a personal matter, neither affecting nor affected by the affairs of the State; and further, that the several latter-day religious movements which were tinged with Western religious thought or Western culture, were also, though perhaps unconsciously, contributing to the crystallization of the modern transition. It was his hope that, with more discrimination between essentials and non-essentials, sectarian bitterness would die out and all would join together in the common task of reappraising and restating, according to modern needs, the content and significance of the ancient Indian culture. With this integrative outlook on the Indian world, and faith in the soundness of its ideals, the Swami arrived in Madras. His wandering life had practically come to an end.

19

IN MADRAS AND HYDERABAD

The beginning of 1893 found the Swami plodding up to Madras from Rameswaram, staff and Kamandalu in hand. This, the thirty-first year of his life, was to be one of the most important in it.

It will be remembered that the Swami had parted from Manmathanath Bhattacharya on reaching Kanyakumari. It so happened that Manmathanath chanced to meet the Swami as the latter journeyed north. He insisted that the Swami travel with him to Madras via Pondicherry and be his guest there. They stayed at Pondicherry for some days, until Mr. Bhattacharya had completed the work for which he had gone there.

It was at Pondicherry that the Swami had a heated discussion with a bigoted pandit on topics relating to Hinduism and its reform. The pandit, being of the old school, opposed the Swami at every turn. He was more bellicose than learned, and he became fierce in his denunciation of the Swami's progressive ideas. The conversation turned to the question of going overseas. The Swami told the pandit that the time had come for Hinduism to take a look at itself; for it to contrast its glories, culture and worth with those of Western civilization; and for it to adjust itself to modern needs and problems, without sacrificing essentials. The pandit met these remarks with violent denunciation, saying that Hinduism was not in need of any reform, that Westerners were all Mlechchhas, and that contact with the West would pervert the Hindu people. Evidently the pandit had seen nothing outside his own province, and knew no better. The Swami felt that it was this narrow conservatism, characteristic of many, that was ruining the country. The argument became bitter, and both contestants excited. "My friend," the Swami cried out at last, "what do

you mean? Upon every educated Hindu devolves the responsibility of submitting the contents of Hinduism to the
test. For this reason we must come out of the limited grooves
of the past and take a look at the world as it moves onwards
to progress at the present day. And if we find that there are
hide-bound customs which are impeding the growth of our
social life or disturbing our philosophical outlook, it is time
for us to advance a step by eschewing them." The Swami
spoke also of the uplift of the masses, and said that the time
was at hand when the Shudras (labouring class) would rise
and demand their rights. He insisted that it was the duty of
educated Indians to help the downtrodden classes by giving
them education, to spread the ideal of social equality, and to
root out the tyranny of priestcraft and the evils that perversion
of the caste system and of the higher principles of religion had
brought about. This was altogether too much for the pandit.
While the Swami was speaking, the man made insulting
gestures, as much as to say, "What can a wandering beggar-
monk know? He [the Swami] is only a child!" He kept inter-
rupting by blurting out "Kadapi na! Kadapi na!"—"Never!
Never!"

It was natural for the pandit to be opposed to reform of
any kind, for he was himself embedded in caste distinctions
and rigid social customs. Nevertheless the Swami did not
let up, but endeavoured to show him how Hinduism itself
sanctioned a broadening of outlook and the breaking down
of social barriers. He spoke of the levelling influence of
Buddhism as the logical development of Hinduism in the
social sphere; for the Vedantic ideal of oneness called for a
social body imbued with the spirit of equality and fraternity:
but of course the groundwork and orientation of reform
were to be strictly Hindu. In the end the pandit was able to
appreciate the force of the Swami's reasoning, though he still
maintained that the Kalapani, or "black water" of the ocean,
was the great dividing-line between the land of the Hindus
and the lands of the Mlechchhas, and was never to be crossed.
It seems that what had particularly annoyed him was that a

young man like the Swami should have dared to question his (the pandit's) learning and orthodox beliefs.

A few days before leaving Pondicherry, Manmathanath had written to a friend in Mysore that the Swami was with him and would be going to Madras. This friend in turn informed his own friends in Madras. So when the Swami arrived with his host in Madras, there were, awaiting his coming, a dozen or so of the city's finest young men; and these in time became his disciples.

Soon, word spread through the city that "a remarkable English-speaking sannyasi has come". Indeed, from the time the Swami reached Madras, he may be said to have been on the high road to public recognition. In Madras many progressive young men became his devoted adherents. The funds for him to go to America were largely secured by them. It was in Madras that his formulation of the ideals of Hinduism was really appreciated, and where the message of his Master gained a ready hearing. It was here, later on, that his work in India in the way of organization and publication was to start. And it was his Madrasi disciples who were to spread his message widely even before his return from the West.

One of the first to meet the Swami on arrival at Madras was G. G. Narasimhachari. In a paper read at Bangalore in 1906, and published in the *Brahmavadin* the same year, he wrote:

My first acquaintance with him [the Swami] began at the beginning of the year 1893 of Chicago Religious Parliament, when he came as a wandering sannyasi to Madras, in the company of one Babu Manmathanath Bhattacharya, the then Deputy Accountant-General of Madras. Mr. Bhattacharya picked him up on his way to [from] Rameswaram as a beggarly sannyasi plodding on the road with a staff and Kamandalu. Forewarned by a kind Mysore friend of ours of a remarkable English-speaking sannyasi travelling in the company of Mr. Bhattacharya at Pondicherry, half a dozen picked friends went to meet him at the Babu's on the day of his arrival at Madras. Each one of my friends may be said to have represented a fair knowledge in a branch of modern Western culture, my humble self a large share of the curiosity to see a modern sannyasi of a new type. The very fact that these young men were very good friends was a proof that they all possessed a decent amount of general culture. After we were welcomed by the Babu and left in the presence of the Swami with a bright smiling face and wonderful flashing, rolling eyes, my friends introduced themselves to the Sadhu through questions. After a few preliminary enquiries of ordinary etiquette, he was hemmed in with all sorts of questions literary and scientific, historical and metaphysical. I was the wisest of the lot; I silently sat and enjoyed the fruits of their conversation. The Swami's pithy and melodious answers came like flashes silencing his questioners. Quotations were freely made from all sorts of classical authors, literary and scientific, historical and philosophical. Late in the evening when my friends returned home, leaving the travel-worn sannyasi to rest, they began to indulge in all sorts of conjectures about his proficiency. . . . From that day onward the house of Manmathanath Babu became a place of daily pilgrimage, to the young and old of the city, till the Swami left for America.

The same disciple, in an earlier issue of the *Brahmavadin*, wrote as follows:

Swamiji was comfortably lodged in Mr. Bhattacharya's residence at St. Thome. Within a few days his intellectual attainments came to be known to all and his first introduction to the Madras Public was in the Literary Society at Triplicane, where a conversazione was held. From that day, he became more and more known. Educated men of all ranks and position began to gather in his room and listen with enrapt attention to the mellifluous discourses of the Swami on all matters. His conversational power was marvellous. Even abstruse metaphysical subjects were handled by him in a very pleasing way and in simple language. . . . Coming again to his discourses in Mr. Bhattacharya's residence, we used to gather there every evening. People whose minds were not settled and who were hating every form of religious faith began to take a peculiarly lively interest in his instructions so much so that from 4 to 10 p.m. there used to be a regular crowd at his residence, people that came to know him being unwilling to miss his company even for a day.

C. Ramanujachari, who was later to devote his life to the work started by the Swami in Madras, remembers the Swami's first visit in these words:

I had three occasions to meet him [the Swami] during my life.

First in February 1893, when he was in Madras as a Parivrajaka [wandering monk]. He was then a guest of one Mr. Bhattacharya, the Accountant General of Madras, who lived in a bungalow called "Rahmat Bhag", on the Beach Road, St. Thome. He was given a suite of rooms in the western portion of the house. We, as students then, had heard of a monk called Satchidananda Swami, who had come from the North, who was remarkably intelligent, and had an amazing personality. We had heard of his having met some young men at Madras—Messrs. M. C. Alasinga Perumal (of the Pachaiyappa's College), G. Venkataranga Rao, D. R. Balaji Rao . . . , G. G. Narasimhachari and some young men, who were members of the Triplicane Literary Society—a very virile association of young men, who had been active in inviting prominent men to speak at the Society's premises. The Swami must have been introduced to them through Mr. Bhattacharya. The Swami spoke at the Literary Society of Triplicane first to a small audience. The impression he created then was that he was a remarkable speaker, and by this chiefly young men were first attracted to him. Then followed immediately the realization by the elders that within this magnificent personality were treasured a prodigious intellect, profound learning, fire of sincere patriotism, sparkling wit and above all unbending spirit of renunciation. Soon Madras came to know that here was a man who had power to lift him above all others, and everybody vied with each other to have a glimpse of him. It was one morning, when he, followed by nearly 15 or 20 young men, was walking majestically, with staff in hand, along the Luz Church Road, Mylapore, towards the west, to Sir S. Subramania Iyer's house to see him and to place before him a proposal of sending him to America for the Parliament of Religions, that I saw him for the first and last time on that occasion. I followed him to the end of the road, but, as he proceeded, a large crowd gathered, who, including myself, had to be kept out when the main party entered Sir S. Subramania Iyer's house. I had no chance to see more of the Swami on that occasion, except hearing that he was a great sadhu, who was being sent to America for the Parliament of Religions.

These reminiscences show that hardly had the Swami settled in his lodging at Madras, when he was besieged by eager enquirers and listeners. The discussions would range over psychology, science, literature, history and other subjects,

besides religion and philosophy. The Swami seemed to gauge
a newcomer's personality at a glance. He was full of ideas.
He had the whole contents of Hinduism held in a grand
perspective made possible by wide learning. One day some of
those who came to the house of Mr. Bhattacharya, finding the
Swami in an exalted mood, which his every thought and word
reflected, asked him, "Swamiji, why is it that in spite of their
Vedantic thought the Hindus are idolaters?" With flashing
eyes the Swami turned on the questioner and answered,
"Because we have the Himalayas!" He meant that, surrounded
by Nature so sublime, man cannot but fall down and adore.

The Swami's personality towered over everything. His
thrilling musical voice, his songs, his strength of soul, his power
of intellect, his luminous and ready replies, his scintillating
wit, his epigrams and eloquence—these all held his hearers
spellbound. Day by day the number of those who came to
the house of Mr. Bhattacharya increased. The Swami combined humility with outspokenness and authority. Now
perhaps he would beg pardon of a pandit who had been insulting to him; at another time he would burst like a hurricane
on his audience, giving them no chance to escape the logic
of his thought; but it was all unostentatious and spontaneous.
He spoke no harsh words against anyone; on the other hand
he did not refrain from criticism when it was necessary. For
example, there was the pandit who asked him if there was
any harm in giving up Sandhyavandana (ritualistic prayers
performed in the morning, noon and evening) because of lack
of time. "What!" exclaimed the Swami, almost ferociously,
"those giants of old, the ancient Rishis, who never walked but
strode, of whom if you were to think but for a moment you
would shrivel up into a moth, they, sir, had time—and you
have no time!" On that same occasion, when a Westernized
Hindu spoke in a belittling manner of the "meaningless
teachings" of the Vedic seers, the Swami fell upon him with
thunderbolt vehemence, crying out, "How dare you criticize
your venerable forefathers in such a fashion! A little learning
has muddled your brain. Have you tested the science of the

Rishis? Have you even as much as read the Vedas? There is the challenge thrown by the Rishis! If you dare oppose them, take it up: put their teachings to the test."

Those in Madras who heard the Swami were amazed. This was the Vedas and Vedanta exhibited as science and at the same time brought to life in personal realization. Each day new gifts and areas of knowledge came to light. Today he would be speaking of Valmiki, Kalidasa and Bhavabhuti in almost the same breath as of Homer and Virgil, Shakespeare and Byron; tomorrow it would be of the Trojans and of the Pandavas, of Helen and of Draupadi. Now he would descant on the idealization of the sensuous in Greek art, and then would go on to contrast it with the whole trend of Hindu art and culture towards the supersensuous. In discussing Hindu psychology he would give his hearers entrée into worlds of heightened perception of which they had not dreamed.

To relieve the strain put on him by the constant influx of people, the Swami used to walk in the evening on the seashore. One day, when he saw the half-starved children of the fishermen working with their mothers, waist-deep in the water, tears filled his eyes, and he cried out, "O Lord, why dost Thou create these miserable creatures! I cannot bear the sight of them. How long, O Lord, how long!" Those who were in his company were overcome and shed tears.

One evening a party was arranged in his honour. The intellectual luminaries of Madras were present. The Swami boldly, almost challengingly, declared himself to be an Advaitin. A group of intellectuals asked him, "You say you are one with God. Then all your responsibility is gone. What is there to check you when you do wrong, and when you stray from the right path?" The Swami replied crushingly, "If I honestly believe that I am one with God, I shall abominate vice and no check is needed."

A few weeks earlier, when the Swami had been at the palace of the Raja of Ramnad, the discussion had taken a similar turn. Someone had ridiculed the assertion that it was possible for a human being to see Brahman, the Unknown. Roused at once, the Swami had exclaimed, "I *have* seen the Unknown!"

Many of the young men who came to the Swami belonged to the social reform movement in Madras. But he saw that they were taking the wrong line, that of sweeping condemnation. Repeatedly he urged on them the need to analyse foreign ideals critically and to guard against assimilating the materialistic foreign culture. They should preserve and make the most of all that was great and glorious in their country's past; otherwise the foundations of the national structure would be undermined. He was not an enemy of social reform; on the contrary, he himself yearned for reform: but it must come from within, not from outside, India; it must be constructive, not destructive.

The Swami held several conversaziones at the Literary Society of Triplicane, a noted and flourishing association; and these introduced him to the public. A report of one of them, one which took place in the third week of January 1893, was given in the *Indian Social Reformer*, a weekly edited by Kamakshi Natarajan, one of the most powerful journalist-writers in India at that time. Although that report is not now to be had, it was extensively quoted in the Madurai *Mail* of January 28, 1893. This latter report (reproduced in *Prabuddha Bharata*, August 1974) began:

A BENGALI SADHU ON HINDU RELIGION AND SOCIOLOGY

A young Bengalee sannyasi of about thirty-two years of age, and a Master of Arts [*sic*] of the Calcutta University was last week interviewed at the Triplicane Literary Society by about a hundred educated Indians among whom was Dewan Bahadur Raghunath Rao. A summary of what was stated by the sadhu is published by the *Indian Social Reformer*, from which we make the following extracts: . . .

The report then summarizes what the Swami said, under the headings of Vedic Religion, Hindu Ideal of Life, Srādha (i.e. Srāddha) Ceremony, Education of Women, and Emancipation of the Hindus. The chairman of the meeting, Dewan

Bahadur Raghunath Rao, was a national figure. Besides being the author of a number of legal treatises, he was for long General Secretary of the Hindu National Social Conference, and had come out strongly in support of the Age of Consent Bill, when even a section of the social reformers had been hesitant about it. That the Swami strongly supported this bill, we have already noted.

These days in Madras were referred to by Kamakshi Natarajan, mentioned above, when he spoke at Bombay on the occasion of the Swami Vivekananda Birthday Anniversary in 1920. The relevant portion of the report of his speech (*Prabuddha Bharata*, March 1920) runs:

Mr. K. Natarajan . . . said that it was his privilege to meet Swami Vivekananda on the very first occasion on which he appeared in Madras as a poor mendicant monk and he took pride in saying that it was Madras that had discovered Swami Vivekananda, after he had wandered all over India and apparently did not feel that his call had come. He then alluded to the vigorous discourse that Swami Vivekananda, then an obscure sannyasi of 28 [*sic*], gave to an audience presided over by Dewan Bahadur Raghunath Rao, in which he expounded upon the Western interpretation of the Eastern culture. It was here that it was decided that the Swamiji should be sent to the Chicago Congress, where the Swamiji showed that his great interest lay in the application of the great spiritual principles to the interpretation of life in terms of modern civilization. . . .

There came to the Swami one day an atheist, the Assistant Professor of Science in the Christian College. His name was Singaravelu Mudaliar. He saw the practical value of Christianity and criticized Hinduism. He. came to argue, but conversation with the Swami changed him into a devoted disciple. The Swami loved him very much, and called him "Kidi". He used to say, "Caesar said, 'I came, I saw, I conquered.' But Kidi came, he saw, and *he* was conquered!" After a time Kidi devoted his life to his Master's cause. When, at the Swami's suggestion, the *Prabuddha Bharata* was started in Madras, Kidi became its honorary manager. He later renounced the world to lead the life of a recluse, and died a saintly death.

V. Subramanya Iyer says that he went with some of his class-fellows to the house of Mr. Bhattacharya, with the idea of having some fun. They found the Swami smoking his hookah in a sort of half-awake, half-dreamy state; in deep contemplation, as it seemed to them. One bolder than the others advanced and asked, "Sir, what is God?" The Swami smoked on as if entirely unconscious of the question. Then he raised his eyes and asked, "Well, my friend, what is energy?" When neither the boy nor his companions were able to give a definition, the Swami, all attention now, exclaimed, "What is this! You cannot define a simple word like 'energy', which you use every day of your life, and yet you want me to define God!" They asked other questions, only to receive equally crushing replies. After a time they left, except for the young Iyer. He, greatly impressed, remained and accompanied the Swami and his disciples on their daily walk to the beach. Casually the Swami asked Subramanya Iyer, "Well, my boy, can you wrestle?" Receiving an answer in the affirmative the Swami said in fun, "Come, let us have a tussle." It was with this athleticism of the Swami in mind that Mr. Subramanya Iyer used to call him "Pahalwan Swami", that is "Athlete Swami".

One day the Swami found Mr. Bhattacharya's cook looking wistfully at the hookah that the Maharaja of Mysore had given him; so he asked the cook, "Would you like to have this?" Seeing the man afraid to say "yes" even after he had repeated the question, the Swami then and there handed it to him. The man could not believe that the Swami had meant what he said. When he actually had the hookah in his own hands, he was grateful beyond words; and to those who came to know of the incident, the Swami's renunciation was manifest, for that hookah was his only comfort. As a matter of fact, it was a custom with him, throughout his life, to give away whatever there was in his possession that anyone specially admired. For instance, in America, a young Mr. Prince Woods coveted the staff which the Swami had used during his wandering days. The latter had brought it all the way from India and prized it for its sacred associations; but he gave it away without hesitation, saying, "What you admire is already yours!" And to Prince's mother, Mrs. Kate Tannatt Woods, of Salem, with whom he stayed for a few days in September 1893, he gave his trunk and blanket.

The Swami had a strange experience about this time. For some days he was bothered by waves of psychic disturbance sent by some spirits. The spirits reported all sorts of false things to make his mind uneasy, which statements he learned later to be untrue. When they had thus annoyed him for some days, he remonstrated with them, whereupon they told him of their miserable condition. The Swami thought over the matter. One day, repairing to the seashore, he took a handful of sand as a substitute for rice and grain, and offered it, praying with his whole heart that these spirits might find rest. After that they ceased to disturb him.

In Madras the Swami drew many who became followers. The experience that he had had in Alwar was repeated here, but in an intensified form. People flocked from all parts of the city to hear him. His strength, purity, and effulgence of soul were more and more manifest; and his personality captivated their hearts even as his ideas captivated their minds. K. Vyasa Rao speaks as follows of the impression the Swami created:

A graduate of the Calcutta University, with a shaven head, a prepossessing appearance, wearing the garb of renunciation, fluent in English and Sanskrit, with uncommon powers of repartee, who sang "with full-throated ease" as though he was attuning himself to the Spirit of the universe, and withal a wanderer on the face of the earth! The man was sound and stalwart, full of sparkling wit, with nothing but a scathing contempt for miracle-working agencies . . .; one who enjoyed good dishes, knew how to appreciate the hookah and the pipe, yet harped on renunciation with an ability that called forth admiration and a sincerity that commanded respect. The young Bachelors and Masters of Arts were at their wits' end at the sight of such a phenomenon. There, they saw the man and saw how well he could stand his ground in wrestling and fencing in

24

the arena of the Universal Soul; and when the hour of discussion
gave way to lighter moods, they found that he could indulge in fun
and frolic, in uncompromising denunciation and in startling *bons
mots*. But everything else apart, what endeared him to all was the
unalloyed fervour of his patriotism. The young man, who had
renounced all worldly ties and freed himself from bondage, had
but one love, his country, and one grief, its downfall. These sent him
into reveries which held his hearers spellbound. Such was the man
who travelled from Hooghly to Tamraparny, who bewailed and
denounced in unmeasured terms the imbecility of our young men,
whose words flashed as lightning and cut as steel, who impressed
all, communicated his enthusiasm to some, and lighted the spark
of undying faith in a chosen few.

The same Vyasa Rao says that when the world discovered
Vivekananda, it discovered Ramakrishna Paramahamsa too:
it was through the disciple that the master was known. The
people of Madras had hopes of Vivekananda not because of
what Shri Ramakrishna had said about him, but because of
what they themselves saw of this young sannyasi, who had not
previously been known to them.

To many the Swami seemed the embodiment of the spirit of
the Darshanas, the Agamas, and the Yogas. He was saturated
not only with the Hindu spiritual experience, but also with
the philosophical and scientific outlook of the West. One
who was highly cultured, and who became his disciple in
these days, spoke of him thus:

The vast range of his mental horizon perplexed and enraptured
me. From the Rig-Veda to *Raghuvamsha*, from the metaphysical
flights of the Vedanta philosophy to modern Kant and Hegel, the
whole range of ancient and modern literature and art and music
and morals, from the sublimities of ancient Yoga to the intricacies
of a modern laboratory—everything seemed clear to his field of
vision. It was this which confounded me, made me his slave.

Another disciple writes:

He frequently had to descend to the level of his questioners and to
translate his soaring thoughts into their language. He would often
anticipate several questions ahead and give answers that would

satisfy the questioners at once. When asked how he so understood them, he would say with a smile that sannyasis were "doctors of men", and that they were able to diagnose their cases before they administered remedies to them.

At times many men's thoughts were his. He would answer scores of questioners at one time and silence them all.

Soft and forgiving as he was to those on whom his grace rested, one had to live in his presence as in the vicinity of a dangerous explosive. The moment a bad thought entered one's mind, it would flash across his also. One could know it from a peculiar smile that lit his lips and from the words that would casually escape from his mouth in the course of conversation.

Already the Swami had announced his intention of going to the West. He said to all those who knew him in Madras: "The time has come for the propagation of our Faith. The time has come for the Hinduism of the Rishis to become dynamic. Shall we stand by whilst alien hands attempt to destroy the fortress of our ancient Faith? Are we satisfied with its impregnability? Shall we remain passive, or shall we become aggressive, as in days of old, preaching unto the nations the glory of the Dharma? Shall we remain encased within the narrow confines of our social groups and our provincial consciousness, or shall we branch out into the thought worlds of other peoples, seeking to influence these for the benefit of India? In order to rise again, India must be strong and united, and must focus all its living forces."

Those who listened understood that the preaching of the Dharma was for him an imperative call. They understood the Swami's intentions in sailing for the West: nay more, they positively exhorted him, saying, "It must be done, Swamiji, and you are the one man to do it. You will work wonders." With that, they went about to raise subscriptions for the purpose. He himself had long had it in mind to attend the Parliament of Religions, but he had taken no definite step in the matter, preferring to wait for the will of the Mother to become evident. Those who went out had soon collected a good amount. About this, G. G. Narasimhachari said:

"When it was three [actually eight] months for the Parliament of Religions to commence its sitting at Chicago, the Swami expressed his desire to attend it to represent Hinduism. A few devoted to him went round to collect subscriptions. A philanthropic gentleman whose official position and rank is the pride of Southern India headed the list with Rs. 500, though another gentleman richer than the one mentioned above refused to give a pie, and even suspected the bona fides of sannyasins in general and Vivekananda in particular. . . ."

But the Swami, when he saw the money, grew uneasy. He said to himself, "Am I following my own will? Am I being carried away by enthusiasm? Or is there a deep meaning in all that I have thought and planned?" He prayed, "O Mother, show me Thy will! It is Thou who art the Doer. Let me be only Thy instrument." He, a sannyasi, inexperienced in the ways of the world, was about to sail, alone and unknown, for distant lands, to meet strange peoples and deliver to them a strange message. And so he said to the astonished disciples, "My boys, I am determined to force the Mother's will. She must prove that it is Her intention that I should go, for it is a step in the dark. If it be Her will, then money will come again of itself. Therefore, take this money and distribute it among the poor." His disciples obeyed him without a word, and the Swami felt as though a great burden had been taken off his shoulders.

The "another gentleman", mentioned by G. G. Narasimhachari, who "refused to give a pie" and even doubted the bona fides of the Swami, was, almost certainly, the Raja of Ramnad. This is known from the reminiscences of Swami Shivananda, the Swami's brother-disciple. In later years (January 1925), Swami Shivananda told a disciple of his that when the Swami had been at Ramnad, the Raja had requested him to attend the Parliament of Religions at Chicago and represent Hinduism. The Raja had promised Rs. 10,000, but the Swami had not accepted anything then. Later on, when the Madras disciples wrote to the Raja for a contribution, he flatly refused, saying, "I am unable to send any money for this purpose."

Not only that, the Raja, swayed by others, even suspected that the Swami, being a Bengali, and an educated one too, might indulge in politics and scheming to his (the Raja's) detriment. We can imagine how pained the Swami was to hear of this. He had had hopes of the Raja of Ramnad: it was therefore natural for him now to feel that his plans had been "dashed to the ground". His response was complete surrender to the Mother's will, as can be seen from the letter he was shortly to write to Alasinga from Hyderabad. It is dated "21st February" 1893; but since the Swami was back in Madras on February 21, it is probable that the letter was written on February 11, the day after his arrival at Hyderabad. He wrote:

Your friend, the young graduate, came to receive me at the station, so also a Bengali gentleman. At present I am living with the Bengali gentleman; tomorrow I go to live with your young friend for a few days, and then I see the different sights here, and in a few days, you may expect me at Madras. For I am very sorry to tell you that I cannot go back at present to Rajputana. It is so very dreadfully hot here already. I do not know how hot it would be at Rajputana, and I cannot bear heat at all. So the next thing I would do, would be to go back to Bangalore and then to Ootacamund to pass the summer there. My brain boils in heat.

So all my plans have been dashed to the ground. That is why I wanted to hurry off from Madras in the beginning. In that case I would have months left in my hands to seek out for somebody amongst our northern princes to send me over to America. But alas, it is now too late. First, I cannot wander about in this heat—I would die. Secondly, my fast friends in Rajputana would keep me bound down to their sides if they get hold of me and would not let me go over to Europe. So my plan was to get hold of some new person without my friends' knowledge. But this delay at Madras has dashed all my hopes to the ground, and with a deep sigh I give it up, and the Lord's will be done! It is my "Praktana" [fate]; nobody to blame. However, you may be almost sure that I shall see you in a few days for a day or two in Madras and then go to Bangalore and thence to Ootacamund to see "if" the Mysore Maharaja sends me up. "If", because you see I cannot be sure of any promise of a Dakshini [southern] Raja. They are not "Rajputs". A Rajput would rather die than break his promise. However, man learns as he lives, and experience is the greatest teacher in the world.

"Thy will be done on earth as it is in heaven, for Thine is the glory and the kingdom for ever and ever."

My compliments to you all,

Yours &c

Sachchidananda

In these days at Madras, waiting for the Mother's call— the "Mother" and the "Lord", mentioned in the above letter, were interchangeable terms with the Swami—the monk of prodigious intellect and patriotic fire was outwardly, as he always was inwardly, the ardent devotee. His soul grew tense with the determination to make Her speak Her will. He carried on with his life of teaching, but prayed to the Mother and the Master for direction. He meditated intensely. Often he would go on singing to the Mother, and be carried away in ecstasy while doing so. Those who were with him would also be caught up in waves of spiritual fervour.

While he was in this devotional state of mind, people in Hyderabad, who had heard of the Swami from their Madras friends, begged him to go there on a brief visit. He readily agreed, thinking that there might be a hidden purpose in this unexpected call. His host at Madras telegraphed to a friend, Babu Madhusudan Chatterjee, Superintending Engineer to His Highness the Nizam, saying that the Swami was to arrive at Hyderabad oh February 10 and would be his guest. On the 9th, a public meeting of the Hindus of Hyderabad and Secunderabad was called to arrange a fitting reception for the Swami; so when he arrived at Hyderabad the following day, he found, to his surprise, about five hundred people assembled on the station platform to receive him, including some very distinguished members of the Court of Hyderabad, several of the nobility, and many pandits, pleaders, and rich merchants. Notable among them were Raja Srinivas Rao Bahadur, Maharaja Rambha Rao Bahadur, Pandit Rattan Lal, Captain Raghunath, Shams-ul-Ulema Syed Ali Bilgrami,

Nawab Imad Jung Bahadur, Nawab Dula Khan Bahadur, Nawab Imad Nawaz Jung Bahadur, Nawab Secunder Nawaz Jung Bahadur, Mr. H. Dorabjee, Mr. F. S. Mundon, Rai Hukum Chand, the bankers Seth Chaturbhuj and Seth Motilal, the host, and the host's son, Babu Kalicharan Chatterjee. The last, who had been known to the Swami in Calcutta, introduced them to him. Garlands of flowers were heaped on the monk. An eye-witness writes:

The Swami, then a young man of robust health, alighted from a first-class compartment, in the robes of a Paramahamsa, a Kamandalu in hand. He was conveyed to the bungalow of Babu Madhusudan, and was followed thither by many of the gentry. Those who could not go to the station came to have interviews at the bungalow. Surely we have not witnessed such crowds before to receive a Swami in Hyderabad. It was a magnificent reception, befitting a reigning Prince.

On the morning of February 11, a committee of one hundred Hindu residents of Secunderabad approached him with offerings of sweets, milk and fruits, and asked him to deliver a lecture at the Mahaboob College in their city. The Swami consented, fixing the 13th as the day. Then he drove with Kalicharanbabu to the fort at Golconda, of historic note and famous for its diamonds. On returning, the Swami found awaiting him a bearer from the Private Secretary to Nawab Bahadur Sir Khurshid Jah, Amiri-i-Kabir, K.C.S.I., the foremost nobleman of Hyderabad and the brother-in-law of His Highness the Nizam, requesting him to come to the palace for an interview the following morning. At the appointed hour the Swami, accompanied by Kalicharanbabu, went to the palace, where he was received by an aide-de-camp of the Nawab. Sir Khurshid Jah was noted for religious tolerance and was the first Muslim to visit all the Hindu places of pilgrimage from the Himalayas to Cape Comorin. He received the Swami warmly and offered him a seat by his side.

For more than two hours the interview lasted, the Swami discussing the contents of Hinduism, Christianity and Islam. The Nawab took exception to the idea of the Personal God as presented in Hinduism, himself believing in the Impersonal Ideal. Then the Swami spoke to him of the evolution of the idea of God, and showed the need for the conception of Him as a Person, since human experience was personal by nature, and therefore the highest conception to which human thought could rise had to be personal. He pointed out that every religion but Hinduism depended on the life of some person as its founder: that Vedanta, on the other hand, was based on eternal principles and did not depend on persons: and that it was on this fact that its claim to universality was founded. The Swami then explained to the Nawab how the whole range of religious ideas arrived at by mankind had arisen from the depths of human nature as a result of its readings of the Truth. All ideals, he said, were true: the religious systems were paths for the attainment of these various ideals: and any one of them, when practised intensely, was certain to make manifest the Divinity already in man. Then, bringing in the Vedantic idea of the Absolute, he stated that man was the greatest of all beings, for it was by the spiritualized human intelligence that the truths of the universe had been discovered. In his essence, man transcended all limitations and was divine.

As the Swami spoke, his eyes were brilliant, his face luminous, and from his personality power emanated. Almost in spite of himself, he gave out his intention of going to the West to preach the Eternal Religion. His eloquence, and what he said, deeply impressed the Nawab, who interrupted to say, "Swamiji, I am ready to help you in your undertaking with one thousand rupees." But the Swami declined to accept the money just then, saying, "Your Highness, the time has not yet come. When the command comes from on high, I shall make you aware of it."

Taking leave of the Nawab, the Swami went to see the Mecca Masjid, Charminar, Falaknama, Nizam's palaces, Bashirbagh, and other places of interest. On the morning of the 13th he met by appointment Sir Ashman Jah, K.C.S.I., the Prime Minister of Hyderabad, the Maharaja Norendra Krishna Bahadur, Peshkar of the State, and the Maharaja

Shew Raj Bahadur; and all these noblemen offered to support his proposed preaching in America. In the afternoon he spoke at the Mahaboob College on "My Mission to the West". Pandit Rattan Lal was in the chair. More than a thousand people attended the lecture, including many Europeans. The Swami's command of the English language, his eloquence, his learning, his power of exposition, were a revelation to all. He spoke of the merits of the Hindu religion, of the greatness of Hindu culture and society in former days, and gave an outline of Vedic and post-Vedic thought. He spoke of the Rishis as the great law-givers, and as the authors and arrangers of the Shastras. He showed how the Puranas incorporated high ethical ideals. Finally he spoke of his mission, "which is nothing less than the regeneration of the Motherland". He declared his feeling that it was imperative on him to go out as a missionary from India to the farthest West, to reveal to the world the incomparable glory of the Vedas and the Vedanta.

On the next day the well-known bankers of the Begum Bazar, headed by Seth Motilal, interviewed him. They promised to help him with his passage money. Some members of the Theosophical Society, and of the Sanskrit Dharma Mandal Sabha, also came. On February 15 the Swami received a telegram from Poona, signed by leading citizens in the name of the Hindu societies of the place, urging him to go there on a visit. He replied that he could not go then, but that he would be happy to go when he could. The next day he went to see the ruins of the Hindu temples, the famous tomb of Baba Saraf-ud-din, and also the palace of Sir Salar Jung.

In Hyderabad the Swami met a yogi famous for his psychic powers. In his lecture on "The Powers of the Mind", delivered at Los Angeles in 1900, he described what happened at this meeting:

Another time I was in the city of Hyderabad in India, and I was told of a Brahmin there who could produce numbers of things from where, nobody knew. This man was in business there; he was a respectable gentleman. And I asked him to show me his tricks. It so happened that this man had a fever, and in India there is a general belief that if a holy man puts his hand on a sick man he will be well. This Brahmin came to me and said, "Sir, put your hand on my head, so that my fever may be cured." I said, "Very good; but you show me your tricks." He promised. I put my hand on his head as desired, and later he came to fulfil his promise. He had only a strip of cloth about his loins, we took off everything else from him. I had a blanket which I gave him to wrap round himself, because it was cold, and made him sit in a corner. Twenty-five pairs of eyes were looking at him. And he said, "Now, look, write down anything you want." We all wrote down names of fruits that never grew in that country, bunches of grapes, oranges and so on. And we gave him those bits of paper. And there came from under his blanket, bushels of grapes, oranges and so forth, so much that if all that fruit were weighed, it would have been twice as heavy as the man. He asked us to eat the fruit. Some of us objected, thinking it was hypnotism; but the man began eating himself—so we all ate. It was all right.

He ended by producing a mass of roses. Each flower was perfect, with dew-drops on the petals, not one crushed, not one injured. And masses of them! When I asked the man for an explanation, he said, "It is all sleight of hand."

Whatever it was, it seemed to be impossible that it could be sleight of hand merely. From where could he have got such large quantities of things?

The Swami studied the man, pondering long over the phenomena that he had witnessed. He came to the conclusion that they were of a subjective character; but the individual mind is part of a universal mind: therefore "each mind is connected with every other mind". Hence the yogi who had "systematically studied, practised, and acquired" these extra-ordinary powers of the mind could cause other minds to perceive what he wished them to perceive.

On February 17 the Swami left Hyderabad. More than a thousand people came to the railway station to bid him farewell. "His pious simplicity, unfailing self-control and profound meditation", writes Kalicharanbabu, "made an indelible impression on the citizens of Hyderabad."

When the Swami returned to Madras, he was accorded an

ovation at the station by his many disciples. He seemed more self-confident. He had tested his oratorical powers before the assembly at the Mahaboob College and found that he could sway large assemblies as well as small gatherings. At Belgaum, it will be remembered, he had told Haripada Mitra that a large audience draws out the powers of a speaker; and this is what had happened on the above occasion.

Back in Madras the Swami continued his religious discourses and his conversations on a wide variety of subjects. Each day brought new disciples and devotees. He became more and more engrossed with the idea of going to America. Sometimes he felt that in America he would be handicapped; at other times he would thrill with the anticipation of extending the field of his work, and with eagerness for new experience. He had at times an intuition of the opportunity and success that awaited him, and he would talk with his disciples about his mission to the West. Those who gave money for the voyage were moved to do so not only by devotion to him, but also by the conviction that he was destined to accomplish great things. They did not know of Shri Ramakrishna's prophecies concerning the Swami's future greatness, for he never spoke of them to these people.

During March and April the Swami's disciples in Madras took definite steps to raise subscriptions for his passage to America. Some went even to Mysore, Ramnad and Hyderabad for the purpose. They visited those whom the Swami had made his disciples, or who were his avowed admirers. Those who had organized themselves into a subscription committee, had, as their leader, Alasinga Perumal, a devoted follower of the Swami. He did not hesitate to beg from door to door. It was he and the young men under him who collected the major portion of the funds. They went for the most part to the middle classes, for the Swami had told them, "If it is the Mother's will that I go, then let me receive the money from the people! Because it is for the people of India that I am going to the West—for the people and the poor!"

From the Swami's letter of May 1893 to the Dewan of

Junagadh, it is clear that by the middle of April the people
of Madras, in conjunction with the Maharaja of Mysore and
the Raja of Ramnad, had contributed the money to send him
to Chicago. We know from a letter of Swami Shivananda
dated February 13, 1894, that the Swami's Madrasi disciples
"collected through subscription about Rs. 4,000". Swami
Shivananda also told one of his disciples years later (January
1925): "Subramanya and Manmathababu paid Rs. 500 each,
and then started collecting from other people." He further
said that when the Raja of Ramnad saw that many big Government officials were contributing, he also sent Rs. 500 at the
request of Manmathababu.

But the Swami was still in a tumult over whether to go at
all. We have noted what steps he took, when he was at Madras
before going to Hyderabad, to force the Mother to tell him
directly Her will. Returning to Madras and finding his disciples eager to collect funds and urging him to go to the West,
he thought, "Well, their readiness is perhaps the first sign."
Then, for some reason, he seems to have passed again through
a period of uncertainty, in spite of being convinced of the
necessity and utility of going.

In this state of mind the Swami prayed again to the Mother
and to his Master for guidance. He felt assured that he ought
to go, but he demanded actual vision: he wanted the direct
command. Several days later, as he lay half-asleep one night,
the command did come, in a symbolic dream. He saw the
figure of his Master, Shri Ramakrishna, walking from the
seashore into the waters of the ocean, and beckoning him to
follow. Peace and joy filled his whole being as he became
fully awake: the order "go" had been impressed on his mind,
as it were. The vision convinced him. He knew it to be a
divine command. His doubts and misgivings were dispelled.

When plans for going to the West were taking shape, the
Swami became disturbed in mind as a result of a dream he had.
Narrating the incident to a disciple five years later, he said:

 Once while I was putting up at Manmathababu's place, I dreamt
one night that my mother had died. My mind became much dis-

tracted. Not to speak of corresponding with anybody at home, I used to send no letters in those days even to our Math. The dream being disclosed to Manmatha, he sent a wire to Calcutta to ascertain the facts of the matter. For the dream had made my mind uneasy, on the one hand; and on the other, our Madras friends, with all arrangements ready, were insisting on my departing for America immediately: yet I felt rather unwilling to leave before getting any news of my mother. So Manmatha, who discerned this state of my mind, suggested our repairing to a man [named Govinda Chetti] living some distance from the town, who, having acquired mystic powers over spirits, could tell fortunes and read the past and future of a man's life. So at Manmatha's request, and to get rid of my mental suspense, I agreed to go to this man. Covering the distance partly by railway and partly on foot, we four of us—Manmatha, Alasinga, myself and another—managed to reach the place. There, what met our eyes was a man with a ghoulish, haggard, soot-black appearance, sitting close to a cremation ground. His attendants used some jargon of a South Indian dialect to explain to us that this was a man with perfect power over ghosts. At first the man took absolutely no notice of us; and then, when we were about to retire from the place, he requested us to wait. Our Alasinga was acting as interpreter, and he explained the request to us. Next the man commenced drawing some figures with a pencil, and presently I found him becoming perfectly still in mental concentration. Then he began to give out my name, my genealogy, the history of my long line of forefathers, and said that Shri Ramakrishna was keeping close to me all through my wanderings, intimating to me also good news about my mother. Furthermore, he foretold that I should have to go very soon to far-off lands to preach religion.

Receiving the good news about his mother, the Swami, with his party, returned to Madras. After arrival there, a wire came from Calcutta saying that his mother was doing well.

During his stay in Madras the Swami spoke at least twice at the headquarters of the Theosophical Society. The news that appeared in *The Theosophist* of March 1893, though it contains a few factual errors, shows that the Swami was making an impression on the educated people of Madras. The report, written by W. R. Old, runs as follows:

During the absence of the President-Founder and Mr. Edge, the monotony of routine work has been agreeably broken by several gatherings of Theosophists and friends upon various occasions. The arrival of Sannyasi Sachchidananda Swami in Madras, and his subsequent visits to the Headquarters of the T.S. [Theosophical Society] has [have] been the cause of much local interest. The sannyasi is possessed of great versatility, a thorough knowledge of Pali [sic], Sanskrit, English, French [sic] and Hebrew [sic] being among his many accomplishments. He is also an M.A. [sic] of the Calcutta University. To these Nature has added a fine stalwart physique and dignified presence. He has travelled a great deal and, among other places, has visited Lhassa and other cities in Thibet [sic]. In his teaching he follows Sri Sankaracharya. But what sets him off from all others of his Holy Order, is the fact that he travels far and wide, mixing freely with the people, holding public meetings and discussions upon religious philosophy. The Sannyasi has had audiences from among the highest intellects in Madras, and has shown himself to be equally facile with arguments from Western philosophy and well versed in modern science.

Sachchidananda expressed himself pleased with some experiments in "localization" and "impression-reading" conducted at Headquarters. . . .

In anticipation of his visit to America, the Swami approached Colonel Olcott, the leader of the Theosophical Society there, for a letter of introduction. This is the account the Swami gave later:

Four years ago, when I, a poor, unknown, friendless sannyasin, was going to America, going beyond the waters to America without any introductions or friends there, I called on the leader of the Theosophical Society. Naturally I thought he, being an American and a lover of India, perhaps would give me a letter of introduction to somebody there. He asked me, "Will you join my Society?" "No," I replied, "how can I? For I do not believe in most of your doctrines." "Then, I am sorry, I cannot do anything for you", he answered.

Even as, when he had first set out on the wandering life he had sought the blessings of the Holy Mother, Sarada Devi so now he yearned for her blessings on this longer journey

Accordingly, he wrote to her for them, requesting her at the same time to be silent about his plans. The feelings of the Holy Mother, when she received her "Naren's" letter, may well be imagined. For many, many months she had not heard from him who had been the most beloved disciple of the Master, and for whom she cherished a special affection. Moreover, she had had a vision regarding him after the passing away of the Master, in which she saw the form of Shri Ramakrishna entering into the body of Narendra, signifying that the Master would thenceforth work in and through his chief disciple. The maternal instinct of the Holy Mother prompted her to prevent the Swami's going to unknown lands: at the same time she recognized that it was the will of the Master. She therefore set her personal feelings aside and sent him her blessings together with loving counsel. She also informed him of the above-mentioned vision that she had had.

When the Swami received the Holy Mother's letter, he alternately danced and wept with joy. He went into his room to conceal his elation, and later on, to the seashore. He said to himself, "Ah! it is all right now. It is the will of the Mother!" When he returned to the house of Manmathababu, he was radiant. Just then quite a number of his disciples had assembled as usual to hear him discourse on religious topics. When the Swami entered, they were surprised to hear him saying, "Yes, now it is the West, the West! Now I am ready. Let us go to work in right earnest. The Mother Herself has spoken!" The disciples were fired with his enthusiasm and eagerly continued their efforts to raise money. As we have noted they had collected a substantial amount.

20

AT KHETRI AND BOMBAY AGAIN

When arrangements for sailing had been made by the Swami's disciples at Madras, Munshi Jagmohanlal, the Private Secretary to the Raja Ajit Singh of Khetri, unexpectedly appeared on the scene, sometime in the second week of April. His appearance put a stop to preparations for the time being.

It will be recalled that nearly two years previously when the Swami had been at Khetri, the Raja there had sought his blessings so that a son might be born to him. On January 26, 1893, a son had indeed been born to him, and been named Rajkumar Jaisingh. The Raja, elated that through the blessings of the Swami, there was now an heir to the ancient Raj of Khetri, wished to celebrate the event, and to have the Swami there for the occasion. Having learnt that the Swami was at Madras, and that his disciples were collecting money for his voyage to the West, he sent Jagmohanlal to bring him to Khetri. He also said that if the Swami fell short of funds, he (the Raja) was prepared to contribute from his personal account, since he heartily agreed with the Swami's intention of going to the West.

Arrived at Madras, Jagmohanlal learnt that the Swami was the guest of Manmathanath Bhattacharya. After much effort he found the residence of this gentleman, but the Swami was not at home. His first question to Mr. Bhattacharya's servant was, "Where is Swamiji?" The man answered, "He has gone to the sea." "What! has he left for the West, then? What do you mean?" cried Jagmohanlal in despair; but the next moment his eyes fell on the Swami's ochre robes hanging on a peg, and he thought, "He cannot have gone." Jagmohan had not understood the servant's meaning. Just then a carriage drew up at the front of the residence, and to his delight he saw the Swami alighting from it: he had gone for an

afternoon drive to the beach with his host. Instantly the
devoted Jagmohanlal prostrated himself full length on the
ground. The Swami was surprised to meet him so unexpectedly.
After having the matter explained to him he said, "Dear
Jagmohan, I am making preparations to embark for America
on May 31st, and hardly a month and a half is left. How can
I go to see the Maharaja now?" But the envoy persisted,
saying, "Swamiji, you must come to Khetri, even if only for a
day. Rajaji will be overwhelmed with disappointment if you
fail to come. You need not trouble yourself further about
making arrangements for your going to the West. The Maharaja himself will see to it. You simply must come with me."
The Swami at length consented, and after some discussion it
was decided that he should sail from Bombay.

When all was ready for him to start for Khetri, there was
a touching farewell scene. His Madras disciples fell prostrate
before him and sought his blessings. They went with him to
the railway station. As the train started, the name of the
Lord, issuing from scores of devotees, rent the air. They saw
him standing at the carriage door with his right hand raised
in benediction.

On his way to Khetri the Swami stopped at Bombay,
Vapingana and Jaipur. At Bombay he stayed at first with a
pandit, at whose house Swamis Brahmananda and Turiyananda unexpectedly came to meet him. In the course of
their pilgrim travels these two had come to Bombay from
Karachi by boat. Thinking that the pandit might not show
proper regard to his brother-disciples, the Swami said, "Haribhai, I won't stay here any more. Let us go to Kalida's house:
he will entertain all of us lovingly." Kalipada Ghosh, a disciple
of the Master, was then living in Bombay because of his employment there. He gladly received them, and showed them
various places in Bombay. One day the Swami said to Turiyananda, "Haribhai, I am going to America. Whatever you
hear of as happening there [meaning preparations for the
Parliament of Religions], is all for this [striking his own chest].
For this [me] alone everything is being arranged."

25

In the evenings many people used to gather round the Swami, and he would discourse on religious topics. One evening the Swami felt unwell; so he asked Turiyananda to speak to the gathering. Very unwillingly the latter spoke a few words. Afterwards the Swami said to him, "Oh, they are all householders! Why did you speak to them about absolute renunciation and dispassion? You may be a monk, but they are all householders. You ought to have told them something that would be useful to them. They will be terrified to hear such things, and their minds will be disturbed. You could have told them something that they could understand and grasp." On being reproached like this, Turiyananda said, "I thought that you were there listening to whatever I said, and so I should not tell them anything at random. In taking that precaution, I became confused."

After staying for a few days at Bombay, the Swami and Jagmohanlal started for Khetri. Brahmananda and Turiyananda went with them as far as Abu Road, and got out there. Khetri was reached about nine in the evening of April 21. The palace was *en fête* and all lit up. Indeed, the festivities had been going on for three or four days, and the whole town was decorated. Singing and dancing were in full swing on all sides. As the carriage bringing the Swami drew up, the guard presented arms. The Raja was at the time in his state barge, which was adorned with jewels, and with flowers, garlands and palms. Seated round him were state guests, some of them princes and chiefs of Rajputana. When Jagmohanlal presented the Swami, the Raja rose and prostrated himself before his guru. The Swami blessed him and, taking him by the hand, raised him up. All present rose to their feet and bowed before the monk. The musicians sang a song of welcome as he was led to a seat of honour. Then the Raja formally introduced him to the assembled guests, and made known to them how the Swami had given his blessing so that a son might be born to him (the Raja of Khetri). He told them also of the Swami's intention of visiting the West to preach the doctrines of the Sanatana Dharma. At this the whole court applauded. Then the babe was brought to receive the blessings of the Swami. The Raja was beside himself with joy.

This time the Swami stayed at Khetri for almost three weeks. He spent much of his time with the Raja, talking on various matters. When, in due course, the Swami told the Raja that he must be leaving for Bombay to make preparations for the voyage, the latter said, "Well, Swamiji Maharaj, it wrings my heart to part with you; but I must bow to Providence. I shall, however, accompany you as far as Jaipur." On the Swami's remonstrating with him, the Raja said, "It is a host's duty to see his guest off, at least to the confines of his residence." The day before his departure, the Swami was taken to the women's apartments in the palace to bless the Rajkumar, the infant prince.

On May 10, with due ceremony observed, the Swami made his departure by the state bullock-cart, accompanied by Jagmohanlal. From the Waqyat Register of Khetri state, it would seem that the Raja did not go to Jaipur, as was earlier thought. Jagmohan had orders to go with the Swami to Bombay, and had been given sufficient money to meet all expenses and to provide him with whatever he needed for the voyage. At the Raja's request the Swami reassumed the name Vivekananda for good, in place of Sachchidananda, which he had been using in South India.

On their way the Swami and Jagmohan stopped off at Abu Road, and spent the night in the house of a railway employee who had put the Swami up in the days of his wandering. Here he met Swamis Brahmananda and Turiyananda again. They had been staying at Mount Abu, in the summer palace of the Raja of Khetri, and, on being informed that the Swami would be passing through Abu Road, had come all the way by bullock-cart to meet him. When they reached the station, the Swami asked, "Oh, you came in a bullock-cart? Did they make a hay mattress for you in the cart?" When the brotherdisciples replied in the negative, and told him that because of the jolting that they had had, their bodies were aching, the Swami took them to task, saying, "Had you paid four annas

to the driver, he would have prepared a soft seat of hay
for you. You do not have such simple common sense as
that!"

On the eve of leaving them, the Swami said to Turiyananda,
"You leave Brahmananda alone and go to the Math. Do the
Master's work there and try for the improvement of the Math."
Of this meeting, Swami Turiyananda said later: "I vividly
remember some remarks made by Swamiji at that time. The
exact words and accents, and the deep pathos with which they
were uttered, still ring in my ears. He said, 'Haribhai, I am
still unable to understand anything of your so-called religion.'
Then with an expression of deep sorrow on his countenance
and intense emotion shaking his body, he placed his hand on
his heart and added, 'But my heart has expanded very much,
and I have learnt to feel. Believe me, I feel intensely indeed.'
His voice was choked with feeling; he could say no more.
For a time profound silence reigned, and tears rolled down his
cheeks." In telling of this incident Swami Turiyananda was
also overcome. He sat silent for a while, his eyelids heavy
with tears. With a deep sigh he said, "Can you imagine what
passed through my mind on hearing the Swami speak thus?
'Are not these', I thought, 'the very words and feelings of
Buddha?' . . . I could clearly perceive that the sufferings of
humanity were pulsating in the heart of Swamiji: his heart was
a huge cauldron in which the sufferings of mankind were
being made into a healing balm."

Swami Turiyananda relates another incident indicative of
the profound love for all men that there was in the Swami's
heart. Although it happened after his first visit to America, it
will be in place to mention it now, while this side of our subject's personality is before us. It took place at Balaram Bose's
home in Calcutta, where the Swami was staying for a time.
Swami Turiyananda said:

I came to see Swamiji and found him walking alone on the veranda
lost in such deep thought that he did not perceive my arrival. I kept
quiet, lest I should interrupt his reverie. After some time Swamiji,
with tears rolling down his cheeks, began to hum a well-known

song of Mirabai. Then, with his face in his hands and leaning on the railings, he sang in anguished tones, "Oh, nobody understands my sorrow! Nobody understands my sorrow!" The sad strains, and Swamiji's dejection, seemed to affect even the objects around him! The whole atmosphere vibrated with the sad melody: "No one but the sufferer knows the pangs of sorrows." His voice pierced my heart like an arrow, moving me to tears. Not knowing the cause of Swamiji's sorrow I was very uneasy. But it soon flashed upon me that it was a tremendous universal sympathy with the suffering and oppressed that was the cause of his mood.

To return to our story: At Abu Road station, before resuming his journey, the Swami had rather an unpleasant experience with a European ticket-collector. A Bengali gentleman, an admirer of the Swami, was sitting with him in the compartment, when the ticket-collector rudely ordered the former out of the carriage, citing an alleged railway regulation. The gentleman, who was also a railway employee, mildly protested and pointed out that there was no regulation requiring him to leave. This only enraged the European all the more. Then the Swami himself intervened. This did not improve matters, for the man turned on him and said sharply "*Tum* kahe bat karte ho?", which means, "Why do you meddle?" The Hindi word "Tum" is used to address intimate friends or inferiors, while "Āp" is used to one's equals and superiors. So at this the Swami became annoyed and said, "What do you mean by 'Tum'? Can you not behave properly? You are attending to first- and second-class passengers, and you do not know manners! Why do you not say 'Āp'?" The ticket-collector, seeing his mistake, said, "I am sorry. I do not know the language well. I only wanted this man. . . . " The Swami interrupted him: "Just now you said you did not know Hindi well. Now I see that you do not even know your own language well. This 'man' of whom you speak is a gentleman!" The ticket-collector, finding himself in the wrong, left the compartment. Speaking of this incident to Jagmohanlal, the Swami said, "You see, what we need in our dealings with Europeans is self-respect. We do not deal with men according to their position, and so they take advantage of us. We must keep our dignity before others. Unless we do that, we expose ourselves to insult."

The Swami had written to his Madras disciples on April 27, confirming his intention of embarking at Bombay, and not at Madras. Alasinga Perumal had therefore come all the way from Madras to see the Swami off to the West. So when his guru, accompanied by Jagmohanlal, reached Bombay from Khetri, Alasinga was at the station to meet them. Jagmohan, as we have noted, had been instructed by the Raja of Khetri to make all necessary arrangements. He now took the Swami to the best shops in the city and bought all manner of things for him. When the Swami found costly silk materials and suiting being ordered for the robes and turbans that he would wear when lecturing in the West, he protested. A simple ochre robe would do, he said: but Jagmohan would hear nothing of the kind. The Swami found himself helpless in face of the well-meaning and devoted intentions of his disciples, and could only submit. The result was that he was fitted out in royal style, and presented with a handsome purse. A first-class ticket had been bought for him on the Japan-bound P. and O. steamer *Peninsular*, Jagmohan maintaining that the guru of a Raja should travel like a Raja. From Japan to Vancouver he was booked in another steamer. Jagmohan seems to have made the arrangements through Thomas Cook and Son. Even after reaching America, the Swami for some time had his letters addressed to him in the United States care of these agents.

The few remaining days were spent in meditation, in going to see friends of earlier days, and in giving religious discourses. But often his mind travelled to Baranagore in far-off Bengal. The Swami wondered how the monastery and his brother-disciples were faring, and hoped that all was well. He did not know that they often spoke of him with loving solicitude, and asked themselves "Where is Naren?"; that they raised their hearts in prayer to the Master for his welfare. All he knew was that he was doing the will of the Master in sailing for the West.

Finally May 31, 1893, the day of sailing, arrived. The ship, the farewells, the uncertainties and formalities of foreign travel, and so many belongings to care for—all these were new to the Swami. Then too, his friends had made him dress in a robe and turban of silk. Like a prince he indeed looked; but in his heart were various emotions. Jagmohan and Alasinga went up the gangway with him and remained on board until the ship's gongs gave warning of imminent departure. There were tears in their eyes as they prostrated themselves at his feet in final salutation, and left the ship. Mr. Chhabildas, who had been one of the Swami's hosts in Bombay, sailed for Japan by the same ship.

The Swami stood on deck and gazed towards land until it faded from sight, sending his blessings to those who loved him and those whom he loved. His eyes were filled with tears, his heart overwhelmed with emotion. He thought of the Master, of the Holy Mother, of his brother-disciples. He thought of India and her culture, of her greatness and her suffering, of the Rishis and of the Sanatana Dharma. His heart was bursting with love for his native land. As the waters of the ocean encompassed him, he murmured under his breath, "Yes, from the Land of Renunciation I go to the Land of Enjoyment!" But it was not to be enjoyment for him. It was to be work, work: arduous, stupendous work attended with much difficulty and self-sacrifice. That work was to shatter his body; he was not to know rest. But nine years of life were left him, and those in service and often in anguish. Now he breathed the names of his Master and of the Mother of the Universe almost audibly. Yes, he, the Seer of the Vedic Wisdom, was always and everywhere the child of the Mother and disciple of his Master. The ship moved on its way southward to Ceylon, while the Swami remained alone with his thoughts and the vastness of the sea.

This chapter can be suitably concluded with the words of a well-known writer. They enable us to see how well the Swami was fitted to represent India and her spiritual culture at the World Parliament of Religions:

During his travels, by turns he realized the essence of Buddhism and Jainism, the spirit of Ramananda and Dayananda. He had become a profound student of Tulsidas and Nischaldas. He had learned all about the saints of Maharashtra and the Alwars and Nayanars of Southern India. From the Paramahamsa Parivrajaka-charya to the poor Bhangi Mehtar disciple of Lalguru he had learnt not only their hopes and ideals, but their memories as well. To his clear vision the Mogul supremacy was but an interregnum in the continuity of Indian national life. Akbar was Hindu in breadth of vision and boldness of synthesis. Was not the Taj, to his mind, a Shakuntala in marble? The songs of Guru Nanak alternated with those of Mirabai and Tansen on his lips. The stories of Prithvi Raj and Delhi jostled against those of Chitore and Pratap Singh, Shiva and Uma, Radha and Krishna, Sita-Ram and Buddha. Each mighty drama lived in a marvellous actuality, when he was the player. His whole heart and soul was the burning epic of the country, touched to an overflow of mystic passion by her very name. He held in his hands all that was fundamental, organic, vital; he knew the secret springs of life. There was a fire in his breast, which entered into him with the comprehension of essential truths, the result of spiritual illumination. His great mind saw a connection where others saw only isolated facts; his mind pierced the soul of things and presented facts in their real order. His was the most universal mind, with a perfect practical culture. What better equipment could one have who was to represent before the Parliament of Religions, India in its entirety—Vedic and Vedantic, Buddhistic and Jain, Shaivic and Vaishnavic and even Mohammedan? Who else could be better fitted for this task than this disciple of one who was in himself a Parliament of Religions in a true sense?

21

ON THE WAY TO AND EARLY DAYS
IN AMERICA

The Swami accustomed himself gradually to life on board ship. At first he was much worried over having to take care of the many things that his voyage made necessary. This proved to be one of his great crosses. He, the wandering monk, going about with his staff and Kamandalu, with hardly any other possessions worth the name, was now burdened with a tourist's outfit of trunks, valises and wardrobe! Aside from this, the Swami enjoyed his novel experiences. His rich imaginative nature saw beauty in a thousand forms, in the swelling and falling of the waters, in every gust of wind, in every cloud. The mighty expanse of ocean, the invigorating air, the carefree atmosphere, and the courtesy of all aboard reconciled him to his new surroundings. He soon accommodated himself to the strange food, strange environment and strange people, and by watching others, he acquainted himself with the manners and customs of the Europeans. As for his fellow passengers, they admired the orange-robed Oriental of luminous countenance and commanding presence. His courtly manner, his intelligent face and manly bearing made him popular with them, and often the Captain, when at leisure, would join the Swami on his solitary walks. He showed him the entire ship, and explained to him the working of the engines.

It was not long before the steamer reached Colombo, where it halted for almost a whole day. The Swami took the opportunity to visit the city. He drove through the streets, visited a temple rich with Buddhist imagery, and was fascinated at seeing the gigantic figure of the Buddha in a reclining posture, entering Nirvana. The next stop was Penang, a strip of land along the sea in the body of the Malay Peninsula. The Swami learned that the Malayans were Muslims and that the place had been infested in olden days with pirates. "But now", he writes, on July 10, 1893, in a letter from Yokohama, "the leviathan guns of modern turreted battleships have forced the Malays to look about for more peaceful pursuits." On his way from Penang to Singapore, he had glimpses of Sumatra, with its high mountains, and the Captain pointed out to him several favourite haunts of pirates in days gone by. The next port was Singapore, then the capital of the Straits Settlements, where he went to see the museum and the Botanical Garden with its beautiful collection of palms. The Swami was happy as a child at seeing these strange new lands.

Next, the ship stopped at Hong Kong, giving him the first glimpse of China. The name conjured up the land of dreams and romance, but he found that there were no people more commercial than the Chinese. He was interested to see the rush of craft that swarmed about the steamer, and was amused by the way their owners implored the travellers in various dialects and in broken English to go ashore in their boats. It was a busy, restless scene. In a humorous vein, the Swami writes in his letter of July 10 mentioned above:

These boats with two helms are rather peculiar. The boatman lives in the boat with his family. Almost always the wife is at the helms, managing one with her hands and the other with one of her feet. And in ninety per cent of cases you find a baby tied to her back, with the hands and feet of the little Chin left free. It is a quaint sight to see the little John Chinaman dangling very quietly from his mother's back whilst she is now setting with might and main, now pushing heavy loads, or jumping with wonderful agility from boat to boat. And there is such a rush of boats and steam-launches coming in and going out. Baby John is every moment in danger of having his little head pulverized, pigtail and all; but he does not care a fig. This busy life seems to have no charm for him, and he is quite content to learn the anatomy of a bit of rice-cake given to him from time to time by the madly busy mother. The Chinese child is quite a philosopher and calmly goes to work at an age when your Indian boy can hardly crawl on all fours. He has learnt the philosophy of necessity too well. Their extreme poverty is one of the causes why the Chinese and the Indians have remained in a state of mummified civilization.

To an ordinary Hindu or Chinese, everyday necessity is too hideous to allow him to think of anything else.

The halt of three days at Hong Kong gave the passengers an opportunity to visit Canton, eighty miles up the Si Kiang river. The Swami's impressions, given in the same letter, continue:

. . . What a scene of bustle and life! What an immense number of boats almost covering the waters! And not only those that are carrying on the trade, but hundreds of others which serve as houses to live in. And quite a lot of them so nice and big! In fact, they are big houses two or three storeys high, with verandahs running round and streets between, and all floating!

. . . Around us on both sides of the river for miles and miles is the big city—a wilderness of human beings, pushing, struggling, surging, roaring.

Canton proved to be a revelation to the Swami. He learned that the high-caste Chinese lady could never be seen and that there was as strict a zenana in China as was then in vogue amongst the Hindus of northern India. He found that even many of the women of the labouring classes had "feet smaller than those of our youngest child, and of course they cannot be said to walk, but hobble". In Canton, the Swami visited several of the more important temples, the largest of which was dedicated to the memory of the first Buddhist Emperor and the first five hundred disciples of the Buddha. Entering the temple he found an imposing image of the Blessed One in the central position; beneath him was the figure of the Emperor in reverent and meditative attitude, and about him were grouped the images of his five hundred disciples. The Swami studied the ancient Buddhist carvings and wondered at the artistry of the wooden images. He noted the points of similarity and dissimilarity between Buddhist and Indian temples, and delighted in the originality that he found here.

But as a monk, his earnest desire was to visit a Chinese monastery. Unfortunately, these monasteries were forbidden ground to foreigners. What could be done? When he asked the interpreter, he was told that a visit was impossible. But this served only to intensify his desire: he must see a Chinese monastery! He said to the interpreter, "Suppose a foreigner should go there, what then?" and received the reply, "Why, sir, they would be sure to maltreat him!" The Swami thought that if the monks knew him to be a Hindu sannyasi, they would not molest him. So he persisted, and finally induced the interpreter and his fellow passengers to tread "forbidden ground", saying laughingly, "Come, let us see if they will kill us!" But they had not gone far when the interpreter cried out, "Away! Away, gentlemen! they are coming, and they are infuriated!" Two or three men with clubs in their hands were approaching rapidly. Frightened at their menacing appearance, all but the Swami and the interpreter took to their heels. When even the latter was on the point of fleeing, the Swami seized him by the arm and said with a smile, "My good man, you must not run away before you tell me the Chinese word for Indian Yogi." Having been told this, the Swami loudly called out that he was an Indian Yogi. And lo, the word for "Yogi" acted like magic! The angry expression of the men changed to that of deep reverence and they fell at his feet. They rose, stretched out their joined palms in most respectful salutation, and then said something in a loud voice, one word of which the Swami understood to be "Kabatch". He thought that it was undoubtedly the Indian word meaning amulet; but to be sure of what they meant, he shouted a question to the interpreter, who stood at a safe distance, confounded at these strange developments—as well he might be, for never in all his experience had he witnessed such a spectacle as this. For an explanation he said, "Sir, they want amulets to ward off evil spirits and unholy influences. They desire your protection." The Swami was taken aback for a moment. He did not believe in charms. Then he took a sheet of paper from his pocket, divided it into several pieces, and wrote on them the word "Om" in Sanskrit, the most holy word of the Vedas and the symbol of the highest truth. He gave them the pieces of paper, and the men, touching them to their heads, led him into the monastery.

In the more isolated portions of the building he was shown many Sanskrit manuscripts, written, strange to say, in old Bengali characters. And then it occurred to him that when he had visited the temple dedicated to the first Buddhist Emperor he had been struck with the unmistakable resemblance between the faces of the Blessed One's five hundred followers and those of Bengalis. These evidences, as also his past study of Chinese Buddhism, convinced him that Bengal and China had at one time been in close communication, that there must have been a great influx into China of Bengali Bhikkhus (Buddhist monks), who brought to that distant country the gospel of the Blessed One, and that Indian thought had influenced Chinese civilization to a significant extent.

From Hong Kong the ship sailed to Nagasaki in Japan, where the Swami was greatly impressed with everything he saw. In the same letter he continues:

The Japanese are one of the cleanliest peoples on earth. Everything is neat and tidy. Their streets are nearly all broad, straight and regularly paved. Their little houses are cage-like, and their pine-covered evergreen little hills form the background of almost every town and village. The short-statured, fair-skinned, quaintly-dressed Japanese, their movements, attitudes, gestures, everything is picturesque. Japan is the land of the picturesque! Almost every house has a garden at the back, very nicely laid out according to Japanese fashion with small shrubs, grass-plots, small artificial waters and small stone bridges.

In order to see the interior of Japan, the Swami left the ship at Kobe and took the land route to Yokohama, where he would be boarding another. He visited three of the larger cities: Osaka, the great manufacturing town; Kyoto, the former capital; and Tokyo, the present capital. During his visit to Japan he penetrated into the essential elements of its national life and acquainted himself with the customs and the culture of the people. But what struck him most was the modern rage for progress, which was spontaneous in every department of knowledge. He writes further:

The Japanese seem to be fully awakened to the necessities of the present times. They have now a thoroughly organized army equipped with guns, which one of their own officers has invented, and which is said to be second to none. Then, they are continually increasing their navy. I have seen a tunnel nearly a mile long, bored by a Japanese engineer.

The match factories are simply a sight to see, and they are bent upon making everything they want in their own country. There is a Japanese line of steamers plying between China and Japan, which shortly intends running between Bombay and Yokohama.

In all these cities he made a point of seeing the important temples and of studying the rituals and ceremonies observed in them. To his amazement he found that here also the temples were inscribed with Sanskrit Mantras in old Bengali characters, though only a few of the priests knew Sanskrit. He found that the modern spirit had penetrated even the priesthood; but he was delighted to discover that "to the Japanese, India is still the dreamland of everything high and good."

In this letter from Yokohama to the group of disciples in Madras, one finds the Swami vigorously denouncing the evils of his own country and trying to rouse Indians from the inertia into which they had sunk through priestcraft and social tyranny. He had done this often before, but once out of India he gained a much clearer perspective and found that a system that disregarded the masses and trampled them underfoot was at the root of all her evils. He did not rant against the Brahmanical culture; indeed, he revered it. What he desired was that Indians should be "men". He wrote in the same letter:

I want that numbers of our young men should pay a visit to Japan and China every year. Especially to the Japanese, India is still the dreamland of everything high and good. And you, what are you? . . . talking twaddle all your lives, vain talkers, what are you? Come, see these people, and then go and hide your faces in shame. A race of dotards, you lose your caste if you come out! Sitting down these hundreds of years with an ever-increasing load of crystallized superstition on your heads, for hundreds of years spending all your energy upon discussing the touchableness or untouchableness of this food or that, with all humanity crushed out of you by the continuous social tyranny of ages—what are you? And what are you doing now? ... promenading the sea-shores with books in your hands— repeating undigested stray bits of European brainwork, and the whole soul bent upon getting a thirty-rupee clerkship, or at best becoming a lawyer—the height of young India's ambition—and every student with a whole brood of hungry children cackling at his heels and asking for bread! Is there not water enough in the sea to drown you, books, gowns, university diplomas, and all?

This intense note of criticism, enthusiasm, and inspiration which came from Yokohama stirred the Swami's disciples in Madras. The letter shows that his heart was always Indian. His outburst is that of a patriot who, finding in other nations a more modern, organized, and self-reliant public life, desires it for his native land.

Having disembarked from the *Peninsular* at Kobe, the Swami now boarded the new 6,000-ton *Empress of India*, which left Yokohama on July 14 and sailed for Vancouver. The voyage was not a comfortable one. Although he had been provided with a handsome wardrobe, it had not occurred either to him or to his disciples that the summer voyage by the northern Pacific would be cold; and so he suffered much from want of warm clothing. From Vancouver, in British Columbia, where the ship landed on the evening of July 25, he travelled to Chicago. His train passed through the scenic Canadian Rockies to Winnipeg and thence down into the rolling lake country of Minnesota and Wisconsin. It was a beautiful trip, but a long one; not until the evening of the fifth day, probably July 30, did he reach his destination.

The state of the Swami's mind when he found himself in a teeming railway station of Chicago can well be imagined. He was burdened with unaccustomed possessions; he did not know where to go; his strange dress made him conspicuous, and prankish boys ran after him in amusement. He was weary and confused. The porters demanded exorbitant charges for having carried his luggage from the train to the waiting-room;

and on all sides there were crowds of people, chiefly visitors to the World's Fair. The Swami at length went with one of the hotel agents, who had assured him that his hotel was the best in every way. Feeling that in a strange land he should put up at a first-class hotel, he consented. After a short drive, he entered the marbled lobby of one of the fashionable hotels and was soon taken up by elevator to his room. When the porters had brought his luggage and he found that he would no longer be interrupted, he sat down amid his luggage and tried to calm his mind.

On the following day he set out to visit the World's Fair. He was struck with amazement at the wonders he saw. Here all the latest products of the inventive and artistic mind of the entire world had been brought to a focus, as it were, for examination and admiration. He visited the various exposition palaces, marvelling at the array of machinery, at the arts and products of many lands, and, above all, at the energy and practical acumen of the human mind as manifested by the exhibits. Yet, among the streams of visitors to the Fair, he at first felt desperately lonely; for in all that vast crowd, indeed in the whole continent of North America, he had not one friend. Soon, however, people now and then approached the Swami, desiring to know who he was. He continued to frequent the Fair, eager to absorb all that was of value. He was fascinated by the splendour and perfect organization of it all.

While he was on the fair-ground one day, a funny incident occurred. It is best narrated in the Swami's own words. In his letter of August 20, 1893, he writes, shortly after leaving Chicago:

The Raja of Kapurthala was here and he was being lionized by some portion of Chicago society. I once met the Raja in the Fair grounds, but he was too big to speak with a poor fakir. There was an eccentric Mahratta Brahmin selling nail-made pictures in the Fair, dressed in a dhoti. This fellow told the reporters all sorts of things against the Raja—, that he was a man of low caste, that those Rajas were nothing but slaves, and that they generally led immoral lives, etc. etc. And these truthful (?) editors, for which

America is famous, wanted to give the boy's stories some weight; and so the next day they wrote huge columns in their papers, giving an elaborate description of "a man of wisdom" from India, meaning me—extolling me to the skies, and putting all sorts of words in my mouth, which I never even dreamt of, and ascribing to me all those remarks made by the Mahratta Brahmin about the Raja of Kapurthala! And it was such a good brushing that Chicago society gave up the Raja in hot haste. . . . These newspaper editors made capital out of me to give my countryman a brushing. That shows, however, that in this country intellect carries more weight than all pomp of of money and title.

Yes, such a conspicuous figure as the Swami was not to escape the notice of news-devouring reporters; inevitably they found him out. Some learned about him from the manager of the hotel where he was stopping; others sought him out on the fair-ground, besieging him with questions.

Gradually the Swami became accustomed to his strange surroundings; yet there were moments when he felt depressed. Those whom he had met were only casual acquaintances; he had made no friendships. Still, beyond both the excitement and the depression of his experiences, he always felt sure in his heart that he had a divine command and that the Lord would guide him.

But his hopes received a rude shock when, after few days in Chicago, he inquired at the Information Bureau of the Exposition as to the details of the Parliament of Religions. To his dismay he learned that it would not open until the second week of September, that no one would be admitted as a delegate without proper references, and that, in any event, the time for being so admitted had gone by. This almost broke the Swami's spirit. To have come all the way from India for nothing! It was too much. He also discovered that he should have come as a representative of some recognized organization. He wondered why he had been so foolish as to have listened to his ingenuous and rhapsodical followers in Madras, who were ignorant of the formalities involved in becoming a delegate. "To their unbounded faith it never occurred",

26

writes Sister Nivedita, "that they [the disciples] were demand-
ing what was, humanly speaking, impossible. They thought
Vivekananda had only to appear, and he would be given his
chance. The Swami himself was as simple in the ways of the
world as these his disciples; and when he was once sure that
he was divinely called to make the attempt, he could see no
difficulties in the way. Nothing could have been more typical
of the unorganizedness of Hinduism itself than this going forth
of its representative unannounced, and without formal credentials, to enter the strongly guarded doors of the world's wealth
and power."

Even to attend the Parliament as a spectator, the Swami
had over a month to wait, and his purse was being rapidly
emptied. The hotel charges were very high; indeed, he found
that in America everything was expensive. To make matters
worse, he had no idea of the value of money and was cheated
right and left wherever he went. Fortunately, he was not
entirely without help; one of his Madras friends, Varada Rao,
wrote to a lady of his acquaintance in Chicago about the
Swami. She and her husband belonged to the highest Chicago
society, and were very kind to the Swami. Thus began a
friendship that lasted as long as the Swami lived. All the
members of the family came to love him dearly, to appreciate
his brilliant gifts, and to admire the purity and simplicity of
his character, to which they often bore loving testimony. We,
however, do not definitely know their names; but in the
opinion of some researchers they were Mr. and Mrs. Milward
Adams.

Meanwhile, he had learned that Boston was the Athens
of America and also that it was much less expensive than
Chicago. So after living in Chicago for twelve days, most
of which he had spent at the Fair, he took the train for
Boston, accompanied by a Mr. Lulloobhoy. Mysterious are
the ways of the Lord! The Swami, who had been helped in a
score of wonderful ways as the wandering monk, was also
helped here. Travelling with him in the same carriage was a
Miss Katherine Abbott Sanborn. Attracted by his noble

bearing, she approached and entered into conversation with him. She was more than interested to know that he was a Hindu monk and had come to America to preach the truths of the Vedanta. She said, "Well, Swami, I invite you to come to my home and live there. Perhaps something will turn up in your favour!" He readily consented and accordingly found himself lodged in a beautiful country house, called "Breezy Meadows", near Metcalf, a town in Massachusetts not far from Boston.

Although in a letter to India the Swami wrote of his hostess as an "old lady", in 1893 she was fifty-four and, by Western standards, more middle-aged than old. Her name was not unknown in America. Kate Sanborn was a lecturer and author of note, and numbered among her friends many prominent thinkers of the time. Her cousin was Franklin Benjamin Sanborn, a well-known journalist, an author of many books, and a philanthropist. As a young boy, Mr. Sanborn had discovered Transcendentalism, then well past its prime, and was profoundly attracted to its ideals. Later he founded the Concord Summer School of Philosophy and became a biographer of many of the famous Transcendentalists of the previous generation, such as Emerson, Thoreau and Alcott. It was only to be expected that he would deeply appreciate the Swami. Through Kate Sanborn, the Swami was to meet not only her cousin but, among others, Dr. John Henry Wright, a professor of Greek classics at Harvard University, who, as we shall see shortly, was to be instrumental in helping him to fulfil the purpose for which he had come half-way round the globe. Indeed, the Swami's trip to New England was, as it turned out, not a move away from the Parliament of Religions but a move toward it.

At first, however, the outlook appeared bleak; the Swami had much difficulty in adjusting to his new environment. Winter was coming on, and he had no warm clothing. Even August in New England seemed cold to him. He was hooted at in the streets of Boston on account of his dress and on one occasion was pursued by a group of ruffians. Indeed, his

Hindu clothes were so conspicuous that his hostess urged him to dress in American fashion. But even moderately-priced winter clothing cost him at least one hundred dollars, leaving him very little margin for living expenses. The financial uncertainty was a great strain upon him, and he sometimes feared he might have to telegraph his Madras disciples for the wherewithal either to remain in America or to return to India. But he would return to India only as a last resort, for he was determined to make every effort to succeed in America, and if he failed there, to try in England; should failure be his in England too, he could then go back to India and wait for further commands from the Lord. In the meanwhile he patiently bore with various difficulties that beset him, knowing that nothing worthwhile was ever accomplished without suffering and sacrifice.

At "Breezy Meadows" his hostess delighted in showing him off as "a curio from India", and many of those who came to see him at her invitation plied him with all sorts of queer and annoying questions, thinking him a "pagan". Yet thoughtful people also came, and here too, as in Chicago, he was learning about the customs and institutions of the West. Among others who called on him at the wish of his hostess was the superintendent of the Women's Reformatory in the near-by town of Sherborn. Later, she invited him to visit the prison, and he was much impressed with that institution. To a disciple he wrote on August 20, giving his thoughts:

They do not call it prison but reformatory here. It is the grandest thing I have seen in America. How the inmates are benevolently treated; how they are reformed, and sent back as useful members of society; how grand, how beautiful, you must see to believe! And oh, how my heart ached to think of what we think of the poor, the low, in India. They have no chance, no escape, no way to climb up. . . .

In the same letter the Swami wrote, "I am here amongst the children of the Son of Mary, and Lord Jesus will help me." He saw that the more sympathetic and thoughtful of his visitors came to see him because of his love for the Prophet of

Nazareth and through that love were able to understand the broadness of Hinduism. He was invited to speak at a large women's club in Boston, the members of which were interested in the Indian-Christian social reformer, Ramabai. Although the supporters of Ramabai were later to oppose him, this lecture was a success, and many people became interested in him.

Slowly the way was opening up. Distinguished persons called on the Swami, among them Mr. Franklin Sanborn, who, sceptical at first, was soon completely won over by his radiant personality and brilliance of mind. Indeed, he was so impressed by the young Hindu monk that he invited him to speak during the first week of September at a convention of the august and scholarly American Social Science Association at Saratoga Springs, New York. In the meanwhile, Professor John Henry Wright, who no doubt had heard a great deal about the Swami from the Sanborns, invited him to spend the week-end of August 26 and 27 at Annisquam, Massachusetts, a small and quiet village resort on the Atlantic seaboard, some thirty miles north-east of Boston, where he and his family were vacationing. The Swami and the professor, whose learning was said to be encyclopaedic, had long conversations at Annisquam, discussing all manner of subjects for hours on end.

The Swami had given up all hope of speaking at the Parliament of Religions, but Professor Wright was so deeply impressed with the Swami that he insisted he represent Hinduism at that important gathering, saying, "This is the only way you can be introduced to the nation at large." The Swami explained his difficulties and said that he had no credentials. Whereupon Professor Wright exclaimed, "To ask you, Swami, for credentials is like asking the sun to state its right to shine!" He then assured the Swami that he would take it upon himself to see that he had a place as a delegate. The professor was acquainted with many distinguished people who were connected with the Parliament. He wrote at once to the Chairman of the Committee for the Selection of Delegates, stating, "Here is a man who is more learned than all our learned professors put together." Knowing that the Swami had very little money, he presented him with the fare to Chicago, and also gave him letters of introduction to the Committee in charge of accommodating and providing for the Oriental delegates. This was, indeed, a godsend! The Swami rejoiced at this indubitable manifestation of Divine Providence. Yes, the purpose for which he had come so far was to be fulfilled in a way that could not have been foreseen.

But before returning to Chicago, he was to spend a busy week in New England. On Sunday, August 27, he delivered his first public lecture in the Western world at the little village church in Annisquam, speaking with such convincing eloquence of the needs of the Indian people for an industrial rather than a religious education that, as Mrs. Wright wrote to her mother with great amusement, these staid New Englanders took up a collection for "a heathen college" in India, "to be run on strictly heathen principles"! With his first lecture, the Swami had carried the day!—a foreshadowing, as it were, of things to come.

We shall give here a vivid description of the Swami in these early days, written by the professor's wife. It is taken from a long sketch Mrs. Wright wrote, using notes that she had made during the Swami's brief visit:

One day, at an unfashionable place by the sea, the professor was seen crossing the lawn between the boarding-house and his cottage accompanied by a man in a long red coat. The coat, which had something of a priestly cut, descended far below the man's knees, and was girded around his waist with a thick cord of the same reddish orange tint. He walked with a strange, shambling gait, and yet there was a commanding dignity and impressiveness in the carriage of his neck and bare head that caused everyone in sight to stop and look [at] him; he moved slowly, with the swinging tread of one who had never hastened, and in his great dark eyes was the beauty of an alien civilization which might—should time and circumstances turn it into opposition—become intolerably repulsive. He was dark, about the colour of a light quadroon, and his full lips, which in a man of Caucasian race would have been brilliant scarlet, had a tint of bluish purple. His teeth were regular, white and sometimes cruel, but his beautiful expressive eyes and the proud wonderful carriage of his head, the swing and grace of the heavy crimson tassels that hung from the end of his sash, made one forget that he was too heavy for so young a man, and that long sitting on the floor had visited him with the fate of the tailor.

... He seemed very young, even younger than his twenty-nine years, and as he seated himself he covered his legs carefully with his flowing robe, like a woman or a priest; but the hoary ancient turn of his thought belied his childlike manner. . . .

... And then, having said his say, the Swami was silent. . . . Occasionally he cast his eye up to the roof and repeated softly "Shiva, Shiva, Shiva!" . . . And a current of powerful feeling seemed to be flowing like molten lava beneath the silent surface of this strange being. . . .

He stayed among them, keenly interested in all practical things; his efforts to eat strange food were heroic and sometimes disastrous to himself. He was constantly looking about for something which would widen the possibilities of feeding his people in times of famine. Our ways seemed to inspire him with a sort of horror, meat-eating cannibals that we seemed to be! But he concealed it, either with absolute dumbness, or by a courteous flow of language which effectually hid his thoughts.

He had been brought up amidst polemics, and his habit of argument was mainly Socratic, beginning insidiously and simply by a story, or clear statement of some incontestable fact, and then from that deriving strange and unanswerable things. All through, his discourses abounded in picturesque illustrations and beautiful legends. To work, to get on in the world, in fact any measure of temporal success seemed to him entirely beside the subject. He had been trained to regard the spiritual life as the real thing of this world! Love of God and love of man! . . . "The love of the Hindu", he told us, "goes further than the love of the Christians, for that stops at man; but the religion of Buddha goes on towards the beasts of the field and every creeping thing that has life."

At sixteen he had renounced the world and spent his time among men who rejoiced in these things and looked forward to spending day after day on the banks of the Ganges, talking of the higher life.

When someone suggested to him that Christianity was a saving power he opened his great dark eyes upon him and said, "If Christianity is a saving power in itself, why has it not saved the Ethiopians, the Abyssinians?" He also arraigned our own crimes, the horror of women on the stage, the frightful immorality in our streets, our drunkenness, our thieving, our political degeneracy, the murdering in our West, the lynching in our South, and we, remembering his own Thugs, were still too delicate to mention them.

... He cared for Thomas a Kempis more than for any other writer and had translated a part of the "Imitation of Christ" into Bengali and written an introduction to it; as for receiving the Stigmata, he spoke of it as natural result of an agonizing love of God. The teaching of the Vedas, constant and beautiful, he applied to every event in life, quoting a few verses and then translating, and with the translation of the story giving the meaning. His mouth, also, was full of wonderful proverbs. "Of what use is the knowledge that is locked away in books?" he said, in speaking of the memories of Hindu boys.

Himself a Hindu monk, he told, once, of a time when he turned into a forest, a trackless forest, because he felt that God was leading him, of how he went on for three days, starving and how he was more perfectly happy than he had ever been before because he felt that he was entirely in the hands of God. "When my time comes," he said, "I shall like to go up the mountain and there, by the Ganges, lay myself down, and with the water singing over me I shall go to sleep, and above me will tower the Himalayas—men have gone mad for those mountains!" There was once a monk, he told us, who went far up into the mountains and saw them everywhere around him; and above his head towered their great white crests. Far below, thousands of feet, was the Ganges—narrow stream at the foot of a precipice. "Shall I then like a dog die in my bed when all this beauty is around me?" the monk thought, and he plunged into the chasm. . . .

All the people of that little place were moved and excited by this young man, in a manner beyond what might be accounted for by his coming from a strange country and a different people. He had another power, an unusual ability to bring his hearers into vivid sympathy with his own point of view. It repelled, in some cases, however, as strongly as it attracted, but whether in support or opposition, it was difficult to keep a cool head or a level judgement when confronted with him.

All the people of all degrees were interested; women's eyes blazed and their cheeks were red with excitement; even the children of the village talked of what he had said to them; all the idle summer boarders trooped to hear him, and all the artists longingly observed him and wanted to paint him.

He told strange stories as ordinary people would mention the wonders of electricity, curious feats of legerdemain, and tales of monks who had lived one hundred, or one hundred and thirty years; but so-called occult societies drew down his most magnificent contempt. . . . He spoke of holy men who at a single glance converted hardened sinners and detected men's inmost thoughts. . . . But these things were trifles; always his thoughts turned back to his people. He lived to raise them up and make them better and had come this long way in the hope of gaining help to teach them, to be practically more efficient. We hardly knew what he needed; money, if money would do it; tools, advice, new ideas. And for this he was willing to die to-morrow. . . .

His great heroine was the dreadful Rani of the Indian Mutiny, who led her troops in person. . . . Whenever he mentioned the Rani he would weep, with tears streaming down his face. "That woman was a goddess," he said, "a Devi. When overcome, she fell on her sword and died like a man."

In quoting from the Upanishads his voice was most musical. He would quote a verse in Sanskrit with intonations and then translate it into beautiful English, of which he had a wonderful command. And, in his mystical religion, he seemed perfectly and unquestionably happy.

. . . And yet, when they gave him money, it seemed as if some injury had been done him and some disgrace put upon him. "Of all the worries I have ever had," he said, as he left us, "the greatest has been the care of this money!" His horrified reluctance to take it haunted us. He could not be made to see why he might not wander on in this country, as in his own, without touching a medium of exchange, which he considered disgraceful, and the pain he showed when it was made clear to him that without money he could not even move, hung round us for days after he left, as if we had hurt some innocent thing or had wounded a soul. . . . And we saw him leave us after that one little week of knowing him, with fear that clutches the heart when a beloved, gifted, passionate child fares forth, unconscious, in an untried world.

By now the Swami had made some friends in New England and was receiving invitations to visit and to lecture. Leaving Annisquam, he went to Salem, Massachusetts, near Boston, where he had been invited by Mrs. Kate Tannatt Woods to be her house guest. Like Miss Sanborn, Mrs. Woods was an energetic lecturer and writer; she was also the founder and president of the Thought and Work Club in Salem, a women's club of high standing. The Swami stayed at Mrs. Woods's home for a week, from August 28 to September 4. During this time he lectured twice: on August 28 before the members of the Thought and Work Club at the Wesley Church, and on the evening of Sunday, September 3, at the East Church. In addition, he spoke one afternoon in Mrs. Woods's garden to a group of children and young people.

Certain reactions to the Swami's first lecture in Salem, in which he told of India's urgent need for a technological education, must have served him as an eye-opener to the more dreary side of America's religious climate. During the course of the lecture he was interrupted many times and questioned in the most acrimonious manner by two members of the Christian clergy. His replies were courteous and unperturbed; yet this brief and unpleasant encounter surely forewarned him of the powerful opposition he would have to face in months to come.

On September 4, the Swami left Salem for Saratoga, New York, where he was to keep his engagement to speak before the convention of the American Social Science Association, of which Mr. Franklin Sanborn was Secretary. He spoke three times before this assembly of eminent men, and twice at a private home at Saratoga. It was a singular honour paid to a young, unknown Hindu monk, whose only credentials were his brilliance of mind and nobility of thought and character. But those qualities were, as Professor Wright had pointed out, credentials enough and to spare. Indeed, the Swami was by no means at a loss to speak before this secular and highly learned gathering, and his subjects were suited to the occasion. The titles of two of his three talks—the third title is not known —were "The Mohammedan Rule in India" and "The Use of Silver in India". (The silver standard was then a critical issue in American politics.)

And now, after some three weeks on the East Coast, the Swami turned back to Chicago and to the Parliament of Religions. He was provided with the necessary credentials, and he was joyful in spirit that the Lord had cleared away the obstacles before him and enabled him to present his message to the people of the West.

It so happened that on the train he met a merchant who promised to direct him to his proper destination. But at the Chicago station the merchant was in such a hurry that he forgot to instruct the Swami how to reach that part of the city where Dr. John Henry Barrows, Chairman of the Parliament's General Committee, had his office; and the Swami, to his dismay, found that he had lost the address! He made inquiries of passers-by, but it being the north-east side of the city where mostly Germans lived, no one could understand him. Night was coming on. He could not even make anyone understand that he wanted a hotel. He was lost and knew not what to do. At length, he lay down in a huge empty box in the railway yards and, trusting to the guidance of the Lord, soon freed himself of all anxieties and fell asleep. Two days later he was to shake America with his address at the Parliament; but now, so destiny decided, he had to sleep like some outcast—unknown, unaided, and despised—or perhaps, more truly, like some sannyasi in his own land, sleeping where the evening found him. Morning came; he arose and "smelling fresh water", as he said, followed the scent and found himself in a short time on Lake Shore Drive, the most fashionable residential avenue in the city, where millionaires and merchant-princes dwelt. He was extremely hungry and, like the true sannyasi he was, commenced begging from house to house, asking for food and for directions to the offices of the Parliament Committee. Because of his strange and rumpled clothes and travel-worn appearance, he was rudely treated; at some houses he was insulted by the servants, at others the door was slammed in his face. His heart sank; he knew nothing of city directories or telephones, so he could not seek help in that way. On and on he trudged. At length exhausted, he sat down on the street-side determined to abide by the will of the Lord.

At this juncture the door of a fashionable residence opposite him opened and a regal-looking woman came across to him. She addressed him in a soft voice and accents of refinement, "Sir, are you a delegate to the Parliament of Religions?" The Swami told her his difficulties. Immediately she invited him into her house and gave orders to her servants that he should be taken to a room and attended to in every way. She promised the Swami that after he had had his breakfast she herself would accompany him to the offices of the Parliament of Religions. The Swami was grateful beyond words. His deliverer was Mrs. George W. Hale; she, her husband, and children became his warmest friends.

A new spirit now took possession of him. He was convinced beyond doubt that the Lord was with him, and with the spirit of a Prophet he awaited the coming of events. With Mrs. Hale he called on the officers of the Parliament, gave his credentials, and was gladly accepted as a delegate. He was housed for a short while with the other Oriental delegates, and later he was assigned a lodging at the house of Mr. and Mrs. John B. Lyon, at 262 Michigan Avenue. He felt with the passing of each moment that the Parliament of Religions would be the great test, the crucial experience for him. The time glided by in prayer, in meditation, and in earnest longing that he might be made the true instrument of the Lord, the true spokesman of Hinduism, the true bearer of his Master's message. He became acquainted with many distinguished persons who were to attend the Parliament. In this grand circle of ecclesiastics he moved as one lost in rapture and in prayer. He had no personal feelings in the matter save as related to the carrying out of the mission entrusted to him by his Master and perceived by him as a command from on high.

22

THE PARLIAMENT OF RELIGIONS

The Parliament of Religions, which was held in connection with the World's Columbian Exposition in the city of Chicago from September 11 to 27, 1893, was undoubtedly one of the great epoch-making events of the world, marking as it did an era in the history of religions, especially in that of Hinduism. From all parts of the world delegates came, representing every form of organized religious belief. It was not only a Parliament of Religions, it was a parliament of humanity. To unify the religious vision of mankind was the motive of the workers who made possible this assembly of religious ideas and creeds, and if the Parliament had done nothing more than make the whole of human society aware of the "Unity in diversity" and the "diversity in Unity" of the religious outlook of man, it would still have been unequalled among ecumenical conventions in character and importance. But it did far more than that. It roused a wave of new awareness in the Western world, causing it to be conscious of the profundity and vitality of Eastern thought. In the language of the Honourable Merwin-Marie Snell, President of the Scientific Section of the Parliament:

One of its chief advantages has been in the great lesson which it has taught the Christian World, especially to the people of the United States, namely that there are other religions more venerable than Christianity, which surpass it in philosophical depth, in spiritual intensity, in independent vigour of thought, and in breadth and sincerity of human sympathy, while not yielding to it a single hair's breadth in ethical beauty and efficiency. Eight great non-Christian religious groups were represented in its deliberations—Hinduism, Jainism, Buddhism, Judaism, Confucianism, Shintoism, Mohammedanism and Mazdaism.

Some of the highest ecclesiastical dignitaries in America had preached the necessity and the advantages of such a Parliament for some time: and when the Chicago World's Fair was being planned, it seemed to be the proper medium and opportunity. In the words of the Rev. John Henry Barrows, one of the principal organizers of the Parliament and Chairman of the General Committee: "Since faith in a Divine Power to whom men believe they owe service and worship, has been like the sun, a life-giving and fructifying potency in man's intellectual and moral development; . . . it did not appear that Religion any more than Education, Art, or Electricity should be excluded from the Columbian Exposition."

News that the Parliament was to be held was heralded to all parts of the globe. Committees of various kinds were formed to organize it on a proper basis, and invitations were sent out to the heads or executive bodies of all acknowledged religious organizations the world over. Stipulations were made and instructions given, and the process of sending delegates was mapped out. Every religious creed was to send its own delegate or delegates, as the case might be, and reception committees were to receive them on their arrival in Chicago. There were many necessary formalities to be observed in order to systematize the movement. Unfortunately, as has been seen earlier, the group of disciples who had sent the Swami as a representative of Hinduism to the Parliament were unaware of these. They had simply recognized the worth of the man and his ideas, and they felt sure that he could introduce himself, as, in one sense, he did.

The historic and unprecedented Parliament of Religions was held in Chicago's newly-constructed and imposing Art Institute on Michigan Avenue. Here, during the seventeen days of the Parliament proper, assembled a great concourse of humanity, which included in its midst many of the most distinguished people of the world: the audience was sprinkled liberally with eminent men of every profession, many of the greatest philosophers of the West were in daily attendance, and among the delegates were high ecclesiastics of various faiths. The main sessions of the Parliament were held morning, afternoon and evening in the large Hall of Columbus, whose floor and gallery had a combined seating capacity of 4,000. Generally, the Hall of Columbus was full to overflowing; indeed, at times the overflow was so great that it nearly filled the adjoining twin Hall of Washington, where the speakers repeated their lectures to a second vast audience. Hundreds of papers and addresses were delivered during the main sessions. In addition, many talks were given before the thirty-five denominational congresses and auxiliary sections, which were held either in the Hall of Washington or in smaller halls of the building. One of the most important auxiliary sections was known as the Scientific Section, where papers and addresses of more scientific and less popular character were delivered, and were often followed by conferences on the topics treated. As will be seen later, the Swami was to speak several times here, in addition to his scheduled addresses and impromptu talks in Columbus Hall.

A noted American author wrote of the Parliament of Religions and of Swami Vivekananda:

Prior to the convention of the Parliament of Religions, adjunct to the World's Columbian Exposition in 1893, which was convened in Chicago, little was known of Vivekananda in this country. On that auspicious occasion, however, he appeared in all his magnificent grandeur. It was on Monday, September 11th, at 10 a.m. . . . On that memorable . . . morning there sat upon the platform of the great Hall of Columbus representatives of the religious hopes and beliefs of twelve hundred millions of the human race. It was indeed impressive. In the centre sat Cardinal Gibbons, highest prelate of the Roman Catholic Church on the Western Continent. He was seated upon a Chair of State and opened the meeting with prayer. On the right and left of him were gathered the Oriental delegates, whose brilliant attire vied with his own scarlet robes in brilliancy. Conspicuous among the followers of Brahma, Buddha and Mohammed was an eloquent monk from India, Vivekananda by name. He was clad in gorgeous red apparel and wore a large turban, his remarkably fine features and bronze complexion standing out prominently in the great throng. Beside him sat Nagarkar of the Brahmo Samaj, representative of the Hindu Theists; next was Dharmapala,

Ceylon's Buddhist representative; next came Mazoomdar, leader of the Theists [Brahmo Samaj] in India. Amongst the World's choicest divines ... many more, whose names would be more or less familiar, must be left out for want of space. This will suffice to show the setting with which our subject was surrounded. "In contact with the learned minds of India we have [been] inspired [by] a new reverence for the Orient." In numerical order Vivekananda's position was number thirty-one.

The Swami himself describes in a letter dated November 2, to his disciple Alasinga Perumal, the opening of the Parliament and his own state of mind in replying to the address of welcome offered to the delegates:

On the morning of the opening of the Parliament, we all assembled in a building called the Art Palace, where one huge, and other smaller temporary halls were erected for the sittings of the Parliament. Men from all nations were there. From India were Mazoomdar of the Brahmo Samaj and Nagarkar of Bombay, Mr. Gandhi representing the Jains, and Mr. Chakravarti representing Theosophy with Mrs. Annie Besant. Of these men, Mazoomdar and I were of course old friends, and Chakravarti knew me by name. There was a grand procession, and we were all marshalled on to the platform. Imagine a hall below and a huge gallery above, packed with six or seven thousand men and women representing the best culture of the country, and on the platform learned men of all nations on the earth. And I who never spoke in public in my life to address this august assemblage!! It was opened in great form with music and ceremony and speeches; then the delegates were introduced one by one, and they stepped up and spoke! Of course my heart was fluttering and my tongue nearly dried up; I was so nervous, and could not venture to speak in the morning. Mazoomdar made a nice speech—Chakravarti a nicer one, and they were much applauded. They were all prepared and came with ready-made speeches. I was a fool and had none, but bowed down to Devi Saraswati and stepped up, and Dr. Barrows introduced me. I made a short speech, ... and when it was finished, I sat down almost exhausted with emotion.

Indeed, that sea of faces might have given even a practised orator stage fright. To speak before such a distinguished, critical and highly intellectual gathering required intense

Prof. John Henry Wright

At the Parliament of Religions

The Art Institute at Chicago

self-confidence. The Swami had walked in the imposing procession of delegates, had seen the huge assembly, the keen,
eager faces of the audience, the shrewd, authoritative and
dignified countenances of the princes of the Christian churches
who sat on the platform. He was, as it were, lost in amazement
by the splendour of it all. What had he, the unsophisticated
wandering monk, the simple Indian sadhu, in common with
this grand function and these high functionaries? As was
shortly to be seen, he had much to do with them. His very
person had attracted the attention of thousands. Among arch-
bishops, bishops, priests and theologians, the people singled
him out, by reason of both his apparel and his commanding
presence. He himself was alternately rapt in silent prayer and
stirred by the eloquence of the speakers who had preceded
him. Several times he had been called upon to speak, but he
had said, "No, not now", until the Chairman was puzzled and
wondered if he would speak at all. At length, in the late afternoon the Chairman insisted, and the Swami arose.

His face glowed like fire. His eyes surveyed in a sweep the
huge assembly before him. The whole audience grew intent;
a pin could have been heard to fall. Then he addressed his
audience as "Sisters and Brothers of America". And with
that, before he had uttered another word, the whole Parliament
was caught up in a great wave of enthusiasm. Hundreds rose
to their feet with shouts of applause. The Parliament had
gone mad; everyone was cheering, cheering, cheering! The
Swami was bewildered. For full two minutes he attempted to
speak, but the wild enthusiasm of the audience prevented it.

When silence was restored, the Swami began his address
by thanking the youngest of nations in the name of the most
ancient order of monks in the world, the Vedic Order of
sannyasins, and by introducing Hinduism as "the Mother of
Religions, a religion which has taught the world both tolerance
and universal acceptance". He quoted two beautiful, illustrative passages, taken from the scriptures of Hinduism: "As the
different streams having their sources in different places all
mingle their water in the sea, so, O Lord, the different paths

27

which men take, through different tendencies, various though
they may appear, crooked or straight, all lead to Thee!" And
the other: "Whosoever comes to Me, through whatsoever
form, I reach him; all men are struggling through paths
which in the end lead to Me!"

It was only a short talk, but its spirit of universality, its
fundamental earnestness and broadmindedness completely
captivated the whole assembly. The Swami announced the
universality of religious truths and the sameness of the goal
of all religious realizations. And that he did so, was because
he had sat at the feet of a Man of Realization, in far-off
Dakshineswar, and had learnt from his Master, through both
his teachings and his life, the truth that all religions were one,
that they were all paths leading to the selfsame goal, the
selfsame God. When the Swami sat down almost exhausted,
as he wrote, with emotion, the Parliament gave him a great
ovation significant of its approval.

Commenting on the reception accorded to the Swami's
first appearance before the Parliament, the Rev. John Henry
Barrows wrote in *The World's Parliament of Religions*, "When
Mr. Vivekananda addressed the audience as 'Sisters and
Brothers of America', there arose a peal of applause that
lasted for several minutes." Another eyewitness, Mrs. S. K.
Blodgett, later recalled: "When that young man got up and
said, 'Sisters and Brothers of America,' seven thousand people
rose to their feet as a tribute to something they knew not
what. When it was over I saw scores of women walking over
the benches to get near him, and I said to myself, 'Well,
my lad, if you can resist that onslaught you are indeed a
God!'"

On September 15, the Swami gave a short address on
"Why We Disagree". Here he pointed out, by referring to
the frog in the well who thought his little well to be the whole
universe, that the insularity of religious outlook was the source
of fanaticism. With the exception of this brief talk, the Swami
did not speak formally before the Parliament proper until
September 19. On this date he read his celebrated paper on

"Hinduism"—a summary of the philosophy, psychology, and general ideas and statements of Hinduism. Though the Swami was not the only Indian or even the only Bengali present, he was the only representative of Hinduism proper. The other Hindu delegates stood for societies or churches or sects, but the Swami stood for Hinduism in its universal aspect. He gave forth the ideas of the Hindus concerning the soul and its destiny; he expounded the doctrines of the Vedanta philosophy, which harmonizes all religious ideals and all forms of worship, viewing them as various presentations of truth and as various paths to its realization. He preached the religious philosophy of Hinduism, which declares the soul to be eternally pure, eternally free, only appearing under the bondage of matter as limited and manifold. He spoke of the attainment of the goal —the perception of Oneness—as the result of innumerable efforts of many lives. He asserted that the soul was never created. And he went on to say that death meant only a change of centre from one body to another, and that one's present was determined by one's past action, and one's future by the present. He said that in order to realize Divinity, the self that says "I" and "mine" must vanish. This, however, did not mean the denial of true individuality; it meant, rather, its utmost fulfilment. By overcoming the small egoistical self, centred in selfishness, one attained to infinite, universal individuality. "Then alone", he said, "can death cease when I am one with life; then alone can misery cease when I am one with happiness itself; then alone can all errors cease when I am one with knowledge itself; and this is the necessary scientific conclusion. Science has proved to me that physical individuality is a delusion, that really my body is one continuously changing mass in an unbroken ocean of matter; and Advaita (Unity) is the necessary conclusion with my other counterpart, the soul." The pervasive spirit of his address was the sense of Oneness. And he insisted that the realization of the Self—that is, becoming and being Divinity—inevitably led to seeing Divinity manifest everywhere.

And inspired with this vision like another Vedic sage, he

addressed the vast mass of humanity before him as "heirs of Immortal Bliss" and exclaimed with apostolic power:

Yea, the Hindu refuses to call you sinners! Ye are the children of God, the sharers of immortal bliss, holy and perfect beings. Ye divinities on earth—sinners? It is a sin to call a man so; it is a standing libel on human nature. Come up, O lions, and shake off the delusion that you are sheep; you are souls immortal, spirits free, blest and eternal; ye are not matter, ye are not bodies; matter is your servant, not you the servant of matter.

Thus it is that the Vedas proclaim not a dreadful combination of unforgiving laws, not an endless prison of cause and effect, but that at the head of all these laws, in and through every particle of matter and force, stands One, "by whose command the wind blows, the fire burns, the clouds rain, and death stalks upon the earth." And what is His nature? "He is everywhere, the Pure and formless One, the Almighty and the All-merciful. . . ." [And the Swami had said earlier:] "Knowing Him alone you shall be saved from death over again", and attain Immortality.

But what of the polytheism in Hinduism? He explained the psychological necessity of lower forms of religious ideas and worship; of prayers and ceremonies as aids to the purification of mind, and image-worship as a help to spiritual concentration. There can be no idolatry where the image stands as an objectified symbol of Divinity. And he said that with the Hindus, moreover, religion is not centred in doctrinal assent or dissent, but in *realization*. Surveyed in this light, forms and symbols and ceremonials are seen to be the supports, the helps of spiritual childhood, which the Hindu gradually transcends as he progresses towards spiritual manhood; even these helps are not necessary for everyone or compulsory in Hinduism. The Swami saw Unity in variety in religion, and said, "Contradictions come from the same truth adapting itself to the varying circumstances of different natures. And these little variations are necessary for purposes of adaptation. But in the heart of everything the same truth reigns." In conclusion he presented the ideal of a universal religion, having no temporal, spatial, or sectarian bounds but including every attitude of the human mind, from the savage to the most enlightened, in a grand synthesis, all going in their own way towards the Goal. The Swami closed his address with the following words:

Offer such a religion and all the nations will follow you. Asoka's council was a council of the Buddhist faith. Akbar's, though more to the purpose, was only a parlour-meeting. It was reserved for America to proclaim to all quarters of the globe that the Lord is in every religion.

May He who is the Brahman of the Hindus, the Ahura-Mazda of the Zoroastrians, the Buddha of the Buddhists, the Jehovah of the Jews, the Father in Heaven of the Christians, give strength to you to carry out your noble idea. The star arose in the East; it travelled steadily towards the West, sometimes dimmed and sometimes effulgent, till it made a circuit of the world, and now it is again rising on the very horizon of the East, the borders of the Sanpo, a thousandfold more effulgent than it ever was before.

Hail Columbia, motherland of liberty! It has been given to thee, who never dipped her hand in her neighbour's blood, who never found out that the shortest way of becoming rich was by robbing one's neighbours, it has been given to thee to march at the vanguard of civilization with the flag of harmony.

Certainly it is not going beyond the bounds of just appreciation to say that the Swami's paper on Hinduism was the most far-reaching and prophetic utterance in the history of religions, pointing out as it did the truth of Oneness, of Realization, and of the Divinity of Man. Its ringing declarations of an all-inclusive ideal sounded the death-knell of the sectarianism which had drenched the earth so often with human blood and barred the progress of civilization in the name of religion. Its unique features were its acceptance of all faiths and creeds as valid paths, and its spirit of religious cooperation and harmony. It had no note of criticism or of antagonism. It went counter to many of the dogmas of the various sects; yet none were attacked; indeed his definition of a universal religion, so startling in its novelty, struck at the very root of all sectarian thought. He spoke with authority, for he was a man of realization. In all the solemnity of direct vision, he preached the realization of spiritual truth as opposed to the blind credulity that most creeds uncompromisingly demand. Through him the whole import and effulgence of Divine consciousness bore in upon the Parliament, and thousands of those who were brought up in a particular religious belief saw on that day the universality of Truth and the oneness of all religious realization.

The Swami was undoubtedly in that hour at the summit of his illustrious career, preaching, through the Parliament, to all peoples of the earth, the sovereignty of human nature, its divinity, and the unity of all souls. And in that hour he was acclaimed by this vast representative assembly of nations an apostle of a new order of religious thought; he became a world figure, his name ever to be associated with the gospel of the divinity of man. He made Christianity itself revalue its contents.

But his greatest service was to India, for by revealing the unity of Indian religious ideals, a unity that had not yet found self-conscious expression in the communal consciousness of Hinduism, he conferred a great dignity upon the Hindu outlook on life. Definitely stated, the principal contribution to Hinduism that the Swami's address embodied was: first, his philosophical and religious synthesis of the faith of his forefathers; second, the idea of the Mother-Church, embracing all the forms, from the lowest to the highest, of its religious vision; and third, though not least, the unshakeable position that he won for Hinduism by his scholarly and spiritual interpretation, thus giving it prestige· among the enlightened thinkers and theologians of the West and raising it in the estimation of the whole Western world. And the most eloquent elements in all these triumphs were his commanding personality, his supreme personal realization, and the unimpeachable authority of his statements.

In her introduction to the *Complete Works of Swami Vivekananda*, Sister Nivedita has with great insight best described the general import of his address at the Parliament:

Of the Swami's address before the Parliament of Religions, it may be said that when he began to speak, it was of the religious ideas of the Hindus; but when he ended, Hinduism had been created. . . .

For it was no experience of his own that rose to the lips of the Swami Vivekananda there. He did not even take advantage of the occasion, to tell the story of his Master. Instead of either of these, it was the religious consciousness of India that spoke through him, the message of his whole people, as determined by their whole past. And as he spoke in the youth and noonday of the West, a nation, sleeping in the shadows of the darkened half of earth, on the far side of the Pacific, waited in spirit for the words that would be borne on the dawn that was travelling towards them, to reveal to them the secret of their own greatness and strength.

Others stood beside the Swami Vivekananda, on the same platform as he, as apostles of particular creeds and churches. But it was his glory that he came to preach a religion to which each of these was, in his own words, "only a travelling, a coming up, of different men and women, through various conditions and circumstances to the same goal." He stood there, as he declared, to tell of One who had said of them all, not that one or another was true, in this or that respect, or for this or that reason, but that "All these are threaded upon Me, as pearls upon a string. Wherever thou seest extraordinary holiness and extraordinary power, raising and purifying humanity, know thou that I am there." To the Hindu, says Vivekananda, "Man is not travelling from error to truth, but climbing up from truth to truth, from truth that is lower to truth that is higher." This, and the teaching of Mukti—the doctrine that "Man is to become divine by realizing the divine," that religion is perfected in us only when it has led us to "Him who is the one life in a universe of death, Him who is the constant basis of an ever-changing world, that One who is the only soul, of which all souls are but delusive manifestations"—may be taken as the two great outstanding truths which, authenticated by the longest and most complex experience in human history, India proclaimed through him to the modern world of the West.

For India herself, the short address forms, as has been said, a brief Charter of Enfranchisement. Hinduism in its wholeness, the speaker bases on the Vedas, but he spiritualizes our conception of the word, even while he utters it. To him, all that is true is Veda. "By the Vedas," he says, "no books are meant. They mean the accumulated treasury of spiritual laws discovered by different persons in different times." Incidentally, he discloses his conception of the Sanatana Dharma. . . . To his mind, there could be no sect, no school, no sincere religious experience of the Indian people—however like an aberration it might seem to the individual—that might rightly be excluded from the embrace of Hinduism. And of this Indian Mother-Church, according to him, the distinctive doctrine is that of the Ishta-devata, the right of each soul to choose its own path, and to seek God in its own way. . . .

Yet would not this inclusion of all, this freedom of each, be the glory of Hinduism that it is, were it not for her supreme call, of sweetest promise: "Hear, ye children of immortal bliss! Even ye that dwell in higher spheres! For I have found that Ancient One who is beyond all darkness, all delusion. And knowing Him, ye also shall be saved from death." Here is the word for the sake of which all the rest exists and has existed. Here is the crowning realization, into which all others are resolvable.

On September 20, the day following his paper on Hinduism, the Swami commented on the fact that it was not religion of which the Indians were in crying need, but bread. It was a short impromptu address—later entitled "Religion Not the Crying Need of India"—but it embodied his solution of India's pressing problems. He stated also, that what had brought him to the far West was to seek aid for his impoverished people. By his forthright words the Parliament was made aware that the man who stood before it was not only a monk, but a patriot as well.

We have seen earlier that in addition to speaking at the plenary session of the Parliament, the Swami gave a number of addresses before the Scientific Section, whose President, the Honourable Merwin-Marie Snell, became a great friend of his and an ardent advocate of Hinduism. The first time the Swami spoke in these conferences, as recorded in the Rev. J. H. Barrows's *The World's Parliament of Religions*, was on the morning of September 22, when he discussed "Orthodox Hinduism and the Vedanta Philosophy". "Hall III was crowded to over-flowing," the Chicago *Interocean* wrote o[n] this occasion, "and hundreds of questions were asked b[y] auditors and answered by the great sannyasi with wonderful skill and lucidity." That same afternoon he spoke on "The Modern Religions of India". Another conference was held on the 23rd on the subject of the foregoing addresses, and on the 25th the Swami spoke in the afternoon session on "The Essence of the Hindu Religion". The reader should know that, in addition, four other addresses in these conferences were given by the Swami.

On the afternoon of September 22 the Swami also spoke on "Women in Oriental Religion" at a special session organized by Mrs. Potter Palmer, President of the Woman's Branch of the Auxiliary, in Hall VII of the Art Institute.

On September 23, the Swami gave a talk before a session of the Universal Religious Unity Congress, one of the congresses held in conjunction with the Parliament. His days were crowded indeed; yet while the Parliament was in session he spoke on invitation at least once outside its halls, delivering on Sunday, September 24, a lecture entitled "The Love of God" at the Third Unitarian Church in Chicago. This was the first of many lectures he was to give from a Unitarian pulpit in the United States.

On the 26th the Swami delivered before the Parliament a short address called "Buddhism, the Fulfilment of Hinduism". He pointed out that Hinduism was divided, as it were, into two branches, one being the ceremonial and the other the purely spiritual. The Buddha interpreted the spiritual elements of the dharma, with their natural social conclusions, to the people. He was the first Teacher in the world to carry on missionary work and to conceive the idea of proselytizing. "Shakya Muni", said the Swami, "came not to destroy, but he was the fulfilment, the logical conclusion, the logical development of the religion of the Hindus." At the close he said, "Hinduism cannot live without Buddhism, nor Buddhism without Hinduism", and he emphasized that the need in India today was to "join the wonderful intellect of the Brahmin with the heart, the noble soul, the wonderful humanizing power of the Great Master".

In addition to delivering addresses before the Parliament at the plenary sessions, the Scientific Section, and the Universal Religious Unity Congresses, to attending, as he undoubtedly did, many other daily sessions, and to lecturing on invitation at the Third Unitarian Church, the Swami was certainly present at the several receptions given in honour of the delegates, thus becoming acquainted with countless eminent men and women of both America and abroad. The first of these gala receptions was held on the evening of the opening day of the Parliament. It was given for the foreign delegates by the Rev. J. H. Barrows at the spacious residence of Mr. and Mrs. Bartlett, the halls and rooms of which were, it is said, "appropriately decorated with many hundreds of flags of all nations". The following evening (September 12) a huge public reception was given by the President of the Parliament, the Hon. Charles C. Bonney, in the halls of the Art Institute. And on Thursday evening, September 14, Mrs. Potter Palmer, President of the Board of Lady Managers of the Columbian Exposition, gave a reception to all the delegates at the Woman's Building of the Fair. On this last occasion, the Swami, in response to Mrs. Palmer's request, gave a short talk on the condition of women in his country. Still another large reception was given to the delegates on Saturday afternoon, September 16, by Mr. and Mrs. E. W. Blatchford at their home on La Salle Avenue. Besides them many other leading residents of Chicago, including prominent Christian ministers and Jewish rabbis, extended their hospitality in their homes and churches to the foreign delegates, and from the Chicago newspaper reports it is evident that the Swami was always one of the notables present on these occasions.

Day after day the Parliament went on, the Swami speaking extemporaneously at its main sessions many times. He was allowed to speak longer than the usual half-hour, and being a popular speaker, he was always scheduled last in order to hold the audience. The people would sit from ten in the morning to ten at night, with only a recess of a half-hour for lunch, listening to paper after paper, in which most of them were not interested, to hear their favourite. Such was their enthusiasm. Months later, the *Boston Evening Transcript* of April 5, 1894, recalled this evidence of the Swami's popularity:

At the Parliament of Religions they used to keep Vivekananda until the end of the programme to make people stay until the end of the session. On a warm day, when a prosy speaker talked too long and people began going home by hundreds, the Chairman would get up and announce that Swami Vivekananda would give a short address just before the benediction. Then he would have the peaceable hundreds perfectly in tether. The four thousand fanning people in the Hall of Columbus would sit smiling and expectant, waiting for an hour or two of other men's speeches, to listen to Vivekananda for fifteen minutes. The Chairman knew the old rule of keeping the best until last.

On September 27, the Swami delivered his "Address at the Final Session", and here he again rose to one of his most prophetic and luminous moods; he declared:

The Christian is not to become a Hindu or a Buddhist, nor a Hindu or a Buddhist to become a Christian. But each must assimilate the spirit of the others and yet preserve his individuality and grow according to his own law of growth. . . .

If the Parliament of Religions has shown anything to the world it is this: It has proved to the world that holiness, purity, and charity are not the exclusive possessions of any church in the world, and that every system has produced men and women of the most exalted character. In the face of this evidence, if anybody dreams of the exclusive survival of his own religion and the destruction of the others, I pity him from the bottom of my heart, and point out to him that upon the banner of every religion will soon be written, in spite of resistance: "Help and not Fight", "Assimilation and not Destruction", "Harmony and Peace and not Dissension".

Thus did the unknown monk blossom into a world figure, the wandering monk of solitary days in India become the Prophet of a New Dispensation!

On all sides his name resounded. Life-size pictures of him were seen posted in the streets of Chicago, with the words "The Monk Vivekananda" beneath them, and passers-by would stop to do reverence with bowed head. "From the day the wonderful Professor [the Swami] delivered his speech, which was followed by other addresses, he was followed by a crowd wherever he went", a contemporary newspaper reported. "In going in and coming out of the building, he was daily beset by hundreds of women who almost fought with each other for a chance to get near him, and shake his hand." The press rang with his fame. The best known and most conservative of the metropolitan newspapers proclaimed him a Prophet and a Seer. Indeed, the *New York Herald* spoke of him in these words: "He is undoubtedly the greatest figure in the Parliament of Religions. After hearing him we feel how foolish it is to send missionaries to this learned nation."

The *Boston Evening Transcript* wrote of him on September 30:

He is a great favourite at the Parliament from the grandeur of his sentiments and his appearance as well. If he merely crosses the platform he is applauded; and this marked approval of thousands he accepts in a childlike spirit of gratification without a trace of conceit.

Other leading newspapers of the United States, such as the *Rutherford American*, the *Press of America*, the *Interior Chicago*, and the *Chicago Tribune*, were eloquent about Swami Vivekananda. Well-known periodicals quoted his talks in full. The *Review of Reviews* described his address as "noble and sublime", and the *Critic* of New York spoke of him as "an orator by Divine right". Similar accounts of the Swami's triumph appeared in other papers too numerous to quote here. Amongst personal appreciations, the Honourable Merwin-Marie Snell wrote some time after:

No religious body made so profound an impression upon the Parliament and the American people at large, as did Hinduism. . . . And by far the most important and typical representative of Hinduism was Swami Vivekananda, who, in fact, was beyond question the most popular and influential man in the Parliament. He frequently spoke, both on the floor of the Parliament itself and at the meeting of the Scientific Section, over which I had the honour to preside, and, on all occasions he was received with greater enthusiasm

than any other speaker, Christian or "Pagan". The people thronged
about him wherever he went and hung with eagerness on his every
word. . . . The most rigid of orthodox Christians say of him, "He
is indeed a prince among men!" . . .

And the Rev. John H. Barrows said, "Swami Vivekananda
exercised a wonderful influence over his auditors." Dr. Annie
Besant, giving her impression of the Swami at the Parliament,
wrote long after:

A striking figure, clad in yellow and orange, shining like the sun
of India in the midst of the heavy atmosphere of Chicago, a lion
head, piercing eyes, mobile lips, movements swift and abrupt—
such was my first impression of Swami Vivekananda, as I met him
in one of the rooms set apart for the use of the delegates to the Parliament of Religions. Monk, they called him, not unwarrantably,
warrior-monk was he, and the first impression was of the warrior
rather than of the monk, for he was off the platform, and his figure
was instinct with pride of country, pride of race—the representative
of the oldest of living religions, surrounded by curious gazers of
nearly the youngest, and by no means inclined to give step, as though
the hoary faith he embodied was in aught inferior to the noblest
there. India was not to be shamed before the hurrying arrogant
West by this her envoy and her son. He brought her message, he
spoke in her name, and the herald remembered the dignity of the
royal land whence he came. Purposeful, virile, strong, he stood out,
a man among men, able to hold his own.

On the platform another side came out. The dignity and the inborn
sense of worth and power still were there, but all was subdued to
the exquisite beauty of the spiritual message which he had brought,
to the sublimity of that matchless evangel of the East which is the
heart, the life of India, the wondrous teaching of the Self. Enraptured,
the huge multitude hung upon his words; not a syllable must be
lost, not a cadence missed! "That man a heathen!" said one, as
he came out of the great hall, "and we send missionaries to his
people! It would be more fitting that they should send missionaries
to us."

Hundreds of enlightened and liberal-minded persons, Emer-
sonians, Transcendentalists, Neo-Christians, Theosophists,
Universalists, Congregationalists, either hearing him per-

sonally while in attendance at the Parliament, or reading the
glowing accounts about him, felt that the Swami was, indeed,
another Oriental Master come to them with a new message.
And so meteoric was the transformation of the Swami from
obscurity to fame, that it can be truly said that he "awoke
one morning to find himself famous".

But to the Swami the recognition of his eloquence and the
glorification of his name, far from touching or elating him,
made him weep like a child at the thought that for him the
joy of the free life of the unknown monk was at an end. In
spite of his hatred of name and fame, he was destined to be
"thrown out" of his quest for forgottenness. He was the monk
with a message and he had been "dragged out" by Divine
Providence. He could no longer be the itinerant monk. There
was to be no more the quiet, solemn peace for him; it was to
be strenuous, ceaseless labour with a terrible and constant
demand upon his time and personality.

But the Swami took himself and his message seriously,
and he was inspired with the courage to fulfil his Master's
will. He had become bold. An incident that occurred in the
Parliament is told in the second volume of *The Times*'s *Historian's History of the World*, on pages 547 and 548. These were
substituted in deference to the violent objection taken by the
Indian subscribers to some serious calumnies that had appeared
in it against Hinduism. The following passage, later reproduced in *Prabuddha Bharata* of June 1908, illustrates the Swami's
boldness of spirit and self-confidence:

A striking illustration of what in another case would be termed
insularity of outlook was brought to view by a noted Hindu when
addressing a vast audience at the World's Congress of Religions in
America, in the city of Chicago, in 1893. Pausing in the midst of his
discourse, the speaker asked that every member of the audience who
had read the sacred books of the Hindus, and who therefore had first-
hand knowledge of their religion, would raise his hand. Only three or
four hands were raised, though the audience represented, presumably,
the leading theologians of many lands. Glancing benignly over the
assembly, the Hindu raised himself to his full height, and in a voice

every accent of which must have smitten the audience as a rebuke, pronounced these simple words, "And yet you dare to judge us!"

The Swami was not only brilliant but strong in the hour of his unparalleled success. Just before reading his paper on Hinduism he again took the Parliament to task. Of this incident the *Chicago Tribune* of September 20 wrote:

Dr. Noble presented Swami Vivekananda, the Hindu monk, who was applauded loudly as he stepped forward to the centre of the platform. He wore an orange robe, bound with a scarlet sash, and a pale yellow turban. The customary smile was on his handsome face and his eyes shone with animation. Said he: "We, who have come from the East, have sat here day after day and have been told in a patronizing way that we ought to accept Christianity because Christian nations are the most prosperous. We look about us and we see England the most prosperous Christian nation in the world, with her foot on the neck of 250,000,000 Asiatics. We look back into history and see that the prosperity of Christian Europe began with Spain. Spain's prosperity began with the invasion of Mexico. Christianity wins its prosperity by cutting the throats of its fellow men. At such a price the Hindoo will not have prosperity. I have sat here today and I have heard the height of intolerance. . . . Blood and the sword are not for the Hindu, whose religion is based on the law of love."

When the applause had ceased, Mr. Vivekananda went [on] to read his paper.

Never catering to popularity, the Swami could assume a severely critical attitude. But his love was too deep and sincere to be misunderstood, and his rebukes were accepted by a large majority of the audience in the same spirit of brotherhood in which he gave them. So also was accepted his valiant defence of Hinduism. He found that India and her spiritual ideas had indeed been misrepresented and felt that he must constantly reveal and uphold the merits of the Hindu religion. He always sought to give Hinduism its rightful status in the West. And to the incredulous jubilation of the Indian people he succeeded.

Though the news about the proceedings of the Parliament

of Religions, and about the Swami, had been coming out in the Indian newspapers since mid-September of 1893, it did not catch the attention of the Indian people till November, when a long article entitled "Hindus at the Fair", first published in the *Boston Evening Transcript* of September 23, appeared in the leading papers of Bombay, Calcutta and Madras. This article, reproduced in the *Indian Mirror* of Calcutta on November 11, contained a behind-the-scenes interview with the Swami. It told of the grandeur of his ideals and mentioned his wonderful oratorical power, which was electrifying the great gathering of the Parliament. The article brought to India the first inkling that something extraordinary was taking place half-way round the globe. It read in part:

There is a room at the left of the entrance to the Art Palace marked "No. 1—keep out". To this the speakers at the Congress of Religions all repair sooner or later. . . . Only delegates are supposed to penetrate the sacred precincts, but it is not impossible to obtain an "open sesame", and thus to enjoy a brief opportunity of closer relations with the distinguished guests than the platform in the Hall of Columbus affords.

The most striking figure one meets in this ante-room is Swami Vivekananda, the Brahmin monk. He is a large well-built man, with the superb carriage of the Hindustanies, his face clean shaven, squarely moulded, regular features, white teeth, and with well-chiselled lips, that are usually parted in a benevolent smile while he is conversing. His finely poised head is crowned with either a lemon-coloured or red turban, and his cassock (not the technical name for this garment), belted in at the waist and falling below the knees, alternates in a bright orange and rich crimson. He speaks excellent English and replies readily to any questions asked in sincerity. . . .

Vivekananda's address before the Parliament was broad as the heavens above us; embracing the best in all religions, as the ultimate universal religion—charity to all mankind, good works for the love of God, not for fear of punishment or hope of reward. He is a great favourite at the Parliament, from the grandeur of his sentiments and his appearance as well. If he merely crosses the platform he is applauded, and this marked approval of thousands he accepts in a childlike spirit of gratification, without a trace of conceit. It must be a strange experience, too, for this humble young Brahmin monk, this sudden transition from poverty and self-effacement to affluence and aggrandizement. . . .

From that time on, as news of Swami Vivekananda's spectacular success at Chicago came from the American Press, it was reprinted in the leading Indian newspapers, notably the *Indian Mirror*, with enthusiastic editorial comments. Some journals, it is true, commented sourly upon the Swami's popularity, their religious affiliations and views being unable, for one reason or another, to accommodate it. But whether the information was given grudgingly or jubilantly, it was not long before all of India knew that a young sannyasi had crossed the ocean, mixed with foreigners, and conquered the great international Parliament of Religions.

Almost daily, articles summarizing the Swami's formal talks at the Parliament, as well as those that had fallen unannounced upon the audience like thunder rolls from some Himalayan sky, were relayed to an astonished Indian public.

On December 6, the *Indian Mirror* editorialized:

. . . But the one figure among the audience, the one Indian representative, on whom were riveted all eyes, and who conquered as he went, was Swami Vivekananda, who appeared in the robes of the sannyasi, of handsome presence, somewhat portly form, and with eyes glittering like large brilliants . . . But when he spoke, when the inner man emerged from the shell, then the power was doubled, and the vast audiences heard his fervid exposition of the Vedic faith of the Hindus with rapture. We can well understand the enthusiasm of the Americans over Swami Vivekananda. . . .

Again, on December 12, after the news of the close of the Parliament of Religions had reached India, the *Indian Mirror* wrote:

Among those who created the greatest stir at Chicago was Swami Vivekananda, a Hindu. His utterances on Hinduism created widespread interest, and some sensation even. The majority of his audiences heard of Hinduism, for the first time, from his lips. Other Hindus also spoke of that [their] religious creeds at Chicago, though their speeches were not listened to, perhaps, with as much interest as

.28

those of Vivekananda. . . . The Parliament of Religions at Chicago is, we believe, the beginning of the movement that will come into greater prominence by and by for unification of all nations into a common religious bond. That was the impression, at least, of all those who attended the Parliament of Religions, and listened intelligently to the presentment of the different religious creeds by their representatives. We must own that the holding of the Parliament of Religions was a splendid idea, splendidly carried out.

As early as November 15, the *Indian Mirror* had identified the Swami as "a Bengali Graduate of the Calcutta University, Norendro Nath Dutt by name, who became a disciple of the late venerable Paramahamsa Ramakrishna of Dakshineswar"; and one cannot but think that his brother-disciples at Alambazar Math had long been well aware that the famous and much-lauded Vivekananda was their own Naren. A letter to the editor of the *Indian Mirror*, printed on December 27 and signed "Trigunatit"—Swami Trigunatita, one of Shri Ramakrishna's monastic disciples—makes it certain that the identity was known to them at least by that date. For the interest of the *Mirror*'s many readers the letter contained quotations in appreciation of the Swami from "*New York Critique*" [the *Critic*] and the *New York Herald*.

Four waves of amazement at the Swami's success rolled over India from the great boulder-splash in Chicago. The first came from the aforesaid eyewitness news of his highly-appreciated talks before the Parliament. The second came two months later on the publication of the Rev. John Henry Barrows's two-volume work, *The World's Parliament of Religions*—an official and detailed history of the event. The book was reviewed exhaustively in the January issue of the American periodical the *Review of Reviews*, which account was, in turn, commented upon at length in an editorial in the *Indian Mirror* of February 21, 1894. The fact that Barrows had given a prominent place to Swami Vivekananda and to his paper on Hinduism in his history put an official and impressive seal on the Swami's great accomplishment. His achievement could no longer be brushed aside as a passing sensation by

Christian missionaries and others to whose interest it was to discredit him. The deep mark he had made was now a matter of solid historical record. The *Mirror*'s editorial read in part:

... Dr. John Henry Barrows, the President of the Parliament of Religions, has just published the official report of the Parliament, and from the pretty exhaustive résumé of the report, which Mr. W. T. Stead gives in the current number of the *Review of Reviews*, it appears that a prominent place has been accorded to Swami Vivekananda in the report. "This speaker", says Dr. Barrows, "is a high-caste Hindu and representative of orthodox Hinduism. He was one of the principal personalities in the Parliament as well as one of the most popular of guests in the Chicago drawing rooms." The report gives select extracts from the address the Swami delivered before the Parliament. ... Dr. Barrows characterizes the Swami's address as "noble and sublime," and it was so much appreciated for its breadth, its sincerity and its excellent spirit of toleration, that the Hindu representative soon came to be as much liked outside the Parliament as within it. .... With the fact before us of this outburst of enthusiasm and admiration for the teachings of Hinduism by hundreds of Americans, shall we not be justified in advancing the opinion that these Christian people have found in the essence of Hinduism a higher and truer ideal of religious life than Christianity could supply them [with]?

Whatever may be the practical outcome of Swami Vivekananda's Mission to America there can be no question that it has already had the effect of immensely raising the credit of true Hinduism in the eyes of the civilized world, and that is, indeed, a work for which the whole Hindu community should feel grateful to the Swami.

Editorials such as the above not only created jubilation and gratitude in the Hindu community as a whole, they also fanned the destructive flames of fear and jealousy which licked at the Swami's mission. But he was never without defenders. Mr. Merwin-Marie Snell, President of the Scientific Section of the Parliament, wrote in the goodness of his heart and the courage of his convictions a long letter to the editor of the *Pioneer*, an Anglo-Indian newspaper of Allahabad. His letter, dated January 30, 1894, was printed in the *Pioneer* on March 8 of the same year. Subsequently it was reprinted in the *Indian Mirror* of March 9 and the *Amrita Bazar Patrika* of March 10, with accompanying editorials in, respectively, agreement and disagreement with its views. This laudatory letter, written by a highly-respected Western scholar, together with editorial reactions to it, constituted the third wave of amazement and journalistic attention relating to the Swami's success at the Parliament of Religions. A passage from Mr. Snell's letter has been quoted earlier in this chapter; other portions read as follows:

There having been an occasional note of discord in chorus of praise which the delegates from India in the World's Parliament of Religions —and especially the Swami Vivekananda—elicited from the American Press and People, I have felt inspired to acquaint your people with the true state of the case, to voice the unanimous and heartfelt gratitude and appreciation of the cultured and broadminded portion of our public, and to give my personal testimony, as the President of the Scientific Section of the Parliament and of all the Conferences connected with the latter, and therefore an eyewitness, to the esteem in which he is held here, the influence that he is wielding and the good that he is doing. . . . Intense is the astonished admiration which the personal presence and bearing and language of Paramahamsa Vivekananda have wrung from a public accustomed to think of Hindus—thanks to the fables and half-truths of the missionaries—as ignorant and degraded "heathen"; there is no doubt that the continued interest is largely due to a genuine hunger for the spiritual truths which India through him has offered to the American people. . . .

All the Hinduizing forces hitherto at work have received a notable impulse from the labours of Swami Vivekananda. Never before has so authoritative a representative of genuine Hinduism—as opposed to the emasculated and Anglicized versions of it so common in these days—been accessible to American inquirers: and it is certain that the American people at large will, when he is gone, look forward with eagerness to his return, or the advent of some of his confrères of the institute of Sankaracharya. . . . America thanks India for sending him.

Mr. Snell's letter was widely circulated, and thus the Swami's achievement, confirmed again and again by highly reputable sources, was becoming deeply impressed upon the mind of the Indian people.

The fourth wave from the Parliament of Religions to sweep

over India was the publication in Madras and Calcutta of the
text of the Swami's paper on "Hinduism"—his official address,
which he had delivered on September 19, 1893. The Calcutta
pamphlet was distributed on March 11, 1894, at Dakshineswar,
on the birthday celebration of Shri Ramakrishna. The Swami's
address created, perhaps, the greatest sensation of all, for it left
no doubt of what, precisely, he had said to the American
people, and in what, precisely, his achievement consisted. On
March 21, the *Indian Mirror* printed a lengthy excerpt from his
paper, commenting in part:

The spirit that reigned over the Parliament and dominated the
soul of almost every religious representative present, was that of
universal toleration and universal deliverance, and it ought to be a
matter of pride to India, to all Hindus specially, that no one expressed, as the American papers say, this spirit so well as the Hindu
representative, Swami Vivekananda. His address, in every way
worthy of the representative of a religion, such as Hinduism is, struck
the keynote of the Parliament of Religions. . . . The spirit of catholicity and toleration which distinguishes Hinduism, forming one of its
broad features, was never before so prominently brought to the notice
of the world, as it has been by Swami Vivekananda, and we make no
doubt that the Swami's address will have an effect on other religions,
whose teachers, preachers and Missionaries heard him, and were
impressed by his utterances.

As the Swami's "Paper on Hinduism" circulated through
India, the tremendous historical significance of his mission
became apparent to all—to the gratification of some, to the
chagrin of others. A correspondent wrote to the editor of the
Mirror in a letter dated April 12, 1894:

I am extremely sorry to see that the unprecedented success of
Swami Vivekananda has created a strong jealousy and heart-burning
among the Christians and the Brahmos, who are trying their best to
damage his reputation. They have commenced regular warfare in
writing and speaking against the Swami in his absence. But they are
fighting a losing battle. Swami Vivekananda is a mighty power now.
His culture, his eloquence and his fascinating personality have given
to the world a new idea of Hindu religion. . . . The Swami's address

on Hinduism, which has been printed and circulated, is a precious
gem. It should be read, pondered over and thoroughly grasped. Every
sentence uttered by him is a museum of thoughts, and it is a wonder
how he succeeded in giving such a remarkable picture in half an
hour's time. . . .

The Swami's epoch-making representation of Hinduism at
the Parliament was to raise India not only in the estimation of
the West but in her own estimation as well, and was eventually
to bring about a profound change in her national life. Years
later, on the Swami's passing from this world, the *Brahmavadin*
commented:

. . . Had the late lamented Swami Vivekananda done nothing
more than attend the Parliament of Religions in Chicago, and
deliver that one speech which brought India and America together
in juxtaposition almost immediately, he will still have been entitled
to our fullest gratitude. That speech compelled attention both in
method and substance. To Swami Vivekananda belongs the undying
honour of being the pioneer in the noble work of Hindu religious
revival.

The Swami's appearance at the Parliament of Religions had
without question made him irreversibly famous throughout the
world. Never again was he to wander alone, unknown through
his beloved country. His world mission in its public aspect had
begun. But in the midst of all the immediate acclaim and popularity that his appearance at the Parliament had brought him,
he had no thought for himself; his heart continued to bleed for
India. Personally he had no more wants. The mansions of some
of the wealthiest of Chicago society were open to him, and he
was received as an honoured guest. On the very day of his
triumph, he was invited by a man of great wealth and distinction to his home in one of the most fashionable parts of the city.
Here he was entertained royally; a princely room fitted with a
luxury beyond anything he could have conceived was assigned
to him. But instead of feeling happy in this splendid environment, he was miserable. Name and fame and the approval of
thousands had in no way affected him; though sumptuously
cared for, he was the same sannyasi as of old, thinking of India's

poor. As he retired the first night and lay upon his bed, the terrible contrast between poverty-stricken India and opulent America oppressed him. He could not sleep for pondering over India's plight. The bed of down seemed to be a bed of thorns. The pillow was wet with his tears. He went to the window and gazed out into the darkness until he was well-nigh faint with sorrow. At length, overcome with emotion, he fell to the floor, crying out, "O Mother, what do I care for name and fame when my motherland remains sunk in utmost poverty! To what a sad pass have we poor Indians come when millions of us die for want of a handful of rice, and here they spend millions of rupees upon their personal comforts! Who will raise the masses in India! Who will give them bread? Show me, O Mother, how I can help them."

Over and over again one finds the same intense love for India shining out in his words and actions. The deep and spontaneous love that welled in his heart for the poor, the distressed and the despised, was the inexhaustible spring of all his activities. From now on, the student of the Swami's life is led into a world of intense thought and work. He will discover that hand in hand with giving the message of Hinduism to the West the Swami was constantly studying, observing, and trying to turn to advantage, every new experience in seeking to solve the problems of his country. Though the dusty roads and the parched tongue and the hunger of his days as a wandering monk were ascetic in the extreme, the experiences he was to undergo in foreign lands were to be even more severe. He was to strain himself to the utmost. He was to work until work was no longer possible and the body dropped off from sheer exhaustion.

23

AFTER THE PARLIAMENT—1

The unknown young wandering monk of India had suddenly become a famous man of his time; but it was not as if Swami Vivekananda had been yearning for name and fame. From his letters written immediately after the Parliament, as well as from his recorded conversations, we learn how often he intensely longed to return to the days of his lonely wanderings, of his meditation and his studies. The divine mandate, however, had ordained otherwise: he was to preach the message of the Lord in various lands as a world teacher—and to sacrifice himself in the process. And behind all his undertakings was his limitless faith in God and his firm resolve to move and act according to His will. Moreover, the question of how to bring about the uplift of India and to remove the poverty of his people always occupied his mind. Thus, although in the early part of his stay in America his accustomed manner of thinking and living was in conflict with Western ways, he soon realized that it was possible to live according to Indian ideals even in this strange environment. On October 2, 1893, he wrote to Professor Wright:

I am now going to be reconciled to my life here. All my life I have been taking every circumstance as coming from Him and calmly adapting myself to it. At first in America I was almost out of my water. I was afraid I would have to give up the accustomed way of being guided by the Lord and *cater* for myself—and what a horrid piece of mischief and ingratitude was that. I now clearly see that He who was guiding me on the snowtops of the Himalayas and the burning plains of India is here to help me and guide me. *Glory unto Him* in the highest. So I have calmly fallen into my old ways. Somebody or other gives me a shelter and food, somebody or other comes to ask me to speak about Him, and I know He sends them and mine is to obey. And then He is supplying my necessities, and His *will be done*!

"He who rests [in] Me and gives up all other self-assertion and struggles I carry to him whatever he needs" (*Gita*).

So it is in Asia. So in Europe. So in America. So in the deserts of India. So in the rush of business in America. For is He not here also? And if He does not, I only would take for granted that He wants that I should lay aside this three minutes' body of clay—and hope to lay it down gladly.

But although the Swami was thus able to remain rooted in the mental attitudes befitting a sannyasi, he had to make changes in the methods of his contemplated work. He wanted to propagate the essential tenets of Indian thought, to remove the prevailing misconceptions about India, and to acquire funds for his Indian work. His actual experience in America, however, made him relinquish for the time being his decision to ask for money in public. In this connection he wrote to Professor Wright from Chicago on October 26, 1893:

You would be glad to know that I am doing well here and that almost everybody has been very kind to me, except of course the very orthodox. Many of the men brought together here from far-off lands have got projects and ideas and missions to carry out, and America is the only place where there is a chance of success for everything. But I thought better and have given up speaking about my project entirely—because I am sure now—the heathen draws more than his project. So I want to go to work earnestly for my own project, only keeping the project in the background and working like any other lecturer.

He who has brought me hither and has not left me yet will not leave me ever I am here. You will be glad to know that I am doing well and expect to do very well in the way of getting money. Of course I am too green in the business but would soon learn my trade. I am very popular in Chicago. So I want to stay here a little more and get *money*. . . .

In other words, the Swami decided to earn money for his contemplated work in India through his own labour, without appealing publicly for contributions.

The first intimation of the character of the Swami's work following the Parliament of Religions was an invitation from the Slayton Lyceum Lecture Bureau to make a tour of America. He accepted it as the best way to enable him broadcast the ideas with which his mind teemed and to disillusion the Western people of their erroneous notions about India and its religion. It was also a way to get funds for the various educational, philanthropic and religious works in India that he had in mind. We now see him travelling here and there in America, visiting numerous cities and towns, telling of the glories of Indian culture. He lectured in most of the larger cities of the eastern, midwestern, and southern states, including Chicago, Iowa City, Des Moines, Memphis, Indianapolis, Minneapolis, Madison, Detroit, Hartford, Buffalo, Boston, Cambridge, Baltimore, Washington, Brooklyn and New York. Unfortunately, our knowledge of the Swami's tour is not yet complete, but as time goes on, more and more information comes to light. In the contemporary daily newspapers, for instance, or in the reminiscences of those who met him and heard him lecture, one finds records of his illuminating utterances or glowing descriptions of his personality. One also discovers details of his itinerary. It is now known, for instance, that through October and most of November of 1893 the Swami remained in Chicago, lecturing in and around that city.

"His stay in Chicago has been a continual ovation", the *Evanston Index* reported on October 7; and as we have seen, nearly three weeks later he himself wrote to his friend Professor Wright, "I am very popular in Chicago." Although surprisingly little is known at present of his lecture engagements in and near the city during these seven or eight weeks, we do know that at the end of September he gave a course of three lectures in near-by Evanston in conjunction with one of the liberal delegates of the Parliament of Religions, a Dr. Carl van Bergen of Sweden. The Swami spoke on "Hindu Altruism" (September 30), "Monism" (October 3), and "Reincarnation" (October 5). On October 7 he lectured in Streator, Illinois, taking as his subject "The Customs of India"; and on October 27 he spoke on "The History of Buddhism" at the Fortnightly of Chicago, one of the most influential women's clubs of the Midwest.

Through these engagements in and outside Chicago some money came to the Swami. He wrote in a letter to Mrs. Tannatt Woods on October 10, from Chicago:

Just now I am lecturing about Chicago—and am doing as I think very well; it is ranging from 30 to 80 dollars a lecture, and just now I have been so well advertised in Chicago gratis by the Parliament of Religions that it is not advisable to give up this field now. To which *I am sure you will agree.* However I may come soon to Boston, but when I cannot say. Yesterday I returned from Streator where I got 87 dollars for a lecture. I have engagements every day this week. And hope more will come by the end of the week. . . .

It does not appear that the Swami had any fixed residence at this time. We have seen earlier that during the Parliament he stayed with Mr. and Mrs. Lyon. But in his letter of October 2, 1893, to Professor Wright he wrote, "I am moving about just now. Only when I come to Chicago, I always go to see Mr. and Mrs. Lyon, one of the noblest couples I have seen here. If you would be kind enough to write me, kindly address it to the care of Mr. John B. Lyon, 262 Michigan Ave., Chicago."

From about the middle of November we find his letters carrying the address of the Hales—541 Dearborn Avenue, Chicago—and thereafter the Hale house became his head-quarters. The members of the Hale family looked upon him as an ever-welcome son and brother; and to him they were like his own. He often spoke of their loving kindness to him. But before this the Swami's permanent address was the Lyons's.

We have already told in some detail of his stay with Mr. and Mrs. Lyon when the Parliament was in session. We have also noted that even after the Parliament, when he moved about lecturing, his relationship with them was not severed; indeed, his letters show that at that later time he visited them at least twice. In her "Memoirs" of Swami Vivekananda, Cornelia Conger, granddaughter of the Lyons, throws some interesting sidelights on the Swami's personality, tastes and character. She wrote in part:

He seemed to feel especially close to my grandmother, who reminded him of his own mother. She was short and very erect, with quiet dignity and assurance, excellent common sense, and a dry humour that he enjoyed. My mother, who was a pretty and charming young widow, and I—who was only six years old—lived with them. My grandmother and my mother attended most of the meetings of the Congress of Religions and heard Swamiji speak there and later at lectures he gave. I know he helped my sad young mother who missed her young husband so much. . . .

My memories are simply of him as a guest in our home—of a great personality who is still vivid to me! His brilliant eyes, his charming voice with the lilt of a slight well-bred Irish brogue, his warm smile! He told me enchanting stories of India, of monkeys and peacocks, and flights of bright green parrots, of banyan trees and masses of flowers, and markets piled with all colours of fruits and vegetables. . . . I used to rush up to him when he came into the house and cry, "Tell me another story, Swami," and climb into his lap. . . . He was always wonderful to me! Yet—because a child is sensitive—I can remember times when I would run into his room and suddenly know he did not want to be disturbed—when he was in meditation. He asked me many questions about what I learned in school and made me show him my school-books and pointed out India to me on the map—it was pink, I recall—and told me about his country. He seemed sad that little Indian girls did not have, in general, the chance to have as good an education as we American children. . . . My grandmother was president of the Women's Hospital at home and he visited it with lively interest and asked for all the figures in infant mortality, etc.

When he began to give lectures, people offered him money for the work he hoped to do in India. He had no purse. So he used to tie it up in a handkerchief and bring it back—like a proud little boy!—pour it into my grandmother's lap to keep for him. She made him learn the different coins and to stack them up neatly and count them.

Once he said to my grandmother that he had had the greatest temptation of his life in America. She liked to tease him a bit and said, "Who is she, Swami?" He burst out laughing and said, "Oh, it is not a lady, it is Organization!" He explained how the followers of Ramakrishna had all gone out alone and when they reached a village, would just quietly sit under a tree and wait for those in trouble to come to consult them. But in the States he saw how much could be accomplished by organizing work. Yet he was doubtful about just what type of organization would be acceptable to the Indian character and he gave a great deal of thought and study how to adapt what seemed good to him in our Western world to the best advantage of his own people. . . . I spoke earlier of his delightful slight Irish brogue. . . . My grandmother used to joke him about it. But Swami said it was probably because his favourite professor was an Irish gentleman, a graduate of Trinity College, Dublin. . . .

After Swami left us, my mother was eager to do some studying along the lines of Oriental philosophy, as she realized she had not enough background to understand his teachings as fully as she wished. A Mrs. Peake held some classes in Chicago that following winter and, in the course of them, mother discovered much to her surprise that if she held a letter torn up into fine bits between her hands, she received a brief but vivid impression of the writer, both physically and mentally. When Swamiji returned to Chicago a year or so later to give lectures, mother asked him about this strange gift and he said, he had it also, and that when he was young he used to have fun doing it to show off, but Ramakrishna had rapped his knuckles and said, "Don't use this great gift except for the good of mankind! Hands that receive these impressions can also bring relief from pain. Use this gift to bring healing!"

Swamiji was such a dynamic and attractive personality that many women were quite swept away by him and made every effort by flattery to gain his interest. He was still young and, in spite of his great spirituality and his brilliance of mind, seemed to be very unworldly. This used to trouble my grandmother who feared he might be put in a false or uncomfortable position and she tried to caution him a little. Her concern touched and amused him and he patted her hand and said, "Dear Mrs. Lyon, you dear American mother of mine, don't be afraid for me! It is true I often sleep under a banyan tree with a bowl of rice given me by a kindly peasant, but it is equally true that I also am sometimes the guest in the palace of a great Maharajah and a slave girl is appointed to wave a peacock feather fan over me all night long! I am used to temptation and you need not fear for me!"

It is said that Western women were sometimes so fascinated by the Swami's personality that some actually proposed marriage to him. One such, an heiress to a fortune, said, "Swami, I offer myself and all my riches at your feet!" His reply was,

"Madam, I am a sannyasin; what is marriage to me! To me all women are as my mother!" Verily, everywhere and in all situations of life, he was a sannyasi.

The Swami was loved not only by the Lyons and Hales but by everyone he visited. His hosts always showed him every consideration, and, aside from the charm and inspiration of his personality, he was a perfect guest, making every effort to fit himself in with Western customs and manners. East and West, so different in all other things, are different also in their forms of etiquette, and it was touching to many who met him in America to see how he would often turn to his host or hostess, questioning with all the simplicity of a child as to the right social form. "How is it?" he would ask: "Does the gentleman or the lady precede in coming up or going down the stairs?" As a guest he was given complete personal liberty. It was understood that at any moment the mood of insight might come upon him, making him oblivious of what was happening about him. As with his Master, even the simplest phenomenon of life would remind him of revelations and spiritual truths. The states of meditation and recollection were always with him. Writes Sister Nivedita of his early days in the West:

The Swami never seemed, it must be remembered, to be doing Tapasya [austerity], but his whole life was a concentration so intense that for any one else it would have been a most terrible Tapasya. When he first went to America, it was extremely difficult for him to control the momentum that carried him into meditation. "When he sits down to meditate," had said one whose guest he was in India, "in two minutes he feels nothing, though his body be black with mosquitoes." With this habit thus deeply ingrained, he landed in America, that country of railroads and tramways, and complicated engagement lists; and at first it was no uncommon thing for him to be carried two or three times round a tram-circuit, only disturbed periodically by the conductor asking for the fare. He was very much ashamed of such occurrences, however, and worked hard to overcome them.

Yet ingrained though the Swami's habit of meditation was, he missed nothing of importance in his surroundings. Just as he

made every effort to give the American people a true picture
of India and Hinduism, so he lost no opportunity to study the
methods of the industrial and economic systems of the West, so
that he could apply them later on in definite and practical ways
to relieve the wants of his own people. Thus while lecturing in
and around the city, he was also gathering all kinds of information regarding the working of Western civilization. Chicago
offered him a broad field of study, for in many respects it was a
representative city of the West, as it continues to be even
today.

Referring to this period of the Swami's life, the Chicago
newspaper *Interocean* wrote in September of 1894, almost a year
after the Parliament:

... Vivekananda lingered in Chicago for several months after the
great Parliament of Religions closed, studying many questions relating
to schools and the material advancement of civilization in order to
carry back to his own people as convincing arguments regarding
America as he brought to this country concerning the morality and
spirituality of his own people.

In Chicago the Swami visited museums, universities, schools
and art galleries, trying to comprehend the spirit of Western
life. Gazing at some work of art, or studying some signal
engineering or architectural achievement, his thought would
leap in admiration of the greatness of the human mind. He
became a keen student of the public and social life in America.
Often he would gaze in wonder at the mad rush of energy on
all sides and view with astonishment the massive, towering
palaces of industry. And the contrast between the pomp and
power of the Western world, with its complicated and highly
sophisticated social and industrial life, and the poverty and
crowded misery of the Indian cities, with here and there some
naked sadhu covered with ashes, would be borne in on him.
The greatness of his spirit enabled him to hold the balance
between the two worlds, the East and the West. He saw each
clearly and to its depths, and the result of his continued and
penetrating observations was later embodied in his two studies,

"The East and the West" and "Modern India", written in Bengali.

Because of the various congresses held in connection with the World's Fair, Chicago was at this period a meeting-place of some of the best minds of the day. Inevitably, the Swami came in contact with many thinkers, famous and influential in their own fields. In September of 1893, immediately following his appearance at the Parliament, he was introduced to a group of noted scientists who had gathered in the city to attend the Electrical Congress, held from August 21 through 25. A vegetarian dinner was given especially in his honour by Professor Elisha Gray, the inventor of electrical equipment, and his wife in their beautiful residence in Highland Park, Chicago. Among the distinguished guests invited to meet him were Ariton Hopitallia, Sir William Thomson, afterwards Lord Kelvin, Professor Hermann von Helmholtz, the last two of whom were eminent in the field of physics. The Swami's knowledge of electricity amazed the scientists, and his shining repartee bearing on matters of science was greeted with sincere pleasure. With one voice they acclaimed him a sympathetic *confrère*.

It was no doubt also in Chicago that the Swami first met the famous agnostic and orator Robert Ingersoll and more than once discussed religious and philosophical matters with him. During the course of these conversations the great agnostic cautioned the Swami not to be too bold and outspoken, to be careful in his preaching of new doctrines and in his criticisms of the ways of life and thought of the people. When asked why, Mr. Ingersoll replied, "Fifty years ago you would have been hanged if you had come to preach in this country, or you would have been burned alive. You would have been stoned out of the villages if you had come even much later." The Swami was surprised; he could not believe that there was so much fanaticism and bigotry in the American nation, and he told Mr. Ingersoll as much. But there was a difference in the approaches of these two great preachers; for Mr. Ingersoll was antagonistic toward all religious ideals, whereas the Swami, though present-

ing a new order of religious thought, was tolerant of all religions
and was a devotee of Christ. The difference between these two
great men is best shown in an anecdote told by the Swami
himself in the course of a class talk: "Ingersoll once said to me,
'I believe in making the most out of this world, in squeezing
the orange dry, because this world is all we are sure of.' I replied,
'I know a better way to squeeze the orange of this world than
you do; and I get more out of it. I *know* I cannot die, so I am
not in a hurry. I know that there is no fear, so I enjoy the
squeezing. I have no duty, no bondage of wife and children
and property; and so I can love all men and women. Everyone
is God to me. Think of the joy of loving man as God! Squeeze
your orange this way and get ten thousandfold more out of it.
Get every single drop!' "

During his first year in America, the Swami met and became
friends not only with philosophers and scientists, but with
artists as well. Madame Emma Calvé, the celebrated opera
singer, who later became his ardent devotee, wrote in her
autobiography (*My Life*, New York: D. Appleton and Co.,
1922) of her first meeting[1] with Swami Vivekananda and of the
profound effect his teaching had had upon her life:

It has been my good fortune and my joy to know a man who truly
"walked with God", a noble being, a saint, a philosopher and a true
friend. His influence upon my spiritual life was profound. He opened
up new horizons before me, enlarging and unifying my religious idea
and ideals; teaching me a broader understanding of truth. My soul
will bear him eternal gratitude. . . . He was lecturing in Chicago one
year when I was there; and as I was at that time greatly depressed in
mind and body, I decided to go to him, having seen how he had

[1] An undated entry in one of the recently discovered travel diaries of Mme
Calvé (*vide Prabuddha Bharata*, 1977, p. 191) has made it rather doubtful when this
first meeting took place. From the description of the Swami given by her in the
autobiography it should have taken place sometime in late March of 1894; but
from what she has written in her diary and from other evidences, it appears to
have taken place on November 28, 1899. The Swami has written in his letter from
Chicago on November 30, 1899 to Mrs. Bull, "Madame Calvé came to see me
day before yesterday. She is a great woman." As the description of the Swami in
her narrative corresponds more to the earlier period, it has been given here.

helped some of my friends. An appointment was arranged for me and when I arrived at his house, I was immediately ushered into his study. Before going I had been told not to speak until he addressed me. When I entered the room, I stood before him in silence for a moment. He was seated in a noble attitude of meditation, his robe of saffron yellow falling in straight lines to the floor, his head swathed in a turban bent forward, his eyes on the ground. After a pause he spoke without looking up.

"My child," he said, "what a troubled atmosphere you have about you! Be calm! It is essential."

Then in a quiet voice, untroubled and aloof, this man who did not even know my name talked to me of my secret problems and anxieties. He spoke of things that I thought were unknown even to my nearest friends. It seemed miraculous, supernatural.

"How do you know all this?" I asked at last. "Who has talked of me to you?"

He looked at me with his quiet smile as though I were a child who had asked a foolish question.

"No one has talked to me," he answered gently. "Do you think it is necessary? I read in you as in an open book."

Finally it was time for me to leave.

"You must forget," he said as I rose. "Become gay and happy again. Build up your health. Do not dwell in silence upon your sorrows. Transmute your emotions into some form of external expression. Your spiritual health requires it. Your art demands it."

I left him, deeply impressed by his words and his personality. He seemed to have emptied my brain of all its feverish complexities and placed there instead his clear and calming thoughts. I became once again vivacious and cheerful, thanks to the effect of his powerful will. He did not use any of the hypnotic or mesmeric influences. It was the strength of his character, the purity and intensity of his purpose that carried conviction. It seemed to me, when I came to know him better, that he lulled one's chaotic thoughts into a state of peaceful acquiescence, so that one could give complete and undivided attention to his words.

He often spoke in parables, answering our questions or making his points clear by means of a poetic analogy. One day we were discussing immortality and the survival of individual characteristics. He was expounding his belief in reincarnation which was a fundamental part of his teaching.

"I cannot bear the idea," I exclaimed. "I cling to my individuality, unimportant as it may be: I don't want to be absorbed into an eternal unity. The mere thought is terrible to me."

"One day a drop of water fell into the vast ocean," the Swami answered. "When it found itself there, it began to weep and complain just as you are doing. The great ocean laughed at the drop of water. 'Why do you weep?' it asked. 'I do not understand. When you join me, you join all your brothers and sisters, the other drops of water of which I am made. You become the ocean itself. If you wish to leave me, you have only to rise up on a sunbeam into the clouds. From there you can descend again, little drop of water, a blessing and a benediction to the thirsty earth.'"

In addition to writing of Swami Vivekananda in her autobiography, Mme Calvé often spoke to her friends of him, revealing in later years her memory of episodes long passed. One of these was a story of an encounter between the Swami and John D. Rockefeller, the fabulously wealthy American financier. Emma Calvé related the incident, which may have taken place in the early part of 1894, to her close friend, Mme Paul Verdier, herself an ardent devotee. The latter's notes, taken down during a conversation with Mme Calvé, read as follows:

Mr. X, in whose home Swamiji was staying in Chicago, was a partner or an associate in some business with John D. Rockefeller. Many times John D. heard his friends talking about this extraordinary and wonderful Hindu monk who was staying with them, and many times he had been invited to meet Swamiji, but, for one reason or another, always refused. At that time Rockefeller was not yet at the peak of his fortune, but was already powerful and strong-willed, very difficult to handle and a hard man to advise.

But one day, although he did not want to meet Swamiji, he was pushed to it by an impulse and went directly to the house of his friend, brushing aside the butler who opened the door and saying that he wanted to see the Hindu monk.

The butler ushered him into the living room, and, not waiting to be announced, Rockefeller entered into Swami's adjoining study and was much surprised, I presume, to see Swamiji behind his writing table not even lifting his eyes to see who had entered.

After a while, as with Calve, Swamiji told Rockefeller much of his past that was not known to any but himself, and made him understand that the money he had already accumulated was not his, that he was only a channel and that his duty was to do good to the world—that God had given him all his wealth in order that he might have an opportunity to help and do good to people.

Rockefeller was annoyed that anyone dared to talk to him that way and tell him what to do. He left the room in irritation, not even saying goodbye. But about a week after, again without being announced, he entered Swamiji's study and, finding him the same as before, threw on his desk a paper which told of his plans to donate an enormous sum of money toward the financing of a public institution.

"Well, there you are," he said. "You must be satisfied now, and you can thank me for it."

Swamiji didn't even lift his eyes, did not move. Then taking the paper, he quietly read it, saying: "It is for you to thank me." That was all. This was Rockefeller's first large donation to the public welfare.

On the morning of November 20, 1893, the Swami left Chicago to begin his arduous lecture tour through the wintry midwestern and southern States. The first city he visited was Madison, Wisconsin, where he lectured on the evening of November 20. The next day one finds him in the much larger city of Minneapolis, Minnesota, where, to his delight, he was at once plunged into the severe midwestern winter. "The day I came here," he wrote to Mrs. Hale on November 24, "they had their first snow, and it snowed all through the day and night, and I had great use for the arctics [a type of winter boot]. I went to see the frozen Minihaha Falls; they are very beautiful. The temperature today is 21 below zero, but I had been out sleighing and enjoyed it immensely though. I am not the least afraid of losing the tips of my ears or nose. The snow scenery here has pleased me more than any other sight in this country. I saw people skating on a frozen lake yesterday."

The Swami spoke twice in Minneapolis at the First Unitarian Church, on 24th afternoon and 26th morning. On November 26th he travelled to Des Moines, the capital city of Iowa. The following excerpt from the *Iowa State Register* of December 3,

1893, shows how appreciatively he was received in Des Moines. One catches a glimpse here also of his personality, sharp as a rapier one moment, warm as a friendly hand the next:

Swami Vivekananda, the Hindu monk, spoke three times in Des Moines. During his stay in the city, which was happily prolonged by the cancellation of engagements farther west, Vivekananda met many of the best people in the city, who found their time well spent discussing religious and metaphysical questions with him. But it was woe to the man who undertook to combat the monk on his own ground, and that was where they all tried it who tried it at all. His replies came like flashes of lightning, and the venturesome questioner was sure to be impaled on the Indian's shining intellectual lance. The workings of his mind, so subtle and so brilliant, so well stored and so well trained, sometimes dazzled his hearers, but it was always a most interesting study. He said nothing unkind, for his nature would not permit that. Those who came to know him best found him the most gentle and lovable of men, so honest, frank, and unpretending, always grateful for the many kindnesses that were shown him. Vivekananda and his cause found a place in the hearts of all true Christians.

Although the Swami's itinerary for December of 1893 and the first part of January of 1894 has not yet been traced, we know that his lecture engagements carried him far and wide. "Necessity makes me travel by rail to the borders of Canada one day, and the next day finds me lecturing in South America!" he wrote in January of 1894 to his brother monks. By "South America" he no doubt meant the southern States of America. And to be sure, in mid-January he travelled as far south as Memphis, Tennessee, where he had been invited by the members of the Nineteenth Century Club, some of whom had heard him lecture at the Parliament of Religions. As in other cities where he stopped over for a week or more, the Swami gave a number of lectures in Memphis to large and enthusiastic audiences and was interviewed at length by the local newspapers. He pleaded, as he did everywhere, for universal acceptance of all religions and for love; he explained the underlying unity of the world's rich variety of creeds, and he emphasized the basic divinity of man. Indeed, wherever he went, he not only spoke of the merits of Hinduism, but, like a great sower, spread his Master's message. "Wherever the seed of his power will fall," he wrote to his brother monks, on October 22, 1894, "there it will fructify, be it today, or in a hundred years." He was always aware that a great power was working in and through him. "I am amazed at His grace", he wrote again to them in the early part of 1894: "Whatever town I visit, it is in an uproar. They have named me 'the cyclonic Hindu'. Remember it is His will—I am a voice without a form."

Almost everywhere the Swami went during his lecture tour, he went as a guest; but despite the cordiality with which he was received in many homes, the tour was not an altogether pleasant experience. Unaccustomed to the severe winters of the Midwest, he suffered intensely from cold; travelling by train from each one-night stand to the next was gruelling; accommodations in small-town hotels, where he sometimes had to stay, were primitive in the extreme. Then, too, the constant demands of the lecture platform told on him. Everywhere he went people flocked about him, and clergymen—particularly Unitarians—beseeched him to lecture from their pulpits. But if the Swami spoke time and again to enthusiastic audiences, he also had to run the gauntlet of innumerable irritating questions that disclosed both a monumental ignorance of Hindu culture and erroneous ideas of Indian life. Some questioners flatly contradicted him on subjects on which they were in entire ignorance; then he fell upon them like a thunderbolt. Or perhaps he would retort with sarcastic humour as he did in Minneapolis when asked if Hindu mothers threw their children to the crocodiles. "Yes, Madam!" he replied: "They threw me in, but like your fabled Jonah I got out again."

Perhaps one of the most trying experiences that the Swami had on his lecture tour occurred when he was visiting a small town in the Midwest. Hearing him speak of Indian philosophy, a number of university men who had taken up ranch life and become cowboys wanted to put him to the test. Did he not say that a person who had realized the Highest is equable under all conditions? So they invited him to lecture to them. When he arrived they escorted him to a wooden tub, which they had placed bottom up to serve as a platform in the public square of their town. The Swami commenced his discourse and soon became absorbed in it. Suddenly there was the deafening noise of firing, and shots whizzed past his ears! But he went on with his lecture to the end, as though nothing had happened. He had withdrawn into that innermost consciousness of which he was speaking. When he had finished, the cowboys crowded round him and in their own boisterous way pronounced him "a right good fellow". If he had shown the faintest sign of being alarmed, they would have branded him "a tenderfoot" —their derisive term for an inexperienced Easterner newly come to the cattle country of the "wild West".

Indeed, the Swami had many odd experiences. One, which he related as a joke on himself, also took place in a small town, in the midwestern States. It was in the days when he was lecturing most strenuously, moving on from one place to another, with only a gladstone bag, sometimes giving as many as three lectures a day, arriving at one place, giving his lecture, and then proceeding immediately to another place. He was exhausted when he arrived at the town in question. The secretary of the reception committee showed him courteously into a small room, which happened to be dark. It contained a rather frail and rickety armchair. Seeing it only dimly, the Swami sat down on it, when, to use his own words, "Lo! it gave way, and that, too, in the most awkward manner possible. I went down backwards and could not for the life of me extricate myself. The more I tried, the more danger there was of my hurting myself and ruining my clothes. So I just had to stay in that uncomfortable position and wait for the secretary to come to escort me to the platform. At last he came, calling, 'Come, Swami, the audience is waiting for you!' 'Well, then,' I cried out, 'it will have to wait till you break this chair and extricate me from the nice plight I am in!' He then helped me to get up, and we had a hearty laugh over it." The manner in

which the Swami told the story on himself sent his friends and
disciples into fits of laughter.

But this amusing incident is complemented by another,
which for its dignity and genuine human touch reveals the
quality of the man. Being an Oriental, his skin seemed dark
to an American, and in the South he was often mistaken for a
Negro. Sometimes he was even insulted. But the Swami invariably received rude remarks and rude glances with a grand
indifference and what one might call a spiritual hauteur. What
was race-prejudice to him who saw in every man his brother?
Once a Negro porter, who had seen him being welcomed by a
reception committee, came up to him and said that in him one
of his own people had become a great man and that he would
like to have the privilege of shaking hands with him. The
Swami warmly clasped his hand and exclaimed, "Thank you!
Thank you, brother!" He related many similar confidences
made to him by Negroes. He never minded being taken for
one of them. In barbers' shops of northern as well as southern
cities, he was for this reason not infrequently shown the door
with scant courtesy. Several times in important cities of the
south he was brusquely refused admittance to hotels because of
his dark colour, but even in such situations he refused to say
that he was an Oriental; whereupon the manager of his tour
would have to make other arrangements for him. When the
hotel proprietors who had turned him away, read of his lectures
in the papers the next morning or heard his name spoken everywhere with deference they would be mortified and hurry to
him to apologize. Long afterwards a Western disciple, referring
to these incidents, asked him in surprise why he had not told
them who he was. "What!" he replied, "rise at the expense of
another! I did not come to earth for that!" Nor was he ever
ashamed of his own race. On the contrary, he was proud that
he was an Indian; and when any Westerner showed a feeling of
his own superiority because of the colour of his skin, he did not
escape the Swami's stern reproof. Sister Nivedita writes:

He was scornful in his repudiation of the pseudo-ethnology of
privileged races. "If I am grateful to my white-skinned Aryan

ancestor," he said, "I am far more so to my yellow-skinned Mongolian ancestor, and most so of all, to the black-skinned Negritoid!"

He was immensely proud, in his own physiognomy, of what he called his "Mongolian jaw", regarding it as a sign of "bulldog tenacity of purpose"; and referring to this particular race-element, which he believed to be behind every Aryan people, he one day exclaimed, "Don't you see? The Tartar is the wine of the race! He gives energy and power to every blood!"

Throughout the course of his lecture tours the Swami found his name blazoned in the papers. Reporters and editors literally besieged him. He was made to answer endless questions with regard to his habits of life, his religion, his philosophy, his views on Western civilization, his plans for future work, his diet, his antecedents, the manners and customs of his people, the political conditions of his land, and a host of other matters. The newspapers acquainted the American public with many details of his personal as well as his country's history—particularly of the latter, for India was his love, and the welfare of his country was his deep concern, of which he never tired of speaking.

Indeed, besides the fundamental, divinely ordained mission of giving his message to the West, about which he rarely spoke, the main object of his coming to America was to further the cause of his people. In his letter of December 28, 1893, to Haripada Mitra, he says:

I came to this country not to satisfy my curiosity, nor for name or fame, but to see if I could find any means for the support of the poor in India. If God helps me, you will know gradually what those means are.

A notable feature of the Swami's addresses at this time, which the newspapers did not fail to notice, was his patriotism. To quote from one of them: "His patriotism was perfervid. The manner in which he speaks of 'My country' is most touching. That one phrase revealed him not only as a monk, but as a man of his people."

The Swami received invitation after invitation to speak in churches and to clubs and private gatherings. Most of these he accepted, thinking each to be an opportunity of spreading the truths of Vedanta, of giving spiritual help, and of presenting the true needs of India before the American people. He gave himself and his time unstintingly in service. He gave and gave, until the mental and physical strain became intense.

Often he had to deliver extempore twelve to fourteen lectures a week, sometimes even more. The exertion was so great that after a time he felt as though he had exhausted himself intellectually. At such times he asked himself, "What is to be done! What shall I say in my lecture tomorrow!" In this difficulty he was aided in wonderful ways. For instance, at dead of night he would hear a voice shouting at him the thoughts that he was to speak on the following day. Sometimes it would come as from a long distance, speaking to him down a great avenue; then it would draw nearer and nearer. Or it would be like someone delivering a lecture alongside of him, as he lay on his bed listening. At other times two voices would argue before him discussing at great length subjects that he would find himself repeating the following day from the platform or the pulpit. Sometimes these discussions introduced ideas that he had never heard of or thought of previously.

He was not, however, puzzled at these strange happenings, and interpreted them as manifestations of the wider powers of the mind. He spoke of them as subjective, as automatic workings of the mind. Given certain forms of thought, the mind naturally works on and enlarges on them, calling to its aid the creative faculties for their perfect presentation and utterance. It was perhaps an extreme case of the mind becoming its own guru. The Swami believed that the Rishis of old must have had such revelations in composing the Upanishads. Commenting upon these experiences to his more intimate disciples, he would remark that they constituted what is generally regarded as inspiration. Yet, though the Swami ascribed only a highly developed subjective character to them, it must be noted that some people living in the same house with him would ask him in the morning, "Swami, with whom were you talking last night? We heard you talking loudly and enthusiastically, and were wondering!" He would smile at their bewilderment and answer in an evasive manner, leaving them mystified; but to his close disciples he would explain that these experiences revealed the powers and potentialities of the self; he would deny that there was anything miraculous about them.

During this time and also later, the Swami felt extraordinary Yoga powers spontaneously manifest in him. He could change, if he so wished, the whole trend of the life of anyone by a simple touch. He could see clearly things happening at a great distance. Some of his intimate disciples, to whom he spoke casually of this fact, prevailed upon him, despite his abhorrence of displaying psychic powers, to allow them to test him, and they invariably found his words to be true. On many occasions his students would find him answering and solving the un-expressed doubts and unasked questions that were troubling them at the moment. He could see a person's past life and read the contents of his mind at a glance. Once a wealthy citizen of Chicago chaffed him rather flippantly about his Yoga powers and challenged him to demonstrate them saying, "Well, sir, if all this that you say be true, then tell me something of my mental make-up, or of my past!" The Swami hesitated a moment, then fixed his eyes upon those of the man as though he would pierce, by some quiet irresistible power, through the body to the naked soul. The man at once became nervous. His flippancy gave way to sudden seriousness and fear, and he exclaimed, "Oh, Swami, what are you doing to me? It seems as if my whole soul is being churned and all the secrets of my life are being called up in strong colours!" But the Swami did not consider these powers to be marks of spirituality, and very rarely did he deliberately exercise them. Whenever he did so, it was for grave reason and always for the benefit of others.

We left the Swami a while back at Memphis, Tennessee. He remained there from January 13, 1894, to the 22nd, when he returned to Chicago. After this, his travels and his stays in various cities and towns have been fairly well traced, leaving but few gaps. In the early hours of the morning of February 13, we find him arriving at Detroit, Michigan, his train seven hours late, having been blocked by snow-drifts on the way. "I enjoyed the novelty", he wrote to Mrs. Hale the following day: "Several men cutting and clearing the snow and two engines tugging and pulling was a new sight to me." In February, from the 13th to the 23rd, and most of March, from the 9th to the 30th, he lectured in Detroit, primarily at the Unitarian Church. During these two periods he was the guest for about four weeks all told of Mrs. John J. Bagley, the widow of the ex-Governor of Michigan and a lady of rare culture and unusual spirituality. Of the Bagley family the Swami wrote to Mrs. Hale on February 14, "They are very rich, kind and hospitable. Mrs. Bagley is especially interested in India. The daughters are very good, educated and goodlooking. The eldest gave me a luncheon at a club where I met some of the finest ladies and gentlemen of the city." On the evening following his arrival in Detroit, Mrs. Bagley, who had met the Swami five months earlier at the Parliament of Religions, honoured her guest with an enormous, gala reception to which the whole town, as it were, was invited. The imposing invitation list included the names of bishops, clergymen, rabbis, professors, the mayor and his wife, and at least three hundred of the cream of Detroit society. The *Detroit Journal* of February 14 reported, "The social lion of the day is Swami (brother) Vive Kananda." Mrs. Bagley often said that during his visit with her he constantly expressed the highest in word and action, and that his presence was a "continual benediction".

When in March the Swami came to Detroit for the second time, he at first stayed for nearly a week with the Honourable Thomas W. Palmer, President of the World's Fair Commission, and formerly United States Senator and Minister of his country to Spain. While the Swami was his guest Mr. Palmer gave a dinner to a group of his friends, each more than sixty years of age, which he called his "old boys' club". "I am pulling on well with old Palmer", the Swami wrote to a friend; and indeed Mr. Palmer, "a spirituous gentleman but very good," made his guest "laugh the whole day" by his conviviality. The

Swami found the following newspaper report the funniest thing said of himself while he was in Detroit:

The cyclonic Hindu has come and is a guest with Mr. Palmer. Mr. Palmer has become a Hindu and is going to India; only he insists that two reforms should be carried out: firstly that the Car of Jaggernath [Jagannath] should be drawn by Percherons raised in Mr. Palmer's Loghouse Farm, and secondly that the Jersey cow be admitted into the pantheon of Hindu sacred cows.

What assurance the Swami could give Mr. Palmer in the matter we do not know. But soon his host was to be sad. On March 17 the Swami wrote to Harriet McKindley of Chicago: "I have returned today to Mrs. Bagley's as she was sorry that I would remain so long with Mr. Palmer. Of course in Palmer's house there was real 'good time'. He is a real jovial heartwhole fellow, and likes 'good time' a little too much and his 'hot Scotch'. But he is right along innocent and childlike in his simplicity. He was very sorry that I came away, but I could not help. . . ."

In February and March of 1894, the Swami lectured three times, in three small towns, outside Detroit. On February 23 he spoke in the Opera house of Ada, Ohio, where his lecture, entitled "Divinity of Man", was attended by a large audience. On March 20 he spoke in Bay City, Michigan, on "Hinduism", and on the following evening (March 21) in Saginaw, Michigan, on "The Harmony of Religions". But the main scene of his activities during the months of February and March was Detroit. In this lively metropolis, where opinions both conservative and liberal were strongly held and emphatically expressed, he became the centre of a swirl of heated controversy. Ever since his triumph at the Parliament of Religions, where the sublimity and breadth of his thought had clearly given the lie to the prevalent misrepresentations of India, resentment toward him had been smouldering among the more orthodox and narrow members of the Christian clergy. From time to time, in the wake of his tour through the Midwest, that resentment had flared up in whispered slander and acrimonious sermons. But in Detroit, as though it could contain itself no longer, the opposition exploded in full and unrestrained force. Ministers of the Gospel openly and vehemently denounced the Swami and "his false doctrines" from their pulpits. The Detroit newspapers flamed with letters to the editors, bitterly attacking him on the one hand, fervently supporting him on the other.

The Swami made no effort to defend himself or to pacify his detractors. On the contrary, he had no patience with small-mindedness or fanaticism. He had great reverence for Christ and his teachings. When a distinguished clergyman wondered how he could understand the Christ Ideal so well, he replied, "Why, Jesus was an Oriental! It is therefore natural that we Orientals should understand Him truly and readily." But he pointed out the faults and defects of Christian civilization in unmistakable terms and occasionally was sternly critical, condemning with remarkable penetration the aggressive and destructive characteristics of Western civilization. "I am a rather plain-spoken man," he once said, "but I mean well. I want to tell you the truth. I am not here to flatter you; it is not my business. If I wanted to do that I would have opened a fashionable church in Fifth Avenue in New York. You are my children. I want to show you the way out of self to God by pointing out to you your errors, your defects, and your vanities. Therefore you do not hear me praising your current Christianity or your ideals of civilization, or the peculiar forms of character and life that are developed by Western ethical standards." An instance of the Swami's straightforwardness may be cited from one of his February 1894 lectures in Detroit:

One thing I would tell you, and I do not mean any unkind criticism. You train and educate and clothe and pay men to do what?—to come over to my country and curse and abuse all my forefathers, my religion and my everything. They walk near a temple and say, "You idolators, you will go to hell!". . . But the Hindu is mild; he smiles and passes on saying, "Let the fools talk." That is the attitude. And then you who train men to abuse and criticize, if I just touch you with the least bit of criticism, with the kindest of purpose, you shrink and cry, "Do not touch us; we are Americans, we criticize, curse and

abuse all the heathens of the world, but do not touch us, we are
sensitive plants." You may do whatever you please, but we are
content to live as we do; and in one thing we are better off—we never
teach our children to swallow such horrible stuff: "Where [Though]
every prospect pleases, and [only] man is vile". And whenever your
ministers criticize us let them remember this: if all India stands up
and takes all the mud that is at the bottom of the Indian Ocean and
throws it up against the Western countries, it will not be doing an
infinitesimal part of that which you are doing to us. And what for?
Did we ever send one missionary to convert anybody in the West? We
say to you, "You are welcome to your religion, but allow us to have
ours!" You call yours an aggressive religion. You are aggressive, but
how many have you converted? Every sixth man in the world is a
Chinese subject, a Buddhist; then there are Japan, Tibet, and Russia,
and Siberia, and Burma, and Siam; and it may not be palatable, but
this Christian morality, the Catholic Church, and many other things
are derived from them. Well, and how was this done? Without the
shedding of one drop of blood! With all your brag and boasting, where
has your Christianity succeeded without the sword? Show me one
place in the whole world. One, I say, throughout the history of the
Christian religion—one; I do not want two. I know how your forefathers were converted. They had to be converted or killed, that was
all. . . . "We are the only one." And why? "Because we can kill
others." The Arabs said that; they bragged. And where is the Arab
now? He is the Bedouin. The Romans used to say that, and where are
they now? And we have been sitting there on our blocks of stone.
"Blessed are the peacemakers; for they shall be called the children of
God!" Such things tumble down; they are built upon sand; they
cannot remain long.

Everything that has selfishness for its basis, competition for its right
hand and enjoyment as its goal, must die sooner or later. If you want
to live, go back to Christ. Go back to Him who had nowhere to lay
His head. . . . Yours is a religion preached in the name of luxury.
What an irony of fate! Reverse this if you want to live; reverse this.
It is all hypocrisy that I have heard in this country. If this nation is
going to live, let it go back to Him. You cannot serve God and
Mammon at the same time. All this prosperity, all this from Christ?
Christ would have denied all such heresies. . . . If you can join these
two, this wonderful prosperity with that ideal of Christ, it is well; but
if you cannot, better go back to Him and give up these vain pursuits.

Better be ready to live in rags with Christ than to live in palaces without Him.

Again in Detroit the Swami mercilessly asked, "Where is your Christianity? Where is there a place for Jesus the Christ in this selfish struggle, in this constant tendency to destroy? True, if He were here today, He would not find a stone whereon to lay His head."

It is no wonder that utterances like these aroused bitter opposition from Christian propagandists. They tried to injure his reputation by abusing and vilifying him. They even went to the length, the Swami said, of tempting him with young women, promising them recompense if they succeeded. They desisted when they found him as simple and pure as a child. It seems almost incredible that they should have gone so far in the name of religion. Sometimes notes and letters that declared that he was not what he represented himself to be, and that contained all kinds of calumnies against him, were sent to persons who had invited him to their homes. Occasionally this malice had the desired effect, and the Swami would find the doors of his hosts-to-be closed to him! But in most instances, the error would be discovered after a time, and those who had rebuffed him would call and apologize and become greater friends than ever.

It should be noted here (although we shall deal with this topic fully in the following chapter) that for many months after the Parliament of Religions the Swami had no united support or recognition from India. An unaccredited delegate to the Parliament, long unrecognized officially by his own country, he stood alone against all opposition and criticism. He was indeed himself the proof of his rightness, but his ostensible position at this time as a religious teacher without credentials gave great advantage to those who would harm him and cast doubt upon his standing in India and upon his honour. Yet amid all these difficulties and distractions the Swami kept his equanimity, trusting the Lord and consoling himself with the thought that the highest-minded Christians—clergymen and distinguished laymen alike—were his avowed admirers. Many espoused his cause and were even his followers. Above all, he knew that if it was the will of God that his message should be broadcast, nothing on earth could stand against him. His was the spirit of the Rishis (sages) of old. Inwardly he remained always the meditative sannyasi, the spiritual genius, the man who had been a wandering monk, the child of the Mother of the Universe, awaiting her commands and guidance. To his many friends who answered his critics and urged him to do likewise, he replied, "Why should I attack in return? It is not the monk's place to defend himself. Besides, Truth will have its way, believe me; Truth shall stand." Sometimes his only reply, when he was told of some baseless assertions newly made against him, would be a prayer.

But while the Swami refused to reply to the malicious charges made against himself, he gave battle over his Motherland, vindicating her in his own terms, in his own way. Unperturbed by critics, he continued in his Detroit lectures to present the religious and social customs of India in their true light and to shower upon his listeners the grand spiritual truths of Hinduism. Through his lectures and talks the generality of Americans were able to see the depth and beauty of Hindu religion and culture for the first time. "I am the one man who dared defend his country," he was to write on May 6, 1895, to an Indian disciple, "and I have given them such ideas as they never expected from a Hindu." Indeed, the Swami was himself a revelation. His powerful and radiant personality was refutation enough of the "benighted-heathen" myth that had become ingrained in nineteenth-century American thinking. Singlehanded, he was able to dispel that national fallacy, for through him worked a power that nothing could withstand. "The power behind me", he was to write later in his letter of July 9, 1897, when speaking of his mission, "is not Vivekananda but He the Lord."

The Swami was, without question, the fiery champion of his Motherland. But to thousands of Americans he was also much more than this, he was a prophet of divine truths, awakening them to the life of the Spirit.

30

People who had listened for years with increasing dissatisfaction to numerous preachers of modern cults, came to hear him and had their souls animated and their spiritual hopes fulfilled. His utterances were authoritative, his realization genuine; he spoke of what he had felt and had himself seen. Those who had knocked long at the gates of wisdom found him opening those gates for them. Those who had him as their guest or came in intimate contact with him, spoke of him as a kaleidoscopic genius, enriching his surroundings with his many-sided greatness; they said that his was a soul of unutterable beauty and grandeur, that he transcended their previous notions of greatness or of saintship.

Of the Swami's first visit to Detroit, Mrs. Mary C. Funke, who was to become his ardent disciple, wrote many years after:

February 14th, 1894, stands out in my memory as a day apart, a sacred, holy day; for it was then that I first saw the form and listened to the voice of that great soul, that spiritual giant, the Swami Vivekananda, who, two years later, to my great joy and never-ceasing wonder, accepted me as a disciple.

He had been lecturing in the large cities of this country, and on the above date gave the first of a series of lectures in Detroit, in the Unitarian church. The large edifice was literally packed and the Swami received an ovation. I can see him yet as he stepped upon the platform, a regal, majestic figure, vital, forceful, dominant, and at the first sound of the wonderful voice, a voice all music—now like the plaintive minor strain of an Eolian harp, again, deep, vibrant, resonant—there was a hush, a stillness that could almost be felt, and the vast audience breathed as one man.

The Swami gave five [actually eight] public lectures and he held his audiences, for his was the grasp of the "master hand", and he spoke as one with authority. His arguments were logical, convincing, and in his most brilliant oratorical flights never once did he lose sight of the main issue—the truth he wished to drive home.

During the five weeks or so that Swami Vivekananda lectured in Detroit, the press made the most of this extraordinary, famous, and controversial visitor from the East. It would be well to quote here what the *Detroit Free Press*, one of the leading journals not only of the city but of the nation, wrote concerning him, for the description of the Swami given in this paper, on February 11, 1894, was typical of what was printed of him throughout his tour:

Since the Parliament he has spoken to immense audiences in many towns and cities, who have but one opinion of praise and are enthusiastic over his magnetic power and his way of giving light and life to every subject he touches upon. Naturally his views of great questions, coming like himself from the other side of the globe, are refreshing and stirring to American people. His hearers are pleasantly astonished when the dark-hued, dark-haired, dignified man rises in rich yellow robes and speaks their own language with fluency, distinctness and correctness.

Commenting on his lecture of February 17, 1894, the same paper reports:

Swami Vivekananda, Hindu philosopher and priest, concluded his series of lectures, or, rather, sermons, at the Unitarian church last night, speaking on "The Divinity of Man". In spite of the bad weather, the church was crowded almost to the doors, half an hour before the Eastern brother—as he likes to be called—appeared. All professions and business occupations were represented in the attentive audience —lawyers, judges, ministers of the Gospel, merchants, a Rabbi—not to speak of the many ladies who have, by their repeated attendance and rapt attention, shown a decided inclination to shower adulation upon the dusky visitor, whose drawing-room attraction is as great as his ability in the rostrum.

The lecture last night was less descriptive than preceding ones, and for nearly two hours Vivekananda wove a metaphysical texture on affairs human and divine, so logical that he made science appear like common sense. It was a beautiful logical garment that he wove, replete with as many bright colours and as attractive and pleasing to contemplate as one of the many-hued fabrics made by hand in his native land and scented with the most seductive fragrance of the Orient. The dusky gentleman uses poetical imagery as an artist uses colours, and the hues are laid on just where they belong, the result being somewhat bizarre in effect, and yet having a peculiar fascination. Kaleidoscopic were the swiftly succeeding logical conclusions, and the deft manipulator was rewarded for his efforts from time to time by enthusiastic applause.

During this period the Swami discovered that the Slayton Lyceum Lecture Bureau was exploiting and defrauding him. For example, at one lecture the returns were $2,500, but he received only $200. At first, in order to hold him, the manager of the lecture bureau had given him as much as $900 for a single engagement, but after a time he lowered the rate until it became apparent, even to one as unworldly as the Swami, that he was being cheated. On February 20, he wrote from Detroit to Mrs. Hale, "I am thoroughly disgusted with this Slayton business and am trying hard to break loose. I have lost at least $5,000 by joining this man.... I hope to do some private lecturing here and then go to Ada [Ohio] and then back to Chicago. . . . President Palmer has gone to Chicago to try to get me loose from this liar of a Slayton. Pray that he may succeed. Several judges here have seen my contract—and they say it is shameful fraud and can be broken any moment, but I am a monk—no self-defence. Therefore I had better throw up the whole thing and go to India." But by the time the Swami returned to Detroit in March, Mr. Palmer had dealt with the lecture bureau and got the fraudulent contract annulled. Thus the Swami's tour with the lecture bureau through the midwestern and southern States of America came to an end between the first and second visits to Detroit, and he was free.

The Swami's break with the lecture bureau marks an important step in his post-Parliament life in America. He returned to Detroit on March 9 and remained until March 30, lecturing now independently. His letters of this period disclose the working of his mind. On March 12, he wrote the Hale sisters from Detroit: "To tell you the truth, the more I am getting popularity and facility in speaking, the more I am getting fed up. My last lecture was the best I ever delivered. Mr. Palmer was in ecstasies and the audience remained almost spellbound, so much so that it was after the lecture that I found I had spoken so long. A speaker always feels the uneasiness or inattention of the audience. Lord save me from such nonsense. I am fed up."

At the peak of his success as a lecturer the Swami was getting "fed up"! This paradox is explained in another letter to the Hale sisters written three days later:

So far all is well; but I do not know—I have become very sad in my heart since I am here—do not know why.

I am wearied of lecturing and all that nonsense. This mixing with hundreds of varieties of the human animal has disturbed me. I will tell you what is to my taste; I cannot write, and I cannot speak, but I can think deep, and when I am heated, can speak fire. It should be, however, to a select, a very select—few. Let them, if they will, carry and scatter my ideas broadcast—not I. This is only a just division of labour. The same man never succeeded both in thinking and in scattering his ideas. A man should be free to think, especially spiritual thoughts.

Just because this assertion of independence, this proving that *man is not a machine*, is the essence of all religious thought, it is impossible to think it in the routine mechanical way. It is this tendency to bring everything down to the level of a machine that has given the West its wonderful prosperity. And it is this which has driven away all religion from its doors. Even the little that is left, the West has reduced to a systematic drill.

I am really not "cyclonic" at all. Far from it. What I want is not here, nor can I longer bear this cyclonic atmosphere. This is the way to perfection, to strive to be perfect, and to strive to make perfect a few men and women. My idea of doing good is this: to evolve out a few giants, and not strew pearls before swine and so lose time, health and energy.

. . . Well, I do not care for lecturing any more. It is too disgusting, this attempt to bring me to suit anybody's or any audience's fads. . . .

It would appear that for a while the Swami thought of leaving America. Continuing in the same letter he wrote, "However, I shall come back to Chicago for a day or two at least before I go out of this country."

But notwithstanding the Swami's weariness and disgust for lecturing, the Divine will did not seem to concur just then with his ideas and provide for "a just division of labour"; he had rather to continue lecturing and scattering his ideas him-

self in wider regions. His desire, rising in his mind like a prophecy, perhaps, to teach "a select, a very select—few" was to
be carried out later, but not until he had fully completed the
first part of his mission—the wide spreading of his message.
Whatever the personal predilections that he might occasionally
give expression to, and whatever remonstrances he might make
against the course of events, he always acted under direct
guidance, even when it went counter to his declared intentions.
On many occasions, particularly in his letters, he mentioned
this fact.

A study of the Swami's post-Parliament life in America as a
preacher, especially during and after his Detroit days of battle,
reveals in him a unique fusion of manliness and resignation to
the Divine will. He has been called a "militant mystic"; but
his powerful manliness looked militant only to the casual
observer: it was seldom divorced from gentleness. Those who
could not see beyond the militant side of him, did not know
that in all his activities he sought and received divine guidance.
In his many letters written from America one finds evidence
enough of his habitual communion with the Lord—a communion in no way incompatible with awareness of his identity
with the Supreme Spirit.

Sometime in 1894 (after he had written to the Hale sisters
as quoted above) he wrote to Swami Ramakrishnananda:

Through the Lord's will, the desire for name and fame has not
yet crept into my heart, and I dare say never will. I am an instrument, and He is the operator. Through this instrument He is rousing
the religious instinct in thousands of hearts in this far-off country.
Thousands of men and women here love and revere me.... "He
makes the dumb eloquent and makes the lame cross mountains." I am
amazed at His grace. Whatever town I visit, it is in an uproar. They
have named me "the cyclonic Hindu". Remember, it is His will—I
am a voice without a form.

The Lord knows whether I shall go to England or any other blessed
place. He will arrange everything. . . .

And in a rare disclosure of specific divine guidance received
or not received, he wrote to Mrs. Hale on July 19, 1894,

"Most probably I will go to England very soon. But between you and me, I am a sort of mystic and cannot move without *orders*, and that has not come yet."

Thus, carried by the will current of the Lord, Swami Vivekananda continued to work on resolutely. Henceforth, though he was to return often to Chicago, he lectured primarily in the eastern States, where he travelled about freely. He accepted with equal willingness invitations to lecture before small private gatherings and before large public audiences, and he exerted as great an influence in private as in public life.

From the Swami's letters it would seem that his programme of visits on the East Coast was probably fixed, at least in part, while he was still in Detroit. On March 15, he wrote from that city to the Hale sisters, "Your mother asked me to write to a lady in Lynn [Massachusetts]. . . . Where is Lynn?" And in his letter of March 30, he wrote to Mary Hale, "Mrs. Breed [the lady in Lynn] wrote to me a stiff burning letter first, and then today I got a telegram from her inviting me to be her guest for a week. Before this I got a letter from Mrs. Smith of New York writing on her behalf and another lady Miss Helen Gould and another Dr. (forgot his name) [Guernsey] to come over to New York. As the Lynn club wants me on the 17th of next month, I am going to New York first and come in time for their meeting at Lynn."

Thus the Swami, without the help of a lecture bureau, was able to make his own way and fix his own engagements. One acquaintance or friendship led to another, one invitation to the next. Even as he went, the path opened, as though by the magic of his walking on it: "There was a certain Mrs. Smith in Chicago", he wrote from New York to Mrs. Hale on April 10; "I met her at Mrs. Stockham's. She has introduced me to the Guernseys. Dr. Guernsey is one of the chief physicians of this city and is a very good old gentleman."

Around the first of April, the Swami arrived in New York where he stayed at the home of his new friends, Dr. and Mrs. Egbert Guernsey, who were shortly to become devoted to him.

Dr. Guernsey was the founder and editor-in-chief of the *Medical Times*, and a founder of the prestigious Union League Club of New York. The Swami remained in New York for almost two weeks, making many other friends, including Miss Helen Gould, the daughter of Jay Gould, one of the fabulously wealthy tycoons of the era. Although the Swami gave no public lectures in New York during this period, he very probably gave a talk to a number of invited guests in Dr. Guernsey's home. Of this he wrote to Mrs. Hale on April 2:

The lady of the house is very very kind and good. They are trying to help me as much as they can, and they will do a good deal, I have no doubt.

Awaiting further developments. This Thursday [April 5] they will invite a number of the brainy people of the Union League Club and other places of which the doctor is a member and see what comes out of it. Parlour lectures are great feature in this city and more can be made by each such lecture than even platform talks in other cities.

As seen above, the Swami had an engagement to lecture in Lynn, Massachusetts, on April 17. Meanwhile, however, he had been invited to lecture at Northampton, Massachusetts, on April 14. Accordingly, he left New York on April 13 and arrived in Northampton the same day. At this quiet college town the Swami put up at a boarding-house where four girls of Smith College were living. Of the deep influence that he everywhere exerted, we get an example on this occasion. One of the girls, Martha Brown Fincke, never forgot his brief stay. Many years later the impression the Swami had made on her mind was still vivid. In her memoirs she wrote:

Of [the Swami's] lecture that evening I can recall nothing. . . . But what I do remember was the symposium that followed. To our house came the College President, the Head of the Philosophy Department and several other Professors, the ministers of the Northampton churches and a well-known author. In a corner of the living-room we girls sat as quiet as mice and listened eagerly to the discussion which followed. . . . One felt that he was being challenged. Surely these leaders of thought in our world had an unfair advantage. . . . How could one expect a Hindu from far-off India to hold his own with

these, master though he might be of his own learning? The reaction
to the surprising result that followed is my purely subjective one, but
I cannot exaggerate its intensity.

To texts from the Bible, the Swami replied by other and more
apposite ones from the same book. In upholding his side of the argument he quoted English philosophers and writers on religious subjects.
Even the poets he seemed to know thoroughly, quoting Wordsworth
and Thomas Gray (not from the well-known Elegy). Why were my
sympathies not with those of my own world? Why did I exult in the
air of freedom that blew through the room as the Swami broadened
the scope of Religion till it embraced all mankind? Was it that his
words found an echo in my own longings, or was it merely the magic
of his personality? I cannot tell, I only know that I felt triumphant
with him.

The repercussion of the triumph that filled me then is with me to
this day.

On the evening of April 14 the Swami spoke at Northampton
City Hall. He started by proving that all races are close cousins
to one another, differing only a trifle in colour, language,
customs and religion. With easy freedom he then passed on to
the customs of the Hindu people, and compared them with
those of the English-speaking nations. He emphasized the point
that the Hindu ideal of womanhood was divine motherhood.
Though the *Northampton Daily Herald* of April 16 could not
agree with the speaker on all points, it approved his "rebuke
to the greed for gain, the national vice of luxury-seeking, self-
seeking, the 'dollar-caste' sentiment which taints the dominant
white European and American races to their mortal danger,
morally and civilly"—a rebuke which was "only too just and
superbly well-put, the slow, soft, quiet, unimpassioned musical
voice embodying its thought with all the power and fire of the
most vehement physical utterance, and [going] straight to the
mark like the 'Thou art the man' of the prophet."

The editorial further conceded: "To see and hear Swami
Vive Kananda is an opportunity which no intelligent fair-
minded American ought to miss if [he] cares to see a shining
light of the very first product of the mental, moral, and spiritual
culture of a race which reckons its age by thousands, where

we count ours by hundreds, and [which] is richly worth the study of every mind."

On the following afternoon, Sunday April 15, the Swami spoke on invitation at the vesper service at Northampton's Smith College, one of America's most famous colleges for women. The *Smith College Monthly* summarized his remarks as follows: We say much of the brotherhood of man and the fatherhood of God, but few understand the meaning of these words. True brotherhood is possible only when the soul draws so near to the All-Father that jealousies and petty claims of superiority must vanish because we are so much above them. We must take care lest we become like the frog in the well of the old Hindoo story, who, having lived for a long time in a small place, at last denied the existence of a larger space.

From Northampton the Swami went to Lynn, Massachusetts, an industrial city some ten miles from Boston, known primarily for its manufacture of shoes and also as the early home of Mary Baker Eddy, the nineteenth-century founder of Christian Science. At Lynn the Swami was the guest of Mrs. Francis W. Breed, wife of a prominent shoe manufacturer, and a distinguished club woman.

The Swami gave two lectures at Lynn. The first, which had as its subject "The Manners and Customs of India", was given on April 17 at the North Shore Club—a woman's club of which Mrs. Breed was president. The second, the subject of which is not known, was given the following evening before the general public in Oxford Hall. At Lynn, as in many other places during 1894, he spoke on the manners and customs of India, answering with the utmost patience, though at times with an irrepressible wit, the questions hurled at him: "Do the people of India throw their children into the jaws of crocodiles?" "Do they kill themselves beneath the wheels of Juggernaut?" "Do they burn their widows alive?" Wherever he went he shed the light of reason and truth onto the West's dark and disfigured picture of his country.

Belonging as much to near-by Boston as to Lynn, Mrs. Breed also ran a home in that city; and thus, during the

week that the Swami was her guest, he visited Boston, where
he not only renewed his friendship with Professor John Henry
Wright, but made some new acquaintances. In a letter of
April 26, written from New York to Isabelle McKindley, the
Swami wrote: "I had a good time in Boston at Mrs. Breed's—
and saw Prof. Wright. I am going to Boston again. . . . I am
going to speak at Cambridge [Harvard] University and would
be guest of Prof. Wright then—they write grand welcomes to
me in Boston papers." In the same letter he gave vent to his
growing dislike of continuous lecturing; but this dislike co-
existed with and was overpowered by his profound urge to
awaken the spiritual consciousness of the American people. He
said incidentally in the letter, "Do not expect to make money
at Boston. Still I must touch the Brain of America and stir it
up if I can."

The Swami did return shortly to Boston to give several
lectures. In the meanwhile, however, he had engagements in
New York where, on April 24 and May 2, he gave his first
talks in that largest and most important city of the United
States.

In the first of these two New York lectures, that of April 24,
the Swami spoke on "India and Hinduism" before Mrs. Arthur
Smith's "Conversation Circle" at the Waldorf Hotel. In report-
ing the lecture the *New York Daily Tribune* of April 25 wrote,
"The theory of reincarnation was discussed. The speaker said
that many clergymen who were more aggressive than learned
asked: 'Why [is one] unconscious of a former life if such a thing
had been?' The reply was that, 'It would be childish to lay a
foundation for consciousness, as man is unconscious of his birth
in this life, and also of much that has transpired.' The speaker
said that 'no such thing' as 'a Judgement Day' existed in his
religion, and that his God neither punished nor rewarded. . . .
The soul, he added, passed from one body to another, until it
had become a perfect spirit, able to do without the limitation
of the body."

The Swami remained in New York from April 24 to May 6,
probably giving informal talks and meeting many people. His

second lecture in the city was given on the evening of May 2 at the home of Miss Mary Phillips, who had been among those present at his lecture at the Waldorf Hotel. Miss Phillips became one of his ardent followers, and he often used her home in New York at 19 West 38th Street as a sort of head-quarters, giving it as his return address on many letters to India.

The subject of the May 2 speech was "India and Reincarnation". As reported in the *New York Daily Tribune* of May 3: "The Karmic Law of cause and effect was explained, also the external and internal values in their close relations to each other. The actions in this world, as governed by previous life and the change to still another life, were dwelt upon in detail."

Among those who attended the Swami's first two lectures in New York City were men and women who were to befriend him and serve his cause loyally when, later on, he started and got established the Vedanta Society of New York—namely, Dr. and Mrs. Egbert Guernsey, Miss Emma Thursby, the famous singer, Miss Mary Phillips, Mrs. Arthur Smith, and Mr. Leon Landsberg.

In his letter of May 1, 1894, to Isabelle McKindley, the Swami wrote, "From 7th to 19th [of May] there are engagements in Boston ... I am going to speak to the students of the Harvard University. Three lectures at Boston, three at Harvard —all arranged by Mrs. Breed." He arrived in Boston from New York on Sunday, May 6, and the next day lectured before the New England Women's Club, of which the famous Mrs. Julia Ward Howe was president. During the following nine days the Swami gave five more lectures in Boston and Cambridge before various groups, drawing large and enthusiastic audiences. "The brahmin monk has become a fad in Boston, as he was in Chicago last year," the *Boston Herald* of May 15 put it, "and his earnest, honest, cultured manner has won many friends for him." Among those who made him welcome in the ultra-conservative city of Boston was not only Julia Ward Howe, the tireless originator and champion of innumerable social reforms, but Thomas Wentworth Higginson, also a famous reformer and one of the last followers of Transcendentalism. There were also, of course, the Swami's friends of his first days in America—Professor John Henry Wright, Franklin B. Sanborn, and others who had recognized his merit when he was still unknown.

On May 8 the Swami spoke on religion to the younger generation of Bostonians at Radcliffe, then a recently founded college for women, associated with Harvard University. His third lecture in Boston was given on May 10 at "Mr. Collidge's Round Table", and on May 14 he spoke at Association Hall on "The Manners and Customs of India". It was characteristic of the Swami that this lecture was given for the benefit of the Tyler-Street Day Nursery, for although at this period he was trying to raise funds for his contemplated work in India, he could never say no to those who asked him to contribute his earnings to various American charities. His lecture of May 16 on "The Religions of India" was also given in aid of the same nursery school. The time of this lecture was "fixed late—from 3:30 till 5:30—so that businessmen may attend." But this gave the Swami little time for rest, for on the same day, May 16, he delivered a second lecture at eight in the evening at Harvard University, in Sever Hall, under the auspices of the Harvard Religious Union. In this talk before the Union the Swami said in part:

There are various sects and doctrines in India, some of which accept the theory of a personal God, and others which believe that God and the universe are one; but whatever sect the Hindoo belongs to he does not say that his is the only right belief, and that all others must be wrong. He believes that there are many ways of coming to God; that a man who is truly religious rises above the petty quarrels of sects or creeds. In India if a man believes that he is a spirit, a soul, and not a body, then he is said to have religion and not till then.

In his lectures in both Boston and Cambridge, the Swami dwelt on the profound spiritual meaning that underlay and suffused every facet of the Hindu's daily life. Nor did he fail during the course of his lectures to point out the implicit immorality of much Western behaviour. Many of his listeners, perhaps particularly those who had stood in judgement on India, smarted under his rebukes, for his aim was true and his arrows penetrating. But his motive was never to condemn or to wound; always it was to awaken and uplift.

During his stay in Boston, the Swami visited Lawrence, Massachusetts, a city some twenty-five miles to the north. Here on the evening of May 15, he lectured on the religion and customs of India, and here also, as the *Lawrence Evening Tribune* remarked, "He did not hesitate to criticize adversely some Western customs, especially some connected with the position of woman." The status and treatment of Hindu women was one of the aspects of Indian society most blatantly and crudely misrepresented in the West. As a consequence, almost everywhere the Swami went he spoke of the purity and selflessness of Indian women and of the respect that was both traditionally and in fact accorded to them. Sometimes, the better to make his point, he would draw a contrasting picture of the Western wife and Hindu mother. But for all this he did not fail to appreciate the virtues and achievements of Western women; on the contrary, he had nothing but admiration for their culture and spirit of independence, and, as will be seen later, he fervently wanted similar opportunities for education and self-development to be given to the women of his own country.

The hot summer season now descended on America, putting a stop in the cities to all social, cultural, and even religious pursuits, sending hundreds of city-dwellers to their country homes or to summer resorts in the mountains or at the seaside. The Swami stayed in Chicago till June 28, living in the house of the Hale family—now a nearly empty house, for some of the family were out of town. In some respects this summer month was not a bright one for him, for, as we are about to see, the circumstances attending his mission in the West were not then altogether favourable.

24

AFTER THE PARLIAMENT—2

The news of the unparalleled success of the Swami in America began to reach India by the beginning of November 1893, about two months after the great Parliament of Religions had commenced in Chicago. As has been seen in a previous chapter, leading Indian journals reprinted the American reports of his talks at the Parliament, and these extracts, quotations and comments were avidly read by Hindus, from Madras to Almora, from Calcutta to Bombay. The general public was transported with joy at the glowing accounts of the welcome accorded to the Swami and to the message of Hinduism that he preached. This was a new experience for India—to receive recognition of her greatness, to be vindicated as "the Spiritual Teacher of the World".

But although the Indian people wholeheartedly applauded the Swami's work in America, their recognition of him as a bona-fide spokesman of Hinduism was more jubilant than organized and was thus generally unknown in the West. Indeed, until far into the second half of 1894 no word had reached the American public that the Swami was honoured in his own country; and this long failure on the part of Hindu society to give united voice to its recognition of him as a true representative of Hinduism caused him many months of anxiety, if not despair; for through the silence of his countrymen his entire mission in the West was jeopardized. Without the backing of his country his standing as an accredited representative of Hinduism remained insecure, and his enemies in both America and India could thus proceed undeterred in their persistent campaign to cut the ground from under his feet.

From the day of the Swami's extraordinary and spectacular success at the Parliament of Religions, when he thrilled the American public with his lofty thought and luminous personality—from that day forward the number of his enemies steadily grew. That a monk of India could stand up before the august Parliament and speak words of the highest moral and spiritual idealism, and this with eloquence and authority, that this young, unknown Hindu could be publicly acclaimed "an orator by divine right", was enough to strike terror into the heart of bigotry. In the preceding chapter we have touched on the almost hysterical reaction of the more narrow sections of the Christian clergy to the Swami's sudden, comet-like appearance on the horizon. Let us here enlarge somewhat on this distasteful theme, for it not only formed a part of the religious climate in which he worked and preached, it constituted as well a chapter of his life that revealed his character in bold relief. As we have pointed out elsewhere, it was not his personality alone that gave the lie to the Christian missionaries' portrayal of India as a benighted land of heathen rites. The Swami did not spare any words in presenting the true picture of his country's highly refined culture. In simple language he beautifully explained the traditions governing the everyday life of the Hindu people—traditions rooted deep in an ancient religious idealism, in which a life of renunciation and self-sacrifice was everywhere more highly honoured than one of kingship or affluence. Nor did the Swami hesitate to criticize openly the proselytizing methods of the Christian missionaries in India. He informed the American people that the money being spent in India to convert the "heathen" to Christianity was bearing little fruit; he pointed out that the most ignorant Indian villager was as rich in religious knowledge and faith as was the Western farmer in political knowledge and opinion. Indeed, in the Swami's every lecture delivered after the Parliament, his startling words at that assembly, "Religion is not the crying need of India", were underscored again and again with unmistakable strokes.

But perhaps the blow that fell most painfully upon the Missionary Societies was the sharp decrease in monetary contributions to their causes. An official statement of the missionaries themselves read: "As a consequence of Vivekananda's success and teaching, the contributions to the Indian missionary funds

have decreased in one year by as much as one million pounds."
This was indeed cause for alarm. But instead of devoting themselves to improving and chastening their methods of work, the
better to serve the Indian people, the Swami's detractors set
themselves to destroy him, employing every means to bring
about his personal ruin and to discredit his teaching. They
attempted to show that he was a man without character and
hence unfit to be a guest in any respectable American home;
simultaneously, they made a concerted effort to prove that his
teachings in America represented his personal religious views
only and not those of any Hindu sect or society, that they were,
in fact, entirely unacceptable to the Hindu and could not,
therefore, be looked upon in the West as representative. The
Swami was, in short, said to be a disreputable charlatan. That
was the burden of the smear campaign against him.

The Christian missionaries were not without their Indian
and American allies. Without conscious effort or intention
on his part, the Swami's dazzling success in America had
eclipsed the influence previously exerted by the Brahmo Samaj
and the Theosophical Society. Of these the latter, though not
a large organization in the United States at the time, was a
growing one and had attained considerable recognition. Among
the leaders of both these groups jealousy of the Swami was
rampant, and their consequent animosity towards him played
directly into the hands of his Christian traducers. In this
connection we may mention Mr. Pratap Chandra Mazoomdar,
a prominent leader of the Nava-vidhan (New Dispensation)
Brahmo Samaj, who had attained great popularity in America
as a preacher of a kind of Indian-flavoured Christianity and
whose book *The Oriental Christ* was well known to the West. At
the Parliament of Religions, where he had represented the
Brahmo Samaj, he had been well received; but it was Swami
Vivekananda, not he, who had swept the Parliament off its feet.

"As it pleased the Lord," the Swami wrote to his brother-
disciple, Swami Ramakrishnananda, in January of 1894, "I
met here Mr. Mazoomdar. He was very cordial at first, but
when the whole Chicago population began to flock to me in

31

overwhelming numbers, then grew the canker in his mind!
Brother, I was astonished to see and hear these things. . . .
Mazoomdar slandered me to the missionaries in the Parliament
of Religions, saying that I was a nobody, a thug, and a cheat,
and he accused me of coming here and pretending to be a
monk. Thus he greatly succeeded in prejudicing their minds
against me. He so prejudiced President Barrows that he didn't
even speak to me decently. In their books and pamphlets they
tried their best to snub me, but the Guru is my help; what could
Mazoomdar say?"

The calumny spread against the Swami did not become
particularly fruitful at the time of the Parliament; indeed, only
by persistent, unscrupulous efforts could his name be smeared
and his teachings somehow discredited, for the Swami was not
without friends in America. The following story provides an
example of the resistance Mazoomdar's campaign encountered.
At an evening gathering where he had been speaking disparagingly of the Swami and his Master, one of the guests
handed him a pamphlet written by him some fifteen years
earlier in high and reverential praise of Shri Ramakrishna.
"Did you not write this?" the guest asked. Mr. Mazoomdar's
reply is not recorded. There was, after all, little he could say.

But Mr. Mazoomdar continued to stoke the flames of his
envy, and after returning to India applied himself in earnest
to vilifying the Swami. In a letter dated March 18, 1894, the
Swami wrote to Mary Hale: "Mazoomdar has gone back to
Calcutta and is preaching that Vivekananda is committing
every sin under the sun in America—especially 'unchastity' of
the most degraded type!!! Lord bless his soul." And to his
Madras disciple Alasinga Perumal, the Swami wrote on April 9
"Of course, the orthodox clergymen are against me; and seeing
that it is not easy to grapple with me, they try to hinder, abuse
and vilify me in every way; and Mazoomdar has come to their
help. He must have gone mad with jealousy. He had told them
that I was a big fraud and a rogue! And again in Calcutta he
is telling them that I am leading a most sinful life in America
specially unchaste! Lord bless him!"

It is clear from his letters that the Swami was by no means unaware of the malicious attacks that were being directed from all sides against his work and against his probity as a man and a religious teacher. Yet for many months he took no action in his own defence. Rather, sannyasi that he was, he depended on the Lord. Indeed it might be said that he had received divine guidance in this matter, as in others, and was well assured that he was divinely protected. One incident that could have served to underscore his innate faith was related by Swami Vijnana-nanda, one of his brother-disciples. At a dinner in Detroit, when the Swami was about to sip from his cup of coffee, he saw Shri Ramakrishna standing by his side, saying, "Don't drink! That is poison!" In an atmosphere so clouded with malice, he could not easily discount that warning; for it would have been a wonder if people so mean-minded as to carry on a smear campaign against a holy man were not bent on destroying his life as well!

The Swami's long imperturbability in the face of such virulence is clearly shown by a letter written to his disciples in Madras on January 24, 1894:

I am surprised that so much about me has reached you. The criticism you mention of the *Interior* is not to be taken as the attitude of the American people. That paper is almost unknown here, and belongs to what they call a "blue-nose Presbyterian paper", very bigoted. Still all the "blue-noses" are not ungentlemanly. The American people, and many of the clergy, are very hospitable to me. That paper wanted a little notoriety by attacking a man who was being lionized by society. That trick is well known here, and they do not think anything of it. Of course, our Indian missionaries may try to make capital out of it. If they do, tell them, "Mark, Jew, a judgement has come upon you!" Their old building is tottering to its foundation and must come down in spite of their hysterical shrieks. I pity them—if their means of living fine lives in India is cut down by the influx of oriental religions here. But not one of their leading clergy is ever against me. Well, when I am in the pond, I must bathe thoroughly.

Gradually, however, the campaign to destroy the Swami

and his mission assumed such menacing proportions that if
unchecked it could defeat the very purpose of his coming to
America. Seeing this, he at last took measures to counteract it.
Even then, he did not become directly involved in publicly
refuting the scandalous charges against his character and
conduct; rather, he asked the Hindu people to vouch for him
with united voice, to announce publicly that his message was
the message of India's soul, and that Hindu society acknowledged his views as its own.

The Swami well knew that the failure of his countrymen to
give official recognition to his accomplishment during and
after the Parliament of Religions was not due to a lack of
appreciation on their part, and that their silence was not by
any means studied. Having lived long under foreign domina-
tion, the Hindus had forgotten the methods of organized action
—had forgotten, indeed, the need for it. Thus the Swami,
seeing his mission jeopardized and his enemies emboldened,
attempted to channel the disorganized enthusiasm and jubilation in India over his American success into a united force. He
was constrained not only to remind the Hindus of their duty
but to advise a way of action. In his letter of April 9, 1894, to
Alasinga he wrote:

One thing is to be done if you can do it. Can you convene a big
meeting in Madras getting Ramnad or any such big fellow as the
President, and pass a resolution of your entire satisfaction at my
representation of Hinduism here, and send it to the *Chicago Herald*,
Inter-Ocean, and *New York Sun*, and the *Commercial Advertiser* of Detroit?
Chicago is in Illinois. *New York Sun* requires no particulars. Detroit is
in the State of Michigan. Send copies to Dr. Barrows, Chairman of
the Parliament of Religions, Chicago. I have forgotten his number,
but the street is Indiana Avenue. One copy to Mrs. J. J. Bagley of
Detroit, Washington Ave.

Try to make this meeting as big as possible. Get hold of all the big
bugs who must join it for their religion and country. Try to get a
letter from the Mysore Maharaja and the Dewan approving the
meeting and its purpose—so of Khetri—in fact, as big and noisy a
crowd as you can.

The resolution would be of such a nature that the Hindu com-

munity of Madras, who sent me over, expressing its entire satisfaction
in my work here, etc.

Now try if it is possible. This is not much work. Get also letters of
sympathy from all parts you can and print them and send copies to
the American papers—as quickly as you can. That will go a long way,
my brethren. The Brahmo Samaj fellows here are trying to talk all
sorts of nonsense. We must stop their mouths as fast as we can.

In this same letter the Swami also advised that efforts be
made to hold similar meetings in Calcutta. He, however,
received no answer to this important letter till the second week
of July. Alasinga's reply, directed to one of the Swami's
temporary addresses, rather than to his headquarters at the
Hales's house in Chicago, was long delayed in reaching him.
"More than two months ago", the Swami wrote to another
Madras disciple on June 28, "I wrote to Alasinga about this
[convening a public meeting in Madras]. He did not even
answer my letter. I am afraid his heart has grown lukewarm."
As far as the Swami knew, his advice had been ignored; and no
public meeting had been held anywhere in his country. No
news of any kind had reached America; and in this prolonged
silence his traducers thrived.

One of the Indian attacks against him had been published in
Unity and the Minister, the organ of the Nava-vidhan Brahmo
Samaj, conducted under the leadership of Mazoomdar. This,
together with other derogatory remarks about the Swami, was
quoted in the *Boston Daily Advertiser* of May 16, 1894, when, as
we have seen, the Swami was lecturing in Boston. The article,
which implied that he was a fraudulent monk who preached
a pseudo-Hinduism, ran as follows:

The Indian Mirror has published several long leaders in praise of the
Neo-Hindu BABU NORENDRA NATH DUTT alias VIVEKHA-
NANDA [*sic*] in some of its late issues. We have no objection to the
publication of such panegyrics on the sannyasi (monk), but since the
time he came to us to act on the stage of the Nava-Vrindavan Theatre
or sang hymns in one of the Brahmo Samajs of this city we knew him
well that no amount of newspaper writing could throw any new light
on our estimate of his character. We are glad our old friend lately

created a good impression in America by his speeches, but we are aware that Neo-Hinduism of which our friend is a representative is not orthodox Hinduism. The last thing which the latter would do is to cross the Kalapani (ocean), partake of the Mlechha food (i.e., food of outcasts, i.e. of Christians and foreigners) and smoke endless cigars and the like. Any follower of modern Hinduism cannot command that respect from us which we entertain for a genuine orthodox Hindu. Our contemporary may try to do his best to promote the reputation of VIVEKHANANDA, but we cannot have patience with him when he publishes glaring nonsense.

The insinuations are clear: although the Swami called himself 'Vivekananda' he was in fact Babu Narendra Nath Dutta. Secondly, he was not a genuine Hindu: he took forbidden food, smoked cigars, crossed the ocean, was a singer and an actor—was, in fine, a wayward Bohemian! But the article suppressed the fact that Keshabchandra Sen had also acted in the same play, which, it so happened, was a religious drama put on by the members of the Brahmo Samaj, of which Keshab was the leader. Narendra, then a member of the rival Sadharan Brahmo Samaj and an accomplished singer, had been persuaded to take the part of a Yogi.

While the Swami, a sannyasi, still scorned to defend himself publicly, he felt that an explanation was due from him to the intimate friends in America who had so generously and trustingly helped and supported him these many months. Indeed, if he did not give them some assurance, his silence could be construed as a tacit admission of fraudulence, and it would be impossible for him to remain in America. Even if for the continuance of his work an explanation was not required the demands of friendship called for one. To Professor John Henry Wright, who had made possible his appearance at the Parliament of Religions by vouching for his fitness to be a delegate, the Swami sent every scrap of favourable Indian testimony that he could gather. Some of it had only recently come into his hands. In May he wrote from his hotel in Boston to the Professor:

By this time you have got the pamphlet and the letters. If you like,

I would send you over from Chicago some letters from Indian Princes and ministers—one of these ministers was one of the Commissioners of the late opium commission that sat under Royal Commission in India. If you like, I will have them write to you to convince you of my not being a cheat. But, my brother, our ideal of life is to hide, to suppress, and to deny. . . . I am morally bound to afford you every satisfaction, my kind friend; but for the rest of the world I do not care what they say—the sannyasin must not have self-defence. So I beg of you not to publish or show anybody anything in that pamphlet or the letters.

At the close of the Swami's letter one finds words that come from his sorrow-stricken heart: "I was never a *missionary*," he wrote, " nor ever would be one—my place is in the Himalayas. I have satisfied myself so far that I can with a full conscience say, 'My God, I saw terrible misery amongst my brethren; I searched and discovered the way out of it, tried my best to apply the remedy, but failed. So Thy will be done.' " But if he could not (as he thought) rescue his mission from the onslaught of his enemies, at least he was able to reassure his friends; for he was not without influential admirers in his own country. The pamphlet mentioned in the letter to Professor Wright quoted above was without doubt the one that he had received two weeks earlier from India. Of this he had written on April 26 to Isabelle McKindley, who had forwarded it to him: ". . . the mail you sent yesterday from India was really . . . good news after a long interval. There is a beautiful letter from Dewanji [Haridas Viharidas Desai, the Dewan of Junagadh and the Opium Commissioner whom Swamiji had mentioned to Prof. Wright]. . . . Then there was a little pamphlet published in Calcutta about me—revealing that once at least in my life the prophet has been honoured in his own country. [It contains] extracts from American and Indian papers and magazines about me. The extracts printed from Calcutta papers were especially gratifying, although the strain is so fulsome that I refuse to send the pamphlet over to you. They call me illustrious, wonderful, and all sorts of nonsense, but they forward me the gratitude of the whole nation."

But Indian articles in praise of Swamiji were not published in the American papers; only those detrimental to him were printed and widely read. As far as the American public knew, the Swami was not honoured in his own country and was as suspect as ever.

It would appear that Professor Wright was not altogether satisfied by the "fulsome" pamphlet and letters that Swamiji sent him; or so the Swami felt. Thus on May 24 he wrote to him again, from Chicago, enclosing further testimony of his being "no fraud". His letter reads in part:

Herewith I forward to you a letter from one of our ruling princes of Rajputana, His Highness the Maharaja of Khetri, and another from the opium commissioner, late minister of Junagad, one of the largest states in India, and a man who is called the Gladstone of India. These I hope would convince you of my being no fraud. . . . I am bound, my dear friend, to give you every satisfaction of my being a genuine sannyasin, but to *you* alone. I do not care what the rabbles say or think about me. . . .

The letter from the Maharaja of Khetri that Swamiji sent to Professor Wright was found years later among the professor's papers. It was written on April 7, 1894, and read in part:

My dear Guroo . . . I see there is no need of advising one who is far more wise, but still I dare say that you ought not to feel disgusted by the backbiting of our countrymen for you should see "*Kraya-vikraya-velayam kachah kachah manih manih*" [At the time of buying and selling, that is, true appraisal, glass is only glass, a jewel is a jewel]. If a man like you would give up your long cherished design for bettering your mother-country by getting some help from the noble civilized people of West, who else could ever attempt to fulfil it ?. . . . My eagerness for seeing your holy self urges me to write to you to come back soon, but at the same time something else checks my pen and makes me write something quite contrary to that i.e. to ask you to remain still there where the people are jewellers of human beings. . . .

As far as we know, the letter the Swami sent to Professor Wright from the Dewanji of Junagadh is no longer extant. But it was to this latter noble friend that the Swami now poured out the despair of his heart. His letter, dated June 20, 1894, read in part:

The backbiters, I must tell you, have not indirectly benefited me; on the other hand, they have injured me immensely in view of the fact that our Hindu people did not move a finger to tell the Americans that I represented them. Had our people sent some words thanking the American people for their kindness to me and stating that I was representing them! Mr. Mazoomdar and a man called Nagarkar from Bombay and a Christian girl called Sorabji from Poona have been telling the American people that I have donned the sannyasin's garb only in America and that I was a cheat, bare and simple. So far as reception goes, it has no effect on the American nation; but so far as helping me with funds goes, it has a terrible effect in making them take off their helping hands from me. And it is one year since I have been here, and not one man of note from India has thought it fit to make the Americans know that I am no *cheat*. There again the missionaries are always seeking for something against me, and they are busy picking up anything said against me by the Christian papers of India and publishing it here. . . . a year has rolled by, and our countrymen could not even do so much for me as to say to the American people that I was a real sannyasin and no cheat, and that I represented the Hindu religion. Even this much, the expenditure of a few words, they could not do! Bravo, my countrymen!

It was perhaps in response to this letter that the Dewanji, Haridas Viharidas Desai, wrote to Mr. G. W. Hale in staunch defence of his beloved Swami Vivekananda. His letter, which was dated August 2, 1894, has come to light only recently. He wrote:

Sir,

I hope you will excuse my troubling you with this letter.

I learn with regret that some people have given out in America that Swami Shri Vivekanandaji is not what he appears to be in public there. Allow me to tell you as a friend of his that the Swami is known to me for some years. I respect and revere him very much. He is sincere to the avocation he has disinterestedly taken up for the good of the people at large. He has given up his family and social connections since about 12 years and has devoted himself entirely to the good of his own soul and that of others. He went to Chicago only with the avowed object of enlightening the American nation with the true religion of the Hindus, the knowledge of which he has acquired so much as to win the admiration of those who are in a position to appreciate it. He is a true friend of the Hindus and a staunch advocate of their religion. I saw his house, mother & brothers in Calcutta where I was in November and December last, to serve as a member of the Royal Commission on Opium. He does not keep any connection with his relations &c, because he has long renounced the worldly connections and—become a sannyasi. I send you by Book Post a small pamphlet, the perusal of which will introduce my humble-self to you.

You are welcome to make use of this letter in any way you think proper for the sake of truth and fair play.

I remain
Yours very faithfully
Haridas Viharidas

"Your kind note to G. W. Hale has been very gratifying," Swamiji was to write in September to the Dewanji, "as I owed them that much." Yet it is doubtful whether Mr. Hale was himself in need of reassurance in regard to the Swami's authenticity and honour. The story goes that once he received an anonymous and scandal-filled letter, warning him to keep his daughters from associating with the Swami. On reading this unsolicited advice, Mr. Hale dropped the letter into the flames of his hearth, as one might drop into the fire some vermin-ridden piece of trash.

But let us return to the dark month of June 1894, when the Swami was living in the Hale house in Chicago. By mid-June, Professor Wright seems to have been satisfied by the many assurances the Swami had given him—if ever he had been in doubt. But now another close friend had, the Swami thought, given him up. On June 18 he wrote to the professor, "I do not know whether I will come to Annisquam or not. . . . Mrs. Bagley seems to be unsettled by that article in the Boston paper against me. She sent me over a copy from Detroit and has ceased correspondence with me. Lord bless her. She has been very kind to me." The article referred to was, of course, that quoted above from the *Boston Daily Advertiser* of May 17,

1894, which had been reprinted in the *Detroit Free Press* of June 11.

The Swami must have been much hurt to think that his good friend and hostess had lost faith to the extent of cancelling an invitation to him to visit her summer home in Annisquam, Massachusetts. Happily, he was mistaken. Only a few days after he had written the above letter to Professor Wright, one finds Mrs. Bagley writing to a friend in eloquent defence of the Swami. Her letter, written from Annisquam, was dated June 22, and read as follows:

You write of my dear friend, Vivekananda. I am glad of an opportunity to express my admiration of his character, and it makes me most indignant that any one should call him in question. He has given us in America higher ideas of life than we have ever had before. In Detroit, an old conservative city, in all the Clubs he is honoured as no one has ever been, and I only feel that all who say one word against him are jealous of his greatness and his fine spiritual perceptions; and yet how can they be? He does nothing to make them so.

He has been a revelation to Christians, . . . he has made possible for us all a diviner and more noble practical life. As a religious teacher and an example to all I do not know of his equal. It is so wrong and so untrue to say that he is intemperate. All who have been brought in contact with him day by day, speak enthusiastically of his sterling qualities of character, and men in Detroit who judge most critically, and who are unsparing, admire and respect him. . . . He has been a guest in my house more than three weeks, and my sons as well as my son-in-law and my entire family found Swami Vivekananda a gentleman always, most courteous and polite, a charming companion and ever-welcome guest. I have invited him to visit us at my summer-home here at Annisquam, and in my family he will always be honoured and welcomed. I am really sorry for those who say aught against him, more than I am angry, for they know so little what they are talking about. He has been with Mr. and Mrs. Hale of Chicago much of the time while in that city. I think that has been his home. They invited him first as guest and later were unwilling to part with him. They are Presbyterians, . . . cultivated and refined people, and they admire, respect and love Vivekananda. He is a strong, noble human being, one who walks with God. He is as simple and trustful as a child. In Detroit I gave him an evening reception, inviting ladies and gentlemen, and two weeks afterwards he lectured to invited guests in my parlour. . . . I had included lawyers, judges, ministers, army-officers, physicians, and businessmen with their wives and daughters. Vivekananda talked two hours on "The Ancient Hindu Philosophers and What They Taught." All listened with intense interest to the end. Wherever he spoke, people listened gladly and said, "I never heard man speak like that." He does not antagonize, but lifts people up to a higher level—they see something beyond man-made creeds and denominational names, and they feel one with him in their religious beliefs.

Every human being would be made better by knowing him and living in the same house with him. . . . I want everyone in America to know Vivekananda, and if India has more such let her send them to us. . . .

The above letter stands as clear evidence that Mrs. Bagley had by no means turned from the Swami, though the very fact that he thought she had, shows how despairing he was at this period of his American mission. As late as the end of June 1894 we find him still without word from India; still without defence in the face of his enemies; still in despair. To one of his disciples in Madras he wrote on June 28:

Now as to my prospects here—it is well-nigh zero. Why, because although I had the best purpose, it has been made null and void by these causes. All that I get about India is from Madras letters. Your letters say again and again how I am being praised in India. But that is between you and me, for I never saw a single Indian paper writing about me, except the three square inches sent to me by Alasinga. On the other hand everything that is said by Christians in India is sedulously gathered by the missionaries and regularly published, and they go from door to door to make my friends give me up. They have succeeded only too well, for there is not one word for me from India. Indian Hindu papers may laud me to the skies, but not a word of that ever came to America, so that many people in this country think me a fraud. In the face of the missionaries and with the jealousy of the Hindus here to back them, I have not a word to say.

. . . I came here without credentials. How else to show that I am not a fraud in the face of the missionaries and the Brahmo Samaj? Now I thought nothing so easy as to spend a few words; I thought nothing would be so easy as to hold a meeting of some respectable persons in Madras and Calcutta and pass a resolution thanking me and the American people for being so kind to me and sending it over officially, i.e. through the Secretary of the function, to America, for instance, sending one to Dr. Barrows and asking him to publish it in the papers and so on, to different papers of Boston, New York, and Chicago. Now after all I found that it is too terrible a task for India to undertake. There has not been one voice for me in one year and every one against me, for whatever you may say of me in your homes, who knows anything of it here?. . .

. . . Every moment I expected something from India. No, it never came. Last two months especially I was in torture at every moment. No, not even a newspaper from India! My friends waited—waited month after month; nothing came, not a voice. Many consequently grew cold and at last gave me up. But it is the punishment for relying upon man and upon brutes, for our countrymen are not men as yet. They are ready to be praised, but when their turn comes even to say a word, they are nowhere.

But while the Swami's countrymen were indeed slow in paying public tribute to him after the Parliament of Religions and in expressing their gratitude to the American people for having so warmly welcomed him, they were not so slow as the delay in news from India had led him to believe. Even as, in this connection, he was writing his first letter known to us of advice to his Madras disciple Alasinga, the thought of holding public meetings in his honour was stirring in India. The idea may have been communicated in some unknown letter of the Swami written to his Madras disciples or the brother-disciples, which might have reached India by March end at the latest. But by whatever medium it was conveyed, the power of Swamiji's thought seems to have awakened his countrymen to their duty. His letter to Alasinga was dated April 9; the response was as swift as thought itself! On April 10—the very next day—the following editorial comment appeared in the *Indian Mirror*, a leading Calcutta newspaper sympathetic to the Swami:

That a prophet is not honoured in his country is a commonplace which is often illustrated in life. It is doubtful whether Swami Vivekananda would have become so widely known, if he had not visited

America. The broad-hearted Americans are to be thanked for whatever success the Swami met with in his exposition of Hinduism in the
Parliament of Religions at Chicago. How far Swami Vivekananda
succeeded in impressing his American hearers with the intrinsic
worth of Hinduism is well known to us. . . . In view of the glorious
success, achieved by Swami Vivekananda in his missionary tour in
America, we think that Hindus will be doing a grateful duty by
presenting an address to the Swami, and also to the organizers of the
Parliament of Religions but for whose help the Swami would have
found it difficult to obtain such a strong footing in America. We hope,
our Hindu brethren all over the country will heartily join the movement. Swami Vivekananda is still in America, and the address ought
to be sent to him there without delay. We must also let our American
friends know that we are not ungrateful for the good offices which
they rendered to our Hindu brother. There should be no loss of time
to get up the addresses, and we should like to have the views of our
Hindu brethren in all parts of the country on the subject.

The people of Madras were the first to arrange such a public
meeting in his honour, under the presidentship of Dewan
Bahadur S. Subramania Iyer, C.I.E., in Pachaiyappa's Hall in
Madras, on Saturday, April 28, 1894—days before the Swami's
letter of April 9 to Alasinga could have reached India. Raja Sir
Ramaswamy Mudaliar and many other distinguished citizens
and scholars took part in this important event, and stirring
speeches were made in official tribute to the Swami. The
proceedings of this public meeting as reported by the local
press in Madras, were later published in the *Indian Mirror* of
September 5, 1894. The account read in part:

A public meeting of the Hindus of Madras was held in Pachaiyappa's Hall on Saturday [April 28, 1894] at 5-30 P.M. to thank Swami
Vivekananda for his representing Hinduism in the Parliament of
Religions at Chicago, and the American public for the cordial reception they accorded to him. The meeting was very largely attended by
many Hindu gentlemen and students. . . . On the motion of Rajah
Sir Ramaswamy Mudelliar, Dewan Bahadur S. Subramania Iyer,
C.I.E., was voted to the chair. The Rajah of Ramnad sent a telegram
and Rai Bahadur S. Seshayya, B.A., and a few other Native gentlemen
wrote sympathizing with the objects of the meeting.

The Chairman, in opening the proceedings of the meeting said that
. . . he had no doubt that all present were agreed that for a long time
to come they must simply be learners and students, and endeavour to
learn and assimilate what was good and excellent in the civilization
of the West. . . . But he believed there was one matter about which
there was so much to be found in Indian literature in this country
which would preclude their having to go to the West for information
for example or for study. . . . He referred to the philosophy and religion of Hindus. He did not mean to pretend that in practice, that
even in the matter of theoretical knowledge the people of this country
generally understood their great philosophy and their great religious
tenets. He only said that however much they might have to learn
from the great civilized nations of the West in other matters, they
would hardly find very much to learn from them in regard to this
great question. . . . If the position which he had taken was agreed to,
they would agree with him in saying that the visit of Swami Vivekananda to America and his work and success there was of the utmost
importance to the Americans and the Hindus. . . . It has become
possible for a son of the soil acquainted with the language of the East
to preach the truth of Vedanta not for the purpose of conversion or
proselytism, but simply to place it before the great American people.
The great advantage in placing such truths before the Western races
was that they examined the matter with great ability and energy
characteristic of them and once they were convinced that they were
well founded they endeavoured to communicate it to all under their
sway and influence. In that view Vivekananda himself was one of the
noble souls that could be entrusted with such a task. It was necessary
that the Western nations should assimilate the truths of Vedanta; for
as the Indian adage says "as is the King, so are the subjects." If the
Western races accepted the philosophy of the East, it seemed to the
Indians the more readily to accept the position. . . . For the reception
given to the Swami in America he found that the time for the endeavour that was being made by Swami was more propitious than it was
half-a-century ago, in the days of Rajah Ram Mohun Roy. With the
above observations the Chairman called upon Mr. C. Ramachandra
Rao Saheb to move the first Resolution, *viz*: "That this meeting
tenders its thanks to Swami Vivekananda for having represented
India at the Parliament of Religions at Chicago, and for his lucid
exposition of Hinduism before the same.". . .

The next proposition was moved by Mr. M. O. Parthsarathy

Iyengar, which ran thus: "That this meeting tenders its thanks to the American people for the cordial and sympathetic reception they have accorded to Swami Vivekananda."

He said: Mr. Chairman and Gentlemen: In moving the proposition I shall presently read to you, I am conscious I am only giving expression to the unanimous feeling of the hearts here assembled. The Chicago Parliament of Religions marks a great epoch in the history of the world—an epoch, the like of which could never be seen in the vast expanse of the past. . . . With what poetic rapture will the future historian record the noble act of generous hearts that cordially welcomed nationalities of every creed—made possible for all religions to meet on common grounds as friends and brethren and to hear with kindly patience the friendly criticisms of co-religionists. Hinduism is mostly criticized without a sufficient preparatory knowledge of its principles. Nobody takes the trouble to study the religion he would gladly scoff at. Few like to give even an opportunity [to] Hinduism to express itself. . . . It was left for Swami Vivekananda, the Americans, the gentlemen assembled at Chicago to make many people realize the fact that Hinduism is well able to hold its own against any religion. . . .

Mr. T. P. Kodanda Rama Iyer, B. L., proposed and Mr. D. R. Balaji Rao, B.A. B.L., seconded "that this meeting requests the Chairman to forward copies of the above Resolutions to Swami Vivekananda, and Dr. Barrows, President of the Parliament of Religions, held at Chicago in 1893." The Resolution was put to the meeting and carried.

As has been seen, throughout the whole of May and June the Swami had no inkling that this meeting had taken place. Meanwhile, another meeting in his honour was held in Calcutta. The inspiration for this, it appears, came from the Buddhist H. Dharmapala, Secretary of the Maha-Bodhi Society of Calcutta, who had been a delegate to the Parliament of Religions and who, unlike Mr. Pratap Chandra Mazoomdar, had been full of admiration for the Swami and enthusiastic over his message to the Western people. Returning to India, Dharmapala had spoken in high praise of the Swami's work. "The Buddhist representative", said the *Indian Mirror* of April 12, "truly remarks that all *Hindus* should be proud of the honour accorded to their representative by the American people, and that blessings and good wishes should be sent to him from every Hindu home. Mr. Dharmapala is of opinion that the success of the Religion Parliament was, to a great extent, due to Swami Vivekananda." In April Dharmapala visited the Swami's brother-disciples at Alambazar Math, no doubt giving them details of their beloved Naren's dazzling success in America. On May 14 he delivered a lecture in Calcutta entitled "Hinduism in America and Swami Vivekananda". This event, at which the Buddhist Archbishop of Japan, His Holiness Utoki, also spoke, was presided over by Maharaja Bahadur Sir Norendra Krishna, K.C.I.E. and attended by many dignitaries of the Hindu community. It took the form of a public meeting in honour of the Swami. A report of the occasion appeared in the *Indian Mirror* of May 18, 1894, and read in part as follows:

The subject of Mr. Dharmapala's lecture at the Minerva Theatre, Calcutta, on Monday evening last, was "Swami Vivekananda and Hinduism in America" and the manner in which the theme was treated, proved the good feeling and friendliness which the Buddhists bear towards the Hindus and Hinduism. . . . The audience, met at the Minerva Theatre, was very large, and by their plaudits showed not only that they relished the discourse, but . . . recognized the signal services which Swami Vivekananda has been rendering to the cause of Hinduism among the great American people. This is all the more pleasant to us, for our own writings on the subject and estimate of the Swami's American work have been now publicly and unmistakably upheld. This is all the more pleasant to us, we say, because most unworthy efforts had been made in some quarters to belittle Swami Vivekananda's brilliant doings in the Parliament of Religions at Chicago and in other important American centres of intellectual activity. Those attempts, miserably as they did originate, have as miserably failed, and this Buddhistic testimony, unsought and unanticipated, as to Swami Vivekananda's worth must make all similar efforts in the future abortive. And not only Mr. Dharmapala has borne testimony to the value of the Swami's work in America, but a far more eminent man, no less a personage than His Holiness the Buddhist Archbishop of Japan, has done the same. . . .

The above reference to "unworthy efforts . . . to belittle
32

Swami Vivekananda's brilliant doings" at the Parliament was, of course, to the efforts of, specifically, Mr. Mazoomdar. Over two years later a letter addressed to the editor of the *Indian Mirror* and dated December 3, 1896, recalled the occasion: "The Calcutta public may remember how he [Mr. Mazoomdar] was frustrated in his malicious attempt by Mr. Dharmapala and a High Priest of Japan, who happened to be in Calcutta at that time. When he was thus exposed before his countrymen, the ignominy of his conduct called forth the denunciation of every right-minded man."

A letter telling the Swami of this Dharmapala's meeting reached him around July 9 and seems to have been the first news of India's public action on his behalf that he had so far received. The letter that he subsequently wrote to the Hale sisters can alone adequately tell of his joy and immense relief:

O My Sisters,

Glory unto Jagadamba [Mother of the Universe]! I have gained beyond expectations. The prophet has been honoured and with a *vengeance*. I am weeping like a child at His Mercy—He never leaves His servant, sisters. The letter I send you will explain all, and the printed things are coming to the American people. The names there are the very flower of our country. The President was the chief *nobleman* of Calcutta, and the other man Mahesh Chandra Nyayaratna is the principal of the Sanskrit College and the chief Brahmin in all India and recognized by the Government as such. The letter will tell you all. O sisters! What a rogue am I that in the face of such mercies sometimes the faith totters—seeing every moment that I am in His hands. Still the mind sometimes gets despondent. Sisters, there is a *God*—a Father—a *Mother* who never leaves His children, never, never, never. Put uncanny theories aside and becoming children take refuge in Him. I cannot write more—I am weeping like a woman.

Blessed, blessed art Thou, Lord God of my soul!

Yours affectionately,
Vivekananda.

Almost simultaneously with the news of Dharmapala's lecture and function of May 14, the Swami received a letter from Alasinga informing him of the Madras Meeting of April 28. On July 11 he wrote in reply:

You must never write to me anywhere else but 541 Dearborn Ave., Chicago. Your last letter travelled the whole country to come to me, and this was only because I am so well known. Some of the resolutions are to be sent to Dr. Barrows with a letter thanking him for his kindness to me and asking him to publish the letter in some American newspapers—as that would be the best refutation of the false charges of the missionaries that I do not represent anybody.

News of the Madras Meeting reached the American public at the end of August 1894, and the event was given full publicity in some of America's leading newspapers, such as the *Boston Evening Transcript*, the *Chicago Interocean*, the *New York Sun*, and the *New York Daily Tribune*. There could no longer be the slightest doubt in America that, however inconvenient the Swami's teachings and influence might be to missionary interests, he was a bona-fide and honoured representative of the mainstream of Hinduism at its highest and best. His voice was the voice of India's soul.

On reading the account of the Madras Meeting in the *Boston Evening Transcript* of August 30, the Swami wrote the following day to Alasinga:

So far you have done wonderfully, my boy. Do not mind what I write in some moments of nervousness. One gets nervous sometimes alone in a country 15,000 miles from home, having to fight every inch of ground with orthodox inimical Christians. You must take those into consideration, my brave boy, and work right along, . . . Rejoice that you have done so much. When you feel gloomy, think what has been done within the last year. How, rising from nothing, we have the eyes of the world fixed upon us now. Not only India, but the world outside, is expecting great things of us. Missionaries or Mazoomdar or foolish officials—none will be able to resist truth and love and sincerity. Are you sincere? unselfish even unto death? and loving? Then fear not, not even death. Onward, my lads! The whole world requires Light. . . . Have faith that you are all, my brave lads, born to do great things! Let not the barks of puppies frighten you—no, not even the thunderbolts of heaven—but stand up and work!

The Swami's name soon became a household word in every province in India. Other large and influential meetings were held in many places in the year 1894 to congratulate him on his success in America and applaud his work in the cause of Hinduism. On August 22 a public meeting was held in Kumbakonam, of which the *Hindu* (as quoted in the *Indian Mirror* of September 1, 1894) wrote in part:

A meeting of the public of Kumbakonam was held in the Porter Town Hall on Wednesday, the 22nd instant, to convey to Paramahamsa Swami Vivekananda their grateful appreciation of his valuable services in America on behalf of Hinduism, and of his spirited defence of Hinduism in the Parliament of Religions at Chicago. There was a large number of students who marked by their presence their sympathy with the objects of the meeting. Dewan Bahadur R. Ragonatha Rao was proposed to the chair.

On the morning of August 26, 1894, a large public meeting was held in Bangalore in the Lecture Hall of the Central College, with Sir K. Seshadri Iyer, K.C.S.I., Dewan of Mysore, in the chair.

Everywhere in India enthusiasm for the Swami's achievements ran high, but in Calcutta, his birthplace, it reached a pitch of frenzy, and it can be said that the public meeting held there in September of 1894 carried the greatest weight of all. Not only was Calcutta the Swami's native city and the then capital of India, it was as well the fountainhead of Mazoomdar's malicious propaganda and its most fertile ground. Recognition of the Swami's achievements could not matter so much from any other city in the whole of India. The great Calcutta Meeting, held to thank the Swami and the American people, took place in the Town Hall on September 5. It was organized by the Swami's brother-disciples, together with the most representative members of the Hindu community, and was attended by some 4,000 people of all shades of opinion. Some of the most well-known pandits as well as members of the landed aristocracy, High Court judges, noted public men, pleaders, politicians, professors and prominent men in many other walks of life took part. It was presided over by Raja Peary Mohun Mookerjee, C.S.I. The following resolutions were made and adopted with eloquent speeches eulogizing the Swami's work and his contribution to the dissemination of Hindu culture among the Western nations:

1. That this meeting desires to record its grateful appreciation of the great services rendered to the cause of Hinduism by Swami Vivekananda at the Parliament of Religions at Chicago, and of his subsequent work in America.

2. That this meeting tenders its best thanks to Dr. J. H. Barrows, the Chairman [of the Parliament of Religions], and Mr. Merwin-Marie Snell, the President of the Scientific Section of the Parliament of Religions at Chicago, and to the American people generally, for the cordial and sympathetic reception they have accorded to Swami Vivekananda.

3. That this meeting requests the Chairman to forward to Sreemat Vivekananda Swami, Dr. Barrows and Mr. Snell copies of the foregoing Resolutions together with the following letter addressed to Swami Vivekananda.

TO SREEMAT VIVEKANANDA SWAMI

Dear Sir,

As Chairman of a large, representative and influential meeting of the Hindu inhabitants of Calcutta and the suburbs, held in the Town Hall of Calcutta, on the 5th of September, 1894, I have the pleasure to convey to you the thanks of the local Hindu community for your able representation of their religion at the Parliament of Religions that met at Chicago in September, 1893.

The trouble and sacrifice you have incurred by your visit to America as a representative of the Hindu Religion are profoundly appreciated by all whom you have done the honour to represent. But their special acknowledgements are due to you for the services you have rendered to the cause they hold so dear, their sacred Arya Dharma, by your speeches and your ready responses to the questions of inquirers. No exposition of the general principles of the Hindu Religion could, within the limits of a lecture, be more accurate and lucid than what you gave in your address to the Parliament of Religions on Tuesday, the 19th September, 1893. And your subsequent utterances on the same subject on other occasions have been equally clear and precise. It has been the misfortune of Hindus to have their religion misunderstood and misrepresented through ages, and therefore they cannot but feel specially grateful to one of them who had the courage and the ability to speak the truth about it and dispel illusions, among a strange people, in a strange land, professing a different religion. Their thanks are due no less to the audiences and the organizers of the meetings, who have received you kindly, given you opportunities for speaking, encouraged you in your work, and heard you in a patient and charitable spirit. Hinduism has, for the first time in its history, found a Missionary, and by a rare good fortune it has found one so able and accomplished as yourself. Your fellow-countrymen, fellow-citizens and fellow-Hindus feel that they would be wanting in an obvious duty if they did not convey to you their hearty sympathy and earnest gratitude for all your labours, in spreading a true knowledge of their ancient faith. May God grant you strength and energy to carry on the good work you have begun!

Yours faithfully,
Peary Mohun Mookerjee,
Chairman.

The lectures that were delivered on the occasion by such prominent men as Mr. Nagendranath Ghosh, Sir Surendranath Banerjee, and others created a great wave of spiritual enthusiasm. It was as if the spirit of the Sanatana Dharma (Eternal Religion of the Hindus) were there, thrilling and electrifying the utterances of the speakers. The following are brief extracts from some of the talks.

On taking the chair, Raja Peary Mohun Mookerjee said:

We are assembled here this evening to express our thankfulness, not to one who has distinguished himself by his meritorious services to the State, or to one who has won the reputation or triumphs of statesmanship; but we assemble in this grand meeting to express our high sense of appreciation and deep gratitude to a simple sannyasin, only thirty years old, who has been expounding the truths of our religion to the great American people with an ability, tact and judgment, . . . which have elicited the highest admiration. Brother Vivekananda has opened the eyes of an important section of the civilized world by explaining the great truths of Hindu religion, and convinced them that the most valuable products of human thought in the region of philosophy and religion, are to be found not in Western science and literature but in our ancient Shastras. . . . I am very glad to find so large and influential a gathering to do honour to such a distinguished benefactor of our country. . . .

Babu Norendra Nath Sen, the editor, *Indian Mirror*, spoke in part as follows:

The present meeting is one which is unique of its kind in this city, as we have met here to honour not a high state functionary, as we usually do, but a Hindu ascetic, who, by crossing the ocean, has done so much to further the cause of Hinduism by his eloquence and learning. . . . Such success has given almost a new lease of life to the Hindus as a nation. It has been a brilliant gleam of light in the dark pages of the contemporary history of the Hindus, and has buoyed them up with hope, such as they never experienced before. Circumstances had, for some time, gone so badly with us that we were driven almost to despair until the triumph, which has been attending the cause of Hinduism in America, through the efforts of a gifted Hindu, relumed our darkened spirits, and fed them with expectant longings. . . .

It is impossible to overestimate the importance of Swami Vivekananda's services to this country; and we should not have deserved to be called Hindus, if we had failed to gather here this evening to testify our respect and gratitude to him. . . .

Rai Jatindra Nath Chowdhury, a landowner of Taki, Bengal, said, during his address, that it had been stated in some quarters that Hinduism was not fully represented at the Parliament; but he thought that a meeting such as they were holding in Calcutta would give the lie direct to a statement like the above. In proposing the resolution, Mr. N. N. Ghose, the editor of the *Indian Nation*, said in part:

. . . No success could be more sudden or brilliant than Vivekananda's. Indeed, there is hardly anything more striking in the history of oratorical achievements. There was a Hindu monk, unknown to fame, addressing, in semi-Oriental costume, an assembly, the majority of whom could hardly pronounce his name, upon a subject removed, as far as possible, from their thoughts, and securing at once their applause and esteem. The merits of the speaker and the performance must have been great and surprising. But let us not forget that credit is at least equally due to those who appreciated him, encouraged him, found opportunities for his speaking, and gave him a patient and kind hearing. . . . I am informed that the delegates had, as a rule, been invited. Vivekananda had not been invited, and therefore it would have been a very easy thing to exclude him on technical grounds from speaking at the Parliament. But Dr. Barrows, by a special act of kindness, waived all technical objections, introduced him to the audience, and permitted him to speak. Vivekananda did not say altogether fine and smooth things about Christianity, but gave occasionally hard knocks. His audience, at any rate the American section of it, nevertheless gave him an indulgent hearing, and were warm in their acknowledgement of his merits. . . .

Vivekananda's achievements in America, remarkable as they have been, I regard, however, rather as promises than as performances. His real work will have to be done in India. The redemption of India, I feel persuaded, lies not through her politics, but through her religion. Politics are in this country a superficial garb, put off and put on at pleasure. They sit loosely on the people. Religion is vital and essential, and inherited with their blood. It reaches the inmost depths of their nature, touches the marrow of their bones. This meeting is only a small testimony to its reality in this town. It has been organized by men unused to the arts of agitation. Most of the active workers have been sannyasins who go about barefooted, in characteristic yellow costume. If they had only known how to employ the machinery, customarily used for getting up political demonstrations, the meeting, large as it is, might have been ten times larger. . . .

These lectures clearly bespoke the attitude of Hindu society toward the Swami's mission and its potentialities. Behind these progressive, far-sighted, and brilliant speakers lay the full support and sympathy of the people at large, who were eager for an onward march. True, as in every society, there existed a handful of people who stood against all change, opposing the flood-tides of progress; but we are not thinking of such people here. The striking fact was that the name Vivekananda rang with acclaim throughout the length and breadth of India; everywhere he was recognized as a great Acharya (Teacher), the man who had come to fill a need. He roused the spirit of Hinduism from the lethargy into which it had fallen; and in these meetings could be discerned the gleam of that approaching dawn when India, as of old, would become conscious of her glory and might, not through warfare and streams of blood, but through the infinitely greater power of the truths enshrined in the Vedas and Vedanta.

The proceedings of the Calcutta Meeting and the lectures that had been delivered were published in brochures, two thousand in number, from the New Calcutta Press. The reports, which were also published in due course in the American papers, greatly pleased the Swami. The resolutions and the President's letter echoed many ideas close to his heart; he was, moreover, exceedingly happy to learn that behind the success of the meeting were the untiring efforts of his brother-disciples— Swami Abhedananda, Swami Ramakrishnananda, and others. Further, the resolution thanking the Swami as a preacher of religion silenced for good the calumny of his detractors in that particular regard. Aside from spreading slander about him, they had circulated the lie that Vivekananda was not preaching religion in America but was politicizing. The Swami, who was aware of this, wrote on September 27, 1894, to Alasinga:

One thing I find in the books of my speeches and sayings published in Calcutta. Some of them are printed in such a way as to savour of political views; whereas I am no politician or political agitator. I care only for the Spirit—when that is right everything will be righted by itself. . . . So you must warn the Calcutta people that no political significance be ever attached falsely to any of my writings or sayings. What nonsense! . . . I heard that Rev. Kali Charan Banerji in a lecture to Christian missionaries said that I was a political delegate. If it was said publicly, then publicly ask the Babu for me to write to any of the Calcutta papers and prove it, or else take back his foolish assertion. This is their trick! I have said a few harsh words in honest criticism of Christian governments in general, but that does not mean that I care for, or have any connection with politics or that sort of thing. Those who think it very grand to print extracts from those lectures and want to prove that I am a political preacher, to them I say, "Save me from my friends.". . .

Tell my friends that a uniform silence is all my answer to my detractors. If I give them tit for tat, it would bring us down to a level with them. Tell them that truth will take care of itself, and that they are not to fight anybody for me.

In another way the meetings held in Madras, Bangalore and

Calcutta were a help to the Swami: they confirmed and put on record that his work in America was successful; thus they indirectly acknowledged the necessity of his continuing the work there. The Swami's devotees, friends and well-wishers in India had repeatedly requested him to return to the Motherland. Referring to this, he wrote to Alasinga on April 9, 1894, "Secretary Saheb writes me that I must come back to India, because that is my field. No doubt of that. But, my brother, we are to light a torch which will shed a lustre over all India. So let us not be in a hurry; everything will come by the grace of the Lord." Though many requests came to the Swami to return to India, he did not deviate from his path. Neither the opposition of his detractors nor the advice of his well-wishing friends could cause him to give up his resolve. He well knew that the poor of India could not, and the wealthy Indians would not, help him financially to translate into action his plans for the uplift of his country; whereas by staying in America he would be able to earn money for his cause. Further, in order tó raise a dependent and weak nation—a nation given to imitating others —it was necessary to give that nation confidence in its own ideals. And one way of doing that was, surely, to make those ideals known to the West, where they would be appreciated and respected. In regard to this last, the Swami wrote on September 13, 1894, to Mrs. Hale in a letter that has only recently come to light:

I do not think the Lord will allow his servant to be inflated with vanity at the appreciation of his countrymen. I am glad that they appreciate me not for my sake but that I am firmly persuaded that a man is never improved by abuse but by praise and so with nations. Think how much of abuse has been quite unnecessarily hurled at the head of my devoted poor country and for what? They never injured the Christians or their religion or their preachers. They have always been friendly to all. So you see, Mother, every *good word* a foreign nation says to them has such an amount of power for good in India. The American appreciation of my humble work here, has really done a good deal of benefit to them. Send a good word, a good thought at least to the down-trodden vilified poor millions of India instead of abusing them day and night. This is what I beg of every nation. Help them if you can, if you cannot at least cease from abusing them.

Thus the public meetings held in India in 1894 to honour the Swami and acknowledge the significance of his mission in the West, well served that mission and were of vital importance to its advancement.

The Swami by no means became "inflated with vanity" at the appreciation of his countrymen. He took the sanction that India had given to his work and message not so much as a personal appreciation of himself, but as an indication that her grasp on the national ideal still remained firm, that the nation's spiritual foundation stood unshaken, strong as ever. He accepted the appreciation of his work in this spirit and replied to the various addresses that were sent to him. The most notable and stirring of his replies was that written to the Hindus of Madras.

Once the various meetings had been held and the ensuing publicity had played its part in aid of the Swami's work, he grew weary of "newspaper blazoning". The avalanche of newspaper clippings from India was hard to stop. In a letter to Mary Hale dated November 1, 1894, he wrote, "I got vexed at getting loads of newspapers from India; so after sending a cart-load to Mother Church and another to Mrs. Guernsey, I had to write to them to stop sending their newspapers. I have had 'boom' enough in India. Alasinga writes that every village all over the country now has heard of me. Well, the old peace is gone for ever and no rest anywhere from heretofore [henceforth]. These newspapers of India will be my death, I am sure." But still they kept coming. Almost two months later the Swami wrote to a Madras disciple, "I have written to you before and I write again, that I shall not pay heed to any criticism or praises in the newspapers. They are consigned to the fire. Do you the same. Pay no attention whatsoever to newspaper nonsense or criticism." And on January 12, 1895, to Alasinga, "I am sorry you still continue to send me pamphlets and newspapers, which I have written you several times not to do. I have no time to peruse them and take notice of them. Please send them *no more*."

Indeed even before news of the public meetings in India had reached the American press the Swami had had enough. In a letter to Mrs. Hale dated August 23, 1894, he wrote:

In India I have become horribly public; crowds will follow me and take my life out. . . . Every ounce of fame can only be bought at the cost of a pound of peace and holiness. I never thought of that before. I have become entirely disgusted with this blazoning. I am disgusted with myself. Lord will show me the way to peace and purity. Why, Mother, I confess to you—no man can live in an atmosphere of public life even in religion without the devil of competition now and then thrusting his head into the serenity of his heart. Those who are trained to preach a *doctrine* never feel it for they never knew *religion*. But those that are after *God* and not after the world feel at once that every bit of name and fame is at the cost of their purity. It is so much gone from that ideal of perfect *unselfishness*, perfect disregard of gain, or name or fame.

Even as the Swami had no use for personal fame, so he had no rancour against those who were jealous of it and tried to destroy it. How much had he not suffered from the malice of Mazoomdar! Yet on July 10, 1894, he could write to Mrs. Hale, "I got the '*Interior*' [a 'blue-nose' Christian periodical] and am very glad to see my friend Mazoomdar's book spoken of so highly. Mazoomdar is a great and good man and has done much for his fellow beings."

Although neither the Swami nor the American people were to learn of India's public recognition of him as a bona-fide representative of Hinduism until the end of August 1894, when news of the Madras Meeting was published in the American newspapers, he became satisfied, as we have seen, in the first part of July that his countrymen were taking at least some action on his behalf. The letter telling him of the well-attended meeting convened by H. Dharmapala in Calcutta had ended his long and harrowing wait. Like the first drops of rain after an oppressive drought, the first sounds of India's acclaim were the breaking of her prolonged and misleading silence. To his friends he could now offer these first clear notes of acclaim as proof that he was not a "fraud". He stood vindicated, and well could he write in his letter of July 9 to the Hale sisters, "The prophet has been honoured and with a *vengeance*."

On June 28, the Swami arrived from Chicago in New York, where he stayed for a few days with Leon Landsberg in the latter's room in the Theosophical Society, and then moved to the residence of Miss Mary Phillips at 19 West 38th Street. From there, on July 1, he wrote to Mrs. Hale, "I am now with Miss Phillips, will move off from here on Tuesday [July 3] to another place." Most of the Swami's friends were out of town in this hot summer month, and he, too, soon left the city, it not being the season for lectures.

We next find him in the middle of July, at Fishkill Landing on the Hudson, New York, at the summer home of his friends Dr. and Mrs. Egbert Guernsey. They, as we have have seen, had met him in April that year and, like many others, had come to look upon him both as a great man of God and as a beloved son. From the Guernseys's home the Swami wrote to Mrs. Hale on July 19, "It is a lovely summer place this Cedar Lawn of the Guernseys'. Miss Guernsey has gone on a visit to Swampscott. I had also an invitation there but I thought better to stay here in the calm and silent place full of trees and with the beautiful Hudson flowing by and mountain in the background."

Soon, however, he visited Swampscott, a seaside resort town in Massachusetts, where he saw once again, among other friends, Mrs. Francis W. Breed of Boston and Lynn. From Swampscott he wrote to Mrs. Hale on July 23, "I am enjoying this place very much; going to Greenacre today or tomorrow." Actually, however, he did not leave Swampscott until Thursday, July 26, arriving at Greenacre, near Eliot, Maine, the same day.

Now took place a highly important episode in the Swami's work and mission in the West. On a wooded acreage by the broad Piscataqua River, the Greenacre Religious Conferences, a symposium of liberal and unorthodox religious groups, had been recently inaugurated by Miss Sarah Farmer, whom the Swami had met in New York. Inspired in part by the Parliament of Religions, the Greenacre Conferences were open to all religious lecturers with something to say and to all men and women with a desire to learn. Many came—earnest teachers and eager students alike—, among them Mrs. Ole Bull, Dr. Lewis G. Janes, and others who were to become dear and close friends of the Swami's. Invited by Miss Farmer, he stayed at Greenacre from July 26 through August 13, 1894. Here he held a series of classes, expounding the Vedanta philosophy to a group of enthusiastic students who sat around him in oriental fashion under a venerable pine tree, since called the "Swami's Pine". As far as is known, this was the first course of classes that the Swami held in the West, and it was a foreshadowing of the shape his American work was later to take. "I teach them all Shivoham, Shivoham," he wrote on July 31 to Mary and Harriet Hale, of his Greenacre classes, "and they all repeat it innocent and pure as they are and brave beyond all bounds." He sometimes took as his text the *Avadhuta Gita*, and according to some recently discovered notes jotted down by a student under the "Swami's Pine", he taught Raja-yoga as well.

The Swami lived and taught at Greenacre for more than two weeks. "Between lecturing-teaching-picnicking and other excitements the time is flying rapidly", he wrote to Mrs. Hale on August 5. He had wanted rest, and though the days were strenuous he had, in a way, found it, for there by the broad river, under the trees, he was doing what he liked best. "I want a little quiet, but it is not the will of the Lord it seems", he wrote again to Mrs. Hale on August 20: "At Greenacre I had to talk on an average 7 to 8 hours a day; that was rest if it ever was! But it [the talk] was of the Lord—and that brings vigour along with it."

On Monday, August 13, he went directly from Greenacre to Plymouth, Massachusetts, where he had been invited to speak that same day before the Free Religious Association, an organization founded by Ralph Waldo Emerson and dedicated to liberalizing contemporary religious thought and practice. Many of the members of the Association were well-known and distinguished men and women, and some were the Swami's friends and admirers. Among them were its President, Thomas Wentworth Higginson, Julia Ward Howe, Ednah Cheney and Dr. Lewis G. Janes. The last, who was to become one of the Swami's most sturdy defenders, was at this time President of the illustrious Brooklyn Ethical Association, of which more later. "The meeting is composed of the best professors of your country," the Swami had written from Greenacre to Mrs. Hale on August 8, "so I must attend it . . ."

From Plymouth the Swami travelled to the seaside village of Annisquam, Massachusetts, around August 16, where almost a year earlier, in the days before the Parliament of Religions, he had been the guest of Dr. and Mrs. J. H. Wright. This time, he visited the summer home of Mrs. John Bagley, his Detroit hostess and ever-loyal friend, where he remained for over two weeks. During that time he made a three-day visit, at the invitation of a Mrs. Percy Smith, to another seaside resort town, named Magnolia, and there delivered a lecture. On Tuesday evening, September 4, he also gave a talk in the little village of Annisquam on "The Religion of India". At this meeting Dr. J. H. Wright, who was there at this time, introduced the Swami to the audience. But for the most part he rested, waiting for the autumn season when he would once again lecture in the cities; he sat for his portrait, painted by a friend; he went boating; and one evening he attended an evening clambake-picnic on the beach.

Around the 6th of September 1894, the Swami left Annisquam. The summer was now over, and a new season of lecturing was about to begin. Without delay, he plunged into work, going directly to Boston to fill three weeks of lecture engagements, both in the city and in outlying towns. Then, wanting, as he said, "a place where I can sit down and write down my thoughts", he accepted an invitation from Mrs. Bull to spend a few days in her Cambridge house at 166 Brattle Street, where she lived with her daughter, a companion, and, generally, many guests. Mrs. Bull, widow of the famous Norwegian violinist and nationalist, was a patron of arts and letters in her own right and was to become one of the Swami's most ardent supporters in America, and a friend on whom he could always count. Her house in Cambridge was to be in some respects a headquarters for him on the East Coast, even as the Hales's house in Chicago was his headquarters in the Midwest.

After a quiet stay from October 2 to 12 in Cambridge, the Swami travelled to Baltimore, Maryland. Here he was the guest of three energetic young ministers known as the Vrooman Brothers, who had invited him to speak at two of their meetings on "Dynamic Religion", on October 14 and 21. The Swami drew large crowds, particularly at the second meeting, when, scheduled as the main speaker, he delivered a talk on Buddhism to an audience that "filled the Lyceum Theatre from pit to dome". "Fully 3,000 persons were present", the *Baltimore Morning Herald* of October 22 reported, and went on to give a brief sketch of the Swami, which enables us to catch a fleeting glimpse of him as he appeared in 1894 to so many thousands of people in concert halls, lecture auditoriums, theatres, and churches throughout a large part of the United States:

The speakers of the evening were seated on the stage, the Rev. Vivekananda being an object of particular interest to all.

He wore a yellow turban and a red robe tied in at the waist with a sash of the same colour, which added to the Oriental cast of his features and invested him with a peculiar interest. His personality seemed to be the feature of the evening. His address was delivered in an easy, unembarrassed manner, his diction being perfect and his accent similar to that of a cultured member of the Latin race familiar with the English language.

From Baltimore, the Swami went to near-by Washington, where he was the guest of Colonel and Mrs. Enoch Totten, the latter, as he wrote to Mrs. Bull, "an influential lady here and a metaphysician". He delivered three lectures in Washington. The first two were given at the People's Church, both on Sunday, October 28—morning and afternoon. Being unplanned, the titles of these two Sunday lectures were unannounced; their subjects, however, were respectively "the common spiritual source of all religions" and "the Aryan race". On November 1 he spoke on "Reincarnation". The following day the Swami returned to Baltimore, where he spoke on "India and Its Religion" at the Harris Academy of Music Concert Hall. He donated the proceeds from this lecture to a proposed "International University", a project of the Vrooman brothers of Baltimore.

The Swami was scheduled to give a lecture in Baltimore on November 5, and one in Washington on November 6. But neither of these were delivered; for on November 4 he returned unexpectedly to New York.

The Swami had by now decided to remain for a while in the West, teaching those who came to him and establishing his work on a firm basis. His one fervent hope was to gain some disciples whose spiritual earnestness and sincerity would form a centre from which his gospel would be disseminated.

As we saw in the preceding chapter, he had for some time wanted to teach "a select, a very select—few", rather than lecture publicly to huge audiences. But the divine Will had been different. He had had to undertake months more of sowing his message broadcast to the American public before he could settle in one place to teach intensively. His desire, however, persisted. "I am going to lecture in New York in Autumn," he had written to Mrs. Hale from Boston on September 13, "but I like teaching small circles better, and there will be enough of that in Boston." Over a month later he was even more definite in respect of his future work. On October 27 he wrote to Alasinga, "I think I have worked enough, now I want rest and to teach a little to those that have come to me from my Gurudeva. . . . Here is a grand field. What have I to do with this 'ism' or that 'ism'? I am the servant of the Lord, and where on earth is there a better field than here for propagating all high ideas?" To present the ideals of the civilization and the religious consciousness of his own race to the peoples of the West, to enhance the spiritual vision of all with whom he came

33

into contact, to enlighten the Western mind with the knowledge of the Advaita Vedanta—these were the ideas which
possessed him. "The whole world requires Light", he had
written at the end of August to the same disciple: "It is expectant! India alone has that Light, not in magic mummeries,
and charlatanism, but in the teaching of the glories of the
spirit of real religion—of the highest spiritual truth. That is
why the Lord has preserved the race through all its vicissitudes
unto the present day. Now the time has come." The spiritual
side of his message was constantly in the foreground, and he
found that though India might be seriously in need of material
aid, the West stood infinitely more in need of spiritual assistance.
So he decided that he should give himself to the West as well as
to the East—that he should give himself, in fact, to the whole
world.

As we have seen before, the Swami returned to New York
from Baltimore on November 4, spent most of the month in
the city, and while there, organized the nucleus of a Vedanta
Society. Its purpose, aside from the immediate one of managing
the organizational and financial aspects of his work, was to
serve as a centre from which the knowledge of Vedanta would
flow outward and into which funds for the educational institutions he wished to start in India might be gathered.

If earlier he had sown the seeds of his message broadcast,
giving abundantly of his power and knowledge wherever he
went, he had done so for one purpose only—the spiritual
uplift of mankind. Now, with the same purpose, he wanted to
remain in one place, establishing a permanent centre, holding
classes, and giving intensive spiritual training to a few earnest
disciples so that his work would strike deep roots and continue
to grow even after he had gone. But of this intensive work we
shall speak later.

Before the Swami settled down in New York in the first part
of 1895 he again visited Cambridge, where Mrs. Bull had
arranged a series of classes for him, from December 5 to 27 of
1894. Speaking about the Swami and his activities of this

period, she wrote on December 27 to her friend Dr. Lewis G. Janes: "We had had him with us three weeks and he has given two lessons daily, and three formal talks. The lessons heard included the eight Upanishads, several renderings from the Gita and from Sankhya books of Realization. The interest awakened has been very unusual and the effect is to be deep and permanent with many. . . . Roman catholics, Sweden-borgians, agnostics, and Episcopalians all paid him the tribute of expressing their best thought; and he has helped students who were bewildered by their course of philosophy at Harvard. . . . We have had a Greenacre annex. Seven lectures with classes. . . . The Greenacre spirit prevailed. . . . Mr. Viveka-nanda as a guest and friend has endeared himself to all. He is so very human and so much of a boy with it all."

In addition to his classes, the Swami gave three formal talks at Mrs. Bull's house, one of which was on "The Ideals of Indian Women". This lecture, given at Mrs. Bull's special request, was deep, stirring and patriotic. It dwelt on the beauty of character and the ideals of Indian womanhood in general and the idea of Indian motherhood in particular. It was as well, though unconsciously, a reply to the remarks that many ignorant or self-interested persons had circulated concerning the "degraded" condition of Indian women. So much impressed was the gathering of Cambridge women with the Swami's address that in the time of the approaching Christmas they sent, unbeknown to the Swami himself, the following letter to his mother, in far-off India, together with a beautiful picture of the Child Jesus in the lap of the Virgin Mary:

To
The Mother of Swami Vivekananda,

Dear Madam,
    At this Christmas-tide, when the gift of Mary's son to the world is celebrated and rejoiced over with us, it would seem the time of remembrance. We, who have your son in our midst, send you greet-ings. His generous service to men, women, children in our midst was laid at your feet by him, in an address he gave us the other day on the

Ideals of Motherhood in India. The worship of his mother will be to all who heard him an inspiration and an uplift.

Accept, dear Madam, our grateful recognition of your life and work in and through your son. And may it be accepted by you as a slight token of remembrance to serve in its true inheritance from God, of Brotherhood and Unity.

Referring to this lecture on "The Ideals of Indian Women", Mrs. Bull has written:

Having given from the Vedas, from Sanskrit literature and the dramas these Ideals, and having cited the laws of today favourable to the women of India, he paid his filial homage to his own mother as having enabled him to do the best he had done, by her life of unselfish love and purity, that caused him by his very inheritance to choose the life of a monk.

It was conspicuous in the Swami that wherever he went he paid the highest tribute to his mother, whenever occasion arose. One of his friends, recalling the few happy weeks that he had spent with the Swami as fellow guest in the house of a common friend, writes:

He spoke often of his mother. I remember his saying that she had wonderful self-control, and that he had never known any woman who could fast so long. She had once gone without food, he said, for as many as fourteen days together. And it was not uncommon for his followers to hear such words upon his lips as: "It was my mother who inspired me to this. Her character was a constant inspiration to my life and work."

The Swami spent Christmas day at Mrs. Bull's home and on December 28 left for Brooklyn, where he had been invited by Dr. Lewis G. Janes, to give a series of lectures before the Brooklyn Ethical Association. When Dr. Janes, who was President of the Association, had met the Swami earlier in the year at Greenacre, he had been much struck by his unusual attainments as well as by his message. On his part, the Swami had deeply appreciated Dr. Janes's sincerity and nobility of character. Thenceforth he and Dr. Janes were fast friends. Later on, in 1896, Dr. Janes resigned from the presidentship of the Ethical

Association and became the Director of the Cambridge Conferences—an annual series of lectures for the comparative study of religion and philosophy that was sponsored by Mrs. Bull. Dr. Lewis Janes was also to become Director of the Monsalvat School of Comparative Religion at Greenacre, a development of the Greenacre Religious Conferences.

Another officer of the Brooklyn Ethical Association who was much interested in the Swami was Mr. Charles M. Higgins, owner of the then well-known Charles M. Higgins & Co., manufacturer of inks and adhesives. As early as July 19, 1894, the Swami had written to Mrs. Hale from Fishkill-on-the-Hudson, where he was visiting Dr. and Mrs. Guernsey, "Mr. Higgins, a rich young lawyer and inventor of Brooklyn is arranging some lectures for me. I have not settled whether I will stop [in America] for them or not." Now in November Mr. Higgins, who was a member of the Association's Committee on Comparative Religion, got out a ten-page pamphlet of American and Indian newspaper articles regarding the Swami and, perhaps by way of sponsoring his coming lectures at the Ethical Association, distributed it "among those interested in the study of Oriental Religions".

The Swami's first lecture before the Brooklyn Ethical Association ensured him immediate success. An overflowing and enthusiastic audience greeted him on that night—the last night but one of the year—to listen to his lecture "The Religions of India", "and as the Swami, in long robe and turban, expounded the ancient religion of his native land, the interest grew so deep that at the close of the evening there was an insistent demand for regular classes in Brooklyn."

On his appearance before the Brooklyn Ethical Association the *Brooklyn Standard Union* wrote on December 31:

It was a voice of the ancient Rishis of the Vedas, . . . that held spellbound every one of those many hundreds who had accepted the invitation of the Brooklyn Ethical Society and packed the large lecture hall and the adjoining rooms of the Pouch Gallery on Clinton Avenue to overflowing on the 30th December 1894. '

. . . Men of all professions and callings—doctors, and lawyers and judges and teachers—together with many ladies, had come from all parts of the city to listen to his strangely beautiful and eloquent defence of the Religion of India. . . .

And they were not disappointed. Swami (i.e. Master or Rabbi or Teacher) Vivekananda is even greater than his fame. . . . He was a splendid type of the famous sages of the Himalayas, a prophet of a new religion combining the morality of the Christians with philosophy of the Buddhists. . . .

The Swami acceded to the demand for regular classes in Brooklyn and agreed also to give a series of three public lectures on the "Religions and Social Customs of India". The lectures were at the Pouch Mansion, where the Ethical Association held its meetings. Their titles and dates were: "Ideals of Womanhood—Hindu, Mohammedan, and Christian", January 20, 1895; "Buddhism as Understood in India", February 3; and "The Vedas and Religion of the Hindus. What is Idolatry?", February 17. According to the announcement of this series, the lectures were given "for the joint benefit of the Swami Vivekananda's Educational Work, and the Publication Fund of the Ethical Association". The Swami gave a fourth lecture in Brooklyn in February of 1895. "The Brooklyn course ended yesterday [Sunday, February 17]", he wrote: "Another lecture I have there next Monday [February 25] . . . Mr. Higgins is full of joy. It was he who planned all this for me and he is so glad that everything succeeded so well."

As for the Swami's Brooklyn classes, little is known of them at the present time. On the afternoon of January 25 he held "an introductory lecture and conversation" entitled "The Upanishads, and Doctrine of the Soul" at the residence of Mrs. Charles Auel, 65 Lefferts Place. We know also that he held another "parlour lecture" in Brooklyn on January 29. But our present knowledge does not extend beyond this bare information.

It seems almost inevitable that the Swami should raise a storm of controversy wherever he lectured, for his ideas certainly did not run in established grooves; they were a force that met head-on the wall of orthodox opinion and misconception and broke through it. Almost everywhere he met with the sounds of collision. In Brooklyn it was the Ramabai Circle that vociferously protested against his portrayal of Indian life, customs, and ideals, particularly in connection with the treatment and condition of women. The followers of the Pandita Ramabai, a Christian convert, had been told by her that the sufferings of the young and childless Hindu widows were unspeakable, and this description they chose to believe. In an attempt to discredit the Swami's statements in regard to Indian women, the usual whispering campaign against him was employed. "I am astonished", he wrote to Mrs. Bull on March 21, "to hear the scandals the Ramabai circles are indulging in about me. Among others, one item is that Mrs. Bagley of Detroit had to dismiss a servant-girl on account of my bad character!!! Don't you see, Mrs. Bull, that however a man may conduct himself, there will always be persons who will invent the blackest lies about him? At Chicago I had such things [spread] every day against me. And these women are invariably the very Christian of Christians!"

Earlier in this chapter we have quoted at length one of Mrs. Bagley's eloquent letters (dated June 22, 1894) written in defence of the Swami. Let us here quote another, dated March 20, 1895, in which she writes to the same friend apropos of the slander spread by the Ramabai Circles:

Let my first word be that all this about Swami Vivekananda is an absolute falsehood from beginning to end. Nothing could be more false. We all enjoyed every day of the six weeks he spent with us. . . . He was invited by the different clubs of gentlemen in Detroit, and dinners were given him in beautiful homes so that greater number[s] might meet him and talk with him and hear him talk . . . and everywhere and at all times he was, as he deserved to be, honoured and respected. No one can know him without respecting his integrity and excellence of character and his strong religious nature. At Annisquam last summer I had a cottage and we wrote Vivekananda, who was in Boston, inviting him again to visit us there, which he did, remaining three weeks, not only conferring a favour upon us, but a great pleasure I am sure, to friends who had cottages near us. My servants, I have had many years and they are all still with me. Some of them went with us to Annisquam, the others were at home. You can see how wholly without foundation are all these stories. Who this woman in Detroit is, of whom you speak, I do not know. I only know this that every word of her story is as untrue and false as possible. . . . We all know Vivekananda. Who are they that speak so falsely?. . .

This dignified and powerful refutation of the scandals circulated against the Swami was supplemented by another letter written on the following day by Mrs. Bagley's daughter Helen. It read:

I am glad to know that the story was not circulated by R . . . . If I find it possible I wish to see Mrs. S . . . and ask her what her authority for such a statement was. I shall do it quietly of course, but I am going to find out for once, if possible, who starts these lies about Vivekananda. These things travel fast, and if once one is uprooted, perhaps these women will stop to think before they circulate a story so readily. If only they would investigate them they would find how false they all are. . . .

So vociferous was the antagonism of the Ramabai Circles against the Swami and, more important to him, against India, that on April 7, 1895, he delivered an additional lecture at the Pouch Mansion in Brooklyn, entitled "Some Customs of the Hindus: What They Mean and How They Are Misinterpreted". To make it quite clear that he had nothing against the aid and education of India's child-widows, as such, the Swami's lecture was given free, with a collection taken for the benefit of Babu Sasipada Banerjee's school for Hindu widows; but the lecture was as clearly a reply to the defamers of his country. During its course, he spoke strongly in defence of India and thundered fearlessly at the West's thoughtless and often malicious criticism of her religions and culture. At the close he cried: "It matters not as long as India is true to herself and to her religion. But a blow has been struck at her heart by this awful godless West when she sends hypocrisy and atheism into her midst. Instead of sending bushels of abuses, car-loads of vituperation and ship-loads of condemnations, let an endless stream of love go forth. Let us all be men!" Although the Swami did not directly retort to the women of the Ramabai Circle, this lecture seems to have effectively silenced them, for one finds no further protests from them in the Brooklyn press.

As we have seen, the Swami's scheduled lectures before the Brooklyn Ethical Association overlapped the start of his classes in New York and Brooklyn; nevertheless they marked the close of the period of his mission during which he had lectured far and wide, defending the religion and customs of India, giving the lie to the Christian critics of this country, and spreading the lofty ideals of Hinduism at its best.

On the New Year's day of 1895, he paid a surprise visit to the Hale family at Chicago. By the third week of January he came to stay for a time in New York, to hold an intensive course of classes, and, as he had long wanted, to train a few disciples. "I did a good deal of platform work in this country last year, and received plenty of applause," he wrote to a friend on April 24, 1895, "but found that I was only working for myself. It is the patient upbuilding of character, the intense struggle to *realize* the truth, which alone will tell in the future of humanity. So this year I am hoping to work along this line—training up to practical Advaita realization a small band of men and women. I do not know how far I shall suceed. The West is the field for work, if a man wants to benefit humanity, rather than his own particular sect or country." Thus early in 1895 began a new phase of Swami Vivekananda's mission in the West.

25

SETTING THE INDIAN WORK IN MOTION

The year 1894 was the most battle-torn of Swami Vivekananda's life in the West. But it was also one of the most creative
years of his mission in regard not only to his American work,
but to the work he was to start in India as well. The early phase
of his work in America has been described; but the way in
which he simultaneously set in motion his future work in India
through the power of his thoughts and words should here be
told, if a gap is not to be left in the story of his life.

This story is unfolded mainly in the letters the Swami wrote
to India from America in 1893–94. Probably no other of his
writings are so charged with apostolic fire as his letters; and of
all his letters, those written at this time to his Indian disciples,
friends and brother-disciples are particularly dynamic. Written
when he was besieged by powerful forces bent on destroying
him and his work, they reveal that his vision remained ever
crystal-clear regarding the mandate that his Master had given
him. Even in the battle at its thickest he never deviated from
the "Mother's work" that he had been commissioned by Shri
Ramakrishna to do and that he had started to do immediately
after the Master's passing away. Although it is not known
whether or not he consciously planned everything he said and
did, one can discover in these letters an evolving pattern of
prophetic leadership, which combined supreme idealism dedicated to the emancipation of mankind with the realistic approach of one who has to deal with the hard facts of the world.
That leadership was steeped in an oceanic love for Man.

The "Mother's work" consisted primarily and essentially in
the communication of spirituality. Once, speaking of Shri
Ramakrishna, the Swami said:

My Master taught me this lesson hundreds of times, yet I often
forget it. Few understand the power of thought. If a man goes into a

cave, shuts himself in, and thinks one really great thought and dies, that thought will penetrate the walls of that cave, vibrate through space, and at last permeate the whole human race. Such is the power of thought; be in no hurry therefore to give your thoughts to others. First have something to give. He alone teaches who has something to give, for teaching is not talking, teaching is not imparting doctrines, it is communicating. Spirituality can be communicated just as really as I can give you a flower. This is true in the most literal sense.

This "communication of spirituality" was the unshakeable aim of the Swami's mission from start to finish. It was not that he was unconversant with the new socio-economic thinking of his times; he was well up in such matters. But he also knew, in accord with ancient Indian wisdom, that whatever system was not built on spirituality—be it religious or social, political or economic—was not built on strong, enduring foundations. Moreover, even before his Master's passing away, he had already become spiritually illumined, knowing reality by direct experience and perceiving the purpose of human life in the light of that experience. It is only the illumined person, fully aware of the dimensions of man, who can understand human problems in right perspective; and Shri Ramakrishna had deliberately, one could say forcibly, turned the mind and heart of the Swami toward humanity, charging him to teach. This was the task laid on him by his guru, and as Shri Ramakrishna had set no limit to this task, it had ultimately to become a global one.

Even before the Master set before him this mission, young Naren had in his days of Sadhana (spiritual practices) at Dakshineswar manifested some predilection for it. After hearing from Shri Ramakrishna the words "not compassion to Jivas but service to them as Shiva", Naren had, in effect, declared, unprompted by anyone, that he had a world mission, namely, as he said, to "proclaim everywhere in the world this wonderful truth that I have heard today".

The mandate that Shri Ramakrishna directly gave his great disciple was along the same lines. A few days before his passing away, he wrote on a piece of paper: "Naren will teach others." Young Naren rebelled; yet in his heart did he not know that his Master could not be denied? That he had renounced the world keenly aware that a great mission awaited him, requiring total sacrifice, is borne out by a letter he wrote from America on January 29, 1894, to Haridas Viharidas Desai, Dewan of Junagadh. The latter, while in Calcutta, had gone to see the Swami's mother and his monastic brothers. The Dewan's report of this visit gave rise to a revelation of the workings of the Swami's mind and heart. He wrote in reply:

You had been to see my poor mother and brothers. I am glad you did. But you have touched the only soft place in my heart. You ought to know, Dewanji, that I am no hard-hearted brute. If there is any being I love in the whole world, it is my mother. Yet I believed and still believe that without my giving up the world, the great mission which Ramakrishna Paramahamsa, my great Master, came to preach would not see the light, and where would those young men be who have stood as bulwarks against the surging waves of materialism and luxury of the day? These have done a great amount of good to India, especially to Bengal, and this is only the beginning. With the Lord's help they will do things for which the whole world will bless them for ages. So, on the one hand, my vision of the future of Indian religion and that of the whole world, my love for the millions of beings sinking down and down for ages with nobody to help them, nay, nobody with even a thought for them; on the other hand, making those who are nearest and dearest to me miserable; I chose the former. "Lord will do the rest." He is with me, I am sure of that if of anything. So long as I am sincere, nothing can resist me, because He will be my help.

Although the Swami renounced the world with an over-powering sense of divine mission, it was to take years for him to be clear in his mind about, and carry into practice the full implications of his Master's command. During those years, in the days of his wandering, he did indeed enter caves and think great, world-moving thoughts; but it was not thus that his mission was to be fulfilled. As he himself said later on, every time he entered a cave, some force before long threw him out, back into the concourse of men—suffering men, seeking men. There was profound meaning in this. Shri Ramakrishna had fashioned him with infinite care so that he would remove the miseries of people and teach mankind, and Shri Ramakrishna was now seeing to it that the disciple did just that.

Moving through India from July 1890 onward the Swami was, just by his presence and the power of his thoughts and words, setting his work in motion. He was even then functioning in the role of a teacher of men and giver of light. His thought and efforts were never for himself, but always for the good of the many, for the happiness of the many. During his wanderings over India the Swami noticed that when a society became stagnant, all kinds of tyranny developed within it. This was the state of Hindu society at that time. Referring to the contemporary situation the Swami wrote to Pandit Sankarlal of Khetri on September 20, 1892:

And over and above all, we must cease to tyrannize. To what a ludicrous state are we brought! If a Bhangi comes to anybody as a Bhangi, he would be shunned as the plague; but no sooner does he get a cupful of water poured upon his head with some mutterings of prayers by a Padri [padre], and get a coat on his back, no matter how threadbare, and come into the room of the most orthodox Hindu—I don't see the man who then dare refuse him a chair and a hearty shake of hands! Irony can go no further. And come and see what they, the Padris, are doing here in the Dakshin [south]. They are converting the lower classes by lakhs; and in Travancore, the most priest-ridden country in India—where every bit of land is owned by the Brahmins . . . nearly one-fourth has become Christian! And I cannot blame them; what part have they in David and what in Jesse? When, when, O Lord, shall man be brother to man?

Even while he was on his way to America the Swami's mind was occupied as much with the regeneration of India as with what he would see or say in a foreign land. From Yokohama he wrote on July 10, 1893, to his Madras disciples and friends:

Come, be men! Come out of your narrow holes and have a look abroad. See how nations are on the march! Do you love man? Do you love your country? Then come, let us struggle for higher and better things; look not back, no, not even if you see the dearest and nearest cry. Look not back, but forward!

India wants the sacrifice of at least a thousand of her young men—men, mind, and not brutes. . . . How many men unselfish, thorough-going men, is Madras ready now to supply, to struggle unto life and death to bring about a new state of things—sympathy for the poor, and bread to their hungry mouths, enlightenment to the people at large—and struggle unto death to make men of them who have been brought to the level of beasts, by the tyranny of your forefathers?

In America, as in India, the urgency of raising his country's submerged millions was always in his mind. His visit to an American reformatory inspired him with nation-building ideas. He communicated some of these to his followers in Madras when, on August 20, 1893, he wrote to Alasinga from Breezy Meadows:

Yesterday Mrs. Johnson, the lady superintendent of the women's prison, was here. They don't call it prison but reformatory here. It is the grandest thing I have seen in America. How the inmates are benevolently treated, how they are reformed and sent back as useful members of society; how grand, how beautiful, you must see to believe! And, oh, how my heart ached to think of what we think of the poor, the low, in India. They have no chance, no escape, no way to climb up. The poor, the low, the sinner in India have no friends, no help—they cannot rise, try however they may. They sink lower and lower every day, they feel the blows showered upon them by a cruel society, and they do not know whence the blow comes. They have forgotten that they too are men. And the result is slavery. Thoughtful people within the last few years have seen it, but un-fortunately laid it at the door of the Hindu religion, and to them, the only way of bettering is by crushing this grandest religion of the world. Hear me, my friend, I have discovered the secret through the grace of the Lord. Religion is not in fault. On the other hand, your religion teaches you that every being is only your own self multiplied. But it was the want of practical application, the want of sympathy —the want of heart. The Lord once more came to you as Buddha and taught you how to feel, how to sympathize with the poor, the miserable, the sinner, but you heard Him not. Your priests invented the horrible story that the Lord was here for deluding demons with false doctrines! True indeed, but we are the demons, not those that believed. And just as the Jews denied the Lord Jesus and are since that day wander-ing over the world as homeless beggars, tyrannized over by everybody, so you are bond-slaves to any nation that thinks it worth while to rule over you. Ah, tyrants! you do not know that the obverse is tyranny, and the reverse slavery. The slave and the tyrant are synonymous.

The Swami envisaged a national regeneration in which all, particularly the downtrodden masses, would be given every opportunity and assistance to achieve all-round progress and well-being. When the Swami wrote in the letter just quoted that the Buddha came to teach us "how to feel, how to sympathize with the poor, the miserable, the sinner", was not the compassion and enlightenment of the Buddha once more finding its way into the national consciousness of India through his words? Was not the same Spirit that worked through the Buddha now working through the Swami? The ultimate goal towards which all were to move, according to both teachers, was spiritual salvation. By and large the world, accustomed to political uprisings devoid of all concepts of spiritual salvation, would take ages to learn the need of spiritual values in social and political movements; but India was, through the Swami, being shown that need. The leader-sage wrote in this same letter of August 20:

A hundred thousand men and women, fired with the zeal of holiness, fortified with eternal faith in the Lord, nerved to lion's courage by their sympathy for the poor and the fallen and the downtrodden, will go over the length and breadth of the land, preaching the gospel of salvation, the gospel of help, the gospel of social raising-up—the gospel of equality.

No religion on earth preaches the dignity of humanity in such a lofty strain as Hinduism, and no religion on earth treads upon the necks of the poor and the low in such a fashion as Hinduism. The Lord has shown me that religion is not in fault, but it is the Pharisees and Sadducees in Hinduism, hypocrites, who invent all sorts of engines of tyranny in the shape of doctrines of Paramarthika [absolute] and Vyavaharika [relative].

When the Swami emphatically wrote "*The Lord has shown me* . . ." he meant what he said. It was the Lord-shown way he was treading and Lord-given words he was speaking. He was ever aware that the Lord stood directly behind his movements. In this letter of August 20, when he had yet to find his bearings in America, he wrote:

A hundred times I had a mind to go out of the country and go back to India. But I am determined, and I have a call from Above; I see no way, but His eyes see. And I must stick to my guns, life or death. . . . Despair not; remember the Lord says in the Gita, "To work you have the right, but not to the result." Gird up your loins, my boy. I am called by the Lord for this.

Across continents and oceans the Swami's mind was always awake at the sick-bed of his Motherland. "There are some", he wrote, "who see, feel, and shed tears of blood in their hearts, who think that there is a remedy . . . and who are ready to apply this remedy at any cost, even to the giving up of life." He who penned these words was himself ready to give up his life without question for the cause. That was why his letters were to those who read and re-read them a galvanizing force. Who could withstand their appeal and charge? Who would not be quickened to the depths of his being, if he had any manhood left in him? And who, among those who had, would not answer the Swami's call to action? To do so was to move forward in spirituality; for purity, sincerity, and selfless love were what his call demanded. They were to work as the instruments of God. In a letter to Alasinga, dated November 2, 1893, he wrote:

Day by day I am feeling that the Lord is with me, and I am trying to follow His direction. His will be done. . . . We will do great things for the world, and that for the sake of doing good and not for name and fame.

"Ours not to reason why, ours but to do and die." Be of good cheer and believe that we are selected by the Lord to do great things, and we will do them. Hold yourself in readiness, i.e., be pure and holy, and love for love's sake. Love the poor, the miserable, the down-trodden, and the Lord will bless you.

And in his earlier letter of August 20, 1893, from Breezy Meadows, the Swami had also told them what was required of them:

Trust not to the so-called rich, they are more dead than alive. The hope lies in you—in the meek, the lowly, but the faithful. Have faith in the Lord; no policy, it is nothing. Feel for the miserable and look up for help—it *shall come*. I have travelled twelve years with this load in my heart and this idea in my head. I have gone from door to door of the so-called rich and great. With a bleeding heart I have crossed half the world to this strange land, seeking for help. The Lord is great. I know He will help me. I may perish of cold or hunger in this land, but I bequeath to you, young men, this sympathy, this struggle for the poor, the ignorant, the oppressed. . . . Vow, then, to devote your whole lives to the cause of the redemption of these three hundred millions, going down and down every day.

Swami Vivekananda, in setting his Indian work in motion, was intent to see that it would not stop until the goal was reached. He did not make his appeal sweet. His demand was total because nothing less would suffice for the task of India's regeneration. In the same letter he continued:

It is not the work of a day, and the path is full of the most deadly thorns. But Parthasarathi [Shri Krishna] is ready to be our Sarathi [charioteer]—we know that. And in His name and with eternal faith in Him, set fire to the mountain of misery that has been heaped upon India for ages—and it shall be burned down. Come then, look it in the face, brethren, it is a grand task, and we are so low. But we are the sons of Light and children of God. Glory unto the Lord, we will succeed. Hundreds will fall in the struggle, hundreds will be ready to take it up. I may die here unsuccessful, another will take up the task. You know the disease, you know the remedy, only have faith. Do not look up to the so-called rich and great; do not care for the heartless intellectual writers, and their cold-blooded newspaper articles. Faith, sympathy—fiery faith and fiery sympathy! Life is nothing, death is nothing, hunger nothing, cold nothing. Glory unto the Lord—march on, the Lord is our General. Do not look back to see who falls— forward—onward! Thus and thus we shall go on, brethren. One falls, and another takes up the work.

This was the call and message that suited India's history and destiny. How thoroughly the Swami had steeped himself in the spirit of India to be sending forth these thoughts and words!

They touched responsive chords in the Indian heart and set the nation growing and achieving.

The Swami's letter to Alasinga of November 2, 1893, was the first known letter to his countrymen in which he reported his success at the Parliament of Religions. He told of the tribute paid him by the American people, but soon turned to the theme of his heart—the uplift of India:

The Hindu must not give up his religion, but must keep religion within its proper limits and give freedom to society to grow. All the reformers in India made the serious mistake of holding religion accountable for all the horrors of priestcraft and degeneration, and went forthwith to pull down the indestructible structure, and what was the result? Failure! Beginning from Buddha down to Ram Mohan Roy, everyone made the mistake of holding caste to be a religious institution and tried to pull down religion and caste all together, and failed. But in spite of all the ravings of the priests, caste is simply a crystallized social institution, which after doing its service is now filling the atmosphere of India with its stench, and it can only be removed by giving back to the people their lost social individuality. Every man born here knows that he is a *man*. Every man born in India knows that he is a slave of society. Now, freedom is the only condition of growth; take that off, the result is degeneration. With the introduction of modern competition, see how caste is disappearing fast! No religion is now necessary to kill it. The Brahmana shopkeeper, shoemaker, and wine-distiller are common in Northern India. And why? Because of competition. No man is prohibited from doing anything he pleases for his livelihood under the present Government, and the result is neck and neck competition, and thus thousands are seeking and finding the highest level they were born for, instead of vegetating at the bottom.

Among the Swami's ideas for the regeneration of India, those that chiefly found expression through these letters to his Indian followers were: (1) the need to raise the masses, giving them opportunities for all-round development "without injuring their religion"; (2) the need to remove untouchability; (3) the need for the well-to-do to assist the suffering millions; (4) the need to give women opportunities for proper education and self-improvement; (5) the need for the universal spread of the right kind of education; (6) the need to cultivate the material sciences; (7) the need for technological and industrial development; and, above all, (8) the need to give freedom to society for its onward movement. On these themes he did not write a thesis; he simply spoke from the depth of his at-one-ment with the suffering millions as occasion required. For example, on India's need to better the condition of her women, he wrote on December 28, 1893:

Do you know who is the real "Shakti-worshipper"? It is he who knows that God is the omnipresent force in the universe and sees in women the manifestation of that Force. Many men here [in America] look upon their women in this light. Manu, again, has said that gods bless those families where women are happy and well treated. Here men treat their women as well as can be desired, and hence they are so prosperous, so learned, so free, and so energetic. But why is it that we are slavish, miserable, and dead? The answer is obvious.

And how pure and chaste are they here! Few women are married before twenty or twenty-five, and they are as free as the birds in the air. They go to market, school and college, earn money, and do all kinds of work. Those who are well-to-do devote themselves to doing good to the poor. And what are we doing? We are very regular in marrying our girls at eleven years of age lest they should become corrupt and immoral. What does our Manu enjoin? "Daughters should be supported and educated with as much care and attention as the sons." As sons should be married after observing Brahmacharya up to the thirtieth year, so daughters also must observe Brahmacharya and be educated by their parents. But what are we actually doing? Can you better the condition of your women? Then there will be hope for your well-being. Otherwise you will remain as backward as you are now.

The main idea, on which pivoted all his other ideas, was the need for freedom of thought and action thoughout Indian society. This basic need he expounded with special clarity in a letter to his disciples in Madras, dated January 24, 1894:

My idea is to bring to the door of the meanest, the poorest, the noble ideas that the human race has developed both in and out of India, and let them think for themselves. Whether there should be caste or not, whether women should be perfectly free or not, does not concern me. "Liberty of thought and action is the only condition of life, of growth and well-being." Where it does not exist, the man, the race, the nation must go down.

Caste or no caste, creed or no creed, any man, or class, or caste, or nation, or institution which bars the power of free thought and action of an individual—even so long as that power does not injure others—is devilish and must go down.

These words of awakening that the Swami spoke to the soul of his nation from afar were to roll through its consciousness as a healing and strengthening power, working from within outward. He continued:

My whole ambition in life is to set in motion a machinery which will bring noble ideas to the door of everybody, and then let men and women settle their own fate. Let them know what our forefathers as well as other nations have thought on the most momentous questions of life. Let them see specially what others are doing now, and then decide. We are to put the chemicals together, the crystallization will be done by nature according to her laws. Work hard, be steady, and have faith in the Lord. Set to work, I am coming sooner or later. Keep the motto before you—"Elevation of the masses without injuring their religion."

Among those whose thoughts have changed the course of history, few perhaps understood the need to improve the lot of people *without injury* to their religious faith. Among modern Indian thinkers, it was Swami Vivekananda who first gave the highest priority to the elevation of the masses through means that would not disturb their inherent spiritual culture. It was he who saw that regeneration of the nation would be otherwise impossible: only a basic, religion-oriented restoration of the downtrodden would do. In the same letter he went on:

Remember that the nation lives in the cottage. But, alas! nobody ever did anything for them. Our modern reformers are very busy about widow remarriage. Of course, I am a sympathizer in every reform, but the fate of a nation does not depend upon the number of husbands the widows get, but upon the *condition of the masses*. Can you raise them? Can you give them back their lost individuality without making them lose their innate spiritual nature? Can you become an occidental of occidentals in your spirit of equality, freedom, work, and energy, and at the same time a Hindu to the very backbone in religious culture and instincts? This is to be done and *we will do it*. You are all *born to do it*. Have faith in yourselves, great convictions are the mothers of great deeds. Onward for ever! Sympathy for the poor, the downtrodden, even unto death—this is our motto.

If the Swami was planning a revolution, it was to be a God-centred revolution in which everyone was to share in the benefits. He did not say just how human society was to be organized. He wanted for every individual a man-making education and freedom of thought and action, so that all might grow and achieve well-being. Provided that people on all levels of society had these opportunities, it did not matter much what shape the socio-political and economic systems took. Institutions—social, political, and economic—were for human beings, not human beings for institutions. Though, in the India of his time, his revolutionary ideas were unsettling to the privileged, they were acceptable to the people at large, and this because he taught like a prophet, with authority. God was always central in his thought and so he spoke in the language of all, from the highest to lowest. He advocated such methods as would be for the good of everyone who adopted them. If some sections of Indian society failed at the time to comprehend the broad, beneficent sweep of his vision, he did not care. In his letter of January 29, 1894, to Haridas Viharidas Desai the Swami wrote:

Many and many in India could not understand me; and how could they, poor men? Their thoughts never strayed beyond the everyday routine business of eating and drinking. I know only a few noble souls like yourself appreciate me. Lord bless your noble self. But appreciation or no appreciation, I am born to organize these young men; nay, hundreds more in every city are ready to join me; and I want to send them rolling like irresistible waves over India, bringing comfort, morality, religion, education to the doors of the meanest and the most downtrodden. And this I will do or die.

In his teachings the Swami anticipated the socio-economic revolutions of the future and suggested measures by which their violence and bloodshed would be avoided. "Three things", he wrote in the same letter, "are necessary to make every man great, every nation great: (1) Conviction of the powers of goodness. (2) Absence of jealousy and suspicion. (3) Helping all who are trying to be and do good."

Fully conversant with the disheartening realities of the Indian situation though the Swami was, his sturdy and reasoned faith in the destiny of the nation never wavered. In the sweep of the gaze that he cast across the oceans from Chicago, India stood, in prospect, resplendent and unshackled. Thus he continues:

Three men cannot act in concert together in India for five minutes. Each one struggles for power, and in the long run the whole organization comes to grief. Lord! Lord! When will we learn not to be jealous! In such a nation, and especially in Bengal, to create a band of men who are tied and bound together with a most undying love in spite of difference, is it not wonderful? This band will increase. This idea of wonderful liberality joined with eternal energy and progress must spread over India. It must electrify the whole nation and must enter the very pores of society in spite of the horrible ignorance, spite, caste-feeling, old boobyism, and jealousy which are the heritage of this nation of slaves.

The Swami's call to action, his marching-orders addressed through certain individuals to the nation, reached India through his letters. And the wonder of it was that these nation-building letters were written in the midst of his hectic lecture tours and drawn-out battle in America. The West was in need of the precious and potent message of Vedanta, and the Swami was giving it; but to do so he was "having to fight every inch of the ground with orthodox inimical Christians". At the same time he was preparing the Indian mind, so long sterile, to receive the seeds of his reawakening message.

II

It was not only to his disciples and friends that the Swami wrote from America. He poured even more energy and fire into the letters written to his brother-disciples at the Baranagore

Math. It was they—the monastic brotherhood of Shri Ramakrishna—who were to form the heart of his Indian work and, of
course, of his world mission as a whole. To them he looked for
total co-operation. To them he expressed his anguish of heart
and his hopes for his country, and to them he wrote in detail
about methods of work, of organization, and about the place
of Shri Ramakrishna and his Order in the future of India. All
of this came upon the monks at Baranagore as a surprise, for
their Naren had not before spoken to them in any detail—if at
all—of these dreams and plans. Certainly, he had not spoken
of these things with such practical seriousness, nor had he
spoken as a leader intent on giving a new shape, a new purpose,
and a new meaning to Indian monasticism.

As readers will recall, he had left the Baranagore Math in
the middle of 1890 to wander through India. Even before
leaving the monastery, he had made it clear to his brothers that
he wanted to be alone. Although in the first phase of his wandering Swami Akhandananda had accompanied him, after a few
months the Swami had insisted on travelling alone. Occasionally, by chance, he had met one or another of his brother-
disciples in the expanses of northern and western India. From
February 1891 onwards he was rarely in touch with them.
Mostly by himself, he roamed over his own country as the
inner spirit guided him, learning, teaching, practising austerities, and witnessing at first-hand the heart-rending condition of
the Indian people. Thus even while he was still in India, his
brother-disciples were so much out of touch with him that they
did not quite know how his mind was working and at what he
was aiming. Nor was the Swami's uncommunicativeness acci-
dental: for had he not written to Swami Saradananda on
July 15, 1890, "I have my own plans for the future, and they
shall be a secret"?

Then again, it was not his brother-disciples who were the
first to hear from him after the news of his success at the Parliament of Religions had burst over India. Rather, as we have
seen above, it was his disciples in Madras to whom he wrote
during his early months in America. The Chicago Parliament

was over on September 27, 1893; his first letter to the monks at Baranagore Math, addressed to Swami Ramakrishnananda, was written not earlier than January of 1894. After this, however, the flow of his letters to his brother-disciples continued until he returned to India in January 1897.

That steady current of written words was a spontaneous welling forth of the Swami's mind, heart, and soul. It brought before the brothers their beloved Naren, but now grown incredibly beyond the greatness of his that was familiar to them. Writing in Bengali, he poured out—now with great depth of feeling, now in prophetic vein, now in powerful exhortation, now with merry humour—a message that was awe-inspiring and soul-stirring. It naturally took them time to understand him rightly.

Even as, in the preceding six months or so, he had been infusing into the hearts of his Madras disciples his own compassion, and awakening in their minds his own keen awareness of the inhumanity of India's prevailing social system, in the same way he now set to work on his brother-disciples. But to them he at once sketched out a remedy in the application of which they were to be the primary instruments. In his first letter to the Baranagore Math from America he told of his vision and his plan. It was his brothers' first inkling of how he intended to carry out the mission laid on him by their Master:

A country where millions of people live on flowers of the Mohua plant, a million or two of sadhus and a hundred million or so of Brahmins suck the blood out of these poor people, without even the least effort for their amelioration—is that a country or hell? Is that a religion, or the devil's dance?. . .

My brother, in view of all this, specially of the poverty and ignorance, I had no sleep. At Cape Comorin sitting in Mother Kumari's temple, sitting on the last bit of Indian rock—I hit upon a plan: We are so many sannyasins wandering about, and teaching the people metaphysics—it is all madness. Did not our Gurudeva [Divine Master] use to say, "An empty stomach is no good for religion"? That those poor people are leading the life of brutes is simply due to ignorance. We have for all ages been sucking their blood and trampling them underfoot.

... Suppose some disinterested sannyasins, bent on doing good to others, go from village to village, disseminating education and seeking in various ways to better the condition of all down to the Chandala, through oral teaching, and by means of maps, cameras, globes, and such other accessories—can't that bring forth good in time? All these plans I cannot write out in this short letter. The long and the short of it is—if the mountain does not come to Mohammed, Mohammed must go to the mountain. The poor are too poor to come to schools and Pathashalas, and they will gain nothing by reading poetry and all that sort of thing. We, as a nation, have lost our individuality, and that is the cause of all mischief in India. We have to give back to the nation its lost individuality and *raise the masses*. The Hindu, the Mohammedan, the Christian, all have trampled them underfoot. Again the force to raise them must come from inside, that is, from the orthodox Hindus. In every country the evils exist not with, but against, religion. Religion therefore is not to blame, but men.

To effect this, the first thing we need is men, and the next is funds. Through the grace of our Guru I was sure to get from ten to fifteen men in every town. I next travelled in search of funds, but do you think the people of India were going to spend money!... Selfishness personified—are they to spend anything? Therefore I have come to America, to earn money myself, and then return to my country and devote the rest of my days to the realization of this one aim of my life.

As our country is poor in social virtues, so this country is lacking in spirituality. I give them spirituality, and they give me money. I do not know how long I shall take to realize my end.... These people are not hypocrites, and jealousy is altogether absent in them. I depend on no one in Hindusthan. I shall try to earn the wherewithal myself to the best of my might and carry out my plans, or die in the attempt. "... When death is certain, it is best to sacrifice oneself for a good cause."

You may perhaps think what Utopian nonsense all this is! You little know what is in me. If any of you help me in my plans, all right, or Gurudeva will show me the way out....

In the summer of 1894 the Swami again wrote to his brother-disciples, now at the Alambazar Math, in regard to the immediate putting into effect of his plan:

I am giving you a new idea. If you can work it out, then I shall know you are men and will be of service.... Make an organized plan.

A few cameras, some maps, globes, and some chemicals, etc., are needed. The next thing you want is a big hut. Then you must get together a number of poor, indigent folk. Having done all this, show them pictures to teach them astronomy, geography, etc., and preach Shri Ramakrishna to them. Try to have their eyes opened as to what has taken place or is taking place in different countries, what this world is like, and so forth. You have got lots of poor and ignorant folk there. Go to their cottages, from door to door, in the evening, at noon, any time—and open their eyes. Books etc., won't do—give them oral teaching. Then slowly extend your centres. Can you do all this? Or only bell-ringing?. . .

Come! Apply yourselves heart and soul to it. The day of gossip and ceremonials is gone, my boy, *you must work now.*

. . . We must electrify society, electrify the world. Idle gossip and barren ceremonials won't do. Ceremonials are meant for house-holders, your work is the distribution and propagation of thought-currents. If you can do that, then it is all right. . . .

. . . He alone is a child of Shri Ramakrishna who is moved to pity for all creatures and exerts himself for them even at the risk of incur-ring personal damnation—"Others are vulgar people". Whoever, at this great spiritual juncture, will stand up with a courageous heart and go on spreading from door to door, from village to village, his message, is alone my brother, and a son of his. This is the test, he who is Ramakrishna's child does not seek his personal good.

In his letters to the brother-disciples one recurring command was: Go from village to village, go from door to door of the poor! Awaken them, teach them, serve them, help them to grow and to solve the problems of their lives. In a letter written in 1894 (probably in March or April) to Swami Akhandananda, the Swami reiterates this theme, combining it with his revolutionary ideas of monastic life:

Go from door to door amongst the poor and lower classes of the town of Khetri and teach them religion. Also, let them have oral lessons on geography and such other subjects. No good will come of sitting idle and having princely dishes, and saying "Ramakrishna, O Lord!"—unless you can do some good to the poor. Go to other villages from time to time, and teach the people the arts of life as well as religion. Work, worship, and Jnana [knowledge]—first work, and your mind will be purified; otherwise everything will be fruitless like pouring oblations on a pile of ashes instead of in the sacred fire. When Gunanidhi comes, move from door to door of the poor and the destitute in every village of Rajputana. If people object to the kind of food you take, give it up immediately. It is preferable to live on grass for the sake of doing good to others. The Gerua robe is not for enjoyment. It is the banner of heroic work. You must give your body, mind and speech to "the welfare of the world". You have read, "Look upon your mother as God, look upon your father as God"—but I say, "The poor, the illiterate, the ignorant, the afflicted—let these be your God." Know that service to these alone is the highest religion.

These unconventional ideas of Hindu monasticism and its purpose flowed from the Swami's pen with bewildering force. They would perhaps have been unacceptable to his brother-disciples, whose lives were tending to become cast in the traditional monastic mould—the practice of austerities and devotions, with no concern for the world—, had it not been that these same letters flamed with proof of their great brother's fathomless devotion and loyalty to Shri Ramakrishna. They could not dismiss his startling ideas as merely the effects of occidental influence on his mind; for they, themselves advanced in spirituality, could read between the lines that Naren's devotion to his Master was without compare, and that the Master's teachings were the unalloyed source of his inspiration.

Moreover, they had not forgotten what Shri Ramakrishna had repeatedly prophesied about Naren's future work and achievements; nor had they forgotten that Naren had been chosen leader of the brotherhood by the Master himself. Though some of the brother-disciples were not fully convinced of the rightness and efficacy of his ideas until he himself cleared their doubts on his return to India in 1897, they by and large believed that he was working as an instrument in the Lord's hands. His letters to them were replete with evidence of his own conviction in this respect, and his convictions were, they knew, characteristically rational and objective in nature. In his letters, such passages as the following could not but carry conviction into the hearts of the brothers who read them:

. . . The priests tried their utmost to snub me. But the Guru is with me, what could anybody do? And the whole American nation loves and respects me, pays my expenses, and reveres me as a Guru. . . . It was not in the power of your priests to do anything against me.

To work, with undaunted energy! What fear! Who is powerful enough to thwart you! "We shall crush the stars to atoms, and unhinge the universe. Don't you know who we are? We are the servants of Shri Ramakrishna." Fear?. . . "It is those foolish people who identify themselves with their bodies, that piteously cry, 'We are weak, we are weak, we are low.' All this is atheism. Now that we have attained the state beyond fear, we shall have no more fear and become heroes. This indeed is the theism which we, the servants of Shri Ramakrishna, will choose.

"Giving up the attachment for the world and drinking constantly the supreme nectar of immortality, for ever discarding that self-seeking spirit which is the mother of all dissension, and ever meditating on the blessed feet of our Guru which are the embodiment of all well-being, with repeated salutations we invite the whole world to participate in drinking the nectar.

"That nectar which has been obtained by churning the infinite ocean of the Vedas, into which Brahma, Vishnu, Shiva, and the other gods have poured their strength, which is charged with the life-essence of the Avataras—Gods incarnate on earth—Shri Ramakrishna holds that nectar in his person, in its fullest measure!" [September 25, 1894]

I am very sorry to hear of Mazoomdar's doings. One always behaves thus in trying to push oneself before all others. I am not much to blame. Mazoomdar came here ten years ago, and got much reputation and honour; now I am in flying colours. Such is the will of the Guru, what shall I do?. . . It is the will of the Lord that people of this land have their power of introspection roused, and does it lie in anybody to check His progress? I want no name—I want to be a voice without a form. I do not require anybody to defend me—who am I to check or to help the course of His march? And who are others also?. . . I am an instrument and He is the operator. Through this instrument He is rousing the religious instinct in thousands of hearts in this far-off country. Thousands of men and women here love and revere me. . . . "He makes the dumb eloquent and makes the lame cross mountains." . . . I am a voice without a form. . . .

A movement which half a dozen penniless boys set on foot and which now bids fair to progress in such an accelerated motion—is it a humbug or the Lord's will? [(Beginning of?) 1894]

We have just noticed the Swami calling the work of himself and his brothers a "movement". That he regarded this movement as dedicated to the service of Shri Ramakrishna, and that he held up Ramakrishna before his brother-servants as a divine manifestation, incarnate for the good of all mankind, were in no way incompatible with his unflinching adherence to Advaita as the movement's philosophy, inspiration, and fulfilment. It was, indeed, Shri Ramakrishna himself who had taught him to experience the ultimate truth of Advaita while being at the same time a lover of God. Further, although the Swami insisted on devotion to the guru as the movement's source of spiritual power, he was anxious that its members should not fall into sectarian narrowness, which was directly opposed to the purpose for which the Master came. He therefore wanted a broad Advaitic catholicity to permeate their understanding and preaching of Shri Ramakrishna. Early in 1894 he wrote to his brother-disciples:

I tell you brother, let everything go on as it is, only take care that no form becomes necessary—unity in variety—see that universality be not hampered in the least. Everything must be sacrificed, if necessary, for that one sentiment, *universality*. Whether I live or die, whether I go back to India or not, remember this specially, that universality—perfect acceptance, not tolerance only—we preach and perform. Take care how you trample on the least rights of others. Many a huge ship has foundered in that whirlpool. Remember, perfect devotion minus its bigotry—this is what we have got to show. Through His grace everything will go all right.

And in the summer of the same year:

Great sages come with special messages for the world, and not for name; but their followers throw their teachings overboard and fight over their names—this is verily the history of the world. I do not take into any consideration whether people accept his [Shri Ramakrishna's] name or not, but I am ready to lay down my life to help his teachings, his life, and his message spread all over the world.

And a little later, on September 25:

We must mix with all, and alienate none. All the powers of good against all the powers of evil—this is what we want. Do not insist upon everybody's believing in our Guru. . . . Wherever you go, you must start a permanent preaching centre. Then only will people begin to change. . . . Always remember that Shri Ramakrishna came for the good of the world—not for name or fame. *Spread only what he came to teach. Never mind his name—it will spread of itself.* Directly you insist on everybody's accepting your Guru, you will be creating a sect, and everything will fall to the ground—so beware! Have a kind word for all—it spoils work to show temper. Let people say whatever they like, stick to your own convictions, and rest assured, the world will be at your feet. They say, "Have faith in this fellow or that fellow", but I say, "Have faith in yourself first", that's the way.

Though the Swami instructed his brother-disciples not to insist on everyone's accepting Shri Ramakrishna, and though his own mission, as he saw it, was to spread "his [Shri Ramakrishna's] teachings, his life, and his message"—not his name —all over the world, he was, as we know, by no means unmindful of the Master's identity. In the winter of 1894 he wrote to Swami Shivananda:

My dear brother, that Ramakrishna Paramahamsa was God incarnate, I have not the least doubt; but then you must let people find out for themselves what he used to teach—you cannot thrust these things upon them—this is my only objection.

Let people speak out their own opinions, why should we object? Without studying Ramakrishna Paramahamsa first, one can never understand the real import of the Vedas, the Vedanta, of the *Bhagavata* and the other Puranas. His life is a searchlight of infinite power thrown upon the whole mass of Indian religious thought. He was the living commentary to the Vedas and to their aim. He had lived in one life the whole cycle of the national religious existence in India.

Whether Bhagavan Shri Krishna was born at all we are not sure; and Avataras like Buddha and Chaitanya are monotonous; Ramakrishna Paramahamsa is the latest and the most perfect—the concentrated embodiment of knowledge, love, renunciation, catholicity, and the desire to serve mankind. So where is anyone to compare with him? He must have been born in vain who cannot appreciate him! My supreme good fortune is that I am his servant through life after life. A single word of his is to me far weightier than the Vedas and the Vedanta. . . . Oh, I am the servant of the servants of his servants. But narrow bigotry militates against his principles, and this makes me cross. Rather let his name be drowned in oblivion, and his teachings bear fruit instead! Why, was he a slave to fame? Certain fishermen and illiterate people called Jesus Christ a God, but the literate people killed him. Buddha was honoured in his lifetime by a number of merchants and cowherds. But Ramakrishna has been worshipped in his lifetime—towards the end of this nineteenth century—by the demons and giants of the university as God incarnate. . . . Only a few things have been jotted down in the books about them (Krishna, Buddha, Christ, etc.). "One must be a wonderful housekeeper with whom we have never yet lived!" so the Bengali proverb goes. But here is a man in whose company we have been day and night and yet consider him to be a far greater personality than any of them. Can you understand this phenomenon?

Whether or not the reader agrees with the Swami's estimate of his Master *vis-à-vis* other world teachers, we have here his uninhibited view of Shri Ramakrishna, expressed in the candid language of his heart and sanctioned by his thoroughly rational intellect. It was indeed Swami Vivekananda who revealed even to his brother-disciples the true proportions of Shri Rama-krishna's greatness; but at the same time he repeatedly and emphatically warned them against sliding into the narrow groove of sectarianism and barren ritualism.

The Swami's concept of worship had little to do with cere-monial piety, but was directed towards the spiritual transfor-mation of the worshipper. It harmonized with the new spirit of monasticism that he was inculcating in his brother-disciples—a monasticism in which the service of man "knowing him as the manifestation of God" was a potent form of spiritual discipline, as meditation and other devotional practices also were. He was fully aware of the important role this new monasticism was to play in the regeneration of India. In fact his "plan" hinged upon it. In his letters, therefore, he wrote of the reorientation of the age-old institution of monasticism that would be needed. He wanted the followers of Shri Ramakrishna to cultivate a new kind of spirituality, at once vigorous and transcendental. To his brother-disciples he wrote in a letter dated 1894:

You have renounced everything. Come! Now is the turn for you to banish the desire for peace, and that for Mukti [liberation] too! Don't worry in the least; heaven or hell, or Bhakti [devotion] or Mukti—don't care for anything, but go, my boy, and spread the name of the Lord from door to door! It is only by doing good to others that one attains to one's own good, and it is by leading others to Bhakti and Mukti that one attains them oneself. Take that up, forget your own self for it, be mad over the idea. As Shri Ramakrishna used to love you, as I love you, come, love the world like that. Bring all together. . . . Remember these few points:

1. We are sannyasins, who have given up everything—Bhakti, and Mukti, and enjoyment, and all.

2. To do the highest good to the world, everyone down to the lowest—this is our vow. Welcome Mukti or hell, whichever comes of it.

3. Ramakrishna Paramahamsa came for the good of the world. Call him a man, or God, or an incarnation, just as you please. Accept him each in your own light.

4. He who will bow before him will be converted into purest gold that very moment. Go with this message from door to door, if you can, my boy, and all your disquietude will be at an end. Never fear— where's the room for fear?—Caring for nothing whatsoever is a part of your life. You have so long spread his name and your character all around, well and good. Now spread them in an organized way. The Lord is with you. Take heart!

Whether I live or die, whether I go back to India or not, you go on spreading love, love that knows no bounds. . . . "When death is so certain, it is better to die for a good cause."

In his Western work, at least in its initial stages, the Swami did not stress the organizational aspect of it, the emphasis characterizing the work and the circumstances attending it being what they were. But he was convinced that for the Indian work a strong organizational structure based on spiritual values was important. The Hindu monasticism that he envisioned was to be *organized*, and this organization was to be founded on utter selflessness and such other spiritual virtues as conduce simultaneously to "the liberation of the spirit and the good of the world". He wanted this organization, moreover, to spread widely. In his letters of 1894 to his brother-disciples, he emphasizes again and again the need to imbue the educated youth of the country with the ideal of monasticism. In September 1894 he writes:

We must work among the English educated young men. "Through renunciation alone some (rare ones) attained immortality." Renunciation!—Renunciation!—you must preach this above everything else. There will be no spiritual strength unless one renounces the world.

And in the summer of 1894:

What is wanted is a power of organization—do you understand me? ... Brother Tarak, Sharat, and Hari [Swamis Shivananda, Saradananda and Turiyananda] will be able to do it. —has got very little originality, but is a very good workman and persevering—which is an essential necessity, and Shashi has great executive ability.... We want some disciples—fiery young men—do you see?—intelligent and brave, who dare to go to the jaws of Death, and are ready to swim the ocean across. Do you follow me? We want hundreds like that, both men and women. Try your utmost for that end alone. Make converts right and left, and put them into our purity-drilling machine. ...

Let character be formed and then I shall be in your midst. Do you see? We want two thousand sannyasins, nay ten, or even twenty thousand—men and women, both. What are our matrons doing? We want converts at any risk. Go and tell them, and try yourselves, heart and soul. Not householder disciples, mind you, we want sannyasins. Let each one of you have a hundred heads tonsured—young educated men, not fools. Then you are heroes. We must make a sensation. Give up your passive attitude, gird your loins, and stand up. Let me see you make some electric circuits between Calcutta and Madras. Start centres at places, go on always making converts. Convert everyone into the monastic order, whoever seeks for it, irrespective of sex, and then I shall be in your midst. A huge spiritual tidal wave is coming —he who is low shall become noble, and he who is ignorant shall become the teacher of great scholars—through HIS grace.

And a little earlier he had written to his brother-disciples:

35

Remember my previous letter—we want both men and women. There is no distinction of sex in the soul. It won't do merely to call Shri Ramakrishna an Incarnation, you must manifest power. Where are Gour-Ma, Yogin-Ma, and Golap-Ma? Tell them to spread these ideas. We want thousands of men and thousands of women who will spread like wild fire from the Himalayas to Cape Comorin, from the North Pole to the South Pole—all over the world. It is no use indulging in child's play—neither is there time for it. Let those who have come for child's play be off now, while there is time, or they will surely come to grief. We want an organization. Off with laziness. Spread! Spread! Run like fire to all places. Do not depend upon me. Whether I live or die, go on spreading, yourselves.

We have mentioned earlier the Swami's emphasis on making possible the elevation of the women of India. In line with this was the importance he gave to the role of women in his Indian work. His idea was that women's monasticism in modern Hinduism would grow with the Holy Mother as its centre, as men's monasticism was already growing with Shri Rama-krishna as centre. Among the disciples of the Master, Swami Vivekananda was the first to realize the greatness of the Holy Mother and her importance for the regeneration of India and all mankind. His words in this connection must have come as a revelation even to his brother-disciples, who were themselves by no means deficient in comprehension of her greatness. He wrote in a letter to Swami Shivananda in 1894:

You have not yet understood the wonderful significance of Mother's life—none of you. But gradually you will know. Without Shakti [Power] there is no regeneration for the world. Why is it that our country is the weakest and the most backward of all countries?—Because Shakti is held in dishonour there. Mother has been born to revive that wonderful Shakti in India; and making her the nucleus, once more will Gargis and Maitreyis be born into the world. Dear brother, you understand little now, but by degrees you will come to know it all. Hence it is her Math that I want first. . . . Without the grace of Shakti nothing is to be accomplished. What do I find in America and Europe?—the worship of Shakti, the worship of power. Yet they worship Her ignorantly through sense-gratification. Imagine then, what a lot of good they will achieve who will worship Her with all purity, in a Sattvika spirit, looking upon Her as their mother! I am coming to understand things clearer every day, my insight is opening out more and more. Hence we must first build a Math for Mother. First Mother and Mother's daughters, then Father and Father's sons —can you understand this?. . . To me, Mother's grace is a hundred thousand times more valuable than Father's. Mother's grace, Mother's blessings are all paramount to me. . . . Please pardon me. I am a little bigoted there, as regards Mother. If but Mother orders, her demons can work anything. Brother, before proceeding to America I wrote to Mother to bless me. Her blessings came, and at one bound I cleared the ocean. There, you see. In this terrible winter I am lecturing from place to place and fighting against odds, so that funds may be collected for Mother's Math. . . . I shall be relieved when you will have purchased a plot of land and established there the living Durga, the Mother. . . . As soon as you can do that, I shall heave a sigh of relief after sending the money.

The Swami repeatedly urged his brother-disciples to purchase a suitable plot of land, promising to send money for it, so that the Holy Mother could have a place of her own. That he gave the establishment of a home for the Holy Mother the highest priority on his schedule of work, revealed how deeply concerned he was about the cause of womanhood in India and, for that matter, in the world at large. He was convinced that women had a vital part to play in the mission of Shri Ramakrishna.

As to his conception of organization, the Swami wrote to his brothers: "The term organization means division of labour. Each does his own part, and the parts taken together express an ideal of harmony." Besides stating the theory of organization, he pointed out the principles governing this division of labour and explained where a spiritual organization's source of strength lay. It lay not in numbers or temporal power, but in the living, dynamic current of spirituality:

Without an unbroken chain of discipleship—Guruparampara— nothing can be done. . . . Nothing, I say, can be done without the chain of discipleship, that is, the power that is transmitted from the Guru to the disciple, and from him to his disciple, and so on.

He impressed on his brother-disciples the knowledge that they were instruments in the Lord's work and as such were irresistible—provided there was perfect unity among them and obedience to leadership. After the Calcutta Town Hall Meeting of September 5, 1894, he wrote to Swami Abhedananda:

May you have exceeding love for one another among yourselves, and it would be enough to have an attitude of indifference towards public criticisms. . . . So long as there is no feeling of disunion amongst you, through the grace of the Lord, I assure you, there is no danger for you, . . . "be it in battle, in the forest, or on the top of mountains". ". . . All noble undertakings are fraught with obstacles." It is quite in the nature of things. . . . So long as you gird up your loins and rally behind me, there is no fear even if the whole world combines against us.

The Swami did not believe in numerical strength if it was at the cost of quality. There must be integrity of character among those who were to form the brotherhood. He had written to Swami Ramakrishnananda at the begining of 1894:

That jealousy, that absence of conjoint action is the very nature of enslaved nations. But we must try to shake it off. . . .
At any cost, any price, any sacrifice, we must never allow that to creep in among ourselves. Whether we be ten or two, do not care, but those few must be perfect characters.

And again on October 22, 1894:

From all of you I want this that you must discard for ever self-aggrandizement, faction-mongering, and jealousy. You must be all-forbearing, like Mother Earth.

And he warned the brothers that sannyasis should beware of pride. In his letter addressed to Swami Ramakrishnananda he had written:

A besetting sin with sannyasis is the taking pride in their monastic order. That may have its utility during the first stages, but when they are full-grown, they need it no more. One must make no distinction between householders and sannyasis—then only one is a true sannyasi. . . .

The Swami exhorted his brother-disciples to be perfect in every respect. For strong souls he used strong language. A little later in 1894 he wrote:

There is no hope for our nation. Not one original idea crosses anyone's brains, all fighting over the same old, threadbare rug—that Ramakrishna Paramahamsa was such and such—and cock-and-bull stories—stories having neither head nor tail. My God! Won't you do something to show that you are in any way removed from the common run of men!—Only indulging in madness! . . . Today you have your bell, tomorrow you add a horn, and follow suit with a chowry the day after; or you introduce a cot today, and tomorrow you have its legs silver-mounted, and people help themselves to rice-porridge, and you spin out two thousand cock-and-bull stories—in short, nothing but external ceremonials. This is called in English imbecility. Those into whose heads nothing but that sort of silliness enters are called imbecile. Those whose heads have a tendency to be troubled day and night over such questions as whether the bell should ring on the right or on the left, whether the sandal-paste mark should be put on the head or anywhere else, whether the light should be waved twice or four times —simply deserve the name of wretches, and it is owing to that sort of notion that we are the outcasts of Fortune, kicked and spurned at, while the people of the West are masters of the whole world. . . . There is an ocean of difference between idleness and renunciation.

Notwithstanding this kind of remorseless but constructive criticism, of which the Swami was a past master, no one knew better than he the spiritual worth of his brother-disciples. It was his profound love for them and his conviction that they were to be instruments for the fulfilment of Shri Ramakrishna's mission that made him speak so mercilessly. He knew for sure, as he himself wrote, that they would catch his fire:

"Arise! Awake!" Great Lord! He is at our back. I cannot write any more.—Onward! I only tell you this, that whoever reads this letter will imbibe my spirit! Have faith! Onward! Great Lord! . . . I feel as if somebody is moving my hand to write in this way. Onward! Great Lord! Everyone will be swept away! Take care, he is coming! Whoever will be ready to serve him—no, not him but his children —the poor and the downtrodden, the sinful and the afflicted, down to the very worm—who will be ready to serve these, in them he will manifest himself. Through their tongue the Goddess of Learning Herself will speak, and the Divine Mother—the Embodiment of all Power—will enthrone Herself in their hearts. Those that are atheists, unbelievers, worthless, and foppish, why do they call themselves as belonging to his fold?. . .

The Swami's words proved true. The brother-disciples who read his letters did imbibe his spirit. The successful meeting organized by them in Calcutta on September 5, 1894, was the first evidence he received that they had begun to imbibe his spirit, that the dynamic spirit that he had been striving to arouse in them had been aroused. Born leader that he was, he sought at once to harness the awakened enthusiasm of his brothers to the fulfilment of the Master's mission. On October 22 he wrote to Swami Ramakrishnananda:

Now you have come to know your own powers. Strike [while the iron] is hot. Idleness won't do. Throw overboard all idea of jealousy and egotism, once for all. Come on to the practical field with tremendous energy; to work, in the fullness of strength! As to the rest, the Lord will point out the way. The whole world will be deluged by a tidal wave. Work, work, work—let this be your motto. I cannot see anything else. . . . You must work in sympathy with all, then only will it lead to quick results. . . .

But he warned his brothers against too much newspaper blazoning of his cause. To Swami Shivananda he wrote late in 1894:

Too much of everything is bad. This newspaper booming has given me popularity no doubt, but its effect is more in India than here. . . . Now try to organize yourselves in India on the lines of these meetings. . . .

Everything will come all right. Be the servant if you will rule. That is the real secret. Your love will tell even if your words be harsh. Instinctively men feel the love clothed in whatever language.

This described the Swami's own method of work. He wrote harsh things in his letters to India, but every word sprang from his love for Shri Ramakrishna, his brother-disciples, and for all mankind; so there was no mistaking that what he meant was for the good for all.

III

Meanwhile, the Swami's letters to his Madras disciples and others flowed forth. And even as his brother-disciples imbibed his spirit, so also did his disciples and friends; for to them he wrote with the same fire. His letters had almost the value of his presence, inspiring all who read them to constructive thought and action. To Alasinga he wrote on May 28, 1894:

I do not know whether I shall go away this summer or not. Most probably not. In the meantime try to organize and push on our plans. Believe you can do everything. Know that the Lord is with us, and so, onward, brave souls! ...

Act on the educated young men, bring them together, and organize them. Great things can be done by great sacrifices only. No selfishness, no name, no fame, yours or mine, nor my Master's even! Work, work the idea, the plan, my boys, my brave, noble, good souls—to the wheel, to the wheel put your shoulders! Stop not to look back for name, or fame, or any such nonsense. Throw self overboard and work. Remember, "The grass when made into a rope by being joined together can even chain a mad elephant." The Lord's blessings on you all! His power be in you all—as I believe it is *already*. "Wake up, stop not until the goal is reached", say the Vedas. Up, up, the long night is passing, the day is approaching, the wave has risen, nothing will be able to resist its tidal fury. The spirit, my boys, the spirit; the love, my children, the love; the faith, the belief; and fear not! The greatest sin is fear.

The Swami believed that only by awakening the higher self in his direct followers, and through them the higher self in many individuals, could his oppressed nation be stirred; and stirred the nation eventually was. At the stage of which we are speaking this was done by giving great ideas from half-way round the world. Continuing in the same letter, he wrote:

My blessings on all. Tell all the noble souls in Madras who have helped our cause that I send them my eternal love and gratitude, but

I beg of them not to slacken. Throw the idea broadcast. Do not be proud; do not insist upon anything dogmatic; do not go against anything—ours is to put the chemicals together, the Lord knows how and when the crystal will form. Above all, be not inflated with my success or yours. Great works are to be done; what is this small success in comparison with what is to come? Believe, believe, the decree has gone forth, the fiat of the Lord has gone forth—India must rise, the masses and the poor are to be made happy. Rejoice that you are the chosen instruments in His hands. The flood of spirituality has risen. I see it is rolling over the land resistless, boundless, all-absorbing. Every man to the fore, every good will be added to its forces, every hand will smooth its way, and glory be unto the Lord!

The Swami's approach to age-old problems was refreshingly modern. The way to the goal lay, he knew, through doing rather than through writing and talking; and he urged the same line of action on his brothers and followers, asking them, at the same time, to be content with small beginnings. The letter continued:

I do not require any help. Try to get up a fund, buy some magic-lanterns, maps, globes, etc., and some chemicals. Get every evening a crowd of the poor and low, even the Pariahs, and lecture to them about religion first, and then teach them through the magic-lantern and other things, astronomy, geography, etc., in the dialect of the people. Train up a band of fiery young men. Put your fire in them, and gradually increase the organization, letting it widen and widen its circle. Do the best you can, do not wait to cross the river when the water has all run down. Printing magazines, papers, etc., are good no doubt, but actual work, my boys, even if infinitesimal, is better than eternal scribbling and talking. Call a meeting at Bhattacharya's. Get a little money and buy those things I have just now stated, hire a hut, and go to work. Magazines are *secondary*, but this is primary. You must have a hold on the masses. Do not be afraid of a small beginning, great things come afterwards. Be courageous. Do not try to lead your brethren, but serve them. The brutal mania for leading has sunk many a great ship in the waters of life. Take care especially of that, i.e. be unselfish even unto death, and work. I could not write all I was going to say, but the Lord will give you all understanding, my brave boys. At it, my boys! Glory unto the Lord!

It was this consecrated, selfless, co-operative, organized work under the banner of the Divine that the Swami prescribed for India, rather than uncoordinated free-lancing. His idea was to organize his monastic and lay followers for conjoint work. Through co-ordination of wills, he said, comes "that accumulation of energy and power that is going to make the future India". "Let me see you make some electric circuits between Calcutta and Madras", he wrote in the summer of 1894 to his brothers at Alambazar Math. And in July to Alasinga:

Try to expand. Remember the *only sign of life* is motion and growth. . . . Keep on steadily. So far we have done wonderful things. Onward, brave souls, we will gain! Organize and found societies and go to work, that is the only way.

Since an organization was to be the central force in the Swami's scheme for future work in India, he carefully taught his lay followers as well as his brother-disciples how to build one, stressing the spirit that should guide it and the methods and responsibilities of its leaders. He wrote to Alasinga on August 31, 1894:

Now organize a little society. You will have to take charge of the whole movement, not as a *leader*, but as a *servant*. Do you know, the least show of leading destroys everything by rousing jealousy?

Accede to everything. Only try to retain all of my friends together. Do you see? And work slowly up. Let G. G. and others, who have no immediate necessity for earning something, do as they are doing, i.e. casting the idea broadcast. G. G. is doing well at Mysore. That is the way. . . .

So the sooner you organize yourselves and you be ready as secretary and treasurer to enter into direct communication with my friends and sympathizers here, the better for you and me. Do that quickly, and write to me. Give the society a non-sectarian name.

On November 30, 1894, the Swami wrote again to Alasinga:

You need not send any more newspaper cuttings. I have been deluged with them. Enough of that. Now go to work for the organization. I have started one already in New York and the Vice-President will soon write to you. Keep correspondence with them. Soon I hope to get up a few in other places.

The Swami's mention of a direct liaison between his followers in India and those in America seems to indicate that he was thinking of an international organization. He continued in the same letter: "We must organize our forces not to make a sect— not on religious matters, but on the secular business part of it. A stirring propaganda must be launched out. Put your heads together and organize."

Further elucidating his idea of organized work, the Swami wrote to Haridas Viharidas Desai in November of 1894:

The secret of success of the Westerners is the power of organization and combination. That is only possible with mutual trust and co-operation and help. Now here is Virchand Gandhi, the Jain, whom you well knew in Bombay. This man never takes anything but pure vegetables even in this terribly cold climate, and tooth and nail tries to defend his countrymen and religion. The people of this country like him very well, but what are they doing who sent him over? They are trying to outcast him. Jealousy is a vice necessarily generated in slaves. Again it is jealousy that holds them down.

"Expansion is life; contraction is death." This was one of the energizing ideas that the Swami transmitted to the soul of his prostrate, stupor-bound country. Elaborating on it, he wrote to Manmathanath Bhattacharya on September 5, 1894:

Keeping aloof from the community of nations is the only cause for the downfall of India. Since the English came, they have been forcing you back into communion with other nations, and you are visibly rising again. Everyone that comes out of the country confers a benefit on the whole nation; for it is by doing that alone that your horizon will expand. And as women cannot avail themselves of this advantage, they have made almost no progress in India. There is no station of rest; either you progress upwards or you go back and die out. The only sign of life is going outward and forward and expansion. Contraction is death. Why should you do good to others? Because that is the only condition of life; thereby you expand beyond your little self; you live and grow. All narrowness, all contraction, all selfishness is simply slow suicide, and when a nation commits the fatal mistake of contracting itself and of thus cutting off all expansion and life, it must die. Women similarly must go forward or become idiots and soulless tools in the hands of their tyrannical lords. The children are the result of the combination of the tyrant and the idiot, and they are *slaves*. And this is the whole history of modern India. Oh, who would break this horrible crystallization of death? Lord help us!

The Swami was himself a powerful agent of God in breaking the "horrible crystallization of death" that had come over India. As early as September 1892 he had written, "So you see, we must travel, we must go to foreign parts. We must see how the engine of society works in other countries, and keep free and open communication with what is going on in the minds of other nations, if we really want to be a nation again." But his mission was not only to gather the riches of technological and sociological knowledge from other nations of the world; it was also to give abundantly of India's vast spiritual treasure. As has been well said, Swami Vivekananda's going forth proved that India was alive not only to survive but also to conquer; and this conquest was not with weapons but with lofty ideas and ideals. Lest any of his countrymen should undervalue the treasures that India already possessed and madly rush after things foreign and exotic, with grievous hurt to themselves, he pointed out in unmistakable terms—even at the risk of being misunderstood—that India had her own strength, had her own lessons to teach. He wrote to Haridas Viharidas Desai in September 1894:

I have been travelling all over this country all this time and seeing everything. I have come to this conclusion that there is only one country in the world which understands religion—it is India; that with all their faults the Hindus are head and shoulders above all other nations in morality and spirituality; and that with proper care and attempt and struggle of all her disinterested sons, by combining some of the active and heroic elements of the West with calm virtues of the Hindus, there will come a type of men far superior to any that have ever been in this world.

This was the Swami's appraisal of the role of India's religion in the future of man. At the same time he was sensible of where

India had erred and of how her faults were to be corrected. He wrote to Alasinga on September 29:

Liberty is the first condition of growth. Your ancestors gave every liberty to the soul, and religion grew. They put the body under every bondage, and society did not grow. The opposite is the case in the West—every liberty to society, none to religion. Now are falling off the shackles from the feet of Eastern society as from those of Western religion.

Each again will have its type; the religious or introspective in India, the scientific or out-seeing in the West. The West wants every bit of spirituality through social improvement. The East wants every bit of social power through spirituality. Thus it was that the modern reformers saw no way to reform but by first crushing out the religion of India. They tried, and they failed. Why? Because few of them ever studied their own religion, and not *one* ever *underwent* the training necessary to understand the *Mother of all religions*. I claim that no destruction of religion is necessary to improve the Hindu society, and that this state of society exists not on account of religion, but because religion has not been applied to society as it should have been. This I am ready to prove from our old books, every word of it. This is what I teach, and this is what we must struggle all our lives to carry out. But it will take time, a long time to study. Have patience and work. "Save yourself by yourself."

It is the Swami who in the present age has most clearly shown the creative role of religion in bringing about the desired evolution of modern civilization, not only in India but in the whole world. This was his most original contribution to modern Indian thought. True, his voice has not yet been fully heard, either in India or abroad; but there are signs that thinkers all over the world are slowly veering round to his views. But even as the Swami was a fervent exponent of the application of essential religion to social problems, he was at the same time a forthright critic of the excessive emphasis laid by Hindu society on certain religious attitudes and traditions. In the postscript to the letter last quoted he wrote:

The present Hindu society is organized only for spiritual men, and hopelessly crushes out everybody else. Why? Where shall they go who want to enjoy the world a little with its frivolities? Just as our religion takes in all, so should our society. This is to be worked out by first understanding the true principles of our religion and then applying them to society. This is the slow but sure work to be done.

This liberal and understanding attitude was that of a man of illumination, of one who had faith in the power of essential religion and in the divine potential within all men.

His simple practical philosophy he stated to Alasinga on October 27, 1894. It is faithful to the highest truth, yet down to earth in its practicality:

I believe in God, and I believe in Man. I believe in helping the miserable. I believe in going even to hell to save others. . . .

I am a Tyagi [detached] monk. I only want one thing. I do not believe in a God or religion which cannot wipe the widow's tears or bring a piece of bread to the orphan's mouth. However sublime be the theories, however well-spun may be the philosophy—I do not call it religion so long as it is confined to books and dogmas. The eye is in the forehead and not in the back. Move onward and carry into practice that which you are very proud to call your religion, and God bless you!. . .

What have I to do with this "ism" or that "ism"? I am the servant of the Lord. . . .

Love never fails, my son; today or tomorrow or ages after, truth will conquer. Love shall win the victory. Do you love your fellow-men? Where should you go to seek for God—are not all the poor, the miserable, the weak, gods? Why not worship them first? Why go to dig a well on the shores of the Ganga? Believe in the omnipotent power of love. Who cares for these tinsel puffs of name? I never keep watch of what the newspapers are saying. Have you love?—You are omnipotent. Are you perfectly unselfish? If so, you are irresistible. It is character that pays everywhere. It is the Lord who protects His children in the depths of the sea. Your country requires heroes; be heroes! God bless you!

The Swami went straight to the root of human ills and there applied remedial measures. And these remedies were not such as would themselves create other problems in the future, as measures based on partial views of reality and lacking in universal love tend to do.

"The only way", he wrote, "is love and sympathy. The only worship is love." The Swami's work sprang from love. Love was its method. And its end was to bring men in all parts of the world to greater love.

In this chapter we have seen how, in the midst of intense activity in America, the Swami set in motion his work in India; and have seen too the lines on which he wanted the work conducted. How it in fact developed after his return there in 1897 will be seen in later chapters. Meanwhile we must resume the interrupted account of his life and mission in the West.

GLOSSARY

Acharya   A religious teacher

Agamas   A traditional sacred writing or a scripture; the Vedas

Bhagavatam   A sacred book of the Hindus, one of the best known of the eighteen Puranas; it contains narrations of the lives and deeds of the Avataras of Vishnu, with particular elaboration of the life of Shri Krishna, and in addition many religious and philosophical discourses. Also called *Srimad-Bhagavata*

Bhakti   Love of God; single-minded devotion to one's Chosen Ideal

Brahmacharin   A spiritual aspirant who has taken the vows of continence, austerity and so on, with a view to leading a spiritual life. It also means a celibate or a student in the first stage of life, who stays with his spiritual teacher for his education and serves him

Charhak   A festival mostly prevalent in Bengal, India, observed on the last day of the Bengali year. On this occasion, Lord Shiva is offered special worship, and there is a ceremonial swinging from a tall pole by the worshippers in fulfilment of certain vows made to Shiva

Chowry   Bushy tail of the Chamari or yak (*Bos Grunniens*) used as a fan in the temple service; also called Chamara

Darshanas   The six systems of orthodox Hindu philosophy; namely the Samkhya, the Yoga, the Vaisheshika, the Nyaya, the Purva Mimamsa, and the Vedanta or Uttara Mimamsa

Dashanami tradition   Ten Orders of the sannyasi followers of Vedanta, organized by Shri Shankaracharya, each having distinguishing features and a name of its own but a common tradition in the background, termed here Dashanami tradition

Dhuni   Sacred fire lighted by holy men

Esraj   A kind of stringed musical instrument having five principal strings and played with a bow

Japa   Repetition of God's name or of a sacred formula given by the spiritual teacher, with mind concentrated on its meaning

Jnana   Knowledge of God gained through reasoning and discrimination

Kayastha   A subsidiary caste of Kshatriyas in Hindu society, generally found in northern India

Khichuri   Indian dish prepared out of lentils, spices and rice

Laddu   A sweetmeat made out of ghee, sugar and powdered pulse

Mahasamadhi   Death of a liberated soul by entering into a deep meditative state

Mantra   Holy Sanskrit text; also the formula sacred to a deity, devotional repetition of which leads to its realization

Narayana   A name of Vishnu, the inner controller of all beings

Pakhawaj   A sort of double drum, percussion shaped almost like a tomtom

Puri   A thin and small saucer-shaped brown bread fried in clarified butter

Purushottama   The highest or Supreme Being, an epithet of Lord Vishnu or Krishna

Rasagolla   A spongy ball-like sweetmeat made of casein and farina

Samadhi   Profound concentration of the mind, in which one experiences oneness with Divine Reality

Sannyasa   The monastic life, the last of the four stages of life according to the Hindu scriptures

Shaktas   The worshippers of divine energy in the form of its female personification generally represented by Durga or Kali

Shraddha   A Hindu religious ceremony in which food and drink are offered to deceased relatives

Sitar   A three-stringed musical instrument

Smritis   Traditional law books subsidiary to the Vedas, containing secular and religious laws for guiding the life and conduct of the Hindus

Tabla   A kind of tabor played along with another semi-circular bigger drum called Baya, as musical accompaniment

Tanpura   A stringed musical instrument that helps a singer sustain a uniform voice

Tantras   Systems of religious philosophy in which Shiva, Vishnu, or the Divine Mother is the ultimate Reality, differentiated respectively as the Shaiva, Vaishnava or Shakta Tantras; also mean the scriptures dealing with these philosophies

Yoga   Union of the individual soul with the Supreme Soul; a particular path by which this union can be attained; also means one of the six schools of Indian philosophy

BIBLIOGRAPHY

Abhedananda, Swami. *Amar Jivankatha* [Bengali]. Calcutta: Ramkrishna Vedanta Math, 1964.

———. *The Complete Works of Swami Abhedananda*. X. Calcutta: Ramakrishna Vedanta Math, 1970.

Abjajananda, Swami. *Swamijir Padaprante* [Bengali]. Belur, West Bengal: Ramakrishna Mission Sarada Pitha, 1964.

Akhandananda, Swami. *Smriti Katha* [Bengali]. Calcutta: Udbodhan Office, B.S. 1357.

Annadananda, Swami. *Swami Akhandananda* [Bengali]. Calcutta: Udbodhan Office, B.S. 1367.

Bandyopadhyay, Asitkumar; Basu, Sankari Prasad; and Sankar. *Visvavivek* [Bengali]. Calcutta: Vak-Sahitya, 1963.

Barrows, J. H. *The World's Parliament of Religions*. I and II. Chicago: The Parliament Publishing Company, 1893.

Basu, Pramathanath. *Swami Vivekananda* [Bengali]. I and II. Bhowanipore, Calcutta: the Author, B.S. 1326.

Basu, Sankari Prasad. *Vivekananda O Samakalin Bharatavarsa* [Bengali]. I, Calcutta: Mandal Book House, B.S. 1382.

———; and Ghosh, Sunil Bhihari; eds. *Vivekananda in Indian Newspapers—1893–1902*. Calcutta: Basu Bhattacharya and Co. (Pvt) Ltd., 1969.

Burke, Marie Louise. *Swami Vivekananda in America: New Discoveries*. Mayavati: Advaita Ashrama, 1966.

———. *Swami Vivekananda: His Second Visit to the West*. Mayavati: Advaita Ashrama, 1973.

Chattopadhyaya, Chandrasekhara. *Sri Sri Latu Maharajer Smriti Katha* [Bengali]. Baghbazar, Calcutta: Suresh Chandra Saha, B.S. 1347.

Datta, Bhupendranath. *Swami Vivekananda: Patriot-Prophet*. Calcutta: Nababharat Publishers, 1954.

Datta, Mahendranath. *Srimat Vivekananda Swamijir Jivaner Ghatanavali* [Bengali]. I. Calcutta: Mahendra Publishing Committee, 1957.

———. *Swami Vivekanander Balya Jivani* [Bengali]. Calcutta: Mahendra Publishing Committee, 1935.

Datta, Narendra Nath; Basak, Baisnav Charan; and Basak, Jnana

Chandra. *Sangita Kalpataru* [Bengali]. Calcutta: Arya Pustaka-laya, 1887.

Datta, Ramachandra. *Paramahamsadever Jivan Vrittanta* [Bengali]. Calcutta: Kankurgachhi Yogodyan, B.S. 1310.

Dhar, Sailendra Nath. *A Comprehensive Biography of Swami Vivekananda.* I. Madras: Vivekananda Prakashan Kendra, 1975.

Eastern and Western Admirers. *Reminiscences of Swami Vivekananda.* Mayavati: Advaita Ashrama, 1964.

Eastern and Western Disciples. *The Life of Swami Vivekananda.* I and II. Mayavati: Advaita Ashrama, 1914.

Gambhirananda, Swami. *History of the Ramakrishna Math and Mission.* Mayavati: Advaita Ashrama, 1957.

———. *Sri Ma Sarada Devi* [Bengali]. Calcutta: Udbodhan Office, B.S. 1360.

———. *Yuganayak Vivekananda* [Bengali]. I (B.S. 1374) and II (B.S. 1376). Calcutta: Udbodhan Office.

Jagadiswarananda, Swami. *Swami Turiyananda* [Bengali]. Calcutta: Udbodhan Office, B.S. 1361.

Joshi, Vasantji Raghavji. *Sri Yashvant Charitra* [Gujarati]. Purva Khanda, Limbdi: the Author, 1896.

'M'. *The Gospel of Sri Ramakrishna.* Translated by Swami Nikhilananda. Madras: Sri Ramakrishna Math, 1974.

Majumdar, Satyendra Nath. *Vivekananda Charit* [Bengali]. Calcutta: Udbodhan Office, B.S. 1337.

Menon, K. P. K. *Chattambi Swamigal—the Great Scholar-Saint of Kerala.* Trivandrum: P. G. Narayana Pillai, 1970.

Nivedita, Sister. *The Master As I Saw Him.* Calcutta: Udbodhan Office, 1918.

Pillai, S. N. Krishna. *Jivancharitra Samuchchaya* [Malayalam].

Prakashachandra, Brahmachari. *Swami Saradananda* [Bengali]. Edited by Devendranath Basu. Calcutta: Basumati Sahitya Mandir, B.S. 1342.

Saradananda, Swami. *Sri Ramakrishna: the Great Master.* Translated by Swami Jagadananda. Madras: Sri Ramakrishna Math, 1970.

———. *Sri Sri Ramakrishna Lilaprasanga* [Bengali]. I and II. Calcutta: Udbodhan Office, B.S. 1360.

Sharma, Beni Shankar. *Swami Vivekananda—A Forgotten Chapter of His Life.* Calcutta: Oxford Book and Stationery Co., 1963.

Sharma, Jhabarmall. *Adarsa Nares* [Hindi]. Jasrapur, Rajasthan:

Sri Jayadeva Sarma, Shekhavati Historical Research Institute, 1940.

Shraddhananda, Swami. *Atiter Smriti* [Bengali]. Belur, West Bengal: Sri Ramakrishna Math, B.S. 1363.

'Sri Ma'. *Sri Sri Ramakrishna Kathamrita* [Bengali]. I to V. Calcutta: Sri Anil Gupta, Kathamrita Bhavan.

Sri Sri Mahapurusjir Katha O Samksipta Jivan-Charit [Bengali]. Calcutta: Udbodhan Office, B.S. 1341.

Swami Brahmananda [Bengali]. Calcutta: Udbodhan Office, B.S. 1348.

Vivekananda, Swami. *The Complete Works of Swami Vivekananda.* I to VIII. Mayavati: Advaita Ashrama.

———. *Swami Vivekanander Bani O Rachana* [Bengali]. VI and IX. Calcutta: Udbodhan Office, B.S. 1369.

Periodicals, Souvenirs and Pamphlets

Brahmavadin, XI (1906): 678 ff; XIII (1908): 565–66.
Calcutta Gazette, Calcutta: Government of Bengal, January 30, 1884.
The Hindu, Madras, January 19, 1964.
Junagadh, Gandhinagar: Directorate of Information and Tourism, Government of Gujarat.
Kerala Kaumudi [Malayalam], January 22, 1963, p. 2.
Mathrubhumi [Malayalam], XL (1963): 48.
Prabuddha Bharata, XIII (1908): 116; XX (1915): 58; XXV (1920): 68–69; XXXV (1930): 338–39; LI (1946): 82; LVIII (1953): 383–86; LX (1955): 311; LXVIII (1963): 273; LXIX (1964): 204; LXXIX (1974): 296–98; LXXXIII (1978): 136–43.
Souvenir of the Grand Lodge of India (No. 1), Calcutta, 1975.
Sri Chattambi Swami Centenary Memorial Souvenir, 1953.
Udbodhan [Bengali], VII (1905): 437; XVII (1915): 440; XXXVI (1934): 634–36; LXXIV (1972): 679.
Vedanta Kesari, XX (1934): 344–45; XXXIX (1952): 73–74; XLVIII (1961–62): 266–67, 384–89, 396–97; LVIII (1971): 151.
Vidyasagar College Satavarsa Smaranika [Bengali], Calcutta, 1972, pp. 350–417.
Vivekananda Centenary Souvenir, Trichur: Sri Ramakrishna Ashrama, 1963.
Vivekananda Sataka Prasasti [Malayalam], Trichur Central Committee's Souvenir, 1963.

Manuscripts

Calcutta. Archives of the Advaita Ashrama. Photostats of Swami Vivekananda's letters; unpublished letters of Swami Vivekananda, Mrs. Boshi Sen's Collection; letter of Mr. G. C. Connor to Mr. Smith of Chicago, dated January 22, 1894, Mrs. Boshi Sen's Collection; Revashankar Anupama Dave's "Reminiscences of Swami Vivekananda in Porbandar".

San Francisco. Archives of the Vedanta Society of Northern California.

INDEX

Abdar Rahaman, Amir of Afghanistan, 260

Abdul Rahaman Saheb, a Muslim Councillor of Mysore State, 322

Abhedananda, Swami (Kali), 159, 166–7, 172, 177, 190, 194–5, 198–9, 204, 206, 210, 236–7, 302, 505, 548; account given in his autobiography regarding Naren's realization, 167; at Gujarat, 292; autobiography, 301–2; meeting Vivekananda at Junagadh and Mahabaleshwar, 292, 301; observation on Vivekananda, 302; suffering from repeated attacks of malaria at Hrishikesh, 232

Absolute, the, 60, 75, 80, 141, 172, 179; Existence and Bliss, ocean of, 205; Existence-Knowledge-Bliss, 139; experience of, 163, 177; realm of, 91; veil covering realization of, 179; idea, progressive unfolding of, 108; of Advaita Vedanta, 60; of Vedanta, 178; state, 177; Truth, 67

Abu Road, 386–7

Abyssinians, 408

Ada, Ohio, 461, 468

Adams, Mr. & Mrs. Milward, 402

Adbhutananda, Swami (Latu, Leto), 159, 168–9, 174, 177, 187, 189–90, 199, 213

Adhikari, Beni, see Gupta, Beni

Adjustment, law of nature, 62; on the spiritual plane was needed in the last century, 62

Advaita, 68, 165; philosophy, 67, 72, 96–7, 140, 307, 419–20; treatises on, 95; see also Non-dualism

Advaita Vedanta, 60, 95, 171, 177, 229, 335; and Sufism, 357; to enlighten the Western mind with the knowledge of, 514; the philosophy and the source of spiritual power of the Ramakrishna-Vivekananda Movement, 541

Advaitananda, Swami (Gopal Senior, Gopal-da), 159, 168, 177–8, 187, 189, 194–5, 199, 204, 211, 219; at Meerut, 259; handed over twelve sets of ochre clothings etc. to Shri Ramakrishna, 177; wish of, 176–7

Advaitic, catholicity and devotion to the Guru are the two main principles of the Ramakrishna-Vivekananda Movement, 541

Advaitin, characteristics of a true, 365

Aesop's Niti Katha (Fables), 297

Afghan gentleman, a refugee Sardar, 260

Afghanistan, 260

Agamas, 338, 370

Age of Consent Bill, Vivekananda on, 367

Agnosticism, 106, 112, 333; had impressed on Naren the meaninglessness of all things, 106; to Naren, was voice of anguish, 111

Agnostics, 515

Agriculture, as a profession for educated Indians, 274

Agra, the city of palaces and tombs, 217; fort, 217

Ahalyabai, the Rani of Indore, 294, 303

"Aham Brahmasmi", 177

Ahmad Khan, 43

Ahmedabad, 288, 298; District, 288

Ahura-Mazda of the Zoroastrians, 421

"Air-eating Father", 229

Ajit Singhji, Raja of Khetri, 281–3, 384; devotion to Vivekananda, 282–5

Ajmer, 258, 278, 281–2, 286–7, 298

Akbar, 264, 278, 421; Hindu in breadth of vision and boldness of synthesis, 392; palace of, 278

Gunas, 170

Gupta, Beni, 43

Gupta, Mahendranath (Mahendra), 162, 168–9, 174, 176, 191–2, 199, 210, 238; account of Narendra by, 205; diary of, 203; question regarding doctrines of Buddha, 174–6; Sharatchandra: Assistant Station Master, Hathras Railway Station, 220–3; his elder brother, 220; his first meeting with Vivekananda, 220; initiated into Sannyasa as Swami Sadananda, 224; reminiscences about Vivekananda, 222–3; renunciation of, 222

Guru, 66, 92, 110, 129, 133, 147–8, 151, 158, 160, 164, 183, 208, 236; and disciple, 84–100; Mahashaya, 22; need for, 55; spiritual teacher, is necessary, 81–2

Hakim, Mohammedan doctor, in Delhi, 258

Haldarpukur, 91

Hale, Mr. George W., 489–90, 509; receiving an anonymous letter about his daughter and Vivekananda, 490; Mr. & Mrs. George W., Chicago, 443, 446, 485, 489, 491; Mrs. George W., 443, 452, 460, 468, 470, 485, 506, 508–10, 513, 517; taking Vivekananda from the street-side into her care, 412; Harriet, 510; Mary, 471, 482, 507, 510; family, 478; house in Chicago, 490, 512; sisters, 468–71, 509

Hall, of Columbus, 415, 432; of Washington, 415

Hallucinations, 85, 95, 113, 189

Hamilton, 112

Hanuman, 17; and his army, 345; mandir and a Muslim shrine on Shatrunjaya mountain, 300

Haramohini (Haramoni), 10

Hardayal Singhji of Jodhpur, 281

Hardwar, 190, 219–20, 258, 260

Hari, 15; "Om Tat Sat", chanting of, 184; Singh, Sardar, of Jaipur: 278; his vision through a touch of Vivek-

ananda, 278; see Turiyananda, Swami

Haridasbhai, the Dewan of Junagadh, 302

Haripal station, 195

Hariprasanna, see Vijnanananda, Swami

Harish, 159, 189, 204

Harmony of Religions, a lecture by Vivekananda, 461

Harris Academy of Music Concert Hall, 513

Hartford, 442

Harvard, Religious Union, 477; University, 403, 476–7

Hastie, William, Principal, 47–8, 107; his estimation of Vivekananda, 48

Hatha Yoga, 233, 236

Hathras, 220, 222, 224; Railway Station, Assistant Station Master, 220

Havishyanna, 93

Hazra, Pratapchandra, 90, 96, 98–9, 162

Hegel, 108, 205, 370

Helen, daughter of Mrs. Bagley, her letter refuting scandals circulated against Swamiji, 520; and Draupadi, 365

Helmholtz, Prof. Hermann von, 448

Hemali, a friend of Swamiji, 120

Hengar, a Muslim saint, 300

'Here', significance of, 173

Hero-worship, 231

Higgins, Charles M., 517–18

Higginson, Thomas Wentworth, President of the Free Religious Association, 476–7, 511

High Court of Calcutta, 5

Highest Reality, 232

Highland Park, Chicago, 448

Himalayas, 219, 223, 227, 241, 243, 247–9, 251–2, 256, 303, 346, 350, 355–6, 364, 375, 487, 546; Vivekananda like the famous sages of, 518

Hindi, 43, 220; bhajan, 265

Hindu, 30, 246, 500; The, newspaper, 319, 500; "Altruism", a lecture by Vivekananda, 442; and Chinese, 394–

tical to, 96; an inspired Bohemian, 107; and a few disciples asked the Master to heal himself, 165; began to tell the story of Jesus, 196; brother-disciples could not escape the magnetism of his personality, 195; did not believe in the forms of God, 162; equated Advaitism with atheism, 96; felt that the cabs and his own self were of one stuff, 97; had a great respect for Western material science and its analytical process, 104; held forth to his brother-disciples on the glory of the wandering life, 211; held that monks should serve mankind in a spirit of worship, 192; himself became restless for pilgrimage, 211; his days of ecstasy at Dakshineswar and Shyampukur, 131–2; his nature was to stand against falsehood, 96; missed no opportunity to ridicule Advaita philosophy, 96; must have had a glimpse of Advaita, 97; often said: "Shri Ramakrishna was the only person who believed in me uniformly", 130; outright denunciation of Advaita by, 96–7; said: "Shri Ramakrishna alone knew how to love another", 130; the spirit of the Master incarnate in, 195; though outwardly a man of Jnana, was full of Bhakti within, 206; world began to appear dreamlike to, 97; see also Bileh, Naren, Naren Babu, Narendranath, Vivekananda

Narendranath, 12, 14, 21, 26, 74, 85, 99, 120, 153, 179–80, 190, 197, 210; brother-disciples looked upon him as their leader, 194–5; combined reason and a wide range of knowledge with a devotional nature, 164; was competent to chide as well as guide, 153–4; early education and glimpses of spirituality, 27–45; gave brother-monks freedom in the matter of wandering, 211; giving advice to brother-disciples on the imminent end of Ramakrishna, 159–60; his

question to Ramakrishna: "Have you seen God, Sir?" 77; his remarkable letter to Swami Brahmananda, 191; his stirring appeal to brother-disciples regarding Ramakrishna's relics, 188; led the procession in the removal of the Master's ashes, 190; only, amongst disciples understood Ramakrishna's greatness, 133; qualities that made him leader of Ramakrishna's disciples, 153–4; replying to certain criticisms regarding Ramakrishna, 152–3; said, "Ramakrishna is a God-like man", 153; saw a vision of Ramakrishna, 189; seemed to be the true mouthpiece of the Master, 194–5; studying for the Law examination, 158; third visit of, to Ramakrishna, 78; was able to arrive at the true spirit of Ramakrishna's teachings, 138; was convinced that religion preached by Ramakrishna would give rise to a new current of thought and culture, 192; was determined that his brother-disciples should lead life of renunciation after Ramakrishna's passing away, 190–1; was looked up to by his brother-disciples, 164; was the first to realise dangers of sentimentalism, 156; see also Bileh, Naren, Vivekananda

Narmada, 211

Natakrishna's reminiscences about Swamiji, 221

Nataraja, King of Dancers, 54; Shiva as known in South India, 54

Natarajan, Kamakshi, a powerful journalist-writer in India, 366; reminiscences about Swamiji, 367

Nath, Kashinath Govind (Natu), 307

Nathnagar temple, holy place of Jaina community, 246

Nation, lives in the cottage, 532

Nature, 110, 177; -worship, 231

Navaratra festival, 284

Nava-vidhan (New Dispensation), 481; Brahmo Samaj, 485

Nava-Vrindavan Theatre, 485; Swami-

the monks in their understanding of his teachings, 191–2; "reconciled the ideal of Bhakti with Vedanta", 139; how he cried aloud, 64–5; ". . . I and the Mother have become one", 169; "I feel great strength when Narendra is with me", 92; ideal of his disciples, 538; ill-treated at the Brahmo Samaj, 89; imminence of his Mahasamadhi, 182–3; in a state of semi-consciousness, 96; initiated Naren with the name of Rama, 160; instructed boys to beg their food from door to door, 163–4; instruction of, to householders different from that given to young boys, 154; intending to initiate Narendra into truth of Advaita Vedanta, 95; intuitive experiences of, 71; "It is better to enter the house by the front door", 137; joined the disciples in merry-making, 132; Kali the giver of immortality to, 70; Kali merged in his realization, in the Impersonal, 70; key to his overwhelming love for Naren, 90; knew the apparent vanity and obstinacy of Naren to be self-reliance, 87; laid bare the living spirit of Hinduism, 140; laid bare the living spirit of realization, 140; last year of his life became slow crucifixion, 150; learned many strange things about Naren, 80; life and teaching of, true to essence of Hinduism, 140; like a child placed implicit trust in Divine Mother, 71; loved his disciples as a mother, 181; made remarkable exception in the case of Naren, 130; Mahasamadhi of, 179–80, 184–5; merged in Impersonal aspect of Divine Mother, 71; met Trailanga Swami, 215; methods of teaching of, 148–9; might have unlocked the treasure-box occasionally for Naren, 179; more than half of the ashes and bones of, transferred, 188; Mother told, those in their last incarnation must come to, 72; Mukti had no meaning for, 71; "My siddhis

(powers) will manifest through you (Naren)", 182; Naren had no body idea, avowed by, 90; Naren, lifted out of the objective conceptions of God by, 97; Naren was indebted for his understanding of Hinduism to, 140–1; Naren was treated with utter indifference by, 98; Naren's all-round development was fostered by, 143–4; "Narendra has the nature of a man . . .", 92; "Narendra is a huge reservoir . . .", 91; "Narendra is a very big receptacle", 91; "Narendra is like a bamboo with a big hollow space inside", 91; "Narendra is like a male pigeon", 91–2; Narendranath played a complementary role for, 74; Narendra seeing a vision of, 189; "Not compassion for others, but rather service . . .", 139; nursing of, 151; of Dakshineswar, 434; of his approaching end gave ample hints, 158; on inebriation resulting from divine love, 141; on the personal level, 75; only Naren could gauge the meaning of Master's message, 139–40; opened the door of Advaita Vedanta to Naren, 177; paid tribute to Saradamani, 69; passed away . . ., August 16, 1886, 184; passionate call of, to his future disciples, 72–3; people waited for miraculous manifestation of, 156; placed his right foot on Naren's body, 78; portions of relics were sent to Hardwar, 190; potentialities in Hinduism revealed in, 140; "power of attorney" given by Girish to, 155; practical commonsense of, 181; practised Bhakti and Tantrika sadhana under the Nun, 66; prayed, "O Mother, may Naren not sink", 146; preserver and rejuvenator of Hindu Dharma, 149; procession to Kankurgachi with ashes of, 190; questioning Naren about Buddha's teachings, 175; reaction to Naren's ecstatic state, 160; reaction to Naren's report on house-

Victoria Terminus, 306

Vidyapati, 265

Vidyasagar, Ishwarchandra, 7, 27, 33, 125; College, Metropolitan Institution, 117

Vijapurkar, Mr., reminiscences of Swamiji's visit to Kolhapur, 307-8

Vijay, *see* Goswami, Vijaykrishna

Vijnanananda, Swami (Hariprasanna), 197, 483

Vilangana river, 254

Village, life, educated people should accept, 274-5; upliftment of, 538-9

Vinata, 25

Vindhya mountains, 40

Viraja-homa, 198-9

Virajananda, Swami, 344

Vireshwar, 12; *see also* Vivekananda, Swami; Shiva, 10; temple of, 3

Virgil, 365

Virgo, 11

Vishishtadvaita, Qualified Non-dualism, 72

Vishnu, 198, 276, 540

Vishwanath, 227-8; temple of, 198, 214

Vivekananda, Birthday Anniversary, 1920, 367; Centenary, Central Committee of Trichur, 328; Souvenir: 328; in Malayalam, published by Ramakrishna Ashrama, Trichur, 329; Mandapam, 344; Rock Memorial Committee, Madras, 344; Rocks, 340; Sataka Prasasti, in Malayalam, published by Ramakrishna Ashrama, Trichur, 329

Vivekananda, Swami, Life and Personality: a funny incident on the fairground, 400-1; a great admirer of Napoleon, 51; a significant incident regarding meditation of, with Girish Ghosh, 180; a strong jaw, evidence of a resolute nature, 144; about Thomas W. Palmer, 460; above name and fame, longing to return to days of wanderings, 440; acceptance of a chillum of tobacco from an outcaste, 218; accepted as a delegate to the Parliament of Religions with

Mrs. G. W. Hale's help, 412; accepting an invitation to the Cambridge house of Mrs. Ole Bull, 511; accommodated with other Oriental delegates, 412; account of Ramakrishna's training his disciples, 131-3; acquainted with eminent men and women of both America and abroad, 426; acquainted with K. Seshadri Iyer, Dewan of Mysore State, 321; acquainted with many distinguished delegates to the Parliament of Religions, 412; acquired the site of Belur Math, carried and installed the Master's relics, 198; acting in a religious drama with Keshab and other Brahmos, 485; activities at Khetri, 281-2; admiration for Gaekwad of of Baroda and the Rajput chief of Khetri, 332; adventures and experiences in his wandering days, 347-58; advice to his Madras disciples to vouch for his representation of Hinduism in America, 484-5; advised Akhandananda to go to a friend's house at Allahabad, and Kripananda to look after him, 256; advised by Robert Ingersoll, 448; advised to be dressed in American fashion, 404; advising his countrymen to counter campaigns against him, 484; alone at Hardwar for hard spiritual practice, 258; alone set out for Rajasthan, 263; ample scope for his study at Junagadh, 291; an incident that was a landmark in his life, 129; an inspiring song sung by, 51; and a noted Austrian musician, 323; and a scholar, 328; and a wealthy citizen of Chicago, 459; and Akhandananda: again with fever, 253; as guests of Ramprasanna Bhattacharya, Nainital, 249; at Sethji's garden-house, Meerut, 259; at the house of Manmathanath Chowdhury, 243; fell ill on the way, 253; in the garden of Amba Dutt, 251; reached Srinagar by Dandi, 253; straight to

Madras disciples his own awareness
of the heartrending condition of
India, 536; insisting on doing rather
than writing and talking, 552; instantly remembered Ramakrishna,
142; intellectual pursuits of, 45; intense aloofness, one of the striking
traits of, 144; intention of embarking
at Bombay and not at Madras, 390;
intention to sail for America, 317;
interest in science at which a laboratory was started in Khetri, 284; interest in any one ceased when "he had
wrung him dry", 144; interesting
journey to Almora, 251; interviewed
by local newspapers at Memphis,
453; intimacy with Sardar Hari
Singh, Commander-in-Chief of Jaipur State, 278; invited by Free Religious Association to speak, 510-11;
invited by Mrs. Wood to be her
house guest, 410; invited by Prof.
John Henry Wright to spend the
week-end at Annisquam, 405; it was
delightful to listen to, 51; itinerant
days of, in Northern India, 209-42;
journey to Badarikashrama, 249;
journey to Garhwal with brother-
disciples, 252-3; keen awareness of
the inhumanity of India's prevailing
social system, 536; keen for adventure,
49; law suits of, 158; learnt a number
of Tamil words, 337; learnt to cook,
36; leaving Hathras for Himalayas,
222; leaving Yokohama for Vancouver, July 1893, 399; left Ajmer
for Mount Abu, April 14, 1891, 279;
left Allahabad for Ghazipur, 228;
left Alwar on March 28, 1891, by
covered bullock-cart, 275-6; left
Bhagalpur for Vaidyanath, 247; left
Hyderabad, 378; left Khetri for
Ajmer, 286; left Salem for Saratoga,
410; left Varanasi for Calcutta to
comfort Balaram Bose's family, 237;
left for Junagadh, 290; living according to Indian ideals even in strange
environment, 440; living in Chicago,

402; living with a family of the
sweeper caste, 354; long imperturbability in the face of virulence, 483;
longing for Himalayas, 224, 241;
longing for Self-realization, 260; love
and devotion to truth, 322-3; love
for his mother, 524; love for the
Prophet of Nazareth, 404-5; many
times he saw Ramakrishna in meditation, 141; many trying experiences
in Central India, 354; mechanical
interest of, 36; meditation on the
rock at Kanyakumari, 339, 342,
344-5; meeting with: a yogi in
Hyderabad, 377-8; a Bhangi, 217; a
Muslim Vakil of the Prince of a
Native State, 279; a noted Sanskrit
grammarian at Jaipur, 277; a relative of the Amir Abdar Rahaman of
Afghanistan, 260; a school master, a
recent convert to Christianity, 254;
an old monk suffering from extreme
cold, 355; Chattambi Swami, Kerala,
327, 329; Gurucharan Lashkar, a
Moulavi Sahib and other people at
Alwar, 264-6; Hridaybabu, a class-
mate, 255; Janakibar Saran, Mahant
of Ayodhya, 249; Munshi Jagmohanlal, Khetri, 280; other persons at
Ghazipur, 230-1; Pavhari Baba,
230; Rajnarayan Bose, the old
Brahmo preacher, 247-8; Sir Ashman
Jah, K.C.S.I., Prime Minister of
Hyderabad, 376; Shri Ramakrishna,
61; Swami Abhedananda at Mahabaleshwar, 301; Swami Akhandananda at Mandvi, 299; Swamis
Brahmananda and Turiyananda,
385-7; Swami Trigunatitananda at
Porbandar, 296; the Bengalis of
Allahabad, 228; the Dewan of Porbandar, 294-5; the learned women
of the royal family of Cranganore,
326-7; the Maharaja of Alwar, 268-
70; the Maharaja of Kolhapur, 307-
8; the Maharaja of Kutch, 294; the
Maharaja of Mysore, 322; the Maharaja of Travancore, 332; the Raja of

Chetti, along with Alasinga and Manmathanath Bhattacharya, 381; restlessness, 295, 302; restlessness at Meerut, 260; rethinking his desire to go to the West, 372–3; return to Badri Sah's house from the solitary cave, 252; returning to Madras, 378; said about Shashi: "Know him to be the backbone of our Math", 211; said of Ramakrishna: "He made me his slave by his great love for me", 146; sailing for the West, May 31, 1893, 391–2; sang songs on the intense spiritual love of Radha, 141; sarcastic humour in an interview in Minneapolis, 454; set out to achieve his spiritual goal, 241; short visits of, to near-by places, 211–12; singing devotional songs and playing Tabla at Margao, 320; solitary monk's life of, 261; some blanks in the life-history of, 212–13; some music teachers of, 43; something always "held him back", 57; sore throat treatment for, 325; sought after by people of all faiths, 322; special purpose of visiting Goa, 319; spending a busy week in New England, 406; spending Christmas Day in Mrs. Bull's house, 516; spent a night in Nilakantha Mahadeva, Tahla, 276; spiritual dissatisfaction and restlessness, 232; spiritual experiences during the period of wandering, 212–13; spiritual visions of, 357; stay at: Baranagore Math for a year, 224; Bombay for two months, 306; Jaipur for two weeks, 277; Khasbag, 308; Khetri House, Jaipur, 283; Poona, with Balgangadhar Tilak, 306–7; Trivandrum at the residence of Prof. Sundararama Iyer, 330; Greenacre, 510; Khetri for three weeks, 387; Thomas W. Palmer, President of the World's Fair Commission, for nearly a week, 460; Leon Landsburg, in the Theosophical Society, New York, 509; the palaces of the Princes or

with their Dewans—the reasons for, 292–3; staying three weeks on the East Coast, 411; still scorned to defend himself publicly, 486; straightforwardness—an instance of, 462–3; strange experience with some evil spirits in Madras, 369; strange vision, 347–8; struggles and hardships of, 116–29; study of French music, 311; study of Panini and French, 295; study of Vedanta literature, 225; subsequent life history of, a confirmation of certain elements of his character and personality, 111; suffering from intense cold, 454; suffering from want of warm clothing, 399; superabundant spiritual energy welling up in him, 257; surrender to the Mother's will, 373; taking measures to counteract the slanderous campaign against him, 484–5; tamer of souls, 111; tendency towards monastic life "in his blood", 4; terrible illness at Hrishikesh, 258; the ideal which became incarnate in, 145; the life of, from 1887 to 1893 reconstructed with some accuracy, 213; the longest time he had to go without food was five days, 213; "the loved and lost", was loved, 111; the man in the making, 113; to the borders of Canada, 453; to those who hold their views obstinately, 317; took back the name Vivekananda on the eve of his departure for the West, 200; took the vow of not touching money, 213; took to vegetarianism, 59; towards Bombay Presidency, 287; towards Jaipur, 277; travel throughout India, 343; tribute of, to Shashi, 201; two dissimilar visions of life that came before his mind, 58–9; underwent a wonderful psychological transformation, 48; unflinching faith in God, 465; unpleasant experience with a European ticket-collector at Abu Road, 389–90; using Miss Phillips' home in New York as a headquarters, 476; vision of his Master walking over the waters, beckoning him to follow, 380; visit to Agra, 217; visit to an American reformatory, 526; visit to Antpur, 224; visit to Ayodhya, 217, 249; visit to Ghazipur and Varanasi, 248; visit to Ghusuree to receive Holy Mother's blessings, 241–2; visit to Goa, 319–20; visit to Japan, 397–9; visit to Kanheri caves, 305; visit to Kanyakumari, 327, 340; "Visit to Kerala", an article published in the *Prabuddha Keralam*, 1918, 340; visit to Lucknow, 217; visit to Simultala, 224; visit to the frozen Minihaha Falls, 452; visit to the women's Reformatory, Sherborn, 404; visit to Vrindavan, 217; visited Hanumanji temple, Pandupol, 276; visiting various places of interest, 400; visiting Kamarpukur with Holy Mother, 224; visiting the Maharaja of Travancore, 332; visits to various native princes and courts, 332; wandering days described in general, 213; wanderings in western India and Kanheri caves, 306; wanted to know the "why" and "how" of every phenomenon, 56; wanted to take the name Ramakrishnananda for himself, 199; warned by Shri Ramakrishna about a poisoned cup of coffee, Detroit, 483; was at all times the monk, the prophet, the teacher, 200; was good not through weakness but through strength, 58; was to become the heart and mind of New India, 75; well fitted to represent India at the Parliament, 391–2; with a family of Tibetans, 356–7; with a Mohammedan saint, Allahabad, 228; with a tourist outfit, 393; with Bahadur Manibhai J., 300; with European officials at Ghazipur, 231; with Har Bilas Sarda at Mount Abu and Ajmer, 282; with Mr. Pennington, Ghazipur, 231; with Mr. Ross, a Government official

at Ghazipur, 231; with Satishchandra Mukherji, Ghazipur, 228; with the Captain of his ship, 393–4; with Robert Ingersoll, 448–9; with the Maharaja and the Prime Minister, Mysore State, 323–5; with the Maharaja of Kutch, 293; with the Raja of Khetri, Ajit Singhji, 281–7; without any warm clothing in New England, 403; without purity and chastity no spiritual life possible, 57; witnessing first-hand the heart-rending condition of the Indian people, 535; worshipping the Mother of the Universe in the daughter of Manmathanath Bhattacharya, 340; writing about the nature of the Indian people, 493; wrote Pramadadas Mitra a number of letters regarding interpretations of Hindu scriptures, 216–17

Vivekananda, Swami, Lectures: address at the Final Session of the Parliament, 427; address before the Parliament: "Buddhism, the Fulfilment of Hinduism", 425; address to the Hindus of Madras, 507; aided in wonderful ways for his lectures, (some strange happenings), 458–9; and his listeners at Trivandrum, 334–6; and public lectures, 336; at Boston to fill three weeks of lecture engagements, 511; at Brooklyn with Dr. Lewis G. Janes to give series of lectures, 516; conversations with Swami Bhaskarananda on the conquest of lust and gold, 215; conversation with the two princes of Cranganore palace in Sanskrit, 326; correspondence with Thakore Saheb, Dewan of Junagadh, 302; delivering a lecture on Buddhism at Lyceum Theatre, Baltimore, 512; delivering addresses before the Parliament, 426; delivering extempore twelve to fourteen lectures a week, 458; discourse on religious topics at Kalipada Ghosh's residence, Bombay, 386; dis-

states of America, 453; lecturing in eastern states, 471-8; lecturing independently, 468-71; lecturing on "The Religion and Customs of India", Lawrence, Massachusetts, 478; lecturing primarily at the Unitarian Church in Detroit, Michigan, 460; lengthy discussions on the Vedantic ideals with Colonel Rivett Carnac, 231; mellifluous discourses on all matters, 362-70; metaphysical and religious discourses to the people, 265-7; one of the lectures in California, 353; other addresses before the Scientific Section, 424; other four lectures at conferences during the Parliament, 425; paper on Hinduism, 431; practice to speak in Sanskrit, 299; receiving invitations to visit and lecture at many places, 410; religious discourses and discussions on various matters with Thakore Saheb, 290; religious discourse with the people at Meerut, 260; second lecture in New York at the house of Miss Mary Phillips, 476; short address on "Why we Disagree", September 15, 1893, 418; short talk and the spirit of universality, 418; showering upon his listners the grand spiritual truths of Hinduism, 465; speaking at Northampton Smith Hall, 473; speaking at Northampton's City College, 474; speaking at the plenary session of the Parliament, 424; speaking of sinners as potential saints, 355-6; speaking of the merits of Hinduism and the basic divinity of man, 454; speaking on the "Divinity of Man", in the opera house of Ada, Ohio, 461; speaking on "Dynamic Religion", October 14 and 21, 1894, Baltimore, 512; speaking on India and Hinduism before the Conversation Circle at the Waldorf Hotel, New York, 475; speaking on religion to young Bostonians at Radcliffe, 477; speaking on "The Manners and Customs of

India", at the Association Hall, Boston, 477; speaking to the members of the Nineteenth Century Club, Memphis, 453; speech on "The Essence of Hindu Religion", 425; subject of lectures in Evanston, 442; talk before a session of the Universal Religious Unity Congress, 425; talk to a number of guests in Dr. Guernsey's home, New York, 472; talk with Jaina Acharyas, 246; talking for three days and nights without a moment's rest, 351-2; talking on "The Ancient Hindu Philosophers and What They Taught", 492; three formal talks at Mrs. Bull's house, New York, 515; tour with the Slayton Lecture Bureau coming to an end, 468; travelling to various American cities and towns telling of the glories of Indian culture, 442-4, 448; two lectures in Minneapolis at the First Unitarian Church, 452

Vivekananda, Swami, Letters: about Bagley family to Mrs. Hale, 460; about his visit to China, July 10, 1893, 394; about the reorientation of the age-old monastic institution, 543-4; about the scandals the Ramabai Circle indulged in, March 21, 1895, 519; after leaving Chicago, August 20, 1893, 400-1; call to action through his letters, 528; first letter to the monks at Baranagore Math, 536; first with the signature of "Swami Sachchidananda", 318-19; from Yokohama, July 10, 1893, 394; from Yokohama to the group of disciples in Madras, 397-8; to a friend on April 24, 1895, 521; to a Madras disciple regarding newspaper criticism and praises, 507; to Alasinga: from Hyderabad, 373; from Breezy Meadows, August 20, 1893, 526-9; describing the opening of the Parliament, 416; of April 9, 1894, 482, 484-5, 493; of May 28, 1894, inspiring his Madras disciples to construc-

honour, 498; from Detroit, 468–9; on July 9, 1894, 509; from America to India, in 1893–94, 522; of 1894, to his brother-disciples on the necessity to imbue the educated with the ideals of monasticism, 545; their influence on his brother-disciples and followers, 550; their influence on Madras disciples, 551

Vivekananda, Swami, Thoughts and Message: about: Christianity, 504; his conception of organization, 547–8; the Holy Mother, 546–7; Japan and its civilization, 397–9; Jesus Christ, 206, 290, 463–4; polytheism in Hinduism, 420–1; Shri Ramakrishna, 542–3; achievements, and its deep impression on the Indian people, 436–7; accustomed to look upon every woman as "Mother", 58; acquaintance with every aspect of life in the West, 447; advice to his followers to found societies and to work, 553; advice to the young Alwaris, 271–3; advised his followers to be content with a small beginning, 552; advising his brother-disciples to start work for the mission, 545; always considered purity the cardinal virtue, 57; always quick to catch what was constructive, 55; and a learned occultist fellow passenger, 350–1; and a nautch-girl at Khetri, 285–6; and a sannyasi at Hrishikesh, 355–6; and a Westernised Hindu, 364–5; and Buddha—feeling for mankind, 388; and Indian women, 531; and John D. Rockefeller, 451–2; and Mother-worship, 266; and Mr. Rama Rao on Indriya-nigraha, 334; and the Bhangi episode, 217–18; and the Moulavi Sahib at Alwar, 267; and the realization of God, 271; and the tiger incident, 352–3; and women's monasticism in modern Hinduism, 546; and young enquirers, 368; asking his brother-disciples to start centres and go on making converts,

545; at a Muslim cemetry, 250–1; attempting to channel enthusiasm in India over his success in America into a united force, 484–5; awakening the higher self in his direct followers, 551–2; awareness of his identity with the Supreme Spirit, 470–1; breaking the horrible crystallization of death in India, 555; Brooklyn classes, 518; caste-consciousness, 217; cherished desire for bettering his mother-country, 488; commentary on and explanation of Upanishads, 304; communion with the Lord, 470–1; completely satisfied himself of the truth of Ramakrishna's teachings, 134; concept of worship and the transformation of the worshipper, 543; conception of a great man and a great nation, 534; conception of Indian national regeneration, 527–8; conception of new monasticism and his brother-disciples, 539; conception of religion-orientation of the down-trodden, 532; continuing to present religious and social customs of India in their true light, 465; criticism of Christian governments in general, 505; decided to remain for a while in the West to consolidate his work, 513; deep and sincere love for humanity, 431; deeply concerned about the cause of womanhood in India, 547; depending on Divine guidance, 483; describing China and her people, 394–5; Divine Mission of, 179; elucidating his ideas of organised work, 554; emphasis on making possible the elevation of the women of India, 546; enquiry into social reform, 225; enlightening the American nation with the true religion of the Hindus, 490; entertainment at the residence of the Moulavi Sahib and devout Muslims at Alwar, 268; epoch-making representation at the Parliament, and its effect on

education and national awakening, 272; on practical patriotism, 338; on race-prejudice and colour-superiority, 456-7; on religion, 308; on science and religion, 333; on social reform movement, 366; on the distinction between the world of gross and fine matter, 333; on the evolution of the idea God, 376; on the idea of the Personal God, 375-6; on the ideals of Sannyasa Ashrama, 315; on the last stone of India, 341; on the merits of Hindu religion, culture and society, 377; on the status and the lower classes, 334; on Western civilization, 407-8; on writing and studying accurate Indian history, 271-2; open criticism of proselytizing methods of the Christian missionaries in India, 480; overwhelming desire to give himself utterly for the good of the Indian people, 343; patriotism and his feeling for the poor masses of India, 438-9; patriotism as revealed to Haripada Mitra, 314; perception of the realities and potentialities of Indian culture, 341; placed positive ideals before young disciples, 159; plan of carrying out the mission laid on him by his Master, 536-8; plan of work for the Indian people, 536-8; plan to go to the West in the name of India's millions, 343; plan to instruct the masses, 552; pleading for universal acceptance of all religions, 453; preaching the ideal of universal religion, 420-1; prescription for India's uplift and progress, 553; presenting the true needs of India before the American people, 458; presenting the true picture of his country's culture, 480; profound urge to awaken the spiritual consciousness of the American people, 475; propagating the essential tennets of Indian thought to remove prevailing misconceptions, 441-2; reawakening message to

the nation, 534; renunciation of desire only way to the vision of God, 59; rousing call to all classes of Indian people, 330; seeking to solve the problems of his country, 439-40; stressing the need of organization, 545; stressing upon the unity among his brother-disciples and followers, and obedience to leadership, 548; striving to arouse the dynamic spirit in his brother-disciples, 550; sturdy and reasoned faith in the destiny of the nation, 534; surrender to the will of God, 374; taking classes in Oriental fashion on Vedanta philosophy, 510; talking with his disciples about his mission to the West, 379; talking of his vision and his plan, to his brother-disciples at Baranagore Math, 536-7; "the man for the regeneration of India", 324; the same sannyasi as of old, thinking of India's poor, 438-40; thinking every woman his mother, 446; thinking of an international organization, 554; thoughts on the Great India, 297; to carry out the great mission Shri Ramakrishna preached, 524-5; to enlighten the Western mind with Advaita Vedanta, 514; to present the ideals of civilization and religious consciousness of his own race to the people of the West, 513-14; to remove the miseries of people and teach mankind, 525; to solve the problems of the soul and of the land he was born in, 241; training up to practical Advaita realization a small band of men and women, 521; throwing the light of reason and truth onto the West's disfigured picture of his country, 474; two most impressive ideas, 246; universal mind with a perfect practical culture, 392; universal sympathy with the suffering and the oppressed, 388-9; valuable services in America on behalf of Hinduism, 500; view on Avataras, 278; vigorously denouncing the evils

40

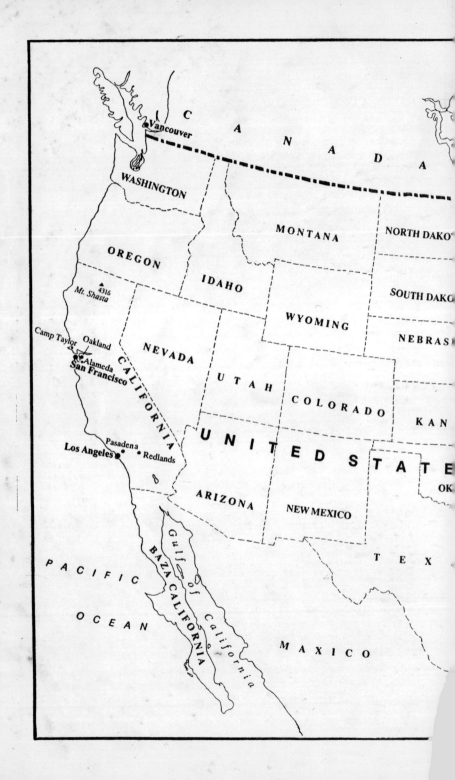